LANDSCAPE
ARCHITECTURE
CONSTRUCTION

LANDSCAPE ARCHITECTURE CONSTRUCTION

Harlow C. Landphair
Fred Klatt, Jr.

Department of Landscape Architecture
Texas A&M University

ELSEVIER
New York · Amsterdam · Oxford

Elsevier Science Publishing Co., Inc.
52 Vanderbilt Avenue, New York, New York 10017

Sole distributors outside the USA and Canada:

Elsevier Science Publishers B.V.
P.O. Box 211, 1000 AE Amsterdam, The Netherlands

Library of Congress Cataloging in Publication Data

Landphair, Harlow C.
    Landscape architecture construction.

    Bibliography: p.
    Includes index.
    1. Building. 2. Landscape architecture.
    I. Klatt, Fred, joint author. II. Title.
TH153.L29   712   78-5518
ISBN 0-444-00264-2

Current printing (last digit)
10 9 8 7

To: Wendie & Deborah

Contents

PREFACE
ACKNOWLEDGMENTS

UNIT I   SHAPING THE LANDSCAPE   1

CHAPTER 1: INTRODUCTION TO GRADING   3

Why Grade?   3
Grading and the Soil   4
Maps for Grading   7
Representation of Land Form   10
Contour Interpretation   12
Classifying the Land Form   17
The Six Cardinal Laws of Contours   23
Contour Manipulation   27
Grading Around Buildings and Structures   27
Grading Evenly Sloped Surfaces   30
Grading Roads and Ways   30
Grading for Drainage   32
Grading Standards   36
Calculating Grades   37
The Grading Plan   59
Calculation of Cut and Fill   64

CHAPTER 2: CIRCULATION DESIGN   75

Design of Streets and Roads   76
Horizontal Alignment   89
Vertical Alignment   96
Superelevation   104
Pedestrian Ways   104
Bicycle Ways   107

CHAPTER 3: DRAINAGE DESIGN   **113**

Contemporary Issues in Drainage Design   113
Estimating Storm Runoff   116
Design of Surface Drainage Systems   120
Design of Open Channels   121
Design of Subsurface Storm Drains   128
Drainage Structures   141
Pipe Bedding and Loading   145
Controlling Runoff   148
Earth Dams   149
Subdrainage Design   152

UNIT II   LANDSCAPE STRUCTURES   157

CHAPTER 4: BASIC PRINCIPLES OF STATICS AND MECHANICS **159**

Force and Stress   159
Moments   160
Equilibrium   160
Reactions   161
Structural Properties of Materials   163
Selecting and Sizing Horizontal Members   164
Selecting and Sizing Vertical Members   168

CHAPTER 5: CARPENTRY AND DESIGN WITH WOOD   **175**

Softwood Lumber Species   175
Lumber and Wood Grading   176
Wood Fasteners   177
Wood Preservatives   184
Frame Construction   186
Structural Design of Wood Landscape Structures   189
Carpentry and Detailing Wood Structures   192

CHAPTER 6: CONCRETE AND MASONRY DESIGN   **199**

Concrete and Masonry Materials   199
Concrete and Masonry Structures   204

UNIT III   SPECIAL SYSTEMS   231

CHAPTER 7: IRRIGATION DESIGN   **233**

Agronomic Principles of Irrigation   233
Irrigation Equipment   234
Basic Irrigation Hydraulics   241
Computation of Pressure Loss and Pipe Sizing   244
Designing the Irrigation System   246

CHAPTER 8: LIGHTING DESIGN   **263**

Lighting Equipment   263
Designing Lighting Systems   266
Designing for Effect   269
Principles of Electricity   271
Wiring and Electrical Plans   274

CHAPTER 9: FOUNTAIN AND POOL DESIGN   **283**

Equipment for Fountains and Pools   283
Basic Hydraulics of Fountains and Pools   287
Pool Construction   290

UNIT IV   LANDSCAPE CONSTRUCTION MANUAL   293

Curb and Gutter Details   294
Concrete Edges and Mowing Edges   298
Brick and Concrete Step Details   302
Brick Paving Details   304
Drain Inlet Details   310
Curb Inlet Details   322
Catch Basin Details   326
Manhole Details   334
Headwall and Endwall Details   336
Retaining Wall Details   338
Visual Screen Details   352
Gate Details   360
Brick Wall Details   364
Deck Details   378
Pool and Fountain Details   390
Light Details   392
Parking Standards   394

APPENDIX   CONTRACT DOCUMENTS AND SPECIFICATIONS   399

The Project Manual   399
Technical Specifications   400
The Uniform System   401

SELECTED BIBLIOGRAPHY   **405**

SOLUTIONS TO PROBLEMS   **409**

INDEX   **425**

Preface

Landscape construction is best defined as the art and technology of building the outdoor human environment. Implicit in this definition is that landscape construction cuts across the boundaries of many other disciplines and depends a great deal on other more established bodies of knowledge.

It is recognized that the landscape architect, or for that matter any other professional, does not operate in a vacuum, for no individual can be expected to be competent in all matters affecting the environment. On the other hand, if a landscape architect or site planner is to affect the plans that are drawn, there must be a broad understanding of the actions necessary to bring them into being. That is the essence of this book.

The content of this book has evolved over several years of teaching landscape construction, research, and practice on the part of both authors. We have also sought the advice and counsel of other working professionals in determining the content. In so far as possible, the material is comprehensive, directed toward what might best be called a minimum professional competence in each area.

The book itself has been organized into four broad units: I—Shaping the Landscape, II—Landscape Structures, III—Special Systems, and IV—The Reference Manual. Each unit has been separated into individual chapters that are mutually supportive but that can also be used without benefit of material from another chapter. This was done to increase the effectiveness of the book as a reference.

Unit I, Shaping the Landscape, concentrates on the technology related to the preparation of a site for use: Grading, Circulation Design, and Drainage. The Grading chapter provides an extensive discussion of the grading process with step-by-step problem illustrations and concludes with a discussion of cut and fill calculations. The chapter of circulation provides a discussion of highway design and the design criteria of other circulation ways. The final chapter deals with site drainage and includes information on open channel flow, storm sewerage, and subdrainage. All of the material in Unit I is presented in both English and metric measure. Where formulas require conversion to metric units, these are featured in metrication blocks.

Unit II, Landscape Structures, is also divided into three chapters: Basic Statics and Mechanics, Design with Wood, and Design with Concrete and Masonry. The Statics and Mechanics chapter is provided to introduce the basic terminology involved in structural design. All the material is highly simplified, but it provides the basis for a more thorough discussion of structures in the other chapters. The chapter on design with wood covers basic material on wood and fasteners, structural design, and general detailing. The Concrete and Masonry chapter discusses materials, structural design, detailing, and retaining wall stability.

Unit III, Special Systems, is composed of three chapters: Irrigation, Lighting, and Fountains and Pools. Because of the rapidly changing technology in each of these areas, the information presented in each chapter is limited to basic principles that are not likely to change rapidly. Likewise, the material is presented at an introductory level rather than trying to provide the detail available in other sources.

The Reference Manual, Unit IV, is designed to complement the written text by providing a ready reference to construction details. The presentation format was developed to give both students and professionals a series of construction details with an explanation of why each detail was developed as it is shown. The order of the detail sheets generally follows the organization of the text.

Readers and students should understand that in an effort to make this book a comprehensive work we have had to make decisions regarding the completeness of coverage of material in each chapter. It has also been necessary to simplify much of the material on structures; however, we feel that this is appropriate since our major objective is to introduce vocabulary and principles.

Acknowledgments

A book of this type is the product of the efforts of many people. We recognize this and wish to express our thanks to everyone included in this effort. First, we would like to express special thanks to Jot Carpenter, Brooks Breeden, Brad Sears, Herrick Smith, and Charles Hix for reading the text and offering advice on the content. We would also like to recognize Bruce Smith and Yvonne Kovar for their help in handling many of the administrative chores, and Susan Koscielniak, "editor extraordinaire," for her guidance, advice, and patience. Also, we wish to thank the students of Landscape Architecture at Texas A & M University who have been the guinea pigs for much of the material as it was developed. In addition, our thanks to the following companies for the courtesy of allowing us to reprint original figures from the following publications: "1977 Irrigation Equipment," Toro Irrigation Division, 5825 Jasmine St., Riverside, CA 92504; "Fountain Components," Kim Lighting, Inc., P.O. Box 1275, 16555 E. Gale Avenue, City of Industry, CA 91749. Finally, we say thank you to our wives and families who have put up with us throughout the project.

LANDSCAPE ARCHITECTURE CONSTRUCTION

UNIT

I

SHAPING THE LANDSCAPE

1

Introduction to Grading

Preparation of land for any use beyond its natural condition involves changing the land form by grading. Grading involves changing the elevations of the existing landscape to accommodate structures, paths, and ways, and to facilitate the removal of surface water. It also considers the installation of subsurface structures for the distribution of water, gas, power, telephone service, and the disposal of waste water and storm runoff.

All construction projects regardless of their size involve some modification of the earth's surface. How and the extent to which the surface is changed will to a large measure determine the success or failure of the project itself. For example, failure to maintain natural drainage systems can cause flooding, accelerate erosion, undermine foundations, and damage desirable vegetation. In essence the grading plan for a project is the foundation that supports all other structures and connects them to their environment.

Grading then is the primary construction skill to be developed by the landscape architect, for if this fundamental skill is weak, no amount of expertise in design or management can make a project succeed. On the other hand, when grading is integrated into the design vocabulary and applied by a skilled, sensitive designer, it can reduce project and maintenance costs and improve the natural setting.

This chapter is presented in five sections. It introduces the grading process and presents the preparation of the final grading plan and calculation of cut and fill. The first is an overview of the theory, procedures, and graphic tools used to prepare grading plans. The second introduces the fundamentals of contour manipulation by developing contour signature recognition and introducing rules of contours.

The third presents standards for grading, basic calculations and the use of spot elevations. The fourth section is a synthesis of the preceding sections that covers the grading process from the preparation of the base map to the final grading plan. The final section explains two methods used for the calculation of cut and fill.

The material introduced in the chapter should be studied and mastered, not just kept for reference.

WHY GRADE?

Many contemporary environmentalists would have us believe that any modification of the natural environment is unnecessarily destructive. This is not, and need not be, true. While it must be acknowledged that a change in the natural system of a site will affect the operation of that system, the effect need not be deleterious. On the contrary, many contemporary ecologists have demonstrated that the proper use and management of a natural system can in fact diversify the system further and even increase its vitality. The key of course is proper management and proper use.

Unfortunately, grading under the guise of economics and functional necessity sometimes becomes the greatest instrument of environmental degradation, disruption, and destruction. This is due largely to a lack of understanding on the part of the designer. Sacrificing the land to keep a road straight, sitting a house on an unstable hill for the sake of view alone, removing a primary sand dune to obtain visual access to the ocean, and filling in the drainage swales to increase lot size or build roads, is rarely justified. Mistakes like these have made construction appear to be a growing cancer on the natural landscape and indeed it is if these practices continue. But these errors need not be condoned nor should they be hidden under the protective rubric of "functionalism." Not so! Designers must learn to grade in sympathy with the natural setting and have imagination enough to work within the natural constraints. This is the essence of creativity and leads to good design.

So what is the answer? Why grade? As a landscape architect or site planner you have a moral and professional obligation to do two things: produce a design solution that will satisfy the client's needs within the budget and at the same time seek to enhance the efficiency of the natural environment. If your solution doesn't do both, you haven't earned your fee. It might appear from the discussion so far that we are advocating the least grading solution. Not so. Many projects may require extensive grade revision to meet the program needs and enhance the environment. The trick is knowing the difference and that's why you must learn to grade.

GRADING AND THE SOIL

The character and composition of the soil is very much a part of how a grading problem should be approached. As a designer it is essential that you consider soil a basic building material and have a basic understanding of its design implications. The soil itself, many times, will directly determine what can and cannot be done, especially when the budget will not permit replacing or extensively modifying the soil.

Soil Formation

Soils are produced by the weathering of rocks. Weathering occurs when rocks become exposed to water, air, and organisms that cause the rock to change or break into successively smaller pieces. Two kinds of weathering are recognized by geologists: chemical weathering and physical weathering.

Chemical weathering involves a change in the chemical make-up of the parent rock material. Typically, chemical weathering is involved in the formation of the clay minerals in soils. Physical weathering is the simple breaking up of the parent rock into smaller particles. Sands and gravels are typically the products of physical weathering processes. No soil, however, is the result of just chemical or physical weathering even though one may be the more dominant process.

For example, in colder climates where frequent freezes and thaws occur, physical weathering processes tend to dominate. On the other hand, chemical weathering will tend to dominate in humid tropical areas and deserts.

Mature soil formations are characterized by distinct layers called horizons. These horizons are designated as A, B, and C. Together these three horizons form the soil profile called the regolith. Figure 1–1

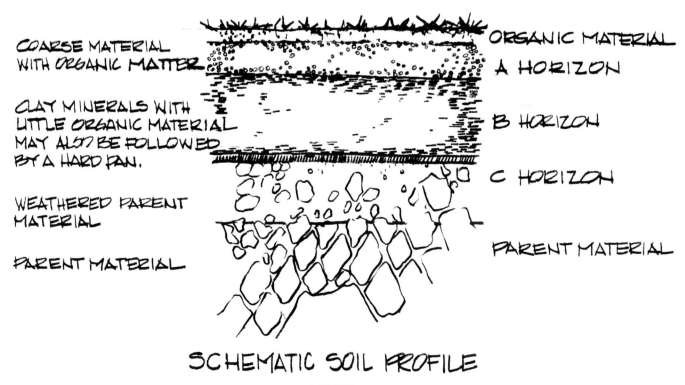

COARSE MATERIAL WITH ORGANIC MATTER

CLAY MINERALS WITH LITTLE ORGANIC MATERIAL MAY ALSO BE FOLLOWED BY A HARD PAN.

WEATHERED PARENT MATERIAL

PARENT MATERIAL

ORGANIC MATERIAL
A HORIZON

B HORIZON

C HORIZON

PARENT MATERIAL

SCHEMATIC SOIL PROFILE

FIGURE 1–1

illustrates the regolith and the characteristics of each major horizon.

A general knowledge of how soils form and the characteristics of the various layers can provide many clues to problems that might be encountered in a development. The relative importance of these characteristics is a function of what you intend to do with the site. For example, some projects require a knowledge of the soil as a growth medium, while others may be concerned with regional land stability. In each instance the concern is with a different set of soil properties. The need to deal with these different soil characteristics has led to three different methods of soil classification.

Soil Classification

Soils are typically classified by agricultural characteristics, geologic characteristics, or engineering characteristics. The agriculturalist is concerned primarily with soil as a plant growth medium, the geologist classifies soils by their physical and morphological properties, and the engineer classifies soils by their mechanical and structural capabilities.

Agricultural soils are classified by a system similar to the system used to classify plant and animal life. Classification begins with a grouping of the broadest characteristics working toward more and more specific characteristics. Table 1–1 illustrates the similarity of the systematic classification of plants to the agricultural soil classification system. A soil is referred to by its series name and the surface soil texture, while a plant is referred to by the genus and species.

A soil series is a group of soils that have formed from a specific parent material with a similar arrangement of horizons, but with different surface soil textures. Soil series are usually named for a place in the area where they were first identified, e.g., Lakewood, Axtell, Houston, Hagerstown, Lakeland, and Norfolk.

Soil textures are based on the relative percentage

TABLE 1–1
Similarity of the Systematic Classification of Plants to the Agricultural Soil Classification

PLANT KINGDOM CLASSIFICATION	SOIL CLASSIFICATION
Kingdom	Order
Phylum	Suborder
Class	Great group
Order	Subgroup
Family	Family
Genus	Series
Species	Type
Variety	Texture (A-Horizon)

of sand, silt, or clay particles in the soil. By definition sand particles are from 2 mm to .05 mm, silt is from .05 mm to .002 mm and clay is less than .002 mm in size. The smallest sand particles, .05 mm, are barely visible to the naked eye. Silt particles are not visible individually, but can be felt when rubbed between your fingers. Clay particles are not visible and feel like powder or flour when dry. When wet, clay will be sticky and can be rolled into a ball. Typical soil texture designations are: silty clay (40–60% clay, 40–60% silt); sandy clay loam (20–35% clay, 0–25% silt and 60–90% sand). Any soil that is 65% clay minerals is classified clay. A loam is a soil that has a percentage of all three particles.

The Soil Conservation Service maps these soil types on aerial photographs and publishes soil surveys for individual counties or parishes throughout the country. These surveys provide information about the land suitability for various agricultural crops, susceptibility to erosion, moisture and drainage characteristics, potential flooding, slopes, and current land use.

In addition to this information, these surveys also include some engineering soil data as well as a land capability classification. In the more recent soil survey publications the land capability considerations are most beneficial to the design disciplines. While a complete examination of the land capability classification system is beyond the scope of this discussion, you should be aware that it exists and that all of this information is available at no cost from the local Soil Conservation Service office. A description of the land capability grouping system is reproduced here from Bexar county, Texas, to give you a better idea of what is considered.

Class I.   Soils that have few limitations that restrict their use. (No subclasses)
Class II.   Soils that have some limitations that restrict the choice of plants or require moderate conservation practices.
   Subclass IIc.   Soils that have some limitations because of climate.
      Unit IIc-1, dryland; I-1, irrigated. — Deep, nearly level, noncalcareous loams; moderately permeable subsoil.
      Unit IIc-2, dryland; I-2, irrigated. — Deep, nearly level, strongly calcareous, medium-textured to fine-textured soils; slowly permeable to moderately permeable subsoil.
   Subclass IIe.   Soils subject to moderate erosion if they are not protected.
      Unit IIe-1, dryland; IIe-1, irrigated. — Deep, nearly level fine sandy loams; slowly permeable to moderately permeable subsoil.
      Unit IIe-2, dryland; IIe-2, irrigated. — Deep, near-

ly level loams; moderately permeable subsoil.

Unit IIe-3, dryland; IIe-3, irrigated. — Deep, nearly level, strongly calcareous, medium-textured to fine-textured soils; slowly permeable to moderately permeable subsoil.

Subclass IIs.   Soils that have moderate limitations of moisture capacity or tilth.

Units IIs-1, dryland; IIs-2, irrigated. — Deep, nearly level, slowly permeable, very hard, calcareous clays that crack when dry.

Subclass IIw.   Soils that have moderate limitations because of excess water.

Unit IIw-1, dryland; IIw-1, irrigated. — Deep, nearly level, moderately permeable fine sandy loams and clay loams on flood plains.

Unit IIw-2, dryland. — Deep, nearly level, calcareous clays on flood plains along creeks and major streams and in depressions on the uplands.

Class III.   Soils that have severe limitations that reduce the choice of plants, or require special conservation practices, or both.

Subclass IIIe.   Soils subject to severe erosion if they are cultivated and not protected.

Unit IIIe-1, dryland; IIIe-1, irrigated. — Deep, nearly level fine sandy loams and clay loams; very slowly permeable subsoil.

Unit IIIe-2, dryland; IIIe-2, irrigated. — Deep, nearly level, slowly permeable, calcareous clays and gravelly clays that crack when dry.

Unit IIIe-3, dryland. — Deep, gently sloping, slowly permeable, calcareous clays and gravelly clays that crack when dry.

Unit IIIe-4, dryland; IIIe-3, irrigated. — Deep, gently sloping fine sandy loams; slowly permeable or moderately permeable subsoil.

Unit IIIe-5, dryland; IIIe-5, irrigated. — Deep, gently sloping, strongly calcareous loams, clay loams, and silty clays; moderately permeable subsoil.

Unit IIIe-6, dryland; IIIe-5, irrigated. — Moderately deep, gently sloping, moderately permeable, strongly calcareous clay loams; eroded.

Unit IIIe-7, dryland; IIIe-6, irrigated. — Shallow to moderately deep, nearly level, moderately permeable clay loams and silty clays.

Unit IIIe-8, dryland; IIIs-1, irrigated. — Level and nearly level, thick loamy fine sands; dense, slowly permeable or very slowly permeable subsoil.

Unit IIIe-9, dryland; IIIs-2, irrigated. — Deep, nearly level and gently sloping, thick loamy fine sands; crumbly, moderately permeable subsoil.

Unit IIIe-10, dryland. — Deep to shallow, gently sloping and sloping, slowly permeable to moderately permeable clays on old alluvial fans and in narrow valleys.

Subclass IIIs.   Soils that have severe limitations of moisture capacity or tilth.

Unit IIIs-1, dryland; IIIs-3, irrigated. — Deep, nearly level fine sandy loams and clay loams; very slowly permeable subsoil.

Unit IIIs-2, dryland; IIs-2, irrigated. — Shallow, nearly level, moderately permeable clay loams, clays, or loams.

Class IV.   Soils that have very severe limitations that restrict the choice of plants, require very careful management, or both.

Subclass IVe.   Soils subject to very severe erosion if they are cultivated and not protected.

Unit IVe-1, dryland; IVs-1, irrigated. — Deep, nearly level, dark-colored clay loams; very slowly permeable subsoil.

Unit IVe-2, dryland. — Deep, gently sloping, dark-colored, noncalcareous clay loams; very slowly permeable subsoil.

Unit IVe-3, dryland. — Deep, gently sloping and sloping, dark-colored, calcareous clays and gravelly clays; slowly permeable subsoil.

Unit IVe-4, dryland. — Deep, gently sloping fine sandy loams; eroded; slowly permeable subsoil.

Unit IVe-5, dryland; IIIe-7, irrigated. — Gently sloping loamy fine sands; eroded; moderately slowly permeable to very slowly permeable subsoil.

Unit IVe-6, dryland; IIIs-4, irrigated. — Deep, nearly level and gently sloping, loose fine sands underlain by sandy clay loam at a depth of 42 to 100 inches or more.

Unit IVe-7, dryland. — Shallow and deep, nearly level and gently sloping, moderately permeable clay loams and silty clays.

Class V.   Soils that are not likely to erode but have other limitations, impractical to remove without major reclamation, that limit their use largely to pasture or range, woodland, or wildlife food and cover.

Subclass Vw.   Soils too wet for cultivation; drainage or protection not feasible.

Unit Vw-1, dryland. — Deep, nearly level, dark-colored, calcareous clays or clay loams on flood plains; frequently flooded.

Unit Vw-2, dryland. — Deep, somewhat granular, noncalcareous fine sandy loams and clay loams on flood plains; frequently flooded.

Class VI.   Soils that have severe limitations that make them generally unsuitable for cultivation and that limit their use largely to pasture or range, woodland, or wildlife food and cover.

Subclass VIe.   Soils severely limited, chiefly by risk of erosion, if protective cover is not maintained.

Unit VIe-1, dryland. — Deep, gently sloping fine sandy loams and clay loams; eroded; slowly permeable or very slowly permeable subsoil.

Unit VIe-2, dryland. — Deep to very shallow,

strongly sloping clays; eroded; slowly permeable subsoil.

Unit VIe-4, dryland. — Deep, gently sloping loamy fine sands; eroded; slowly permeable subsoil.

Subclass VIs.   Soils generally unsuitable for cultivation and limited for other uses by low moisture capacity, stones, or other soil features.

Unit VIs-1, dryland. — Moderately deep and shallow, noncalcareous stony clays and cherty clay loams; slowly permeable subsoil.

Unit VIs-2, dryland. — Very shallow, dark-colored stony clays and stony clay loams over chalk and hard limestone bedrock.

Unit VIs-3, dryland. — Very shallow, rolling and hilly, dark-colored stony clays and stony clay loams over hard limestone bedrock.

Class VII   Soils that have very severe limitations that make them unsuitable for cultivation without major reclamation, and that restrict their use largely to grazing, woodland, or wildlife.

Subclass VIIs.   Soils very severely limited by moisture capacity, stones, or other soil features.

Unit VIIs-1, dryland. — Very shallow, sloping and strongly sloping, light-colored, calcareous gravelly to stony clay loams over soft limestone bedrock interbedded with hard limestone.

Unit VIIs-2, dryland. — Very shallow, hilly or moderately steep, light-colored, calcareous gravelly to stony clay loams over soft limestone bedrock interbedded with hard limestone.

Unit VIIs-3, dryland. — Deep gullies, hilly gravelly to stony clay loams over soft limestone bedrock interbedded with hard limestone.

Unit VIIs-3, dryland. — Deep gullies, hilly gravelly land, and outcrops of caliche.

Class VIII.   Soils and landforms that, without major reclamation, have limitations that preclude their use for commercial production of plants and restrict their use to recreation, wildlife, water supply, or aesthetic purposes. (There are no class VIII soils in Bexar County.)

The geologic classification of soils concerns itself with the mineral composition of the crustal material and how it was formed and deposited. This means that geologist's definition of soil is broader in the sense that any mass of unconsolidated surface material would be considered soil.

The geologic soil classification has three major soil groups: pedalfers, laterites, and pedocals. Pedalfers have high aluminum and iron content with a noted lack of calcium. These soils are typical of the temperate zones. The pedocals form in warm, dry climates and will be high in calcium because of a lack of moisture. These soils are typical of the arid and desert regions. Laterites are deep soils composed mostly of aluminum and iron oxides. Since the soils are leached of calcium, silica, and minerals they have very low fertility. These soils are typical of the tropics.

The engineering soil classification is also concerned with the physical composition of a soil. However, the major concern is the structural bearing capacity of the soil profile. The engineering soil classification system is broken into 15 groups based on their suitability as a foundation material for different kinds of construction. The 15 classifications are given in Table 1-2 with their general structural characteristics.

These broad classifications provide excellent guidelines for determining what site restrictions might exist. But these values should never be considered absolute, or substituted for actual test boring data, even for light construction. This fact will be pointed out several times in later chapters and cannot be over emphasized.

A quick glance at Table 1-2 shows that sands and gravels tend to be the best foundation soils. Nonplastic clays and silts are also generally acceptable. The plastic clays and silts on the other hand are troublesome soils for any kind of construction.

A limited amount of engineering soil data is usually available in the county soil survey. Other sources of engineering soil information include city and county or parish engineers offices and state highway departments.

From this brief discussion it can be seen that soils will greatly influence what can or cannot be done with a site. This is particularly true with respect to how the land is reshaped in the grading process. As a designer you must always include soil data as a part of the site inventory and analysis, and be aware of its implications.

MAPS FOR GRADING

The basic tool used to record and display information about land form is a topographic map. Without getting involved in a lengthy discussion of cartographic terminology and theory, there are several general things that the designer should know about using maps.

Map Scales

Maps can be classified as large scale or small scale. The large-scale map is used for site specific work that requires fine detail. The small-scale map is used for a general data display covering large land areas. Rough grading can be accomplished on small-scale maps, but for finished grading plans large-scale maps are a necessity.

The actual scale used for a grading plan is largely a function of the project complexity, budget, and pref-

TABLE 1–2 Characteristics of Soil Groups in United Soil Classification System[1]

MAJOR DIVISIONS	GROUP SYMBOL	SOIL DESCRIPTION	VALUE AS FOUNDATION MATERIAL[2]	VALUE AS BASE COURSE DIRECTLY UNDER BITUMINOUS PAVEMENT	VALUE FOR EMBANKMENTS
Coarse-grained soils (*less than 50 percent passing No. 200 sieve*):	GW	Well-graded gravels and gravel-sand mixtures; little or no fines.	Excellent	Good	Very stable; use in previous shells of dikes and dams.
Gravels and gravelly soils (*more than half of coarse fraction retained on No. 4 sieve*).	GP	Poorly graded gravels and gravel-sand mixtures; little or no fines.	Good to excellent.	Poor to fair	Reasonably stable; use in previous shells of dikes and dams.
	GM	Silty gravels and gravel-sand-silt mixtures.	Good	Poor to good	Reasonably stable; not particularly suited to shells, but may be used for impervious cores or blankets.
	GC	Clayey gravels and gravel-sand-clay mixtures.	Good	Poor	Fairly stable; may be used for impervious core.
	SW	Well-graded sands and gravelly sands; little or no fines.	Good	Poor	Very stable; may be used in pervious sections; slope protection required.
Sands and sandy soils (*more than half of course fraction passing No. 4 sieve*).	SP	Poorly graded sands and gravelly sands; little or no fines.	Fair to good	Poor to not suitable.	Reasonably stable; may be used in dike section having flat slopes.
	SM	Silty sands and sand-clay mixtures.	Fair to good	Same	Fairly stable; not particularly suited to shells, but may be used for impervious cores or dikes.
	SC	Clayey sands and sand-clay mixtures.	Fair to good	Not suitable	Fairly stable; use as impervious core for flood-control structures.
Fine-grained soils (*more than 50 percent passing No. 200 sieve*):	ML	Inorganic silts and very fine sands, rock flour, silty or clayey fine sands, and cleyey silts of slight plasticity.	Fair to poor	Not suitable	Poor stability; may be used for embankments if properly controlled.
Silts and clays (*liquid limit of 50 or less*).	CL	Inorganic clays of low to medium plasticity, gravelly clays, sandy clays, silty clays, and lean clays.	Fair to poor	Not suitable	Stable; use in impervious cores and blankets.
	OL	Organic silts and organic clays having low plasticity.	Poor	Not suitable	Not suitable for embankments.
	MH	Inorganic silts, micaceous or diatomaecous fine sandy or silty soils, and elastic silts.	Poor	Not suitable	Poor stability; use in core of hydraulic fill dam; not desirable in rolled fill construction.
Silts and clays (*liquid limit greater than 50*).	CH	Inorganic clays having high plasticity and fat clays.	Poor to very poor.	Not suitable	Fair stability on flat slopes; use in thin cores, blankets, and dike sections of dams.
	OH	Organic clays having medium to high plasticity and organic silts.	Same	Not suitable	Not suitable for embankments.
Highly organic soils	Pt	Peat and other highly organic soils	Not suitable	Not suitable	Not used

[1]Based on information in The Unified Soil Classification System, Technical Memorandum No. 3–357, Volumes 1, 2, and 3, Waterways Experiment Station, Corps of Engineers, 1953. Ratings and ranges in test values are for guidance only. Design should be based on field survey and test of samples from construction site.

COMPACTION: CHARACTERISTICS AND RECOMMENDED EQUIPMENT	APPROXIMATE RANGE IN A.A.S.H.O. MAXIMUM DRY DENSITY[3]	FIELD (IN-PLACE) CBR	SUBGRADE MODULUS, K	DRAINAGE CHARACTERISTICS	COMPARABLE GROUPS IN A.A.S.H.O. CLASSIFICATION
	Lb/cu. ft.		*Lb./sq. in./in.*		
Good; use crawler-type tractor, pneumatic-tire roller, or steel-wheel roller.	125–135	60–80	300+	Excellent _____	A–1.
Same_____	115–125	25–60	300+	Excellent _____	A–1.
Good, but needs close control of moisture; use pneumatic-tire or sheepsfoot roller.	120–135	20–80	200–300+	Fair to practically impervious_____	A–1 or A–2.
Fair, use pneumatic-tire or sheepsfoot roller.	115–130	20–40	200–300	Poor to practically impervious_____	A–2.
Good; use crawler-type tractor or pneumatic-tire roller.	110–130	20–40	200–300	Excellent _____	A–1.
Same_____	100–120	10–25	200–300	Excellent _____	A–1 or A–3.
Good, but needs close control of moisture; use pneumatic-tire or sheepsfoot roller.	110–125	10–40	200–300	Fair to practically impervious _____	A–1, A–2, or A–4.
Fair, use pneumatic-tire roller or sheepsfoot roller.	105–125	10–20	200–300	Poor to practically impervious_____	A–2, A–4, or A–6.
Good to poor; close control of moisture is essential; use use pneumatic-tire or sheeps-foot roller.	95–120	5–15	100–200	Fair to poor_____	A–4, A–5, or A–6.
Fair to good; use pneumatic-tire or sheepsfoot roller.	95–120	5–15	100–200	Practically impervious_____	A–4, A–6, or A–7.
Fair to poor; use sheepsfoot roller.[4]	80–100	4–8	100–200	Poor _____	A–4, A–5, A–6, or A–7.
Poor to very poor; use sheepsfoot roller.[4]	70–95	4–8	100–200	Fair to poor_____	A–5 or A–7.
Fair to poor; use sheepsfoot roller.[4]	75–105	3–5	50–100	Practically impervious_____	A–7.
Poor to very poor; use sheepsfoot roller.[4]	65–100	3–5	50–100	Practically impervious_____	A–5 or A–7.
in embankments, dams, or subgrades for pavements				Fair to poor_____	None.

[2]Ratings are for subgrade and subbases for flexible pavement.
[3]Determined in accordance with Designation: T 99–49, A.A.S.H.O.
[4]Pneumatic-tire rollers may be advisable, particularly when moisture content is higher than optimum.

erence of the individual designer. Popular scales for grading plans are 1 in = 30 ft, 1 in = 20 ft, and 1 in = 10 ft English, 1:300, 1:500, and 1:1000 metric.

Availability of Maps

Area maps can be obtained from many sources. Cities or governmental jurisdictions will usually have topographic maps of the land within its political boundaries. Engineering supply houses often publish similar maps for sale to the public. Another source of maps is the United States Geological Survey (USGS). These maps, sometimes called "quad" sheets, are published and updated periodically. The scales are usually 1:12000, 1:24000, and 1:62500. Before using any USGS map be sure to check the date of publication to be sure the information is not outdated.

REPRESENTATION OF LAND FORM

One of the biggest sources of anguish to most students of grading is mastering the two-dimensional graphic techniques used to represent three-dimensional land form. This is understandable, since you are expected to visualize reality in reduced scale with the vertical dimension removed. It need not be a source of worry though; with a little work you can master the basic signatures of various land forms and the methods used to record them.

Probably the oldest method used to represent land form is called hachures. Hachures are evenly spaced lines drawn parallel to the lines of steepest slope, with breaks at equal increments of vertical change in elevation. As illustrated in Figure 1–2, hachures give an excellent feel for the shape of the land. However, because they cover the sheet so completely, recording other information is most difficult, to say nothing of the time required to prepare the base map. In practice, the most practical use of hachures is for presentation plans. They have little application in construction drawings.

The most popular method of representing land form is the use of contour lines. Contour lines are the same elevation along their entire length and have the same vertical separation, as illustrated in Figure 1–2.

In other words, the line in Figure 1–2 labeled 10, is 10 units above some known point of elevation called a datum. Any point on that line is exactly 10 units above that plane. This principal is very easy to visualize if we think of putting an object in water, as in Figure 1–3.

If water is added in one foot increments, and a line traced around the object at the water surface, each point on that line will be the same elevation. Then if the object is represented in plan, the lines show up

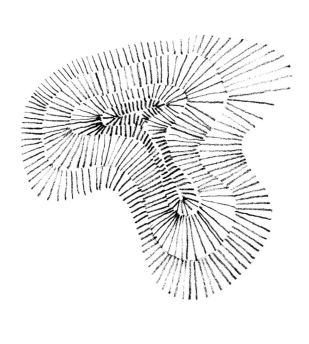

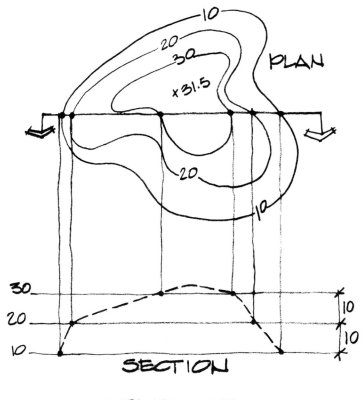

HACHURES   CONTOURS

FIGURE 1–2

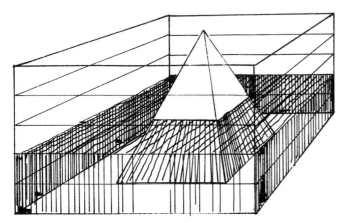

FIGURE 1–3

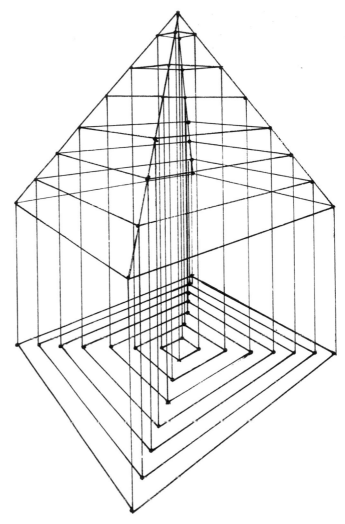

FIGURE 1–4

as contour lines representing a vertical change in elevation of one foot between the two lines, as in Figure 1–4.

Further, it is possible to determine the approximate elevation of any point between the contours by simple interpolation. For example, a point halfway between the 20 and 21 contour would be elevation 20.5. A point three-tenths of the distance between the 23 and 24 contour would be elevation 23.3 units above the datum.

Contours are the most popular and widely used method because they allow the display of other information on the same map. Along with this advantage, they also allow the designer to approximate intermediate elevations with relative accuracy. You will also find that with a little practice they give a very good visual feel for the overall land form.

Representing Land Form in Elevation

Just as elevations are important to visualizing the final form of a structure, land form can be studied using drawings representing the vertical configuration. The drawings used for this are called profiles or sections. Sections are normally associated with either an existing or proposed condition whereas a profile indicates both the existing and the proposed conditions.

While grading information is usually displayed on a plan, much of the information recorded there was either generated or checked on some type of sectional drawing. Therefore the importance of the section and profile cannot be overly stressed.

A section is a two-dimensional plane taken perpendicular to the earth's surface. It indicates the vertical configuration of the earth's surface along its entire length but only on that line. There is no indication of what takes place on either side of the plane. This is important, since a section taken at the wrong point may give a false picture of the conditions. Where sections should be taken and their use will be discussed in more detail with respect to their specific applications.

What is of importance here is the preparation of the sectional drawing and its relationship to the corresponding plan. There are several important steps in preparing a section, illustrated in Figure 1–5.

- The plane of the section must be clearly shown on the plan and labeled.

- The section sheet is prepared with the vertical elevation increments labeled on both sides of the sheet and the horizontal dimensions indicated as 100 ft (30 m) stations. The subscripts N, S, E, W are added to indicate the compass direction of increasing horizontal measure if a series of sections is being prepared.

- The scales, horizontal and vertical, are clearly labeled. It is common to exaggerate the vertical scale by five to ten times when doing most sectional drawings that involve land form.

- The points where the contour lines intersect the plane of the section are projected down to the appropriate elevation line on the sectional drawing. When it is not possible or convenient to project

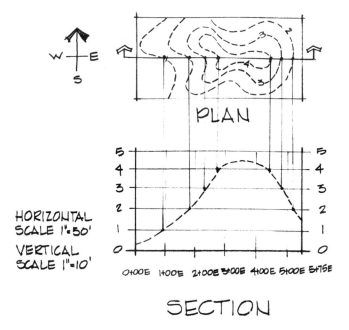

PLAN

HORIZONTAL
SCALE 1"=50'

VERTICAL
SCALE 1"=10'

SECTION

FIGURE 1-5

directly, a "tick-sheet" is used to transfer the information.

• The points are then connected with a smooth freehand line to depict the vertical configuration of the surface.

CONTOUR INTERPRETATION

The ability to interpret and visualize land form from contours is as essential as being able to read, write, or speak effectively. Skill in reading topography from a contour map can never be substituted for actually visiting the site, but when the two are combined, the information that can be gathered and recorded is indispensable to the designer. Before actually beginning to study a contour map, several things should be checked first to be sure of the proper interpretation.

Check the contour interval. This will be recorded somewhere in the legend or near the scale notation on the map. Common contour intervals are 1 ft, 2 ft, 5 ft, and 10 ft English, and .3 m, .5 m, 1 m, and 2 m metric. This means that the vertical distance between each pair of contour lines is 1 ft, 2 ft, 5 ft or 10 ft, respectively or .3 m, .5 m, 1 m, and 2 m metric.

Check the scale of the map. This will be recorded graphically, by a notation of one inch equals so many feet or by a unit equivalent notation. The unit equivalent is always used in the metric system and simply means that for each unit of measure on the map it equals so many in the field. For example, a scale of 1:24000 means that each inch on the map equals 24,000 inches in the field or for the same map 1 mm equals 24000 mm. To convert this to a scale of so many feet per inch, divide by 12. Thus a scale of 1:24000 converted to feet per inch is: 24000/12 = 2000 or 1 in = 2000 ft.

Check the data source. This will usually be shown by a note or in the legend. Field surveys will usually be more accurate than maps interpreted from aerial photographs. Also note the date that the map was done to be sure the information is current.

These three things directly effect the accuracy of the map and thus the accuracy of your interpretation. Small-scale maps with 5–10 foot contour (1 to 2 m) intervals are much less dependable than maps of larger scale. As a general rule of thumb, map accuracy can be taken as one half of the contour interval, horizontally and vertically. Thus a map with a one foot interval should be accurate to ±6 in while a map with a 10 ft interval will only be accurate to ±5 ft. After you have checked the map and have some idea of how accurate the data are, you are ready to begin your study.

In the beginning, it is best to start your interpretation systematically. Later, with more practice, you will undoubtedly develop a system more comfortable to you. But until you develop your proficiency, the system presented here will help you get started.

Orient the map with north to the top of the sheet. Then, identify focal points such as buildings, towers, power lines, or other man-made objects that will help you stay oriented. Observe the road and railroad patterns. They establish boundaries that are easily recognized, and major highways and railroads usually follow the ridgelines.

To effectively read topography you need to develop a vocabulary of land form. This is much the same as learning a graphic alphabet that describes land form, for in fact all similar land forms will be depicted the same way again and again. The contour pattern that describes a particular land form is referred to as the *contour signature*. Our objective here is to develop a working vocabulary of contour signatures and the associated land form. Once this is mastered the job of analysis becomes quite easy.

Ridge and Valley Contour Signatures

The contour signature for a ridge or valley is similar and easily identified. Both are repetitions of U-shaped lines as illustrated in Figure 1–6. If the bottom of the U-shaped points to a contour of lower elevation, it is a ridge (Figure 1–7). On the other hand if the bottom of a U-shaped contour points to a contour of higher elevation, it is a valley (Figure 1–8).

Usually ridge contours will be rounded, much less arrow-shaped than those of a valley. This is caused by the more intensive weathering and erosion that occurs in a valley. The small section from a USGS map (Figure 1–9) illustrates this very clearly.

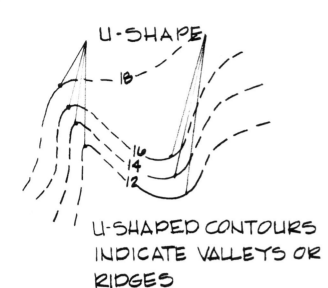

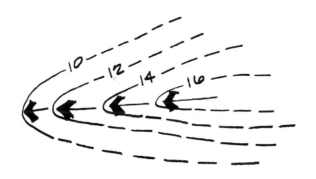

U-SHAPE

18

16
14
12

U-SHAPED CONTOURS
INDICATE VALLEYS OR
RIDGES

10 12 14 16

FIGURE 1-6

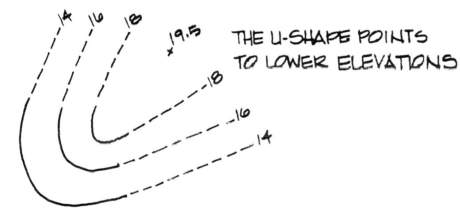

14 16 18

×19.5

THE U-SHAPE POINTS
TO LOWER ELEVATIONS

18

16

14

RIDGE SIGNATURE

FIGURE 1-7

16
14
12

THE U-SHAPE POINTS
TO HIGHER ELEVATIONS

12 14 16

VALLEY SIGNATURE

FIGURE 1-8

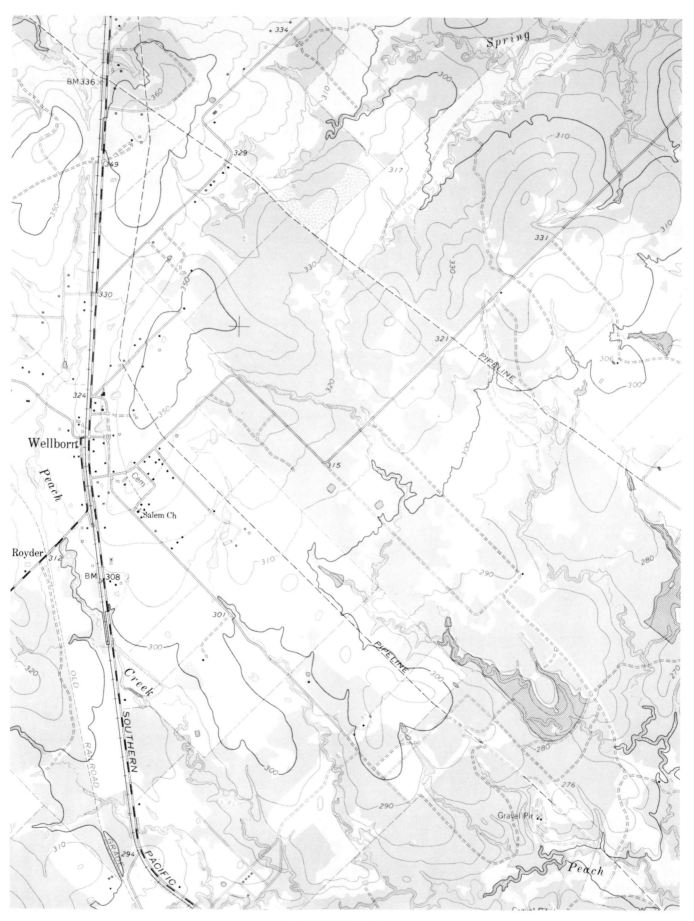

FIGURE 1-9

14

Once the ridge and valley lines have been identified, consider what we know about the site at this point. Notice that if you move away from the ridge line in any direction you will be going to a point of lower elevation. Likewise, if you move away from a valley line you are moving to a higher elevation. This all seems elementary, but it is important. A valley channel carries all the runoff from the land area up stream from any point between the ridge lines. What we have accomplished in this step is an identification of the natural drainage pattern as well as the high and low elevation points.

These ridge and valley associations are commonly called *watersheds*. More specifically, a watershed is the total land area that contributes runoff to a stream or group of streams.

Examining the Character of the Land Form

Observe the spacing of the contours in Figure 1–10. Contours that are closely spaced indicate steep slopes while widely spaced contours indicate flat, gently sloped land.

Steep slopes should generally be avoided for development since extensive grading will probably be

required. In addition, any modification of the surface vegetation will accelerate erosion and markedly increase runoff. Likewise, be suspicious of very flat terrain. Too little slope is just as bad as too much, because drainage will be sluggish and flooding becomes a distinct possibility.

Now observe how the contours are arranged in terms of spacing over a distance. This tells a lot about the overall character of the land itself. Contours closely spaced at the top of a slope and more widely spaced at the bottom are the signature of a concave slope, as can be seen in Figure 1–11. Contours spaced closely at the bottom of a slope and spread at the higher elevations, as in Figure 1–12, are the signature of a convex slope. Contours that are evenly spaced throughout are the signature of a uniform slope (see Figure 1–13). Contours that completely close within the limits of the map are the signatures of hills or depressions, as shown in Figure 1–14.

Now we can take this basic information a step further and begin to develop a catalog of land forms that will place these groups of contour signatures in a more meaningful vocabulary. None of these terms is new; in fact they are rather old-fashioned, and for

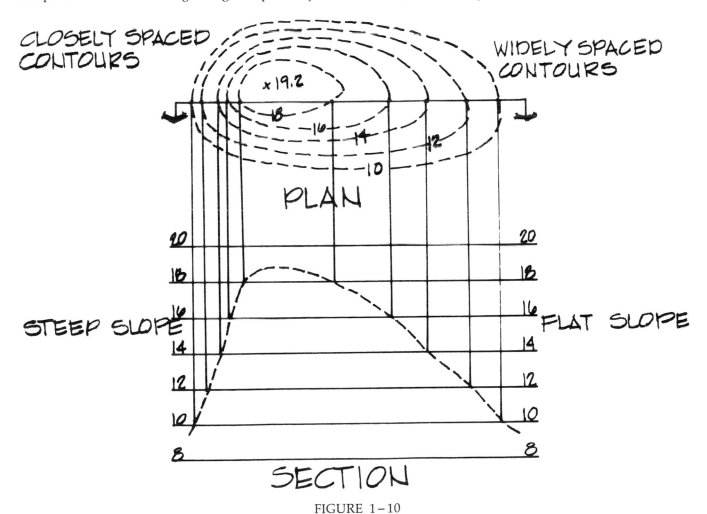

FIGURE 1–10

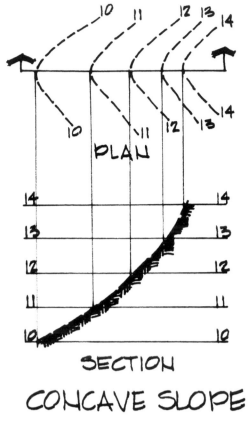

PLAN

SECTION

CONCAVE SLOPE

FIGURE 1–11

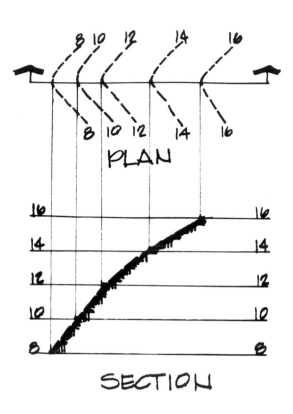

PLAN

SECTION

CONVEX SLOPE

FIGURE 1–12

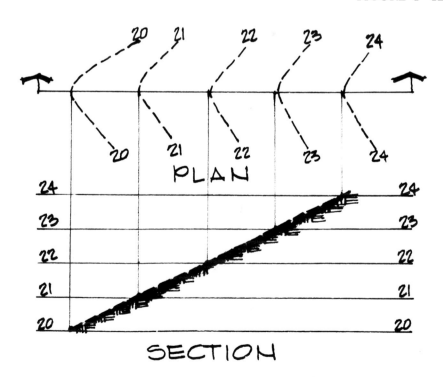

PLAN

SECTION

UNIFORM SLOPE

FIGURE 1–13

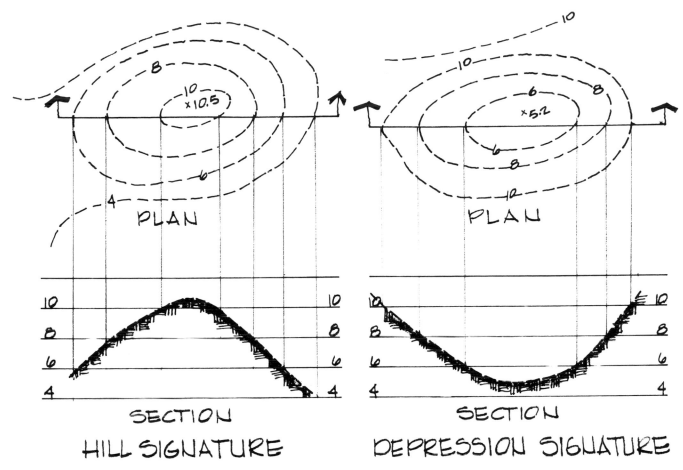

FIGURE 1–14

some reason they seem to have been lost to our more contemporary engineering conditioned vocabularies.

CLASSIFYING THE LAND FORM

In this step we think about the contour pattern in terms of the visual image it presents. What follows is a vocabulary that describes and characterizes the various shapes.

Terms Associated with Land Areas Bounded by Ridge Lines—Valleys

Glen or dale   A small narrow valley usually bounded by gently sloped concave sides (Figure 1–15).

Ravine   A deep valley bounded by steep slopes with little flat land at the base, usually only a stream bed (Figure 1–16).

Flood plain   A broad, flat to gently rolling land area bounded by distant distinct ridge lines (Figure 1–17).

Types of Hills and Ridge Lines

Hogs back   A long distinct ridge line, characterized by concave slopes at the sides (Figure 1–18).

Knoll   A hill usually round to oval-shaped with convex slopes (Figure 1–19).

Knob   An abrupt hill with concave slopes and a rounded top (Figure 1–20).

Camel back ridge   Paired knolls of near equal size that occur along a ridgeline (Figure 1–21).

Butte   A steep sided formation with a nearly flat top. These are usually igneous rock intrusions that have been exposed by the forces of erosion (Figure 1–22).

General Terms

These general terms describe topographic features that occur as points or as complete landscape units.

Bay and promontory   A bay is shaped by a ridge line, and the promontory is the dominant upland feature that shapes the bay (Figure 1–23).

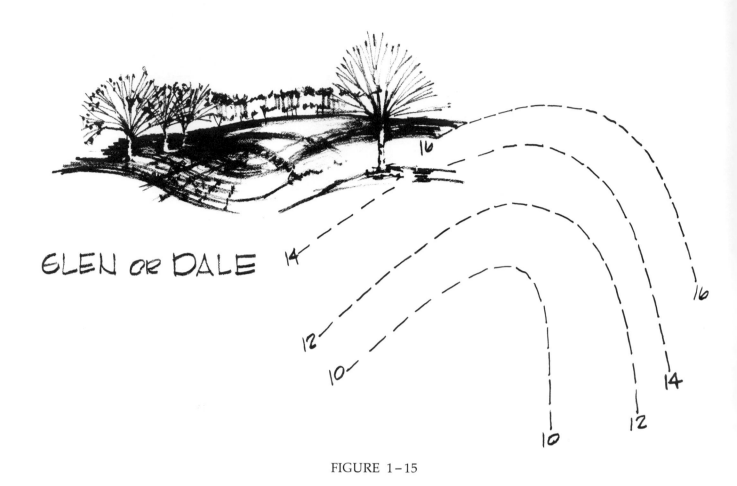

GLEN or DALE

FIGURE 1–15

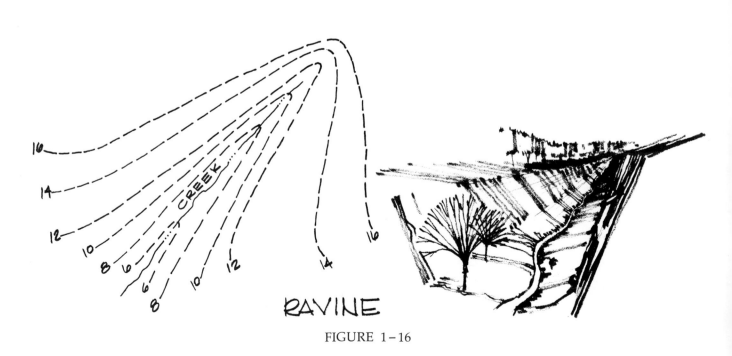

RAVINE

FIGURE 1–16

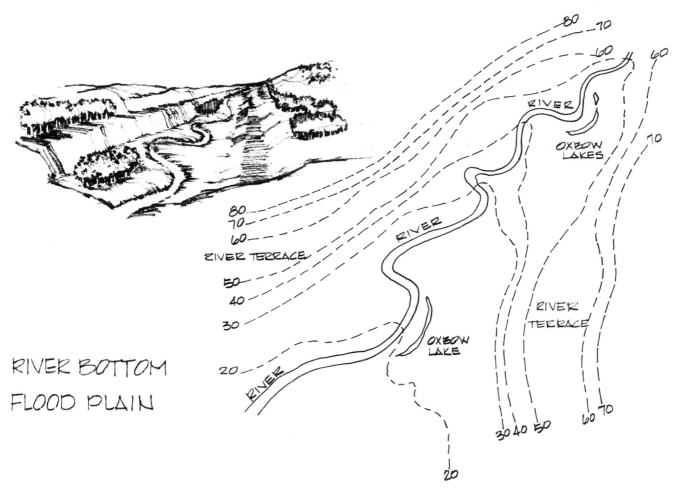

RIVER BOTTOM
FLOOD PLAIN

FIGURE 1–17

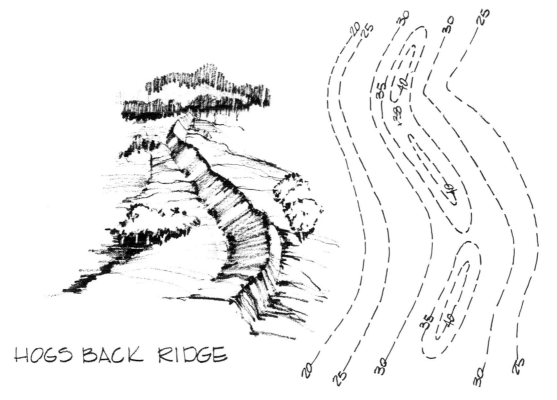

HOGS BACK RIDGE

FIGURE 1–18

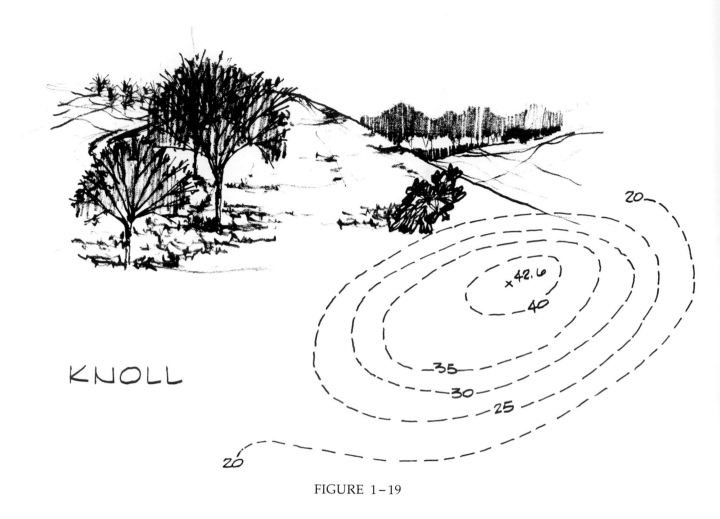

KNOLL

×42.6

40

35

30

25

20

20

FIGURE 1–19

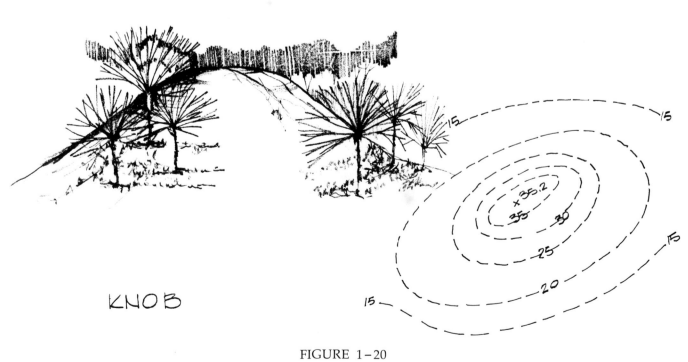

KNOB

×35.2

35

30

25

20

15

15

15

15

FIGURE 1–20

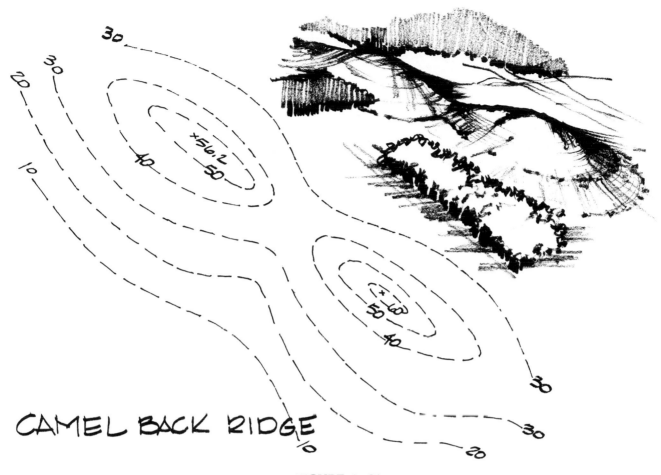

CAMEL BACK RIDGE

FIGURE 1–21

BUTTE

FIGURE 1–22

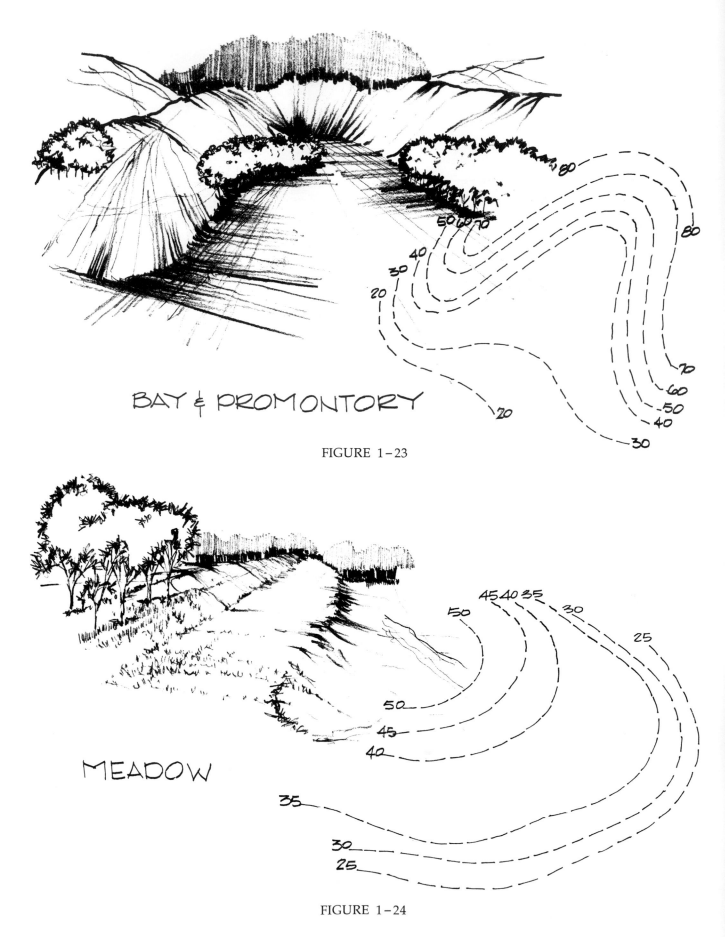

BAY & PROMONTORY

FIGURE 1-23

MEADOW

FIGURE 1-24

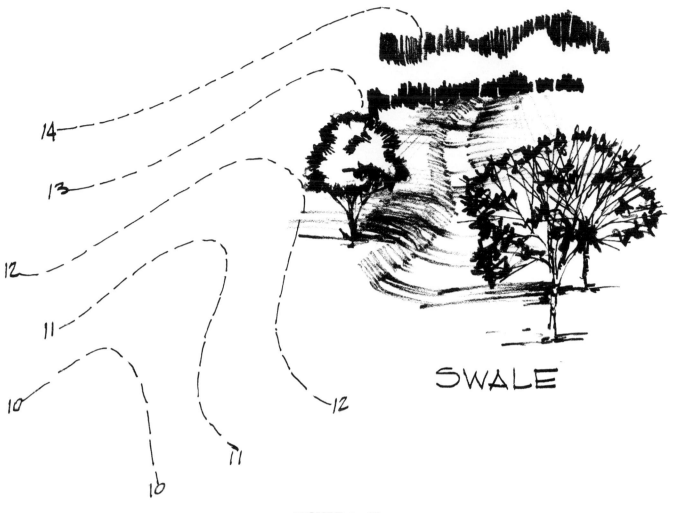

14

13

12

11

10

12

11

10

SWALE

FIGURE 1-25

Meadow   A flat to gently rolling plain that occurs on a hillside or along a ridge line (Figure 1–24).

Swale   A shallow lineal depression with a parabolic cross section and gently sloped sides (Figure 1–25).

Fan (alluvial fan)   A nearly flat deposition of water transported soil at the base of a watershed. The fan will usually be dissected by several water courses rather than a single stream as shown (Figure 1–26).

Toe (of the slope)   The toe is the point where the slope of a hill changes from its steep downward face to more gently sloped terrain. Where a structure is involved it may refer to the base of the cut or fill (Figure 1–27).

Saddle   The low point between two domes or knolls along a ridge line. This feature is sometimes referred to as a pass as well (Figure 1–28).

Crest   The point of highest elevation on a hill. This point is usually always marked on a topographic map by a spot elevation (Figure 1–29).

Military crest   The point on the slope of a hill that will not allow any person or object to be silhouetted against the horizon and also allows full view of the slope below (Figure 1–30).

This list is by no means all inclusive, nor is it meant to be. However, it can be most beneficial to beginning students to have a basic vocabulary of land form that helps associate contour signature with a mental image. Use of this vocabulary and a little practice will have you on your way to reading contour maps with little difficulty.

THE SIX CARDINAL LAWS OF CONTOURS

The following six contour characteristics are called laws because any deviation from them is not possi-

FAN

FIGURE 1-26

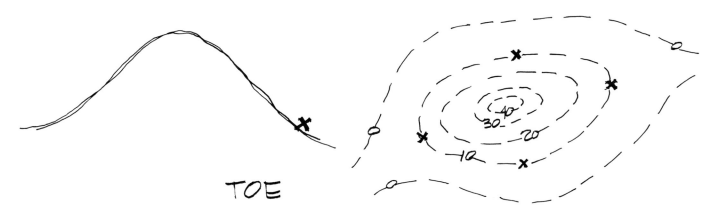

TOE

FIGURE 1-27

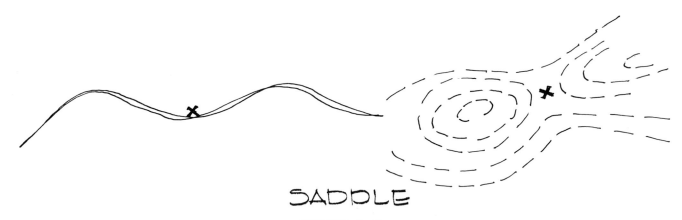

SADDLE

FIGURE 1-28

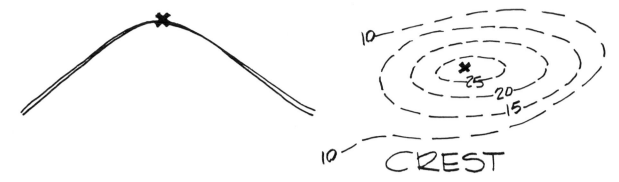

FIGURE 1-29

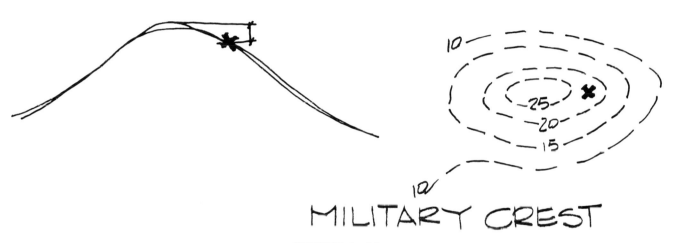

FIGURE 1-30

ble. Any time a plan indicates something contrary to these laws, it is wrong.

- Contours Always Occur in Pairs. Contours that indicate a ridge or depression will always close; therefore, on a map if you cross a 50 ft contour moving uphill, you must cross another 50 ft contour in making the transition to a downhill direction as shown in Figure 1-31.

- Contours Never Cross. Contour lines never cross each other unless an overhanging ledge is indicated. The situation shown in Figure 1-32 will sometimes occur on U.S.G.S. maps, but if it should occur on a site plan it is suspect.

- Contours Have Equal Vertical Separation. Contour lines always indicate equal change in vertical measure. In some unusual cases maps will be made with intermediate contours, but these are carefully marked and should be noted in the map legend.

The principle of equal separation is shown in Figure 1-33.

- All Contour Lines Close on Themselves. All contour lines will close some place on the face of the earth, even though they may not appear to on an individual map. This principle is illustrated in Figure 1-34. Those at 13 and 14 ft close, but the 12 ft contour appears to end at the edge of the sheet when in fact it closes as do the 11 ft and 10 ft contour lines.

- Contours Do Not Merge. Since contours must always occur in pairs they cannot merge as shown in top part of Figure 1-35. Contours must always be continuous and close on themselves.

- The Steepest Slope Is a Line Perpendicular to the Contour. This principle is illustrated in Figure 1-36. This point is important because water will always flow along the line of steepest slope.

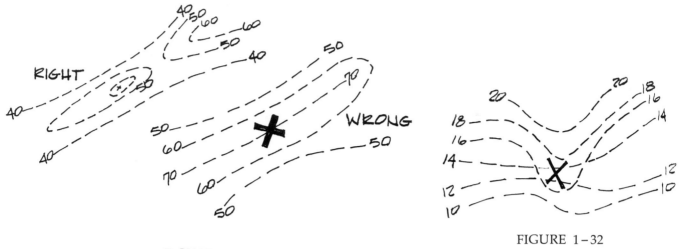

FIGURE 1-31

FIGURE 1-32

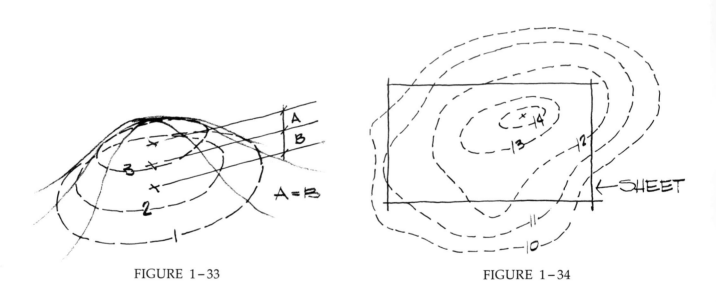

FIGURE 1-33

FIGURE 1-34

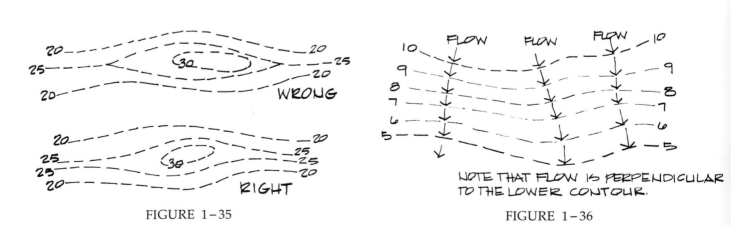

FIGURE 1-35

NOTE THAT FLOW IS PERPENDICULAR TO THE LOWER CONTOUR.

FIGURE 1-36

CONTOUR MANIPULATION

To this point we have developed a basic vocabulary for identifying natural land form. You have no doubt noticed that most of the natural contour signatures are smooth-flowing lines with no sharp angles or perfectly straight lines. These irregular forms while pleasing to the eye in their natural state are seldom satisfactory for use as a building site without some revision.

Revised contour patterns have typical signatures that are as easily identified and related to as natural signatures. In this section we will concentrate on developing skill in recognizing and applying these typical signatures to grading solutions. In essence, all grading solutions will involve a combination of these typical signatures blended together as a working unit. Once the mechanical necessities are satisfied, the designer is free to add finishing touches that will enhance the finished appearance.

All grading problems can be put in four broad categories: grading around buildings and structures (building floors and deck surfaces), grading evenly sloped surfaces, grading for roads and paths, and grading for drainage.

GRADING AROUND BUILDINGS AND STRUCTURES

Solutions to a grading problem are probably best studied and most easily visualized by manipulating the contour lines and preparing several rough grading plans. All preliminary studies and final grading plans should show both existing and revised contours, so the designer has a ready reference to how much the grade has been changed. By convention, the existing contours are shown as dashed lines and proposed contours are shown as solid lines.

Building floors are level planes of the same elevation over the entire surface. This elevation is usually given by the symbol "FF" meaning finished floor. Grading around a level plane can only be handled in four ways: by cutting, by filling, by cutting and filling, and by staying within the limit of the plane using retaining walls.

Grading Around a Level Area by Cutting

To achieve the proposed contour in Figure 1–37 by cutting, the following steps were used. First, the lowest contour adjacent to the slab is selected as the

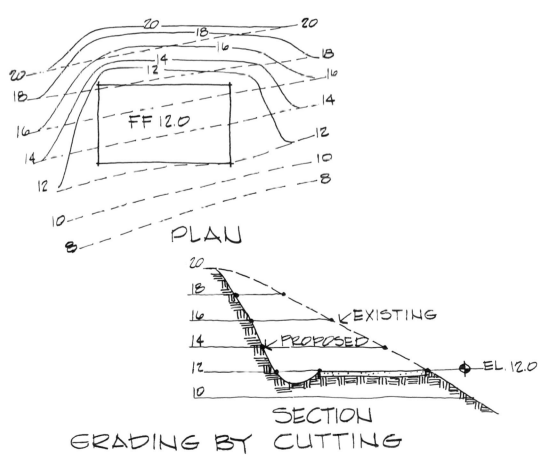

FIGURE 1–37

finished elevation of the slab surface. Then that contour (12 ft) is moved to the back or uphill side of the slab. The remaining contours are then adjusted around the 12 ft contour until none of the new lines cross existing lines. The reason the 12 ft contour moves to the back side is to provide positive drainage. This has the effect of generating a small drainage channel (swale) between the slab and the adjacent ground.

Grading Around a Level Area by Filling

Figure 1–38 shows a plan to grade an area by filling. The proposed contour is accomplished by first selecting the contour of the highest elevation (15 ft) as the finished elevation of the slab, and then adjusting it slightly to shed water away from the slab. The remaining contours are then moved to the downhill side of the slab and adjusted until none of the existing contours are crossed. Once again notice that the contour equal to the slab elevation occurs uphill of the slab to provide positive drainage. If this were not done, water flowing down the hill would run across

the slab. To say the least, this is undesirable if the slab is to support a house.

Grading Around a Level Area Using Cut and Fill

The objective of the cut and fill situation shown in Figure 1–39 is to balance the soil quantities on the site, thus eliminating the need to acquire or dispose of fill material. This is accomplished by establishing a slab elevation that is approximately between the highest and lowest contours adjacent to the slab, in this case 13 ft. With 13 ft as the FF of the slab, the 16 ft contour is moved to the uphill side. The 12 ft contour is then moved to the downhill side as illustrated. Then, as before, the remaining contours are adjusted until no existing lines are crossed.

Grading Around a Level Area
Inside the Limit of a Plane Using Retaining Walls
to Hold Existing Conditions

In this grading solution to the problem shown in Figure 1–40, the foundation wall of the slab or floor

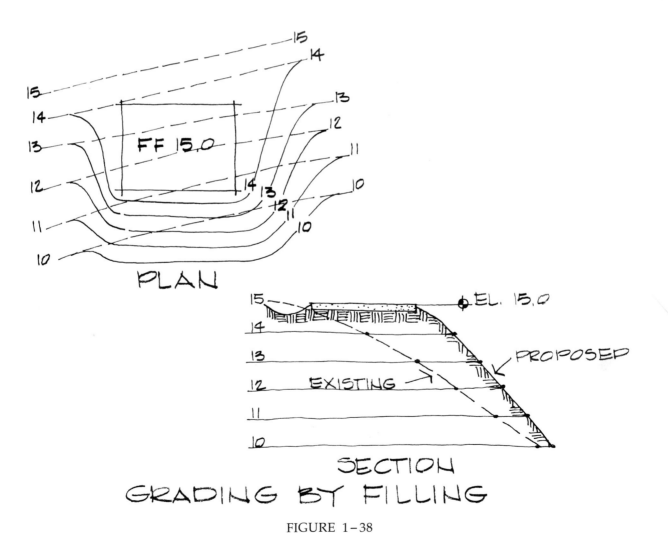

PLAN

SECTION

GRADING BY FILLING

FIGURE 1–38

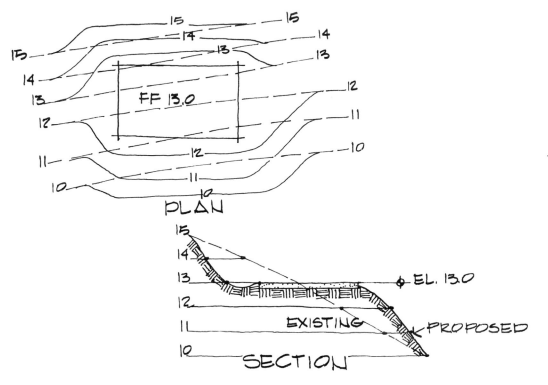

PLAN

SECTION

EXISTING   PROPOSED

φ EL. 13.0

GRADING BY CUTTING & FILLING

FIGURE 1-39

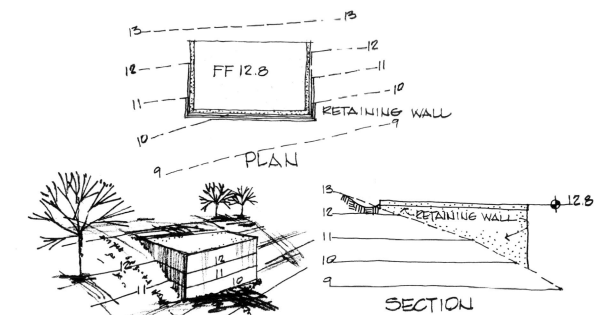

FF 12.8

RETAINING WALL

PLAN

PERSPECTIVE

SECTION

RETAINING WALL

φ 12.8

GRADING WITH RETAINING WALLS

FIGURE 1-40

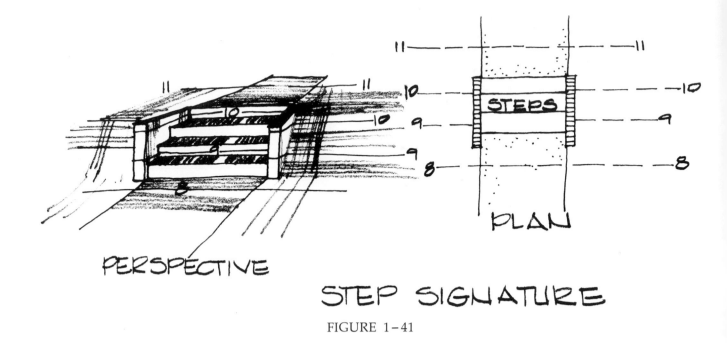

PERSPECTIVE

PLAN

STEP SIGNATURE

FIGURE 1–41

plane becomes exposed and acts as a retaining wall at its inside or outside surface. For many situations this solution is the most practical, but it seems to be the most difficult for the beginning student to visualize in plan because the contour lines appear to violate the law that says contours do not merge.

The following example should be studied carefully and the principle mastered because it will occur frequently. Contours 10, 11, and 12 in Figure 1–40 are shown as heavy lines to illustrate their revised condition only. This would not be shown on a grading plan. Note that if the plan is drawn contours 10, 11, and 12 appear to dead-end into the slab and merge with each other; but as you can see from the perspective, they are in fact on the face of the wall still separated vertically by a foot. Steps are also a good example of this. In plan the contour lines appear to dead-end into the cheek walls, but in fact the contours continue around the walls as shown in the perspective in Figure 1–41.

GRADING EVENLY SLOPED SURFACES

Many exterior surfaces that are exposed to the weather at first glance appear flat but in fact are uniformly sloped planes to shed water. Patios, terraces, athletic fields, and parking lots most commonly fall in this category. The only difference between the contour signature for this condition and the previous conditions is that the revised contours will cross the plane of the surface. The shape of the contour signature is dependent on two things: cross-section and the slope of the surface. The following examples are typical grading solutions that involve sloping surfaces. Each example should be studied in relation to the fixed cross-section, the uniform slope and the resulting contour signatures they generate.

In the first condition (shown in Figure 1–42), the surface slopes in one direction only, remaining level over its longitudinal dimension. Note that the contours are straight mechanical lines parallel to the longitudinal dimension of the surface. They are also evenly spaced on the surface because of the fixed cross-section.

Figure 1–43 illustrates a situation where both the cross-section and the longitudinal surface are sloping lines. When this occurs, the contours will cross the surface diagonally. But, as long as the slope and cross-section remain fixed, the contours will be equally spaced and parallel.

Anytime a valleyed section is used the contour signature develops a chevron pattern as illustrated in Figure 1–44 with the top or point of the chevron always pointing to the higher elevation.

GRADING FOR ROADS AND WAYS

Grading for roads and ways is similar to the situations encountered for evenly sloped slabs. The major difference is the different cross-sections used. This of

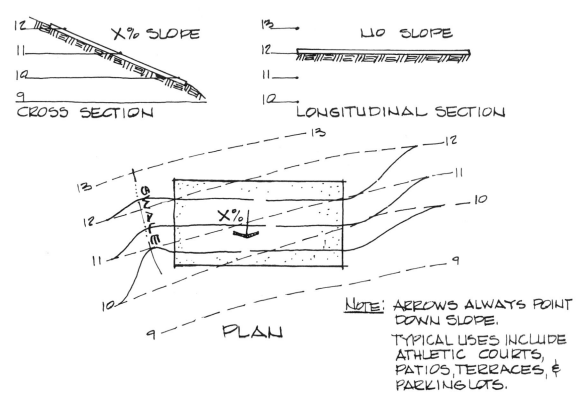

SHEET DRAINAGE - SINGLE SLOPE

FIGURE 1-42

NOTE: ARROWS ALWAYS POINT DOWN SLOPE.

TYPICAL USES INCLUDE ATHLETIC COURTS, PATIOS, TERRACES, & PARKING LOTS.

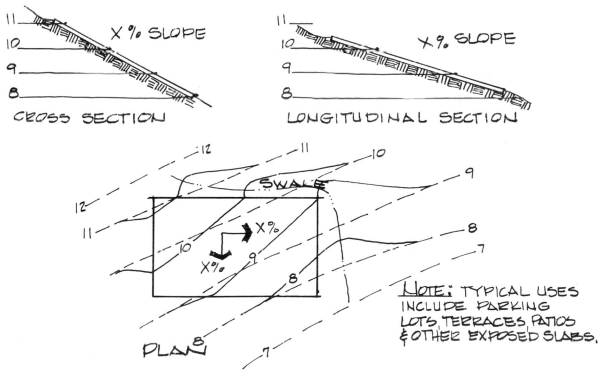

SHEET DRAINAGE - DOUBLE SLOPE

FIGURE 1-43

NOTE: TYPICAL USES INCLUDE PARKING LOTS, TERRACES, PATIOS & OTHER EXPOSED SLABS.

course changes the contour signature. As in the previous section each contour signature should be studied in terms of its appearance in plan and its related cross-section. One thing should be kept in mind at this point, when dealing with contour signatures that are the result of two lines of slope the flatter the slope the more exaggerated the contour will become.

Typical Street with Curb and Gutter

The typical signature of this condition is a W shape becoming more exaggerated as the slope decreases as shown in Figure 1–45. Note also that the middle of the W at the centerline of the street points toward the lower elevation.

Typical Roadway with Drainage at Both Edges

The signature of this condition is very similar to the curb and gutter condition because it is still a W

form pointing toward the lower elevation along the centerline (see Figure 1–46).

A variation of this condition occurs when roads are cut into a hillside. This causes a ditch on one side with the hill sloping away on the other. This is illustrated in Figure 1–47.

GRADING FOR DRAINAGE

In essence grading for drainage is the transition element that will connect the contour signatures of the previous elements. In other words, water will be directed away from buildings and outdoor surfaces and channeled to some collector. Frequently this will be the street, but it can be an existing water body, stream, or drainage inlet.

Generally speaking, there are only two types of surface channels; the swale and the ditch. A ditch is usually 2 or more feet deep with steep sides. A swale is shallow, but sometimes very wide, and usually has

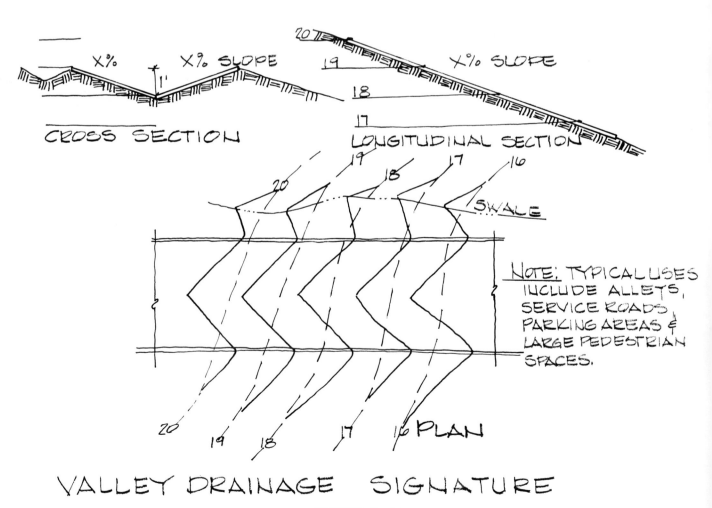

VALLEY DRAINAGE SIGNATURE

FIGURE 1–44

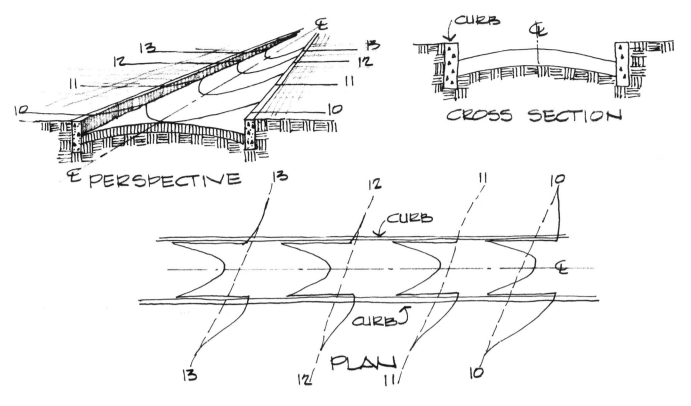

13 12 11 10

£ PERSPECTIVE

CURB £ CROSS SECTION

13 12 11 10

CURB

£

CURB

13 12 11 10

PLAN

CURB & GUTTER STREET SIGNATURE

FIGURE 1-45

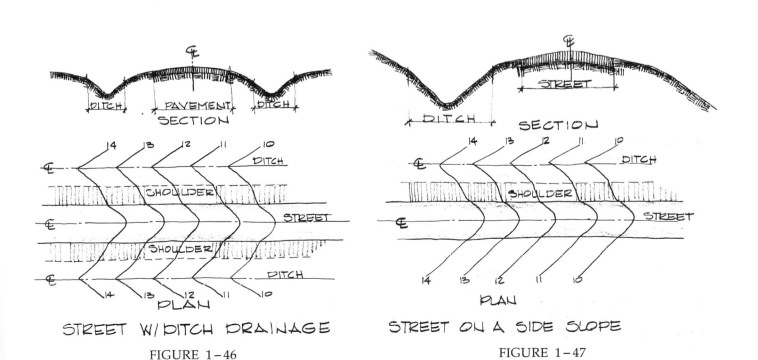

£

DITCH PAVEMENT DITCH
SECTION

14 13 12 11 10

£ DITCH

SHOULDER

£ STREET

SHOULDER

£ DITCH

14 13 12 11 10

PLAN

£

STREET

DITCH SECTION

14 13 12 11 10

£ DITCH

SHOULDER

£ STREET

14 13 12 11 10

PLAN

STREET W/DITCH DRAINAGE

FIGURE 1-46

STREET ON A SIDE SLOPE

FIGURE 1-47

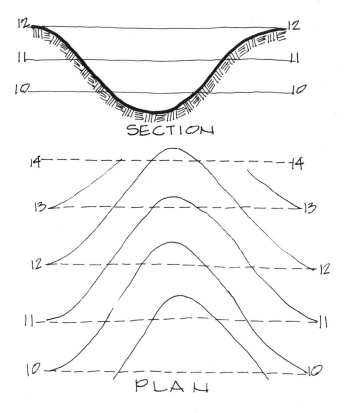

DRAINAGE DITCH SIGNATURE

FIGURE 1–48

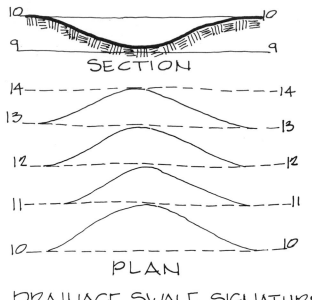

DRAINAGE SWALE SIGNATURE

FIGURE 1–49

a parabolic section. The contour signatures are easily recognized as illustrated in Figures 1–48 and 1–49, respectively.

While these two signatures are easily recognized, many beginning students have problems handling transitions to swales around buildings and what happens when roads or ways cross swales and ditches. The small sketches that follow in Figures 1–50 to 1–54 are some typical examples of how these transitions are made.

Figure 1–50 illustrates a curved swale. This condition most frequently occurs around a building foundation. Figure 1–51 illustrates the use of curved swales in conjunction with a foundation slab. Figure 1–52 illustrates the contour signature that results when a street crosses a drainage swale. The head wall and end wall of the culvert act as a retaining wall. Notice that the 14 ft contour appears to dead-end at each wall. Actually the contour continues through the culvert on the wall of the pipe.

Figures 1–53 and 1–54 illustrate the contour signatures that occur at low points and high points on roads. At a low point (Figure 1–53), the contours on the centerline point to the low elevation; at a high point (Figure 1–54), the contours point away from the high elevation.

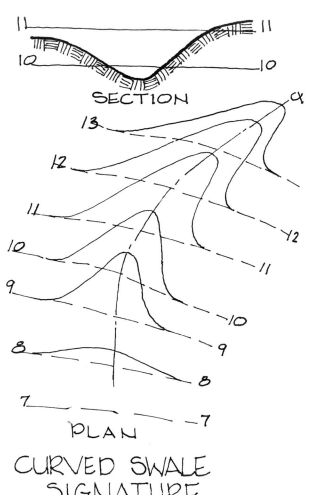

CURVED SWALE
SIGNATURE

FIGURE 1–50

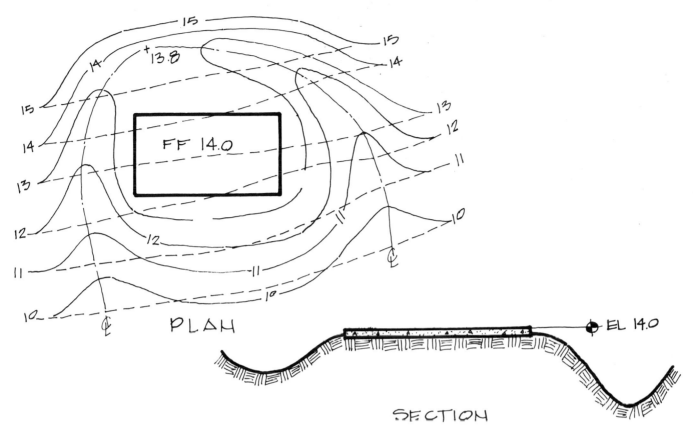

PLAN

SECTION

SWALE TRANSITION AROUND A SLAB

FIGURE 1-51

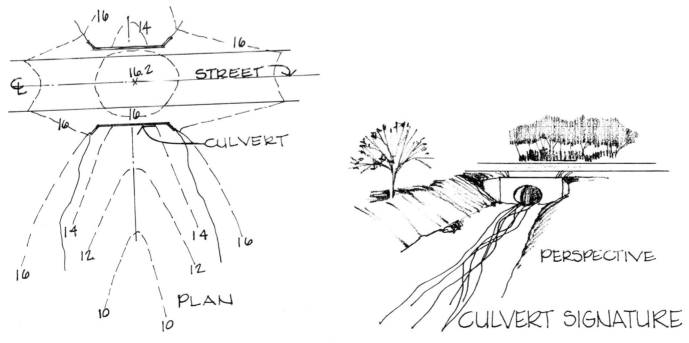

PLAN

PERSPECTIVE

CULVERT SIGNATURE

FIGURE 1-52

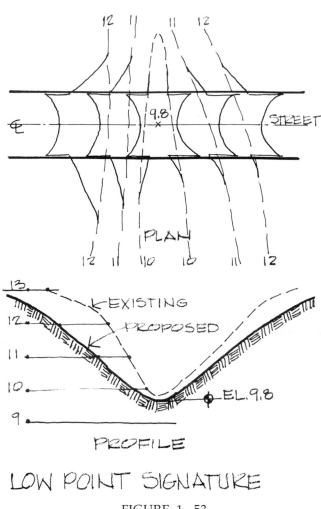

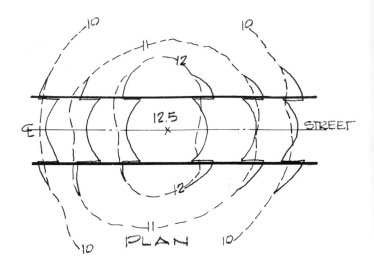

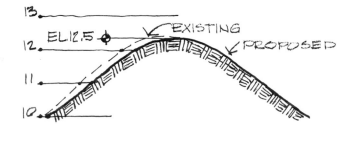

LOW POINT SIGNATURE

FIGURE 1–53

HIGH POINT SIGNATURE

FIGURE 1–54

GRADING STANDARDS

To this point in our discussion we have concentrated on recognition of contour signatures for natural and revised conditions. By now you should be able to quickly recognize ridge and valley patterns, steep and shallow slopes, as well as the signatures of man-made features such as roads, parking areas, flat areas around structures, drainage swales, and their variations. In this section we will work on expanding these interpretive skills into a decision-making vocabulary that can be used to develop solutions to grading problems.

In the beginning it should be emphasized that when we are discussing grading solutions for specific situations and applying a recommended standard, that a standard is not an absolute. Guides for standard practice are just that, guides. When you see a recommended standard with an upper and lower limit, you can be sure that the most desirable condition will be about the middle. The range is given merely to establish an upper and lower limit for practical use and minimum restriction. The final decision as to what is or is not acceptable must rest with the designer, there is no 100% right or wrong solution. So what we are giving you here is a set of tools that will help you make valid, workable, design decisions.

Standards for Grading

Good grading practice is based on many considerations. Probably the most important are: climate, character of the existing topography, soil and subsoil properties, and visual context. These four criteria will largely establish the upper and lower limits of what will be an acceptable solution. For example, it is usually desirable to keep the grade or slope on residential streets to 8% or less. But in demanding mountainous terrain, it is not uncommon to find slopes in excess of 14%. Again, the designer has the final responsibility of deciding the acceptable limits.

As we have already discussed there are four types of grading situations involved in all construction work: grading around the structures, grading the surface of adjacent land, grading for roads and paths, and grading for drainage.

Grading Around Structures

Figure 1–55 and Table 1–3 present acceptable guidelines for grading around structures. The primary concern for this situation is to be sure that the structure is accessible to vehicles and people, as required, and that surface water is channeled around and away from the structure.

The distance from the building to the centerline of the swale should be 10 ft or more if possible, but never less than 5 ft. The width of the swale and its depth will be determined by the volume of water it will be required to carry. This will be discussed in more detail in Chapter 3.

Grading Adjacent Land

The grading that occurs away from buildings and structures is no less important than what occurs immediately next to the building. This is all too often overlooked until the last minute and can have disastrous effects on the success of a project. Figure 1–56 and Table 1–4 provide accepted guidelines for the more common situations.

Grading Paths and Ways

The grading standards for streets are somewhat involved depending on the situation. However, Figure 1–57 and Table 1–5 give some general standards. Detailed standards for street grading will be developed further in Chapter 2. Table 1–5 also provides standards for grades on sidewalks, unpaved roads, and trails.

Grading for Drainage

Figure 1–58 and Table 1–6 give some accepted practices for grading to provide surface drainage. Drainage channels like streets and highways have some critical design parameters that govern their exact dimensions. These will be developed further in Chapter 3. Nonetheless, the information in Table 1–6 is very useful in making initial grading decisions.

The suggested standards given in Tables 1–3 to 1–6 have been compiled from figures published in reference manuals, standard specification outlines, U.S. government publications, and building codes. You will no doubt, in your course of study and work, encounter standards that conflict with those presented here. Do not be alarmed; as mentioned earlier there are no absolute values.

CALCULATING GRADES

Natural contour signatures are the result of geological weathering processes. Like anything else created by nature each feature is unique. The shape of a revised contour signature, however, is the result of preestablished values for either the slope (gradient), horizontal distance (length) or the vertical difference in elevation. These elements have an exact mathematical relationship represented by the algebraic expression:

$$D = G \times L,$$

where:

D = Vertical difference in elevation in feet

L = Horizontal distance in feet

G = Slope or the gradient as a percent

This is easily visualized as a basic right triangle (Figure 1–59). (See bottom of page 41.)

As with any three-term relationship, when any two terms in the expression are known the other can be found. Thus if

$$D = G \times L,$$

solve for G by dividing by L:

$$\frac{D}{L} = \frac{G \times L}{L}, \qquad G = \frac{D}{L}.$$

Solve for L by dividing by G:

$$\frac{D}{G} = \frac{G \times L}{G}, \qquad L = \frac{D}{G}.$$

This relationship is an indispensable tool to the grading design process and should be committed to memory. You will use it time and time again.

To demonstrate how final grading solutions are calculated, let's work back through the contour signatures of the four broad categories of grading solutions and see how they are calculated mathematically. It is recommended that when you begin your study of this section you sketch the problem on paper and work out the solutions to each situation as it is described in the text. The illustrations for each situation will have a series of figures that illustrate the step-by-step development of the solution. The calculations will be worked out for each step.

Grading for Drainage

Since practically all grading plans involve channeling surface water around and away from structures, let us investigate this situation first. The most common method of handling surface water is to develop

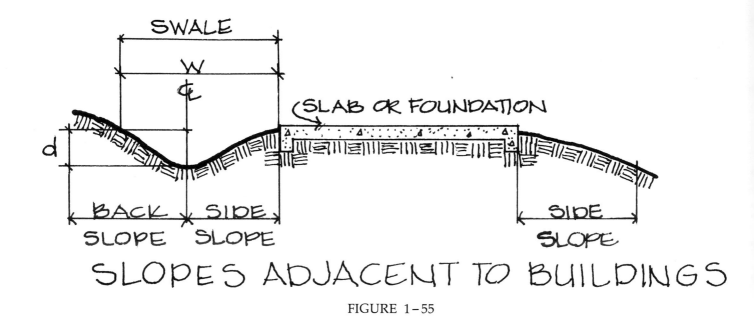

SLOPES ADJACENT TO BUILDINGS

FIGURE 1–55

TABLE 1–3
Guidelines for Grading Around Structures

CONDITION	MAXIMUM		MINIMUM		RANGE PREFERRED
Side slopes with vehicular access	10%	10:1	0.5%	200:1	1–3%
Back slopes with vehicular access	15%	6.66:1	0.5%	200:1	1–5%
Side slopes without vehicular access	15%	6.66:1	0.5%	200:1	1–10%
Back slopes without vehicular access	20%	5:1	0.5%	200:1	1–10%

Note: Upper limits should be avoided where icing is frequent. Flat slopes should also be avoided in wet climates.

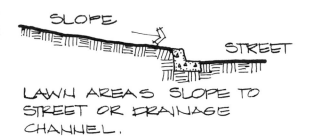

SLOPE   STREET

LAWN AREAS SLOPE TO
STREET OR DRAINAGE
CHANNEL.

SLOPE

CROWNED SECTIONS ARE
USED FOR ATHLETIC FIELDS,
PLAY AREAS & TRAFFIC ISLANDS.

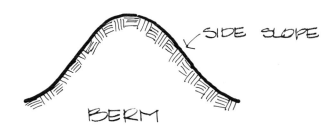

SIDE SLOPE

BERM

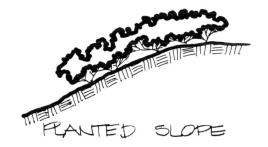

PLANTED SLOPE

THE SIDE SLOPES OF BERMS
AND PLANTED SLOPES MUST
BE SELECTED CAREFULLY
DEPENDING ON THE SOIL AND
THE PLANT COVER.

SLOPES OF GENERAL LANDSCAPE AREAS

FIGURE 1–56

TABLE 1–4
Standards for Grading Adjacent Lands

CONDITION	MAXIMUM		MINIMUM		PREFERRED
Lawns and grass areas	25%	4:1[a]	1%	100:1	1.5–10%
Grassed athletic fields	2%	50:1	0.5%	200:1	1%
Berms and mounds	20%	5:1	5%	20:1	10%
Mowed slopes	25%	4:1[a]	—		20%
Unmowed grass banks	Material ∠ of repose		—		<25%
Planted slopes and beds	10%	10:1	0.5%	200:1	3–5%[b]

[a]25% is approximately the maximum slope that mowing machinery can work.
[b]Slopes covered only by shrub material will tend to erode above 10%.

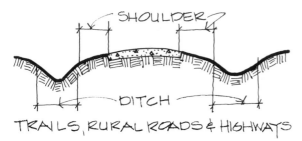

TRAILS, RURAL ROADS & HIGHWAYS

URBAN STREETS & PUBLIC PARKING

LOCAL AND FEEDER STREETS

VALLEY SECTION

PARKING AREAS, UTILITY & SERVICE ROADS.

SLOPES OF STREETS & WAYS

FIGURE 1-57

TABLE 1-5
Standards for Grading Streets and Ways

CONDITION	MAXIMUM		MINIMUM		PREFERRED	
Crown of improved streets	3%	33⅓:1	1%	100:1	2%	50:1
Crown of unimproved roads	3%	33⅓:1	2%	50:1	2.5%	40:1
Slide slope on walks	4%	25:1	1%	100:1	1-2%	
Tree lawns	20%	5:1	1%	100:1	2-3%	
Slope of shoulders	15%	66⅔:1	1%	100:1	2-3%	
Longitudinal slope of streets	20%	5:1	0.5%	200:1	1-10%	
Longitudinal slope of driveways	20%	5:1	0.25%	400:1	1-10%	
Longitudinal slope of parking areas	5%	20:1	0.25%	400:1	2-3%	
Longitudinal slope of sidewalks	10%	10:1	0.5%	200:1	1-5%	
Longitudinal slope of valleyed section	5%	25:1	0.5%	200:1	2-3%	

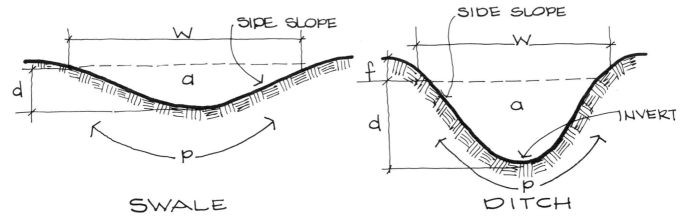

SWALE   DITCH

TERMS

W - WIDTH OF THE CHANNEL
d - DEPTH OF THE CHANNEL
a - AREA OF THE CROSS SECTION
p - WETTED PERIMETER
f - FREEBOARD
INVERT - BOTTOM ELEVATION OF THE CHANNEL

SLOPES OF DRAINAGE CHANNELS

FIGURE 1-58

TABLE 1-6
Standards for Drainage Channels

CONDITION	MAXIMUM		MINIMUM		PREFERRED
Swale side slopes	10%	10:1	1%	100:1	2%
Longitudinal slope of swales					
a) grass invert	8%	12.5:1	1%	100:1	1.5-2%
b) paved invert	12%	8.33:1	0.5%	100:1	4-6%
Ditchside slopes	∠ of repose		—		20-25%
a) grass invert	8%	12.5:1	1%	100:1	2-3%
b) paved invert	10%		—		5-6%

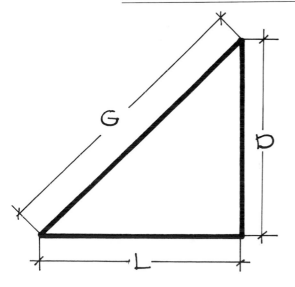

G - GRADIENT

D - VERTICAL DIFFERENCE

L - HORIZONTAL DISTANCE

FIGURE 1-59

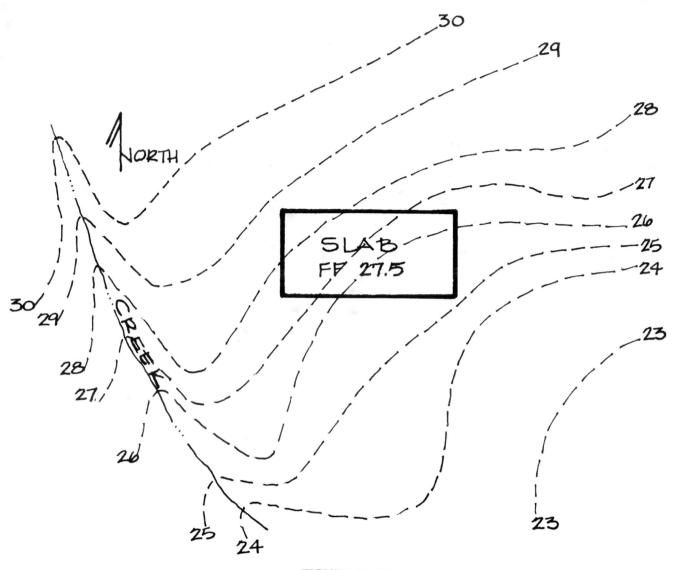

FIGURE 1–60

a swale that collects the water and moves it to a disposal point, such as a catch basin, lake, or creek. If a swale is not used the land is usually just sloped uniformly toward some linear disposal point, such as a creek, ditch, or street.

To demonstrate the construction of a drainage swale, consider Figure 1–60. The slab is to have a finished floor elevation of 27.5 ft. The problem is to construct drainage swales to carry water around the slab and downhill toward the creek. The following criteria have been selected by the designer:

- Slope of the swale centerline 2%;
- Side slopes maximum of 10%, minimum of 2%;
- Back slopes maximum of 20% and minimum of 2%;
- The swale is to be 20 ft from the edge of the slab;
- Hold the 27 ft elevation around the base of the slab.

First construct the centerline of the swale 20 ft from

the back edge of the slab. Notice that the natural drainage is to the right, so the swale will begin at the upper left-hand corner and run around the slab to the right.

The centerline is extended to a 45° construction line and the elevations of the beginning point and the corner intersection are calculated as shown in Figure 1–61:

Point A   Use the minimum 2% slope for 20 ft and assume a ground elevation of 27.0 ft. Find D if:

$$L = 20 \text{ ft}, \quad G = .02,$$
$$D = G \times L = 20 \times .02 = .4 \text{ ft.}$$

Elevation of point A = 27.0 − .4 = 26.6 ft.

Point B   Scales about 70 ft from point A. Therefore:

$$L = 70 \text{ ft}, \quad G = .02,$$
$$D = G \times L = .02 \times 70 = 1.4 \text{ ft.}$$

Elevation of point B = 26.6 − 1.4 = 25.2 ft.

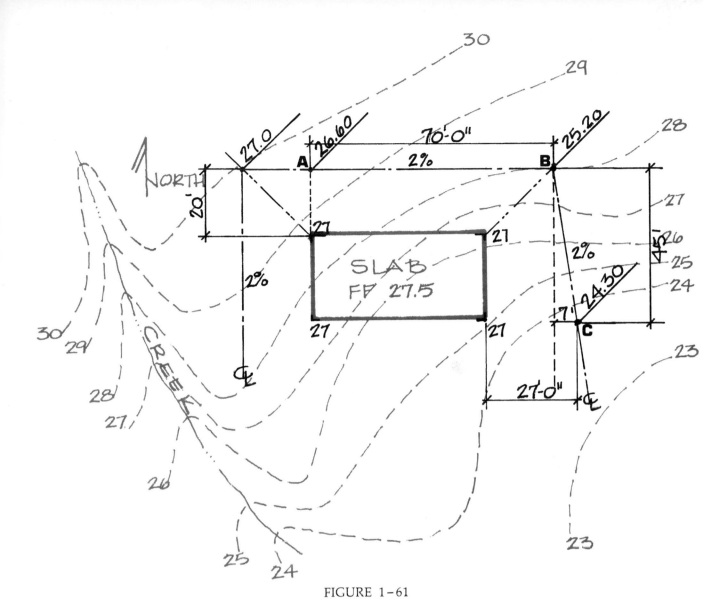

FIGURE 1–61

Point C With this information recorded, extend the centerline along the right side of the slab to the front edge and calculate its elevation as follows. The distance from B to C scales 45 ft. Thus:

$$L = 45 \text{ ft}, \qquad G = .02,$$
$$D = G \times L = .02 \times 45 = .9 \text{ ft}.$$

Elevation of point C = 25.2 − .9 = 24.3 ft.

Next check to see how far away from the front edge of the slab this elevation must be to maintain the maximum 10% side slope. The difference in elevation is 27 − 24.3 = 2.7. Now find L if:

$$D = 2.7 \text{ ft.}, \qquad G = .1,$$
$$L = \frac{D}{G} = \frac{2.7}{.1} = 27 \text{ ft}.$$

Thus the 24.3 ft elevation should occur 27 ft from the slab to hold a 10% side slope. Plot this information on the plan and proceed to locate the even contours. First locate the points of equal elevation on

the centerline of the swale designated as points D and E.

Point D The even 26 ft elevation lies between points A and B. Therefore:

$$D = .6 \text{ ft}, \qquad G = .02,$$
$$L = \frac{D}{G} = \frac{.6}{.02} = 30 \text{ ft}.$$

Point E The even 25 ft elevation occurs between points B and C.

$$D = .2 \text{ ft}, \qquad G = .02,$$
$$L = \frac{D}{G} = \frac{.2}{.02} = 10 \text{ ft}.$$

Now, since the wide slope is 10% opposite point C, the contours will be spaced 10 ft apart at that corner so the 26 ft and 25 ft contours are plotted on that side as shown in Figure 1–62.

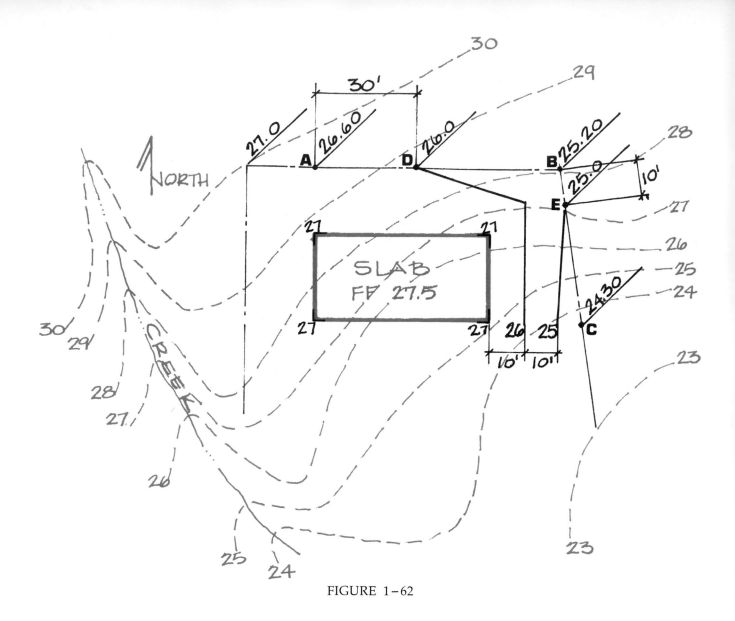

FIGURE 1–62

The 25 ft contour is extended to point E, and the 26 ft contour is extended to the construction line and then to point D. This is shown in Figure 1–61.

Point F In Figure 1–63 the contours are plotted on the back slope as follows. First locate the even 26 ft elevation uphill from point B as:

$$D = .80 \text{ ft } (26 - 25.2 = .80),$$
$$G = .20 \text{ (20\% back slope allowed)},$$

$$L = \frac{D}{G} = \frac{.80}{.20} = 4 \text{ ft.}$$

The contour is 4 ft uphill of point B and is designated as point F.
Next find the spacing of 1 ft contours at a slope of 20%.

$$D = 1.0 \text{ ft}, \qquad G = .20,$$

$$L = \frac{L}{G} = \frac{1}{.20} = 5 \text{ ft.}$$

This means that the 26 ft contour is located 5 ft from point E and all other contours are parallel to each other 5 ft apart. To plot them, construct a series of parallel lines 5 ft apart on either edge and extend each set of lines until they intersect. The information plotted so far is summarized in Figure 1–63. Notice that the contours on the right side of the slab stop where they meet the existing contours.

Point G On Figure 1–64 notice that there is a high point of 27 ft at the upper left-hand corner of the slab, designated point G.

Point H From here we will drop the centerline of the second swale meeting the same criteria of a 2% slope. So the elevation of point H is calculated as:

$$L = 45 \text{ ft}, \qquad G = .02,$$
$$D = G \times L = .02 \times 45 = .90 \text{ ft.}$$

Elevation of point H = 27 − .90 = 26.10 ft.

44

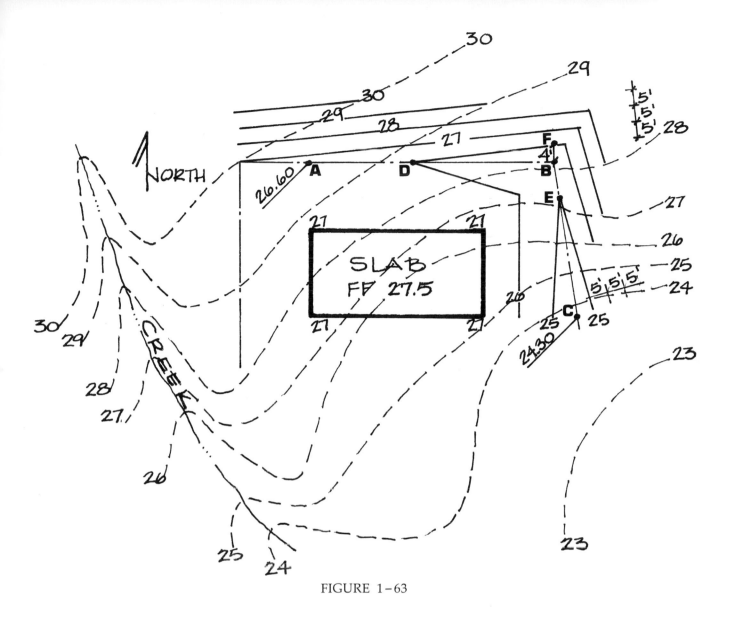

FIGURE 1-63

With this known, locate the 27 ft contour opposite point H and plot the remaining contours on the back slope as follows: Find L (the distance from point H to the 27 ft contour) if:

D = .90 ft (difference between 26.10 and 27),
G = .20 (allowed back slope),

$$L = \frac{D}{G} = \frac{.90}{.20} = 4.5 \text{ ft.}$$

The remaining contours, 28, 29, and 30 are evenly spaced 5 ft apart and parallel to 27 as shown. They are extended until they intersect the lines uphill.

Next locate the even 26 ft contour on the centerline and connect it to the existing conditions as shown. From point H, find L if:

D = 1.0 ft, G = .20,

$$L = \frac{D}{G} = \frac{1.0}{.20} = 5 \text{ ft.}$$

Since a side slope of 10% is required, the contours passing in front of the slab are evenly spaced 10 ft apart and parallel to the slab. There lines are now constructed and the plan is complete as illustrated in Figure 1-64.

In Figure 1-64 notice that the 24 ft contour was simply extended uphill until it met the old 24 ft contour to maintain the 10% slope on the right side of the slab. This solution is technically correct at this point, but it is not a finished solution for two reasons. First, it would be very difficult to shape the ground in such a regimented form and expect it to remain. Second, even if it were possible, the result would be visually distracting. Thus, as illustrated in Figure 1-65, the contours are generalized to a smoother, more natural form. This will help blend the changes back into the landscape.

The centerline of the swale was also generalized to a freehand line and spot elevations are shown at important points. The desired side slopes and back slopes are then noted as a ratio of horizontal distance

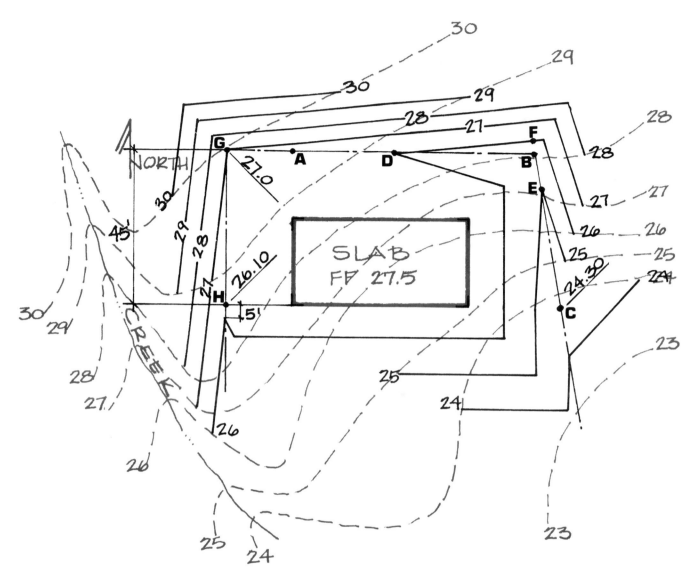

FIGURE 1–64

to vertical difference. In this case 5:1 (20%) and 10:1 (10%).

Keep in mind that in the field situation it is the spot elevations and slope notations that are used to translate the drawing into a finished product. The contour lines only serve as an auxiliary tool to depict form.

Grading Around Buildings

The problem of grading around buildings is essentially the same as the situation encountered in grading for drainage. The objective, once again, is to move the water away from the foundation slab. In our last problem though we used slopes that were a little too steep for normal work, so in this example we will use more realistic criteria.

- All slopes within 60 ft of the structure maximum 5%;
- Slope of the swale centerline 2%;
- The ground elevations around the building can vary as required;
- Slopes from the building to the swale should be 2%.

To solve the problem proceed as in Figure 1–66. Plot the centerline of the swale 10 ft from the edge of the slab and calculate the high point elevation and the elevations of A to D as follows:

High Point:

$$L = 10 \, \text{ft}, \qquad G = .02,$$
$$D = G \times L = 10 \times .02 = .20 \, \text{ft}.$$
$$\text{High Point} = 20 - .20 = 19.80 \, \text{ft}.$$

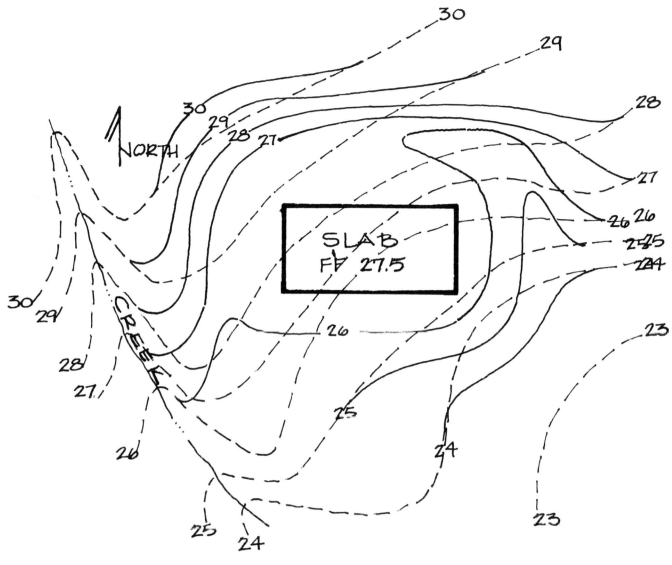

FIGURE 1-65

The swale is to drain in both directions away from this high point so the elevations of points A and B are the same and C and D are also.

Points A and B:

$$L = 25 \text{ ft}, \qquad G = .01,$$
$$D = G \times L = 25 \times .01 = .25 \text{ ft}.$$
$$A \text{ and } B = 19.80 - .25 = 19.55 \text{ ft}.$$

Points C and D:

$$L = 30 \text{ ft}, \qquad G = .01,$$
$$D = G \times L = .01 \times 30 = .30 \text{ ft}.$$
$$C \text{ and } D = 19.55 - .30 = 19.25 \text{ ft}.$$

With these elevations recorded on the plan as shown in Figure 1–66, move to Figure 1–67 and calculate the distance to the 20 ft contour at points A, B, C, and D.

Distance to 20 ft contour at A and B is:

$$D = .45 \text{ ft } (20 - 19.55), \qquad G = .05,$$
$$L = \frac{D}{G} = \frac{.45}{.05} = 9 \text{ ft}.$$

Distance to the 20 ft contour at C and D is:

$$D = .75 \text{ ft } (20 - 19.25), \qquad G = .05,$$
$$L = \frac{D}{G} = \frac{.75}{.05} = 15 \text{ ft}.$$

The distance from the high point to the 20 ft contour is:

$$D = .20 \text{ ft } (20 - 19.80), \qquad G = .05,$$
$$L = \frac{D}{G} = \frac{.20}{.05} = 4 \text{ ft}.$$

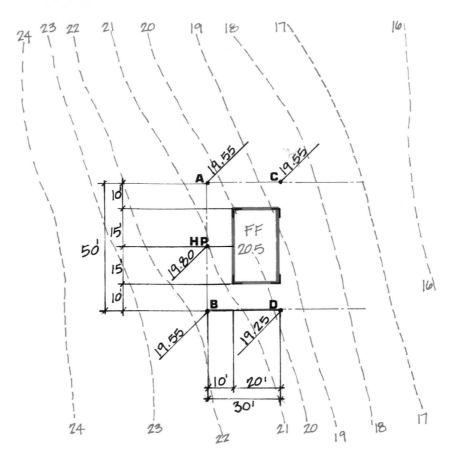

FIGURE 1-66

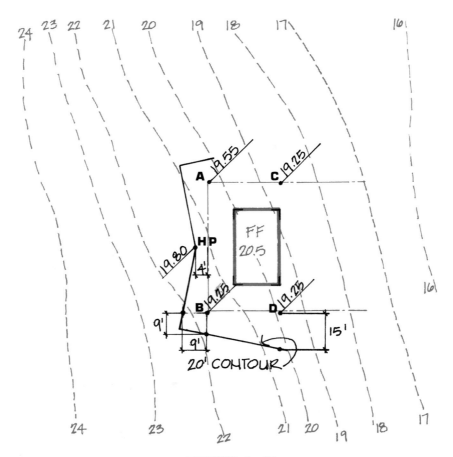

FIGURE 1-67

48

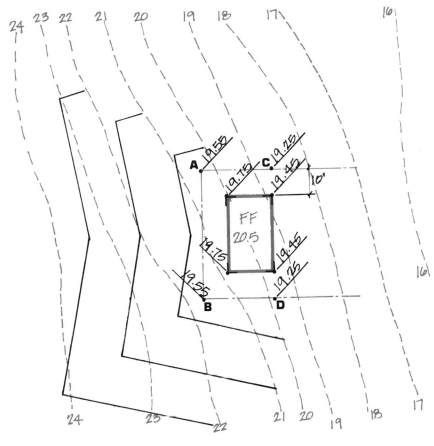

FIGURE 1–68

With this information known, the 20 ft contour can be drawn around the building as shown by the dashed construction lines.

With this known, we can construct the other contours uphill of the building parallel to the 20 ft contour. The distance between 1 ft contours at a 5% slope is:

$$D = 1 \text{ ft}, \qquad G = .05,$$

$$L = \frac{D}{G} = \frac{1}{.05} = 20 \text{ ft}.$$

The contours are drawn in as shown in Figure 1–68.

Next, from the known elevations in the swale calculate the ground elevations adjacent to the corners of the building holding the 2% slope required. The elevations opposite A and B are:

$$L = 10 \text{ ft}, \qquad G = .02,$$
$$D = G \times L = 10 \times .02 = .20 \text{ ft}.$$
$$A \text{ and } B = 19.25 + .20 = 19.45 \text{ ft}.$$

D for the points opposite C and D is also .20 ft so the elevation at the uphill corners is:

$$19.55 \text{ ft} + .20 \text{ ft} = 19.75 \text{ ft}.$$

This information is plotted as shown in Figure 1–68.

Proceed by calculating the distance to the 19 ft contour from each of the known elevations at the front of the building at the allowed 4% slope.

First, find L when:

$$D = .25 \text{ ft } (19.25 - 19), \qquad G = .04,$$

$$L = \frac{D}{G} = \frac{.25}{.04} = 6.25 \text{ ft}.$$

Find L when:

$$D = .45 \text{ ft } (19.45 - 19), \qquad G = .04,$$

$$L = \frac{D}{G} = \frac{.45}{.04} = 11.25 \text{ ft}.$$

This is now plotted on the plan and the 19 ft contour constructed as shown. Then the 18 ft and 17 ft contours are constructed parallel 20 ft apart.

Finally, the 23 ft and 24 ft contours must be adjusted to fit the situation. In this case we are assuming the border is our working limit, so it will be impossible to maintain an even 4% slope. In this case it was necessary to use a 20% slope to go back to grade. This

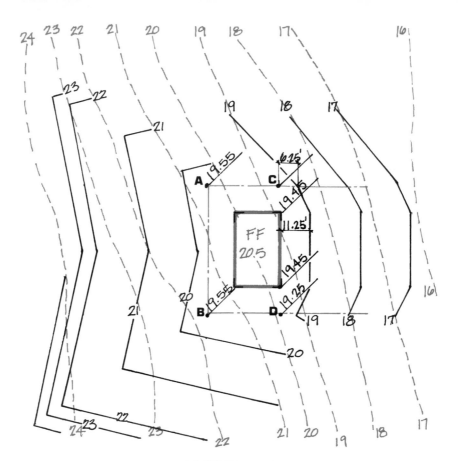

FIGURE 1-69

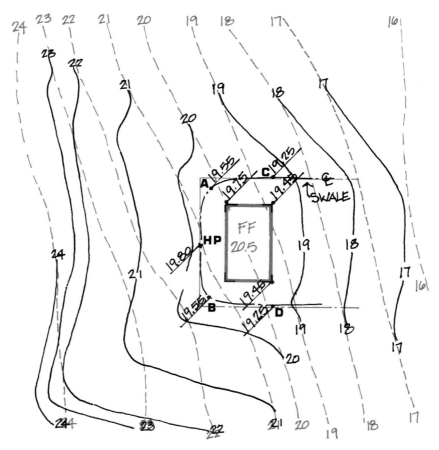

FIGURE 1-70

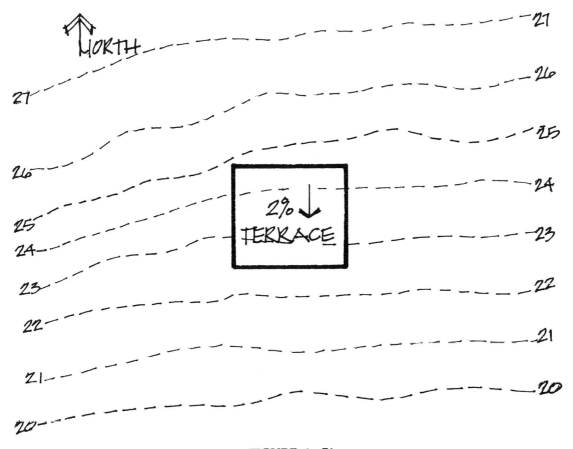

FIGURE 1–71

means the contours are parallel to the 22 ft contour, 5 ft apart as shown in Figure 1–69.

Once again we have generated a technically correct solution but it is not satisfactory visually. So as shown in Figure 1–70 the plan is refined by blending the contours naturally, the centerline of the swale is drawn in, spot elevations fixed, and the desired slopes are specified in ratio form.

Grading Evenly Sloped Surfaces

Consider the evenly sloped terrace in Figure 1–71. In this case we have an exposed surface pitched to shed water. This means that contour lines will cross the surface of the slab, whereas before they went around the slab. The criteria selected for this problem are as follows:

- Slope of the slab is 2%
- Side slopes 5% maximum

Note that in this case we have not specified a swale at the uphill side. This is a design decision. In some cases it might be a good idea to provide a swale to keep trash from washing onto the slab in heavy

rains. The 23.5 ft elevation was selected since it appears to offer the best balance of cut and fill (see Figure 1–72).

To solve the problem we proceed to calculate the grades at the corners of the slabs, designated A to D as follows:

A and B are equal, preset as mentioned above. Points C and D are also equal, so find D when:

$$L = 40 \text{ ft}, \qquad G = .02,$$
$$D = G \times L = .02 \times 40 = .80 \text{ ft}.$$

Therefore, the elevations at points C and D are 23.5 ft − .80 ft = 22.7 ft. This is recorded on the plan as shown in Figure 1–72.

Notice that the even 23 ft elevation is located somewhere on the slab, so L is calculated for:

$$D = .5 \text{ ft } (23.5 - 23), \qquad G = .02,$$
$$L = \frac{D}{G} = \frac{.5}{.02} = 25 \text{ ft.}$$

Thus the 23 ft contour is 25 ft from the uphill edge of the slab and is plotted as shown. The 23 ft contour is almost in its original location.

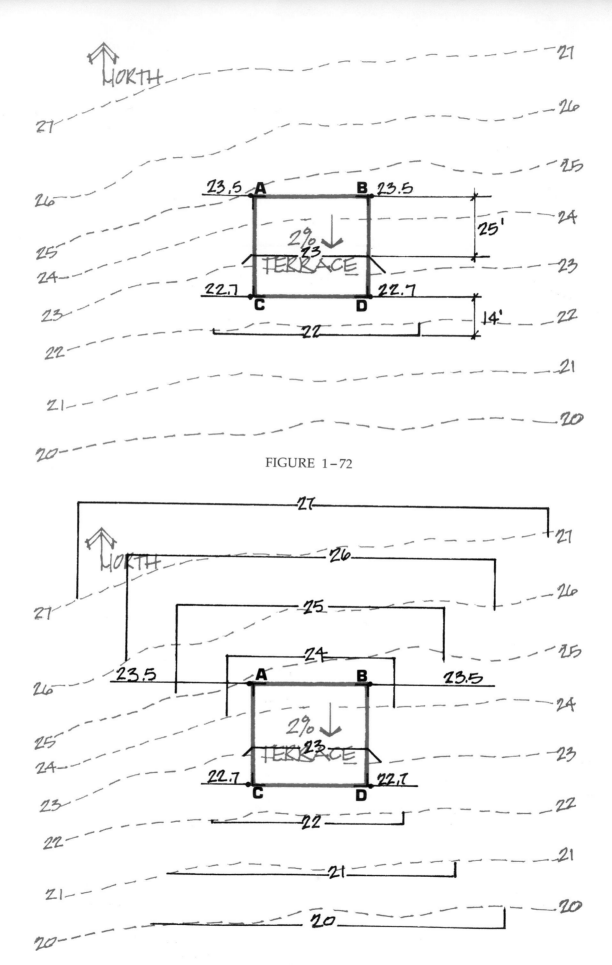

FIGURE 1–72

FIGURE 1–73

52

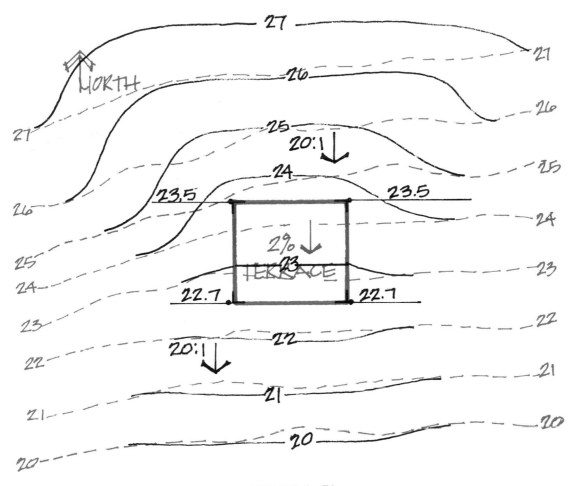

FIGURE 1-74

Now find the distance to the 22 ft contour from the front edge. Find L if:

$$D = .70 \text{ ft} \ (22.7 - 22 = .7), \qquad G = .05,$$

$$L = \frac{D}{G} = \frac{.70}{.05} = 14 \text{ ft}.$$

The 22 ft contour is plotted as shown in Figure 1-72. Next, find the 24 ft contour on the uphill side.

$$D = .51 \text{ ft}, \qquad G = .05,$$

$$L = \frac{D}{G} = \frac{.5}{.05} = 10 \text{ ft}.$$

The 24 ft contour is now plotted as shown in Figure 1-73. The remaining contours are plotted at a 5% slope. In other words, the contours are 20 ft apart and parallel to those already plotted. With this accomplished, the plan is now refined to a final grading plan as shown in Figure 1-74. This is all done freehand, exercising design judgment.

Grading Streets and Ways

The grading of streets, paths, driveways, sidewalks, and other circulation channels is an essential part of most projects. Usually the landscape architect encounters short street additions or streets and paths that occur in large-site development projects and subdivisions. Major street layout will be discussed in more detail in Chapter 2. However, before we begin our discussion of the actual grading plans, it is essential that we look at how the contour patterns are calculated for streets.

Beginning students are usually confused by the contour signatures of curb and gutter streets. This is understandable since we are working with two lines of slope at once, plus the drop of the gutter which is a low retaining wall. But once you work through a few problems such as the example that follows, you will soon find that grading streets poses very little problem.

To illustrate the actual calculations, consider Figure 1-75. A 200 ft cul-de-sac is proposed to enter an existing street. The existing street is curbed, which will require that the old curb be removed and that the new street meet the pavement at the existing grade. Our first task is to establish the existing conditions in the gutter of the old street and work from them.

First calculate the elevations at points A to C. The

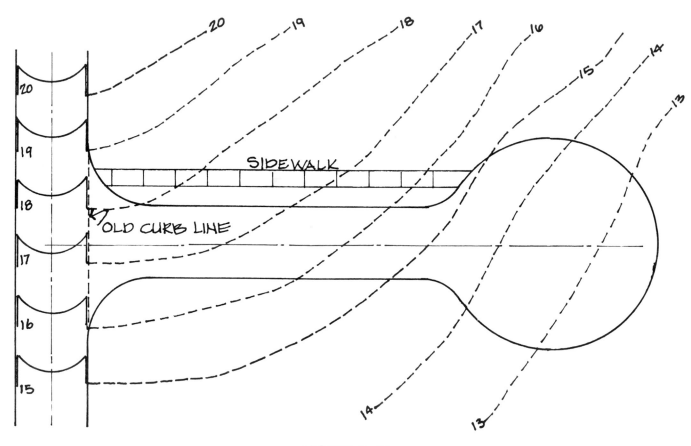

FIGURE 1–75

distance between the contours on the existing street is 20 ft. Therefore the gradient is:

$$D = 1.0 \text{ ft}, \qquad L = 20 \text{ ft},$$

$$G = \frac{D}{L} = \frac{1}{20} = .05 \text{ or } 5\%.$$

The crown of the road is 2% and the pavement width is 24 ft. So the difference in elevation opposite the centerline will be as follows.

Find D if:

$$G = .02, \qquad L = \frac{24}{2} = 12 \text{ ft},$$

$$D = G \times L = .02 \times 12 = .24 \text{ ft}.$$

Thus the gutter elevation opposite each even elevation on the centerline is .24 ft lower. With this information we calculate A, B, and C as follows.

Point A is 6 ft downhill from the 19 ft contour the elevation opposite the even 19 ft elevation is $19 - .24$ ft or 18.76 ft. The difference between the gutter elevation of 18.76 ft and point A is:

$$L = 6 \text{ ft}, \qquad G = .05,$$
$$D = G \times L = 6 \times .05 = .30 \text{ ft}.$$
$$\text{Point A} = 18.76 - .30 = 18.46 \text{ ft}.$$

Point B is 3 ft downhill from the 17 ft contour. The elevation opposite the even 17 ft elevation is 17 ft − .24 ft = 16.76 ft. The difference between the 16.76 ft gutter elevation and point B is:

$$L = 3 \text{ ft}, \qquad G = .05,$$
$$D = G \times L = 3 \times .05 = .15 \text{ ft}.$$
$$\text{Point B} = 16.76 - .15 = 16.61 \text{ ft}.$$

Likewise, point C lies 4 ft downhill from the even 16 ft elevation. The gutter elevation opposite 16 ft elevation on the center line is: $16 - .24 = 15.76$ ft. The difference between 15.76 and point C is:

$$L = 4 \text{ ft}, \qquad G = .05,$$
$$D = G \times L = .05 \times 4 = .20 \text{ ft}.$$
$$\text{Point C} = 15.76 - .2 = 15.56 \text{ ft}.$$

This information is recorded as shown in Figure 1–76.

Next estimate the existing grade along the proposed centerline to see if it must be changed drastically. Note the distance from point B to the even 13 ft contour is 178 ft. The elevation difference between point B and the even 13 ft contour is: $16.61' - 13 = 3.61$ ft.

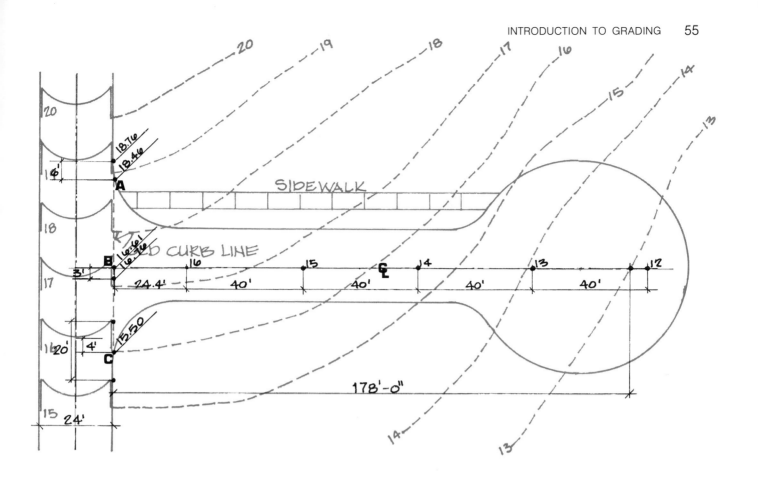

FIGURE 1-76

Therefore find the existing grade if.

$$D = 3.61 \text{ ft}, \qquad L = 178 \text{ ft},$$

$$G = \frac{D}{L} = \frac{3.61}{178} = .0202.$$

Slightly over 2% which is satisfactory in all respects. So, for this example we will use a design slope of 2½% (.025), along the centerline and a 2% crown for the road.

With these criteria established, proceed to locate the points of equal elevation on the centerline of the new street. First locate the even 16 ft elevation by finding L if:

$$D = .61 \text{ ft} (16.61 - 16), \qquad G = .025,$$

$$L = \frac{D}{G} = \frac{.61}{.025} = 24.40 \text{ ft}.$$

Now find the distance between even 1 ft contours when:

$$D = 1.0 \text{ ft}, \qquad G = .025,$$

$$L = \frac{D}{G} = \frac{1.0}{.025} = 40 \text{ ft}.$$

The even elevations are now plotted on the centerline as shown in Figure 1-77.

We now proceed to locate points of equal elevation in the gutter. Keep in mind that once we have calculated one contour the other contours will be the same since the slope and cross-section are uniform. First find the difference in elevation between the centerline and gutter as:

$$L = 12 \text{ ft}, \qquad G = .02,$$
$$D = G \times L = 12 \times .02 = .24 \text{ ft}.$$

Points of equal elevation will occur uphill so find L, if

$$D = .24 \text{ ft}, \qquad G = .025 \text{ (slope of the centerline)},$$

$$L = \frac{D}{G} = \frac{.24}{.025} = 9.6 \text{ ft}.$$

The contours are now plotted to the gutterline as shown. Since the crown is a parabolic section, the contours are also parabolic. Also notice that the contours loose their parabolic shape as they spread in the cul-de-sac.

Next find the point of even elevation on top of the

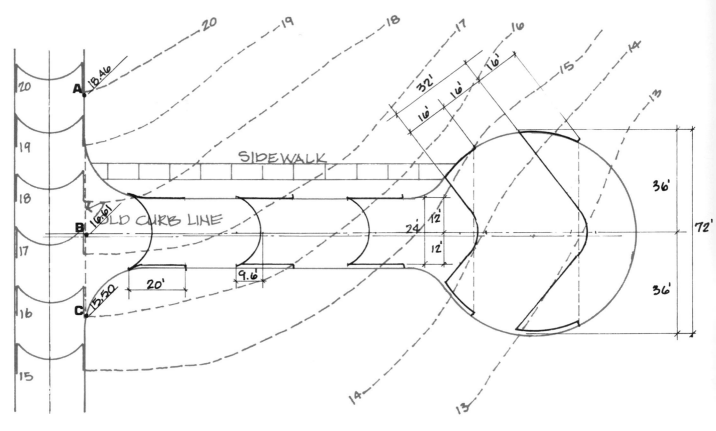

FIGURE 1–77

curb. This point lies downhill of the even gutter elevation and since standard curb heights are 6 in (.5 ft):

$$D = .5 \text{ ft}, \qquad G = .025,$$

$$L = \frac{D}{G} = \frac{.5}{.025} = 20 \text{ ft} \text{ (or } \tfrac{1}{2} \text{ the distance between the contour lines. This is always the case if a 6 in curb is used.)}$$

Now plot the contours to the top of the curb as shown. Observe how the equal points of elevation were constructed on the curb in the cul-de-sac.

Another problem that often baffles the student is how to handle the grade transition at the intersection with the existing street. This can be handled in several ways. One solution is to ignore it and let the construction people handle it in the field. This is not recommended since it usually results in a rough intersection caused by the rapid warp of the surface back to existing grade. Notice in Figure 1–78 the line drawn between point A (elevation 18.46 ft) and point D (elevation 16.0 ft). The difference in elevation is

2.46 ft and they are 28 ft apart. The gradient between A and D then is:

$$G = \frac{D}{L} = \frac{2.46}{28} = .088 \text{ or } 8.8\%.$$

This amount of difference can provide a pretty good jolt if the curve is negotiated at any rate of speed. So what we need to do is begin warping the surface up from a point further down the new road. To do this, construct a line between the even 15 ft elevation in the gutter and point A. The line scales 60 ft. Now checking the slope find that:

$$D = 3.46 \text{ ft } (18.46 - 15), \qquad L = 60 \text{ ft},$$

$$G = \frac{D}{L} = \frac{3.46}{60} = .0576.$$

This is still steeper than desirable (standards for determining desirable differences in slope are given in Table 1–5). So a third line is constructed from point A to the 14 ft elevation in the gutter. It scales 96 ft, so find G if:

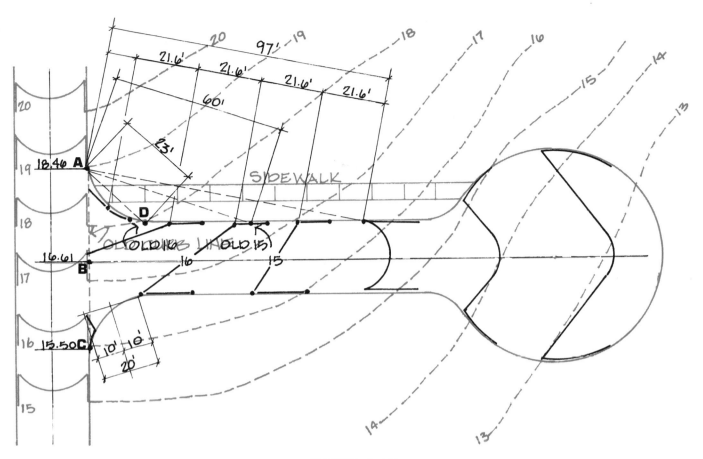

FIGURE 1–78

$$D = 4.46 \text{ ft } (18.46 - 14), \qquad L = 96 \text{ ft,}$$

$$G = \frac{D}{L} = \frac{4.46}{96} = .0464.$$

This value is satisfactory. Next find the distance between 1 ft contours at a gradient of .0464 if:

$$D = 1.0 \text{ ft,} \qquad G = .0464,$$

$$L = \frac{D}{G} = 21.6 \text{ ft.}$$

Using this information replot the contours on the uphill side of the street as shown in Figure 1–78.

What happens here is the street on the uphill side is sloping up faster than the downhill side. The new proposed contours reflect this condition and the crown is removed in the grade transition.

Now check the transition at the downhill side. There are two points of equal elevation since the slope is downhill in both directions. This means that a high point will occur halfway between them. The exact elevation of this point is not important since we can tell visually that the slope transition at this

side is satisfactory. The contour locations were constructed geometrically as shown.

The remaining task is to blend the contours back to existing conditions and grade the walks. This is illustrated in Figure 1–79 and described below.

First select the side slopes for the treelawn, and sidewalk and calculate the location of these points. In this problem 2% was selected for the treelawn, and 1% for the walk. The longitudinal slope of the walk and treelawn follows the street. So from the 18 ft contour to the even 15 ft contour, the slope is .0464. And from the even 15 ft contour to the end of the street, the slope is .025. The calculations are as follows:

Find D if

$$L = 12 \text{ ft,} \qquad G = .02,$$
$$D = G \times L = .02 \times 12 = .24 \text{ ft.}$$

Then find L if

$$D = .24 \text{ ft,} \qquad G = .0464,$$

$$L = \frac{D}{G} = \frac{.24}{.0464} = 5.17 \text{ ft.}$$

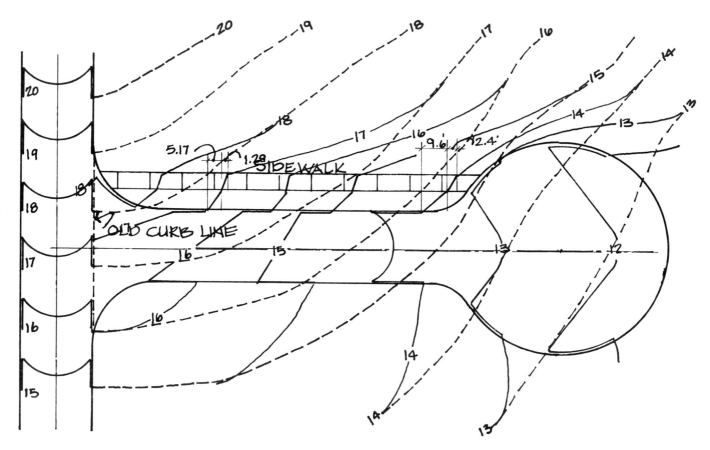

FIGURE 1–79

This is the distance for the 16 ft, 17 ft, and 18 ft contours. Next find L if

$$D = .24 \text{ ft}, \qquad G = .025,$$

$$L = \frac{D}{G} = \frac{.24}{.025} = 9.6 \text{ ft.}$$

Now find the difference in elevation across the sidewalk. Find D if

$$L = 6 \text{ ft}, \qquad G = .01,$$
$$D = G \times L = .01 \times 6 = .06 \text{ ft.}$$

Next find the distance downhill to even elevations at the back of the walk.

Find L if

$$D = .06 \text{ ft}, \qquad G = .0464,$$

$$L = \frac{D}{G} = \frac{.06}{.0464} = 1.29 \text{ ft.}$$

Find L if

$$D = .06 \text{ ft}, \qquad G = .025,$$

$$L = \frac{D}{G} = \frac{.06}{.025} = 2.4 \text{ ft.}$$

With this information plot the contours to the back

of the walk. Then the contours are blended back into the existing grade with freehand lines as shown. Note in the example that slopes of 18% occur at the end of cul-de-sac. This might cause some trouble with lot access depending on the orientation of the lot lines. This could be adjusted by changing the longitudinal slope of the street to 2% rather than the 2½% used.

In this section we have covered four common and typical grading situations. Only the numbers change. These examples by no means cover all the things that can happen. Every new project will be a little different and demand a different approach to the grading. This brings us back to a point mentioned earlier in this section that should be reemphasized.

The solution to a grading problem is largely the result of conscious decisions made by the designer. Furthermore, the first decision is not always correct. This was illustrated in the street problem just completed. In this case it was necessary to abandon the symmetrical contour pattern originally tried to avoid the abrupt change in elevation at the intersection that would have resulted. So a second alternative was explored and rejected. Finally the third alternative proved feasible and the final solution was prepared

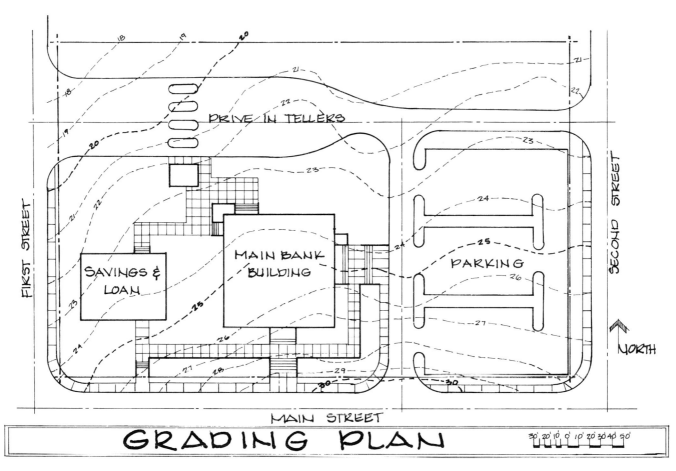

GRADING PLAN

FIGURE 1–80

from there. So to repeat the opening remarks, the final decision concerning what is or is not acceptable rests with the designer. There is no 100% solution, only shades of good or bad.

THE GRADING PLAN

The previous sections have discussed the basic grading problems and presented the methods for solving them as independent situations. However, these kinds of situations do not occur independently in the field. Rather, they occur as parts of an overall project solution. To illustrate how these work together into a completed grading plan we will work through the entire process of developing and refining a grading plan. Once again, it is suggested that you work through the process as it is presented in the text.

Before beginning the example, it should be pointed out that a grading solution is part of the design process. There is no magic rule of thumb method for doing a grading plan. Like design, it is accomplished by taking pencil and paper in hand and probing for a satisfactory solution. Also, keep in mind that the so-

lution presented here is not the only solution, nor are the means used to arrive at the solution necessarily the only way. Insofar as possible, we will explain each decision and why it was made.

The Problem

We are to develop a grading plan for a banking complex that occupies half a city block (see Figure 1–80). The site is bounded by three existing streets. Main street is the major street and is above the mean elevation of the site.

Step One

Where to begin is usually the hardest part of the whole process. This is the one place that we can say that there is a rule of thumb that will apply. Always check the site and determine the fixed conditions. Some things that should be checked are:

- Fixed elevations such as streets, around desirable trees, and utility lines.

- Check for access to storm and sanitary sewers. Be

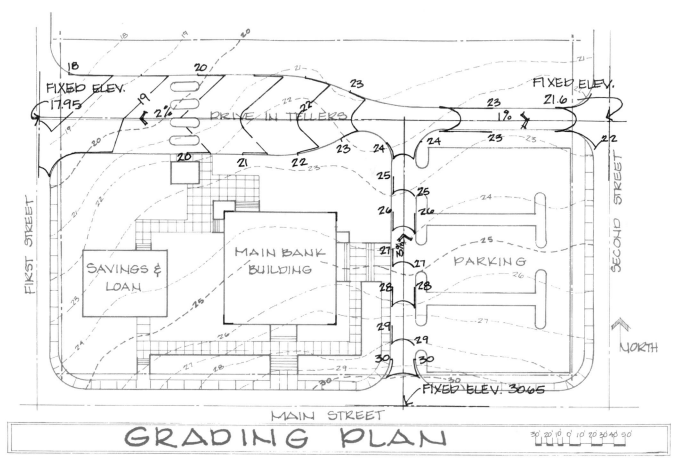

GRADING PLAN

FIGURE 1–81

sure that you get accurate elevations at the access points, do not assume.

- Check building code restrictions. For example, some codes may require that finished floor elevations be above street level.

Once the fixed conditions have been determined, you are ready to begin the first trial solution. In this case our only fixed conditions are the existing streets. These cannot be changed so they are a logical place to begin.

It is recommended that you develop a grading plan in sections at first. Later as you improve your skill, you will be able to think further ahead. In our example we elected to begin at a known point of elevation on Main Street and established the grades on the centerline of the driveway adjacent to the main bank building. Then we worked out the driveway across the back of the bank. The average slope along the driveway centerline is slightly over 3%, so 3% was selected as the slope. The contours for that section were then computed and roughed in as in Figure 1–81.

Notice that the drive is on fill over its entire length.

This is not always the best solution. In this case, it was done to avoid a steeper slope entering Main Street (slopes greater than 3% should be avoided at intersections). The east–west driveway had to be split into two sections. The eastern side was set at a 1% slope and the western side set at 2%. The contour signatures were calculated by the same method illustrated in Figures 1–76 to 1–79.

Step Two

With the street and driveway pattern resolved, the parking lot seemed the next logical step. To do this, the elevations along the street and parkway were fixed at the same slope as Second Street which is 2.5%.

The next step was to decide what type of cross-section would be best for the parking lot. To do this we connected the points of known elevation on the right and left of the parking lot. This produced a sheet pattern with an east–west slope of about 2% (see Figure 1–82). This was a satisfactory slope so the sheet section was selected.

However, it was then decided that we should use

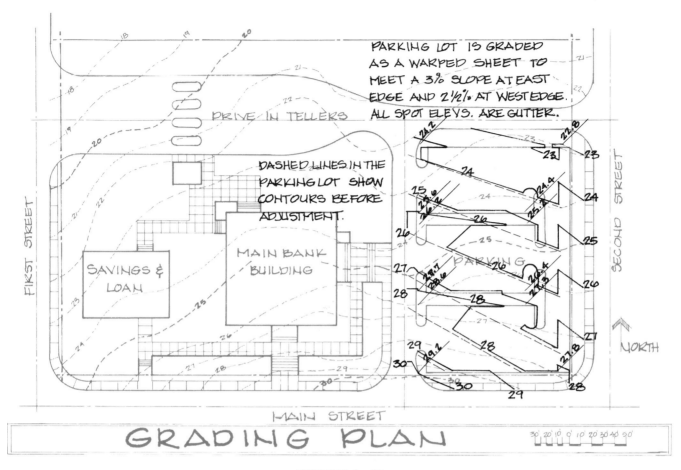

PARKING LOT IS GRADED AS A WARPED SHEET TO MEET A 3% SLOPE AT EAST EDGE AND 2½% AT WEST EDGE. ALL SPOT ELEVS. ARE GUTTER.

DRIVE IN TELLERS

DASHED LINES IN THE PARKING LOT SHOW CONTOURS BEFORE ADJUSTMENT.

FIRST STREET

SAVINGS & LOAN

MAIN BANK BUILDING

PARKING

SECOND STREET

NORTH

MAIN STREET

GRADING PLAN

30 20 10 0 10 20 30 40 50

FIGURE 1–82

only a single drain inlet in the extreme northeast corner of the lot. This meant that two of the parking bays had to be warped up to prevent water collecting in them, see Figure 1-82. Two percent was selected as the gradient for this situation.

The elevations for these changes were then calculated and the dashed contours were adjusted in the two uphill parking bays. Note that these two bays are now valleyed sections. The dashed contours were adjusted to indicate the raised medians. Once the contours were plotted, spot elevations were calculated for all important points in the parking lot and recorded.

Step Three

With the streets and parking lot worked out, the next step is to move the building site. Here several hard decisions had to be made. There is little doubt that it would have been desirable to set the main bank above street grade. But, if you study the elevations of the drive along the back of the bank, this would have put the building 7 to 8 feet above the drive. It would also mean several feet of fill under the building. The driveway grades through the area to

the back worked well with the existing conditions, so the decision was made to set the building lower than the street and use a retaining wall to make the transition to the building. This is shown in Figure 1–83.

Initially, a finished floor elevation of 25.5 ft was tried for the main bank, but this was rejected since the entrance door facing Main Street would have been 5 ft below the sidewalk; thus, 26.5 ft was selected for the bank, 24.5 ft was selected for the savings and loan branch, and 20.5 ft was used for the drive-in teller building.

Since the southeast corner of the building was surrounded by retaining walls, we elected to use a drain inlet in this area and take the storm water out underground. We did consider letting the water run over the walks, but that was rejected. Also note that if the drain inlet happens to get stopped up that the water will run out over the walks and not into the building. From there we proceeded to calculate spot elevations for all walls and paved areas. Two percent was chosen as the gradient (see Figure 1–83).

We have not gone through any detailed explanation of the calculations in this example since these have all been covered in a previous section of this

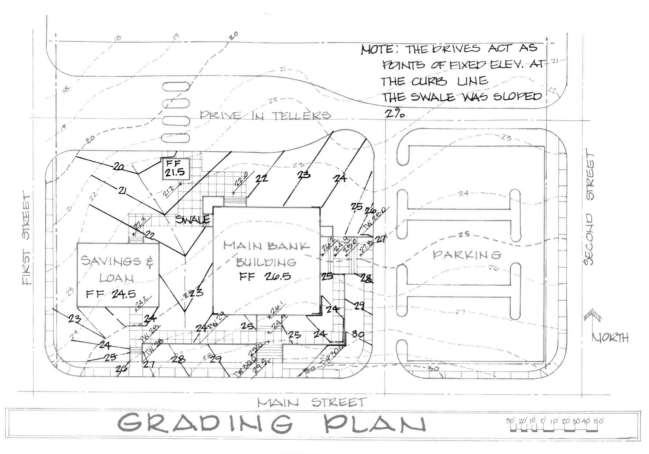

FIGURE 1–83

chapter. Sometimes, however, the beginning student has a great deal of trouble understanding the contour pattern that results from a grading solution. Figure 1–84 has been included here to illustrate where each contour is in relation to all the others. If you compare this sheet to each of the previous sheets, you should be able to visualize what is actually happening to the land form. This is never used for a final grading plan, but it serves to illustrate the basic relationships. Remember that the contour lines shown around the buildings and retaining walls would not show in a plan because they follow the vertical plane of the walls.

Step Four

If we proceeded to draw up a final grading plan from the worksheets as shown so far, the solution would be technically correct but the site would not have any visual appeal. The next step requires that we exercise some aesthetic judgment and refine the solution. This is done by overlaying the plan and graphically studying what can be done to blend the new conditions back into the old conditions.

In this example there are only two areas that can be improved over the basic mechanical solution. First, the lawn area between the savings and loan building and the bank can be smoothed out by rounding the swale contours and blending them back to the building foundation walls, as shown on the final grading plan Figure 1–85. Then the lawn area north of the main bank was shaped to a fanlike slope flowing toward the rear entrance to the main bank and the drive-in teller. Notice that this treatment results in a slope of about 10% along the cheekwall of the steps entering the main bank building. This condition could be unsatisfactory if open growing plant materials were selected in the planting plan. This is just one example of the things that the designer must be looking for in refining the grading plan.

After reaching a satisfactory scheme for refinement, the solution should be checked to see if there is an acceptable balance between the cut and fill qualities. This will be explained in the last section of this chapter.

Step Five

Once it has been determined that there is a satisfactory balance of cut to fill, the finished grading plan is prepared. The grading plan is a working

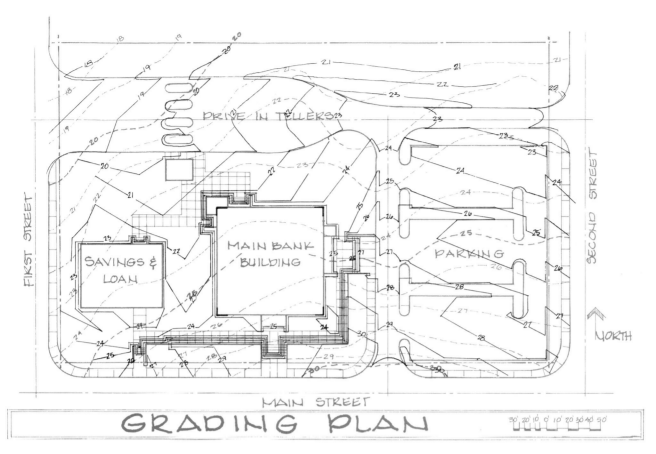

GRADING PLAN

FIGURE 1–84

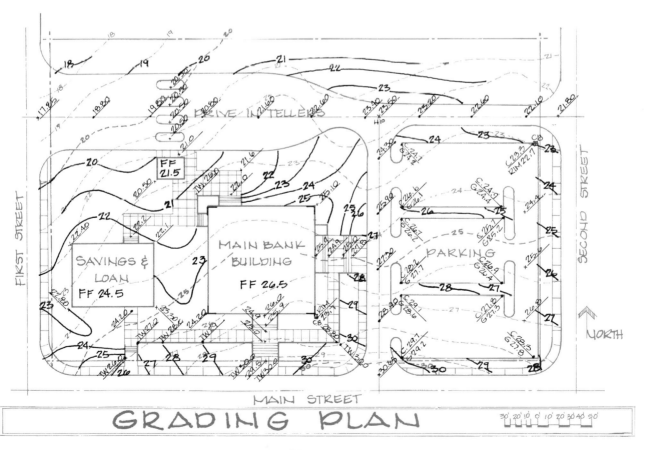

GRADING PLAN

FIGURE 1–85

drawing. For this reason, it must be a carefully draft-ed, accurate drawing.

The grading plan is the document that establishes the vertical dimensions of the site, just as the dimensioned site plan controls the horizontal layout. In the case of the site plan, written dimensions are used by field personnel to stake out the work. Likewise, the grading plan provides written dimensions in the form of spot elevations to control the work. Contour lines are of little value to field personnel in the beginning stages of construction. Their chief value is to convey some idea of finished land form when the final grading is accomplished. For this reason, contour lines are sometimes omitted on parking lots, streets and driveways, terraces, etc. These are controlled by spot elevations placed along centerlines, curb lines, or at important corners. Occasionally, you will see contour lines shown on these kinds of construction, but it is used primarily as a visual guide.

Figure 1–85 is a final grading plan for the bank project. Notice that the contour lines have been omitted from all areas that are paved and spot elevation used to control elevation and shape. The driveways have been controlled by spot elevations at 50 ft intervals along the centerlines. The parking lot has been controlled by spot elevations given for the curb and gutter at each corner. Around the buildings spot elevations are placed at building corners, entrance points, steps, and on the top of the retaining wall. Notice that the wall steps down with the grade. Spot elevations should be used at any high point, low point, or other important points. For example, the drive-in teller medians should have spot elevations. Be liberal in the use of spot elevations; remember it is difficult to give too much information.

The format of a grading plan is a matter of preference. There is no one correct way of doing it. Figure 1–85 is just an example of how it might be done. The important thing is to be sure that it is accurate and legible.

CALCULATION OF CUT AND FILL

A grading solution cannot be considered complete until the volumes of cut and fill have been estimated. As we have mentioned throughout our earlier discussions of grading, one of the major objectives of any solution is to reach a reasonable balance of cut to fill. What determines a reasonable balance depends largely on the overall project objectives, the original site conditions, and the soil type.

There is no way to generalize the first two determinants. For example, if an original site is low, like so many sites are in coastal regions, filling may be the only solution. Mountainous or hilly topography,

likewise, may require removal of a considerable volume of soil material. By and large, these are design decisions that must be made during the formative stages of the work.

In the case of soil type, however, there are some things to keep in mind. Clay soils are usually compacted tightly in their undisturbed condition and expand somewhat in volume during the handling process. Sandy soils, on the other hand, tend to be more stable and will decrease in apparent volume when they are disturbed.

When soil is moved there is actually a net volume loss in the total material caused by erosion and spilling. Depending on the soil type, the net volume loss will run between 5% and 10% of the total volume. In tight clay soils, we would expect the apparent loss to be somewhat less than in a sandy soil, depending on the depth of the fill and the specified compaction. Since estimations of volume are basically educated guesses anyway, an allowance of 10% shrinkage is good practice. In other words, if a solution requires 500 cubic yards of fill, the amount of cut generated should be 10% greater or about 550 yards of cut to balance.

The volumes of cut and fill can be estimated by any number of methods. The two methods most commonly used in office practice are the average end-area method and the planimeter method. Other methods that might be encountered are the average depth method and computer models. The latter methods are potentially more accurate than the average end-area or planimeter methods, but extreme accuracy is not usually required for most projects. The average depth method is a rather laborious manual technique, and the computer methods are expensive in terms of hardware.

The Compensating Polar Planimeter

The planimeter is an indispensable tool for estimating cut and fill volumes. It is an ingenious instrument that measures the area of irregular shapes by simply tracing over the outline. Keep in mind that a planimeter is a precision instrument and if it is abused, dropped, or misused, it will not perform accurately. A good planimeter, properly adjusted and used carefully, is capable of 1% accuracy. This means that any measurement should be accurate to $\pm$ .01 in². This can be critical if you are working on small-scale maps. For example, .01 in² at a scale of 1 in = 2000 ft equals almost a one-acre error per square inch.

The planimeter is composed of two basic parts, a pole arm and a tracing arm, as illustrated in Figure 1–86. The carriage is attached to the pole arm and houses the compensating mechanism that measures the figure. The wheels and gears in the carriage should be kept clean and should never be tampered with.

The carriage has three scaled dials used to read out the measurements as illustrated in Figure 1–87. The revolution wheel is calibrated in tens of square inches or tens of thousands square millimeters. The measuring wheel reads in square inches, or thousands of square millimeters, and tenths of square inches or hundreds of square millimeters.* The ver-

*The English units given assume a standard planimeter adjusted or set to read square inches. The metric units given assume a planimeter set to read in SI units thus millimeters rather than centimeters are proper.

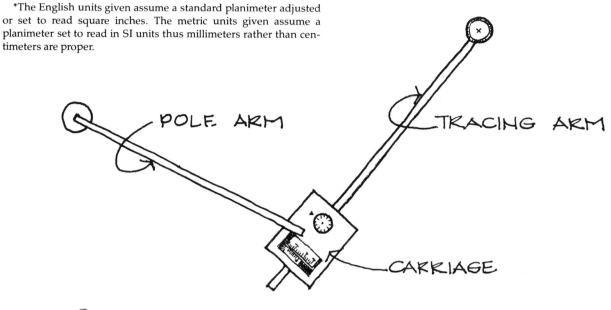

COMPENSATING POLAR PLANIMETER

FIGURE 1–86

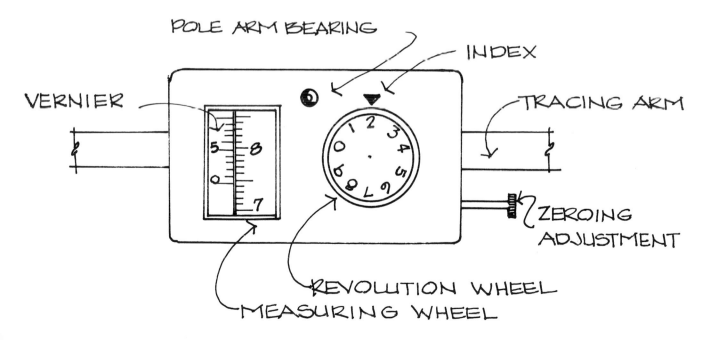

PLANIMETER CARRIAGE

FIGURE 1–87

nier scale reads in hundredths of square inches or tens of square millimeters.

To read the planimeter, begin by reading the revolution wheel, then the measuring wheel and the vernier. For example, the reading illustrated in Figure 1–87 is as shown in the accompanying table.

	ENGLISH	METRIC*
The revolution wheel = 1 + (tens)**		1 – 10 thousands**
The measuring wheel = 74 + (ones and 10ths)		7 – thousands
	4 tenths	5 – hundreds
The vernier = 5 (hundredths)		5 – tens
The reading is: 17.54 in²		17,550 mm²
		(175.5 cm²)
In English measure the decimal goes between the middle digits.		In metric measure a comma goes between the two middle digits and a zero is used for the ones place.

*May vary among instruments.

**While the arrow appears to read 2, 1 (one) is the proper interpretation since a reading of greater than 5 appears on the measuring wheel. This kind of interpretation is frequently necessary.

To operate the planimeter, you should work on a clean, level surface. Don't leave eraser dust or other foreign material on the surface; it will effect the accuracy. Place the weighted pole outside the figure and rest the pole arm in the bearing of the tracing arm. Move the tracing arm to a designated beginning point on the figure to be measured and zero the instrument if it has a zero setting feature. If not, record the planimeter reading; be sure the tracing arm can cover the whole area. Then carefully trace the figure in a clockwise direction and read the planimeter. For the instrument without the zero setting feature, subtract the first reading from the latter to find the area.

When areas are too large to be traced completely, they should be broken into smaller figures and accumulated. Never overextend the tracing arm trying to get everything at once; the results will not be accurate. If extreme accuracy is required, it is recommended that each figure be traced three times and the results averaged.

The Average End-Area Method for Calculating Cut and Fill

Both the average end area method and the planimeter method of cut and fill calculation are based on the assumption that the volumes can be assumed to approximate prismoid masses. A prismoid is a volume with parallel sides or ends that have unequal areas as illustrated in Figure 1–88.

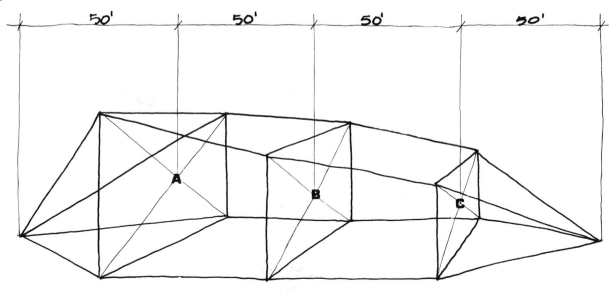

FIGURE 1–88

Average End Area Method For Cut & Fill Calculation

FIGURE 1–89

TABLE 1–7
Cut & Fill, Average End Area Method

LINE	SECTION	1 PLANIMETER	2 VOLUME (yd³)	3 AVERAGE	VOLUME CUT	1 PLANIMETER	2 VOLUME (yd³)	3 AVERAGE	VOLUME FILL
A	0 + 00	—	—			—	—		
B	0 + 50	.52	288	A + B ÷ 2	144	.38	211	A + B ÷ 2	105
C	1 + 00	.64	355	B + C ÷ 2	321	.42	233	B + C ÷ 2	222
D	1 + 50	1.04	577	C + D ÷ 2	466	.21	116	C + D ÷ 2	174
E	2 + 00	.97	538	D + E ÷ 2	557	.56	311	D + E ÷ 2	213
F	2 + 50	.87	483	E + F ÷ 2	510	.91	505	E + F ÷ 2	408
G	3 + 00	—	—	F + G ÷ 2	241	1.13	627	F + G ÷ 2	566
H	3 + 50	.36	200	G + H ÷ 2	100	.46	255	G + H ÷ 2	441
I	4 + 00	.56	311	H + I ÷ 2	255	.13	72	H + I ÷ 2	163
J	4 + 50	.24	133	I + J ÷ 2	222	.10	15	I + J ÷ 2	43
K	4 + 64	—	—	J + K ÷ 2	18″	—	—	J + K ÷ 2	7″
		Total Cut (yds)	2834			Total Fill (yds)	2342		

"The last section is multiplied by 14 ft not 50 ft to obtain the volume. The difference is 410 yd³ or 17% more cut than fill.

The areas of planes B, C, and D are all different but the distance between them is equal. Thus, if we average the area of the plane and multiply by the distance between them, the volume can be determined. Now, if we consider planes A, B, and C as sections through a site taken at equal intervals with the points of the prismoid occurring at the property lines that are points of no cut and no fill, we can calculate the volume by writing the expression.

$$V = 50\,\frac{A}{2} + 50\,\frac{A + B}{2} + 50\,\frac{B + C}{2} + 50\,\frac{C}{2}.$$

To illustrate how this method is applied to a field situation, the cut and fill has been calculated using this method for the bank project. Figure 1–89 shows sections taken at 50 ft intervals across the site. The existing conditions are shown in a dashed line and the proposed condition in a solid line. The areas of cut and fill were then measured with a planimeter and the planimeter readings were recorded in Table 1–7.

The planimeter readings were then converted into volume in cubic yards, column two, Table 1–7. The conversion factor of 555.55 was obtained by first finding the equivalent area of one square inch with a horizontal scale of 1 ft = 30 ft and a vertical scale of 1 ft = 10 ft; 30 × 10 = 300, so each square inch was equal to 300 ft². Then, since the distance between sections is 50 ft, 300 ft² × 50 ft = 15000 ft³. This is converted to cubic yards by dividing by 27. Therefore:

$$\frac{15000}{27} = 555.55 \text{ yd}^3.$$

Conversion of the areas to volumes in the table is preferred to the operation of averaging square-foot areas and multiplying by the distance between sections. The result is the same regardless.

This calculation was run on the early grading plan and shows a 17% overage of cut. In the final grading plan, the excess was used around the main bank building and along the rear property line to blend the street back to existing conditions.

The average end-area method is most commonly used to estimate volumes on linear projects like roads and highways. The sections are taken on 50 ft intervals perpendicular to the centerline. This method is probably more accurate than the planimeter method when contour intervals are in excess of 1 ft.

The Planimeter Method

This method is probably the most popular and practical method since it utilizes the plan and does not require drawing sections. The logic behind this method is the same as the average end-area method. Consider Figure 1–90. The contour interval is comparable to the distance between sections and the area between the old contour and the new contour is analogous to the area of the cross-section. Therefore, if the areas of the sections A, B, C, and D are known, we can apply the average end-area method as follows:

Area

$A = 100 \text{ ft}^2,$
$B = 120 \text{ ft}^2,$
$C = 160 \text{ ft}^2,$
$D = 150 \text{ ft}^2,$

$1 = $ Contour interval

$$V = 1\left(\frac{A}{2} + \frac{A + B}{2} + \frac{B + C}{2} + \frac{C + D}{2} + \frac{D}{2}\right)$$

$$= 1 \times (50 + 110 + 140 + 155 + 75)$$

$$= 530 \text{ ft}^3$$

$$= \frac{530}{27} = 19.6 \text{ yd}^3.$$

Notice that the sum of the averaged areas is equal to the sum of the areas. 100 + 120 + 160 + 150 = 530 × 1 = 530 ft³. Thus, if the plan has a 1 ft contour interval, the sum of the areas between the old and the new contours is equal to the volume in cubic feet.

To illustrate how this method is used, the cut and fill for the bank project was also done using this method. To avoid confusion in using this method, it is recommended that each contour be traced on sketch paper as illustrated in Figure 1–91. The information can then be tabulated in the form shown in Table 1–8. Notice that the totals using this method are less by almost 200 yd³ in each case. This can be accounted for in the scale of the drawings and the accuracy of using the planimeter. Acceptable accuracy for this kind of work is usually ±10%.

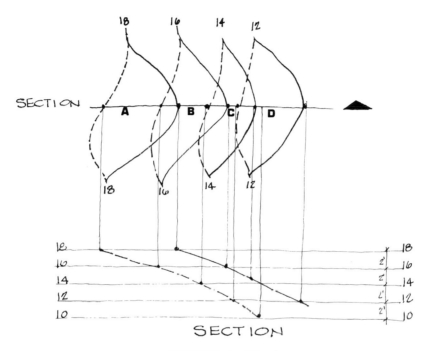

FIGURE 1–90

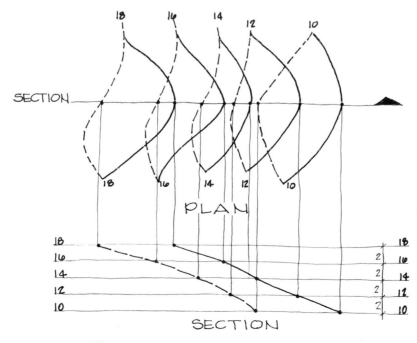

FIGURE 1–91

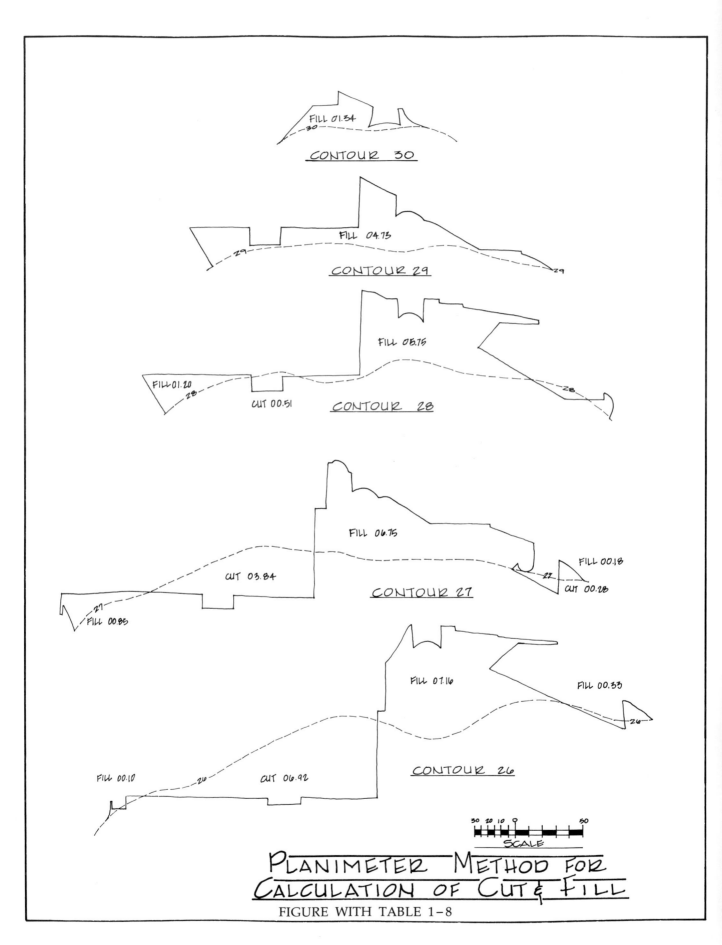

FILL 01.34
30
CONTOUR 30

FILL 04.73
29
29
CONTOUR 29

FILL 05.75
FILL 01.20
28
CUT 00.51
CONTOUR 28
28

FILL 06.75
CUT 03.84
FILL 00.18
27
CONTOUR 27
CUT 00.28
27
FILL 00.85

FILL 07.16
FILL 00.33
26
FILL 00.10
26
CUT 06.92
CONTOUR 26

30 20 10 0   50
SCALE

PLANIMETER METHOD FOR
CALCULATION OF CUT & FILL
FIGURE WITH TABLE 1-8

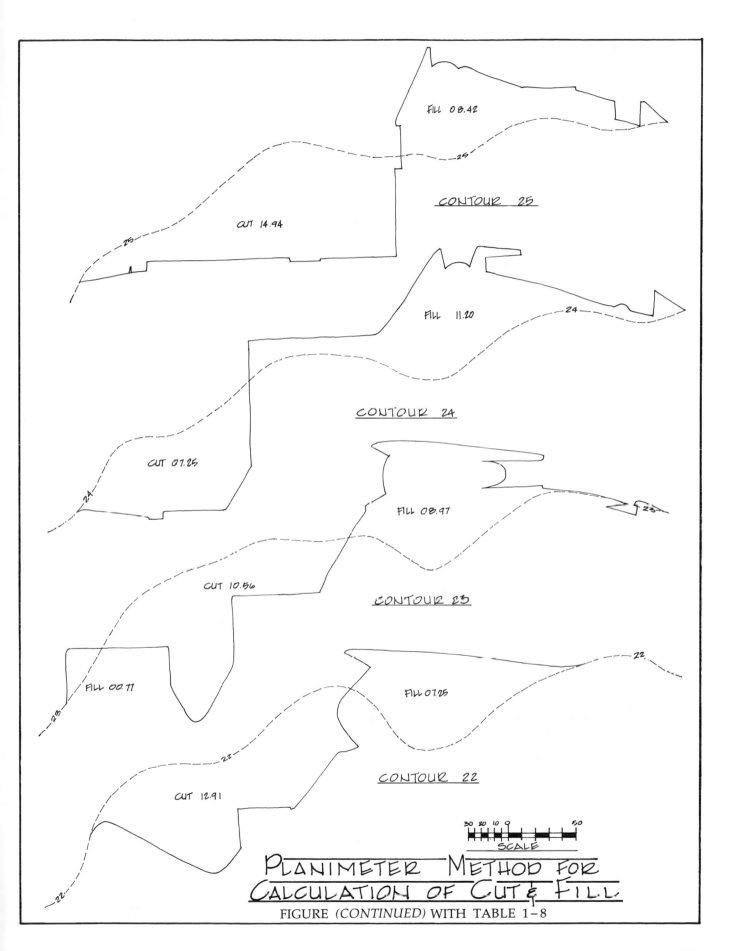

FILL 08.42

CONTOUR 25

CUT 14.94

FILL 11.20

CONTOUR 24

CUT 07.25

FILL 08.97

CUT 10.56

CONTOUR 23

FILL 00.77

FILL 07.25

CONTOUR 22

CUT 12.91

SCALE

PLANIMETER METHOD FOR
CALCULATION OF CUT & FILL

FIGURE (CONTINUED) WITH TABLE 1–8

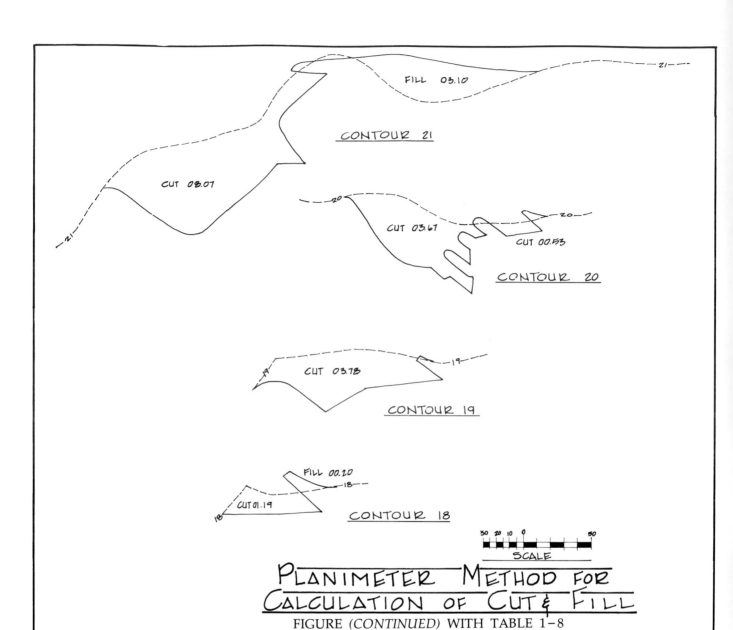

FILL 03.10

CONTOUR 21

CUT 08.07

CUT 03.67

CUT 00.53

CONTOUR 20

CUT 03.78

CONTOUR 19

FILL 00.20

CUT 01.19

CONTOUR 18

SCALE

PLANIMETER METHOD FOR CALCULATION OF CUT & FILL

FIGURE (CONTINUED) WITH TABLE 1–8

TABLE 1–8

	CUT			FILL		
CONTOUR	PLANIMETER READING (in²)	AREA (ft²) × 900	VOLUME (yds³)	PLANIMETER READING (in²)	AREA (ft²) × 900	VOLUME (yds³)
18	1.19	1071	39	.20	180	7
19	3.78	3402	126	—	—	—
20	4.20	3780	140	—	—	—
21	8.07	7263	269	3.10	2790	103
22	12.19	10971	406	7.25	6525	242
23	10.56	9504	352	9.74	8766	325
24	11.20	10080	373	7.25	6525	242
25	14.94	13446	498	8.42	7578	281
26	6.92	6228	230	7.59	6831	253
27	4.12	3708	137	7.78	7002	260
28	.51	459	17	6.95	6255	232
29	—	—	—	4.73	4257	157
30	—	—	—	1.34	1206	45
	Total Cut (yd³)	2587			Total Fill (yd³)	2140

PROBLEMS

1. Find the gradient for the following:
   (a) $L = 265.72$ ft; $D = 2.71$ ft.
   (b) A slope that rises 4.5 ft in 68 ft.
   (c) A 32 ft long sidewalk that drops 1.6 ft.
   (d) A driveway that slopes down 2 ft, 3 in in 50 ft.
   (e) A road that drops 2.821 m in 269 m.

2. What is the horizontal distance for the following:
   (a) $G = .025$; $D = 35$ m.
   (b) A walk with a 2% slope that drops 10 m.
   (c) A road that rises 7 ft at a .03 gradient.
   (d) A slab that slopes at 1.5% and drops 2 ft.
   (e) Between the 50 ft contour and the 55 ft contour at 2%.

3. What is the difference in elevation for the following:
   (a) $L = 25$ ft; $G = .15$.
   (b) A 25 ft long walk that slopes 4%.
   (c) A road that has a .045 gradient for 230 m.
   (d) A terrace that slopes .02 ft/ft for 30 ft.
   (e) A 2,000 m ski slope with a .086 gradient.

4. Plot the contours for a four way intersection as shown in Figure P1–1.

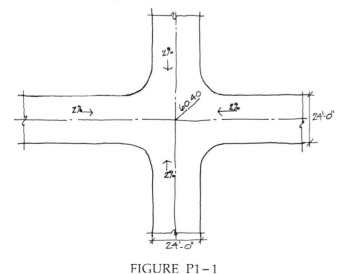

FIGURE P1–1

5. Provide a swale 20 ft off the foundation slab in Figure P1–2 using the following criteria: side slopes 10%, back slopes 15%, slope of the centerline 2½%.

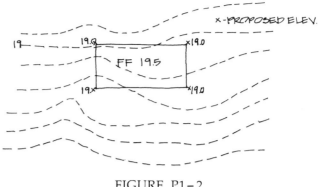

FIGURE P1–2

6. Give the proper planimeter reading in both English and metric measure for each example in Figure P1–3.

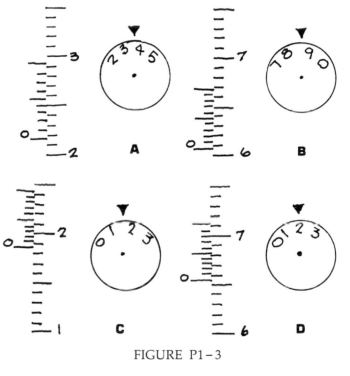

FIGURE P1–3

7. Assuming the English planimeter readings represent areas from a drawing at a scale of 1 in = 30 ft − 0 in with a 1 ft contour interval, section A and B are cut, C and D are fill. What is the total cut and fill in cubic yards?

8. Assume that the metric readings in Figure P1–4 are the areas of four sections taken 10 m apart. All areas represent cut. The scale of the sections is 1:500 horizontal and 1:50 vertical.

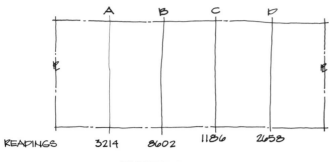

READINGS   3214   8602   1186   2658

FIGURE P1-4

9. Calculate the cut and fill by the average end-area method for Figure P1-5.

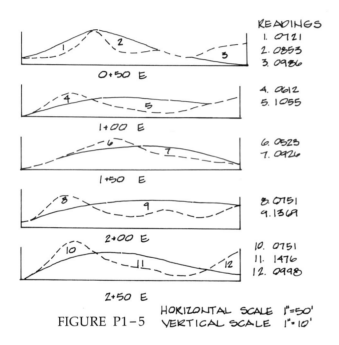

READINGS
1. 0721
2. 0853
3. 0986

4. 0612
5. 1055

6. 0523
7. 0926

8. 0751
9. 1369

10. 0751
11. 1476
12. 0998

FIGURE P1-5   HORIZONTAL SCALE 1"=50'
VERTICAL SCALE 1"=10'

10. Calculate the cut and fill for the following in Figure P1-6.

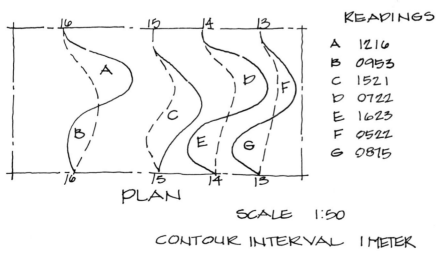

READINGS

A 1216
B 0953
C 1521
D 0722
E 1623
F 0522
G 0875

PLAN

SCALE   1:50

CONTOUR INTERVAL   1 METER

FIGURE P1-6

2
Circulation Design

The single most costly part of any site development will usually be the installation of the streets, paths, trails, and vehicular storage. In addition to the monetary cost, it is potentially the most costly to the visual and natural environment.

There is little doubt that adequate provision for circulation of vehicles to and from a site is a must. Likewise, adequate provision for the maneuvering and storage of vehicles, service and circulation of pedestrians, and other vehicles on site is equally important. But, if the system designed to provide circulation and storage of vehicles is mechanically inefficient or unsympathetic to the site, it will detract measurably from the finished product.

Too frequently the design of the circulation system is relegated to a secondary position in the list of priorities. This is usually because some designers think of circulation ways as mechanical elements rather than primary form generators. For example, a road must be of a certain width, with proper radii for curves, certain fixed slopes, and so on. In addition, since the utility systems (gas, sewer, water, and the like) go with the street, it would seem to tie the hands of the designer even tighter. This kind of thinking, unfortunately, has been the root of many unsuccessful, unsightly, environmentally damaging design solutions.

If we think of just the aesthetic implications of a street and parking lot system for a moment, it becomes rather obvious that the street itself is one of the single most powerful form generators in the landscape. Our buildings are oriented to streets, our sidewalk systems usually parallel streets, the shapes of individual lots in a subdivision are related directly to the streets, utility corridors follow the streets, etc. Since so many elements of a project relate to the street, it is folly to relegate the design of such a powerful form generator to a secondary position in the design hierarchy.

While our purpose in this chapter is to explore the area of circulation design from a technical viewpoint, the design implications must be recognized. So before beginning the technical decision of circulation systems, let's take a little time to consider the major elements of the system in a design context. All circulation systems have two basic components: vehicular and pedestrian. Each of these components is a linear space scaled to facilitate movement to and among various activity nodes.

Vehicular Systems

Vehicular systems are a major force in shaping the visual landscape of the city. Regardless of the kind or order of the vehicle hierarchy, people tend to relate their experience of city spaces in terms of the vehicular circulation pattern. For example, people don't relate the location of an activity center by giving a block number; it is usually given by the street location. Kevin Lynch's work in *The Image Of The City*[1] demonstrates this very clearly by noting how people draw maps of a city. For this reason, the designer must realize that the layout of the street pattern within a project is not just a matter of functional criteria and cost. Design image is also important; good design should help the users understand where they are and how to use the system to safely get where they want to go. If the system functions this way, it will probably provide a pleasant experience as well.

---

[1]Lynch, Kevin. *The Image of the City*. Cambridge, Mass.: The MIT Press, 1960.

Secondary vehicular circulation systems for bicycles, off-the-road vehicles, motorcycles, and other specialized vehicles are usually less dominant form-generating elements for cityscapes, but they are no less important. When possible, separate circulation systems for different kinds of vehicles are desirable. Aside from the safety benefits of traffic separation, the scale of the lineal space is much different. This scale difference is a major contributor to the uneasiness experienced by bicyclists on major streets.

Pedestrian Systems

Just as the vehicular system is the force that shapes the cityscape, the pedestrian circulation system is a major force in shaping the landscape at the project scale. The way a site or group of buildings is perceived is largely a function of the position of the viewers as they move through the circulation system.

The scale of the pedestrian spaces is much smaller than that of the vehicular circulation system and, because movement through them is much slower, detail becomes increasingly important. Much more attention is required in the definition of the movement corridors, views, transition spaces, and access points. Mechanical considerations are no less important with respect to steepness of slopes, transition grades with ramps and steps, intersections, and the materials used in construction.

In the remaining portion of this chapter we will be discussing the more mechanical aspects of circulation design, particularly the design of vehicular circulation systems. This technical information is essential to insure that the design proposals accomplish the task at hand. Much of the material will at first seem to preclude creative thinking; however, this is not the case. This information is but another set of design tools that can be used by skillful designers to generate a better, more manageable landscape.

DESIGN OF STREETS AND ROADS

Classifications of Streets

Street systems are almost universally discussed in a hierarchy of six classes. These classes are based on maintenance requirements, traffic volumes, speed, and general design requirements. The most frequently used terms for these six classes are freeways, expressways, arterial, collector, local, and cul-de-sac.

The freeway is characterized by the interstate highway system. It is a limited-access highway with grade separated interchanges. Its primary function is to move vehicles between cities and across urban areas.

The expressway is usually a multilane divided highway with controlled access. Not all interchanges will be grade separated, and some direct property access is provided. The usual means of controlling access to the expressway is by a boundary road that collects traffic at the side and moves it to selected access points.

Arterial streets are major intercity streets. They provide direct property access at their boundaries but on-street parking is usually not permitted. Traffic control is usually accomplished by signalized intersections.

Collector streets are interneighborhood streets. They pick up the traffic from local streets and transfer it to arterial streets. Traffic control will usually be provided by stop signs on the side streets and on-street parking may be permitted.

Local streets are short streets that discourage through traffic. They provide direct access to residential properties and permit on-street parking.

The cul-de-sac is a short dead-end street with a turnaround provided at the end.

Aside from these six street classifications, there are other design terms that you should be familar with which are concerned with designing for traffic loads at specific times. The most widely used measure of traffic volume is ADT, average daily traffic. This is the 24-hour traffic volume average for a 1-year period. Another measure frequently used is DHV, design hourly volume. This is an estimated value based on a projection system or traffic model. The actual method of projection varies from area to area and basically it all boils down to an educated guess.

The DHV is usually given as total vehicles and will be accompanied by a T factor. This will be the number of trucks in the traffic stream expressed as a percent. For example, for a DHV of 8000 and a T of .10 we would expect 7200 automobiles and 800 trucks.

For most of your work, you will not be greatly concerned with ADT or DHV; this is mostly the bailiwick of traffic and transportation planners. However, these measures of volume are very important for planning intersection locations and the number of intersections. They also become important if you become involved in major land subdivision work.

Design Standards for Streets

To be functional, streets must meet some very basic design criteria. As with grading standards and other rules of thumb, the materials presented here are not absolute; they are general guidelines.

A street is essentially a geometric line composed of arcs (parts of circles) and tangents (straight lines) with a fixed cross section. But before the actual configuration of the line and cross section can be fixed, several things must be considered. It is important to remember that the street is a circulation path for machines that have limitations. Thus, we are designing not only for human performance, but for the performance of the machine as well. The basic criteria that must be determined are how fast the traffic can move (design speed), and the number and types of vehicles that will use the street.

The design speed is the maximum safe speed at which an average vehicle can be expected to negotiate the curves and grade of the street. At low design speeds, the curves can be sharper and the gradients steeper. As operating speeds increase, the curves must be longer and slopes decreased. Design speed is usually determined by the road classification; for example, expressway, arterial, or local. The minimum recommended design speeds for the various classifications are given in Table 2–1. The design speed is then used to establish the minimum standards for horizontal and vertical alignment of the street.

The types and numbers of vehicles will primarily determine the pavement design. Large volumes of heavy trucks will require much heavier pavements than would be required by automobile traffic, and such volumes will also modify the criteria used in conjunction with design speed.

Horizontal Alignment

Horizontal alignment is the configuration of the street in plan. The minimum controls established for horizontal alignment are (1) the minimum curve radius or (2) the degree of curve. The minimum curve radius is the tightest curve that can be safely negotiated at a given design speed. The degree of curve is an alternate method of expressing the same information. Degree of curve refers to the number of degrees required to subtend an arc length of 100 ft (30.48 m). Thus, as the radius of a curve decreases, the degree of curve will increase. For example, a

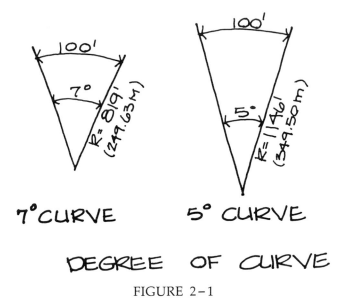

DEGREE OF CURVE

FIGURE 2–1

$7°$ curve has a radius of 819 ft (249.6 m) and a $5°$ curve has a radius of 1146 ft (349.30 m) as shown in Figure 2–1.

Vertical Alignment

Vertical alignment is the configuration of the street in section and reflects what is happening to the street as it moves uphill and downhill. The controls established for vertical alignment by the design speed are the minimum length of vertical curve, maximum gradient, and minimum foreward sight distance.

The vertical curve length refers to the horizontal distance required to move vehicles from one gradient to another without a bump or jolt. Basically, as the design speed increases, the distance required to make a smooth transition in grade increases. Actual calculation of vertical curves is discussed later in the chapter.

Maximum Gradient

The maximum gradient is the steepest gradient that the vehicles utilizing the street can be expected to negotiate in a normal operating mode. The application of this standard requires some design judgment, because a great deal depends on properly estimating the types of vehicles and understanding weather limitations. For example, the gradients on streets subject to frequent icing will have to be flatter than those in a subtropical climate. Table 2–2 summarizes the operating capabilities of the various classes of vehicles for dry pavement conditions.

Sight Distances

Sight distance is measured from a point 4 in (100 mm) above the pavement to a point 4.5 ft (1.37 m) above the pavement. The critical points occur at ei-

TABLE 2–1
Minimum Recommended Design Speeds for Various Highway Classifications

HIGHWAY CLASSIFICATION	DESIGN SPEEDS	
	mph	kph
Freeway	60–70	96–112
Expressway	55–70	88–112
Arterial	35–45	56–72
Collector	25–30	40–48
Local	20–25	32–40
Cul-de-sac	–	–

TABLE 2–2
**Maximum Gradients for Various Vehicle Classes
on Dry Pavement**

VEHICLE TYPE	MAXIMUM GRADIENT IN HIGH GEAR[a]	MAXIMUM GRADIENT IN LOW GEAR[b]
Heavy trucks	3% — 33½:1	5% — 20:1
Heavy trucks	3% — 33⅓:1	7% — 14:1
Light trucks	4% — 25:1	17% — 6:1
Automobiles	7% — 14:1	25% — 4:1

[a]The maximum gradient considered safe for operation in iced conditions is 5% for all vehicles.

[b]Gradients of as much as 32% are encountered on local streets in mountainous areas. These cannot be considered all-weather facilities though.

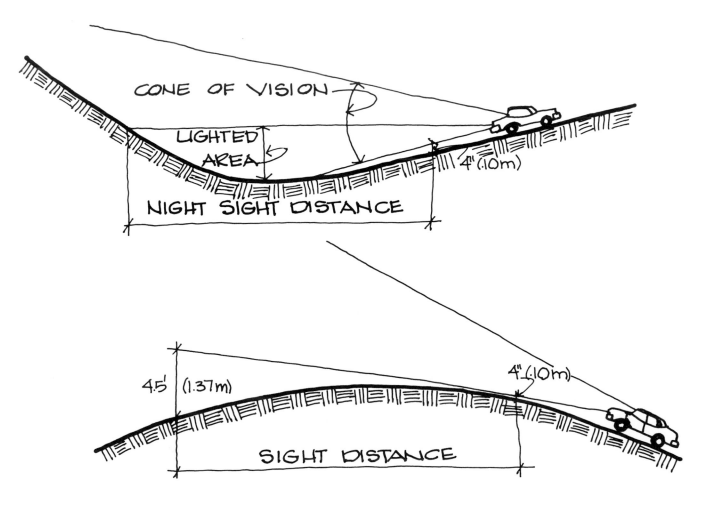

SIGHT DISTANCE

FIGURE 2–2

TABLE 2-3
Road Design Criteria as a Function of Design Speed

DESIGN	SPEED	MINIMUM EVEN DEGREE OF CURVE			MINIMUM RADIUS		MINIMUM SIGHT DIST. (NO PASSING)		MINIMUM SIGHT DIST. (PASSING)		MINIMUM VERTICAL CURVE LENGTH FOR EA. 1% ALGEBRAIC DIFFERENCE		MAXIMUM GRADIENT	
mph	kph	°'s	ft	m	ft	m	ft	m	ft	m	ft	m	%	ratio (ft)
20	32	57	100.53	30.64	100	31	150	46	500	153	10	4	15	6⅔:1
30	48	22	260.45	79.39	250	77	200	61	600	183	20	7	12	8⅓:1
40	64	12	477.50	145.54	450	138	275	84	1100	336	35	11	8	12.5:1
50	80	7	818.57	249.50	750	229	350	107	1600	488	70	22	6	15⅔:1
60	96	5	1146	349.30	1100	336	475	145	2300	702	150	46	5	20:1
70	112	3	1910	582.17	1600	488	600	183	3200	976	200	61	3	33⅓:1

ther a transition to an upgrade or a downgrade. At first glance a downgrade would not seem critical since the cone of vision includes the uphill portion of the road as shown in Figure 2-2. However, at night the headlights of a vehicle would not reach the uphill portion of the road.

Table 2-3 summarizes the various design criteria in relation to design speed. Keep in mind that the criteria given as minimum are just that. Most frequently it will be desirable to exceed these minimum values. For example, the minimum curve radius for a design speed of 20 mph (32 kph) is 100 ft (30.5 m). While a curve with a radius of 100 ft (32.5 m) can be negotiated at 20 mph (32 kph), it is not visually pleas-ant or comfortable. Thus, when it is possible, a longer radius should be used.

Street Widths

Street width varies widely with the type of traffic, the estimated DHV, the street classification, and the local restrictions. Highways in the freeway and expressway classification will usually be multilane divided facilities. Streets in the arterial class are not usually divided, but may be multilane. Collectors, local streets, and cul-de-sacs are usually two-lane undivided facilities. Table 2-4 summarizes and illustrates the cross-sectional dimensions of streets by classification.

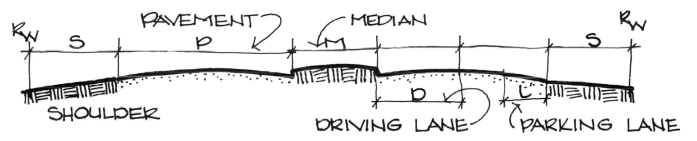

FIGURE WITH TABLE 2-4

TABLE 2-4
Cross-Sectional Dimensions of Streets by Highway Class

	P		D		L		S		M		ROW	
	ft	m	ft	m	ft	m	ft	m	ft	m	ft	m
Freeway	24	7.32	12	3.66	—	—	10	3.05	20+	6.10	200+	61
Expressway	24	7.32	12	3.66	—	—	10	3.05	6+	1.83	200+	61
Arterial	24	7.32	12	3.66	—	—	10	3.05	—	—	120+	37
Collector	24	7.32	12	3.66	8	2.44	8	2.44	—	—	80	25
Local	20	6.10	10	3.05	8	2.44	8	2.44	—	—	60	19

CROWN

VALLEY

SHEET

TYPICAL PAVEMENT SECTIONS

FIGURE 2–3

Design of the Cross Section

Plans and profiles of streets must be supplemented by a cross-section of the facility before the design can be built in the field. All too frequently the cross section is thought of only in terms of the actual pavement cross section. This kind of thinking can lead to some rough problems in construction, such as steep intersection slopes and inaccessible lots. The cross section should not only include the normal pavement data, but should also set some reasonable standards for how the transition is to be made to the right-of-way line and then to the adjacent properties. There are three basic cross sections used for street and parking lot pavements: the crowned section, the valleyed section, and the sheet section. These are illustrated in Figure 2–3.

The crowned section is a parabolic curve, which means the slope becomes progressively steeper as the edge of the pavement is reached. The crowned section is used for street and driveway pavements of all types. It is most efficient in keeping the pavement dry without producing the uncomfortable tilting feeling that would result from an even-side slope.

The valleyed section is most frequently used for parking lots, minor interior streets, and service alleys. It allows the use of single drainage inlets along the centerline rather than requiring two inlets as the crowned section does. Valleyed sections should not be used with flexible asphaltic pavements because of the possible damage to the base caused by standing water in the low spots along the centerline.

The sheet section is also used for minor service roads and parking lots, because it has the advantage of directing water to single drainage inlets. It can be used with flexible asphaltic pavements, since there is little danger of standing water on the paved surface.

Handling of pavement edges can vary from no treatment at all to very elaborate curb and gutter details. The type of treatment used at the edge of a street depends a great deal on the type of pavement, the drainage system, and the purpose of the street. Typical curbs are shown in Figure 2–4.

Concrete does not require a great deal of treatment at the edge of the pavement because it is a rigid monolithic material. Usually a slight thickening of the edge of the slab and backfill that will prevent undermining of the pavement are sufficient. Flexible pavements such as asphalt will require more attention to prevent moisture penetration at the edges, causing the material to sluff off. Rural roads usually rely only on a well-stabilized shoulder that will carry the water away. On urban streets this is not a satisfactory solution due to the volume of traffic moving over the edge of the pavement. The only satisfactory solution to this problem is to finish the edge with some type of curb structure. The curb can be anything from a flush concrete header to an extruded asphalt curb. Some frequently used curb details are illustrated in Figure 2–4 and in the Reference Manual.

The type of curb used on a street is a function of the drainage system and the adjacent land use. If a storm sewer system is used to carry storm runoff, a vertical curb of some type will be used to channel the water in the street to a collection point. If drainage ditches are used to collect storm water, then a flush header will be used for asphalt pavements, or no curb at all for concrete pavements.

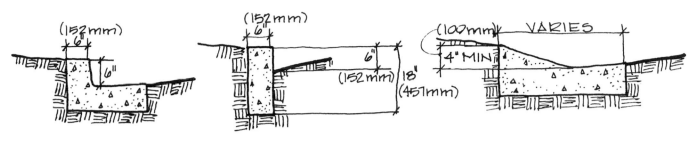

CURB & GUTTER   HEADER CURB   MOUNTABLE CURB

TYPICAL CURBS

FIGURE 2-4

Vertical curbs are classified in two ways: (1) mountable curbs and (2) nonmountable curbs. Mountable curbs are preferred in residential subdivisions where frequent driveway cuts would be required. This allows access to all properties without the need to break out and rework the existing curb. Nonmountable curbs are used for most commercial, collector, and arterial streets to provide a barrier as well as a more positive drainage channel. The height of nonmountable curbs may run as high as 10 in. (254 mm) for extreme cases, but heights over 6 in. (152 mm) are seldom justified.

From the edge of the pavement to the right-of-way line, several things must be taken into account. This area is usually occupied by utility lines, sidewalks, trees, and light fixtures, plus any access drives that connect adjacent properties. For most situations, any back slope greater than 10% in this area will cause problems. Automobiles bottom turning into drive-

ways, sidewalk installation is difficult, and erosion becomes a problem. However, most of these problems can be avoided if the differences between existing and proposed conditions are well-balanced on the profile sheets. Figure 2-5 shows some typical highway sections.

Street Location

Street location is governed by two basic criteria: access and topography. Each of these basic criteria have far-reaching implications that the designer must understand. As we have already pointed out, the street corridor provides not only a vehicular channel, but is also utilized by other utility services as well. Beyond the mechanical considerations, street corridors also carry with them visual and environmental problems. In most cases, if the two basic criteria are handled properly, all the problems created by a street can be solved economically.

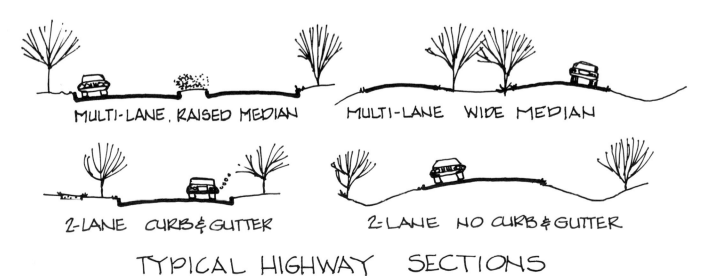

MULTI-LANE, RAISED MEDIAN   MULTI-LANE WIDE MEDIAN

2-LANE CURB & GUTTER   2-LANE NO CURB & GUTTER

TYPICAL HIGHWAY SECTIONS

FIGURE 2-5

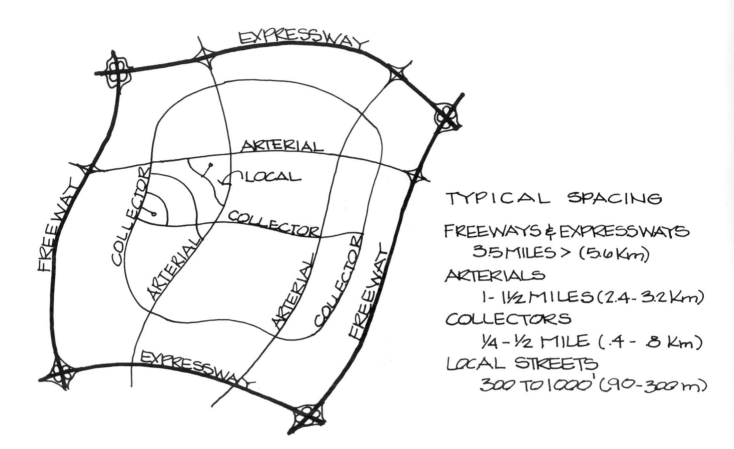

TYPICAL SPACING

FREEWAYS & EXPRESSWAYS
   3.5 MILES > (5.6 Km)
ARTERIALS
   1 - 1½ MILES (2.4 - 3.2 Km)
COLLECTORS
   ¼ - ½ MILE (.4 - .8 Km)
LOCAL STREETS
   300 TO 1000' (90 - 300 m)

TYPICAL SPACING OF STREETS

FIGURE 2-6

First and foremost, a street must provide vehicular access. For example, a freeway should provide access to expressways and arterial streets; collector and local streets should provide direct access to adjacent properties. Figure 2–6 illustrates the generally accepted standards for the spacing and location of the various street classifications.

In addition to providing access for the general public, access must be convenient for service and emergency vehicles. This is why most codes and ordinances will specify maximum block lengths and permissible lengths for cul-de-sacs. The gridiron pattern of our older cities usually provided blocks 250 ft (76.2 m) to 300 ft (91.44 m) long. This arrangement provided excellent accessibility to adjacent properties and land parcels that were easiy marketed. As development costs for streets and other utilities increased, it became desirable to reduce the street frontage to save money. This led to what is usually called the "super block" concept. In some cases blocks were as long as 3000 ft (915 m) between cross streets. Blocks this long have proved unac-

ceptable for emergency vehicle access. The general rule of thumb today is block lengths are limited to no more than 1000 ft (305 m) and cul-de-sacs are usually limited to 500 ft (152 m) depths.

One of the most frequently overlooked elements of accessibility is the visual coherence of a street pattern. The gridiron pattern probably provides the most visually coherent pattern because it is so easy to catalog mentally. But it is also visually sterile. It is therefore incumbent on the designer to reach some balance between a mental image and visual quality in the development of a street pattern (see Figure 2–7).

The accessibility criteria must also be balanced with the topography of the site. As the topography becomes more severe, the location of streets will be more and more influenced by it. The reason for this is pure economics. Road construction costs will rise proportionately to the amount of cut and fill necessary to complete the job. Steep cuts or fills also decrease the accessibility of the adjacent property, which in turn will decrease the value of the land. The

DISORDER

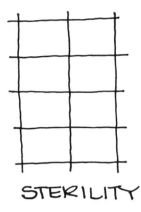
STERILITY

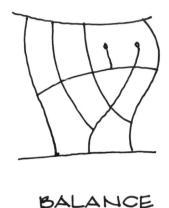
BALANCE

FIGURE 2-7

actual topographic placement of streets depends on their classification.

Freeways, expressways, and arterial streets are best located along major ridge lines. A quick look at any large-scale topographic map will confirm this. The major reason for this is that the ridge will have the least overall variation in vertical elevation. This minimizes the grading required to fit the road to the landscape. It also minimizes the need for bridges and other major drainage structures.

Collector streets, local streets, and cul-de-sacs, on the other hand, are best located along the lines of natural drainage ways. This is because these streets usually make up an integral part of the surface drainage system. The streets themselves will collect water from abutting properties and transfer it to collection points along the way.

The final location is a balance of visual and environmental concerns. As we have already mentioned, if the access and topographic considerations have been properly handled, the other problems should fall within the realm of economic feasibility. The importance of these criteria should not be taken lightly. There are literally volumes of information dealing with just the visual and environmental problems of streets. Many of these problems are regional or political concerns and cannot be dealt with effectively in the scope of this text.

Intersections

To this point we have only been looking at the street as a lineal corridor moving between two points. We have not as yet considered how access to a street is handled. The simplest method of gaining access to a street is the at-grade intersection. This is the cheapest, most practical solution for most local and collector streets; but as volumes of traffic increase the intersection design becomes more complex. The lowest level of traffic control at intersec-

tions utilizes the at-grade intersection with some type of control device, such as stop signs or traffic signals. Some of the control systems used for major intersections are quite sophisticated, utilizing metal sensing devices and computers for traffic control.

The next level is the channelized intersection that provides separate lanes for through traffic and lanes for right- and left-turning movements.

A variation of the channelized intersection is the rotary. This type of intersection has been widely used in European countries since the Renaissance, but has not been widely used in this country. The reason it is not more widely used is that the average driver is probably not familiar with it and does not use it properly. Since we have had the technological ability to build grade-separated interchanges, rotaries have never been popular.

The grade-separated intersection removes the turning conflicts generated by an at-grade intersection. This is the highest level of control. Grade separations are very efficient and very expensive. Because of the high expense factor, grade-separated interchanges are used only on streets with extremely high design volumes, usually expressways and freeways. Figure 2-8 illustrates some typical intersections.

Things that must be taken into account in the design of an intersection are (1) the ease of turning movements and (2) safety. The ease of the turning movement depends on the vehicle and the radius of the corner. The maneuvering characteristics of vehicles and recommended turning radii for intersections are discussed later in the chapter. The safety of an intersection is primarily a function of visibility. If all parts of the intersection are visible the intersection should be safe. Criteria that will help ensure visibility are outlined in Figure 2-9. For all but the most demanding situations, these criteria should be considered absolute requirements.

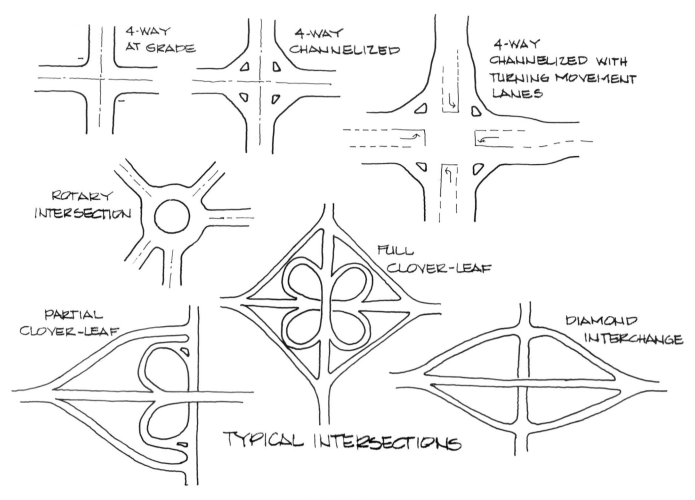

FIGURE 2–8

Parking and Service Facilities

A street does not terminate at the right-of-way line. Like any utility, it is connected to adjacent properties by means of access drives, parking lots, or service areas. These facilities also have some very specific design criteria that must be met if they are to operate successfully.

The design of a functional parking or service facility will be governed by the characteristics of the vehicles that will use it. There are four types of vehicles that must be considered: automobiles, automobile and trailer combinations, long-wheelbase trucks and busses, and tractor-trailor rigs.

The design standards for turning radii, lane width, maneuvering space, and vertical clearance will always be determined by the largest vehicle that requires access to the space. The vehicles that require the least maneuvering space are automobiles. Long-wheelbase vehicles like busses require the greatest area for maneuvering.

When designing for large vehicles, tractor-trailers,

and busses, the best practice is to avoid backing movements. This is particularly true in the case of boat trailers and recreation vehicles. Backing movements in these vehicles require skills that the average driver does not have. Even if the operator of the vehicle does have the necessary skill, backing should still be avoided since the driver's visibility is limited and the movement is not safe. When backing movements will be required of trailer combinations, be liberal with the maneuvering area. If possible, avoid any backing movement over 100 ft long.

Since there is so much variation in the performance of vehicles, and because the actual performance depends largely on the operator, it is impossible to design for all possible combinations of circumstances. The standards presented here will cover a majority of the common situations, but there is never a substitute for checking the actual conditions.

Parking facilities are classified by the angle between the curb and the parking stalls. The angles used are 90°, 60°, 45°, and 30°. Usually the decision of which angle is best depends on the available space

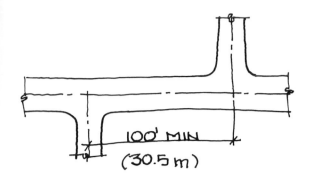

ALLOW 100' BETWEEN ALL
INTERSECTIONS

100' MIN
(30.5 m)

GRADES AT INTERSECTIONS
SHOULD BE 3% OR LESS
FOR 100'.

100'
(30.5m)

100'
(30.5m)

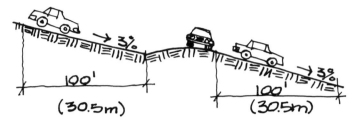

AVOID INTERSECTIONS BELOW
THE BROW OF A HILL

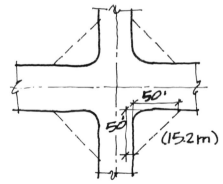

A 50' TRIANGLE ON ALL SIDES
OF AN INTERSECTION SHOULD
BE CLEAR OF VISUAL OBSTRUCTIONS

50'
50'
(15.2m)

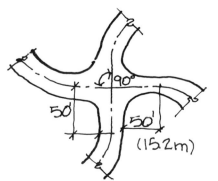

INTERSECTIONS SHOULD ENTER
AT 90° WITHIN 50' EACH
DIRECTION. ANGLED INTER-
SECTIONS ARE SELDOM
JUSTIFIED.

90°
50'
50'
(15.2m)

FIGURE 2-9

for parking and the number of vehicles that will require storage. Figure 2–10 below and on page 87
illustrates the four basic parking arrangements.

Parking schemes of 30° and 45° are most frequently
used when the width of the parking area is restrict-

ed. 30° parking with double bays can be accomplished comfortably in a space as narrow as 46 ft
(14 m), 45° parking requires a 50 ft (15.2 m) width.
The circulation for 30° and 45° parking will normally be one-way. Maneuvering in and out of 30° or

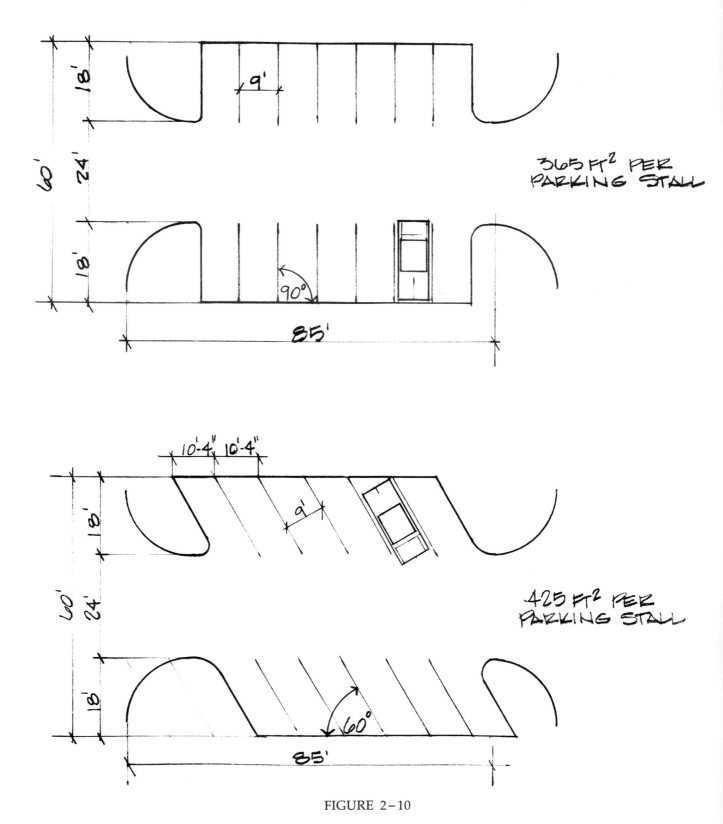

FIGURE 2–10

45° spaces is easy for the average driver and visibility to the rear is good. The major disadvantage of these solutions is that they require more paving for the number of vehicles stored, 430–520 ft² (40–48 m²) per car.

Probably the most popular parking scheme is 60° parking, for several reasons. It lends itself to either one-way or two-way traffic patterns, maneuvering in and out of the spaces is easier than the 90° for most drivers, visibility is usually good for the backing

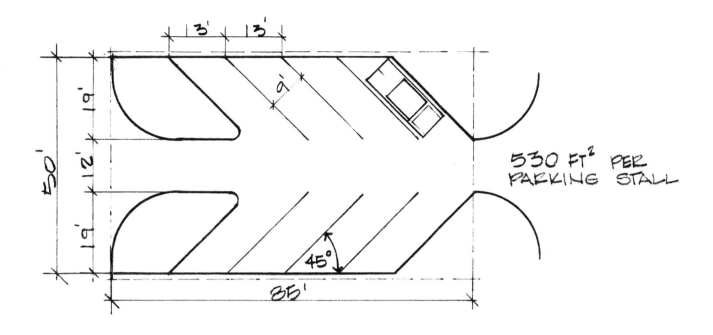

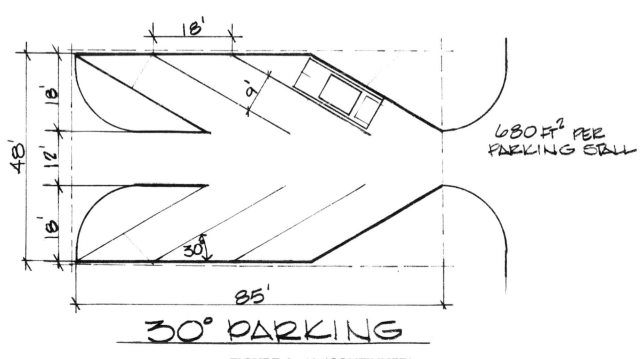

30° PARKING

FIGURE 2–10 *(CONTINUED)*

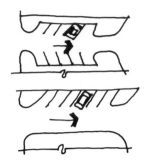

PARKING STALLS SHOULD BE PROVIDED ON BOTH SIDES OF THE DRIVING ISLE IF POSSIBLE TO REDUCE THE COST PER VEHICLE STORED.

"DEAD HEAD" PARKING LOTS SHOULD BE AVOIDED. THE TURN AROUND CUT IS AN OPEN INVITATION FOR PARKING AND MANEUVERING IS DIFFICULT.

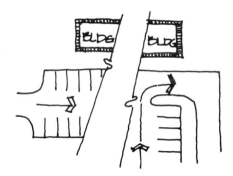

THE CIRCULATION PATTERN SHOULD ALWAYS BE PERPENDICULAR TO THE STRUCTURE BEING SERVICED TO PROVIDE SAFE ACCESS.

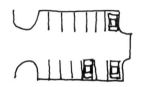

PARALLEL PARKING SHOULD BE AVOIDED ON AN ISLE WITH 90 PARKING.

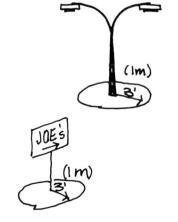

SIGNS, LIGHT FIXTURES AND OTHER FURNITURE IN A PARKING AREA SHOULD BE PROTECTED BY A RAISED CURB WITH A 3' (1m) RADIUS.

NOTES ON PARKING

FIGURE 2-11

TABLE 2–5
Recommended Turning Radii for Various Locations

LOCATION	RADIUS	
	ft	m
Expressway intersections	50	15
Arterial intersections	46	14
Collector intersections	35	11
Local intersections	20	7
Residential driveways	12	4
Public drives and parking lot entrances	18	6
90° parking aisles	20	7
60° parking aisles	18	6
45° parking aisles	12	4
30° parking aisles	12	4

maneuver, and it has a reasonable pavement-to-vehicle-stored ratio, 350–425 ft² (32.5–39.5 m²) per car.

Ninety degree parking is usually selected when the number of spaces per square foot of pavement is the critical consideration. From this standpoint it is the most efficient. It should always be designed with a two-way traffic pattern because the aisle widths must be 20 ft (6 m) for the backing movement and one-way circulation is hard to control.

Some general things to remember when laying out parking facilities are illustrated in Figure 2–11. Table 2–5 summarizes the recommended turning radii for various street intersections and parking lots.

HORIZONTAL ALIGNMENT

The term horizontal alignment refers to the configuration of a street in the horizontal plane, or the plan configuration. The alignment is controlled by a desired design speed, which in turn establishes other minimum design criteria (Table 2–3). As mentioned earlier, the horizontal configuration of a street is composed of arcs, portions of circular curves, tangents, and straight lines. Not all combinations of arcs and tangents are acceptable just because they meet the minimum criteria. For example, two curves in the same direction are called a brokenback curve. This combination frequently occurs in subdivisions, but a brokenback curve is visually awkward, and if design speeds are greater than 30 mph (48 kph), it becomes cumbersome and dangerous. Figure 2–12 illustrates the various curve combinations and outlines some criteria that should be observed for various situations.

Horizontal Control in the Field

Straight lines pose no real problem in the field. Circles, on the other hand, are quite another matter. The layout of a circular curve requires some precise calculations and specific information must be given on the plans. All layout information is always referenced to the centerline of the street. Pavement width,

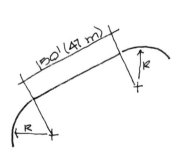

BROKEN BACK CURVE

BROKEN BACK CURVES ARE VISUALLY AWKWARD AND SHOULD BE AVOIDED. IF IT BECOMES NECESSARY TO USE ONE IT SHOULD BE CONNECTED BY A 150' (47 m) TANGENT

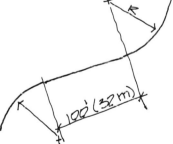

REVERSE CURVE

REVERSE CURVES ARE PLEASANT IF LARGE FLOWING RADII ARE USED. REVERSE CURVES SHOULD BE SEPARATED BY A MINIMUM TANGENT OF 100' (32 m)

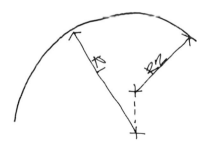

COMPOUND CURVE

COMPOUND CURVES ARE POTENTIALLY DANGEROUS AND SHOULD BE USED ONLY WITH LOW DESIGN SPEEDS.

FIGURE 2–12

intersections, and other structures are referenced to the centerline by plan and typical cross section.

Since the centerline will be composed of some curved lines, conventional straight-line dimensioning will not work. Dimensions are therefore given by a universal system called stationing. A station designation is simply a lineal measurement along the centerline from some known point. In standard practice, a plus sign (+) is placed between the 10's and 100's place of the dimension. For example, a dimension of 250 ft (76.2 m) from the beginning point is designated as station 2 + 50. The beginning point is referenced as 0 + 00.

The horizontal alignment data required to layout a street in the field are a referenced point of beginning, bearings of the tangent lines, curve lengths, the angles of the curves, the curve radii, and the terminal station. With this information on a plan, a survey party can accurately position a street for construction.

Calculation of Horizontal Curves

To understand the calculation of a horizontal curve it is important to understand the basic geometry of the curve. Once the basic relationships are clear, the actual calculations are simple, and in fact they can be accomplished many different ways. In this text we have used machine formulas where possible to facilitate the use of a calculator. Also, where it seems important we have noted other formulas that are used to obtain the same information.

The basic geometry of the circular curve is illustrated in Figure 2–13 along with the basic formulas and definition of the algebraic terms.

L Curve length is usually designated by the letter L or called out as arc. Its dimension is in lineal feet or meters to the nearest hundredth of a foot or 10 mm, respectively.

$$L = \frac{IR}{57.3}, \qquad L = \frac{2\pi RI}{360}, \qquad L = \frac{I\pi D}{360}, \qquad L = \frac{I\pi R}{180}$$

I The included angle is designated by the letter I or the Greek letter Δ (delta). It is usually given to the nearest 30" (seconds). The Δ/I included angle is the angle formed by the intersection of the entering and departing tangents and is equal to the angle subtended by the arc.

$$I = \frac{57.3L}{R \ (\text{English})}.$$

R The radius is represented by the letter R and is given in feet to the nearest hundredth, or meters to the nearest 10 mm.

$$R = \frac{5730}{D \ (\text{English})}, \qquad R = \frac{1746.5}{D \ (\text{metric})}.$$

$D/\Delta°$ The degree of curve is the included angle required to subtend an arc length of 100 ft for a given radius.

$$D = \frac{5730}{R \ (\text{English})}, \qquad D = \frac{1746.5}{R \ (\text{metric})}.$$

PC Point of curvature. This is the point where the arc departs from the entering tangent line.

PT Point of tangency. The point where the arc becomes tangent with the departing tangent line.

PI Point of intersection. The point where the entering and departing tangent lines intersect.

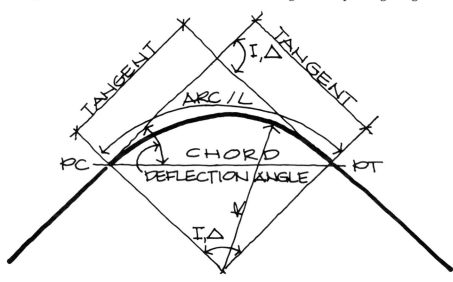

THE CIRCULAR CURVE

FIGURE 2–13

Chord   A line drawn from PC through PT.

$$C = 2R \sin \frac{I}{2}.$$

Deflection angle   The angle between a tangent line and a chord. The deflection angle is always equal to one half of the included angle.

Tangent   The portion of the entering or departing tangent lines that lie between PC or PT and PI.

$$T = R \tan \frac{I}{2}.$$

Laying Out the Street

In the initial design of any project, the roads *should* be laid out freehand to take full advantage of the land form. Every effort should be made to preserve trees and natural features of the landscape. After this is done, the roads can be mechanically drafted. This is usually done on a plan-profile sheet that has a blank area at the top of the sheet for the plan and a grided section at the bottom for the road profile.

If the rough plan is at a working scale (1 in. = 50 ft, or 1:500 metric, or larger), overlay the plan with the blank part of the plan-profile sheet, getting as much of the road as possible on each sheet. Next, lightly draw a series of tangent lines that conform to the desired road alignment. Reference the north arrow and beginning point. When this is done, some initial decisions must be made about the road design. First, establish a reasonable design speed. This will establish a minimum radius for curves and minimum site

distance. Remember, these are minimums and can be exceeded.

Then, bisect the angle between the tangents. Any radius point, regardless of its length, will lie on this line. To bisect any angle geometrically, set your compass at any convenient opening, put the point in the PI and tick both tangent lines. From each tick mark draw arcs that intersect inside the angle and connect the PI and this mark with a line. All radius points fall on this line. From here any number of radii can be tried to achieve the desired configuration. Sometimes it will take several trial runs to establish the desired configuration.

When the desired configuration is reached, you are ready to record the length of each radius and number the curves in the direction of stationing. This is usually left to right on the sheet. The next step is to calculate each curve and station the centerline. To illustrate how this is done consider the example in Figure 2–14.

First, a freehand sketch was drawn approximating the road alignment desired. Next, the three tangent lines were drawn to the approximate centerline and the angles were measured with a protractor. These angles were then used to establish the bearings required for field reference.

A design speed of 20 mph was considered satisfactory, since the street is a short local street. At 20 mph (32 kph) the minimum radius required for any curve was 100 ft (32 m) (see Table 2–3). Then the angles were bisected and radius dimensions selected that would conform as closely as possible to the freehand line. Several trials yielded a radius of 260.45 ft (79.35

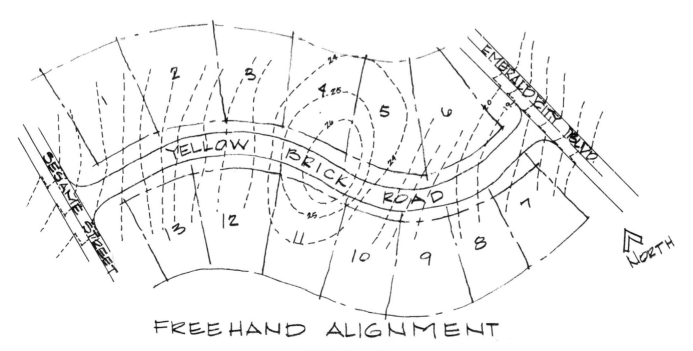

FREEHAND ALIGNMENT

FIGURE 2–14

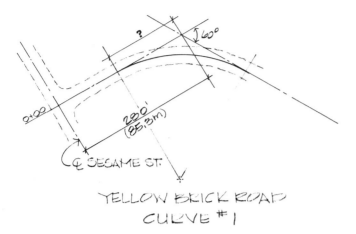

YELLOW BRICK ROAD
CURVE #1

FIGURE 2-15

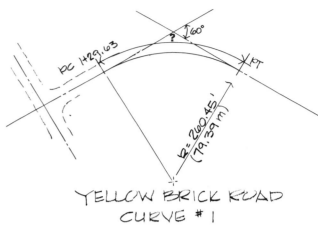

YELLOW BRICK ROAD
CURVE #1

FIGURE 2-16

m) for curve #1, and 191 ft (58.2 m) for curve #2. Remember, the 100 ft (32 m) radius was minimum, and it is perfectly all right to exceed this value.

Once the basic layout is completed as described, the next task is to calculate and record the curve data. The horizontal alignment data for the problem are worked out step by step in the following paragraphs. Keep in mind that these steps apply to any horizontal alignment problem.

First, establish the exact location of station 0 + 00. Next, the length of each tangent line is scaled and recorded. For the example problem they are 280 ft (85.3 m), 350 ft (106.7 m), and 250 ft (76.2 m), respectively.

The first calculation is made to establish the exact station of the PC of curve #1. To do this, calculate the tangent of curve #1 and subtract that value from the length of the entering tangent as shown in Figure 2-15.

$$T = R \tan \frac{I}{2}$$

$$T = 260.45 \tan \frac{60}{2}$$

$$T = 260.45 \tan 30°$$
$$T = 260.45 \times 57735$$
$$T = 150.37 \text{ ft } (45.8 \text{ m})$$

The tangent length of curve #1 (150.37 ft or 45.8 m) is subtracted from the entering tangent line of 280 ft (85.3 m) to establish the station of PC.

$$280 - 150.37 = 129.63$$
$$PC \#1 = 1 + 29.63 \text{ ft}$$

The next calculation is made to determine the station of PT #1. Figure 2-16 involves calculating the curve length (L) and adding this value to the station of PC #1.

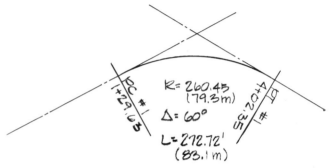

YELLOW BRICK ROAD
CURVE #1

FIGURE 2-17

$$L = \frac{IR}{57.3}$$

$$L = \frac{60 \times 260.45}{57.3}$$

$$L = \frac{15627}{57.3}$$

$$L = 272.72 \text{ ft}$$
$$PT = 129.63 + 272.72 = 402.35 \text{ ft}$$
$$PT \#1 = 4 + 02.35$$

This completes the calculations for curve #1 and the curve data can be recorded on the plan as shown in Figure 2-17.

Now notice that the station of PC #2 will be the remaining length of the second tangent line that lies between PT #1 and PC #2 as shown in Figure 2-18.

We know that the tangent of curve #1 is 150.37 ft (45.83 m) and that the length of the original tangent line was 350 ft (106.68 m); therefore, the distance from PT #1 to PC #2 is 350 ft (106.68 m) less the

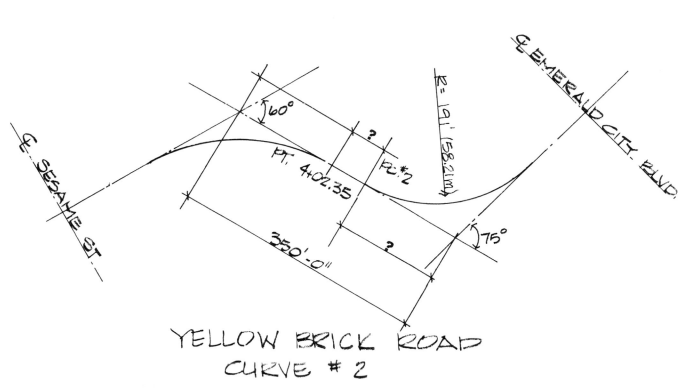

YELLOW BRICK ROAD
CURVE # 2

FIGURE 2-18

length of the tangents of curve #1 and curve #2. Find the tangent of curve #2 and PC of curve #2 as follows.

$$T = R \tan \frac{I}{2}$$

$$T = 191 \tan \frac{75}{2}$$

$T = 191 \tan 37.5°$
$T = 191 \times .7673269$
$T = 144.56$ ft (44.67 m)
PC #2 = 150.37 + 146.56 = 296.93 ft
350 − 296.93 = 53.07 ft
PC #2 = 402.35 + 53.07 = 455.42 ft (138.81 m)
(see Figure 2-19)

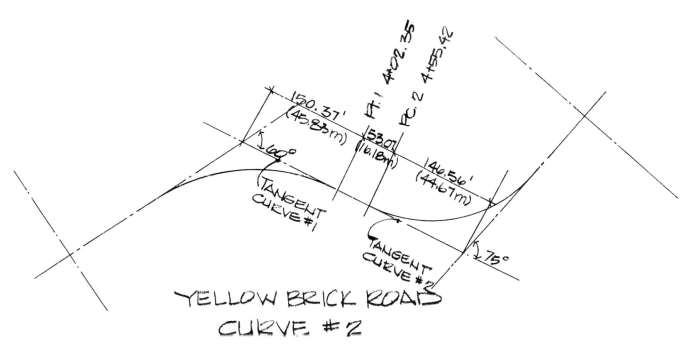

YELLOW BRICK ROAD
CURVE # 2

FIGURE 2-19

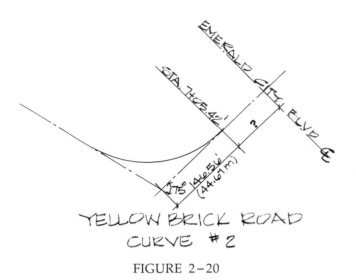

YELLOW BRICK ROAD
CURVE #2

FIGURE 2–20

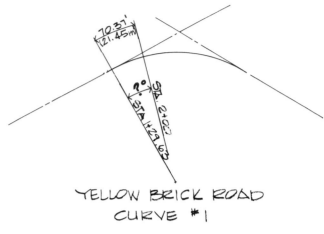

YELLOW BRICK ROAD
CURVE #1

FIGURE 2–22

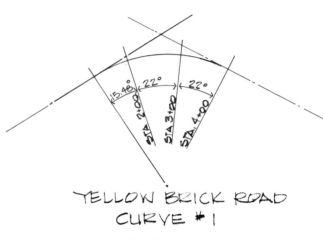

YELLOW BRICK ROAD
CURVE #1

FIGURE 2–23

With the station of PC #2 known, the curve length (*L*) is calculated and added to the PC to determine PT #2 as follows:

$$L = \frac{IR}{57.3}$$

$$L = \frac{75 \times 191}{57.3}$$

$$L = \frac{14325}{57.3}$$

$$L = 250 \text{ ft } (76.2 \text{ m})$$

PT #2 = 455.42 + 250 = 705.42 ft (215.01 m)
PT #2 = 7 + 05.42

The terminal station is then determined by subtracting the tangent of curve #2 from the 250 ft (76.2 m) tangent line and adding this to the station of PT #2 as shown in Figure 2–20.

The terminal station is:

$$250 - 146.56 = 103.44$$
$$705.42 + 103.44 = 808.86 \text{ ft } (246.54 \text{ m})$$
$$\text{Terminus} = 8 + 08.86$$

The horizontal alignment data is usually drafted on a plan-profile sheet as illustrated in Figure 2–21. The curve data is customarily shown inside the curve, toward the radius point as in the illustration. All even stations are shown as well as the stations of PCs and PTs. (Figure 2–21 is on page 95.)

Notice that several of the even-number stations fall on the curved portions of the road. In some cases it may be desirable to locate these points exactly. This can be accomplished by calculating the number of degrees required to subtend an arc of the desired length. For example, the PC of curve #1 is at station 1 + 29.63 and station 2 + 00 lies on the curve 70.37 ft

(21.45 m) from that point. Therefore, to locate station 2 + 00 exactly, we need to calculate the number of degrees required to subtend an arc of 70.37 ft (21.45 m) as illustrated in Figure 2–22.

The included angle (*I*) can be found by:

$$I = \frac{57.3L}{R}.$$

So, for the example,

$$I = \frac{57.3 \times 70.37}{260.45}$$

$$I = \frac{4032.201}{260.45}$$

$$I = 15.48° \ (15°28'48'')$$

Even station 2 + 00 can be plotted by turning off 15.48° from PC #1. Since we laid out curve #1 as a 22° curve, even stations 3 + 00 and 4 + 00 can be plotted by turning 22° for each point as shown in Figure 2–23. From this example the advantage of using even degree curves should be evident.

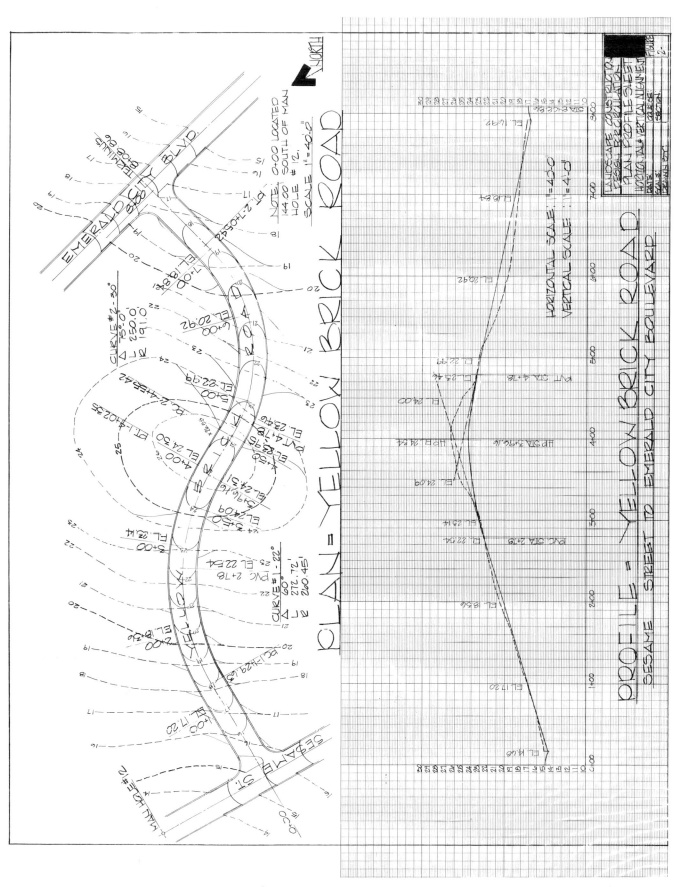

FIGURE 2-21

VEHICLE MAY BECOME
AIR BORNE

EFFECTS OF GRADE TRANSITION

FIGURE 2-24

VERTICAL ALIGNMENT

Establishing the horizontal configuration of a street is only half the job. To actually build the street, finished elevations must be established on the centerline so the grading can be accomplished. The term vertical alignment refers to the location of the street in the vertical plane referenced to some datum plane.

Vertical alignment is quite similar to horizontal alignment in that it is a series of tangent lines connected with curves. The difference is in the curve itself. In horizontal alignment circular curves were used, but parabolic curves are used for vertical curves. A parabolic curve differs from a circular curve because it starts very shallow and gets progressively steeper toward its apex, then becomes shallow again as it reaches the point of tangency. This provides the smoothest possible transition between lines of differing slope.

Consider for a moment what could happen if no consideration were given to vertical alignment. The average automobile for example will actually drag the ground if the change in grade is more than 9% as illustrated in Figure 2-24. If this condition occurs in reverse, the automobile in effect will become airborne. This is dangerous to say the least, and is best left to stunt drivers at a speedway. Even when slopes are less severe, there will still be a jolt if some sort of transition is not provided.

To avoid a bump or jolt, it is recommended that a minimum vertical curve be provided anytime the difference in slope is greater than 3%. The minimum length of the curve can be determined from Table 2-3. For example, if a street has two vertical tangents, one at +5% and one at -4%, the algebraic difference is 9%. If the design speed is 40 mph, we find from Table 2-3 that 35 ft (10.67 m) of curve are required for each 1% of difference. Therefore 9 × 35 = 315, so 315 ft (96.01 m) of vertical curve will be required to join two lines.

Calculation of Vertical Curves

Once again it is important to understand the relationships of the basic parts of the curve. The basic geometry of parabolic curves is illustrated in Figure 2-25.

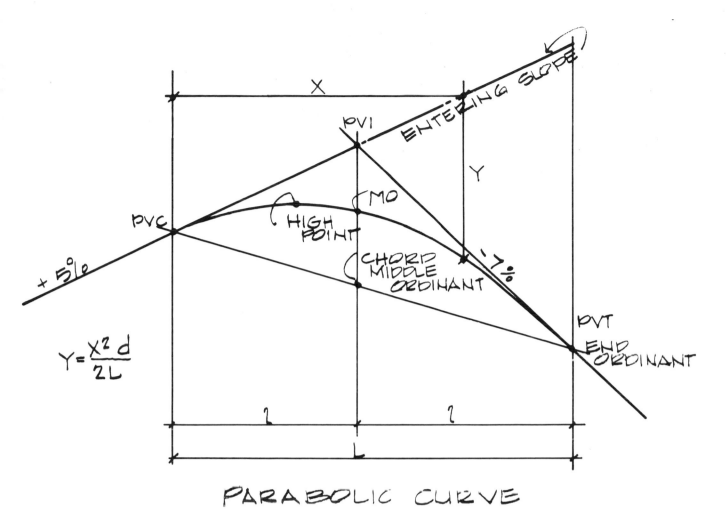

$$Y = \frac{X^2 d}{2L}$$

PARABOLIC CURVE

L - LENGTH OF THE CURVE.

ℓ - ½ THE CURVE LENGTH.

MO- MIDDLE ORDINANT OF THE CURVE.

PVC- POINT OF VERTICAL CURVATURE.

PVI - POINT OF VERTICAL INTERSECTION.

PVT- POINT OF VERTICAL TANGENT.

X - ANY HORIZONTAL DISTANCE FROM PVC.

Y - THE VERTICAL DISTANCE FROM THE
ENTERING SLOPE LINE TO THE CURVE.

d - THE ALGEBRAIC DIFFERENCE OF
THE INTERSECTING SLOPE LINES.

FIGURE 2-25

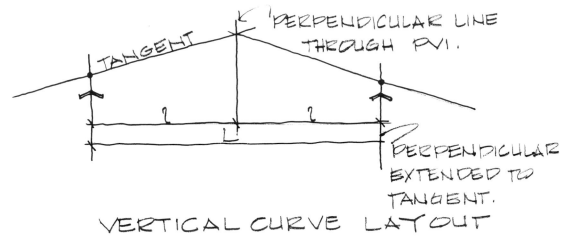

VERTICAL CURVE LAYOUT

FIGURE 2–26

H   The distance from the PVI of the two tangents to the middle ordinant or the chord;

h   ½ *H*;

A   The vertical distance from the middle ordinant of the curve to PVT;

a   ½ *A*;

X   Any horizontal distance measured from PVC;

y   The vertical distance from the entering slope line to the curve for a given horizontal distance *X*; $y = x^2d/2L$.

L   Length of horizontal curve;

l   ½ *L*;

d   The algebraic difference between the two lines of slope;

PVC   Point of vertical curvature;

PVT   Point of vertical tangency;

PVI   Point of vertical intersection;

MO   Middle ordinant;

Chord   A line from PVC through PVT.

The high point (HP) or low point (LP) of the curve measured from PVC is

$$\text{HP or LP} = \frac{\% \text{ of entering slope} \times L}{d}.$$

A vertical curve such as the one illustrated is actually composed of two different parabolic sections. This is usually always the case and is the result of different entering and departing slope lines, with different angles between the chord and tangent lines.

In terms of the basic geometry of the parabola, there are two important things to notice. First, the middle ordinant of the curve will always have an elevation halfway between the middle ordinant of the chord and the PVI elevation. Second, the middle ordinant of the chord will always have an elevation halfway between the PVC and PVI at the middle ordinant unless the curve is symmetrical. If the curve is symmetrical, PVC, PVT, and the chord MO elevations are all equal.

To lay out a vertical curve the intersecting tangent lines are laid out and a perpendicular line is dropped through the PVI. Half of the curve length is measured out on either side of the perpendicular line and these points are projected vertically until they intersect the tangent lines as shown in Figure 2–26. This establishes the PVC and PVT.

The next problem is to determine the actual elevations on the curve itself so these can be plotted on the final drawings. To do this it is common practice to use plan-profile paper. This brings together the vertical and horizontal data on a single sheet. To demonstrate how these data work together we will use the problem here to illustrate horizontal alignment and complete a plan-profile sheet for it.

The plan with the horizontal alignment data and the existing contours is drawn on the top of the sheet. Then a profile of the existing conditions along the centerline is plotted on the graph portion of the sheet as shown. This profile is always drawn with an exaggerated vertical scale. The exaggeration will usually be on the order of 5 to 10 times the horizontal scale. In the example an exaggeration of 10 times was used.

When the street is curved as it is in this example, it is convenient to use a tick sheet to transfer the data from the plan to the profile sheet. To make a tick sheet any old piece of paper will do as long as it has a straight edge and is long enough. Start by making one edge (corner) 0 + 00, then mark on the sheet where each contour crosses the road. To do this around a curve, make a light tick on the paper and

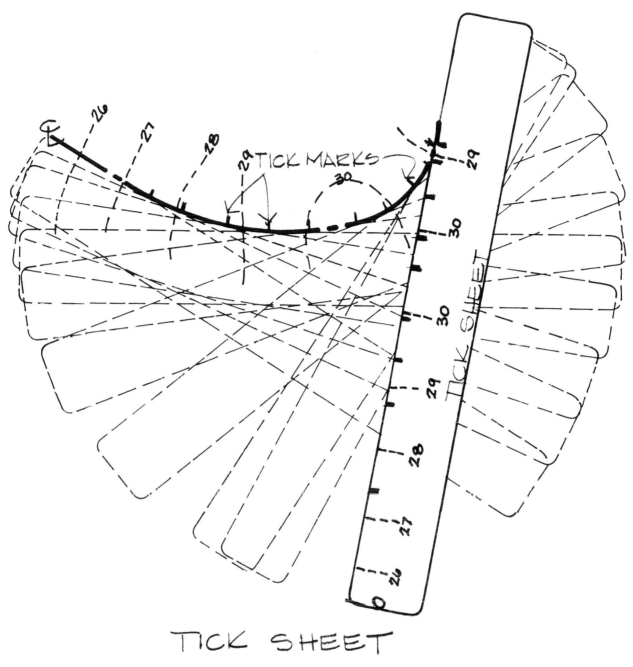

TICK SHEET

FIGURE 2-27

one on the plan. Then rotate the paper keeping these marks matched until you have a line along the curve. Again, reference this and continue rotating the tick sheet this way marking the contours as you go as illustrated in Figure 2–27.

When the tick sheet is done it can be taped under the profile grid and the elevations of each contour point referenced to the proper line. Then the points are connected with a smooth dashed line indicating the existing condition as shown in Figure 2–28.

Next, generalize the topography to a series of in-

tersecting tangent lines. These lines should correspond closely to the existing condition if possible. Next determine the difference in slope between each pair of lines and lay out the required vertical curves as shown in Figure 2–29.

For the example, the entering grade line was set at an even 3%, which is the maximum recommended slope at an intersection. A second line was drawn that intersects the entering grade line at station 3 + 78.00 and connects the existing 16.92 ft gutter elevation of Emerald City Blvd. at station 7 + 92.86.

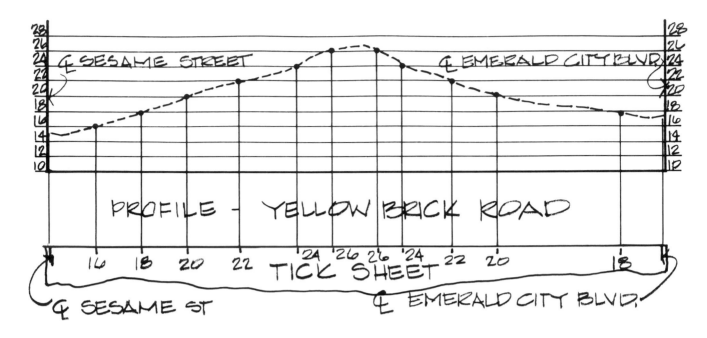

PROFILE PROJECTION FROM TICK SHEET

FIGURE 2-28

Then the slope of the second line was calculated as follows.

The distance from the apex to station 7 + 92.86 is

$$792.86 - 378 = 414.86 \text{ ft } (126.45 \text{ m})$$

The difference in elevation is

$$25.54 - 16.92 = 8.62 \text{ ft } (2.63 \text{ m})$$

$$G = \frac{8.62}{414.86} = .020778.$$

In verticle alignment problems the gradients should be carried out to several places to be sure rounding errors don't cause discrepancies in computed elevations over long distances.

The algebraic difference in the two lines is $(+.03) - (-.020778) = .50778$. From Table 2-3 we find that 10 ft (3.04 m) of vertical curve are required for each 1% of difference.

The minimum curve length then is

$$5.0778 \times 10 = 50.778 \text{ ft}$$

For example, however, we elected to use a 200 ft (60.8 m) curve to generate a smoother, visually pleasant transition of gradients.

The elevations were then computed on a vertical curve computation sheet, shown in Figure 2-30 (pages 100 and 101). Computation forms of this type are a convenient way of handling the data required for multiple calculations. They also make checking the computations easier. For the example problem the computations for each blank on the sheet will be worked in detail.

Design speed 20 mph.

Apex station 3 + 78 read from the plan-profile sheet.

d **(algebraic difference)** $(+.03) - (-.020778)$, $d = .050778$.

Curve length 200 ft (60.8 m) this length was a design decision as noted earlier.

PVC station The PVC station is the apex station less ½ the curve length. PVC station = 378 − 100 = 278. PVC = 2 + 78.

PVT station The PVT station is the apex station plus ½ the curve length. PVT station = 3 + 78 + 100 = 478 ft. PVT = 4 + 78.

PVC elevation The gradient = .03 the distance from the existing 14.68 elevation on Sesame Street to the apex is 262 ft.
$D = G \times L$
$D = .03 \times 262 = 7.86$ ft
$14.68 + 7.86 = 22.54$
PVC elevation = 22.54

Entering grade line elevation at PVT The distance from PVC to PVT is 200 ft (60.8 m). The gradient is still .03; therefore, $D = .03 \times 200$ ft (60.8 m) = 6 ft (1.82 m).
Elevation = 22.54 + 6 (1.82 m) = 28.54 ft (8.70 m).

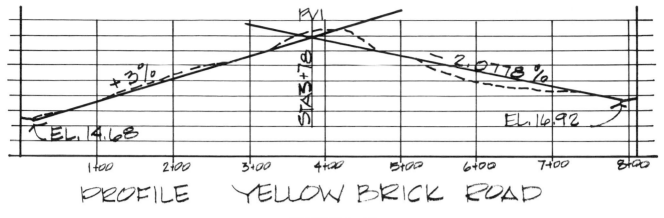

PROFILE YELLOW BRICK ROAD

FIGURE 2-29

Apex elevation The apex is 100 ft (30.8 m) from PVC and the gradient is .03. $D = .03 \times 100 = 3$ ft (.91 m). Apex elevation $= 22.54 + 3$ (.91 m) $= 25.54$ ft.

PVT elevation The departing slope line has a gradient of .020778. The distance from the apex to PVT is 100 ft (30.8 m).

$D = G \times L$

$D = .020778 \times 100 = 2.0778$ ft

PVT elevation $= 25.54 - 2.0778 = 23.46$ ft.

y of end ordinant

$$y = \frac{dL}{2} = \frac{.050778 \times 200}{2}$$

$$y = \frac{10.1556}{2} = 5.0778 \text{ ft}$$

$$y = 5.08 \text{ ft}$$

y of middle ordinant

$$y = \frac{dL}{8}$$

$$y = \frac{.050778 \times 200}{8} = \frac{10.1556}{8} = 1.27 \text{ ft}$$

Distance to HP or LP from PVC

$$HP = \frac{GL}{d}$$

$$HP = \frac{.03 \times 200}{.050778} = \frac{6}{.050778}$$

HP $= 118.16$ ft (36.15 m)

HP station $= 278 + 118.16 = 3 + 96.16$

The columns in the data sheet are then completed and the grades for selected stations are computed. For vertical curves it is customary to calculate elevations for all even 50 ft or 20 m stations that fall on the curve plus the elevations of PVC, PVT, and the high or low point. Therefore, the stations for this problem

are 2 + 78, 3 + 00, 3 + 50, (PVC); 3 + 96.16 (HP); 4 + 00, 4 + 50, 4 + 78 (PVT). These stations are entered in column one.

Column two is the distance of the station from PVC. For the example each station is subtracted from 278.

Column three is the elevation of the entering grade line at each of the selected stations. To obtain this value multiply column two by the gradient of the entering slope line. For example, D for station 3 + 50 is $72 \times .03 = .03 = 2.16$ ft.

Column four is the grade of the entering slope line at the selected station. This is obtained by adding or subtracting the value of column three to the elevation of PVC. For example, the entering slope grade at 4 + 00 is

$$22.54 + 3.66 = 26.2.$$

Column five is the square of the values in column two.

Column six is the distance (y) from the entering grade line to the curve. The value is found by multiplying column five by D and dividing by twice the curve length. For example, the y for station 4 + 50 is

$$y = \frac{29,584 \times .050778}{400} = \frac{1502.216352}{400}$$

$$y = 3.75 \text{ ft (1.14 m).}$$

Column seven is the elevation of the curve at the station. It is obtained by subtracting or adding the value of column six to column four. For example, the elevation on the curve at station 3 + 00 is

$$23.2 - .061 = 23.14 \text{ ft.}$$

Using this information, the parabola can be accurately plotted on the plan-profile sheet, and accurately staked in the field. The completed vertical curve sheet is shown here, and the completed plan-profile sheet is shown in Figure 2-30.

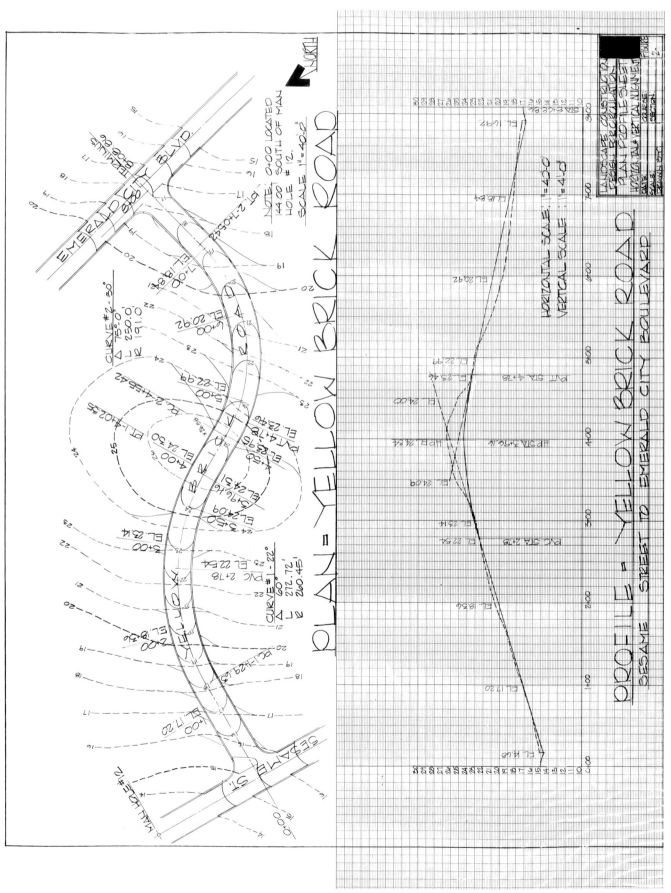

PLAN - YELLOW BRICK ROAD

PROFILE - YELLOW BRICK ROAD
SESAME STREET TO EMERALD CITY BOULEVARD

FIGURE 2-30

102

VERTICAL CURVE DATA

CURVE #1 YELLOW BRICK ROAD

DESIGN SPEED   30 MPH   PVI STA 3+78

DIFFERENCE (d) 5.0778   CURVE LENGTH (L) 200'

PVC STA. 2+78   PVT STA 4+78

PVC ELEV 22.54   PVI ELEV 25.54

ELEV OF ENTERING SLOPE LINE AT PVT 28.54

PVT ELEV. 23.46

END ORDINATE $\left(\frac{dL}{2}\right)$ 5.0778

Y OF MIDDLE ORDINANT $\left(\frac{dL}{8}\right)$ 1.27

DISTANCE TO HP OR LP FROM PVC $\left(\frac{ENTERING\ SLOPE \times L}{d}\right)$ 118.16

STATION	DISTANCE FROM PVC	RISE OR DROP OF ENT SLOPE LINE	GRADE OF ENT. SLOPE LINE	X^2	Y $Y = \frac{X^2 d}{2L}$	CURVE ELEV.
2+78	0	0	22.54	0	0	22.54
3+00	22	.66	23.20	484	.06	23.14
3+50	72	2.16	24.70	5184	.66	24.04
HP 3+96.16	118.16	3.54	26.08	13961.78	1.77	24.31
4+00	122	3.66	26.20	14848	1.88	24.32
4+50	172	5.16	27.70	29584	3.75	23.95
4+78	200	6.0	28.54	40000	5.0778	23.46

FIGURE 2-30 (Continued)

As we mentioned in the first chapter it is not usual practice to show revised contours on a final construction plan for streets. This is because they don't really provide any information necessary to build the street in the field. All the information required by the field personnel is given in the specifications, the cross section, and by spot elevations on the plan. In fact, showing the contours can actually confuse the issue.

On the other hand, you will find that it helps sometimes to go ahead and rough in the new contour lines just to help you visualize what is happening adjacent to the right of way. Sometimes you can pick up some grading revisions that would fit the street to the landscape better, and sometimes mistakes are easier to spot. Figure 2–30 shows the existing and proposed conditions on the plan-profile sheet.

SUPERELEVATION

Superelevation is the rotation of the pavement surface around the centerline to counteract the centrifugal force of the vehicle. Superelevation is rarely a consideration at low design speeds associated with residential subdivisions and small site projects. However, when you are involved with collector streets or long access roads that might be encountered in major park design or planned unit developments (PUDs), superelevation must be considered.

The most widely accepted standards for superelevation are those established by the American Association of State Highway Officials (AASHO) in *A Policy on Geometric Design of Rural Highways*. The AASHO standards are based on the equation

$$e + f = \frac{V^2}{15R},$$

where

e = superelevation in ft/ft (gradient);
f = the side friction factor (the ability of the vehicle to hold the pavement at an average speed and pavement condition);
V = the vehicle speed in mph;
R = the radius of the curve.

Metrication Block
Superelevation

$$e + f = \frac{V^2}{127.4R},$$

where

e = superelevation in m/m;
f = side friction factor;
V = velocity (design speed) in kph;
R = radius in meters.

TABLE 2–6
Superelevation Values for Selected Speeds and Selected Values of f

DESIGN SPEED		e		f		$e = f$	
mph	kph	ft/ft	cm/m	ft/ft	cm/m	ft/ft	cm/m
40	65	.06	6	.15	15	.21	21
		.10	10	.15	15	.25	25
50	80	.06	6	.14	14	.20	20
		.10	10	.14	14	.24	24
60	96	.06	6	.13	13	.19	19
		.10	10	.13	13	.23	23

Source: Adapted from AASHO data, *A Policy on Geometric Design of Rural Highways.*

The value of the side friction factor is a function of the design speed of the curve. The maximum value of e, the superelevation, is a function of development adjacent to the street that might limit speed, and climate. The values of f and the maximum recommended values of e are given in Table 2–6.

To illustrate the application of superelevation to a design situation consider Figure 2–31. A park access road to a boat ramp makes a 72° bend and is connected with a 12° curve ($R = 477.5$) which is the minimum curve for a speed of 40 mph. In this case superelevation should be considered.

To determine the value of e use the superelevation formula as follows:

$$e + f = \frac{V^2}{15R} \text{ (From Table 2–6 find } f = .15 \text{ for a speed of 40 mph.)}$$

$$e + f = \frac{40^2}{15 \times 477.5} = \frac{1600}{7162.5}$$

$$e + f = .2234$$
$$e = .2234 - .15 = .07 \text{ ft/ft}$$

Since there is no development along the road that would tend to limit the speed the calculated value is satisfactory.

The full superelevation begins at the PC station and continues to the PT station. The transition to full superelevation is made in the straight pavement sections approaching the curve. These transition sections are called runoff zones. There is no set standard for the length of the runoff zone but 300 ft (91.44 m) should be considered minimum to avoid an abrupt transition. Figure 2–32 illustrates the sectional transition to full superelevation for the example.

PEDESTRIAN WAYS

The design of a pedestrian circulation system is much less exacting than designing for vehicles, but no less important. If you will think for a moment,

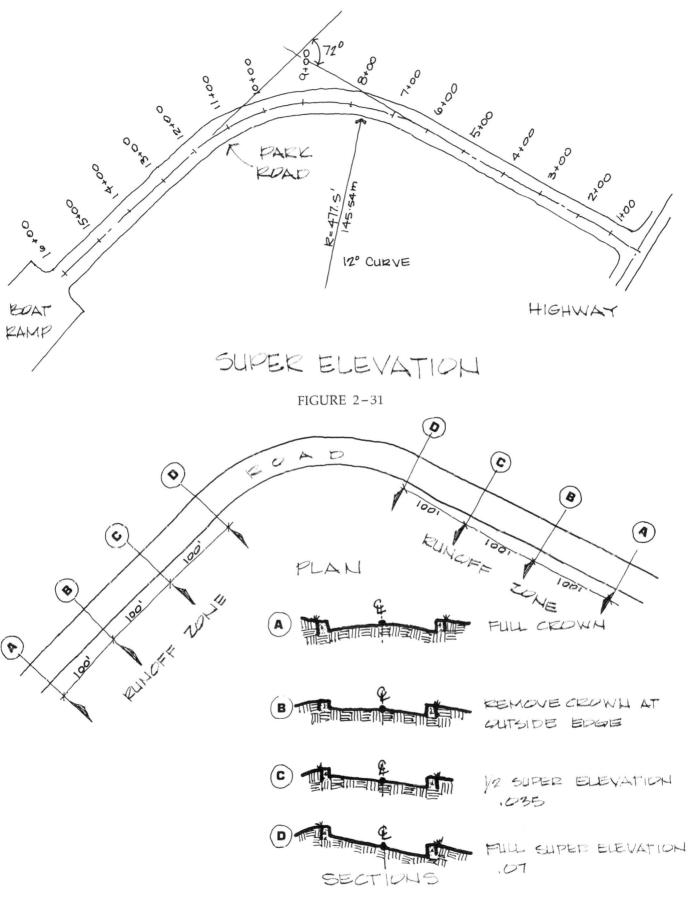

SUPER ELEVATION

FIGURE 2-31

SUPER ELEVATION

FIGURE 2-32

most major projects are experienced as a pedestrian. How we feel about a park or a group of buildings, such as a campus or a shopping center is largely a function of how we get to it. If the access is obstructed or circuitous, if the walks are steep and steps are uncomfortably proportioned the experience of the project is less than pleasant. On the other hand, if the system of access is well done, with attention to details, the experience of arriving can be pleasant or even exciting.

A second major consideration in the design of the pedestrian circulation system is providing access for the handicapped person. The law now requires that all new construction be barrier free. Barrier-free design is a study in itself and is beyond the scope of our discussion here. But you should know that these requirements are the responsibility of the designer, and that the term barrier-free design goes far beyond providing ramps for wheelchairs and cantilevered drinking fountains.

The most important design elements of the pedestrian system are the slopes of the walks, steps, ramps, and the construction materials.

Longitudinal slope   The most comfortable slopes for walks are between 1–3%; above 5% the average pedestrian will notice the grade (see Figure 2–33).

Maximum longitudinal slope   Long walks with slopes in excess of 5% should be avoided. 10% is the maximum recommended slope on walks where ice and snow are not a problem. 6% is the recommended maximum for ice and snow (see Figure 2–34).

Side slope   Side slopes on walks should be less than 3%. Slopes in excess of 3% are noticeable and uncomfortable for the average pedestrian (see Figure 2–35).

Steps   Outdoor steps should be proportioned larger than steps used inside buildings (see Figure 2–36). The maximum recommended riser height is 6 in. (150 mm) with a 14½–15 in. (380 mm) tread. A rule of thumb that is frequently used for step proportioning is The riser + the tread = 21 in. (530 mm). This is not an absolute and many nice combinations of tread and riser relationships can be developed.

Steps should occur in pairs   For safety, there should always be two or more steps. A single step might not be seen and can be a hazard (see Figure 2–37).

More than nine risers should be broken by a landing   When more than nine risers are required to achieve the desired change of grade the steps should be separated by a landing (see Figure 2–38). The landing provides a break, helps the pedestrian stay oriented, and adds interest to the experience.

Best ramp slope   The desirable slope for ramps is 6%. This allows easy access for mothers with strollers, wheelchairs, and older people (see Figure 2–39).

Maximum ramp slope   The maximum ramp slope is 10% but it is extremely difficult for a wheelchair to negotiate (see Figure 2–40).

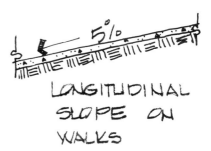

LONGITUDINAL SLOPE ON WALKS

FIGURE 2–33

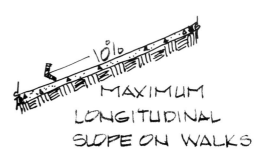

MAXIMUM LONGITUDINAL SLOPE ON WALKS

FIGURE 2–34

SIDE SLOPE ON WALKS

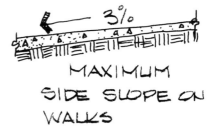

MAXIMUM SIDE SLOPE ON WALKS

SLOPE ON WALKS

FIGURE 2–35

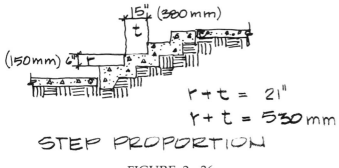

STEP PROPORTION

FIGURE 2-36

STEPS SHOULD OCCUR
IN PAIRS

FIGURE 2-37

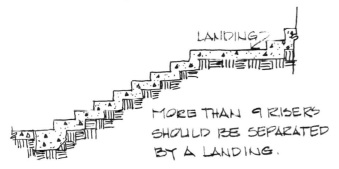

MORE THAN 9 RISERS
SHOULD BE SEPARATED
BY A LANDING.

STEPS

FIGURE 2-38

PREFERD SLOPE
FOR RAMPS

FIGURE 2-39

MAXIMUM
SLOPE FOR RAMPS
FOR SHORT DISTANCES

RAMPS

FIGURE 2-40

The materials used for pedestrian ways are also important. Smooth surfaces such as steel, trowled concrete, trazzo, and small smooth aggregates become very slick when wet and should never be used outside. They should especially be avoided as finishes on steps.

Also keep in mind that feet are very sensitive, and walks must be designed as a tactile experience. For example, loose material may be appealing visually, but it is not a pleasant walking experience. Likewise large or sharp aggregates, $3/4-1\frac{1}{4}$ in. (20-30 mm), are unpleasant surfaces.

BICYCLE WAYS

The bicycle has become increasingly popular as a means of transportation in this country and accommodation of the bicyclist is a major problem. Unfortunately the bicycle does not mix well with either the pedestrian or the automobile. The automobile presents a danger to the cyclist and the cyclist is a hazard to the pedestrian. Obviously the best solution to this problem is the provision of a separate circulation system for bicycles, but the cost of providing a separate system is usually prohibitive. We would suggest, however, that the reason the costs seem prohibitive now is because bicycles are not considered as a program element in the development of most new projects. If the designer will begin with the bicycle as a major element in the program stage, the cost of the separate system can be minimized.

Currently there are several publications that deal with the development of bike trails and paths. Most of these publications deal with the problem by painting bike lanes on existing streets, signing, etc. From a design standpoint these must be considered stopgap measures only. As a designer and a site planner you are encouraged to avoid these and search for real solutions within the individual project.

Some innovative ideas that are already being explored include the provision of bicycle ways along major drainage ways, using the park system as a skeleton for the bike way system, and developing connecting links between existing parks. Other opportunities exist in the form of active or abandoned railroad rights of way and old alley rights of way.

Some elements that should be considered in the design of bike ways include the slopes of the path, the width, and the construction materials.

Longitudinal slope Long gradients in excess of 5% should be avoided if possible. Any grade between 3% and 5% will put a strain on the cyclist (see Figure 2-41).

Side slope Side slopes should be held to 2%, values greater than 2% are uncomfortable for the average cyclist (see Figure 2-42).

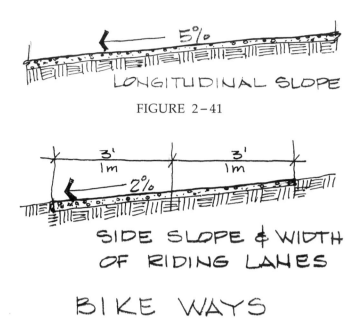

LONGITUDINAL SLOPE

FIGURE 2-41

SIDE SLOPE & WIDTH
OF RIDING LANES

BIKE WAYS

FIGURE 2-42

Width   3 ft (1 m) should be provided for each riding lane. 7 ft (2 m) is preferred for a path with two-way traffic (see Figure 2–42).

The materials used for bike paths should be smooth, not slick. Steel trowel concrete finishes are dangerous to the cyclist when wet. Expansion and control joints should be perpendicular to the flow and as narrow as possible. Drainage inlets and other structures on the path should have very small openings so narrow wheels will roll over them easily. Rough aggregate finishes or masonry units should be avoided on bike paths.

PROBLEMS

1. Calculate the horizontal alignment data in Figure P2–1 for the following proposed center line. Use a 200 ft radius.

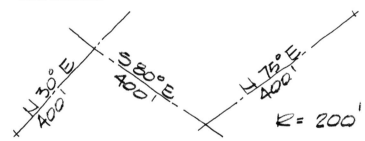

FIGURE P2–1

2. Calculate the horizontal alignment data in Figure P2–2 for the proposed centerline, use a 300 ft radius and provide the stations for PCs, PTs and all even stations.

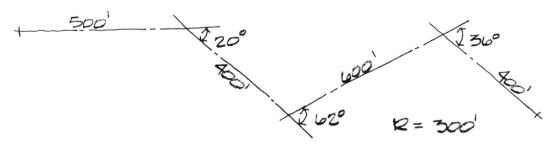

FIGURE P2–2

3. Calculate the horizontal alignment data in Figure P2–3 for the proposed centerline using a 10° curve. Provide all PC and PT stations as well as even stations.

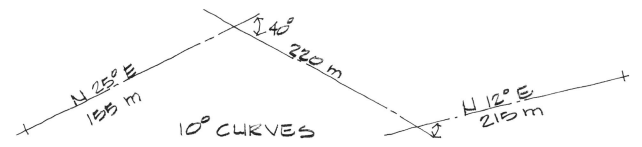

FIGURE P2–3

4–7. Prepare a vertical curve sheet (see blank Vertical Curve Data sheet on page 111 for style) for each of the following proposed profiles based on the data given.

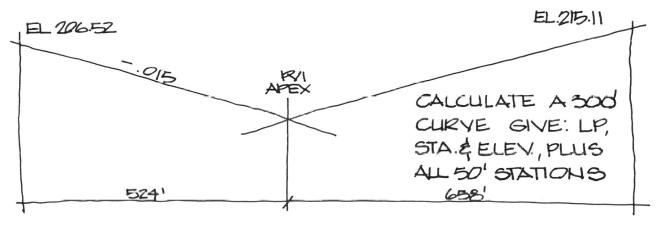

FIGURE P2–4

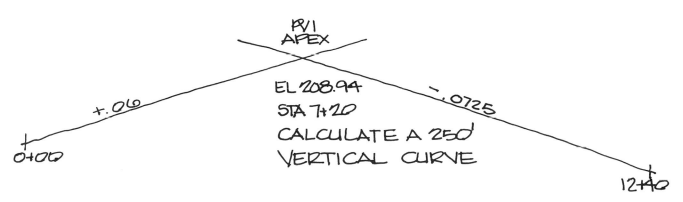

FIGURE P2–5

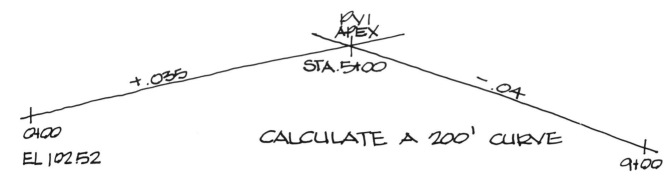

FIGURE P2–6

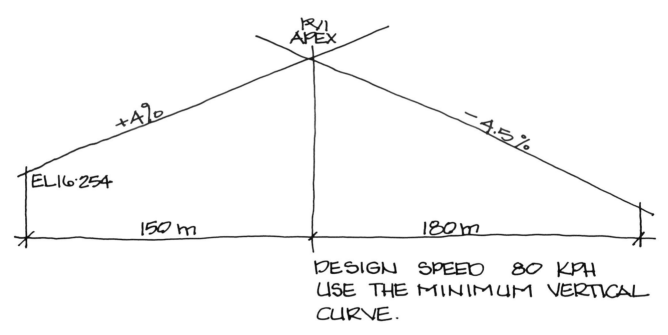

FIGURE P2–7

8. Calculate the superelevation for a 12° curve with a design speed of 40 mph.

9. Calculate the superelevation for a curve with R = 750 ft.

10. Calculate the superelevation for a 3° curve with a design speed of 70 mph. Ice and snow are factors.

11. Calculate the superelevation for a 7° curve at a design V of 80 kph.

12. Calculate the superelevation for a radius of 335 m.

VERTICAL CURVE DATA

CURVE# _____

DESIGN SPEED	PVI STA
DIFFERENCE (d)	CURVE LENGTH (L)
PVC STA	PVT STA.
PVC ELEV	PVI ELEV

ELEV. OF ENTERING SLOPE LINE AT PVT _____

PVT ELEV _____

END ORDINATE $\left(\frac{dL}{2}\right)$ _____

Y OF MIDDLE ORDINATE $\left(\frac{dL}{8}\right)$ _____

DISTANCE TO HP OR LP FROM PVC $\left(\frac{\text{ENTERING SLOPE} \times L}{d}\right)$

STATION	DISTANCE FROM PVC	RISE OR DROP OF ENT SLOPE LINE	GRADE OF ENT. SLOPE LINE	X^2	Y $Y=\frac{X^2 d}{2L}$	CURVE ELEV.

3
Drainage Design

The surface and subsurface drainage systems are an integral part of the final form of a project. As we mentioned earlier, circulation paths, roads, trails, highways, and streets, exercise a broad influence on the conceptualization of final form. Likewise, the drainage system of a site exercises a similar control over the evolution of site form. Each of these systems, circulation and drainage, are linked together by functional and operational necessities that require design sensitivity and technical competence.

In the initial stages of site analysis one of the first steps is an analysis of the site hydrography and hydrology. This analysis is done to identify the elements of the existing drainage system that will impose limitations on the final project form. At the same time we are looking for those elements that can, or possibly should, be changed.

Depending on the scope and nature of the project we may be interested in not only the on-site surface conditions but in off-site conditions and subsurface conditions as well. In recent years our laws and attitudes regarding rights to surface and subsurface water have changed considerably. The need to conserve and protect our water supplies has become an increasing concern that requires a more thorough understanding of water practice on the part of the designer.

Thus in our study of drainage we are not only concerned with often-stated objectives of collecting, conducting, and disposing of the water, we are concerned with preservation of existing water flow, the quality of the runoff, effects of erosion and silting, the effects on ground water recharge, etc. All of these major concerns are tied directly to our ability to interpret and skillfully design site drainage.

It is fairly obvious that in a text of this scope we will not be able to cover in depth all of the issues raised in the introductory remarks. Our mission here is to lay a framework of basic knowledge that will help you understand the problems and set the stage for more detailed study as it is required.

CONTEMPORARY ISSUES IN DRAINAGE DESIGN

Before we begin our technical discussion of on-site drainage considerations we would like to preface it with a brief discussion of the broad scope of drainage issues that confront the designer. In a purely academic sense drainage can be broken into two categories: surface and subsurface drainage. Surface drainage deals with the management, control, transportation, storage, and disposal of water on the surface. Subsurface drainage deals with the management, control, and protection of underground water.

The issue of surface drainage is one that will become increasingly important over the coming decades, because we are turning more and more to surface water impoundments for fresh water supply. The politics of impounding water upstream and cutting off the supply to the downstream users has already become an issue in the western states and between the United States and Mexico. The Texas Water Plan, for example, proposes diverting water from the Mississippi River to the northwest part of the state. These and many other projects proposed are underway and will all have a profound effect on our future approach to the concept of surface drainage. The problem is not a local or even a national problem; it's global, and projects involving only small areas will have an effect on the total system.

Some of the important pieces in the current puzzle

worth mentioning are the concept of zero runoff, flood control, stream and creek channelization, and surface erosion control.

The concept called zero runoff addresses several recent concerns. The term itself is a misnomer because zero runoff schemes usually maintain the estimated current runoff quantities from a site. In other words there is no net increase or decrease in runoff quantity permitted because of construction. In very simple terms, if a site is built to have zero runoff, some on-site provision must be made to store excess runoff from structures and paved areas allowing it to percolate into the ground as it would have before construction. Figure 3–1 illustrates the basic principles of zero runoff.

Another major issue involved in the problem of surface drainage is the whole concept of flood control. Flood control is traditionally accomplished in two ways: channelization or impoundment. Over the years, the Army Corps of Engineers and the Soil Conservation Service have been engaged in massive flood control efforts that involve the smallest water sheds to efforts as large as controlling the Mississippi River. The efforts to date have no doubt resulted in saving billions of dollars in lost lives and property. On the other hand, the environmental costs of these efforts now seem questionable. For example, there is a definite correlation between the problems of beach erosion in coastal areas and upstream impoundments for flood control. Likewise channelization results in similar environmental costs in the destruction of marine habitat and upstream ecosystems.

The solution to this set of problems is still probably many years away. Our current thinking seems to lean in the direction of some logical balancing of flood control measures and recognition of land suitabilities in major drainage basins. A step in this direction has been the national program of flood insurance. This program provides insurance against flood damage for structures outside the intermediate regional flood plane. In order to be eligible for the program a community must adhere to planning principles restricting construction that might increase flood potential in an area. Figure 3–2 illustrates the principles of the flood insurance program.

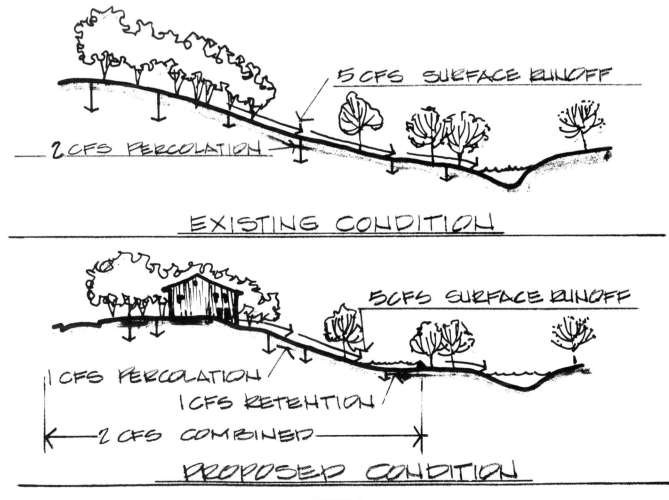

FIGURE 3–1

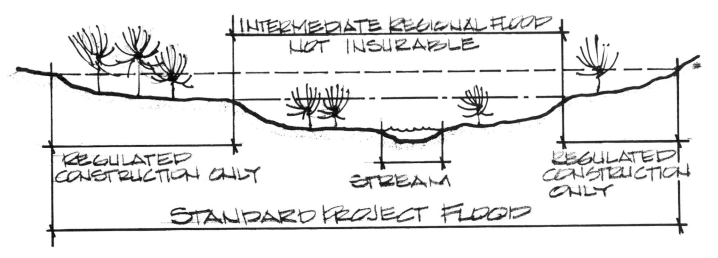

FIGURE 3-2

A final issue that must be considered in the surface drainage design strategy is erosion and siltation. Sheet erosion of fine, organic topsoils is a danger and a problem during all construction. In the past this problem was frequently written off as being only a temporary condition that occurs during the construction period. This kind of rationalization is not at all acceptable in light of our current understanding. Highway construction, for example, can lay bare acre upon acre of land for up to four years. This four-year period is more than enough time to loose all of the top soil to sheet erosion, increase sediment loads in streams beyond reasonable limits and all but prevent an economic reforestation of the roadside environment.

The effects of cultivated agricultural lands, especially where high concentrations of fertilizer and pesticide materials are encountered, also enter the drainage picture. Runoff from these areas is just as bad if not worse than the runoff from urban land.

Subsurface drainage is no less important to our discussion, although it is frequently ignored. This is particularly true when high water tables are not a factor in construction. Runoff is not just a surface phenomenon. There is also subsurface runoff. Subsurface runoff travels vertically as well as horizontally in the earth's crust. When water encounters an impervious layer in the crust it will collect and travel along that layer to the lowest point. Figure 3-3 illustrates the basics of subsurface runoff.

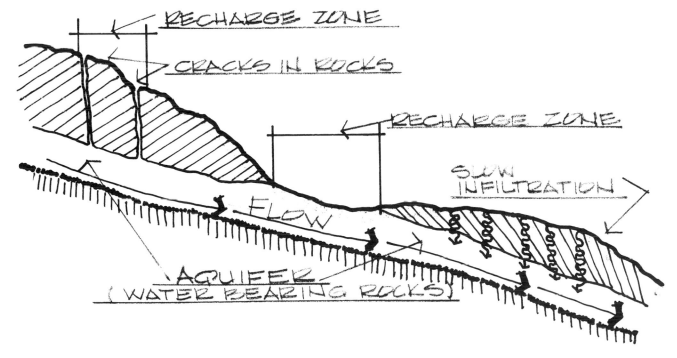

FIGURE 3-3

Today much of our potable water is drawn from these subsurface reservoirs. The problem is the ability of the recharge areas to supply the volume of water being withdrawn, as well as maintaining the quality of the recharge water. When the withdrawal demand on an aquifer exceeds the recharge capacity, several unpleasant things can happen. Salt water can begin to move into the strata replacing the fresh water being removed. If the salt water can't move in, there is a loss of subsurface volume and the surface will settle. This phenomenon is called subsidence. This usually occurs in the form of regional subsidence such as the problem in Houston, Texas where extensive water withdrawal has resulted in subsidence of as much as 4 ft (1.5 m) in 10 years. At other times the settling is a localized disaster known as a sink-hole where the surface collapses into a large hole taking everything on the surface with it. This condition occurs frequently in Florida and other areas supported by limestone.

Some other issues that are more site specific relate to subdrainage. These include groundwater pollution, recharge reduction, and modification of the microenvironment in the soil.

The first two issues go hand in hand because construction on or upstream of a recharge area does two things. First, it will effect the volume of surface water that reaches the recharge area. Upstream construction can increase the volume somewhat but the recharge soil may not be able to effectively absorb the excess. Construction on the recharge area will usually effectively decrease the water moving into the soil and reduce the recharge capability of the aquifer. Along with the reduction in recharge the construction will usually decrease the water quality by introducing added pollutants at the surface. These pollutants enter the soil and further decrease the potability of the groundwater supply.

Subdrainage is frequently used where high water tables are encountered and has a high environmental cost. The natural vegetation that exists on such a site will typically be a moisture-loving species. If the soil is modified by installing extensive subdrainage, the plant environment has been changed, and the vegetation must exist in an overstressed state or die.

A study of these issues can be expanded far beyond this brief discussion. Our major concern is that we have placed the technical discussion of drainage in a design issue context. In other words, the technological means at our disposal to solve drainage problems efficiently are many and varied, but the proof of their efficiency must be measured against the broad objectives of the design situation and the environmental costs.

ESTIMATING STORM RUNOFF

The first step in solving a drainage problem involves making an estimate of the runoff volume. While there are many different methods employed to estimate volumes of surface runoff, the most popular and widely accepted of these empirical formulas is the rational formula. The rational formula is represented by the expression:

$$Q = CiA$$

where

Q = The peak runoff rate in cubic feet per second or cubic meters per second;

C = The coefficient of runoff;

i = The rainfall intensity in inches per hour for a design peak rainstorm adjusted to a duration equal to the "time of concentration" of the watershed;

A = Area of the watershed in acres or hectares.

Metrication Block
Rational formula in metric units

$$Q = .00277\ CiA$$

where

Q = Runoff volume in m³/sec;

i = Rainfall intensity in mm/hr

C = Runoff coefficient (dimensionless)

A = Area in hectares (ha)

The rational formula is based on two assumptions. First, it is assumed that rainfall will occur at a uniform intensity for a time equal to the time of concentration of the watershed, the time of concentration being the time it takes for all areas in the watershed to contribute water to the outlet. The second assumption is that the rainfall will occur at a uniform intensity over the entire watershed. If these assumptions are true, then the relationship of runoff to rainfall can be represented by the graph in Figure 3–4.

These two assumptions are based on the statistical records of rainstorms. The records show that storms of short duration are of high intensity and storms of long duration are of low intensity. This being the case, it is reasonable to assume that a storm of shorter duration than the design time of concentration would not produce runoff greater than Q. This is because all areas of the watershed are not contributing simultaneously to the runoff. This fact compensates for the anticipated higher intensity. If a storm occurs with a duration greater than the design time of concentration, runoff will still be less than Q be-

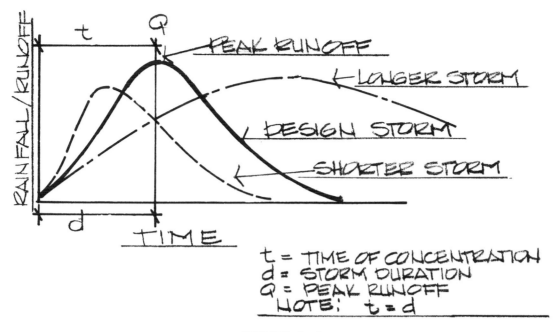

FIGURE 3–4

cause it will be of lower intensity. Curves that illustrate the effects of storms of longer or shorter duration are also shown in Figure 3–4.

It is recognized that this reasoning is a gross oversimplification of a much more complicated process. Nonetheless, the results obtained are well within acceptable limits for watersheds up to 5 square miles or 12 square kilometers, for formal construction practice.

The unit most critical to the successful application of the rational formula is the time of concentration (t_c). In recent years there have been several different methods developed for calculating t_c. Some are presented in graphic form as in Figure 3–5 adapted from *Design*, by Seelye.[1]

Another method is a formula developed for airport drainage design. It is probably more accurate than the nomograph since the designer can adjust the runoff coefficient (C) more accurately to simulate the site conditions. The time of concentration (t_c) can be estimated by the expression:

$$t_c = .619(1.1 - C) L^{.5}S^{-.33},$$

where

t_c = the time of concentration in minutes;
C = the coefficient of runoff;
L = the distance from the outlet to the furthest point in the watershed in feet;
S = the average gradient of the watershed.

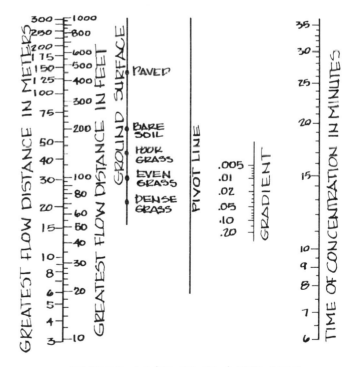

OVERLAND FLOW TIMES

ADAPTED FROM GRAPH IN DESIGN: DATA BOOK FOR CIVIL ENGINEERS. SEELYE

[1]See Selected Bibliography, Chapter 3, reference 12.

FIGURE 3–5

> **Metrication Block**
> $t_c = 1.12 (1.1 - C) .3048L^{.5}S^{-.33}$;
> C = the runoff coefficient;
> L = the distance from the outlet to the most distant point in the watershed in meters;
> S = the average gradient of the watershed.

The rainfall intensity (i) will be estimated based on the design storm intensity. In other words, what is the most intense storm likely to occur once in a given time span. This is a design decision based on the relative value of the property to be protected balanced by the expense of providing the protection.

For example, using a 100-year design storm for a residential subdivision can hardly be justified because the cost of providing such a system would increase the development cost beyond reason. Thus in the design process we must decide what level of protection to provide and what level of flooding is tolerable. Going back to the residential subdivision, we would probably design for a 10- or 25-year storm since some minor flooding of lawns, streets, and driveways can be tolerated.

The value of i is best obtained from local governmental agencies and may be specified by code or ordinance. In lieu of any local standards i can be estimated from rainfall records obtained from the U.S. Weather Bureau, and other technical reference books. If these sources are not available i can be estimated by the Steel formula. The Steel formula is represented by the expression:

$$i = \frac{k}{t_c + b}$$

where

i = the rainfall intensity in inches per hour for a design storm frequency;

k and b = constants that are based on rainfall frequency characteristics and region. These values are given in Table 3–1 and the regions are depicted in Figure 3–6;

t_c = the time of concentration in minutes.

> **Metrication Block**
> Since k and b are constants and t is in minutes, the conversion to millimeters involves multiplying the equation by 25.4. Thus
> $$i = 25.4 \left(\frac{k}{t_c + b} \right)$$
> which yields rainfall intensity in millimeters per hour.

The runoff coefficient C is the ratio of peak runoff to the intensity of rainfall. In other words, the percentage of rainfall that actually becomes runoff. These values are related specifically to the infiltration rates of the soil, surface cover, channel and surface storage capacity, and rainfall intensity. The value of C is usually assumed by the designer based on some knowledge of the existing field conditions and the proposed structures. Table 3–2 is a compilation of runoff coefficient values taken from a number of sources and summerized. These values can be used as guidelines if local jurisdictions do not have established standards.

To illustrate the application of the rational method for estimating runoff consider the following problem, shown in Figure 3–7. The problem is to find the value of Q based on a 10-year design storm fre-

TABLE 3–1
Rainfall Intensity by Region Values of k and b for Steel Formula

DESIGN STORM YEAR	COEFFICIENTS	REGION (SEE FIGURE 3–6)						
		1	2	3	4	5	6	7
2	k	206	140	106	70	70	68	32
	b	30	21	17	13	16	14	11
5	k	247	190	131	97	81	75	48
	b	29	25	19	16	13	12	12
10	k	300	230	170	111	111	122	60
	b	36	29	23	16	17	23	13
25	k	327	260	230	170	130	155	67
	b	33	32	30	27	17	26	10
50	k	315	350	250	187	187	160	65
	b	28	38	27	24	25	21	8
100	k	367	375	290	220	240	210	77
	b	33	36	31	28	29	26	10

TABLE 3–2
Approximate Values of C for Stated Condition

CONDITION	VALUE OF C
Roofs	.95 – 1.00
Pavement (concrete and asphalt)	.90 – 1.00
Roads (clay and gravel)	.30 – .90
Bare soils	
Sand	.20 – .40
Clay	.30 – .75
Grassed surfaces	
Sand	.05 – .40
Clay	.15 – .60
Developed areas	
Commercial areas	.60 – .75
High density residential	.55 – .65
Low density residential	.30 – .55
Parks and open space (developed)	.10 – .30

quency for a 255 ha watershed in Lowneds County, Georgia.

First find the value of t using the formula

$$t_c = 1.12 (1.1 - C) .3084 L^{.5} S^{-.33}$$

Calculate the slope(s) as:

$$G = \frac{D}{L}$$

$$D = 275.025 - 258.386 = 16.642 \text{ m}$$
$$L = 350 \text{ m}$$

$$G = \frac{16.642}{350.00} = .0475$$

Assume $C = .55$. Using Table 3–2 as a guide we would estimate the runoff coefficient as .55 taking the high value for suburban residential areas. The high value was selected based on the high slope of almost 5%.

$$t_c = 1.12 (1.1 - .5)(.3048 \times 350)^{.5} .0475^{-.33}$$
$$t_c = 1.12 \times .6 \times 10.329 \times 2.733$$
$$t_c = 18.970 \text{ (19 min)}$$

Next estimate i for a 10-year design storm frequency with $t_c = 19$ min as follows.

Lowneds County, Georgia is in extreme south Georgia, zone one, on the map for the Steel formula.

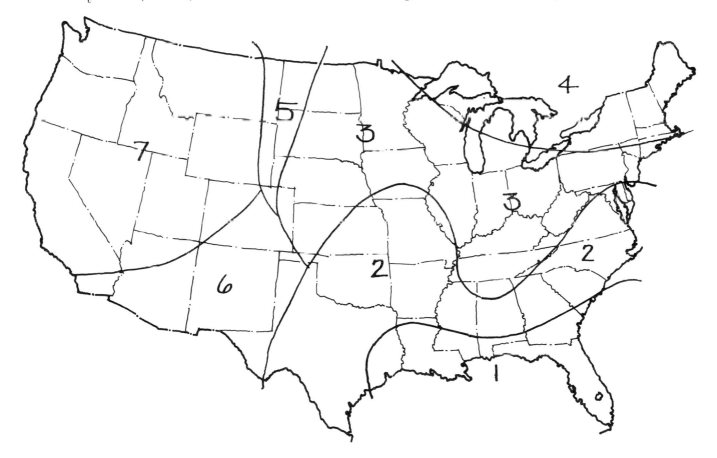

RAINFALL REGIONS FOR THE STEEL FORMULA

FIGURE 3–6

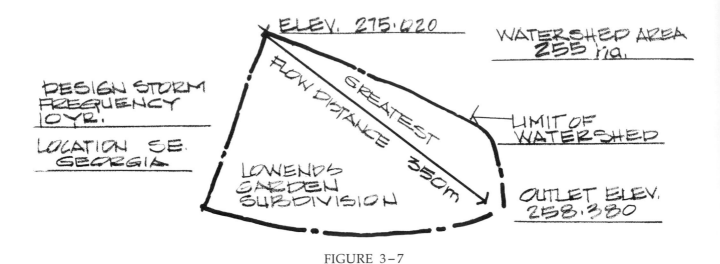

FIGURE 3–7

The zone one coefficients for a 10-year storm are $K=$ 300 and $b=$ 36. Substituting into the equation find that

$$i = 25.4 \left(\frac{300}{19 + 36} \right)$$

$$i = 25.4 \times 5.455$$
$$i = 138.545 \text{ mm/hr.}$$

Now, substituting into the rational formula find Q

$$Q = .00277 \, (CiA) = .00277 \, (.55 \times 138.545 \times 255)$$
$$Q = 53.82 \text{ m}^3/\text{sec}$$

You will find in practice and further study that there are several other methods and tables that can be used to estimate runoff as well as the other terms used in the equation. These tables and formulas will give slightly different values in each instance. The method used in practice is usually based on field experience and judgment. What has been presented here is the methodology believed to be the most commonly accepted and widely utilized for small-site design.

DESIGN OF SURFACE DRAINAGE SYSTEMS

Surface drainage systems are composed of surface swales and ditches, used to collect, transport, and dispose of surface runoff. The ability of a storm drainage system to function efficiently is related directly to the channel's size, shape, and the fluid behavior of water.

Fluid Behavior

It is essential before we begin a technical discussion of drainage design that we develop some basic understanding of fluid behavior. In this instance we are particularly interested in the properties of water behavior as it is influenced by gravity.

Hydraulics is an exacting science that deals with the behavior of liquid materials. However, the natural conditions encountered in the field are the aggregation of so many variables that it is impossible to consider each detail. Essentially the hydraulic techniques that we will use for site design are all empirical models that have been developed by experimentation and observation. They are in fact methods that allow good guesses to be made about how water will behave under given conditions.

Water under the influence of gravity will move toward the lowest possible elevation, taking the shape of its container. Once it reaches this low point it becomes static, or displays no directional motion. It will then continue to collect in the container raising the surface elevation of the water (Figure 3–8).

The properties of water that we are most interested in are volume, weight, and velocity of flow. Water volume is expressed in gallons (liters) and weight is expressed in pounds (kilograms). Velocity measures are expressed in cubic feet per second (cfs) or cubic meters per second (m³/sec).

For our purposes we assume that water cannot be compressed; therefore, the volume of water that is placed in a system is always constant as is the weight: 64.4/ft³ (1 kg/liter). Velocity, however, is variable depending on the external influences of slopes, gravitational acceleration called velocity head, and the resistance of the surface to the flow of water.

Velocity of flow in a drainage system is important for many reasons. First the velocity of flow is directly proportional to the volume of water transported in a system. In other words as velocity increase, volume increases. Velocity also is related to erosion, scower, and sedimentation. High velocities in a pipe or a drainage channel will cause accelerated rates of erosion and scour. Excessive scour will result in the weakening and eventual failure of pipe joints or

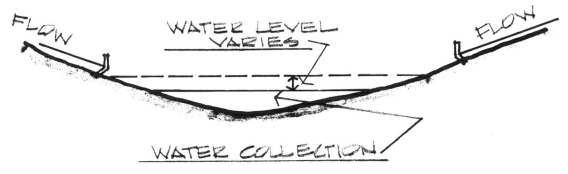

FIGURE 3-8

other structures in the channel. High velocities in vegetated drainage channels will destroy the vegetation and lead to severe erosion. Low velocities bring with them an equally distressing set of problems. If velocities are too low, solid materials in the water will settle out in the form of silt and sedimentation. These materials will eventually build up and block the flow of water in the channel.

Uniform Flow

Theoretically, as water begins to flow in a pipe or channel it should continue to accelerate at a constant rate. This does not occur, however, since the channel surface resists the flow and the water slows down. In actuality, water in a channel flows at several different velocities as illustrated in Figure 3-9. The reason for this is that liquids have very low resistance to shear stress. Therefore, water in contact with the channel flows slower than water near the center of the channel. The important thing to realize is that when we speak of velocities in an open channel we are referring to the mean velocity of the entire cross section.

Design for storm drainage is concerned first with an understanding of the overall design objectives. These in large measure will establish the constraints on the type of drainage system that is most appropriate. Once this is fixed we must be able to estimate the velocity of flow and the most appropriate section for the drainage channel. The rest of this chapter will concentrate on the technical aspects of determining these two variables.

DESIGN OF OPEN CHANNELS

An open drainage channel is any drainage course that is open to the atmosphere. Normally we associate this term with vegetated swales and open ditches. However, a pipe that is flowing partly full is open to the atmosphere and the water will behave the same as in other open channels.

Drainage channels that have constant cross sections and slopes will have uniform flow. If the slope of the hydraulic surface (the water surface) is equal to the slope of the invert (Figure 3-10), the discharge of the channel will be related directly to the velocity of flow.

This relationship of velocity of flow to cross-sectional area and volume is expressed as:

$$Q = Va$$

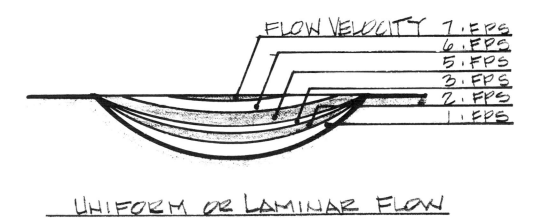

FIGURE 3-9

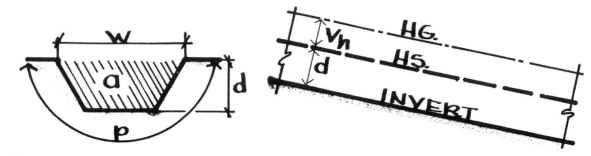

CROSS SECTION   LONGITUDINAL SECTION

W   CHANNEL WIDTH
a   CROSS SECTIONAL AREA
P   WETTED PERIMETER
d   DEPTH OF FLOW
HG. HYDRAULIC GRADIENT
HS. HYDRAULIC SURFACE
Vh VELOCITY HEAD

PROPERTIES OF HYDRAULIC SECTIONS

FIGURE 3–10

where

Q = Volume of flow in cubic feet per second or cubic meters per second;

V = Velocity in feet per second (average) or meters per second;

a = The cross-sectional area of the channel in ft² or m².

The depth of flow in a channel is represented by the algebraic term d. This is the vertical distance between the invert of the channel and the water surface. The length of the channel cross section (circumference) in contact with the water is represented by the algebraic term p, the wetted perimeter. The term hydraulic radius is the ratio between the cross-sectional area a and the wetted perimeter p. This is given by the expression

$$r = \frac{a}{p}$$

where

r = The hydraulic radius,
a = The cross-sectional area,
p = The wetted perimeter.

All of these relationships are illustrated in Figure 3–10. These terms are important because they are basic to all drainage systems.

As we have already discussed, the volume of water that a drainage channel will carry is a function of slope, the channel's resistance to the flow, the velocity of flow of the cross-sectional area of the ditch, and the length of the wetted perimeter of the pipe in relation to the cross-sectional area. To this point we have presented ways of calculating all of these variables except velocity.

Velocity, like runoff, can be calculated by any number of empirical equations. The most popular of all these is called the Manning formula. The Manning formula is an algebraic approximation of a more complex formula called the Kutter formula. Like all empirical models the Manning formula is not absolutely accurate but it provides an acceptable approximation of what will actually happen. The formula is written

$$V = \left(\frac{1.486}{n}\right) r^{.67} S^{.5}$$

where

V = Mean velocity in ft/second or m/sec;
r = The hydraulic radius in ft or meters;
S = The mean gradient of the watershed;
n = Friction coefficient of the channel.

The only new term in this equation is n, the friction coefficient. The friction coefficient is a measure

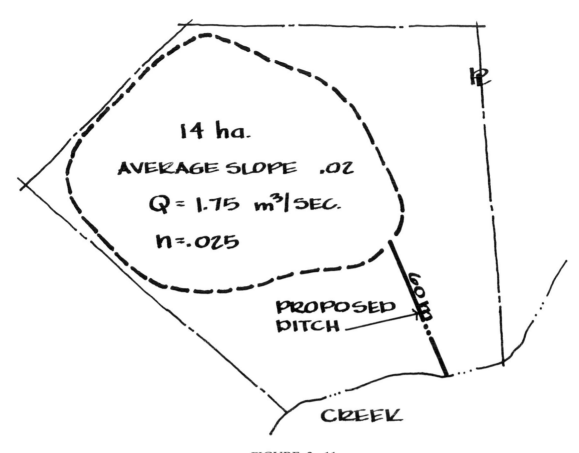

FIGURE 3-11

of the channels resistance to the flow of water. Table 3-3 gives several suggested values for n in various situations. All of these values are empirically estimated and require that the designer exercise judgment in determining its value for each situation.

To illustrate how all of these variables fit together in a system consider the watershed illustrated in Figure 3-11. Our task is to design a drainage chan-

TABLE 3-3
Common Design Values of n
for Use with Manning Formula[a]

CHANNEL SURFACE	VALUE OF n
Cast iron pipe	0.012
Corrugated steel pipe	0.032
Clay drainage tile (agtile)	0.014
Cement grout surfaces	0.013
Concrete pipe (R.C.P.)	0.015
Open concrete inverts	0.016
Uniform earth ditches	0.0225
Rock cut channels	0.033
Winding channels (clear)	0.025

[a]Adapted from *Design: Data Book for Civil Engineers*, by Elwin E. Seelye.

nel to carry the water from the watershed in the northwest part of the site to the creek at the southeast boundary. As we have already seen, the hydraulic efficiency of a channel will be dependent on n, the friction coefficient, the slope of the channel, s, and the hydraulic radius, r. Since there are an infinite number of combinations of these variables, any number of ditch sections could theoretically be devised to do the job. However, the velocity of travel is the critical consideration. The normally acceptable range of velocities is 2-4 ft/sec (.6-1.22 m/sec) in turf channels and 2-8 ft/sec (.6-2.44 m/sec) in paved or piped channels.

The process of designing a ditch is trial and error. It involves selecting trial cross sections and testing them to see if they will be big enough and operate within acceptable velocity limits. A quick way of selecting a trial section is by using the graph in Figure 3-12. This graph relates velocity and flow to the typical sections in Figure 3-13. These were adapted from tables in *Design* by Seelye to read in both English and metric units. To illustrate how the graph and tables are used, we will work through the example problem step by step.

For our purposes in this example we will use an n value of .025. Note that the graph in Figure 3-12

PROPERTIES OF COMMON DITCH SECTIONS

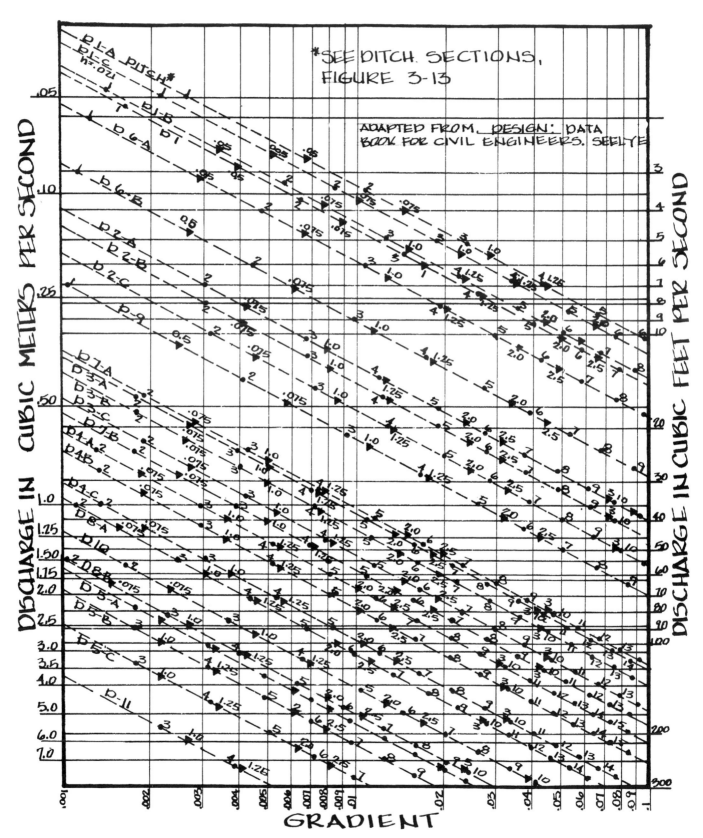

FIGURE 3-12

used an n value of .030, so Q will have to be adjusted to employ the graph.[2]

$$Q = 1.75 \text{ m}^3/\text{sec}$$
$$S = .02$$
$$n = .025$$

Adjust Q by:

$$\frac{.030}{n} = \frac{.030}{.025} = 1.2$$

$$Q = 1.75 \times 1.2$$
$$Q = 2.1$$

The adjusted value of Q is 2.1 m³/sec (6.89 ft/sec).

Enter the table along the discharge line of 2.1 m³/sec (6.89 ft/sec) until it intersects the .02 slope line. The point occurs between ditch section D-3C and D-3B. D-3C would be selected since it has the larger cross section. However, notice that the velocity is approximately 2 m/sec (6.89 ft/sec). This is greater than the 1.22 m/sec recommended. Therefore, it will be necessary to reduce the slope of the ditch to something less than the existing slope of the ground.

Looking back in the table we find that the desired velocity occurs at the intersection of D-8A and a slope of approximately .0045. So, for our trial section we would select section D-8A. The dimensions of this section are given in Table A of Figure 3–13 (see page 126), and illustrated in Figure 3–14.

To be sure this section will work as intended the section should be checked by the Manning formula to determine the velocity. Then check for capacity of flow as follows:

$$V = \frac{1.0032}{n} r^{.67} S^{.5}$$

$$V = \frac{1.0032}{.025} (.4083)^{.67} (.0045)^{.5}$$

$$V = (40.128)(.5487)(.067)$$
$$V = 1.48 \text{ m/sec}$$

Note that this velocity is somewhat higher than recommended, but still satisfactory since the value of n will tend to vary in time.

Next check the volume of flow by

$$Q = Va$$
$$Q = 1.48 \times 1.67$$
$$Q = 2.47 \text{ m}^3/\text{sec}$$

This value is greater than the 2.1 m³/sec estimated, so the ditch should be satisfactory. It is always desirable to have a larger cross section than required to provide additional freeboard.

Most drainage problems encountered can be

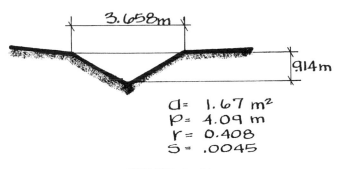

$$a = 1.67 \text{ m}^2$$
$$p = 4.09 \text{ m}$$
$$r = 0.408$$
$$S = .0045$$

FIGURE 3–14

solved with this method. In the event that unusual conditions do arise the cross sections must be designed entirely by trial-and-error testing, using the Manning formula and the formulas for calculating the hydraulic properties of typical cross sections, given in Figure 3–15 (see page 127).

To illustrate how this method works, consider the following situation. Suppose we had to design a ditch to carry 40 cfs at a slope of no more than ½% (.005), but we wish to limit the section depth to no more than 18 in. A quick glance at the charts shows that none of the shallow ditch sections will carry the volume. However, notice that the ditch sections that fit the 40 cfs volume have an area of 12 ft². Using this as a guide we can design a trial section with an area of 12 ft² as follows.

Assume a parabolic section 18 in deep with an area of 12 ft² as shown in Figure 3–16. From Figure 3–15 the formula for the width of a parabolic section is:

$$W = \frac{a}{.67d} = \frac{12}{(.67)(1.5)}$$

$$W = \frac{12}{1.005}$$

$$W = 11.94 \text{ ft (12 ft)}$$

Next calculate the hydraulic properties of the section so the velocity and capacity can be calculated based on $a = 12$ ft².

From Figure 3–15, we find the formula for p of a parabolic section is

$$p = W + \frac{8d^2}{3W}$$

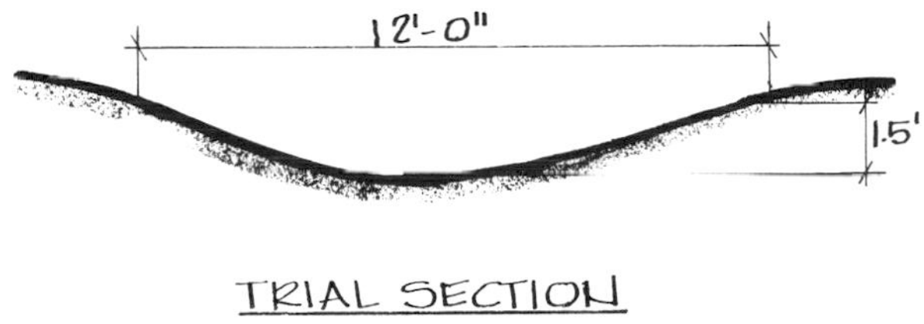

TRIAL SECTION

FIGURE 3–16

PROPERTIES OF COMMON DITCHES*

No.	SIDE SLOPES	DIMENSIONS						HYDRAULIC PROPERTIES					
		B		H		W		a		P		R	R
		FT	m	FT	m	FT	m	FT²	m²	FT	m	ENGLISH	METRIC
D-1	—	—	—	6½"	.165	5'-0"	1.52	1.84	.171	5.16	1.57	0.356	0.109
D1-A	.083 & .5	—	—	6"	.152	7'-0"	2.13	1.75	.163	7.14	2.18	0.245	0.075
D1-B	.083 & .5	—	—	±5"	.127	7'-0"	2.13	1.64	.152	7.08	2.16	0.232	0.070
D1-C	.04	—	—	4½"	.114	10'-0"	3.05	1.68	.156	10.38	3.16	0.162	0.049
D2A	.67	2'-8"	.61	1'-0"	.305	5'-0"	1.52	3.50	.325	5.61	1.70	0.624	0.191
·B	.50	2'-0"	.61	1'-0"	.305	6'-0"	1.83	4.0	.371	6.47	1.97	0.618	0.188
·C	.33	2'-0"	.61	1'-0"	.305	8'-0"	2.45	5.0	.464	8.32	2.54	0.601	0.183
D3A	.67	3'-0"	.91	1'-6"	.457	7'-6"	2.29	7.88	.732	8.41	2.56	0.937	0.286
·B	.50	3'-0"	.91	1'-6"	.457	9'-0"	2.74	9.00	.836	9.71	2.96	0.927	0.282
·C	.33	3'-0"	.91	1'-6"	.457	12'-0"	3.66	11.25	1.05	12.49	3.81	0.901	0.276
D4-A	.67	3'-0"	.91	2'-0"	.610	9'-0"	2.74	12.00	1.11	10.21	3.08	1.175	0.360
·B	.50	3'-0"	.91	2'-0"	.610	11'-0"	3.35	14.00	1.30	11.94	3.64	1.173	0.357
·C	.33	3'-0"	.91	2'-0"	.610	15'-0"	4.57	18.00	1.67	15.65	4.77	1.150	0.350
D5A	.67	4'-0"	1.22	3'-0"	.914	13'-0"	3.96	25.50	2.37	14.82	4.52	1.721	0.524
·B	.50	4'-0"	1.22	3'-0"	.914	16'-0"	4.88	30.00	2.79	17.42	5.31	1.722	0.525
·C	.33	4'-0"	1.22	3'-0"	.914	22'-0"	6.70	39.00	3.62	22.97	7.00	1.698	0.517
D6A	.50	—	—	1'-0"	.305	4'-0"	1.22	2.0	.186	4.47	1.36	0.447	0.136
·B	.33	—	—	1'-0"	.305	6'-0"	1.83	3.0	.279	6.32	1.93	0.475	0.145
D7A	.50	—	—	2'-0"	.475	8'-0"	2.45	8.0	.743	8.94	2.72	0.895	0.273
·B	.33	—	—	2'-0"	.475	12'-0"	3.66	12.00	1.11	12.65	3.86	0.949	0.302
D8A	.50	—	—	3'-0"	.914	12'-0"	3.66	18.00	1.67	13.42	4.09	1.341	0.408
·B	.33	—	—	3'-0"	.914	18'-0"	5.49	27.00	2.51	18.97	5.78	1.423	0.434
D-9	.14	—	—	1'-0"	.305	14'-0"	4.27	7.00	.650	14.14	4.31	0.495	0.151
D-10	.14	—	—	2'-0"	.475	28'-0"	8.53	28.00	2.60	28.28	8.62	0.990	0.302
D-11	.14	—	—	3'-0"	.914	42'-0"	12.80	63.00	5.85	42.43	12.93	1.485	0.452

*ADAPTED FROM DESIGN: DATA BOOK FOR CIVIL ENGINEERS. SEELYE

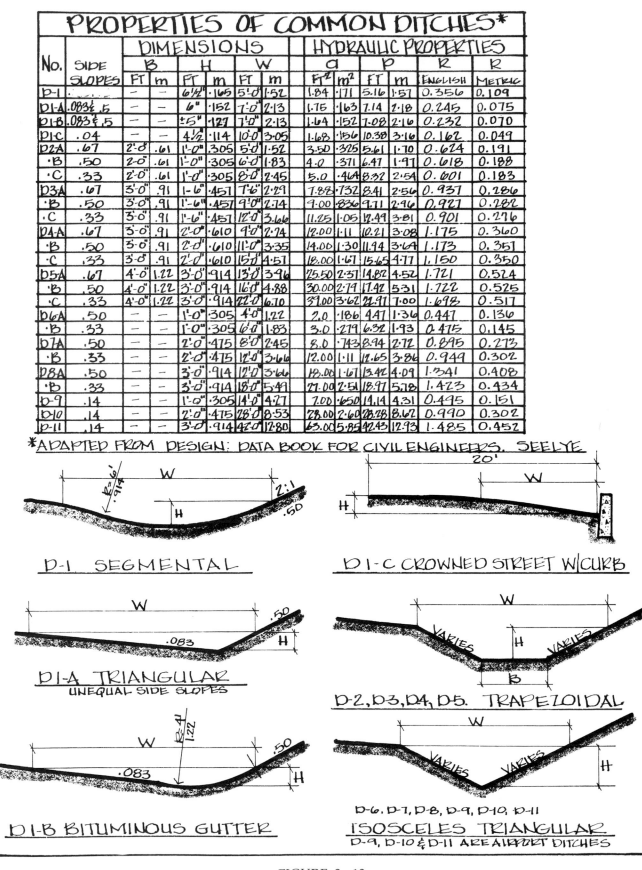

D-1 SEGMENTAL

D1-C CROWNED STREET W/CURB

D1-A TRIANGULAR
UNEQUAL SIDE SLOPES

D-2, D3, D4, D5. TRAPEZOIDAL

D1-B BITUMINOUS GUTTER

D-6, D-7, D-8, D-9, D-10, D-11
ISOSCELES TRIANGULAR
D-9, D-10 & D-11 ARE AIRPORT DITCHES

FIGURE 3-13

HYDRAULIC PROPERTIES OF TYPICAL SECTIONS

TYPE SECTION	WIDTH W	BASE b	DEPTH d	AREA a	WETTED PERIMETER p	HYDRAULIC RADIUS A/p
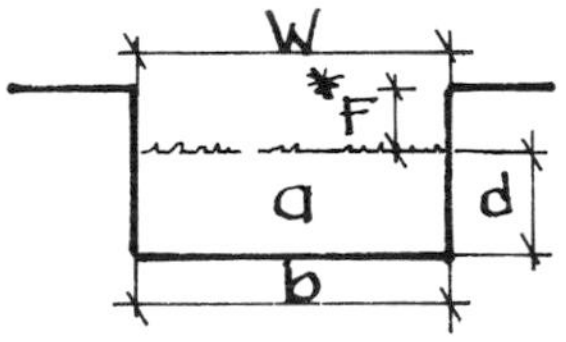 RECTANGULAR	b or $\dfrac{a}{d}$	W or $\dfrac{a}{d}$	$\dfrac{a}{b}$	Wd	$W+2d$	$\dfrac{d}{1+\dfrac{2d}{W}}$
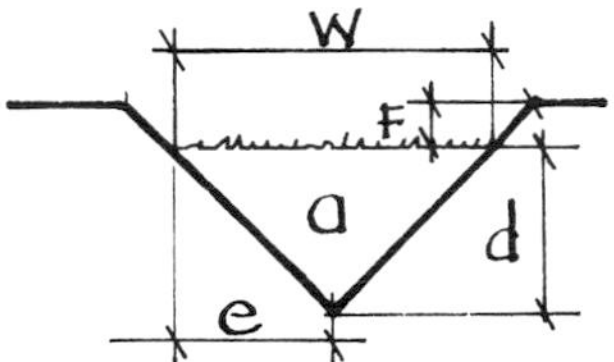 TRIANGULAR	$2e$		$\dfrac{a}{e}$	ed	$2\sqrt{e^2+d^2}$	$\dfrac{ed}{2\sqrt{e^2+d^2}}$
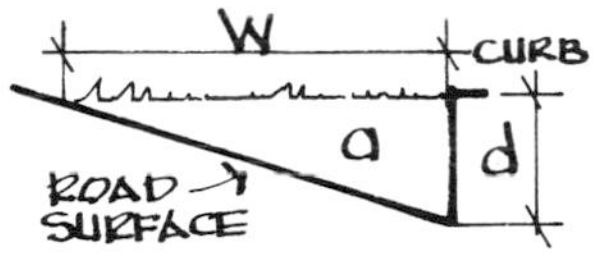 TRIANGULAR CURB & GUTTER	$\dfrac{2a}{d}$		$\dfrac{2a}{W}$	$\dfrac{Wd}{2}$	$d+\sqrt{d^2+W^2}$	$\dfrac{2Wd}{d+\sqrt{e^2+W^2}}$
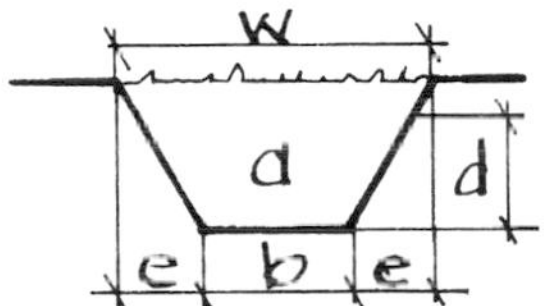 TRAPEZOIDAL EVEN SIDES	$b+2e$	$W-2e$	$\dfrac{a}{b+e}$	$d(b+e)$	$b+2\sqrt{e^2+d^2}$	$\dfrac{d(b+e)}{b+2\sqrt{e^2+d^2}}$
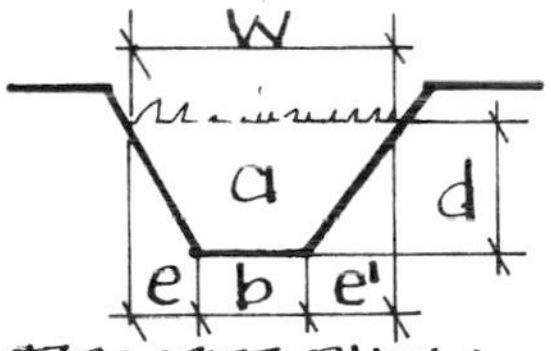 TRAPEZOIDAL UNEVEN SIDES	$b+e+e'$	$W-(e+e')$	$\dfrac{a}{b+\left(\dfrac{e+e'}{2}\right)}$	$d\left(b+\dfrac{e+e'}{2}\right)$	$b+\sqrt{e^2+d^2}+\sqrt{e'^2+d^2}$	$\dfrac{d\left(b+\dfrac{e+e'}{2}\right)}{b+\sqrt{e^2+d^2}+\sqrt{e'^2+d^2}}$
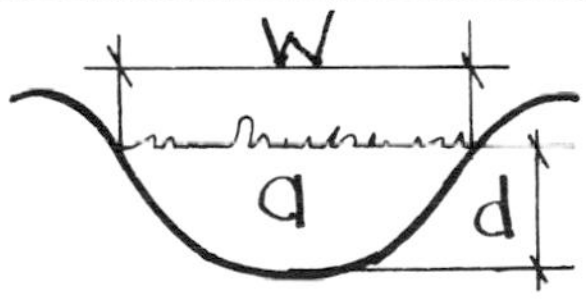 PARABOLIC	$\dfrac{a}{0.67d}$		$\dfrac{a}{0.67W}$	$0.67Wd$	$W+\left(\dfrac{8d^2}{3W}\right)$	$\dfrac{a}{W+\left(\dfrac{8d^2}{3W}\right)}$

NOTE: .3' TO .5' RECOMENDED FREEBOARD (F)

TAKEN FROM: THE HANDBOOK OF LANDSCAPE ARCHITECTURAL CONSTRUCTION CARPENTER, ED. BRADSEARS

FIGURE 3–15

$$p = 11.94 + \frac{(8)\,(1.5)^2}{(3)\,(11.94)}$$

$$p = 11.94 + \frac{18}{35.82}$$

$$p = 11.94 + .50$$

$$p = 12.44 \text{ ft}$$

Find r

$$r = \frac{a}{p}$$

$$r = \frac{12}{12.44}$$

$$r = .9646$$

Next find the mean velocity of flow by the Manning formula. Assume $n = .025$

$$V = \frac{1.486}{n}\, r^{.67}\, S^{.5}$$

$$V = \frac{1.486}{.025} \times (.9646)^{.67}\,(.005)^{.5}$$

$$V = 59.44 \times .9761 \times .071$$
$$V = 4.12 \text{ ft/sec}$$

This velocity is tolerable if the swale has good grass cover, but in erosive soils it would not be well suited.

Now to be sure of the volume find Q by

$$Q = Va$$
$$Q = 4.12 \times 12$$
$$Q = 49.44 \text{ cfs}$$

This capacity is satisfactory since it is greater than the 40 cfs estimated. This means that the section will have adequate freeboard and the velocity will be somewhat less since the section is not flowing full.

DESIGN OF SUBSURFACE STORM DRAINS

Subsurface storm drains are sealed conduits that collect water at surface inlets and transport the water underground to disposal points. The conduits are usually round, reinforced concrete, clay, or corrugated steel pipe. These materials are more efficient because the friction coefficients can be determined accurately and remain relatively constant. Likewise, the durability of the materials permits the use of higher design velocities which further increases the capacity. Design velocities for pipe range from a minimum of 2 ft/sec (.60 m/sec) to 16 ft/sec (4.9 m/sec). Velocities as high as 20 ft/sec (6.1 m/sec) may be used depending on the pipe material and pipe joints, but they are not recommended.

The design methodology used to determine the size of a pipe is essentially the same as sizing open channels. The primary difference is in hydraulic characteristics of a circular pipe. To illustrate the differences, compare the hydraulic properties of the circular section with the triangular section in Figure 3–17.

Notice that when the circular section is flowing half full the hydraulic characteristics of area, wetted perimeter, and discharge are exactly half of the value for the pipe flowing full. This is not the case in the triangular section, however.

In sections other than circular, the values of the hydraulic characteristics increase with the depth of flow. Figure 3–18 is a graph showing the relationship of hydraulic properties to the depth of flow. It is interesting to note that a circular pipe reaches a maximum velocity at about 82% of its depth and has its greatest discharge at 93% of its depth. This fact can be very important in large drainage systems since the higher velocities generated could damage the pipe.

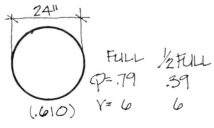

CIRCULAR PIPE

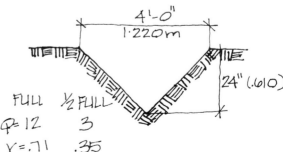

TRIANGULAR SECTION

FIGURE 3–17

Water Turbulence

Another consideration important to this discussion is what happens to water when it moves from a surface channel into a subsurface pipe through a drain inlet, passes through a manhole, or changes slope, channel material, or direction of flow.

As the water moves from the surface into the pipe the conditions of uniform flow are disrupted by turbulence. This results in a loss of energy causing a decrease in velocity. The reduced velocity causes the water level to increase at the pipe entrance momentarily. Then, as the water moves into the pipe the velocity increases under the influence of gravity as shown in Figure 3–19. The water will continue to accelerate until a new balance is reached and uniform flow occurs again.

In these flow transition zones the slope of the hydraulic surface and hydraulic gradient are not equal to the slope of the invert. The actual mechanics of these changes are beyond the scope of our discussion. However, the fact that these differences occur is important when setting finished invert elevations and should be considered. In very simple terms the design objective is to match the hydraulic gradients of all components in the system. The net result of this is that quite often the invert elevations of storm drains don't match. To illustrate this point, consider the two examples most frequently encountered on landscape construction projects, as shown in Figure 3–20.

In case one, a pipe is entering an existing lake or stream. In this situation the objective is to match the existing water surface elevation or the estimated elevation at peak storm flow. In case two, the hydraulic gradients of the two pipes should be matched. In a situation where information is not available as to the HG of the existing pipe it is usually acceptable to assume the crown elevation (top of the pipe) as the

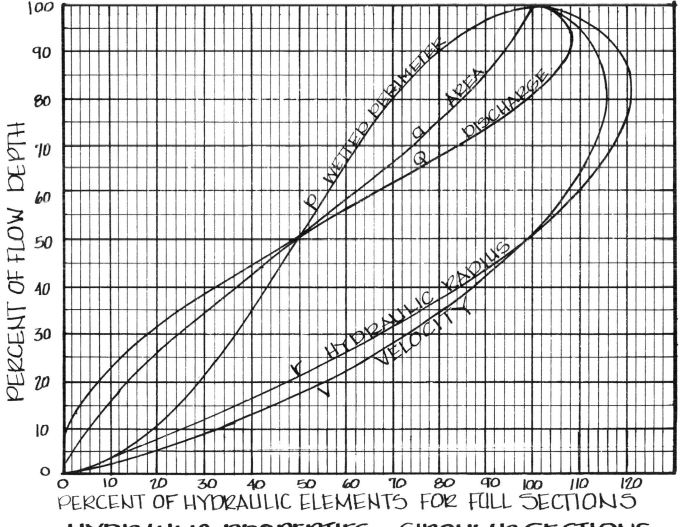

HYDRAULIC PROPERTIES - CIRCULAR SECTIONS

FIGURE 3–18

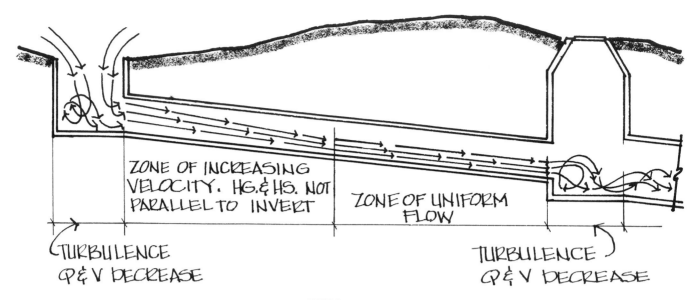

ZONE OF INCREASING VELOCITY. HG.& HS. NOT PARALLEL TO INVERT

ZONE OF UNIFORM FLOW

TURBULENCE Q & V DECREASE

TURBULENCE Q & V DECREASE

FIGURE 3-19

HG elevation. The reason for this is that most storm drainage systems are designed to flow full.

Compensating for Turbulence

Since a storm sewer will hardly ever flow full because of storm variation, it is customary to make an arbitrary allowance for these head losses rather than doing a more detailed hydraulic analysis. An accepted method used to adjust for the head loss in various structures involves dropping the invert of the discharge pipe by some estimated value. This value depends on the pipe sizes and the configuration of the manhole or junction box. Figure 3-21 illustrates three common situations and the invert adjustments recommended for each situation. To illustrate the application of these principles we will work through a suggested design procedure for storm drains.

The layout and design of all storm drainage systems should be done on a series of plan-profile sheets. The preparation of plan-profile sheets is discussed in Chapter 2. These sheets should be done at a scale of 1 in = 100 ft (1:1000) or 1 in = 40 ft (1:500), depending on the amount of detail that will be required and the size of the system. The vertical scale on drainage profiles should be exaggerated ten times (1 in = 10 ft or 1 in = 4 ft English). This large vertical exaggeration is helpful since drainage gradients are typically low. For new construction work the highway alignment and drainage design can be combined on the same plan-profile sheets.

To be complete the plan-profile sheets should show the topography, all proposed structures, vegetation, and all existing proposed utilities. Consider the example problem shown in Figure 3-22. In this case all of the runoff calculations have been made,

and the layout of the drainage system is complete. Our task is to determine the appropriate pipe sizes and establish the invert elevations.

It is helpful to record your calculations on gridded paper or use a drainage computation sheet similar to the one illustrated in Figure 3-23. This keeps all your figures together, helps prevent computational errors and facilitates checking the work.

To begin the calculations, start at the upstream end of the system and work each section of pipe out individually and proceed to the next section. In some instances sections may require several trial calculations if high velocities are encountered.

Trial pipe sizes are selected from the nomograph for circular pipes flowing full shown in Figure 3-24. These sizes are then checked to determine the actual velocity. For the example problem, concrete pipe will be used so n will be .015. The detailed calculations are as follows:

- Determine the pipe size for a design volume (Q) of 2 cfs. Since the existing ground is at a .022 slope use that value for the slope (G). Align the slope of 2.2 with a n of .015 with 2 cfs on the discharge line, finding that a 10 in pipe is required.

- From the nomograph determine the capacity of a 10 in pipe flowing full and the corresponding velocity at a slope of .022. Align the 10 in pipe with the .022 slope and n equals .015. Read the discharge as 2.7 cfs and the velocity is 5 ft/sec.

- Calculate the discharge ratio by dividing the design volume (Q) by the volume flowing full (Q_2).

$$\frac{Q}{Q_2} = \frac{2}{2.7} = .74$$

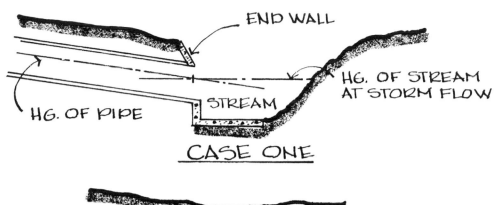

CASE ONE

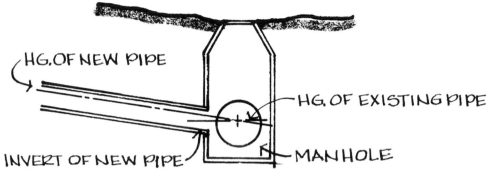

CASE TWO

FIGURE 3-20

• Determine the design velocity. This is the actual velocity of the water when the pipe is flowing at the design volume of 2 cfs.

Go to the graph of hydraulic elements of circular sections. Enter the graph on the hydraulic elements line (bottom) at 74%. Read vertically to the ordinate on the discharge line. Then read horizontally (right) to the velocity curve and then vertically (down) to the hydraulic elements line (bottom). Read 110%. This means the velocity in the pipe at 2 cfs will be 110% of the velocity flowing full or

(% of velocity at full flow) × (full flow velocity)
1.10 × 5 = 5.5 ft/sec

Calculate the invert elevations. For this problem we will set the top of all pipes 3 ft below the surface. In the first section there is no invert adjustment needed. Therefore, the upstream invert is the surface elevation less the pipe diameter (in feet) less the depth of cover. The upstream invert is:

$$(51.0) - (.83) - (3.0) = 47.17 \text{ ft}$$

The downstream invert is the upstream invert less the total difference in elevation for a slope of .022 and a pipe length of 300 ft.

$$D = G \times L = .022 \times 300$$
$$D = 6.6 \text{ ft}$$

The downstream invert is:

$$47.17 - 6.6 = 40.57 \text{ ft}$$

All of this information is recorded in sequence on the storm drain computation sheet. Figure 3-25 shows the information for the example and describes the method for obtaining the information in each blank.

Now proceed to the second section of pipe between manhole #2 and manhole #3. Complete the computation sheet for this section following the same steps used for the first section. These are outlined on Figure 3-26.

The invert calculations for this section require that the invert of the 21 in pipe be lowered to compensate for head loss in the manhole. In this instance the pipe changes direction in the manhole so we would apply the correction for condition C in Figure 3-21. The information required for this calculation is shown in Figure 3-27.

The radius of the connection is 4.8 ft and $2 \times D_1 = 1.66$ ft. Therefore the adjustment to be applied is $V^2/258$. The design velocity (V_2) is 5.7 ft. Therefore

$$\frac{V^2}{258} = \frac{(5.7)^2}{258} = \frac{32.49}{258} = .13 \text{ ft}$$

The adjustment is .13 ft.

SUGGESTED ALLOWANCES FOR HEAD LOSS

<u>CONDITION</u>

<u>SUGGESTED ALLOWANCE</u>

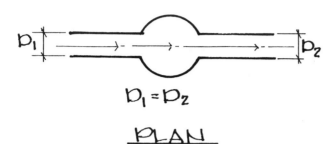

$D_1 = D_2$

<u>PLAN</u>

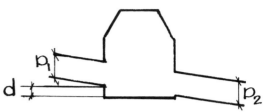

DROP DISCHARGE
INVERT .04'-.08'
12-24 mm

A   <u>SECTION</u>

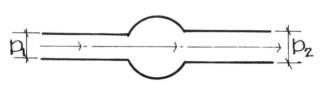

$D_1 < D_2$

<u>PLAN</u>

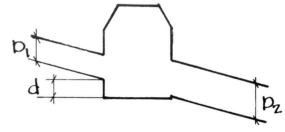

$d = D_2 - D_1$

B   <u>SECTION</u>

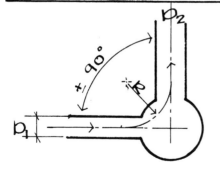

CHANGES OF DIRECTION

<u>PLAN</u>

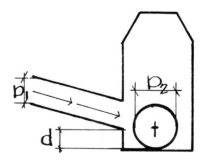

IF $R = < 2D_2$ ALLOW: $d = \dfrac{V^2}{129}$

IF $R = > 2D_2$ ALLOW: $d = \dfrac{V^2}{258}$

C   <u>SECTION</u>

FIGURE 3-21

132

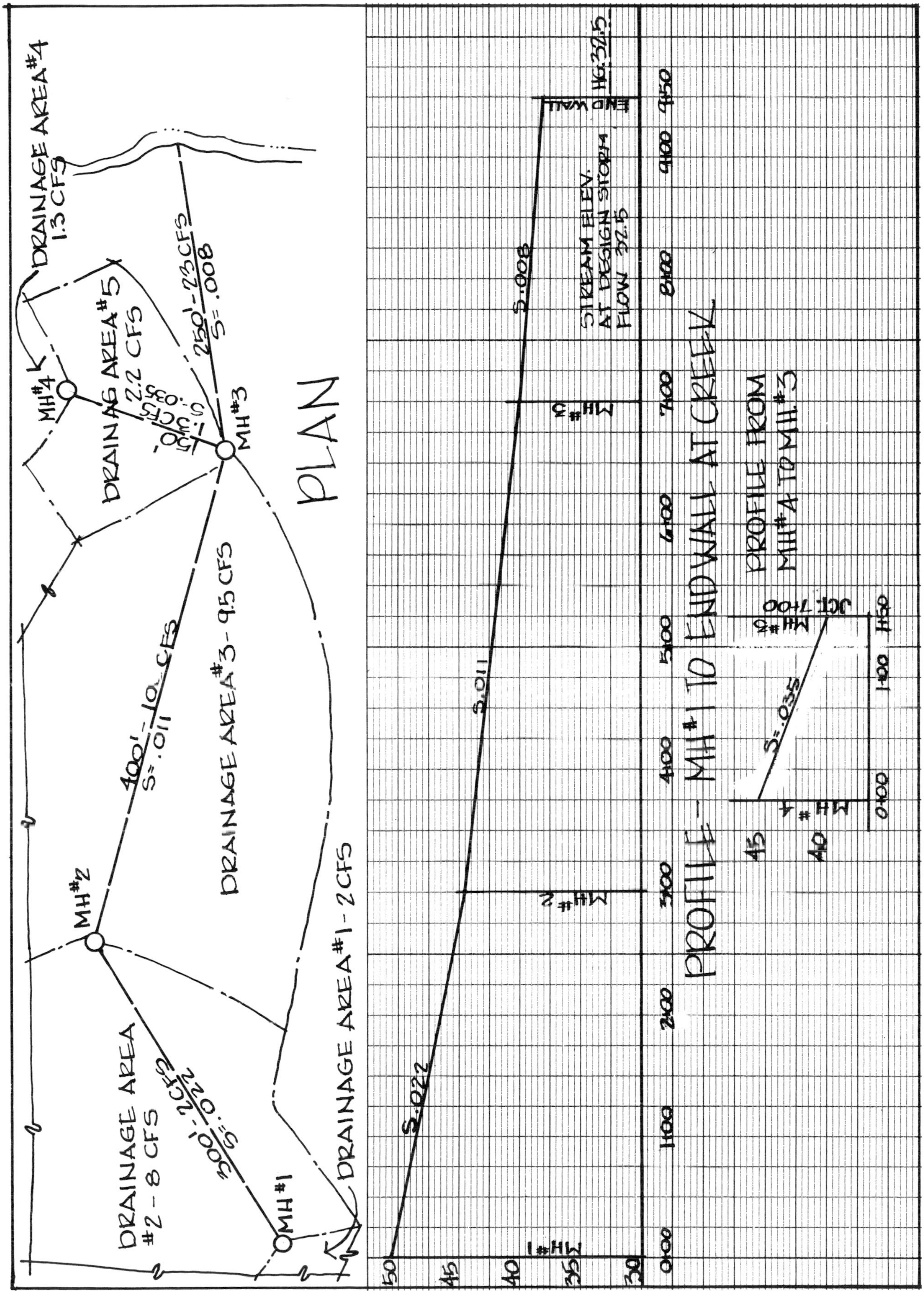

PLAN

DRAINAGE AREA #4
1.3 CFS

DRAINAGE AREA #5
2.2 CFS

MH#4

250'-2.3CFS
S=.008

1.3CFS
150'
S=.035

MH#3

DRAINAGE AREA #3 - 9.5 CFS

400'-10.CFS
S=.011

DRAINAGE AREA #1 - 2 CFS

MH#2

DRAINAGE AREA
#2 - 8 CFS

200'-2CFS
S=.022

MH#1

PROFILE - MH#1 TO END WALL AT CREEK

END WALL

STREAM ELEV.
AT DESIGN STORM
FLOW 32.5

HG 32.5

S=.008

MH#3

PROFILE FROM
MH#4 TO MH#3

MH#2

S=.011

MH#3
0C1 7+00

S=.035

MH#4

S=.022

MH#1

FIGURE 3-22

133

COMPUTATION SHEET FOR STORM DRAINS

PIPE SECTION		DRAINAGE AREA	DESIGN DISCHARGE Q_1	PIPE SLOPE G	FRICTION COEFFICIENT n	PIPE SIZE-FT. d	PIPE SIZE MILLIMETERS	DISCHARGE FLOW FULL Q_2	VELOCITY FULL V_1	DISCHARGE RATIO Q/Q_2	DESIGN VELOCITY V_2	PIPE LENGTH L	ELEVATION DIFFERENCE D	OTHER ELEV. DIFF.	UPSTREAM INVERT	DOWNSTREAM INVERT
FROM	TO															

FIGURE 3-23

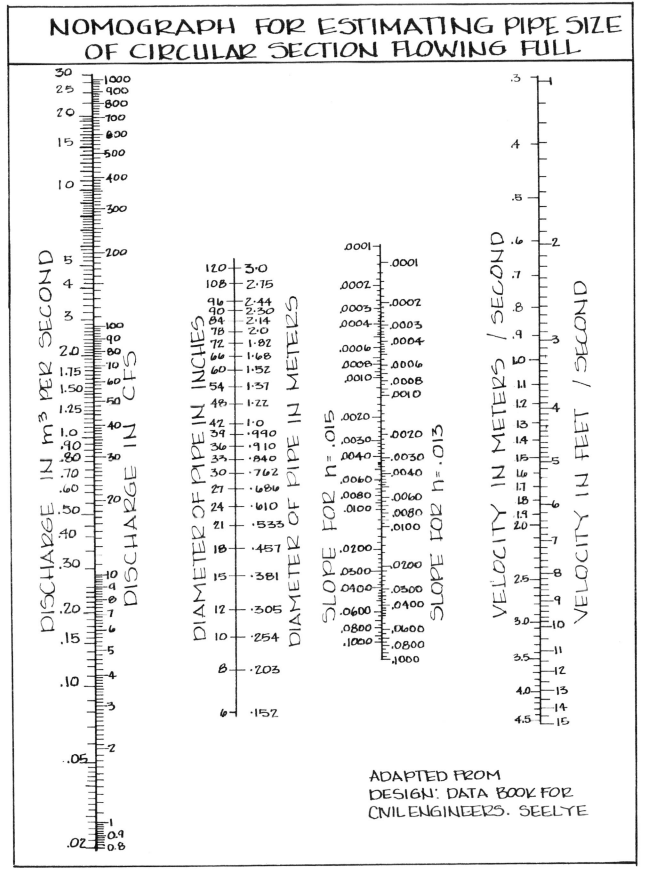

NOMOGRAPH FOR ESTIMATING PIPE SIZE OF CIRCULAR SECTION FLOWING FULL

ADAPTED FROM
DESIGN: DATA BOOK FOR
CIVIL ENGINEERS. SEELYE

FIGURE 3-24

COMPUTATION SHEET FOR STORM DRAINS

(1) PIPE SECTION		(2) DRAINAGE AREA	(3) DESIGN DISCHARGE	(4) PIPE SLOPE	(5) FRICTION COEFFICIENT	(6) PIPE SIZE-FT.	(7) PIPE SIZE MILLIMETERS	(8) DISCHARGE FLOW FULL	(9) VELOCITY FULL	(10) DISCHARGE RATIO	(11) DESIGN VELOCITY	(12) PIPE LENGTH	(13) ELEVATION DIFFERENCE	(14) OTHER ELEV. DIFF.	(15) UPSTREAM INVERT	(16) DOWNSTREAM INVERT
FROM	TO	A	Q_1	G	N			Q_2	V_1	Q_1/Q_2	V_2	L	D			
0 + 00	3 + 00	1	2	.002	.015	$\frac{17}{12}$ .83	253	2.7	5	.74	5.5	300	6.6	$\varnothing$	47.17	40.57

1.-2. Read from Plan Fig. 3-22.
3. Read from Plan Fig. 3-22. Calculated by rational method.
4. Read from Plan Fig. 3-22. Calculated by $G=D/L$.
5. Given concrete pipe n=015. Found in table 3-2.
6. Estimated form nomograph Figure 3-24. Divide by 12 to obtain size in feet.
7. Multiply size in feet by 304.8 to obtain size in mm.
8. Estimate from nomograph Figure 3-24.
9. Estimate from nomograph Figure 3-24.
10. Divide design discharge (Q_1) by the discharge at full flow. (Q_2) Q_1/Q_2

12. Read from the Plan Figure 3-22.
13. Calculate by $D=G \times L$ given in column 4 and column 12.
14. This column is used for adjustment of invert elevations necessary for head loss in structures.
15. Pipe cover + the pipe diameter subtracted from the surface elevation.
16. The elevation difference subtracted from the upstream invert.

FIGURE 3-25

COMPUTATION SHEET FOR STORM DRAINS

(1) PIPE SECTION		(2) DRAINAGE AREA	(3) DESIGN DISCHARGE Q_1	(4) PIPE SLOPE G	(5) FRICTION COEFFICIENT n	(6) PIPE SIZE - FT.	(7) PIPE SIZE MILLIMETERS	(8) DISCHARGE FLOW FULL Q_2	(9) VELOCITY FULL V_1	(10) DISCHARGE RATIO Q_1/Q_2	(11) DESIGN VELOCITY V_2	(12) PIPE LENGTH L	(13) ELEVATION DIFFERENCE D	(14) OTHER ELEV. DIFF.	(15) UPSTREAM INVERT	(16) DOWNSTREAM INVERT
FROM	TO															
0+00	3+00	1	2	.022	.015	.83	253	2.7	5	.74	5.5	300	6.6	0	47.17	40.57
3+00	7+00	1 - 2	10	.011	.015	1.75	533	13.5	5.2	.74	5.7	400	4.4	.13	40.44	36.04
														SEE TEXT		

1. **Columns 1 - 5**
   This information is taken from the profile sheet or was given in the problem.

2. **Columns 6 - 9**
   This information is read directly from the nomograph Figure 3 - 24.

3. **Column - 10**
   Divide the design discharge(Q_1) by the full discharge. (Q_2).

4. **Column 11**
   Read the design velocity per cent from Figure 3 18 and multiply it by the velocity flowing full. $V_1 \times \%$

5. **Column 12 - 13**
   Read L from the profile sheet and calculate D = GxL.

FIGURE 3-26

137

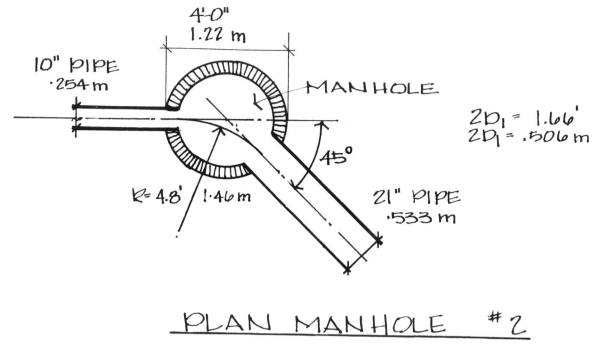

4'-0"
1.22 m

10" PIPE
·254 m

MANHOLE

$2D_1 = 1.66'$
$2D_1 = .506\ m$

45°

R= 4.8' / 1·46 m

21" PIPE
·533 m

PLAN MANHOLE #2

FIGURE 3-27

The invert of the 21 in pipe in manhole #2 is 40.57 ft.

The invert of the entering pipe less the adjustment gives the upstream invert as 40.57 − .13 = 40.44 ft

The downstream invert is the upstream invert less the elevation difference.

$$40.44 - 4.40 = 36.04\ ft$$

The next section that must be designed is the 150 ft run of pipe from manhole #4 to manhole #3. A profile of this section is shown in Figure 3−22. Once again the information for this pipe section should be worked out on the computation sheet as shown in Figure 3−28. Notice that the invert of the 8 in pipe is above the invert of the 21 in pipe in manhole #3. This is satisfactory. However, if it had been below the 36.04 ft elevation, that section would have to be adjusted.

With this section complete, the final pipe section from manhole #3 to the creek can be calculated. Once again the invert of this pipe will have to be adjusted to allow for the head loss in the manhole. Complete the computation sheet as shown in Figure 3−29. Notice that all drainage areas are carried in the last pipe section from manhole #3 to the creek. Figure 3−30 is a detail of manhole #3 showing the information required to calculate the invert adjustment for column 14.

The radius is again greater than twice the diameter of the largest pipe. Therefore the adjustment recommended is $V^2/258$.

The velocity of the 27 in pipe (V_2) is 7.26 ft/sec. Therefore

$$\frac{V^2}{258} = \frac{(7.26)^2}{259} = \frac{52.71}{258} = .20\ ft$$

This is recorded in the table and the invert elevations are calculated as follows:

The upstream invert is found by subtracting .20 from the lowest invert in the manhole, 36.04. The upstream invert is

$$36.04 - .20 = 35.84\ ft$$

The downstream invert is found by the total elevation difference from the upstream invert elevation. The downstream invert is

$$35.84 - 2.0 = 33.84\ ft$$

This elevation is above the HG elevation of the stream which is satisfactory.

Other Pipe Shapes

Before we leave the subject of pipe and subsurface channels it should be pointed out that there are other pipe shapes available for use in special situations. These different shapes are used to alter the flow characteristics to compensate for low flow periods, high velocities, and for situations where it is difficult to get sufficient depth to cover the pipe. Figure 3−31 illustrates some of the pipe sections that are available. These varied cross sections are usually more expensive than circular pipe.

COMPUTATION SHEET FOR STORM DRAINS

(1) PIPE SECTION FROM	(1) TO	(2) DRAINAGE AREA	(3) DESIGN DISCHARGE Q_1	(4) PIPE SLOPE G	(5) FRICTION COEFFICIENT n	(6) PIPE SIZE-FT.	(7) PIPE SIZE MILLIMETERS	(8) DISCHARGE FLOW FULL Q_2	(9) VELOCITY FULL V_1	(10) DISCHARGE RATIO Q_1/Q_2	(11) DESIGN VELOCITY V_2	(12) PIPE LENGTH L	(13) ELEVATION DIFFERENCE D	(14) OTHER ELEV. DIFF.	(15) UPSTREAM INVERT	(16) DOWNSTREAM INVERT
0+00	JGT 7+00 MH #3	4	1.3	.035	.015	67	203	1.8	5.5	.72	5.9	150	5.25	0	41.54	36.29

1. Columns 1 - 5
   All of this information is read from the profile sheet or given in the problem.

2. Columns 1 - 9
   This information is read from the nomograph, Figure 3 - 24.

3. Column - 10
   The discharge ratio is Q_1 divided by Q_2.

4. Column - 11
   This is read from the graph in Figure 3-18 and calculated.

5. Column 12 - 14
   These figures are found by D-GxL and there is no invert adjustment required.

6. Columns 15 - 16
   The upstream invert is: the rim elevation less 3' of cover less the pipe diameter.

6. Columns 15 - 16 (cont'd)
   $45.21 - 3.00 - .67 = 41.54$

   The down stream invert is: the upstream invert less the elevation difference.
   $41.54 - 5.25 = 36.29$

FIGURE 3-28

139

(1) PIPE SECTION		(2) DRAINAGE AREA	(3) DESIGN DISCHARGE Q_1	(4) PIPE SLOPE G	(5) FRICTION COEFFICIENT N	(6) PIPE SIZE-FT. D	(7) PIPE SIZE MILLIMETERS	(8) DISCHARGE FLOW FULL Q_2	(9) VELOCITY FULL V_1	(10) DISCHARGE RATIO Q_1/Q_2	(11) DESIGN VELOCITY V_2	(12) PIPE LENGTH L	(13) ELEVATION DIFFERENCE D	(14) OTHER ELEV. DIFF.	(15) UPSTREAM INVERT	(16) DOWNSTREAM INVERT
FROM	TO															
7+00	9+50	1-5	23	.008	.015	2.25	686	23.5	6	.98	7.26	250	2	.20	35.84	33.84
														SEE TEXT	SEE TEXT

COMPUTATION SHEET FOR STORM DRAINS

1. Columns 1 – 5
   These figures are read from the profiles or are given in the problem.

2. Columns 6-9.
   This information is read from the nomograph, Fig. 3-24.

3. Column 10
   The discharge ratio is Q_1/Q_2.

4. Column 11
   Read from the graph in Fig. 3-18 and calculated.

5. Columns 12 - 13
   Calculated by $G = D \times L$

6. Columns 14 - 16
   See text for detailed calculations.

FIGURE 3-29

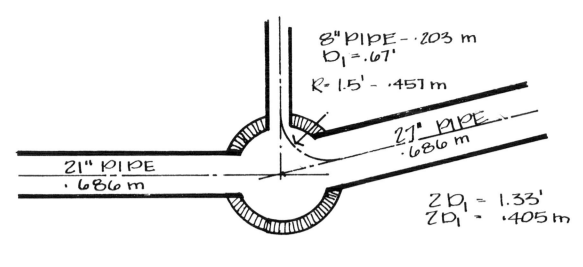

8" PIPE - .203 m
$D_1 = .67'$
$R = 1.5' - .457$ m

21" PIPE
.686 m

21" PIPE
.686 m

$2 D_1 = 1.33'$
$2 D_1 = .405$ m

PLAN - MANHOLE #3

FIGURE 3-30

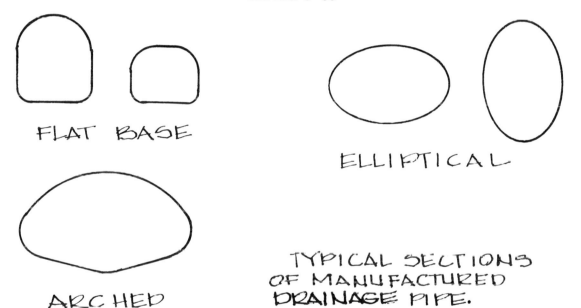

FLAT BASE

ELLIPTICAL

ARCHED

TYPICAL SECTIONS
OF MANUFACTURED
DRAINAGE PIPE.

FIGURE 3-31

DRAINAGE STRUCTURES

There are several types of drainage structures that enter into a completed storm drainage system. Each structure is designed to perform a specific task and these structures are just as important as the pipe or ditch.

Headwalls and Endwalls

A headwall is used where a natural channel enters a closed conduit. Typically headwalls will occur at the entrance to culverts that carry drainage water under roads. The task of the headwall is to make the transition from a rough channel to a smooth channel with minimum head loss.

Endwalls are used at the discharge ends of pipes at the downstream end of culverts or storm drain systems. In most cases the endwall has the responsibility of making the transition back to natural channel flow.

In this situation velocities are typically high and the water will frequently fall free for some distance. Therefore, endwalls will include design features that reduce velocity and prevent erosion from high velocities (see Figure 3-32).

141

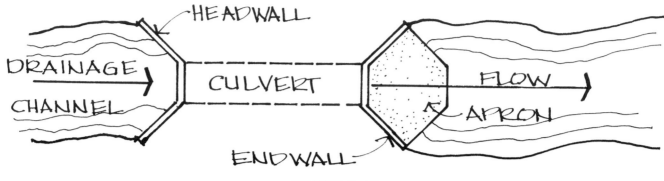

FIGURE 3–32

Storm Drainage Inlet Structures

There are basically only two structures used to collect surface runoff and transfer it to the pipe. The classification is based on how the water is transferred to the pipe below and is not related to the configuration of the surface collection structures.

Drop inlets collect water at the surface and transfer it directly to the pipe at the bottom. The shape of the bottom of the structure is smooth to maintain self-cleaning flow velocities.

Catch basins are designed with a sediment basin at the bottom of the structure. This basin is used to collect heavy sediment material that might build up in the pipe. Catch basins require periodic maintenance and should be used only if the maintenance will be available. Also keep in mind that water will stand in the structure and can be objectionable if mosquito control is a problem.

The shape of the inlet grate at the top of the structure varies depending on local practice and availability. Some typical drainage inlet structures are shown in Figure 3–33.

More critical to the design of an entrance structure than its shape is the size of the opening. The opening must have an area large enough to allow the design runoff volume to move into the system. It should be apparent that if the opening is too small at the design volume flooding will result. The formula used to estimate the required open area of the grate is

$$Q = .66CA \ (64.4 \ h)^{.5}$$

where

Q = The design volume at the inlet in cfs;
C = Orifice coefficient (.6 for square edges, .8 for round edges);
A = The required opening in ft²;
h = The allowable depth of the water over the inlet in ft.

Metrication Block
Standard orifice formula

$$Q = .66CA \ (19.63 \ h)^{.5}$$

where

Q = The design volume at the inlet in m³/sec;
C = Orifice coefficient (.6 for square edges, .8 round edges);
A = The required orifice opening in m²;
H = The allowable depth of the water over the inlet in meters.
19.63 is the value of Q^2 in meters;
.66 is the orifice clogging allowance;

The area obtained from this equation should be considered approximate because the design of the grate itself will effect the hydraulic performance, so it is suggested that manufacturer's literature be consulted.

To illustrate the application of the formula, find the area of grate required for a design runoff of 3.2 cfs. In this case, allow an h value of 4 in (.33 ft) and assume round edges on the grate. Therefore:

$$Q = .66CA \ (64.4h)^{.5}$$
$$3.2 = .66 \times .8 \times A \times (64.4 \times .33)^{.5}$$
$$3.2 = .528 \times A \times 4.609$$
$$3.2 = 2.434A$$
$$A = 1.31 \ ft^2 \ or \ 189.32 \ in^2$$

Figure 3–34 is a table of common grate sizes. Based on our calculations a grate 29¾ in × 21¾ in would be large enough for this condition.

Access Structures

There are two types of access structures placed in sewer systems that allow access for periodic maintenance: manholes and cleanouts.

INLET

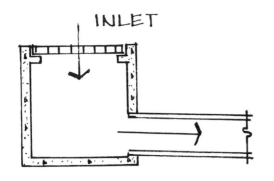

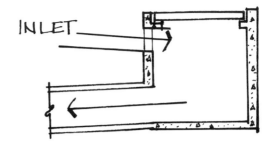

GRATE INLET

CURB INLET

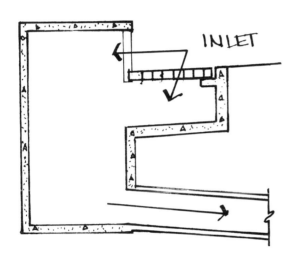

INLET

INLET

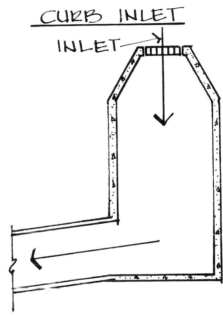

INLET

COMBINED CURB & GRATE

GRATE INLET & MANHOLE

INLET

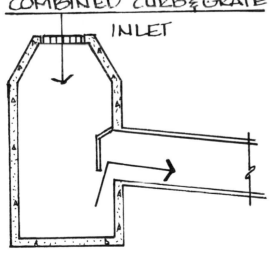

TYPICAL DRAINAGE
INLET STRUCTURES

CATCH BASIN

FIGURE 3-33

143

COMMON INLET GRATES

TYPE	OPENING SIZE		GRATE AREA	
	ENG	METRIC	IN²	m²
1	24 x 18¾	610 x 476	145	.09
	29¾ x 21¾	756 x 552	210	.14
	35 x 21¾	889 x 552	240	.15
	47¾ x 21¾	1·21 x 552	400	.26
	49½ x 29¾	1·26 x 755	630	.41
	47¾ x 43½	1·21 x 1·11	800	.52
2	21½" ⌀	462		
	24" ⌀	604		
	30" ⌀	762		
	36" ⌀	914		
	42" ⌀	1·07		
3	11¾ x 22¾	298 x 578	100	.06
	18 x 24	457 x 609	185	.12
	21¾ x 35¾	552 x 908	273	.18
	26 x 38	660 x 965	366	.24
4	26 x 26	660 x 660		
	32 x 32	812 x 812		
	38 x 38	965 x 965		
	44 x 44	1·12 x 1·12		
	50 x 50	1·27 x 1·27		

INFORMATION ADAPTED FROM; DESIGN: DATA BOOK FOR CIVIL ENGINEERS. SEELYE.

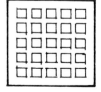

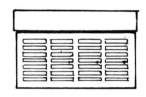

TYPE 1   TYPE 3

CURB INLET W/ GRATE. FOR HIGH VELOCITY CURB FLOW

RECTANGULAR GRATE UNEVEN FLOW DIRECTIONS.

TYPE 2   TYPE 4

CIRCULAR GRATE EVEN DIRECT FLOW

SQUARE GRATE EVEN DIRECT FLOW

FIGURE 3-34

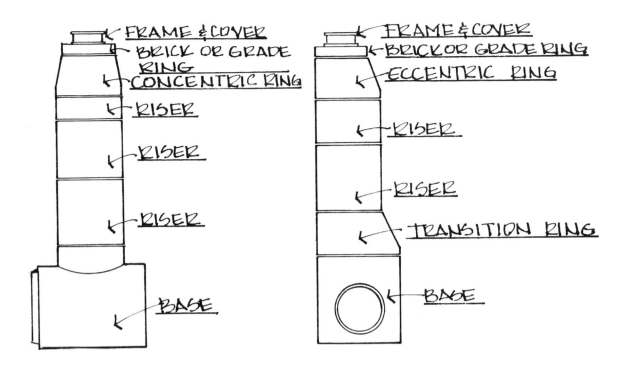

PRECAST MANHOLE SECTIONS

FIGURE 3-35

Manholes are structures large enough to provide access for a maintenance worker. The diameter of a manhole is usually 4 feet (1.250 m) at the base. They can be constructed of masonry units or composed of precast units as illustrated in Figure 3-35.

Cleanouts are usually a pipe riser connected to the line by a Y fitting. They permit access for cleaning equipment and visual inspection of the lines. Figure 3-36 is a typical cleanout detail.

PIPE BEDDING AND LOADING

Pipe used for drainage systems is manufactured from a number of different materials. The most common materials are noted below with a brief description about their use.

Clay Pipe

This is often referred to as agricultural tile or clay tile. It is one of the weakest materials and is usually used for septic tank drain fields, subdrainage and minor surface drainage systems not subject to heavy loads.

Asbestos Cement Pipe

This material is composed of portland cement and asbestos fiber for strength. It is somewhat stronger than clay, has good chemical resistance character,

and is reasonably priced. It is used in most all drainage and sewer applications.

Vitrified Clay Pipe

This is a glazed clay material that is stronger and more serviceable than common clay pipe. It is particularly prized for its resistance to chemical damage. Much of the clay pipe market has been taken over by concrete pipe but it still has application where caustic ground and waste must be reckoned with.

Concrete Pipe

Concrete pipe is available in plain concrete or steel-reinforced concrete. Concrete pipe has reached wide acceptance for all drainage and sewer applications as well as potable water transmission. It is strong and quite durable in normal applications.

Corrugated Steel Pipe

Corrugated steel pipe is manufactured in a wide variety of sizes and shapes. Its primary use is for culvert construction. However, it can be employed for other drainage systems.

Most pipe manufactured for drainage is capable of supporting loads that would be encountered in small culverts or drainage systems if they are properly installed. The key, however, is proper installation. If

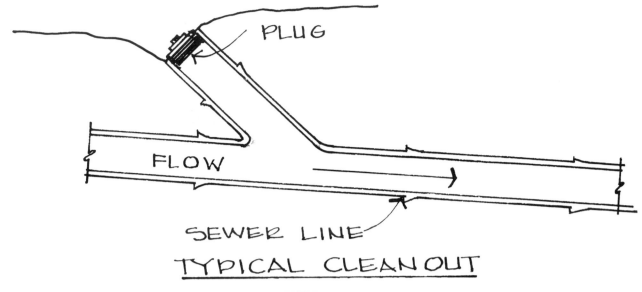

FIGURE 3-36

the pipe is laid on an uneven surface and the backfill is not properly placed, the pipe may be crushed.

A lengthy discussion of load transfer in trenches and the bedding properties of circular sections is not appropriate here. What is important is that pipe loading be considered in the design. It is probably the best practice to obtain loading and bedding data sheets from the manufacturer of the pipe that is being specified and follow their recommendations.

To illustrate how this might be done let's work an example assuming vitrified clay pipe as the material and using the design information from the Engineering Manual published by the National Clay Pipe Institute. The manual contains information on pipe strength, bedding data, load factors, loads generated by various kinds of backfill on pipes of different diameters, and data on live load transfer to the pipe at various depths. Figures 3-37(a-d) provide this data for vitrified clay pipe.

Next consider the following problem. A 24 in pipe will be installed in a 3 ft wide trench 7 ft deep (average) using Class C bedding. The backfill will be sand and gravel weighing 110 lb/ft³ and the maximum live load is estimated to be 20,000 lb wheel loads from construction equipment (Figure 3-38).

First determine the earth load on the pipe for a 3 ft (.914 m) wide trench for a cover of 5 ft over the top of the pipe using sand and gravel backfill. From the Figure 3-37(a) find that the load is 1250 lb/lf for backfill weighing 110 lb/ft³.

From the table showing the percentage of wheel loads transmitted to underground pipes, Figure 3-37(b), determine the live load on the pipe as follows. From the table find that 3.9% of the wheel load is transferred to the pipe with 5 ft of backfill;

therefore:

$$.039 \times 20,000 = 780 \text{ lb/lf}$$

The sum of the live and earth loads is:

$$\begin{array}{r} 1250 \text{ lb/lf} \\ + \ 780 \text{ lb/lf} \\ \hline 2030 \text{ lb/lf} \end{array}$$

Most manufacturers recommend that this figure be adjusted upward to allow for inequities in field conditions. In this case 5% is recommended.

$$2030 \times .50 = 101.50$$
$$2030 \times 101.5 = 2131.5 \text{ lb/lf}$$

Therefore, the pipe must be capable of carrying a 2131.5 lb/lf load in this situation. From the table of minimum crushing strengths of standard strength vitrified clay pipe find that a 24 in pipe will support 2600 lb/lf, Figure 3-37(d). This value must now be adjusted to allow for the bedding class. Class C bedding, Figure 3-37(c), has a load factor of 1.5; therefore, the field strength is found by multiplying the minimum strength by 1.5 as follows:

$$1.5 \times 2600 = 3900 \text{ lb/lf}$$

At this point no safety factor has been considered. The safety factor is the ratio of the minimum supporting strength to the calculated load, therefore:

$$\frac{\text{Field strength}}{\text{Calculated load}} = \frac{3900 \text{ lb/lf}}{2131.5 \text{ lb/lf}} = 1.83$$

Most manufacturers recommend a safety factor of 1.3 to 1.5 depending on the installation. In this case a safety factor of 1.4 to 1.5 was suggested, so the solution is satisfactory.

24″ LOADS ON 24″ VITRIFIED CLAY PIPE IN POUNDS PER LINEAL FOOT CAUSED BY BACKFILLING WITH VARIOUS MATERIALS 24″

Bold print figures represent trench loads on pipe for each width of trench. Italicized figures represent maximum loads on pipe at and beyond transition width.

Transition Width Column represents the critical width where trench loads reach their maximum and are equal to the embankment load.

SAND AND GRAVEL
AVERAGE WT. = 110 LBS./CU. FT.

DEPTH OF BACKFILL OVER TOP OF PIPE (feet)	\multicolumn{8}{c}{TRENCH WIDTH AT TOP OF PIPE (feet)}	Transition Width
	3'0"	3'6"	4'0"	4'6"	5'0"	6'0"	7'0"	8'0"	
5	1250	1540	1805	*1980*					4' 3"
6	1430	1760	2055	*2420*					4' 6"
7	1595	1960	2310	*2715*	*2895*				4' 9"
8	1735	2145	2530	*3005*	*3335*				5' 0"
9	1870	2340	2760	*3265*	3675	*3815*			5' 2"
10	1990	2505	2970	*3520*	3980	*4290*			5' 3"
11	2100	2650	3170	*3750*	4300	*4750*			5' 4"
12	2200	2780	3345	*3995*	4620	*5205*			5' 6"
13	2275	2890	3525	*4180*	4860	*5685*			5' 8"
14	2350	3000	3660	*4355*	5095	*6150*			5'10"
15	2415	3115	3790	*4520*	5300	*6600*			5'11"
16	2475	3205	3915	*4675*	5480	6985	*7085*		6' 1"
17	2530	3285	4050	*4815*	5645	7240	*7535*		6' 2"
18	2580	3355	4120	*4940*	5810	7480	*8030*		6' 3"
19	2625	3420	4210	*5070*	5950	7735	*8470*		6' 4"
20	2660	3475	4280	*5180*	6085	7940	*8945*		6' 5"
21	2695	3525	4365	*5290*	6215	8150	*9405*		6' 7"
22	2725	3575	4440	*5395*	6370	8395	*9900*		6' 8"
23	2750	3620	4510	*5500*	6490	8590	*10360*		6' 9"
24	2780	3660	4570	*5585*	6590	8780	*10800*		6'10"
25	2805	3695	4630	*5665*	6690	8965	*11310*		7' 0"
26	2825	3735	4685	*5740*	6795	9140	11550	*11750*	7' 1"
27	2845	3760	4740	*5810*	6905	9295	11770	*12210*	7' 2"
28	2860	3785	4795	*5880*	6995	9440	11970	*12705*	7' 3"
29	2875	3805	4850	*5940*	7095	9570	12175	*13145*	7' 4"
30	2895	3835	4905	*5995*	7170	9690	12375	*13640*	7' 5"

SATURATED TOPSOIL
AVERAGE WT. = 115 LBS./CU. FT.

DEPTH OF BACKFILL OVER TOP OF PIPE (feet)	\multicolumn{8}{c}{TRENCH WIDTH AT TOP OF PIPE (feet)}	Transition Width
	3'0"	3'6"	4'0"	4'6"	5'0"	6'0"	7'0"	8'0"	
5	1380	1680	*1900*						3'11"
6	1560	1900	2220	*2360*					4' 3"
7	1735	2130	2495	*2840*					4' 6"
8	1900	2325	2760	3210	*3325*				4' 8"
9	2035	2530	3000	3495	*3855*				4'10"
10	2180	2705	3220	3795	*4325*				5' 0"
11	2300	2875	3440	4065	4715	*4785*			5' 2"
12	2410	3020	3635	4290	5005	*5280*			5' 4"
13	2490	3165	3820	4525	5245	*5750*			5' 6"
14	2590	3280	3970	4740	5465	*6210*			5' 8"
15	2670	3405	4130	4945	5695	*6715*			5'10"
16	2755	3495	4270	5105	5900	*7215*			5'10"
17	2820	3590	4405	5280	6095	*7735*			5'11"
18	2885	3680	4530	5430	6300	8225			6' 0"
19	2945	3760	4645	5570	6485	8510	*8685*		6' 2"
20	2990	3840	4750	5705	6695	8740	*9145*		6' 3"
21	3035	3935	4840	5835	6865	9000	*9660*		6' 4"
22	3070	3990	4945	5955	7015	9230	*10120*		6' 5"
23	3105	4050	5025	6070	7190	9460	*10640*		6' 6"
24	3140	4100	5105	6175	7335	9660	*11100*		6' 7"
25	3170	4140	5175	6260	7465	9860	*11560*		6' 8"
26	3200	4185	5245	6370	7590	10065	*12075*		6' 9"
27	3220	4225	5315	6465	7705	10235	*12535*		6'10"
28	3235	4255	5380	6545	7820	10410	*13055*		7' 0"
29	3255	4280	5435	6625	7935	10550	13340	*13515*	7' 1"
30	3265	4300	5475	6695	8050	10695	13570	*13975*	7' 2"

FIGURE 3–37 (a)

Figures 3–37 (a)–(d) courtesy of the National Clay Pipe Institute, Crystal Lake, Illinois.

PERCENTAGE OF WHEEL LOADS
TRANSMITTED TO UNDERGROUND PIPES*

Tabulated figures show percentage of wheel load applied to one lineal foot of pipe.

Depth of Backfill Over Top of Pipe in feet	Pipe Size Inches	6"	8"	10"	12"	15"	18"	21"	24"	27"	30"	33"	36"	39"	42"
	Outside Diam. of Pipe in Feet (Approx.)	.64	.81	1.0	1.2	1.5	1.8	2.1	2.4	2.7	3.0	3.3	3.5	3.9	4.2
1		12.8	15.0	17.3	20.0	22.6	24.8	26.4	27.2	28.0	28.6	29.0	29.4	29.8	29.9
2		5.7	7.0	8.3	9.6	11.5	13.2	15.0	15.6	16.8	17.8	18.7	19.5	20.0	20.5
3		2.9	3.6	4.3	5.2	6.4	7.5	8.6	9.3	10.2	11.1	11.8	12.5	12.9	13.5
4		1.7	2.1	2.5	3.1	3.9	4.6	5.3	5.8	6.5	7.2	7.9	8.5	8.8	9.2
5		1.2	1.4	1.7	2.1	2.6	3.1	3.6	3.9	4.4	4.9	5.3	5.8	6.1	6.4
6		0.8	1.0	1.1	1.4	1.8	2.1	2.5	2.8	3.1	3.5	3.8	4.2	4.3	4.4
7		0.5	0.7	0.8	1.0	1.3	1.6	1.9	2.1	2.3	2.6	2.9	3.2	3.3	3.5
8		0.4	0.5	0.6	0.8	1.0	1.2	1.4	1.6	1.8	2.0	2.2	2.3	2.5	2.6

*These figures make no allowance for impact.

FIGURE 3–37 (b)

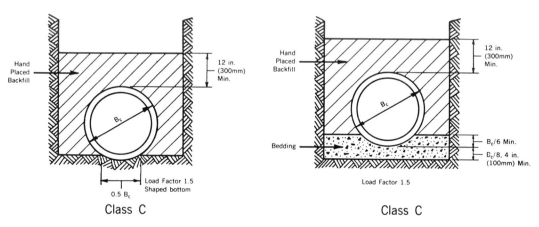

Class C   Class C

FIGURE 3–37 (c)

CONTROLLING RUNOFF

As mentioned in the introduction to this chapter, many urban areas are now requiring all new developments to control the excess runoff generated by new construction. Sometimes this is referred to as a zero runoff requirement. This is really a misnomer because new construction will always generate more runoff than a site in its native state. What they are requiring is that excess runoff be controlled by on-site measures so that discharges are no greater than the existing conditions. These requirements are aimed at reducing the risk of overtaxing the drainage system, thus reducing the risk of flooding.

There are many different methods than can be employed to retain excess storm water on-site and control its release. The effectiveness of these measures is difficult to accurately assess, but research is underway to gather more accurate data. Some of the most widely used techniques for reducing runoff are cistern storage and distribution to the subsoil by drain fields; using porous pavements (asphalt and gravel) for parking lots, walks, and streets; and ponding and retention structures.

Some methods for delaying runoff are allowing ponding on large flat roofs by using constricted down-spouts, using grass strips on paved areas and rough vegetated waterways, and increasing the length and storage capacity of drainage channels.

Currently one of the most widely used methods for controlling runoff is the ponding or retention structure. These structures are similar to farm ponds used

MINIMUM CRUSHING STRENGTH (3-EDGE BEARING STRENGTH)

Nominal Size, in.	Extra Strength Vitrified Clay Pipe		Standard Strength Vitrified Clay Pipe	
	lbf/linear ft	kN/linear m	lbf/linear ft	kN/linear m
3	2 000	29.2	. . .	. . .
4	2 000	29.2	1 200	17.5
6	2 000	29.2	1 200	17.5
8	2 200	32.1	1 400	20.4
10	2 400	35.0	1 600	23.4
12	2 600	37.9	1 800	26.3
15	2 900	42.3	2 000	29.2
18	3 300	48.2	2 200	32.1
21	3 850	56.2	2 400	35.0
24	4 400	64.2	2 600	37.9
27	4 700	68.6	2 800	40.9
30	5 000	73.0	3 300	48.2
33	5 500	80.3	3 600	52.5
36	6 000	87.6	4 000	58.4
39	6 600	96.3	. . .	. . .
42	7 000	102.2	. . .	. . .

FIGURE 3–37 (d)

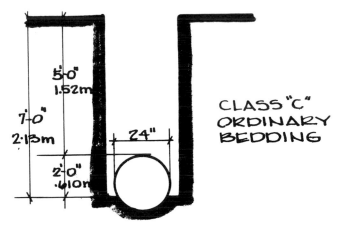

FIGURE 3–38

for stock watering and erosion control. The objective of the retention structure is to intercept runoff from a site and release it at a rate equal to the flow that existed before construction.

For example, assume a 30 acre (12.14 ha) site in its original condition generated a base runoff of 27 cfs (.84 m³/sec) and after construction it was estimated that the same site would generate 74 cfs (2.10 m³/sec). The objective would be to design a retention structure with enough storage capacity to reduce the discharge to the old rate of 27 cfs (.84 m³/sec).

Retention structure size can be estimated using the table in Figure 3–39. This table was taken from the Soil Conservation Service, Technical Release No. 55, and was developed at Pennsylvania State University. To illustrate how it can be applied, consider the following example, shown in Figure 3–40. For the conditions shown determine the storage capacity required of a retention structure to maintain the base flow of 27 cfs if the peak flow is 74 cfs.

First determine the peak flow ratio for the structure.

$$\text{Peak flow ratio} = \frac{Q_o \text{ (design discharge)}}{Q_i \text{ (peak runoff)}}$$

$$\frac{Q_o}{Q_i} = \frac{27}{74} = .36$$

From the graph in Figure 3–39 read the storage to rainfall ratio V_s/V_r to be .39. Notice that the dimensions of these elements are given in inches. Find the required storage in inches (V_s).

V_r = Design storm volume in inches.

$$V_s = V_r \times \frac{V_s}{V_r}$$

$$V_s = 4.3 \times .39$$
$$V_s = 1.68 \text{ in/acre}$$

The total storage capacity required in acre-feet is

$$V_s = \frac{30 \times 1.68}{12} = 4.2 \text{ acre-ft}$$

This process can be followed if the dimensions are given in metric units. For example, assume a design discharge rate (Q_o) of 3 m³/sec and a peak runoff (Q_i) of 5.5 m³/sec with a rainfall of 90 mm/hr and an area of 8 ha.

The Q_o/Q_i ratio is 3/5.5 = .55. The V_s/V_r ratio is .26. Therefore

$$V_s = .26 \times 90$$
$$V_s = 23.4 \text{ mm/ha}$$

The required volume of the retention structure is:

$$V_s = 10 \times 23.4 \times 8 = 1872 \text{ m}^3$$
$$(1 \text{ mm/ha} = 0.1 \text{ m}^3, \quad 10 \text{ mm/ha} = 1 \text{ m}^3).$$

EARTH DAMS

Creation of retention structures usually requires the construction of earth dams. An earth dam is a low head (low pressure) structure that is usually built from materials on the site to minimize the expense. Several things have to be considered in developing the design of an earth dam. First, the soils in the ponding area must be checked for permeability. Highly permeable soils may be satisfactory for retention ponds if part of the design objective is ground water recharge. However, if a water level is to be

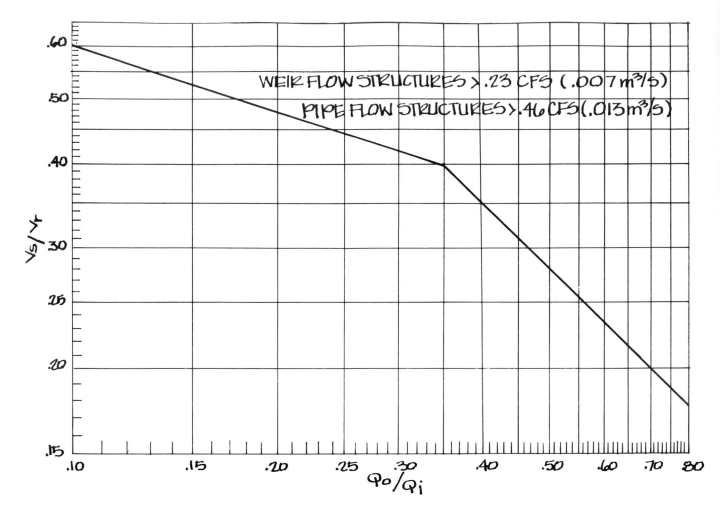

APPROXIMATE SINGLE STAGE STRUCTURE ROUTING FOR TYPE II DISTRIBUTION & 24 HR. RAINFALL

ADAPTED FROM S.C.S TECHNICAL RELEASE NO. 55, JAN. 1975

FIGURE 3-39

maintained for aesthetic or mechanical reasons, i.e., air-conditioning cooling, then impermeable soils are necessary, or some method of sealing the pond will be required.

The foundation characteristics of the soil under the dam are also important. Rock, for example, might seem like a good foundation, but if it is cracked or broken, as in the case of many limestone formations, water seepage from the pond could undermine the dam and cause it to fail. Likewise, sandy materials or any uniform materials, such as fine clay or silt, are undesirable as a foundation material because of seepage or erosion characteristics. The best materials are mixtures of gravel, sand, and clay; sand-silt; and sand-clay mixtures.

The material incorporated into the dam itself is also very important. The ideal material is one that compacts tightly to provide the necessary strength and is impermeable. Sands and gravels will allow excessive seepage through the structure, and may eventually cause failure.

Soils in the spillway area are also critical. Materials that are easily eroded cannot be used since relatively high water velocities will be encountered frequently. If the spillway does erode this will result in a loss of storage capacity and may even cause the dam to fail. Because the materials that make up a dam are so critical, and since the consequences of failure can be great, the materials should be throughly tested. The necessary testing can be done by a soils engineering laboratory or for some projects testing services may be available through the Soil Conservation Service.

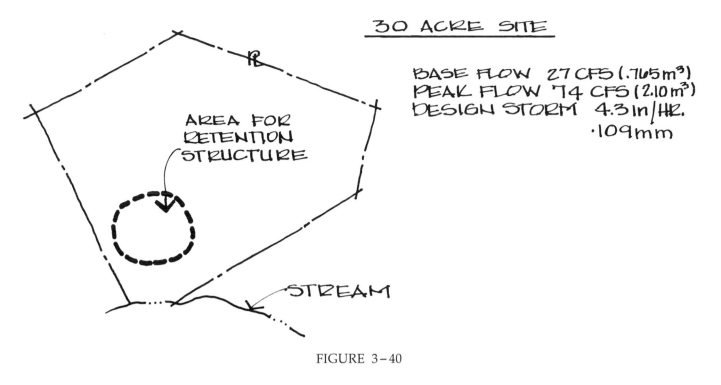

30 ACRE SITE

AREA FOR RETENTION STRUCTURE

STREAM

BASE FLOW 27 CFS (.765 m³)
PEAK FLOW 74 CFS (2.10 m³)
DESIGN STORM 4.3 in/hr.
.109 mm

FIGURE 3-40

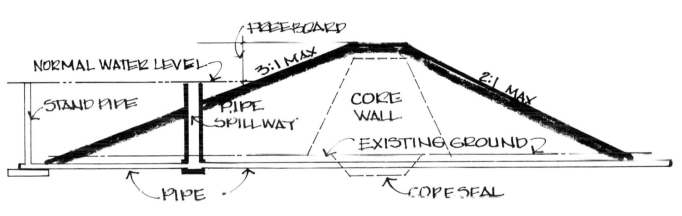

FREEBOARD

NORMAL WATER LEVEL

3:1 MAX

STAND PIPE

PIPE SPILLWAY

CORE WALL

2:1 MAX

EXISTING GROUND

PIPE

CORE SEAL

TYPICAL SECTION-EARTH DAM

FIGURE 3-41

The details of a typical earth dam are illustrated in Figure 3–41. The waterproof core shown in the illustration may not be required in all structures depending on the material available.

One of the major considerations in completing the design of a dam is the spillway. Most dams are designed with two spillways, one established to maintain the designed base flow, and a second spillway for emergency flow. The spillway for base flow is usually a drop inlet or trickletube type shown in Figure 3–41. The emergency spillway is usually an excavated spillway located near one end of the dam. Several tables have been developed by the Soil Conservation Service that can be used to determine the required spillway dimensions for estimated base and emergency flows. According to the SCS literature these tables can be used for flows up to 300 cfs (8.5 m³/sec). For design discharges greater than 300 cfs (8.5 m³/sec) it is recommended that two spillways be utilized or that a mechanical spillway be designed specifically for the conditions.

Keep in mind that high water velocities will be encountered in the downstream sections of all spillways regardless of the type. This will require that special attention be given to the treatment of the natural channel in the transition zone to prevent erosion or undermining of the dam. Protection should always be provided until the stream has reached a uniform flow condition as discussed for open channels.

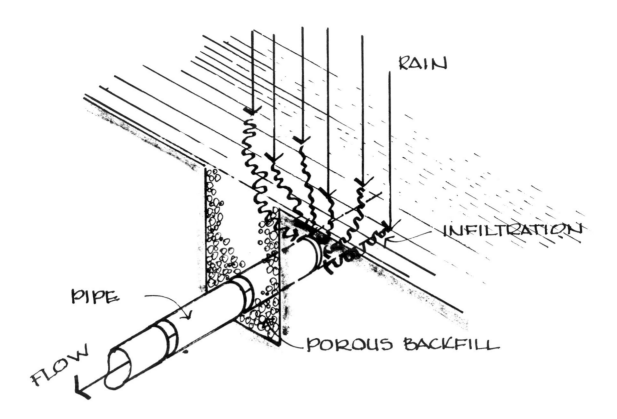

TYPICAL SUBDRAIN

FIGURE 3–42

SUBDRAINAGE DESIGN

Runoff is not just a surface phenomenon. Part of the water that falls to the surface infiltrates the soil and becomes groundwater. The movement of this water below the surface is called subsurface runoff. The movement of subsurface runoff is much slower and much less predictable than surface water, and in many cases it is a more costly problem to deal with than surface water.

Problems with subsurface runoff and groundwater are directly related to soil conditions of the site. As we have mentioned earlier soils are not uniform in cross section. They usually have distinct horizons (layers) that vary in particulate size, compaction, and mineral composition. These differences have a direct bearing on how water will move through the soil. Likewise, the existence, absence, or a change in the amount of water in the soil can cause the soil to change its properties. It is interesting to note that swelling soils alone account for more than $2.5 billion a year in damages to roads, buildings, and other structures. This is more damage per year than the damage caused by floods, hurricanes, tornados, and earthquakes put together.

The primary tool available to the landscape architect and site planner for controlling groundwater relationships is subdrainage. A subdrain is quite simple, consisting of a trench, porous backfill, and an open conduit. The water moving through the soil is collected in the porous material, transferred to the conduit and conducted to the disposal point, as shown in Figure 3–42. The pipe depth and spacing are more critical considerations than the pipe size in most cases.

The depth of the pipe is decided by determining how far the groundwater level must be dropped. For example, if the subdrain is being installed to prevent frost heave the pipe should be laid below the frost line. The line will then intercept the capillary water moving up through the soil. If the subdrain is installed to control the soil moisture in expansive soils, it should be set just below foundation level. Deeper drains are more efficient than shallow drains because the natural head generated will force the water into the drain.

TABLE 3–4
Recommended Depth and Spacing of Subdrains by Soil Type

SOIL CHARACTER	SILT	CLAY	DEPTH ft	DEPTH m	SPACING O.C. ft	SPACING O.C. m
Sand with >20% fine gravel and sand	0–15%	0–10% <20% total	5	1.5	200	60
Sandy loam with >20% fine gravel and sand	10–35% >20%	5–15% <50%	4	1.2	120	36
Fine sandy loam with <20% fine gravel and sand	10–35% >20%	— <50%	3.5	1	100	30
Loam	0–55% >50%	15–25%	4	1.2	75	22
Clay loam	25–50% >50%	25–35%	3	0.9	45	14
Clay	— >60%	35–100%	3	0.9	25	8

The spacing of the drainage lines is related to soil texture. The finer soils require closer spacing to overcome the adhesive force of the soil. The information given in Table 3–4 can be used as a general guide in determining trench spacing and depth for most subdrainage applications.

There are three soil conditions the designer must be alert for that usually require subdrainage: Soil-climate relationships, soil-layering relationships, and soils with high shrink–swell relationships.

In areas that have frequent and prolonged freezes a condition called frost heave is common. This is the result of water traveling upward in the soil by capillary action and freezing. As the ice crystals expand the soil expands or heaves.

In the process of soil formation, soils are laid down in layers of different particle size or may be underlain by an impervious layer called a hard pan. Either of these cases can result in saturated soil. In the case where the soil layers are composed of different particle sizes a perched water table will occur if the top layer is finer than the bottom layer. This is due to the higher adhesive nature of the fine material. When a hard pan is present it prevents the water from moving away from the surface by gravity and again the topsoil will remain saturated.

Expansive soil conditions are usually associated with clay soils. However, just because the soil has a high clay content does not mean that it is highly expansive. Many of the kaolinites are in fact quite well behaved. On the other hand, mountmorrillonite clays can be very destructive. This group of clay minerals has a great chemical affinity for water and will undergo extreme volume changes in the presents of water. When any of these conditions are present on a site the use of a subdrainage system should be considered.

Designing the Subdrainage System

Four things must be determined in the design of a subdrainage system: pipe size, pipe depth, spacing, and the type of backfill material. The pipe size required for most subdrainage systems rarely exceeds 4 inches (100 mm), because the time required for the water to reach the drain is much longer. The backfill material used in a subdrainage system should be a coarse sand and gravel mixture, if possible. If the project is large enough and coarse fill material is not available on site, larger pipe should be used to compensate for the loss of the trench area.

Subdrainage systems should be laid out with slopes that generally conform to the natural ground. A minimum slope of .001 is recommended. The pattern of the drainage field should conform to the existing topography. In most cases one of the patterns shown in Figure 3–43 will fit the conditions.

Several kinds of pipe materials are employed in subdrainage systems. Some of the more popular materials include agricultural clay tile, perforated clay pipe, perforated plastic pipe, and perforated asphalt-coated fiber pipe. The material selected for a specific system is usually a function of cost and local availability.

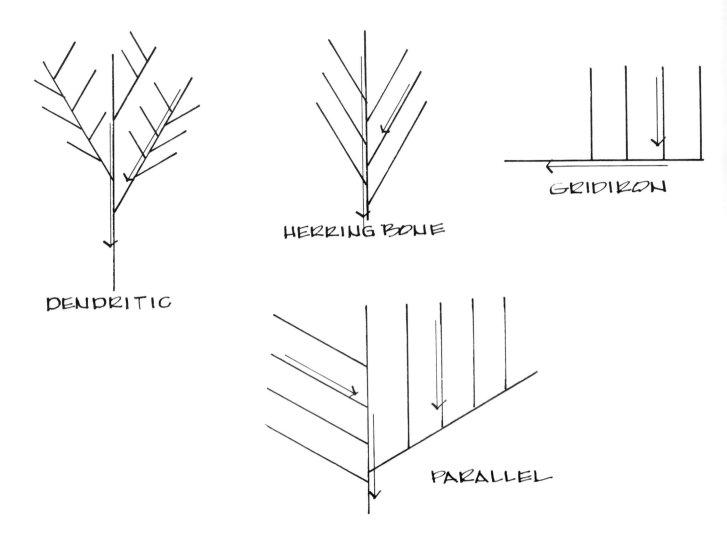

TYPICAL SUBDRAINAGE LAYOUT

FIGURE 3–43

PROBLEMS

1. Estimate the runoff for a 10 acre development for a 5 year design storm in Columbus, Ohio based on the following:

    Q_1 35% Building Cover C .90
    Q_2 40% Streets and Parking C .95
    Q_3 25% Landscape Surface C .35
        $L = 425$ ft $S = .032$ ft/ft

2. What is the estimated runoff for a 5 ha watershed for a 10 year design storm given $C = .78$, $t_c = 18$ min and the watershed is in region 5.

3. What is the estimated velocity of flow in a ditch with a 7.5 ft cross section if it has to carry 4 cfs? Is V satisfactory?

4. What is the maximum flow that can be carried in a triangular ditch 2 ft deep and 16 ft wide. (Assume the ditch is symmetrical and maximum velocity is 4 ft/sec.)

5. What is the triangular ditch size required to carry a volume of 20 cfs at a maximum slope of .008 and a maximum velocity of 3 ft/sec with $n = .025$?

6. Assume that you wish to limit the depth of the ditch in Problem 5 to 1 ft. How wide will the ditch have to be to still keep the velocity below 5 ft/sec?

7. What is the maximum allowable slope for a trapezoidal ditch that must carry 10 cfs given

n = .025 and these ditch dimensions: base 2 ft, depth 1 ft, width 8 ft, and maximum V of 4 fps?

8. What size triangular ditch is required to carry 7 cfs? Assume n = .025, S = .012, and maximum V = 4 fps.

9. Assuming that all pipes are designed to flow full what is the hydraulic gradient (HG) elevation of the following: (a) a 12 in pipe invert 126.49; (b) a 600 mm pipe invert 3.263; (c) a 36 in pipe invert 152.97; (d) a 300 mm pipe invert 5.873?

10. If two 12 in pipes enter a manhole and the invert of the entering pipe is 246.97 ft what should the invert of the discharge pipe be to compensate for head loss?

11. Using the tables and nomograph what should the pipe size be for the following (assume concrete pipe): (a) 12 cfs at a 2% slope; (b) 25 cfs at a .001 slope; (c) 15 cfs at a .008 slope; (d) 60 cfs at a .005 slope?

12. Are the velocities in the above pipes acceptable?

13. Three lengths of pipe connect three drain inlets. Each inlet contributes 5 cfs. How large should the pipe be from the: (a) first to the second inlet; (b) second to the third inlet; (c) third inlet to the discharge? Assume n = .013 and S = .006.

14. If a new 24 in pipe is being installed in an existing manhole that has a discharge invert of 116.72 in and the discharge line is a 42 in pipe, what should the invert of the new pipe be if no allowance is made for head buildup?

15. What is the invert of a 24 in storm line that runs to a manhole 352 ft downstream if it has an inlet invert of 127.62 in and a slope of .002 in?

16. What is the actual velocity of an 18 in concrete storm line, carrying 6 cfs at a slope of .006?

UNIT
II
LANDSCAPE STRUCTURES

4
Basic Principles of Statics and Mechanics

The purpose of this chapter is to introduce the student to some of the basic principles of statics and mechanics that have direct application to the design of landscape structures. Of necessity much of what is presented here is simplified, but a basic understanding of the principles and vocabulary presented here is essential to the design of landscape structures, and it will provide a base for further study.

The science of mechanics is the study of the action of a force on a mass. Statics is concerned with the principles of mechanics that hold a mass stationary. Statics then is concerned with a combination of mechanical events that will not produce motion.

FORCE AND STRESS

Force is an external influence acting on a mass or structure that could cause the mass to move. For example, if we push on a concrete block that is not cemented to a foundation it will move. The action of pushing is a force. Stress is the ability of a mass or a structure to resist a force. For example, if we begin squeezing an egg the shell will initially set up a resistance to the pressure. The resistance of the shell is stress, but once the pressure exceeds a certain point the shell collapses and we have a mess.

Types of Force

There are two principal types of force: compressive force and tensile force. Compressive forces are forces that tend to shorten a member. For example, if a concrete block is placed on a post the weight of the block will tend to squeeze the wood fibers together and

shorten the post. Tensile forces tend to lengthen a member. For example, if we sit on a swing seat suspended by two ropes the ropes tend to lengthen.

Types of Stress

When a force is applied to a mass three types of stress occur in the mass: compressive stress, tensile stress, and shear stress. Compressive stress is the reaction to a compressive force. Tensile stress is the result of a tensile force. Shear stress is the result of forces acting in different directions that tends to cause the particles of a material to slide across each other. For example, if two steel plates were connected by a bolt and then placed in a vise, and the vise were tightened, the two steel plates would act like scissors trying to cut the bolt in half.

Properties of a Force

To properly identify a force three things must be identified: the magnitude of the force, the direction of the force, and the corresponding line of action. The magnitude of a force is expressed by units of weight, either pounds or kilograms. The direction of a force is expressed as being toward or away from a point of reference, usually the centroid of a section. The line of action refers to the force being perpendicular or at an angle to a plane.

Units of Force and Stress

While forces are measured in terms of weight the magnitude of the force is usually spread over an area. For this reason we usually refer to forces and stresses in terms of weight per unit area, e.g., pounds per square inch, pounds per square foot. The basic formula for unit force or unit stress is

$$f = \frac{P}{A}$$

where

f = Unit force/stress;
P = The magnitude of the force/stress in units of weight;
A = The area over which the force/stress is distributed.

To illustrate this relationship consider a deck structure resting on four posts, each post is 6 in × 6 in and carries ¼ the weight of the deck. If the deck weighs 2000 lb, what is the unit force exerted on the ground by each post? The area of each post is 36 in² (6 in × 6 in) and ¼ of 2,000 lb is 500 lb. Substituting in the formula find

$$f = \frac{P}{A} = \frac{500 \text{ lb}}{36 \text{ in}^2}$$

$$f = 13.89 \text{ lb/in}^2$$

The concept of units of force is an important one because all building materials will have strength limits and these will be expressed as units of force. Concrete, for example, is frequently called out as 2,000 lb concrete. This means that after the 28 day curing period the concrete should be able to stand a compressive force of 2,000 lb/in² before it fails.

MOMENTS

Moment is the tendency of a force to cause rotation about an axis and is the product of a force and a distance. For example, if a force is applied to a board resting on a dowel the board will tend to rotate around the dowel as illustrated in Figure 4–1. The axis of the system is the dowel which is referred to as the center of moments. The distance from the center of moments to the point where the force is applied is called the lever arm.

To illustrate this principle, consider the system in Figure 4–2. The moment of force acting around axis A is 50 lb × 10 ft = 500 ft-lb. The moment acting around axis B is 50 lb × 5 ft = 250 ft-lb. As you can see from this example the moment will increase or decrease in proportion to any change in force or length of the lever arm.

EQUILIBRIUM

For a structure to be sound all of its parts must be in equilibrium. In order to achieve equilibrium in a

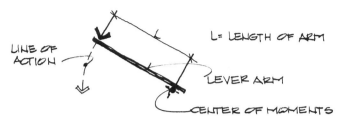

MOMENT PRINCIPLE

FIGURE 4–1

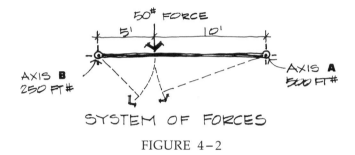

SYSTEM OF FORCES

FIGURE 4–2

SYSTEM OF FORCES

FIGURE 4–3

structure the sum of all moments must equal zero. This principle is referred to as the law of equilibrium.

To illustrate this principle consider the system of forces illustrated in Figure 4–3. The figure shows a simple beam being acted on by two concentrated forces of 500 lb each. If point A is designated the center of moments we can calculate all of the downward moments as follows.

The moment for lever arm A-B is

4 ft × 500 lb = 2,000 ft-lb

The moment for lever arm A-C is

12 ft × 500 lb = 6,000 ft-lb

As shown in Figure 4–3 the support at point D is acting in the opposite direction equal to half the load or 500 lb. The moment for A-D then is

16 ft × 500 lb = 8,000 ft-lb

Since the line of action of A-D is opposite to the lines of action of A-B and A-C we will designate the

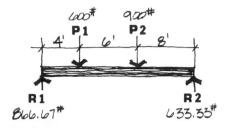

SYSTEM OF FORCES

FIGURE 4-4

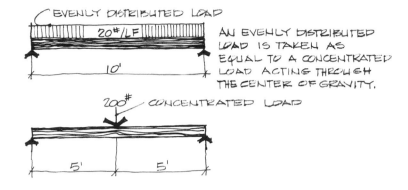

EVENLY DISTRIBUTED LOADS

FIGURE 4-5

clockwise direction as positive and the counterclockwise direction as negative, and the sum of the moments is written as follows.

$$(+2000 \text{ ft-lb}) + (+6000 \text{ ft-lb}) + (-8000 \text{ ft-lb})$$
$$= 8000 \text{ ft-lb} - 8000 \text{ ft-lb} = 0$$

Thus the sum of the moments is zero. The sum of the moments would have been the same if point D had been designated the center of moments.

REACTIONS

When a structural member is acted on by a force it must have an equal but opposite reaction if the system is to remain in equilibrium. In the previous problem the reactions of the supports were equal because the beam was symmetrically loaded. However, if a beam is loaded unevenly the reaction required at the support will not be equal. To illustrate this point consider the condition shown in Figure 4-4.

A simple beam is loaded with two unequal forces that are 4 ft and 6 ft from the left support respectively, $P_1 = 600$ lb and $P_2 = 900$ lb. Based on the law of equilibrium we know that the sum of the moments must equal zero; therefore it is possible to determine the reaction at each support by writing an equation of moments. For the example we will designate R_1 as the center of moments and write the equation as follows:

$$0 = (+4 \text{ ft} \times 600 \text{ lb}) + (+10 \text{ ft} \times 900 \text{ lb})$$
$$+ (-18 \text{ ft} \times R_2)$$

Once again notice that the direction of R_2 is opposite to the direction of P_1 and P_2; therefore it is designated as a negative while P_1 and P_2 are positive. This expression can be more simply written as

$$18R_2 = (4 \text{ ft} \times 600 \text{ lb}) + (10 \text{ ft} \times 900 \text{ lb})$$

$$R_2 = \frac{(4 \text{ ft} \times 600 \text{ lb}) + (10 \text{ ft} \times 900 \text{ lb})}{18}$$

$$R_2 = \frac{2400 \text{ ft-lb} + 9000 \text{ ft-lb}}{18 \text{ ft}}$$

$$R_2 = 633.33 \text{ lb}$$

Next find the reaction at R_1 by designating R_2 as the center of moments and solving for R_1 as follows:

$$0 = (+8 \text{ ft} \times 900 \text{ lb}) + (+14 \text{ ft} \times 600 \text{ lb})$$
$$+ (-18 \text{ ft} \times R_1)$$

$$18R_1 = (8 \text{ ft} \times 900 \text{ lb}) + (14 \text{ ft} \times 600 \text{ lb})$$

$$R_1 = \frac{(8 \text{ ft} \times 900 \text{ lb}) + (14 \text{ ft} \times 600 \text{ lb})}{18}$$

$$R_1 = \frac{7200 \text{ ft-lb} + 8400 \text{ ft-lb}}{18}$$

$$R_1 = 866.67 \text{ lb}$$

Reactions for Evenly Distributed Loads

The reaction for any evenly distributed load is calculated by assuming that the total load acts as a concentrated load at the center of gravity. For example, consider Figure 4-5. A simple 10 ft beam has an evenly distributed load of 20 lb per linear foot over the entire beam. The total load is 200 lb and would be taken the same as a 200 lb force acting at the center of the beam as shown. This principle applies if there is an evenly distributed load over only a portion of the beam as shown in Figure 4-6. In this case the total load is 300 lb and would be treated as a 300 lb force acting at a point 10 ft from the left support.

Reactions with Combined Loads

The reactions with combined loads can be found by moments the same way that they are calculated for several concentrated loads. To illustrate this principle consider the system of forces shown in Figure 4–7.

In this example a simple beam has an evenly distributed load of 40 lb per linear foot centered 2 ft from each support and a concentrated load of 800 lb acting 2 ft from the right support. The evenly distributed load is taken as a concentrated force of 240 lb acting at the center of the beam. Therefore if we designate R_1 the center of moments we can solve for R_2 as follows:

$$0 = (+5\text{ ft} \times 240\text{ lb}) + (+8\text{ ft} \times 800\text{ lb})$$
$$+ (-10\text{ ft} \times R_2)$$

$$10R_2 = (5\text{ ft} \times 240\text{ lb}) + (8\text{ ft} \times 800\text{ lb})$$

$$R_2 = \frac{1200\text{ ft-lb} + 6400\text{ ft-lb}}{10}$$

$$R_2 = \frac{7600\text{ ft-lb}}{10\text{ ft}}$$

$$R_2 = 760\text{ lb}$$

Next solve for R_1 by writing:

$$0 = (+2\text{ ft} \times 800\text{ lb}) + (+5\text{ ft} \times 240\text{ lb})$$
$$+ (-10\text{ ft} \times R_1)$$

$$10R_1 = (2\text{ ft} \times 800\text{ lb}) + (5\text{ ft} \times 240\text{ lb})$$

$$R_1 = \frac{1600\text{ ft-lb} + 1200\text{ ft-lb}}{10}$$

$$R_1 = \frac{2800\text{ ft-lb}}{10\text{ ft}}$$

$$R_1 = 280\text{ lb}$$

Reactions for Overhanging Beams

An overhanging beam is different from a simple beam because the supports are not at the outside edge of the beam as illustrated in Figure 4–8. The major difference between this condition and a simple beam is that the lever arm of R_1 and R_2 is constant and the overhang portion is only considered as a component of the moments around each axis. Thus to solve for R_2 we let R_1 be the center of moments and write:

$$0 = (+2\text{ ft} \times 300\text{ lb}) + (+7\text{ ft} \times 400\text{ lb})$$
$$+ (+15\text{ ft} \times 400\text{ lb}) + (-12R_2)$$

$$12R_2 = (2\text{ ft} \times 300\text{ lb}) + (7\text{ ft} \times 400\text{ lb})$$
$$+ (15\text{ ft} \times 400\text{ lb})$$

$$R_2 = \frac{600\text{ ft-lb} + 2800\text{ ft-lb} + 6000\text{ ft-lb}}{12}$$

$$R_2 = \frac{9400\text{ ft-lb}}{12\text{ ft}}$$

$$R_2 = 783.33\text{ lb}$$

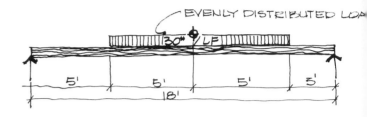

EVENLY DISTRIBUTED LOADS

FIGURE 4–6

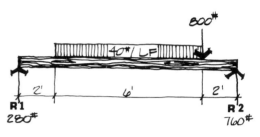

COMBINED LOADS

FIGURE 4–7

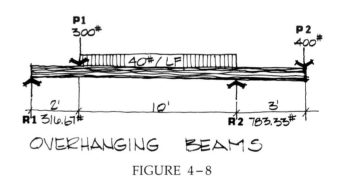

OVERHANGING BEAMS

FIGURE 4–8

Next solve for R_1. In this case notice the 400 lb force, P_2, would cause a rotation around R_2 opposite to P_1 and the evenly distributed load; therefore it is negative. So we write

$$0 = (+10\text{ ft} \times 300\text{ lb}) + (5\text{ ft} \times 400\text{ lb})$$
$$+ (-3\text{ ft} \times 400\text{ lb}) + (-12R_1)$$

$$12R_1 = (10\text{ ft} \times 300\text{ lb}) + (5\text{ ft} \times 400\text{ lb})$$
$$+ (-3\text{ ft} \times 400\text{ lb})$$

$$R_1 = \frac{3000\text{ ft-lb} + 2000\text{ ft-lb} - 1200\text{ ft-lb}}{12}$$

$$R_1 = \frac{5000\text{ ft-lb} - 1200\text{ ft-lb}}{12}$$

$$R_1 = \frac{3800\text{ ft-lb}}{12\text{ ft}}$$

$$R_1 = 316.76\text{ lb}$$

TABLE 4–1
Recommended Working Stresses of Common Landscape Materials

Material	WEIGHT (LB/FT³)	MODULUS OF ELASTICITY E	ULTIMATE STRENGTH (LB/IN²)			WORKING UNIT STRESS (LB/IN²)			
			TENSION	COMPRESSION	SHEAR	TENSION	COMPRESSION	SHEAR	f_b
Cypress	35	1,320,000							
Southern Pine		1,700,000	10,000	8000	500		360	120	1300
No. 1	37						390	120	1450
No. 2		1,600,000					390	105	1200
Redwood	35	1,320,000					320	95	1300
Concrete	150	3,000,000		1500			625	70	
Brick Masonry	120			2000			100		
Steel	490	29,000,000	70,000	70,000	55,000	22,000		14,500	
Aluminum						15,000			
(6061 – T6)	170	10,000,000	38,000		30,000				12,000

We can check the validity of our reasoning by the law of equilibrium that states that all reactions must be opposite and equal. In other words, the sum of the loads must equal the sum of the reactions. Thus for the previous problem the loads are P_1 = 300 lb, and P_2 = 400 lb, the concentrated load is 400 lb, and the reactions are 783.33 lb and 316.67 lb. Therefore

$$300 \text{ lb} + 400 \text{ lb} + 400 \text{ lb} = 783.33 \text{ lb} + 316.67 \text{ lb}$$
$$1100 \text{ lb} = 1100 \text{ lb}$$

STRUCTURAL PROPERTIES OF MATERIALS

To this point we have assumed that the materials used in a force system were capable of withstanding the stress caused by the loads placed on them. This can never be assumed, however, because the stability of a structure depends on the ability of the material to withstand the stress caused by loading.

You will also recall from our earlier discussion that when a force is applied to a mass it sets up an internal reaction called stress. We also introduced the term "unit stress" to describe the magnitude of the stress for each unit of cross-sectional area.

Strength of Materials

The strength of a building material is its ability to withstand the three principal stresses: shear, tension, and compression. The strength of a material is expressed as a maximum unit stress that can be tolerated by the cross section. For example, we have already mentioned that some concretes have an ultimate strength of 2,000 lb/in² in compression. This value represents the maximum compressive stress that the cured material can sustain just before it fails. The working stress of a material however is always lower than maximum to allow a margin of safety.

Table 4–1 gives the values for recommended working stress in common landscape construction materials.

The terms used in the table are important to an understanding of the materials and concepts presented later in the chapter. At this point we will look at a general definition of each term, and later in the chapter we will illustrate the application of each term.

Weight All building materials have variations in weight. Wood for example is much lighter than 2,000 lb concrete but it is actually stronger in compression. Material weight as we will see later also plays a major roll in structural stability.

Modulus of Elasticity Modulus of elasticity is a measure of how much a material deforms in relation to the load applied. For example, if a wood block and a steel bar of the same size are squeezed in a vice the wood will deform much more than the steel. Thus steel has a much higher modulus of elasticity than wood.

Ultimate Strength The ultimate strength of a material is the stress measured in the material at the instant it fails. For reasons of safety the ultimate strength of a material is not a major consideration in construction design.

Working Stress Working stress is the design stress value considered safe for a given material. For example, in Table 4–1 you will notice that concrete has an ultimate strength of 2,000 lb/in² in compression, but it has a recommended working stress of 500 lb/in². This is a safety factor of 4.

Extreme Fiber Stress in Bending, f_b Extreme fiber stress in bending refers to the maximum allowable stress on the wood fiber at the greatest distance from the neutral surface measured in lb/in². The significance of this term will be explained in more detail in our discussion of beams and wood construction.

Deflection   The tendency of a member to deform when placed under a load. It is present in all structures regardless of the material or magnitude of the load.

Elastic Limit   As mentioned earlier, when a building material is loaded the material deforms; this is true even though it is not visible. Then, if the load is removed, the material will return to its original shape. All materials have some point, beyond which the material will no longer return to its original shape; it will be permanently deformed. This point is called the elastic limit. Since the elastic limit occurs in most materials well before the ultimate strength is reached it is more significant than the ultimate strength.

SELECTING AND SIZING HORIZONTAL MEMBERS

The landscape architect is concerned primarily with the stability of two broad groups of structural members: horizontal and vertical. Horizontal structural members are most frequently referred to as beams, but the family also includes joists, stringers, girders, plates, and purlins. Vertical members are most frequently called columns but this family includes other members called posts, piers, studs, and pilings. The design of vertical members will be discussed in the next section.

Beam Failure

Beams can fail in a number of ways: horizontal shear, vertical shear, or bending. Figure 4–9 illustrates the three kinds of failure.

Horizontal shear occurs when the wood fibers slide across each other at right angles to the load. Vertical shear is the tendency of the beam to drop between the supports. Failure in bending is a rupture of the member at the point of greatest bending moment. Notice in Figure 4–9 that the material in the top part of the beam is in compression, the material at the bottom of the beam is in tension, while the material at the center is neutral. The plane that cuts the beam where there is no tensile or compressive stress is called the neutral surface.

While a beam may fail by horizontal or vertical shear, it is not likely in simple structures such as decks, kiosks, and others common to landscape projects. Failure in bending is the primary concern. The reason for this is that the shear stress does not become critical in landscape materials loaded and used in accordance with accepted practice. For this reason we have only considered bending in this discussion.

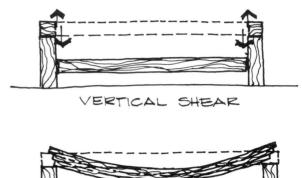

VERTICAL SHEAR

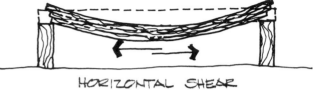

HORIZONTAL SHEAR

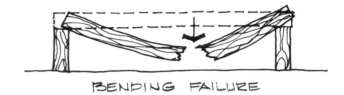

BENDING FAILURE

TYPICAL BEAM FAILURE
FIGURE 4–9

Structural Classification of Beams

The structural classification of beams is based on how the beam is supported. To this point in our discussion we have only considered simple and overhanging beams. However, there are several other types of beam that you should be familiar with, illustrated in Figure 4–10.

The reason we must consider how a beam is supported is that the stress pattern in the beam is a direct result of the support. To illustrate this point consider Figure 4–11. In the simple beam the stress is compressive at the top surface of the beam and tensile at the bottom surface. This stress pattern is the opposite in the cantilever, and in the continuous beam it changes along the length of the beam.

Maximum Bending Moment

Bending moment is stress resulting from the forces acting on the beam and the reaction of the supports. The bending moment at any section in the beam is the sum of the moments on either side of the section. To illustrate this relationship consider Figure 4–12.

If we calculate the moment to the left of section A, we find that there is a single reaction of 333.33 lb with a lever arm of 4 ft. Thus the bending moment is

$$4 \text{ ft} \times 333.33 \text{ lb} = 1,333.33 \text{ ft-lb}$$

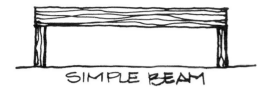

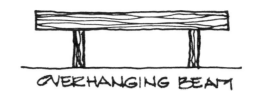

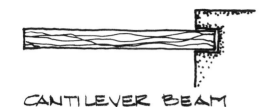

BEAM CLASSIFICATION

FIGURE 4–10

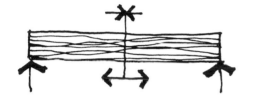

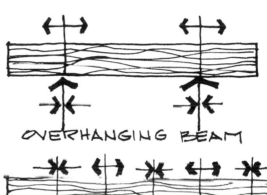

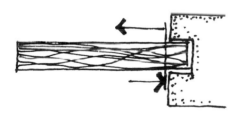

STRESS PATTERNS IN BEAMS

FIGURE 4–11

This will also be true if we consider the load to the right of the section. In this case we have a reaction of 666.67 lb and a concentrated load of 1000 lb. First calculate the moment of the 1000 lb force as

4 ft × 1000 lb = 4000 ft-lb

The moment of the reaction is

8 ft × 666.67 lb = 5,333.33 ft-lb

Since the moments are in opposite directions we will designate the moment of the reaction as a negative

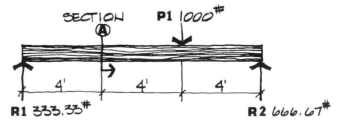

BENDING MOMENT

FIGURE 4–12

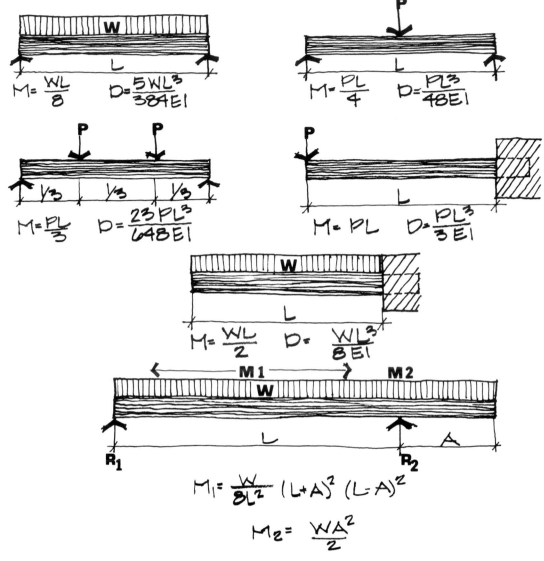

MAXIMUM MOMENT & DEFLECTION OF TYPICAL BEAMS

FIGURE 4–13

moment and the moment of the force as positive and write

$$(+4000 \text{ ft-lb}) + |(-5,333.33 \text{ ft-lb})| = 1,333.33 \text{ ft-lb}$$

Therefore it makes no difference which side of the beam you work from the value of the bending moment will be the same.

Figure 4–13 gives the formulas for determining the maximum bending moments in beams under different load conditions. Always be sure that your calculations are made using the proper formula for load and support conditions.

To illustrate how maximum bending moment can be obtained using these formulas, consider the problem illustrated in Figure 4–14. This is typical of

a condition that might be encountered building a wood deck flush with an existing building. From Figure 4–13 find that the maximum bending moment can occur at two points: it may occur at some point in the beam or it may occur directly over R_2. Which moment is the greatest depends on the length of the overhanging portion of the beam. Thus to find the maximum bending moment calculate the maximum moment in the beam and the moment at R_2 as follows.

The maximum moment in the beam (M_1) is

$$M_1 = \frac{W}{8L^2} \cdot (1 + A)^2 \cdot (1 - A)^2$$

$$M_1 = \frac{600 \text{ lb}}{8 \times (12 \text{ ft})^2} (12 \text{ ft} + 3 \text{ ft})^2 (12 \text{ ft} - 3 \text{ ft})^2$$

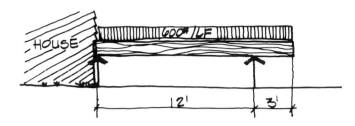

EVENLY DISTRIBUTED LOAD ON
AN OVERHANGING BEAM

FIGURE 4-14

$$M_1 = \frac{600 \text{ lb}}{1152 \text{ ft}^2} \times 225 \text{ ft}^2 \times 81 \text{ ft}^2$$

$$M_1 = .5208 \times 225 \times 81$$
$$M_1 = 9{,}492.19 \text{ ft-lb}$$

The moment at R_2 (M_2) is

$$M_2 = \frac{WA^2}{2}$$

$$M_2 = \frac{600 \text{ lb} \times 3 \text{ ft}^2}{2}$$

$$M_2 = \frac{5400 \text{ ft-lb}}{2}$$

$$M_2 = 2700 \text{ ft-lb}$$

In this condition the maximum moment occurs to the left of R_2 in the main span of the beam with a magnitude of 9492.19 ft-lb.

Moment of Inertia and Section Modulus

The moment of inertia is an abstract measure that is described as the sum of the products of all infinitely small areas times the square of their distance from the neutral surface of the beam. Since both terms used in finding the moment of inertia are expressed in in^2 the products obtained are in inches to the fourth power (in^4).

The value of the moment of inertia for any rectangular cross section can be found by the formula[1]

$$I = \frac{bd^3}{12},$$

where

I = the moment of inertia in inches to the fourth (in^4);
b = The base (width) of the beam parallel to the neutral surface in inches;
d = The depth of the beam in inches.

---

[1]This formula applies only to rectangular beam sections of a homogeneous material about the neutral axis.

Thus the moment of inertia for a standard 2×8 (actual size $1\frac{1}{2}$ in $\times$ $7\frac{1}{2}$ in) is

$$I = \frac{1.5 \text{ in} \times (7.5 \text{ in})^3}{12} = \frac{1.5 \times 421.875}{12}$$

$$I = 52.73 \text{ in}^4$$

Note that $\text{in}^3 \times$ in equals inches to the fourth power (in^4).

The section modulus is the ratio of the moment of inertia to the distance of the most remote fiber in the beam. This relationship is expressed as

$$S = \frac{I}{C}$$

where

S = the section modulus in in^3;
I = the moment of inertia in in^4;
C = the distance to the most remote fiber of the section in inches.

Since the neutral surface of a rectangular section is located at half the depth of the beam, C can be described as $C = d/2$. This relationship is handy because the section modulus of any rectangular section can be found directly without first calculating the moment of inertia. Since $S = I/C$ we can also write

$$S = \frac{\dfrac{bd^3}{12}}{\dfrac{d}{2}} = \frac{bd^3}{12} \times \frac{2}{d}$$

$$S = \frac{bd^{3^2}}{12_6} \times \frac{2}{d}$$

Thus[1] $S = \dfrac{bd^2}{6}$

Now consider the 3 in $\times$ 10 in beam shown in Figure 4-15. The section modulus of this beam can be calculated as follows:

$$S = \frac{bd^2}{6} = \frac{3 \text{ in} \times (10 \text{ in})^2}{6}$$

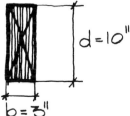

BEAM SECTION

FIGURE 4-15

NOTE: THE BEAM IS BUILT UP WITH 2- 2"X10"'s. 2"X10" IS A NOMINAL MEASURE AND SHOULD BE TAKEN AS ½" LESS ON EACH SIDE.

FIGURE 4-16

$$S = \frac{3 \text{ in} \times 100 \text{ in}^2}{6} = \frac{300 \text{ in}^3}{6}$$

$$S = 50 \text{ in}^3$$

Remember that the section modulus is always in cubic inches as shown.

The Flexure Formula

The flexure formula is the formula used to determine the required section modulus to resist the maximum bending moment calculated for a beam. The flexure formula is written

$$S = \frac{M}{f_b}$$

where

S = the required section modulus in cubic inches;
M = the maximum bending moment of the beam in in-lb;[2]
f_b = the maximum extreme fiber stress in bending expressed in lb/in².

To illustrate the application of this formula consider the following problem shown in Figure 4-16.

If the beam is to be of #1 southern pine, we find from Table 1-4 that the permissible extreme fiber stress in bending (f_b) is 1,500 lb/in². From Figure 4-13 we find that the maximum bending moment for a simple beam with an evenly distributed load is found by:

$$M = \frac{WL^2}{8}$$

Therefore

$$M = \frac{400 \times 10^2}{8}$$

[2]When using the flexure formula remember that moments expressed in ft-lb must be converted to in-lb by multiplying by 12.

$$M = \frac{400 \times 100}{8} = \frac{40,000}{8}$$

$$M = 5,000 \text{ ft/lb}$$

The flexure formula is then applied to find the required section modulus of the beam. Thus[3]

$$S = \frac{M}{f_b}$$

$$S = \frac{5,000 \text{ ft/lb} \times 12 \text{ in/ft}}{1,500 \text{ lb/in}^2}$$

$$S = \frac{60,000 \text{ in/lb}}{1500 \text{ lb/in}^2}$$

$$S = 40 \text{ in}^3$$

The required section modulus is 40 in³. From this point we could calculate the section modulus of a trial beam to see if it has the required section modulus or we can look up the section modulus in a manufacturer's table, such as the one shown in Table 4-2.

In Table 4-2 find that a single 2 in × 10 in beam has a section modulus of 21.39 in³ Therefore, two 2 in × 10 in beams equal 21.39 ×2 = 42.78 in³, which is satisfactory. This can be confirmed by the formula as follows:

$$S = \frac{bd^2}{6} = \frac{3 \text{ in} \times (9.25 \text{ in})^2}{6}$$

$$S = \frac{3 \text{ in} \times 85.5625 \text{ in}^2}{6}$$

$$S = \frac{256.6875 \text{ in}^3}{6}$$

$$S = 42.78125 \text{ in}^3$$

The sequence of calculations just illustrated is a basic tool used by the designer over and over again to determine the size of horizontal members. This material will be expanded and further illustrated in Chapter 6.

SELECTING AND SIZING VERTICAL MEMBERS

As mentioned earlier vertical members are usually referred to as columns, posts, piers, studs, and pilings. These members are designed to carry loads parallel to their longitudinal axis rather than perpendicular to it.

In simple structures such as decks, simple foot bridges, kiosks, shelters, and docks, all column loads can be taken to act as a concentrated load at the cen-

[3]Ft-lb must be converted to in-lb.

TABLE 4–2
Properties of Sections

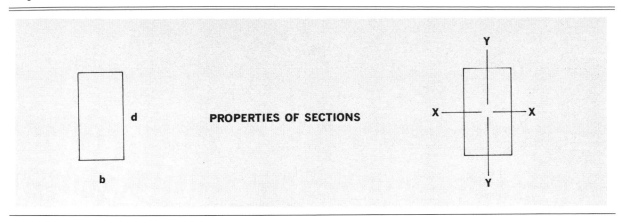

PROPERTIES OF SECTIONS

Nominal Size Inches b d	Actual Size Inches b d	Area In.²	AXIS XX S In.³	AXIS XX I In.⁴	AXIS YY S In.³	AXIS YY I In.⁴	Board Measure per Lineal Foot	Weight per Lineal Foot Lbs.
2 x 2	1-1/2 x 1-1/2	2.25	.56	.42	.56	.42	.33	.63
3	2-1/2	3.75	1.56	1.95	.94	.70	.50	1.05
4	3-1/2	5.25	3.06	5.36	1.31	.99	.67	1.46
2 x 5	1-1/2 x 4-1/2	6.75	5.06	11.39	1.69	1.27	.83	1.87
6	5-1/2	8.25	7.56	20.80	2.06	1.55	1.00	2.29
8	7-1/4	10.88	13.14	47.63	2.72	2.06	1.33	2.98
10	9-1/4	13.88	21.39	98.93	3.57	2.62	1.67	3.87
12	11-1/4	16.88	31.64	177.98	4.23	3.18	2.00	4.68
14	13-1/4	19.88	43.89	290.77	4.97	3.75	2.33	5.50
3 x 3	2-1/2 x 2-1/2	6.25	2.61	3.25	2.6	3.24	.75	1.73
4	3-1/2	8.75	5.10	8.93	3.64	4.56	1.00	2.43
6	5-1/2	13.75	12.60	34.66	5.73	7.16	1.50	3.82
8	7-1/4	18.13	21.90	79.39	7.56	9.53	2.00	5.03
10	9-1/4	23.13	35.65	164.88	9.63	12.16	2.50	6.44
12	11-1/4	28.13	52.73	296.63	11.75	14.79	3.00	7.83
14	13-1/4	33.13	73.15	484.63	14.91	17.34	3.50	9.18
4 x 4	3-1/2 x 3-1/2	12.25	7.15	12.50	7.14	12.52	1.33	3.39
6	5-1/2	19.25	17.65	48.53	11.23	19.64	2.00	5.34
8	7-1/4	25.38	30.00	111.15	14.82	26.15	2.67	7.05
10	9-1/4	32.38	49.91	230.84	18.97	33.23	3.33	8.98
12	11-1/4	39.38	73.82	415.28	23.03	40.30	4.00	10.91
14	13-1/4	46.38	102.41	678.48	27.07	47.59	4.67	12.90
★ 6 x 6	5-1/2 x 5-1/2	30.25	27.73	76.25	27.73	76.25	3	8.40
8	7-1/2	41.25	51.56	193.35	37.81	103.98	4	11.46
10	9-1/2	52.25	82.73	392.96	47.89	131.71	5	14.51
12	11-1/2	63.25	121.23	697.07	57.98	159.44	6	17.57
14	13-1/2	74.25	167.06	1127.67	68.06	187.17	7	20.62
★ 8 x 8	7-1/2 x 7-1/2	56.25	70.31	263.67	70.31	263.67	5.33	15.62
10	9-1/2	71.25	112.81	535.86	89.06	333.98	6.67	19.79
12	11-1/2	86.25	165.31	950.55	107.81	404.30	8	23.96
14	13-1/2	101.25	227.81	1537.73	126.56	474.61	9.33	28.12
★ 10 x 10	9-1/2 x 9-1/2	90.25	142.89	678.75	142.89	678.75	8.33	25.07
12	11-1/2	109.25	209.39	1204.03	172.98	821.65	10	30.35
14	13-1/2	128.25	288.56	1947.80	203.06	964.25	11.67	35.62
★ 12 x 12	11-1/2 x 11-1/2	132.25	253.48	1457.51	253.48	1457.51	12	36.74
14	13-1/2	155.25	349.31	2357.86	297.56	1710.98	14	43.12
★ 14 x 14	13-1/2 x 13-1/2	182.25	410.06	2767.92	410.06	2767.92	16.33	50.62

Source: Southern Yellow Pine; Southern Forest Products Association.
★ *Note: Properties are based on minimum dressed green size which is ½ inch off nominal in both b and d dimensions.*

troid of the columns cross section. For example, consider the simple beam supported by two columns shown in Figure 4–17. Each column would carry half the load (2500 lb) and is taken to act at the longitudinal axis of the column.

Column Failure

Simple columns can fail in two ways. Failure can occur by buckling or it can fail by crushing. In most cases landscape structures are light and carry very light loads; thus for most cases the major concern is the column's ability to withstand buckling (see Figure 4–18).

Slenderness Ratio

The ability of a column to withstand buckling stress is related directly to the length of the column and cross-section dimensions. This relationship is called the slenderness ratio and is expressed as:

$$R = \frac{12\,l}{d}$$

where

R = the slenderness ratio;
l = the unsupported length of the column in feet;
d = the smallest dimension of the column's cross section in inches.

For example, the slenderness ratio of a standard 4 in × 4 in, 8 ft long beam is:

$$R = \frac{12 \times 8}{3.5} = 27.42$$

Maximum Axial Loading of Columns

The column material most important in landscape construction is probably wood and for this reason is the only material considered here. In the event a design solution calls for the use of concrete, steel, or masonry it is unlikely that structural investigation will be required since aesthetic considerations and standard practice will usually exceed minimum structural requirements. However, if a structure is required to carry heavy loads or has unusual load distributions, you should have the structural design checked by a qualified engineer.

A standard formula has been developed to determine the maximum allowable, compressive, axial load on wood columns, based on the ratio of the modulus of elasticity to the slenderness ratio. This formula provides a conservative solution and is accepted by most building codes. The basic formula is

$$f_c = \frac{0.3E}{\dfrac{(12*l)^2}{d}}$$

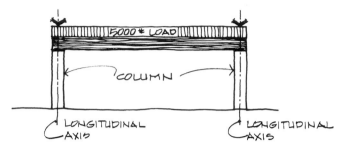

COLUMN LOADING

FIGURE 4–17

f_c = the maximum allowable compressive axial load expressed in lb/in²;
d = the smallest dimension of the column cross section in inches;
l = the unsupported length of the column;
E = Modulus of elasticity for the wood grade specified.
*12 is included where the column length is in feet.

To illustrate the application of the formula consider the problem shown in Figure 4–18.

From Table 5–2 (Chapter 5) find that the modulus of elasticity (E) of #2 Southern Pine is 1,600,000, substitute into the equation as follows:

$$f_c = \frac{0.3\,E}{\dfrac{(12\,l)^2}{(d)}} = \frac{0.3 \times 1,600,000}{\dfrac{(12 \times 6)^2}{(5.5)}}$$

$$f_c = \frac{480,000}{\dfrac{(72)^2}{(5.5)}}$$

$$f_c = \frac{480,000}{942.55}$$

$$f_c = 509.26 \text{ lb/in}^2$$

CRUSHING

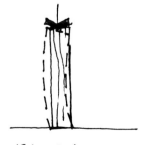

BUCKLING

TYPES OF COLUMN FAILURE

FIGURE 4–18

Thus the maximum allowable compressive load parallel to the grain of the column in 509.26 lb/in² for a buckling condition. Next it is necessary to find the actual unit stress on the column. This is found by:

$$f = \frac{P}{A}$$

For the example $P = 8,000$ lb and the area is $(5.5)^2$ or 30.25 in²; thus

$$f = \frac{8000}{30.25} = 264.45 \text{ lb/in}^2$$

Determining the safety factor we divide f_c by f and find:

$$\frac{f_c}{f} = \frac{509.26 \text{ lb/in}^2}{264.45 \text{ lb/in}^2} = 1.93$$

This is considerably more than necessary, in fact, a 4 × 4 or less would be satisfactory as far as the danger of failure in buckling is concerned. However, to complete our investigation of the columns suitability we must check its resistance to crushing. This is found by looking up the wood material's working stress in compression parallel to the grain also designated f_c. From Table 5–2 we find that f_c for crushing is 1000 lb/in². Thus the column is safe in terms of its ability to withstand crushing as well.

Keep in mind that the expression f_c is used for the *maximum allowable* compressive stress perpendicular to the grain. The working stress indicated in Table

5–2 is the ability of a column to resist crushing. The value of f_c obtained from the formula

$$f_c = \frac{0.3 \text{ E}}{(12 \text{ } l)^2}$$
$$(d)$$

determines the columns ability to resist buckling. The discrepancy in the two values is a function of the slenderness ratio. To illustrate this point, what if we substituted a 2 × 4 for the column we just investigated? The f_c for load perpendicular to the gram given in Table 5–2 is still 1,000 lb/in². But, if we check f_c in buckling we find

$$f_c = \frac{\dfrac{0.3 \times 1,600,000}{(12 \times 6)^2}}{1.5 \; (= d \text{ for a } 2 \times 4)}$$

$$f_c = \frac{\dfrac{480,000}{(72)^2}}{1.5} = \frac{480,000}{2304}$$

$$f_c = 208.33$$

From the previous calculation we found that the actual unit stress on the column was 264.45 lb/in²; therefore the 2 × 4 would fail in buckling.

This brief discussion of basic statics and mechanics has been presented to give the reader a basic understanding of the structural design vocabulary These principles are the basis of more detailed discussions of landscape structures in the next two chapters.

PROBLEMS

Reactions

Determine the reactions of the supports for the following figures by moments. Check your answers.

1. Figure P4–1.

2. Figure P4–2.

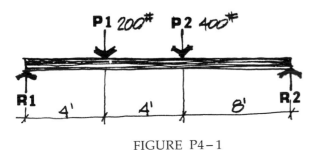

FIGURE P4–1

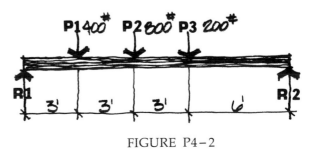

FIGURE P4–2

3. Figure P4–3.

4. Figure P4–4.

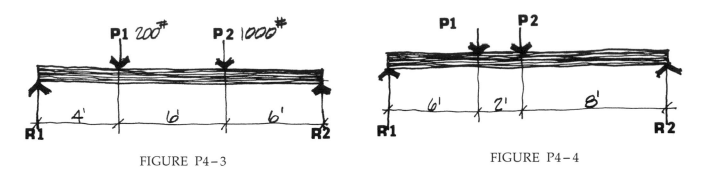

FIGURE P4–3

FIGURE P4–4

Find the reactions of the supports for the following combined loads.

5. Figure P4–5.

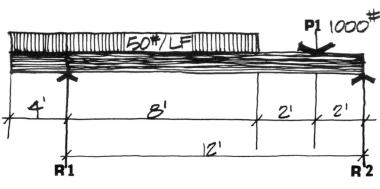

FIGURE P4–5

6. Figure P4–6.

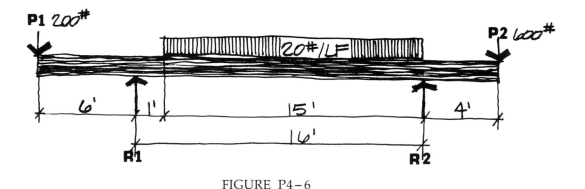

FIGURE P4–6

Moment of Inertia and Section Modulus

Find the moments of inertia I for the following beam sections. Assume that all lumber dimensions are ½ in less than the nominal dimension. All wood is southern pine #1.

7. Find I for a 3 in × 10 in beam sections.

8. Find I for a beam composed of three 2 in × 6 in beam sections.

9. Find I for a 4 in × 12 in beam sections.

10. Find I for a 6 in × 6 in beam sections.

Find the section modulus *S* for the following beam sections. Assume all dimensions are ½ in less than nominal. All material is southern pine #1.

11. Find *S* for a 2 in × 10 in beam.
12. Find *S* for a beam composed of four 2 in × 6 in beam sections.
13. Find *S* for a 6 in × 6 in beam section.
14. Find *S* for a 2 in × 12 in beam section.

Sizing Beams with the Flexure Formula

All beams will be southern pine #1.

15. What is the required *S* for a 10 ft long simple beam supporting 350 lb/lf over the entire length?
16. What is the required *S* for an overhanging beam supporting 400 lb/lf between the two supports if the span between supports is 16 ft and the overhand is 4 ft?
17. What is the minimum combination of 2 in nominal material required to support a load of 600 lb/lf, for a simple beam having a 14 ft span?
18. What is the smallest timber required to support a concentrated load of 5,000 lb at the center of a 12 ft span?

19. Will a 2 in × 10 in beam support a load of 150 lb/lf if it has to span 13 ft 6 in?
20. What is the maximum span for a 2 in × 10 in beam if it must carry 2,000 lb/lf loaded as a simple beam?

Sizing Posts and Columns

Assume all material is southern pine #1. *E* = 1,600,000.

21. What is the maximum unit stress allowable on an 8 ft, 4 in × 8 in column?
22. Will a 6 ft standard 4 in × 4 in column support an axial load of 13,000 lb?
23. What is the maximum total load that can be supported by a 6 in × 6 in column 9 ft long?
24. If a beam spans 16 ft between 6 ft posts and supports a concentrated load of 15,000 lb centered 4 ft from the left post, will a 4 in × 4 in post carry the load?
25. If a beam spans 18 ft with an evenly distributed load of 400 lb/lf and rests one column 4 ft long at the left and a second column 12 ft long at the right, will 4 in × 4 in columns satisfy the requirement?

5
Carpentry and Design with Wood

Wood and wood products are used extensively in all types of landscape project work. Wood appears most frequently in simple structures like shelters, benches, and fences, but wood is also used as a paving material, for planters, and even for retaining walls. In short, wood has applications in the landscape limited only by the imagination of the designer. However, if a designer is to use wood effectively as a construction material, it is essential to have a working knowledge of the structural properties of wood, its endurance qualities, available species, wood grades, and construction practices.

Wood materials used in construction are usually softwoods. This is wood obtained from narrow leaf trees (gymnosperms), such as pine, cedar, fir, and cypress. Wood obtained from broadleafed trees (angiosperms) is called hardwood. Hardwoods are most frequently used in furniture, finished millwork, and for decorative purposes. Since landscape use of hardwoods is limited, they will not be considered in any detail.

SOFTWOOD LUMBER SPECIES

Many different species of softwood are utilized in the manufacture of lumber and availability of some species varies widely with the geographic region. The important thing to remember is that each wood species varies in its workability, structural quality, appearance, hardness, and durability. To give you a better idea of the variation among the species a brief description is provided of the more popular softwood lumber species.

Cedars

Cedars (northern white cedar, western red cedar) are characteristically soft, low density woods. They are very easy to work and do not warp easily. In terms of structural properties, they are among the weakest of the softwood species, and do not hold nails well. Aesthetically, cedars are very pleasant; they are smooth-grained woods and range in color from a deep red to a very pleasant off white. Some cedar species tend to be very knotty and good clear boards may be hard to obtain. Cedars are naturally resistant to rot and are highly prized as a shingle material. In fact, the majority of the cedar harvested each year is used for shingles. Cedar is also known for its distinct fragrance.

Overall, cedar has much to offer as a landscape construction material because of its resistance to rot and aesthetic appeal when allowed to weather naturally. In many cases cedar could be considered as a possible alternative to redwood, so long as strength and nail-holding ability are not critical factors.

Cypress

Cypress (southern) is a tough, medium-density wood with good workability. It is resistant to shrinkage and is not easily warped. Structurally, it is reasonably strong in most sectional properties. Because its growth characteristics, most cypress is very knotty, but the knots are usually small and tight. Cypress, like cedar, is naturally decay resistant and requires little treatment to insure its longevity. Aesthetically cypress varies in color from a pale white to deep tan.

It is a medium-grained wood and holds paint well. If the wood is left unfinished, it will weather to a dark gray or almost black. Then, with age, it becomes a more uniform silver gray.

Cypress is an excellent landscape construction material because of its natural decay resistance, and its finish characteristics. Its most frequent applications are in docks, decks, siding, shingles, and exterior trim. Its major disadvantages are price and availability.

Douglas Fir

Douglas fir is a hard, dense wood and somewhat difficult to work because of its density. It has moderate resistance to shrinkage and warping if it is properly cured. As a structural material, douglas fir is one of the strongest of the popular lumber species, but it only has moderate resistance to rot. Therefore, fir will require the use of some wood preservative if it is used in outside structures. Aesthetically, fir is a medium- to fine-grained wood that has a pleasant off-white to light tan color and the knots are usually small and tight. Douglas fir does not hold paint well, however, so it is not usually preferred as an exposed material. In most cases douglas fir is best used as a structural framing material.

Pine

Pine (southern yellow) is a hard, dense wood and rather difficult to work. It also has a high pitch content and is subject to shrinkage and warping if not carefully cured. On the other hand, pine is the strongest of the softwood species and can be treated with preservatives to achieve a high decay resistance. Aesthetically, pine is somewhat lacking. It frequently has large- to medium-sized knots that may be surrounded by pitch. The wood color varies from white in the spring wood to a dark red or brown in the summer wood. The wood is medium- to coarse-grained and it does not hold paint well. However, it will take penetrating strains very well.

From a landscape construction point of view, pine is still an excellent material because of its strength, nail-holding qualities, ability to take stains and its availability. Pine is frequently used in decks, small shelters, for miscellaneous furniture like bench slats and picnic tables, and for fences.

Redwood

Redwood is a moderately dense wood that is easily worked. It resists shrinkage and is not easily warped. Redwood has good structural properties and a natural resistance to rot and insect attack. Redwood is characteristically knotty but the knots are usually small and tight. Redwood is probably the most popular of all the softwood species for landscape construction work. It has a pleasant range of color that goes from almost white to a dark sienna red. Its rot resistance and structural properties are particularly attractive, and it requires little or no finishing to preserve the wood. The chief drawbacks to the use of redwood are its cost and availability. If cost poses no problem redwood is good for everything.

Hardwoods

Because railroad ties are popular as a landscape material, we might point out here that railroad ties are usually made of hardwood species. Probably the most popular genus is oak. The actual species depends on the availability in a particular region, but the more popular species are white oak, red oak, and pin oak.

LUMBER AND WOOD GRADING

Wood materials manufactured for construction are classified by size as boards, lumber, or timber. Boards are less than 2 in thick, lumber is from 2 in to 5 in thick, and timber is material greater than 5 in thick. The dimensions of classified lumber are "nominal dimensions," that is, the nominal dimensions are larger than the actual dimensions of the wood. For most lumber the nominal dimension refers to the approximate size of the piece cut from the saw log.

When wood is first cut from a saw log it is called rough lumber. The rough lumber is then planed down to obtain a smooth even surface on all sides, and a uniform cross section. After planing the lumber is called dressed lumber. The dressed lumber is then stacked on pallets to allow good air circulation and placed in a drying yard or in drying kilns.

During the curing process the wood will shrink more reaching its final dressed dimensions. Since wood is an organic material the shrinkage from water loss will vary from piece to piece. But for most commercial lumber the dressed dimensions can be taken as $1/2$ in less for 2 in nominal material up to 8 in wide and $1/4$ in less for 1 in nominal material. For example, a 2 in × 6 in is approximately $1\frac{1}{2}$ in × $5\frac{1}{2}$ in, and a 1 in × 8 in would be $3/4$ in × $7\frac{1}{2}$ in.

Construction lumber is graded in two general categories of interest to the landscape architect, common yard lumber and stress-graded lumber.

Common Yard Lumber

Common yard lumber is visually graded in accordance with standards agreed upon by the industry for a particular species. Yard lumber has two broad classifications: select and common lumber. Each of these is broken down into numbered grades.

Select lumber is broken into grades 1 through 4. Select grades #1 and #2 are smooth, knot-free boards or lumber used for natural finished surfaces. Grades #3 and #4 are smooth boards or lumber which may have a few small tight knots but are excellent for painted surfaces.

Common lumber is the material most frequently used in all landscape construction. It is usually always available in the standard board and lumber dimensions in lengths of 8 ft, 10 ft, 12 ft, and 16 ft. Common lumber grades are #1 through #5, although in many areas the grades are called #1, #2, #3, stud and utility grades. The grades of common lumber are shown in Table 5–1 with their most appropriate uses.

Stress-Graded Lumber

The second important type of wood grading is stamped, stress-graded lumber. These grades are established either by visual inspection or mechanically by nondestructive testing. The grading procedures and grade classifications are agreed upon by the industry and grade standards established for each species. An example of the classification and grade markings is given in Table 5–2 for southern pine and California redwood. For most landscape construction the use of stress-graded lumber is not justified. The major application of stress-graded lumber is in heavy construction, prefabricated structural members like trusses and in multistory wood structures. Some applications in the landscape would be in small bridges or heavy-duty decks.

Lumber Measurement

All lumber is sold in units called a board foot. A board foot is 12 in $\times$ 12 in $\times$ 1 in or 144 cubic inches nominal. For example, the board footage of a piece of lumber 2 in $\times$ 4 in $\times$ 12 ft is found by dividing the cubic inches of wood by 144 as follows:

$$2 \times 4 \times 12 \times 12 = 1152 \text{ in}^3$$

$$b_F = \frac{1152}{144} = 8 \text{ b}_F$$

When prices are quoted on lumber they are most usually given in "feet, board measure" meaning so many board feet, usually 100 b_F or 1000 b_F.

WOOD FASTENERS

A very basic and important part of all wood construction is the fasteners used to hold a structure together. The fasteners used to assemble a wood struc-

TABLE 5–1
Common Yard Lumber

GRADE	USE
#1	Framing and exposed finished surfaces
#2	Framing and unexposed surfaces
#3	Light and temporary construction where appearance is not a factor
#4/stud	Light framing and temporary structures
#5/utility	Batter boards, stakes, forming, and general utility work

ture fall into four broad classifications: nails, bolts, screws, and special fasteners. Nails are the most common fastener, but bolts and screws are very important when "weathering" or "racking" of the structure may cause "nail withdrawal."

Nail withdrawal is a condition that occurs when a nail is used on a surface exposed to frequent wetting and drying. The moisture that penetrates the nail hole will cause dry rot, and the natural expansion and contraction of the two materials will cause the nail to back out of the hole.

Nails

Nails are most frequently used for connecting the basic framing elements to the superstructure, and for attaching siding, shingles, and decking. Nails are available in aluminum alloys or steel, bright finish nails, and hot dipped galvanized nails. Bright finish nails can be used for unexposed framing, but galvanized or alloy nails are best for most outside applications. Bright finish nails are undesirable because they will rust; this contributes to withdrawal and the rust will cause an objectionable stain.

Figure 5–1 illustrates some of the most common types of nails used in construction. Table 5–3 provides information on the sizes available and how they are used. Notice that nail sizes can be given by standard wire gauge or by the standard trade designation d or pennyweight. In other words a 20 penny common nail is designated as a 20d nail.

Screws

Screws are classified as either wood screws or as lag screws. Screws are used to fasten wood parts that are subject to frequent use, or heavy loads that might cause nails to pull out. They are available in many sizes and with different head configurations. Figure 5–2 illustrates many of the common wood screws. Table 5–4 gives the size designation and dimensions of common wood screws.

Wood screws are manufactured from a number of different materials and are usually available in plain

TABLE 5–2
Allowable Unit Stresses for Structural Lumber—Visual Grading
(The allowable unit stresses listed are for normal loading conditions. See other provisions of Part II for adjustments of tabulated stresses.)

GRADING RULES AGENCY, SPECIES, AND COMMERCIAL GRADE	SIZE CLASSIFICATION	ALLOWABLE UNIT STRESSES IN POUNDS PER SQUARE INCH					
		EXTREME FIBER IN BENDING[3] "F_b"	TENSION PARALLEL TO GRAIN "F_t"	HORIZONTAL SHEAR "F_v"	COMPRESSION PERPENDICULAR TO GRAIN "$F_{c\perp}$"	COMPRESSION PARALLEL TO GRAIN "F_c"	MODULUS OF ELASTICITY "E"
SOUTHERN PINE INSPECTION BUREAU[1-3]							
SOUTHERN PINE (Moisture content not over 15 percent)[1,2]							
No. 1 KD	2" thick only	1700	1150	105	405	1350	1,900,000
No. 1 Dense KD	"	2000	1350	105	475	1600	2,000,000
No. 2 KD	"	1500	1000	90	405	1150	1,700,000
No. 2 Dense KD	"	1750	1150	90	475	1400	1,800,000
Special KD	"	1200	800	75	305	950	1,300,000
No. 3 KD	"	700	475	80	335	550	1,300,000
No. 3 MG KD	"	825	550	90	405	650	1,500,000
No. 3 Dense KD	"	975	650	90	475	775	1,600,000
KD Stud	"	700	475	80	335	550	1,300,000
No. 1 SR KD	2½" to 4" thick	1700	1150	125	405	1600	1,900,000
No. 1 Dense SR KD	"	2000	1350	125	475	1850	2,000,000
No. 2 SR KD	"	1500	1000	105	405	1150	1,700,000
No. 2 Dense SR KD	"	1750	1150	105	475	1400	1,800,000
Dense Structural 86 KD	2" to 4" thick	3000	2000	160	475	2350	2,000,000
Dense Structural 72 KD	"	2500	1650	135	475	2000	2,000,000
Dense Structural 65 KD	"	2250	1500	120	475	1800	2,000,000
Dense Std. Fac. KD (T&G)	2" to 4" thick decking	2000	1350	105	475	1850	2,000,000
No. 1 Dense Fac. KD (T&G)	"	1750	1150	90	475	1400	1,800,000
No. 1 Fac. KD (T&G)	"	1500	1000	90	405	1150	1,700,000
No. 2 Dense Fac. KD (T&G)	"	1750	1150	90	475	1400	1,800,000
No. 2 Fac. KD (T&G)	"	1500	1000	90	405	1150	1,700,000
Select Dense KD (DT&G)	3" to 4" thick decking	2000	1350	105	475	1850	2,000,000
Select KD (DT&G)	"	1700	1150	105	405	1600	1,900,000
No. 1 Dense KD (DT&G)	"	1750	1150	90	475	1400	1,800,000
No. 1 KD (DT&G)	"	1500	1000	90	405	1150	1,700,000
No. 2 KD (DT&G)	"	1750	1150	90	475	1400	1,800,000
No. 2 KD (DT&G)	"	1500	1000	90	405	1150	1,700,000

SOUTHERN PINE (Moisture content not over 19 percent)[1,2]

Grade	Size						
No. 1 Dry	2" thick only	1600	1050	100	405	1150	1,800,000
No. 1 Dense Dry	"	1850	1250	100	475	1350	1,900,000
No. 2 Dry	"	1350	925	90	405	1000	1,600,000
No. 2 Dense Dry	"	1600	1050	90	475	1200	1,700,000
Special Dry	"	1100	725	70	305	800	1,200,000
No. 3 Dry	"	650	425	75	335	475	1,300,000
No. 3 MG Dry	"	775	500	90	405	575	1,400,000
No. 3 Dense Dry	"	900	600	90	475	650	1,500,000
Stud Dry	"	650	425	75	335	475	1,300,000
No. 1 SR Dry	2½" to thick	1600	1050	120	405	1350	1,800,000
No. 1 Dense SR Dry	"	1850	1250	120	475	1600	1,900,000
No. 2 SR Dry	"	1350	925	100	405	1000	1,600,000
No. 2 Dense SR Dry	"	1600	1050	100	475	1200	1,700,000
Dense Structural 86 Dry	2" to 4" thick	2750	1850	150	475	2050	1,900,000
Dense Structural 72 Dry	"	2300	1550	125	475	1700	1,900,000
Dense Structural 65 Dry	"	2100	1400	115	475	1550	1,900,000
Dense Std. Factory Dry	2" to 4" thick	1850	1250	100	475	1350	1,900,000
No. 1 Dense Factory Dry	"	1600	1050	90	475	1200	1,700,000
No. 1 Factory Dry	"	1350	925	90	405	1000	1,600,000
No. 2 Dense Factory Dry	"	1600	1050	90	475	1200	1,700,000
No. 2 Factory Dry	"	1350	925	90	405	1000	1,600,000

SOUTHERN PINE (Unseasoned)[1,2]

Grade	Size						
No. 1 SR	2½" & thicker	1250	850	110	270	925	1,600,000
No. 1 Dense SR	"	1500	1000	110	315	1050	1,600,000
No. 2 SR	"	1100	725	95	270	675	1,400,000
No. 2 Dense SR	"	1300	850	95	315	775	1,500,000
Dense Structural 86	2½" & thicker	2200	1450	140	315	1350	1,600,000
Dense Structural 72	"	1850	1250	120	315	1150	1,600,000
Dense Structural 65	"	1650	1100	105	315	1000	1,600,000
Dense Std. Factory	2¼" to 5" thick	1500	1000	110	315	1050	1,600,000
No. 1 Dense Factory	x	1300	850	95	315	775	1,500,000
No. 1 Factory	"	1100	725	95	270	675	1,400,000
No. 2 Dense Factory	"	1300	850	95	315	775	1,500,000
No. 2 Factory	"	1100	725	95	270	675	1,400,000

(continued)

TABLE 5–2 (continued)

GRADING RULES AGENCY, SPECIES AND COMMERCIAL GRADE	SIZE CLASSIFI- CATION	EXTREME FIBER IN BENDING³ "F_b"	TENSION PARALLEL TO GRAIN "F_t"	HORIZONTAL SHEAR "F_v"	COMPRESSION PERPENDICULAR TO GRAIN "$F_{c\perp}$"	COMPRESSION PARALLEL TO GRAIN "F_c"	MODULUS OF ELASTICITY "E"
REDWOOD INSPECTION SERVICE⁴⁻⁷ CALIFORNIA REDWOOD (Unseasoned)							
Clear Heart-Clear Structural	2" & thicker	1950	1300	135	305	1600	1,240,000
Select Heart-Select Structural	"	1750	1200	135	305	1250	1,240,000
Construction Heart-Construction Structural	"	1450	1000	125	305	1050	1,240,000

Footnotes Applicable to Southern Pine Inspection Bureau Grades of Southern Pine.

[1]All stress-rated grades for Southern Pine Lumber are established on a basis that permits cutting graded members to shorter lengths without impairment of stress ratings in the shorter pieces. In addition, the stresses apply to members used either flat or on edge. Grade restrictions apply the entire length of each piece, and each piece is suitable for use in continuous spans, over double spans, or under concentrated loads, without the necessity of regrading for shear or other stress requirements.

[2]If lumber is in service under wet conditions of use, or where the moisture content is at or above the fiber saturation point, as when continuously submerged, (a) the allowable unit stresses for "F_b" "F_t," "F_v," and modulus of elasticity shall be limited in all thicknesses to the stresses listed for the corresponding unseasoned grade; (b) the allowable unit stresses for "F_c" shall be limited in all thicknesses to 90 percent of the allowable unit stresses for thicknesses of 5" and up; and (c) the allowable unit stresses for "$F_{c\perp}$" shall be reduced one-third.

[3]For lumber 4" and less in thickness, the tabulated values for "F_b" may be increased 15 percent to provide for Repetitive Member Uses.

Footnotes Applicable to Redwood Inspection Service Grades of California Redwood.

[4]For lumber seasoned below the fiber saturation point (approximately 30 percent moisture content) before full design load is applied, and which will remain dry in service, the tabulated modulus of elasticity may be increased 2 percent, and the tabulated "F_c" values may be increased 10 percent.

[5]For lumber 4" and thinner, where the moisture content in service will not exceed 19 percent, the tabulated values may be increased as follows:

Fiber stress in bending, "F_b," and tension parallel
to Grain "F_t," .... 24 percent
Horizontal shear, "F_v," .... None*
Compression perpendicular to grain, "F_c," .... 50 percent
Compression parallel to grain, "F_c" .... 45 percent
Modulus of elasticity .... 11 percent

[6]For lumber 4" and thinner, kiln dried to 15 percent maximum moisture content, the tabulated values may be increased as follows:

Fiber stress in bending, "F_b," and tension parallel
to grain "F_t," .... 34 percent
Horizontal shear, "F_v," .... 13 percent
Compression perpendicular to grain, "$F_{c\perp}$" .... 50 percent
Compression parallel to grain, "F_c" .... 68 percent
Modulus of elasticity .... 15 percent

[7]For lumber 4" and less in thickness, the tabulated values for Engineered Uses for "F_b" may be increased 10 percent to provide for Repetitive Member Uses.

*For lumber manufactured at or below 19 percent moisture content, the tabulated "F_v" values may be increased 8 percent.

TABLE 5-3
Wire Nails—Kinds and Quantities Required (American Steel & Wire Company Manual of Carpentry)

POUNDS PER 1000 FEET B.M. ON CENTER AS FOLLOWS (POUNDS)

LENGTH IN INCHES	AM. STEEL & WIRE CO'S STEEL WIRE GAUGE	APPROX. NO. TO LBS.	NAIL-INGS	SIZES AND KINDS OF MATERIAL	TRADE NAMES	12"	16"	20"	36"	48"
2½	10¼	106	2	1×4 Used square	8d common	60	48	37	23	20
2½	10¼	106	2	1×6 edge, as plat-	8d common	40	32	25	16	13
2½	10¼	106	2	1×8 forms, floors,	8d common	31	27	20	12	10
2½	10¼	106	2	1×10 sheathing or	8d common	25	20	16	10	8
2½	10¼	106	3	1×12 shiplap.	8d common	31	24	20	12	10
4	6	31	2	2×4 When used	20d common	105	80	65	60	33
4	6	31	2	2×6 D. & M. blind	20d common	70	54	43	27	22
4	6	31	2	2×8 nailed, only	20d common	53	40	53	21	17
4	6	31	3	2×10 ½ quantity	20d common	60	50	40	25	20
4	6	31	3	2×12 named	20d common	52	41	33	21	17
6	2	11	2	3×4 required.	60d common	197	150	122	76	61
6	2	11	2	3×6	60d common	131	97	82	52	42
6	2	11	2	3×8	60d common	100	76	61	38	34
6	2	11	3	3×10	60d common	178	137	110	70	55
6	2	11	3	3×12	60d common	145	115	92	58	46
2½	12½	189	2	Base, per 100 ft. lin.	8d finish	–	1	–	–	–
2½	10¼	106	2	Bracket lath	8d common	–	48	–	–	–
2½	12½	189	1	Ceiling, ¾×4	8d finish	18	14	–	–	–
2	13	309	1	Ceiling, ½ and 5/8	6d finish	11	8	–	–	–
2½	12½	189	2	Finish, 7/8	8d finish	25	12	–	–	–
3	11½	121	2	Finish, 1⅛	10d finish	12	10	–	–	–
2½	10	99	1	Flooring, 1×3	8d floor brads	42	32	–	–	–
2½	10	99	1	Flooring, 1×4	8d floor brads	32	26	–	–	–
2½	10	99	1	Flooring, 1×6	8d floor brads	22	18	–	–	–
4	6	31	} Framing, 2×4, to 2×16 requires 3 or more sizes and vary greatly.		20d common	20	16	14	–	–
3½	8	49			16d common	10	10	8	–	–
3	9	69			10d common	8	6	5	–	–
6	2	11		Framing, 3×4 to 3×14	60d common	30	25	20	–	–
2½	11½	145	2	Siding drop, 1×4	8d casing	45	35	–	–	–
2½	11½	145	2	Siding, drop, 1×6	8d casing	30	25	–	–	–
2½	11½	145	2	Siding, drop, 1×8	8d casing	23	18	–	–	–
2	13	309	1	Siding, bevel, ½×4	6d finish	23	18	–	–	–
2	13	309	1	Siding, bevel, ½×6	6d finish	15	13	–	–	–
2	13	309	1	Siding, bevel, ½×8	6d finish	12	10	–	–	–
				Casing, per opening	6d & 8d casing	About ½ pound per side.				
1¼	14	568	12" o.c.	Flooring, ⅜×2	3d brads	About 10 pounds per 1000 sq. ft.				
1⅛	15	778	16" o.c.	Lath, 48"	3d fine	6 pounds per 1000 pieces.				
1¼	13	429	–	Shingles[a]	3d shingle	4½ pounds; about 2 nails each 4 inches.				
1½	12	274	–	Shingles	4d shingle	7½ pounds; about 2 nails to each 4 inches.				

[a]Wood shingles vary in width. Regardless of width 1000 shingles are the equivalent of 1000 pieces 4 inches wide.

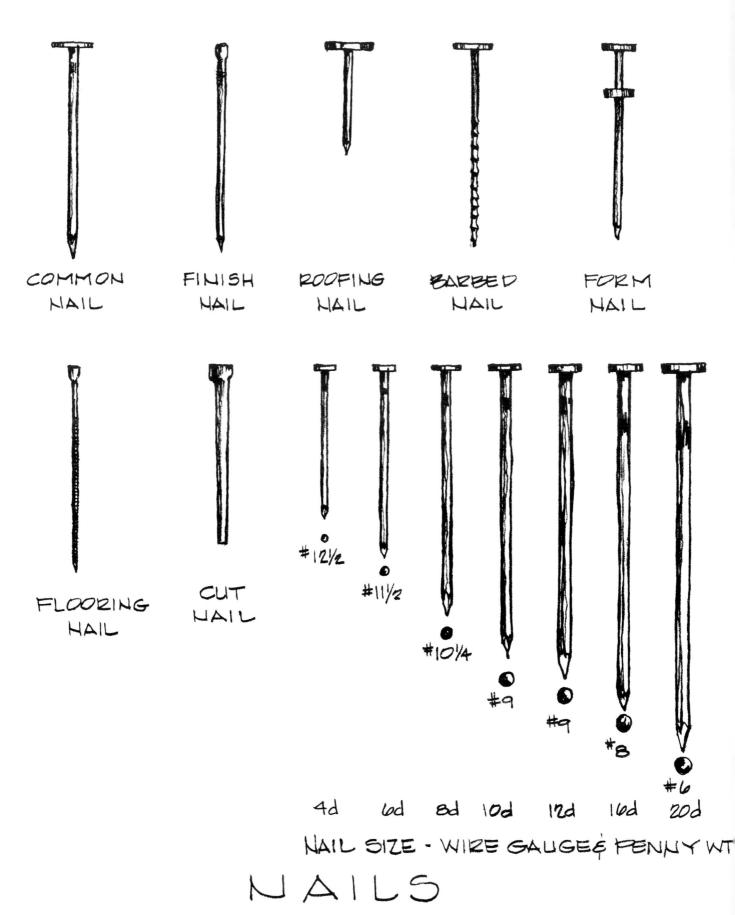

COMMON NAIL   FINISH NAIL   ROOFING NAIL   BARBED NAIL   FORM NAIL

FLOORING NAIL   CUT NAIL

#12½   #11½   #10¼   #9   #9   #8   #6

4d   6d   8d   10d   12d   16d   20d

NAIL SIZE - WIRE GAUGE & PENNY WT

NAILS

FIGURE 5–1

TABLE 5–4
Wood Screws: Properties and Sizes

SIZE	SHANK DIAMETER (D)	ROOT DIAMETER (²/₃ D)	LENGTHS
0	.060	.040	¼ – ³/₈
1	.073	.049	¼ – ½
2	.086	.057	¼ – ¾
3	.099	.066	¼ – 1
4	.112	.075	¼ – 1½
5	.125	.083	³/₈ – 1½
6	.138	.092	³/₈ – 2½
7	.151	.101	³/₈ – 2½
8	.164	.109	³/₈ – 3
9	.177	.118	½ – 3
10	.190	.127	½ – 3½
12	.216	.144	⁵/₈ – 4
14	.242	.161	¾ – 5
16	.268	.179	1 – 5
18	.294	.196	1¼ – 5
20	.320	.213	1½ – 5
24	.372	.248	3 – 5

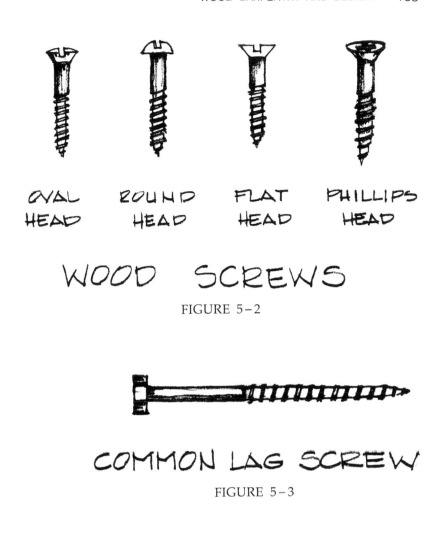

WOOD SCREWS

FIGURE 5–2

COMMON LAG SCREW

FIGURE 5–3

steel, galvanized steel, chrome-plated steel, and brass. Plain screws should not be used on exposed surfaces since they will rust; chrome-plated or galvanized steel are probably the best choice when screws will be exposed.

Lag screws are large, heavy screws with hex, bolt-type heads. They are used to assemble heavy-duty structural members where nail withdrawal would be a problem. Figure 5–3 illustrates a common lag screw and Table 5–4 gives the standard sizes. Lag screws are available in either bright finish or hot dipped galvanized finish.

Bolts

Bolts are used to fasten major construction members together, such as beams to columns, or fastening wood to steel plates. The kinds of bolts most frequently used are carriage bolts and machine bolts as illustrated in Figure 5–4. The sizes are given in Table 5–5. Bolts are also available in bright and hot-dipped galvanized finishes. For most landscape construction the hot-dipped galvanized finish is preferred.

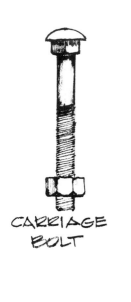

CARRIAGE
BOLT

MACHINE
BOLT

HEX HEAD
BOLT

BOLTS

FIGURE 5–4

TABLE 5–5
Bolts: Sizes and Lengths

DIAMETER (IN)	LENGTHS (IN)
$1/4$	$1/2-8$
$5/16$	$3/4-10$
$3/8$	$3/4-12$
$7/16$	$1-12$
$1/2$	$1-16$
$5/8$	$1-16$
$3/4$	$1-16$
$7/8$	$1 1/2-16$
1	$1 1/2-16$
$1 1/8$	$3-16$
$1 1/4$	$3-16$

Specialized Fasteners

Other types of fasteners used for assembling wood structures are illustrated in Figure 5–5. The Trip-L-Grip anchors are used for bracing and adding extra strength to construction joints. They are a good investment in any structure that could be subject to frequent "racking." They are also a convenience if it is desirable to set joists flush with beams, and for making post-to-beam attachments.

Explosive-driven fastenings are an almost indispensable tool for attaching wood stringers and beams to aluminum, light steel, or concrete. They can also be used to assemble heavy timber structures. They are an expensive alternative to bolts but they usually make up for the additional cost in labor saving.

WOOD PRESERVATIVES

Woods that do not have a natural resistance to rot are frequently treated to increase their longevity. The chemicals used for wood preservation are either petroleum-base or water-soluble chemicals.

The most popular petroleum-base preservative is creosote. It is widely used to treat posts, bridge timbers, and poles. Creosote-treated wood is usually long lived but it cannot be painted and it shouldn't be used where people will come in contact with the surface. Another popular oil base chemical is pentachlorophenol (penta). Penta is also a caustic material but it can be painted if it is properly cured and finished.

The water soluble chemicals are complex compounds that contain copper, zinc, arsenic, chrome, or chloride as the major preservative. Most of the lumber treated with these chemicals can be painted and many of them will take penetrating stains very well.

Application of Preservatives

Preservatives are applied in several different ways. The simplest method is to apply the preservative directly to the wood with a mop or brush. This method only puts a thin veneer on the surface and it will not be as long-lived as materials applied by other methods.

Creosote is most frequently applied by dipping the material into a tank filled with creosote. This method also only treats the outside surface. A variation of the dip method involves dipping the wood in a tank of heated creosote. This causes the cells to expand and absorb the creosote. Then the wood is dipped in a tank of cool creosote, which causes the cells to contract and drive the material deeper into the wood.

The most sophisticated treatments involve application of the chemical preservatives under pressure. These pressure treatment methods force the chemical preservatives into the wood under pressure to get a deep penetration into the wood cells. Pressure processes are classified as either a full-cell method or the empty-cell method. The full cell method involves completely filling the wood cells with preservative. The empty cell method involves filling the wood cells under pressure and then drawing the material out of the cells leaving only the preservative that has penetrated the cell walls.

The full cell method is preferred for wood that will be in constant contact with moisture. The empty cell

TRIP-L-GRIP FASTENERS

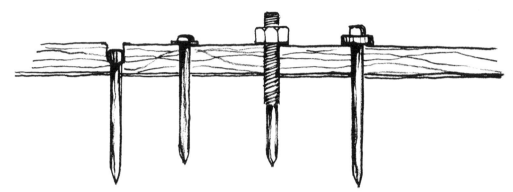

EXPLOSIVE DRIVEN FASTENERS

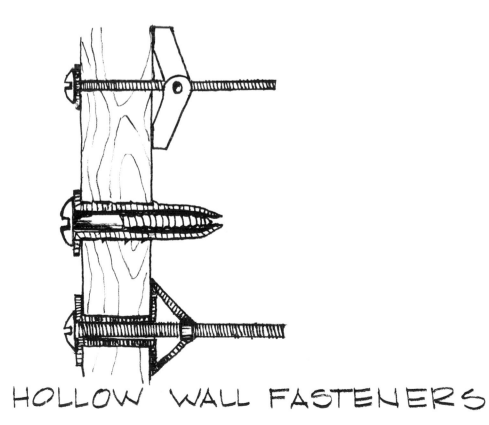

HOLLOW WALL FASTENERS

FIGURE 5-5

TABLE 5–6
Pressure Treatments

PRESERVATIVE	Symbol	MINIMUM RETENTION OF SOLID PRESERVATIVE, LB/CU FT	
		In Contact with Ground A	Not in Contact with Ground B
Oil-borne preservatives			
Clean and paintable water repellent pentachlorophenol[a]	Penta-WR	0.50	0.30
Water-borne preservatives[b]			
Celcure (Acid copper chromate) Fed. Spec. TT-W-546 or AWPA Standard P-5	ACC	1.00	0.50
Chemonite (Ammoniacal copper arsentie) Fed. Spec. TT-W-549 or AWPA Standard P-5	ACA	0.50	0.30
Greensalts, erdalith (Chromated copper arsenate, Type I) Fed. Spec. TT-W-550 or AWPA Standard P-5	CCA-I	0.75	0.40
Boliden K-33 osmose K-33 (Chromated copper arsenate, Type II) Fed. Spec. TT-W-550 or AWPA Standard P-5	CCA-II	0.45	0.25
Chromated zinc chloride Fed. Spec. TT-W-551 or AWPA Standard P-5	CZC	1.00	0.75
Tanalith, wolman salts (Fluor chrome arsenate phenol mixture, Type I)	FCAP-I	0.50	0.35
Osmosalts (Fluor chrome arsenate phenol mixture, Type II) Fed. Spec. TT-W-535 or AWPA Standard P-5	FCAP-II	0.50	0.35

Recommendations in accordance with Fed. Spec. TT-W-571-h and AWPA Standards.

[a]Treatment is with pentachlorophenol in a specially selected solvent with a water repellent added and then seasoned or conditioned after treatment to remove objectionable residues.

[b]Water-borne preservatives are used for installations off the ground and to a limited extent in ground contact where clean, odorless, paintable wood is required. Lumber treated with water-borne preservative should *always* be *redried* to the same moisture content before it was treated.

method is used for most exposed construction material that is not in contact with the ground. A summary of pressure treatments prepared by the Southern Pine Association is given in Table 5–6.

Column A indicates the recommended minimum retention of preservatives for wood processed by the full-cell method. Column B gives the minimum recommended retention of preservative material for wood processed by the empty-cell method.

A further discussion of the effectiveness of any particular chemical or chemical process would serve very little purpose at this point since local availability of materials will vary widely. The best practice is to contact local contractors and material suppliers to find out what is available. It is also worthwhile to contact owners of older projects, if possible, to find out how the materials have held up.

FRAME CONSTRUCTION

Landscape structures that employ wood are usually designed using the plank-and-beam framing system or some variation of the platform framing system. The platform system is an old standard that has been used in residential construction since precut, dressed lumber became common. The plank-and-beam system is of later origin and became very popular in the late forties and early fifties.

The platform system has three basic structural parts: the flooring (decking), joists, and beams. The beams may be supported by columns or piers, or they may be carried by larger horizontal members called girders. The girders then act as larger beams that transfer the loads to heavy columns. In addition to the three major construction members there are several other small parts that are equally important. Figure 5–6 is a cutaway view of the platform framing system as it is commonly used in landscape construction. The terms shown are those most frequently used to identify the individual parts.

The plank-and-beam system is more simple than the platform system because the joists and cross-bridging are eliminated. This system utilizes planks of 2 in or greater nominal thickness to span beams, spaced 4 to 8 feet apart. At first it might appear that this system would result in a substantial saving in material; this is not the case, however. In fact, the material costs increase somewhat because it requires large nominal-dimension lumber of better quality than the platform frame. On the other hand, it does result in some labor savings since there is less material to assemble in the field. The plank-and-beam system is illustrated in Figure 5–7.

The merits of using either system is largely a matter of designer preference. From an aesthetic viewpoint, the plank-and-beam system has a lighter, more contemporary feel than the platform frame. On the other hand, the platform system can be used to

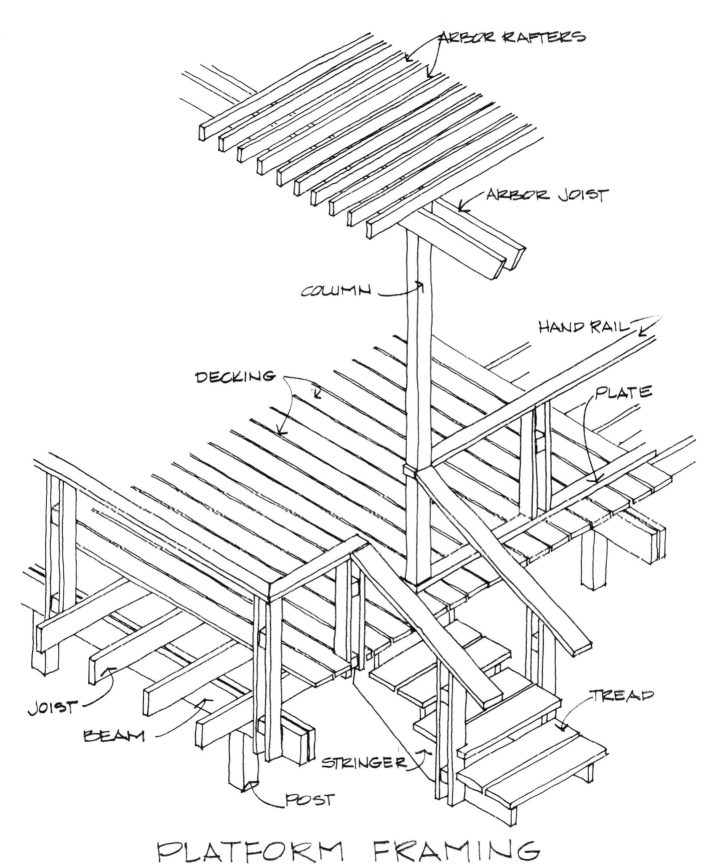

ARBOR RAFTERS

ARBOR JOIST

COLUMN

HAND RAIL

DECKING

PLATE

JOIST

BEAM

TREAD

STRINGER

POST

PLATFORM FRAMING

FIGURE 5–6

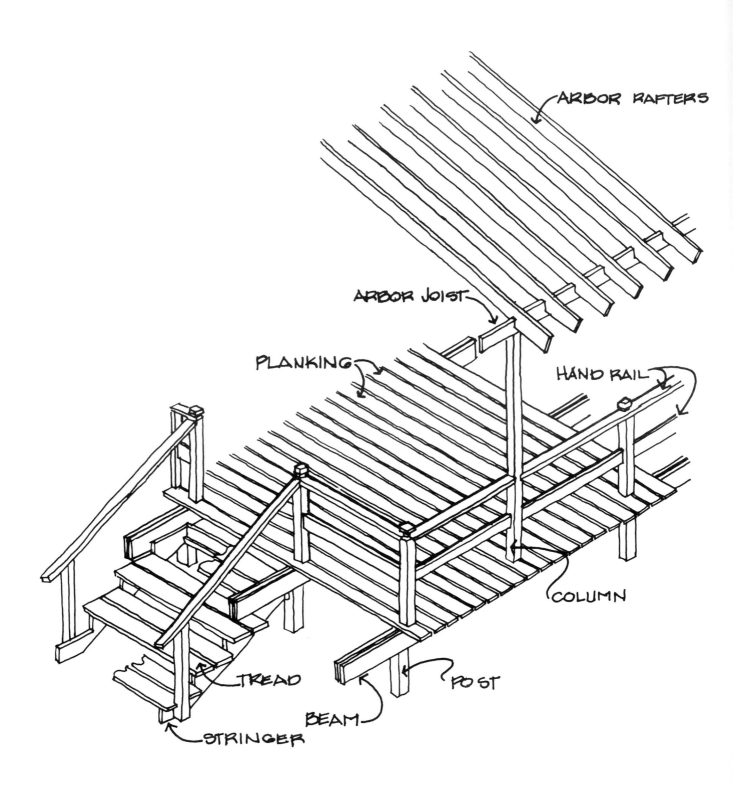

ARBOR RAFTERS

ARBOR JOIST

PLANKING

HAND RAIL

COLUMN

TREAD

STRINGER

BEAM

POST

PLANK & BEAM FRAMING

FIGURE 5-7

good advantage where a heavier, more stable appearance is desirable. Another factor that may weigh heavily in selecting the platform system is the availability of 3 in decking material which is preferred for beam spans over 4 feet.

STRUCTURAL DESIGN OF WOOD LANDSCAPE STRUCTURES

When the design decisions have been made regarding the framing system and the lumber species, the next step is to estimate the loads the structure will have to carry. In some instances the design loads may be spelled out in the local building code but more often you will find that the codes do not consider landscape construction and these decisions will be left to the designer. In these cases, Table 5–7 can be used as a general guideline in establishing live loads. These figures have been compiled from information published by the Southern Forest Products Association, and the American Standards Association in *The American Standard Building Code Requirements for Minimum Design Loads in Buildings and Other Structures.*

In addition to the vertical live loads that act on a structure, the horizontal wind load must also be considered on vertical surfaces. This is particularly important for fences that provide no openings for air circulation. The methods for estimating wind loads on vertical surfaces will be discussed in more detail in Chapter 6. The principles discussed there also apply to wood structures.

After the live loads on the structure have been determined, a preliminary framing plan is prepared. To illustrate the complete process we will work through a typical deck design problem. For this example the platform framing system was chosen, and #1 southern pine was selected as the construction material. Now consider the preliminary framing plan illustrated in Figure 5–8. The proposed deck is supported by beams spaced 12 ft 6 in on center. The longest span of the beams is 12 ft 6 in. The beams support joists spaced 16 in on center and the joists have a 12 ft 6 in span. The deck is being designed for a live load of 40 lb/ft².

The first step is to determine the size of the joists. This is accomplished using Table 5–8 for the allowable span for floor joists based on a 40 lb/ft² load. These tables were developed for southern yellow pine by the Southern Forest Products Association and similar tables are available for other wood species.

From Table 5–8 we find that #1 pine 2 × 6's 16 in o.c. will span only 9 ft-8 in, 2 × 8's will span 12 ft-9 in. Therefore, 2 × 8's are selected for the joists. Next, the sizes of the beams must be determined. Here we must determine the load being carried by each beam.

TABLE 5–7
Recommended Live Load Values for Landscape Structures

VALUES ARE FOR EVENLY DISTRIBUTED LIVE LOADS ON HORIZONTAL SURFACES.	
Residential decks, light duty	40 lb/ft²
Public decks, heavy duty	80 – 100 lb/ft²[a]
Roofs, flat	20 – 40 lb/ft²[a]
Bleacher seating	100 lb/ft²
Foot bridges	100 lb/ft²
Light vehicular bridges	200 – 300 lb/ft²

[a]The higher value should be used for northern areas subject to snow loading.

Since in theory a live load is considered an evenly distributed load, each beam will carry half the load of the deck surface it supports. Therefore beam A carries ½ the load of the area designated section 1 (Figure 5–8). However, beam C carries ½ the load of section 1 plus half the load of section 3. The remaining beams carry only ½ the load of a single section, similar to beam A.

The critical factors in sizing a beam are its strength in bending and the beam deflection.

Bending moments have already been discussed in Chapter 4, but deflection has not yet been discussed. Any beam will deflect (bow) as a result of the load placed on it. This is usually not the major consideration in sizing a beam unless the beam is visible, or will be finished on the underside, or will be subject to large shifting loads, such as a crowd moving across a large deck. In these instances the beam might well be large enough to support the load, but the deflection would be so great that it would be noticeable to the eye, cracks would develop in the plaster or other rigid finishes, and people moving over the structure would experience a springing sensation. Thus when any of these points becomes a design consideration beams should be investigated for deflection as well as maximum bending moment. In any case where design is governed by deflection, deflection should be less than 1/360th of the span.

To proceed with the investigation we have simple beams supporting an equally distributed load. For this situation the maximum bending moment equals $WL/8$. The maximum bending moment is then used to determine the required section modulus (S) for the beam. Section modulus is found by the flexure formula.

$$S = \frac{M}{f}$$ (See Chapter 4 for further explanation of section modulus and the flexure formula.)

M = Maximum bending moment in in-lb
f = Extreme fiber stress in bending

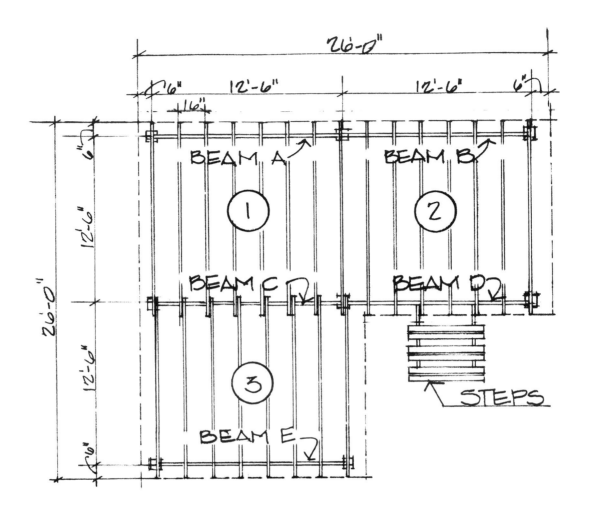

DECK FRAMING PLAN

FIGURE 5–8

The calculations for beams A, B, D, E are as follows. Determine W (the total load).

$$W = \frac{12.5 \text{ ft} \times 12.5 \text{ ft} \times 40 \text{ lb/ft}^2}{2} = \frac{6,250 \text{ lb}}{2}$$

$$W = 3,125 \text{ lb}$$

Next determine M (the maximum bending moment).

$$M = \frac{WL}{8} \quad \frac{3,125 \text{ lb} \times 12.5 \text{ ft}}{8} \quad \frac{39062.5 \text{ ft-lb}}{8}$$

$$M = 4,882.8 \text{ ft-lb}$$

Moment is then converted to inch-pounds, because f (extreme fiber stress) is given in lb/in².

$$M = 58,593.8 \text{ in-lb}$$

Substituting into the flexure formula find S if $f = 1600$ lb/in².

$$S = \frac{M}{F} = \frac{58,593.8 \text{ in-lb}}{1600 \text{ lb/in}^2}$$

$$S = 36.62 \text{ in}^3$$

Since the beams will be used on edge this is the minimum section modulus for the beams on the X–X axis. Looking at Table 4–2 we find that a 3×10 has the closest value to the minimum 36.62 in³ section modulus. This is an unusual size however, so a built-up beam using two 2×10's would be the best choice. This is equivalent to one 3×10 with a section modulus of 54.53 in³.

To proceed with the investigation we must first select beams that are safe in bending. In this case we next calculate the deflection of the beam. From Figure 4–13 find the formula for the maximum deflection of a simple beam supporting an evenly distributed load:

$$D = \frac{5WL^3}{384EI}$$

TABLE 5–8

FLOOR JOISTS — 40 psf live load. All rooms except sleeping rooms and attic floors. Spans shown in light face type are based on a deflection limitation of *l*/360. Spans shown in bold face type are limited by allowable extreme fiber stress in bending of the grade and include a 10 psf dead load.

Size and Spacing in	Grade in. o.c.	Dense Sel Str KD and No. 1 Dense KD	Dense Sel Str, Sel Str KD, No. 1 Dense and No. 1 KD	Sel Str, No. 1 and No. 2 Dense KD	No. 2 Dense, No. 2 KD and No. 2	No. 3 Dense KD	No. 3 Dense	No. 3 KD	No. 3
2 x 5	12.0	9-3	9-1	8-11	8-9	**8-3**	**8-0**	**7-8**	**7-4**
	13.7	8-11	8-9	8-7	8-5	**7-9**	**7-6**	**7-2**	**6-11**
	16.0	8-5	8-3	8-2	8-0	**7-2**	**6-11**	**6-7**	**6-5**
	19.2	7-11	7-10	7-8	7-6	**6-6**	**6-4**	**6-0**	**5-10**
	24.0	7-4	7-3	7-1	7-0[1]	**5-10**	**5-8**	**5-5**	**5-3**
2 x 6	12.0	11-4	11-2	10-11	10-9	**10-1**	9-9	9-4	9-0
	13.7	10-10	10-8	10-6	10-3	**9-5**	9-2	8-9	8-5
	16.0	10-4	10-2	9-11	9-9	**8-9**	8-6	8-1	7-10
	19.2	9-8	9-6	9-4	9-2	**8-0**	7-9	7-4	7-1
	24.0	9-0	8-10	8-8	8-6[1]	**7-1**	6-11	6-7	6-4
2 x 8	12.0	15-0	14-8	14-5	14-2	**13-3**	12-11	12-4	11-11
	13.7	14-4	14-1	13-10	13-6	**12-5**	12-1	11-6	11-1
	16.0	13-7	13-4	13-1	12-10	**11-6**	11-2	10-8	10-3
	19.2	12-10	12-7	12-4	12-1	**10-6**	10-2	9-9	9-5
	24.0	11-11	11-8	11-5	11-3[1]	**9-5**	9-1	8-8	8-5
2 x 10	12.0	19-1	18-9	18-5	18-0	**16-11**	16-5	15-8	15-2
	13.7	18-3	17-11	17-7	17-3	**15-10**	15-5	14-8	14-2
	16.0	17-4	17-0	16-9	16-5	**14-8**	14-3	13-7	13-1
	19.2	16-4	16-0	15-9	15-5	**13-5**	13-0	12-5	12-0
	24.0	15-2	14-11	14-7	14-4[1]	**12-0**	11-8	11-1	10-9
2 x 12	12.0	23-3	22-10	22-5	21-11	**20-7**	20-0	19-1	18-5
	13.7	22-3	21-10	21-5	21-0	**19-3**	18-9	17-10	17-3
	16.0	21-1	20-9	20-4	19-11	**17-10**	17-4	16-6	16-0
	19.2	19-10	19-6	19-2	18-9	**16-3**	15-10	15-1	14-7
	24.0	18-5	18-1	17-9	17-5[1]	**14-7**	14-2	13-6	13-0

1. The span for No. 2 grade, 24 inches o.c. spacing is: 2x5, **6-10**; 2x6, **8-4**; 2x8, **11-0**; 2x10, **14-0**; 2x12, **17-1**.

where

D = total deflection in inches;
W = total load;
L = span of the beam;
E = modulus of elasticity (see Chapter 4 and Table 4–1);
I = moment of inertia (see explanation Chapter 4).

Substituting into the equation the deflection of the beam is as follows. [Remember that all units must be in inches.]

First calculate the moment of inertia. [Discussed in Chapter 4.]

$$I = \frac{bd^3}{12} \quad \frac{3 \text{ in} \times (9.5 \text{ in})^3}{12} = \frac{2572.13}{12}$$

$$I = 214.34 \text{ in}^4$$

Next substitute into the deflection equation as follows:

$$D = \frac{5\,WL^3}{384\,EI} = \frac{5 \times 3125 \times (12.5 \times 12)^3}{384 \times 1,600,000 \times 214.34}$$

$$D = \frac{15,625 \times 3,375,000}{614,400,000 \times 214.34} = \frac{5.273^{10}}{1.317^{11}}$$

$$D = .40 \text{ in}$$

The total deflection is equal to .4 in. Next find the maximum allowable deflection based on 1/360th of the span. Once again be sure that the span is converted to inches because the deflection is in inches. The maximum allowable deflection is found as follows:

$$\frac{1}{360} = (12.5 \text{ ft} \times 12) = \frac{12.5 \times 12}{360} = \frac{150}{360} = .42 \text{ in}$$

Since the maximum allowable deflection (.42) is greater than the actual deflection the beam is safe in both deflection and bending.

Next calculate S for beam C as follows:

$$W = (12.5 \times 12.5 \times 40 \text{ lb/ft}^2) = 6,250 \text{ lb}$$

Next find M if

$$W = 6,250 \text{ lb}$$
$$L = 12.5 \text{ ft}$$

$$M = \frac{WL}{8} = \frac{6,250 \text{ lb} \times 12.5 \text{ ft}}{8} = \frac{78125 \text{ ft-lb}}{8}$$

$$M = 9765.6 \text{ ft-lb}$$
$$M = 117,187.5 \text{ in-lb}$$

Find S if

$$M = 117,187.5 \text{ in-lb}$$
$$f = 1600 \text{ lb/in}^2$$

$$S = \frac{M}{F} = \frac{117,187.5 \text{ in-lb}}{1600 \text{ lb/in}^2}$$

$$S = 73.24 \text{ in}^3$$

In Table 4-2 find that a 6 × 10 has a section modulus of 82.73 in³. Therefore, beam C would be built up of three 2 × 10's, which are approximately equivalent to a 6 × 10.

To this point, no mention has been made of the decking material. Structurally the material selected for the decking can be anything with a 1 in nominal thickness or more. The selection should be made based on the available material, the desired finished appearance, and the amount of traffic anticipated on the deck that might cause extreme deflection.

Since we decided to limit the design by deflection, once again we must find D as before.

First calculate I.

$$I = \frac{bd^3}{12} = \frac{6 \times 9.5^3}{12} = \frac{5144.25}{12}$$

$$I = 428.69 \text{ in}^4$$

Find the deflection as

$$D = \frac{5\,WL^3}{384\,EI} = \frac{5 \times 6255 \times (12.5 \times 12)^3}{384 \times 1,600,000 \times 428.69}$$

$$D = .40$$

Since the beam span has not changed the maximum allowable deflection is still

$$\frac{12 \times 12.5}{360} = .42 \text{ in}$$

Thus the beam is also satisfactory if deflection governs.

In most cases it is advisable to use 2 in nominal material on decks if the joist spacing is greater than 12 in. One inch material spaning more than 12 in will deflect enough to be noticeable.

To complete the design of the structure the size of the columns that support the deck must be determined. This can be accomplished using the formula explained in Chapter 4.

For the example, assume a maximum column length of 4 ft and for the first trial use a #2 southern pine 4 × 4 for the column.

First, determine the maximum allowable unit stress on the column. From Table 5-2 find that the modulus of elasticity for #2 pine is 1,700,000. Then substituting into the equation find (remember to convert to inches)

$$f_c = \frac{0.3E}{\frac{l^2}{d}} = \frac{0.3 \times 1,700,000}{\frac{(4 \times 12)^2}{3.5}}$$

$$= \frac{510,000}{658.29} = 774.73 \text{ lb/in}^2$$

Thus, for a 4 ft, 4 × 4 the maximum allowable compressive stress is 774.73 lb/in².

Next determine the unit stress on the column with the heaviest load. Referring to Figure 5-8 column A would be one of the columns under the heaviest load, carrying ½ of the load of beam C and ½ the load of beam D. The total load on beam C is 6,250 lb. The load on beam D is 3,125 lb. Thus

$$\frac{3,125}{2} + \frac{6,250}{2} = 4,687.5 \text{ lb}$$

The unit stress on the column is:

$$\frac{4687.5 \text{ lb}}{3.5^2} = \frac{4687.5 \text{ lb}}{12.25}$$

$$\text{Unit stress} = 382.65 \text{ lb/in}^2$$

This is well within the limit of 774.73 lb/in² established by the formula.

These same procedures can be followed for investigating the loads in other simple structures.

CARPENTRY AND DETAILING WOOD STRUCTURES

The details of how a wood structure is assembled are just as important to the longevity and serviceability of the structure as its ability to support the design loads. Improper placement of the wood, the use of poor joint techniques, improper to inadequate fasteners, or poor foundation supports will contribute measurably to early deterioration of the structure. Aside from the purely functional aspects, construction details can also add or detract from the appearance of the structure.

Construction detailing is often thought of as a purely mechanical operation that involves selecting an appropriate detail and "redoing" it to fit the job. This idea can be likened to a person trying to design a house by pasting it together from clippings out of the Sunday home section of the newspaper. It just isn't a successful answer to the problem.

Construction detailing is an integral part of the total design process. It is just as much a challenge to the designer's ability as the site plan or basic layout. Attention to these fine details often adds that last bit of sparkle to a job that means success or failure.

Because detailing is largely a matter of design decision the material presented here is intended to provide an elementary vocabulary of carpentry terms and practices. These are not necessarily the best methods; they are provided only to illustrate the major detail considerations.

Piers and Footings

When wood is used as the primary support for a structure, the major concern is the longevity of the wood. The primary zone of deterioration in a wood support occurs where the wood comes in contact with trapped moisture or soil moisture, usually the ground surface or at joints. These areas are subject to frequent wetting and drying cycles that cause dry rot.

There are two basic methods for preventing dry rot. First use a wood material that has been treated, preferably by the full-cell method, to prevent moisture penetration of the wood, or use a material with natural decay resistance. The alternative is to design a footing that will hold the wood support off the ground so that direct contact with moisture is avoided. Figure 5–9 illustrates some common footing and pier details used in wood construction. You will notice in the solutions where wood is set below grade that extra provision has been made to drain off excess moisture.

Post-and-Beam Connections

There is a great deal of variation in how a beam can be attached to a post. Most of the variation occurs because the design of a beam is so flexible and because the post-and-beam connection is frequently featured as a design detail. In most cases, however, the attachment is made with some combination of nails, lag screws, bolts, and/or steel plates. The primary concern in these joints is the prevention of moisture penetration into the fastener holes or between the wood and the plates. Figure 5–10 illustrates some typical post-to-beam connections.

Joist-to-Beam Connections

Joists can be set directly on top of the beams or placed between the beams to reduce the thickness of the structure. These basic connections are usually made by toe-nailing the joist to the beam. (Toe-nailing is driving a nail diagonally through the side of a member). Joists set between the beams are usually rested on a ledger strip or in joist hangers to take the vertical load off the toe-nailed joist.

Another consideration in deciding the joist attachment scheme is how to finish outside edges of the structure. Placing the joists between the beams eliminates the exposed ends of the joists. Two methods for finishing the edges when the joists are attached to the top of the beams are illustrated in Figure 5–11.

Finish Details

The term finish detail is intended here much the same as basic carpentry. That is, how does the designer go about describing physically and graphically how the structure is put together so it gives a finished, workmanlike appearance. At first thought this may seem a matter of trivia, but a little practice will prove that it is not. A thorough understanding of the alternative methods of assembly is almost essential to accomplishing a good design.

Basically the key to good finish detailing is an understanding of how the wood can be put together. If you understand how to turn corners, how to join pieces, which side of the wood should be up or down, and the names of the basic techniques, you have what might be called a design palate. In other words, you have the means to create unique solutions to the problems at hand.

Probably the most important part of the design detail vocabulary of wood is how the individual pieces can be joined. Most of the vocabulary refers to either the fastener arrangement or how the wood is cut. Figure 5–12 gives some of the typical joint techniques that refer to the fastener arrangement.

Nailing Techniques

Toe-nailing is used when the arrangement of members is such that nails can't be driven at a 90° angle or when very thick pieces are being joined. Toe nailing is most commonly used to attach joists to beams, studs or posts to plates, and for securing rafters. Blind nailing is similar to toe-nailing because the nails are driven at an angle. The most frequent application of this technique is for attaching hardwood floors or decking when exposed nailheads would be undesirable (see Figure 5–12).

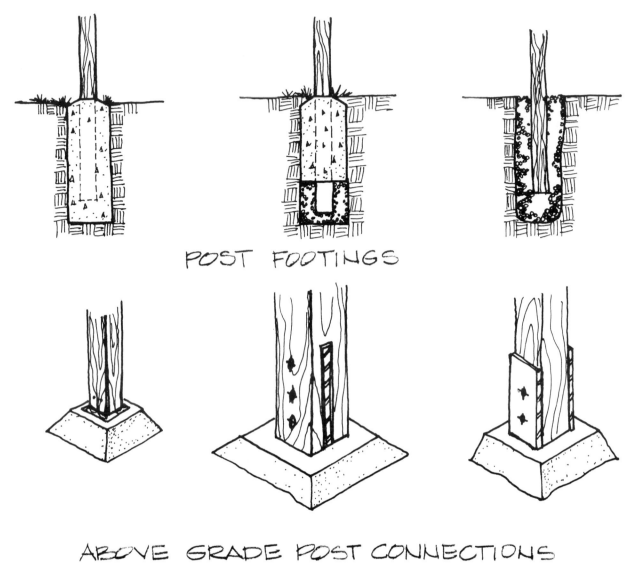

POST FOOTINGS

ABOVE GRADE POST CONNECTIONS

FIGURE 5–9

Joints

The mitered joint is used at corners and at other angular joints, where a lapped joint or butt joint would be objectionable. Most frequently, mitered joints are used in hand railings, at angled joints in decking or steps, and at the corners of fascia details.

Butt joints usually occur only in framing or fence details. It is a weak joint because it relies totally on the fasteners to transfer the loads across the joint. Because of this liability many building codes in hurricane or seismically active areas require the use of Trip-L-Grip fasteners on butt joints.

Routed, rabbet, or slotted joints require more labor and workmanship but the finished appearance is usually worth the extra cost. This is especially true of details like hand railings. The recent development of power handtools to do the routing has made this a much more viable solution. One disadvantage to these joints is that they will collect moisture and this can be a liability in humid areas where dry rot is a problem.

The dovetail joint has limited application to landscape structures. Usually this joint is employed more in cabinet work and furniture. However, where strength and finished appearance are primary concerns the dovetail joint has no equal.

Tongue-and-groove materials are manufactured for use as decking, siding, and roofing. Since the individual pieces fit together they have the advantage of providing a stronger, more uniform surface. Their primary use in the landscape is for decking when spaces between planks are objectionable. The reason for using tongue-and-groove (T&G) material in this case is not so much the more uniform strength but the resistance to warping caused by moisture.

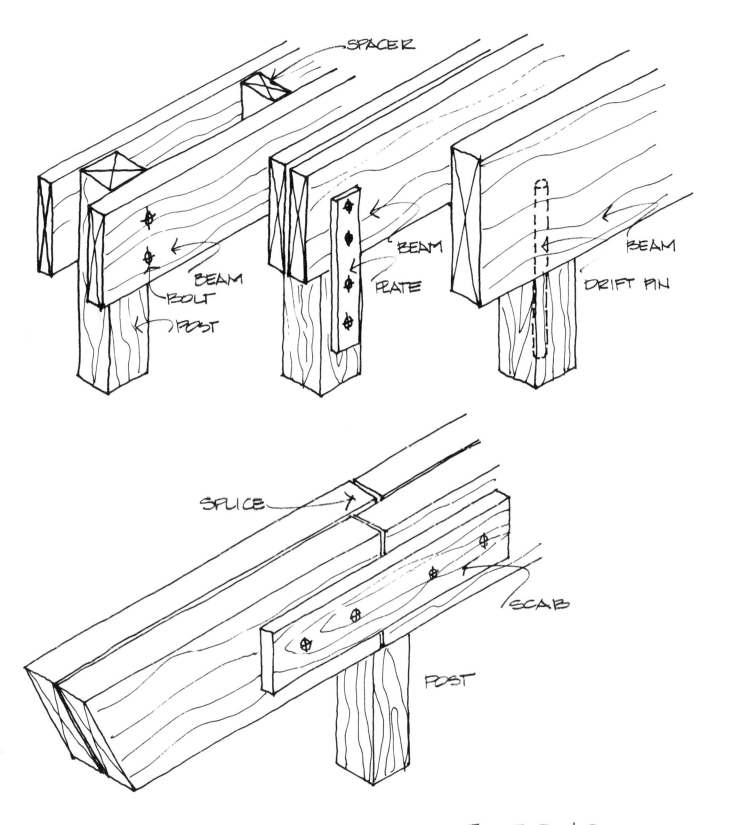

SPACER

BEAM
BOLT
POST

BEAM

PLATE

BEAM

DRIFT PIN

SPLICE

SCAB

POST

POST TO BEAM CONNECTIONS

FIGURE 5–10

195

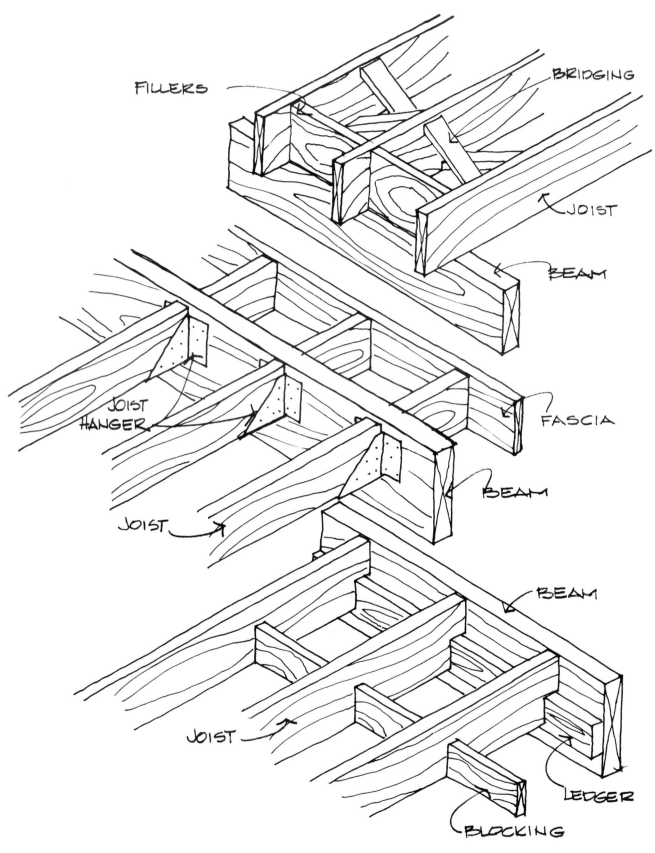

FILLERS

BRIDGING

JOIST

BEAM

JOIST
HANGER

FASCIA

BEAM

JOIST

BEAM

JOIST

LEDGER

BLOCKING

JOIST TO BEAM CONNECTION

FIGURE 5-11

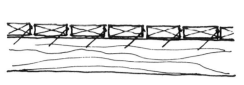
BLIND NAILING

TOE NAILING

MITERED

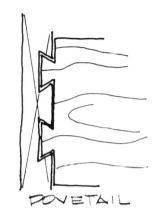
DOVETAIL

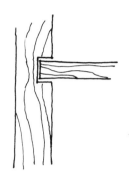
SLOTTED

TONGUE & GROOVE

BUTT

CHAMFER

NAILING & FINISH JOINTS

FIGURE 5-12

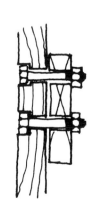
COUNTERSUNK

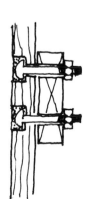
PLUGGED

DOWELED

FASTENER JOINTS

FIGURE 5-13

Chamfer refers to cutting or rounding the edges of a member. Aside from the purely aesthetic considerations the chamfer is a particularly useful finish technique that will discourage splintering. This can be particularly important on bench edges, hand railings, and the edges of step risers.

Joints are shown in Figure 5–12 (see page 197).

Fastener Details

Bolt, screw, and nailheads can sometimes be a problem especially on a wearing surface. In these cases the head may be countersunk to keep the head flush with the surface. The countersunk holes have the disadvantage of collecting extra moisture and should probably be filled if dry rot is a major problem.

Doweled or pegged joints employ wood dowels driven into predrilled holes as a fastening device. This method requires skilled workmen and it is expensive. However, the technique can be used to good advantage as a finish detail for special cases (see Figure 5–13 on page 197).

This brief discussion of details is by no means comprehensive. It is intended to help the student develop a vocabulary of terms and techniques that can be intergrated into the design process. Perfecting a knowledge of construction detailing comes with practice and a keen eye for detail.

PROBLEMS

1. What size should the joists be for a deck at 40 lb/ft² with a beam span of 16 ft if joists are to be 16 in o.c.?

2. What spacing must be used to allow the use of 2 in × 6 in joists to span 16 ft at a load of 40 lb/ft² using southern pine #2?

3. What is the total load on each of two beams that support a deck 16 ft × 16 ft assuming a live load of 40 lb/ft²?

4. What is the maximum bending moment in a beam that must support 5,120 lb if it is a simple beam with a 16 ft span?

5. For the beam condition in problem 4 what is the required section modulus of the beam if $f = 1,600$ lb/in²?

6. What is the actual deflection of 6 in × 10 in beam 16 ft long that carries a total load of 5,120 lb? Assume $E = 1,600,000$.

7. What is the maximum allowable deflection of the beam in Problem 6 if the design is to be limited by deflection?

8. If four posts support a structure 18 ft × 12 ft with a live load of 60 lb/ft², what is the load carried by each column and what is the unit stress put on the ground if 4 × 4's are used?

9. If six posts support a rectangular structure 16 ft × 32 ft and the structure has a live load of 100 lb/ft², what is the load carried by one of the center posts?

10. What is the weight carried by the middle beam of a 10 ft × 20 ft rectangular deck supported by three beams carrying a live load of 70 lb/ft²?

6

Concrete and Masonry Design

Concrete and unit masonry are among the most versatile and widely used materials in landscape construction. Concrete or masonry units are used for most paved surfaces, such as walks, driveways, patios, and terraces. They are used for walls, planters, steps, pools, fountains, and as sculptural features.

Of the two materials concrete is possibly the most versatile material since it can be poured and formed in almost any shape the designer can imagine. The finishing of the material is equally flexible, providing the designer the opportunity to vary line, textural quality, and to a lesser degree the color of the structure. When we consider that concrete has been used for everything from bridges, dams, and buildings to boats and barges the applications of concrete appear to be almost limitless.

Stone and masonry units are also quite flexible because the individual units themselves can be cut or cast in almost any shape, size, color, and finish that can be imagined. Various types of building stone, for example, can be quarried, shaped, planed, and polished to meet the needs of the situation. Likewise masonry units can be cast or formed into any shape the designer desires since the basic materials are plastic prior to processing. Thus, the varieties of color, textural quality, and possible combinations of material makes masonry an equally attractive tool.

Some factors that will frequently limit the flexibility of concrete and masonry are availability, the skill of the craftsmen, and climate. For example, concrete blocks are manufactured in many shapes and sizes as illustrated in Figure 6–1. But from one trade area to another you will find that many of the shapes illustrated are not readily available. You will also find that the block themselves will range widely in color, surface texture, weight, and porosity.

These problems also occur with brick and clay units. Brick size, for example, will differ from place to place depending on the manufacturer, the available raw materials, and local building customs. The color and hardness of clay units are also highly variable.

These are situations that must be faced by the field practitioner and solved on a job-to-job basis, but the key to making a wise decision in such matters boils down to a thorough understanding of the materials, and knowing how to put the materials together to obtain the desired results. Therefore, our preliminary discussion is designed to give you an appreciation of the materials, what they are, how they are used, and what their limitations are. Then we will discuss the structural considerations involved in the most frequent landscape applications of the individual materials.

CONCRETE AND MASONRY MATERIALS

Concrete

All structural concrete is classified as either plain concrete or steel-reinforced concrete. Plain concrete is concrete that is reinforced to resist only temperature change and shrinkage. For this reason the majority of all landscape structures that employ concrete are plain concrete. This is so even though they may contain large quantities of deformed steel reinforcement. The actual placement of steel reinforcement and sizing of the bars will be discussed in the section on masonry structures.

Steel-reinforced concrete is engineered to take advantage of the strong points of each material. The concrete is used to resist high compressive loads and the steel resists the high tensile loads. The two mate-

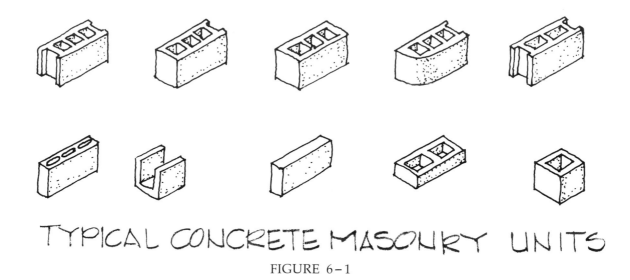

TYPICAL CONCRETE MASONRY UNITS

FIGURE 6-1

rials are most compatible in this respect since they have approximately the same rates of expansion and contraction. However, steel-reinforced concrete theory applies only if the loads and actual stresses can be predicted and measured as in a building or a bridge. When slabs, footings, retaining walls, and other similar structures are placed on grade there is no way to actually predict stresses in the structure since the actual points of support cannot be defined.

Concrete Composition

Concrete is composed of three essential materials: portland cement, water, and some inert material, such as silica sand or gravel, called aggregate. The portland cement and water form a cementitious paste that fills the voids between the aggregate materials binding it together in a single, rocklike mass.

Portland cement is a man-made material, processed from lime, silica, and alumina. The raw materials are processed, mixed in the proper proportions, and then fired and reduced to clinkers. The clinkers are then cured and processed to regulate color, curing time, and heat discharge, and then they are ground into a fine powder. When water is added to portland cement a chemical reaction called hydration takes place causing the paste to set. Usually this initial set takes about 45 minutes and a final set is reached in about 10 hours. The concrete will then harden for an indefinite period getting harder all the time. The base measure of hardness or what is called the cured strength of the material is reached in 28 days.

Portland Cements

Portland cements are manufactured and blended for all sorts of work: there is white portland cement, used for exposed grout and for trazzo; there are spe-cial blends for mortar and pointing and others for plaster and stucco. Portland cements used in concrete fall into two broad categories: plain portland and air-entraining portland cement.

There are five types of plain portland cement. Type I is general purpose cement used for most general construction such as paving, buildings, and bridges. Type II is a lower heat cement than Type I and is used where the heat release caused by hydration may be a factor. Concretes made with Type II cement cure more slowly. Type III is a high, early-strength material used when it is necessary to shorten the time allowed for curing and is frequently employed in winter construction. Type IV is a low heat cement, much lower than Type II. It is used when large masses of concrete are required, such as in a dam, and heat might cause uneven curing. Type V is a sulfate resistant cement used where soils have high alkali or sulfur concentrations.

Air-entraining cements have high durability and are particularly suited to harsh winter environments. The air-entraining additive in the cement causes millions of small air bubbles to be trapped in the cement and act as natural insulation. Any time a concrete structure will be exposed to severe winter conditions and subject to the effects of salt used for snow and ice removal air-entrained cement should be used.

Water Used in Concrete

The water used in concrete must be free of minerals, acids, alkali, or other foreign material. Usually water suitable for drinking is considered satisfactory for concrete.

The quantity of water used in concrete is related directly to the final strength of the concrete. The amount of water required to satisfy the hydration process is actually much less than the amount required to make the mixture workable. However, when more and more water is added, the cement paste becomes diluted with a corresponding reduction in the strength of the material. The water–cement ratio can be checked in the field by a very simple test called a slump test. A sample of the concrete is worked into a 12 in high cone with a 8 in diameter base and a 4 in diameter top. When the cone is removed the material will settle or "slump." The distance from the top of the cone to the top of the concrete sample is the amount of slump. For most general construction work a slump of 2 in – 5 in is considered satisfactory.

Aggregates Used in Concrete

The aggregates used in a concrete mix are usually determined by what raw materials are available locally, and whether or not the aggregate will be exposed in the structure. In some cases, aggregates of a special size, color, or weight will be required, but unless there is a special need to specify the aggregate material, the batching plants will proportion and grade the aggregate material to meet the specified cured strength.

Concrete Strength

Cured strength is a most important consideration to the designer. Cured strength refers to the ultimate compressive strength of the material reached in 28 days. Concrete strength is determined in a laboratory by compressing 12 in × 6 in concrete cylinders until they fail. In most cases, the strength specified for general site work is 2,000 or 2,500 psi concrete. For heavier work, like paving, footings or slabs on expansive soil 3,000 psi concrete will be used. Specifying strengths greater than this is rarely if ever justified for most landscape construction.

Mortar

Mortars, while similar to concrete, are actually quite different and perform a different job. The overriding consideration for masonry mortars is the strength of the bond developed between the individual masonry units, not necessarily the strength of the mortar itself. In fact, it is interesting to note that mortars with higher water–cement ratios generally bond better than stiffer mixtures. This, of course, is just the opposite with concrete.

Masonry mortars are of two basic types according to their material composition. There are portland cement–lime mortars and masonry cement mortars. The portland cement–lime mortars are mixtures of portland cement, hydrated lime or lime putty, sand, and water. Masonry cement mortars are premixed

Table 6–1
Recommended Proportions and Strengths of Various Mortar Mixes

MORTAR TYPE	MIX[a]	STRENGTH (psi) TENSION	COMPRESSION
M	1:¼:3	457	5492
S	1:½:4½	300	2758
N	1:1:6	180	1173

[a]Cement, lime, sand.

materials marketed by various manufacturers that are mixed directly with sand and water.

The American Society for Testing Materials lists five classifications of masonry mortar based on their mixture proportions, and their compressive and tensile properties. They are designated by the letters M, N, S, O, and K. Of primary interest are types M, N, and S.

Type N mortar is a moderate-strength material that can be made up as a portland cement–lime mix or from masonry cement materials. It is best suited for exterior work subject to extreme weather and non-load bearing walls.

Type S mortar is most commonly made up as a cement–lime mortar and has one of the highest bonding strengths of all mortars. This mortar is recommended for use where the mortar is relied upon to bond a facing material to the backing. The best example of this would be bonding ceramic tile to a wall face.

Type M mortar is the strongest of all the mortars and can be made up of masonry cement or a cement–lime mix. It is used primarily in unreinforced masonry, masonry below grade, and high load-bearing structures like foundation walls, retaining walls, and manholes.

The recommended proportioning and approximate strength developed by each type of mortar is given in Table 6–1.

Stone

Stone is a natural material used widely in the landscape. It appears as a paving material, as a veneer surface on walls, as dry stone retaining walls, as natural steps, and sometimes as a purely decorative feature. Like any other natural material, stones vary widely in their composition, color, and structural properties. For the most part stones used in the landscape will be one of three broad types: granites, sandstones, and limestones. However, these are by no means the only kinds of stone that will be encountered for there may be occasions when materials like "feather-rock," marble, or slate will be justified. For most work the stone used will depend on what is available locally and sandstone, limestone, and granite are usually the most plentiful.

Granites

Granites are harder and more dense than other common building stones. Because of their weight and extreme hardness they are very difficult to work, but, because they are very hard, most granites are well suited to surfaces that are exposed to extreme weathering conditions and in areas of heavy traffic. It must be pointed out that not all granites are good materials when exposed to extreme weathering, because of differences in the mineral and chemical composition of the stone. For this reason, some granites, if exposed, may be subject to high rates of chemical weathering. The only way to be sure of how a granite will perform is by checking on previous applications of the particular stone.

In the landscape, granites are most commonly used as paving and curb materials, as riprap, and as a stone building veneer. Small granite blocks, roughly 2¾ in × 2¾ in × 3½ in are frequently seen as a paving material where granite is available. Granite can also be polished to a high gloss surface that is durable and easily cleaned.

Limestone

Limestones vary widely in their hardness and color but most generally they will range from an eggshell white to a light gray. Since limestones are primarily calcium carbonate, they are highly susceptible to chemical weathering. This characteristic has become a major problem in many urban areas since acid-forming compounds are carried freely in the air.

In comparison to granites, limestones are very easy to work. They can be cut with saws, planes, and lathes or worked with handtools. Because of its workability, it can be cut into thinner sheets and used for paving and wall veneer more easily than granite.

In many parts of the country limestones appear as independent stones and boulders floating free in the upper soil profiles. This material is usually referred to as field stone and is much sought after as a landscape material. The stones themselves vary a great deal in their shape and character and range in size from mammoth boulders to small cobbles and pebbles.

As a rule, limestones will be employed as a coping material for walls, paving stone, veneer stone, or in its native state for dry stone walls and as a landscape subject.

Sandstones

Sandstones are widely distributed in most parts of the country. They have good workability and are quite durable. The most common sandstones are earthen color, ranging from a deep ocher to deep sienna or umber. Other less common colors include dark gray, blue, and green. Blue stone and brown stone are names commonly associated with sandstones found in the east and midwest.

Sandstones are similar to limestone in their application and workability. However, they are probably more durable than the limestone. Usually the factors that will determine whether to use sandstone or limestone are the desired color and the local availability. Given current transportation costs and the cost of installation, it is not feasible on most jobs to utilize materials other than those available locally.

Brick and Clay Unit Masonry

Common clay brick and clay unit pavers are probably among the most readily available and most versatile materials used in landscape construction. Clay masonry units are used in practically every imaginable landscape structure from pools and fountains to paving, steps, and walls.

Clay masonry units are molded from moist clay and then fired in a kiln. The color and hardness of the brick will be determined by clay material used and the amount of exposure to the direct heat of the kiln. The greater the heat the harder the brick and darker the brick will be. Bricks that are exposed to extremely high temperatures will be burned to the point of warping and cracking; these bricks are called clinkers. Brick that is cured evenly without excessive warping is called hard brick. Other brick, not exposed to sufficient heat to completely cure, is called soft brick.

Soft brick is of little practical use outside because it will not stand traffic or extreme weather conditions. Hard brick is best suited to general applications in the landscape. Clinkers, while usable, are not generally recommended since they are difficult to lay and very dark in color.

Like any building material that is essentially made up of natural or organic components, brick will vary markedly in its structural properties and color. This is particularly true of brick and clay products. Clay masonry units are usually produced by small independent plants that service a rather limited geographic area. For this reason, you will find that the brick produced for a given trade area will be manufactured to withstand the local climate and furnished in sizes and shapes to meet local practice.

Brick Grades

Even though brick will vary, the clay products industry does have an industry-wide grading system for brick used in buildings. These standards are based on the brick's resistance to weathering and hardness. Since most landscape construction is exposed to extreme weathering conditions, the designer should be aware of these grading standards. There are three grades listed by the American Society for Testing Materials (ASTM C 62).

1. Grade SW is intended for use where a high degree of resistance to frost and freezing action is required. Examples of this are brick used in retaining walls and as paving materials.

2. Grade MW is intended for use where the brick will be exposed to freezing temperatures but is not likely to be saturated with water. Examples of permissable uses of grade MW are freestanding walls above grade, veneered retaining walls, and well-drained paved surfaces.

3. Grade NW is a soft brick that should only be used as a backup material that will not come into contact with a moisture bearing surface. As a general rule grade NW brick is not satisfactory for landscape construction.

Brick Dimensions

Brick dimensions are probably the most variable of all building materials; thus any discussion of size standards could be misleading. In most areas of the country you will find two sizes of brick in use. One is the so-called American Standard Brick, which is usually about 2¼ in × 3¾ in × 8 in; it is suggested that you check with a local supplier, however, to be sure of the actual dimensions locally. The other brick frequently encountered is the modular SCR brick; it is 2⅛ in × 5½ in × 11½ in. It was designed as a primary structural unit and sized to increase the speed and efficiency of the mason. The United States has not adopted a metric brick as yet but the sizes adopted by Australia are: modular, 300 × 100 × 100 mm, standard, 240 × 120 × 86 mm (see Figure 6–2 for common brick types).

Concrete Masonry Units

Concrete masonry units are manufactured from portland cement, relatively fine-graded aggregates, and sand. Most standard concrete units are rather heavy when compared to clay. However, lightweight units are produced by using lightweight aggregates such as cinders, shale, or slag.

The types and sizes of concrete masonry units were illustrated in Figure 6–1. Most of these materials have smooth, fine-textured surfaces, and range in color from almost white to dark gray. In some areas concrete units may also be available with a buff or a light egg-shell color depending on the aggregate material used. Likewise concrete units may be available with artificially colored surfaces or finished with a ceramic glaze.

The most frequently used concrete unit is the concrete block. It is universally employed as a basic building material in structures and in general landscape construction. Its most usual application is in walls, planters, or small pools. In most of these applications it is used as the backup material for some type of veneer, usually brick or stone. While concrete block is not very attractive by itself, the possibilities of using concrete block as a primary building material should not be overlooked.

One word of caution: concrete masonry units are very porous. For this reason any concrete masonry structure should be sealed to prevent unwanted moisture seepage. This can usually be accomplished

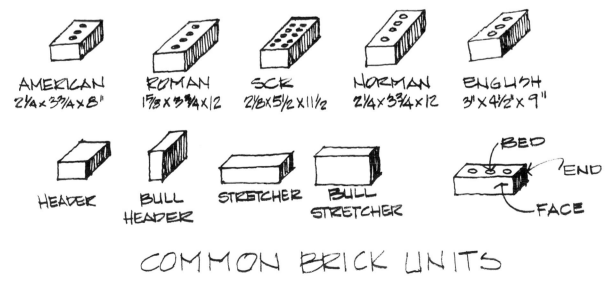

AMERICAN
2¼×3¾×8"

ROMAN
1⅝×3¾×12

SCR
2⅛×5½×11½

NORMAN
2¼×3¾×12

ENGLISH
3"×4½"×9"

HEADER

BULL HEADER

STRETCHER

BULL STRETCHER

BED
END
FACE

COMMON BRICK UNITS

FIGURE 6–2

with a stucco surfacing or some type of bituminous waterproofing material.

Asphalt and Bituminous Concrete

Asphalt and bituminous concretes are materials manufactured from petroleum distillates called bitumens and inert aggregates. The bituminous material bonds the aggregates together to make a concrete-like mass. Since the bituminous cementing material does not cure to a hardened state like portland cement, bituminous materials are classified as flexible pavements.

Bituminous materials are water repellent and frequently used in their raw states as a waterproofing material. However, it has some distinct disadvantages in this regard. First, since asphalt is a petroleum-base product, it is soluble in gasoline, kerosene, or other petroleum solvents. Thus a paved surface can be dissolved and its worth as a waterproof agent is destroyed. Asphalts also become liquid when subjected to high temperatures and pavements can "creep" or "washboard" when exposed to heavy loads at high temperatures. This sort of action also serves to destroy the waterproof qualities of the pavement.

The importance of maintaining the waterproof property of asphalt cannot be overstressed. Because of its flexible nature, asphalt pavements will deform to correspond to the shape of the base. Thus an asphalt pavement is only as good as the base. The majority of failures in asphalt pavements can be directly attributed to water penetrating the base resulting in failure of the base under heavy loads or frost and freeze damage in the winter months.

Most asphalt cements require that they be heated to a liquid consistency before they are mixed with the aggregate materials. These are called hot-mix asphalts. Other asphaltic cements are manufactured in liquid form that require no heat for mixing and are called cold-mix asphalts. Such cold-mix compounds are widely marketed for tennis court surfacing, other athletic courts, and for walk surfacing. Cold-mix

materials are not generally as strong as hot-mix asphalts and not generally suited to pavements that carry vehicular traffic.

Asphalt paving is the least expensive of all the basic paving materials and constitutes approximately 70% of all paving done for highways, airports, trails, and parking lots. Some of its price advantage is lost, however, on facilities like walks, tennis courts, tracks, and small trails because specialized machinery is required to place the material.

CONCRETE AND MASONRY STRUCTURES

This section discusses the four basic types of concrete and masonry structures. Under each type of construction we will look at the structural considerations, application to structures in the landscape, and accepted installation techniques. The five structures to be reviewed are slabs and paving, masonry paving, footings, masonry walls, and retaining walls.

Slabs and Paving

Bituminous Pavements

Depending on the load to be carried, bituminous pavements are typically installed in four layers: a subbase, base course, leveling course, and the wearing course as illustrated in Figure 6–3. In some cases for surfaces that carry very light loads, the leveling and wearing course are combined.

The subbase is usually the native subsoil material that has been graded, shaped, and compacted to an optimum density. (The term "optimum density" simply means a specified percentage of compaction relative to the soils fully compacted state, usually 90 to 95% of optimum.) When highly expansive clays are encountered, the subbase may be treated with lime or other basic materials to reduce the shrink–swell ratio of the soil. In extreme cases, the soil may even be removed from the site and replaced by another material. Muck for example must be evacuated and replaced.

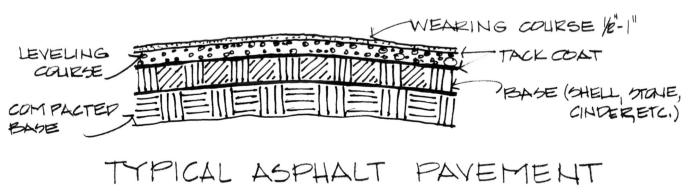

TYPICAL ASPHALT PAVEMENT

FIGURE 6–3

The base course is usually made of construction materials available locally such as crushed rock, sand, and gravel, limestone, shell, nonexpansive clays stabilized with lime, soil cement, or bituminous stabilized materials. This base course is the primary foundation of the asphalt paving because it is the surface that carries the load placed on the pavement.

When the base course is in place, it is covered with a prime coat or sealer course. This is a liquid asphalt slurry that helps waterproof the base and prevent moisture penetration.

The leveling course is an asphaltic concrete composed of coarsely graded aggregates. Its primary function is to level the surface and fill in any uneven spots in the base course. The wearing surface is then applied over another tack coat that helps waterproof the pavement and bind the two layers together. The wearing surface is thinner than the leveling course and made with finely graded aggregates to produce a smooth, fine-grained surface.

This is essentially the process followed for all asphalt pavement regardless of the ultimate use of the facility. To a large measure, modifications to this basic section are at the discretion of the designer and local practice.

Concrete Slabs and Paving

Concrete is the most versatile and widely used landscape paving material. It can be placed in small areas not easily accessible by large machines. It is durable, and can be finished in any number of ways. On the other hand, concrete does have some liabilities that should be considered by the designer before using it. Plain concrete is almost white after it has been cured and directly exposed to the sun. It is highly reflective and a very glaring surface in the summer months. Because of its low tensile strength, it is extremely sensitive to differential soil move-

ments and will crack easily, often becoming unsightly and dangerous. Concrete has a very low resiliency that makes it uncomfortable to stand on for long periods; and, because it lacks resiliency, it is not the best material for play surfaces or athletic courts.

The design of a concrete slab or pavement involves three considerations: preparation of the subgrade, placing and finishing, and reinforcement.

Preparation of the Subgrade for Concrete

When designing and specifying any concrete slab that is poured on grade, it is most important that the character of the soil be known, since this will directly affect how the base is prepared and how the slab will be reinforced. Sandy soils provide a very good base for concrete. They require very little preparation outside of stripping the vegetation and grading the surface. The addition of gravel or other porous materials is usually not necessary.

Clays, silts, and organic soils, however, may require extensive subgrade preparation. Organic soils should be completely removed since they will not support the slab properly. Clays and silts, because of their particle size, tend to swell when they are wet and shrink when they are dry. This kind of movement can completely destroy a concrete slab in a very short time. The best way to handle this problem is to provide a base under the slab that will tend to equalize the moisture relationships of the soil. This can be done with either a subdrainage system or by using gravel or sand under the slab; each method accomplishes the same thing as shown in Figure 6–4. These same precautions should be taken for slabs that are exposed to extreme weather conditions and frost. As with any pavement, the base is the key to the success or failure of the pavement.

A last consideration in the preparation of the base for concrete is moisture protection. If the surface is to be painted or finished with some type of wearing surface, a moisture barrier should be placed between

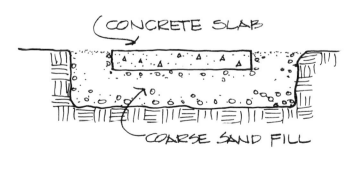

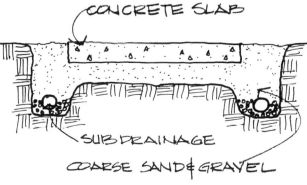

BASE PREPARATION FOR CONCRETE SLABS

FIGURE 6–4

the slab and the ground to prevent ground moisture penetration.

Placing and Finishing

Depending on the situation and soil type, concrete may or may not require forms. Many times the soil can be cut to the desired shape and depth using the soil itself as the form. Concrete should never be poured in freezing temperatures or in frozen forms. If it is necessary to work in freezing conditions, special precautions must be taken to be sure that the concrete does not freeze until it has cured.

When concrete is placed in the forms, the ground and forms should be moist or the water will be drawn out of the concrete and it will not cure properly. It is also necessary to carefully work the concrete into the forms by vibrating or working it with hand-tools to be sure that no air pockets are left in the slab. Voids like this are called honeycombs and can lead to failure of the pavement. After the concrete reaches its initial set, it can then be finished. The possible finishes are almost limitless, so only a few of the more common methods will be mentioned here.

Probably the most common finishes are steel trowel, wood float, and broom or brush finishes. The steel trowel finish is a very smooth, almost slick finish. It is not generally used outside because it can be very slippery when wet. The wood float finish is also smooth, but not as slick as the steel trowel finish. The broom or brush finish is rather coarse and probably the most practical for outside surfaces because it provides a better footing when it is wet.

The broom finish is done after the slab has reached its initial set. Usually the surface will have been finished with a wood float, then it is brushed with a stiff bristle broom to slightly groove the surface. The brushing can be light or heavy, depending on the roughness desired.

Exposed aggregate is probably the most popular decorative concrete finish. Exposed aggregate finishes are obtained by first pouring the concrete and finishing it with a float. Then while the concrete is still plastic, decorative aggregates are applied to the surface and gently tamped into the surface. The surface is then floated again to fill the voids around the aggregates with grout and level the surface. Then before the concrete is completely set, the surface is washed and brushed to expose this decorative material.

Another popular finish used around pools and on patios is called a "keystone" finish. The keystone material is applied as a plaster or mortar coat to a finished slab. First, the slab is floated and then broomed to a very rough surface to insure a good bond. Then a mortar is prepared that is almost a liquid consistency and spread unevenly over the slab.

When the material is almost set it is leveled with a steel trowel, leaving some smooth and some rough places. When properly applied keystone is a very attractive surface and provides excellent footing when wet.

Reinforcement of Paving and Slabs

As noted earlier, landscape structures that utilize concrete as the primary material are essentially made of what is classified plain concrete. The reinforcement placed in the concrete is there principally to resist temperature influences and shrinkage. However, since the steel is in the pavement, some common sense in placing the steel can serve to further increase the strength of the slab or pavement.

The steel used for concrete reinforcement is welded wire mesh or deformed steel reinforcement (rebars).

Wire mesh is standard AWG wire welded together in a mat. It is called out by the spacing of the wire in the mat and by the wire gauge, e.g., $6 \times 6 \times 10 \times 10$ mesh has a 6 in $\times$ 6 in grid of 10 gauge wire.

Deformed steel means that the surface of the bars is rough, having small deformations along the surface of the bar. This ensures a good bond with the concrete and prevents the bar from slipping.

It is important to remember that reinforcing steel will rust if it is not adequately protected by the concrete. If the steel begins to rust, the bond between the concrete and steel will be broken and the reinforcing properties will be lost. Most generally 2 in of concrete should be provided between the rebars and the ground.

Reinforcing bars are specified by number beginning with a #2 bar that has a $1/4$ in diameter to a #11 bar which has a $1\frac{3}{8}$ in diameter. Beginning with the #2 bar, the sizes increase in $1/8$ in increments; a #3 is $3/8$ in, a #4 is $1/2$ in and so on. The #3 and #4 bars are the ones most commonly specified.

When considering how much steel and where it should be placed in a slab, it is important to understand what is likely to happen under it. Essentially, there are two types of failure that will occur because of differential movement of the soil: end lift or center lift. End lift occurs as a result of soil moisture in very expansive soils and from frost. Center lift is most frequently caused by soil expansion as shown in Figure 6–5.

It is important to note in these illustrations the portion of the slab that is in tensile stress. In end lift it is the base of the slab that is in tension and with center lift it is the top of the slab in tension. Since it is rarely possible to predict which condition is most likely to occur, it is recommended in most cases that the top of the slab be protected from center lift. This is most logical since cracks in concrete only become

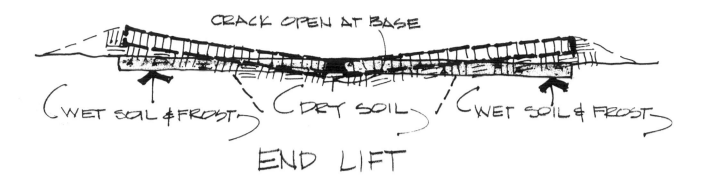

END LIFT

CENTER LIFT

FIGURE 6-5

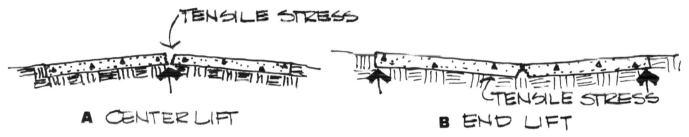

A CENTER LIFT   **B** END LIFT

FIGURE 6-6

dangerous and unsightly on the tensile side of the slab. Because of concrete's high compressive strength, cracks are much less likely to show in compression. In Figure 6–6 notice that the crack is quite obvious in (A) but will be less noticeable in (B).

The amount of steel placed in a slab should be .25% (.0025) of the cross-sectional area of the slab and since the force of the soil acts in all directions, the steel should run both ways.[1] For example, consider a driveway slab 6 in thick and 16 ft wide. The area of the section is:

$$.5 \text{ ft} \times 16 \text{ ft} = 8 \text{ ft}^2$$

The steel required for this condition would be

$$.0025 \text{ ft} \times 8 \text{ ft} = .020 \text{ ft}^2$$

Thus, the total steel required if #4 rebars are used is

$$\frac{\text{sq. ft. req} \times 144}{\text{rebar area}} = \frac{.020 \text{ ft}^2 \times 144 \text{ in}^2/\text{ft}^2}{.20 \text{ in}^2}$$

$$= \frac{2.880 \text{ in}^2}{.20 \text{ in}^2} = 14.4$$

Thus, 14 to 15 #4 bars are required for normal temperature and shrinkage reinforcement. Therefore, we would probably specify #4 bars 12 in on center which would equal 16 bars as shown in Figure 6–7, a total of .022 ft².

It should be noted that #3 bars on 8 in centers would provide 2.64 in² just under the amount required, and on 6 in centers #3 bars would have been satisfactory. The ½ in bars are probably the best answer, however, since there will be less material to handle in the field.

---

[1]This is recommended by the National Building code; other recommendations may differ.

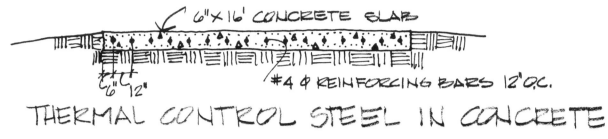

THERMAL CONTROL STEEL IN CONCRETE

FIGURE 6-7

In many parts of the country this amount of reinforcing is considered unnecessary. For example, in the southern states where frost and temperature variations are moderate, reinforcement may be limited to a single layer of welded wire mesh, usually 6 in × 6 in × #10 × #10, or #4 bars on 3 ft to 4 ft centers. In the case of sidewalks, the reinforcement is often omitted completely.

Because these variations in practice exist, it is almost impossible to give any hard and fast rules. The best practice is to be familiar with the local code and observe local building customs. The Reference Manual provides several examples of pavement cross sections and provides a comparison of usage.

Expansion, Construction, and Control Joints

Expansion joints are spaces between independent units of concrete or other materials filled with some type of elastic material to allow for different rates of expansion or contraction. Expansion joints should always be provided where slabs or pavements meet existing or proposed structures. It is also a good idea to provide expansion joints in walks, roads, and large slabs at about 30 ft intervals maximum. Depending on the soil conditions, it may also be desirable to place steel dowels across the expansion joints to prevent independent vertical movement at the expansion joints.

Construction joints are joints that occur between pours. Control joints are cut into the surface of a slab with a jointing tool right after the concrete reaches its initial set. They are about 1/4 in to 3/8 in wide and about 1/2 in deep. The purpose of the control joint is to provide a weak place in the concrete so that cracking from shrinkage will occur at the joint, not randomly in the slab. Since control joints also add pattern to the finished appearance of the slab, they should be considered as an integral part of the overall design. In most cases designers will indicate patterns of control joints in square or rectangular modules. It is recommended that the greatest dimension of the modules not exceed 20 ft.

Some typical placements of expansion joints and control joints are illustrated in Figure 6-8.

Unit Masonry Paving

Masonry units provide an interesting and flexible alternative to bituminous or concrete pavements. The use of masonry units as the primary paving surface adds color and a touch of scale that is almost unobtainable with other materials. However, the cost of unit masonry pavements will run higher than the cost of concrete or asphalt primarily because of the cost of installing the surface.

Like any pavement, a masonry surface will only be as good as its base, so the problems will be the same as for concrete and asphalt. When masonry units are placed directly on grade without mortar joints, they respond as a flexible surface. They will move independently with the soil and each unit must distribute the loads placed on it to the ground independently of other units. If the masonry units are placed on a slab as a veneer, it then becomes a rigid pavement that will not move independently with movements of the soil. Decisions regarding which type of installation to use should be based on three things: the load to be placed on the pavement, weather and temperature variation, and the soil.

Masonry pavements that will be subject to high loads, such as driveways and pavements in public areas, or subject to hard freezes and expansive soils should be designed as rigid pavements. Where the pavement is used as a walk, or residential terrace or patio, laying the units on grade is a satisfactory solution.

When masonry units are laid on grade it is desirable to excavate a bed about 4 in to 6 in deep and backfill it with a clean sand material for the base. The sand base will facilitate drainage and provide a stable, easily worked material to lay the units on.

Rigid unit masonry pavements should be laid on concrete slabs designed to carry the live load and withstand the soil conditions. Walks and light-duty surfaces usually require a 4 in base, and 6 in is usually satisfactory for heavy-duty surfaces. The units can then be laid in a 3/8 in to 1/2 in mortar bed and the joints grouted and tooled to suit the situation.

The design of the base slab and placement of ex-

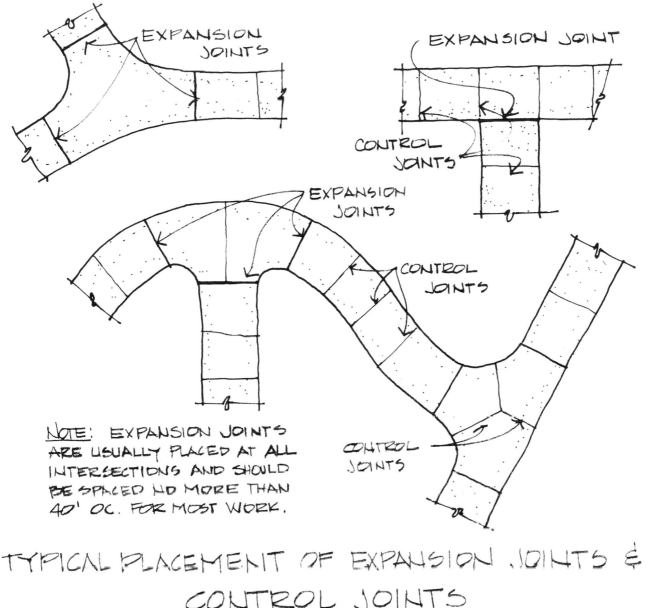

NOTE: EXPANSION JOINTS ARE USUALLY PLACED AT ALL INTERSECTIONS AND SHOULD BE SPACED NO MORE THAN 40' OC. FOR MOST WORK.

TYPICAL PLACEMENT OF EXPANSION JOINTS & CONTROL JOINTS

FIGURE 6-8

pansion joints is handled the same as for any concrete slab as discussed in the previous section. Details of some typical masonry pavements are discussed in more detail in the Reference Manual.

Foundations

Foundations have the sole purpose of transferring the loads above them to the soil below. Most structures in the landscape such as walls, small buildings, and retaining walls will utilize a footing of some sort. A footing is simply a wide concrete band under the support member or wall above.

It must be noted at this point that the footing prin-

ciples set forth here are for simple, lightweight structures in normal soil conditions. There are conditions under which the use of a footing as the main foundation would be ill-advised. For example, footings are not advisable in expansive clay soils, organic unstable soils, or on deep fills. The reason for this is that the soils beneath the footing will be subject to irregular movement causing uneven support of the footing. When this occurs, the concrete will crack and begin to shift, leading to failures in the structure above. The most common solution for these conditions is the use of pilings and grade beams. They will be discussed later in this section.

The size and dimensions of a footing depend

TABLE 6–2
Weights per Cubic Foot of Common Landscape Materials

MATERIAL	lb/ft³
Concrete	150
Brick masonry	120
Rubble masonry	160
Timber	40

TABLE 6–3
Bearing Capacities of Common Soil Types

SOIL TYPE	lb/in²
Soft clay	14
Wet sand	28
Fine sands	42
Coarse sand	56
Gravel	84
Shale	140

on the weight of the structure above and the load-bearing capacity of the soil. Tables 6–2 and 6–3 give the weights per cubic foot of common landscape construction materials and the loadbearing capacities of common soil types. Since most landscape structures are very light by comparison to other structures, the values given here are probably safe for most work. However, it is always advisable to check local soil data if any extensive work is planned.

As an example of how this information would be used to size a footing, let's consider a free standing stone rubble wall, 12 in thick, having a total height of 8 ft and to be built on a soft, nonexpansive clay. First, the weight of the wall would be calculated using 1 linear foot as being typical of the entire length of the wall. Therefore:

$$1 \times 8 = 8 \text{ cubic feet of masonry}$$
$$8 \times 160 = 1280 \text{ lb total weight}$$
$$\frac{1280}{144} = 8.88 \text{ lb/in}^2$$

Now we notice in Table 6–3 that the bearing capacity of the soft clay is 14 lb/in². Thus, a footing for this wall is not actually necessary. However, since any masonry wall is highly sensitive to soil movement, a footing would help stop cracking in the masonry joints. Therefore, a 12 in footing would be satisfactory.

The reason for this example was to illustrate the theory and purpose of a footing. In actual practice, footings should always be provided under a wall or structure to help ensure its long-term durability, regardless of the necessity. You will also note that the conditions used were severe. It is most unlikely that

any landscape structure will ever exceed a soil's bearing capacity if the footing is designed to be twice the width of the wall, and you will find this is a widely accepted practice (see Figure 6–9). Footings should always be placed below the frost line, and have a thickness of 8 in. Thicker footings may be justified in poor bearing soils and areas subject to hard freeze.

Longitudinal reinforcements for temperature should also be provided in the footing equal to .0050 of the cross-sectional area. It is recommended that #4 bars be used to provide the required steel and it should be placed 2 in from the bottom of the footing as shown in Figure 6–10.

Many times a wall will occur on or with a paved deck area and it may be convenient to incorporate the footing with the slab. This will eliminate the need for an expansion joint at the wall and the concrete work can be done in a single pour. This is called a haunch footing and is illustrated in Figure 6–11.

As mentioned earlier, there are occasions when the use of a simple footing is not advisable because of expansive soil conditions. In this situation, it is common to use a pier-and-beam foundation to support the structure above.

The principal of this method is to set the piers in stable material and allow them to distribute the load. The structure above is rested on a steel-reinforced concrete beam, called a grade beam, that spans the piers. The success of this system relies on two important things. First, the piers must be set at a sufficient depth and large enough to distribute the load to the ground and not be affected by soil movement. Second, the grade beam must be supported only by the piers. If contact with the soil is permitted under the grade beam, the value of the system is lost. A typical pier and beam system is illustrated in Figure 6–12.

Freestanding Walls

Freestanding walls are one of the most frequently employed tools for architectural definition of space in the landscape. Freestanding walls are used as screens, background, physical barriers and sometimes just as decorative elements in a total composition.

While there is an infinite variety of material and material combinations available to the designer, the basic elements involved in the structural design of the wall will be the same. A wall will be some combination of masonry units, or plain concrete with a masonry veneer, or plain concrete cast in place. All of these combinations are structurally classified as exterior non-loadbearing, nonreinforced walls. However, as noted in the discussion of concrete, the classification of nonreinforced does not mean that steel reinforcement is not necessary and not used. On the contrary, steel reinforcement is necessary to tie the wall

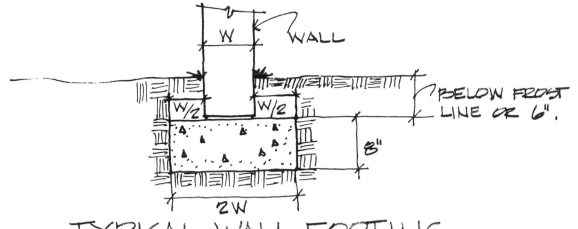

TYPICAL WALL FOOTING

FIGURE 6-9

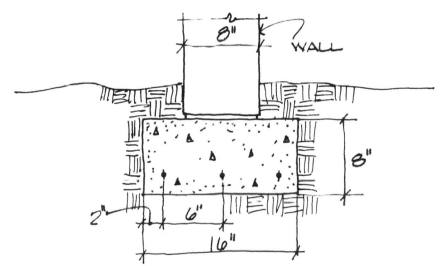

STEEL PLACEMENT IN FOOTINGS

FIGURE 6-10

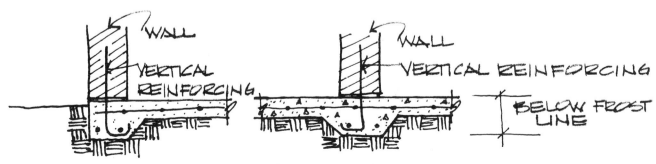

SLAB EDGE HAUNCH   MID-SLAB HAUNCH

SLABS WITH HAUNCH FOOTINGS

FIGURE 6-11

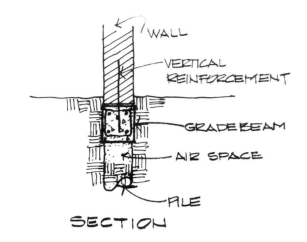

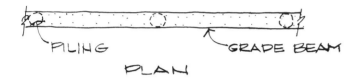

PIER & BEAM
FOOTING SYSTEM

FIGURE 6-12

to the foundation system and compensate for normal temperature and shrinkage effects.

The configuration of a wall and its height will have a direct bearing on the structural design, how it is supported, and its thickness. For example, a straight wall that has a length of 35 or 40 feet will require lateral support and may have to be thicker than a short wall or a wall with frequent angles. This is much like bending a thin strip of paper in a zigzag pattern. When this is done it will stand on its own, whereas that same piece of paper would not stand on its own in a straight line. Common terms used to describe the types of walls and the parts of the wall are illustrated in Figure 6-13.

Structural Design of Freestanding Walls

The discussion and examples in this section refer specifically to unit masonry construction. However, these same principles apply equally to any type of wall construction, e.g., concrete walls or fences.

A freestanding wall or fence is classified as a nonloadbearing wall. Structures in this class carry only their own weight plus any lateral wind loads. In some areas, codes may require that earthquake forces and shock from blasting also be taken into account. If this is the case, the code will usually specify the means for investigating those additional loads; they are not considered here.

Since freestanding walls are usually built from materials with high compressive strength, it is not usually necessary to check the wall for working stresses except in cases of extreme height over 25 feet. The two types of wall failure that are of the most concern are footing failure and overturning. Footing failure usually results from extreme eccentric loads on the footing which exceed the allowable tensile stress of the material. This is illustrated in Figure 6-14 (a). Failure by overturning occurs when the overturning moment exceeds the righting moment of the wall or if the bearing pressure of the soil is exceeded as shown in Figure 6-14 (b).

Since concrete and masonry have very high compressive strength and relatively low tensile strength, the design objective is to keep all stress compressive. This is accomplished by applying the "principle of the middle third." The principle of the middle third simply means that so long as the resultant load of the structure acts in the middle third of the footing, all forces and stresses are compressive (see Figure 6-15). In this situation, the weight of the wall is evenly distributed over the entire cross-sectional area of the footing. Thus all stresses are equal and compressive.

Now assume that the wall is moved a slight distance e from the center of the footing as shown in Figure 6-16. This condition is called eccentric loading and the forces are no longer evenly distributed in the system. The actual pressure exerted by either side of the footing can be determined by the expression:

$$f = \frac{P}{A}\left(1 \pm \frac{6e}{d}\right)$$

where

f = is the force exerted at either edge of the footing in pounds/in²;

P = weight of the wall for a typical 1 ft section in pounds;

A = the area of the footing for a typical 1 ft section in in²;

e = distance between centerline of wall and centerline of the footing in inches;

d = width of the footing in inches.

For example, let's consider Figure 6-17. An 8 in thick concrete block wall 6 ft tall is offset 2 in to the right of its footing. Find f for each side of the footing as follows.

Find P.

Concrete block weighs 100 lb/ft³, so

P = 1 ft × 6 ft × .66 ft × 100 lb/ft³ = 396 lb

Find A.

16 in × 12 in = 192 in²

e = 2 in

d = 16 in

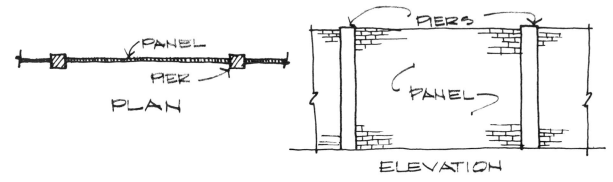

PLAN

PIERS

PANEL

ELEVATION

PIER & PANEL WALL

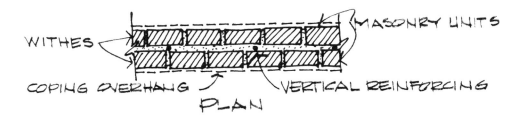

WITHES

MASONRY UNITS

COPING OVERHANG

VERTICAL REINFORCING

PLAN

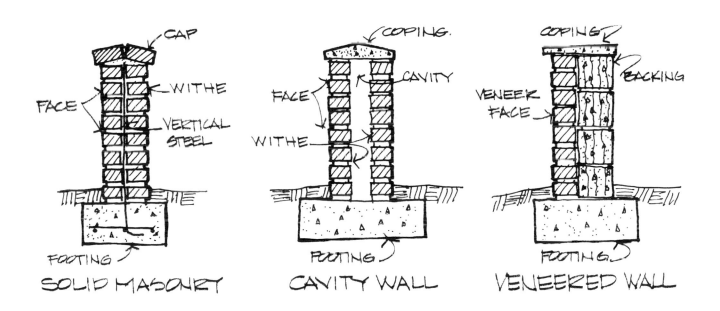

CAP

WITHE

FACE

VERTICAL STEEL

FOOTING

SOLID MASONRY

COPING.

FACE

CAVITY

WITHE

FOOTING

CAVITY WALL

COPING

BACKING

VENEER FACE

COPING

FOOTING

VENEERED WALL

SINGLE MASONRY WITHE

SERPENTINE WALL

FREESTANDING WALLS

FIGURE 6–13

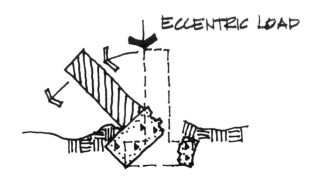

ECCENTRIC LOAD

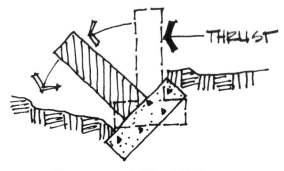

THRUST

A FOOTING FAILURE

B OVERTURNING

WALL FAILURE

FIGURE 6–14

W

IF THE LOAD IS CENTERED ON THE FOOTING ALL STRESS IS EQUAL & COMPRESSIVE

COMPRESSIVE STRESS IN WALLS

FIGURE 6–15

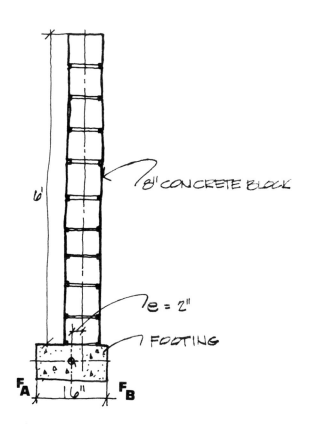

6'

8" CONCRETE BLOCK

e = 2"

FOOTING

F_A 16" F_B

FOOTING STRESS WITH ECCENTRIC LOADING

FIGURE 6–17

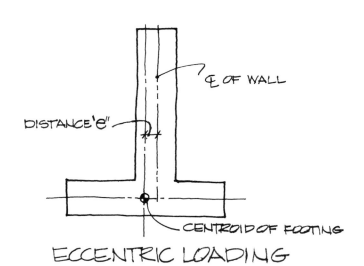

℄ OF WALL

DISTANCE 'e"

CENTROID OF FOOTING

ECCENTRIC LOADING

FIGURE 6–16

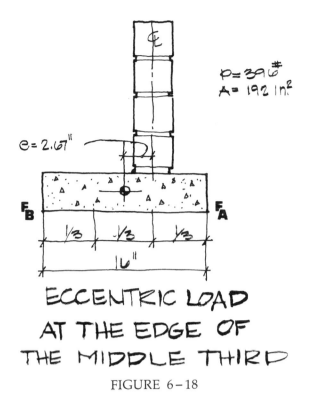

e = 2.67"

P = 396 #
A = 192 in²

ECCENTRIC LOAD
AT THE EDGE OF
THE MIDDLE THIRD

FIGURE 6-18

Find f_A as:

$$f_A = \frac{P}{A}\left(1 - \frac{6e}{d}\right)$$

$$f_A = \frac{396}{192}\left(1 - \frac{6 \times 2}{16}\right)$$

$$f_A = 2.06 \times .25$$

$$f_A = .515\ \text{lb/in}^2$$

Find f_B.

$$f_B = \frac{396}{192}\left(1 + \frac{6 \times 2}{16}\right)$$

$$f_B = 2.06\left(1 + \frac{12}{16}\right)$$

$$f_B = 2.06 \times 1.75$$

$$f_B = 3.61\ \text{lb/in}^2$$

Next let's consider the same condition with the wall centered directly over the outside of the middle third as shown in Figure 6–18. Find f_A and f_B as follows.

Find f_A as:

$$f_A = \frac{396}{192}\left(1 - \frac{6 \times 2.67}{16}\right)$$

$$f_A = 2.06\left(1 - \frac{16}{16}\right)$$

$$f_A = 2.06 \times 0$$

$$f_A = 0$$

Find f_B as:

$$f_B = \frac{396}{192}\left(1 + \frac{6 \times 2.67}{16}\right)$$

$$f_B = 2.06\left(1 + \frac{16}{16}\right)$$

$$f_B = 2.06 \times 2$$

$$f_B = 4.12\ \text{lb/in}^2$$

There are two important points illustrated in this discussion of the middle third. First, notice that as the wall moves away from the center of the middle third, the footing pressure and stress in the footing increase in the direction of movement. Once the wall is centered at the outer edge of the middle third the pressure and stress at the near edge of the footing is twice the average stress and 0 at the far edge. If the wall moves outside the middle third, tensile stress would then develop in the footing and could contribute to the failure of the wall. Also notice that with the wall over the outside of the middle third, the pressure on the soil is twice the average pressure. This means that in extreme cases with heavy wall loads, it would be possible to exceed the soil bearing pressure and the wall could overturn.

In the case of a non-loadbearing wall, we would not expect eccentric loading to be significant for most soils since footing pressures are so light, but the possibility must be considered.

Righting Moments and Overturning Moments

The next consideration in the design of a freestanding wall is the overturning moment of wind pressure. Notice in Figure 6–19 that a freestanding wall is essentially a cantilever beam that is supporting an evenly distributed load caused by air movement.

The weight of a wall and footing times the distance from the vertical axis to the edge of the footing is called the righting moment (M_r). The total wind load on the wall times the distance from the base of the footing to the point of action of the wind load is called the overturning moment (M_o).

Average wind loads may be specified in local codes. However, if no code stipulation exists, wind loads may be obtained from Figure 6–20 which was taken from material published by the United States of America Standards Institute.

For a free standing wall to be considered stable the righting moment must be greater than the overturning moment. To illustrate this point consider the example in Figure 6–21.

To calculate the righting moment (M_r) find the combined weight of the wall and multiply by half the width of the footing. For an investigation of this type we will consider a typical 1 ft section of the wall only.

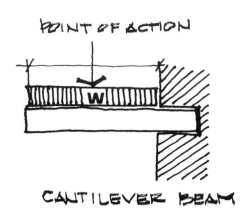

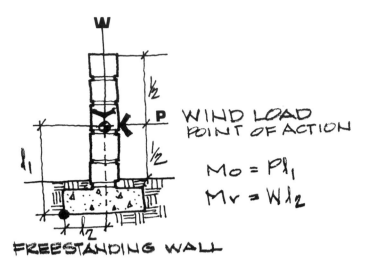

HORIZONTAL LOADING-FREESTANDING WALLS

FIGURE 6-19

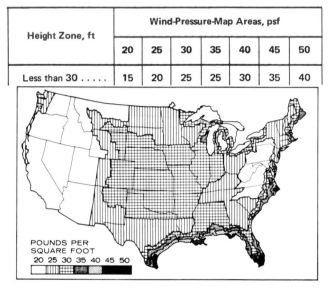

FIGURE 6-20

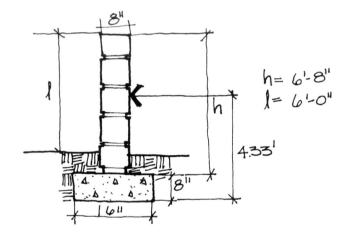

LATERAL STABILITY

FIGURE 6-21

The combined weight is as follows: concrete weighs 150 lb/ft³; block masonry weighs 100 lb/ft³.

The footing weight is

.67 ft (8 in) × 1.33 ft (16 in) × 1 ft × 150 lb
= 133.67 lb

The weight of the masonry wall is

.67 ft (8 in) × 6.67 ft (6 ft 8 in) × 1 ft × 100 lb
= 446.89 lb

Total weight P = 446.89 lb + 133.67 lb = 580.56 lb

Half of the footing width is 8 in or .67 ft. Therefore

$$M_r = 580.56 \text{ lb} \times .67 \text{ ft} = 388.98 \text{ ft-lb}$$

Next find the overturning moment assuming the wall is located in Central Oregon. From Figure 6-20 find that the wind load is 40 lb/ft². The exposed portion of the wall is 6 ft tall and 1 ft wide so the wind pressure is

$$W = 6 \text{ ft} \times 1 \text{ ft} \times 40 \text{ lb/ft}^2 = 240 \text{ lb}$$

The distance from the bottom of the footing to the point of action of the wind load is 4.34 ft (.67 ft + .67 ft + 3 ft). Therefore, M_o is

$$M_o = 4.34 \text{ ft} \times 240 \text{ lb} = 1{,}041.60 \text{ ft-lb}$$

Since M_r the righting moment is only 388.98 ft-lb, the wall is very much in danger of overturning if

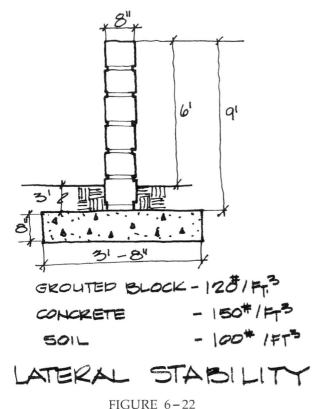

GROUTED BLOCK - 128#/FT.³

CONCRETE   - 150#/FT³

SOIL   - 100#/FT³

LATERAL STABILITY

FIGURE 6-22

winds of the specified magnitude are encountered.

However, there are several ways to insure that the wall will be stable. First, we have assumed that the wall is not supported at either end, if such support is available: another wall perpendicular to the wall at either end or a building into which the wall is tied will provide the necessary extra lateral support. If this kind of support is not available, then it is necessary to widen the footing to increase the lever arm component of the righting moment.

A quick way to determine how much to spread the footing is to divide the overturning moment by the weight of the wall; this yields the lever arm required to offset the lateral pressure. The extra weight added by the footing is usually enough then to provide a safety factor. To illustrate this, let's complete the example problem.

The overturning moment calculated was 1,041.60 ft-lb. This is divided by the weight of the wall: 580.56 lb.

$$\frac{1,041.60 \text{ ft-lb}}{580.56 \text{ lb}} = 1.79 \text{ ft or about 1 ft 10 in}$$

Therefore, to insure wind stability the footing should be widened to 3 ft 8 in as shown in Figure 6-22. To prove out the adjustment calculate M_o and M_r for the revised section.

The weight of the masonry wall portion is still 446.89 lb. The weight of the footing is

.67 (8 in) × 3.67 ft (3 ft 8 in) × 1 × 150 = 368.84 lb

Total Weight = 368.84 lb + 446.89 lb = 815.73 lb.

M_r = 1.83 ft (1 ft 10 in) × 815.73 lb = 1492.79 ft-lb

Since the basic dimensions of the wall have not changed M_o still equals 1,041.60 ft-lb. Thus the safety factor is

$$S_f = \frac{1492.79}{1041.60} = 1.43$$

This is sufficient and the wall can be considered stable.

Wind Loads on Fences

Wind loads on fences pose a problem that is a little different than that for freestanding walls since they are supported only by posts. This means that their stability under wind loads is a function of how deep the post is set in the ground, and the properties and condition of the soil. For most cases a good rule of thumb for post embedment that will satisfy most landscape conditions is that the embedment be 1/3 the height of the fence for wind loads up to 30 lb/ft² and 1/2 the height for loads over 30 lb/ft² for posts placed on 8 ft centers.

Lateral Support of Walls

To this point in our discussion we have considered only a 1 foot section of a wall. Masonry walls will also require lateral support from piers, pilasters, or other walls. The maximum distance between supports can be determined from the length to thickness ratio. Table 6-4 provides length to thickness ratios that are satisfactory for most landscape construction (see also Figure 6-23).

To illustrate how this is applied, let's continue with the example of the 6 ft high, 8 in block wall and

TABLE 6-4
Length-to-Thickness Ratios to Determine Lateral Support of Masonry Walls

WIND PRESSURE (lb²/ft²)	DESIGN MAXIMUM L/T RATIO
5	35
10	25
15	20
20	18
25	16
30	14
35	13
40	12

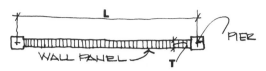

L - LATERAL DISTANCE BETWEEN PIERS

T - WALL THICKNESS

LENGTH-THICKNESS RATIO OF WALLS

FIGURE 6-23

determine the maximum allowable span between supports. In the example, we had designed for a wind load of 40 lb/ft². From the table we find that the maximum L/T ratio recommended is 12. Therefore, if

$$L/T = 12 \text{ in} \quad \text{and} \quad T = 8 \text{ in}$$

then

$$\frac{L}{8} = 12$$
$$L = 8 \times 12$$
$$L = 96 \text{ in or 8 ft}$$

The maximum distance between supports then is 8 ft.

Reinforcing Freestanding Walls

Non-loadbearing masonry and concrete walls are not designed as reinforced structures; however, reinforcing is necessary to compensate for thermal effects and differential soil movements. The recommended standard for this is that reinforcing be provided equal to .005 of the cross-sectional area of the wall, and the reinforcing should be both horizontal and vertical.

With respect to actual placement, overlap, and installation of reinforcing steel in a wall, see the details in the Reference Manual. It is difficult, if not impossible, to say what arrangement is best since most details of this type are not subject to exact structural investigation.

Other Freestanding Walls

Before closing our discussion of freestanding walls, there are two other types of walls mentioned in the introduction that have somewhat different structural requirements than the common wall. One is the pier-and-panel wall and the other is the serpentine wall.

The pier-and-panel wall consists of piers that support a single withe of masonry units between them. The panels themselves are suspended between the piers and rely on the bond between the units, reinforcing, and piers for support. All of the loads, dead load plus wind load, are transferred to the ground through the piers. Details and design requirements

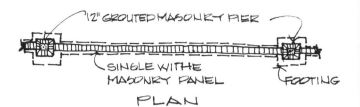

PLAN

PIER & PANEL WALL

FIGURE 6-24

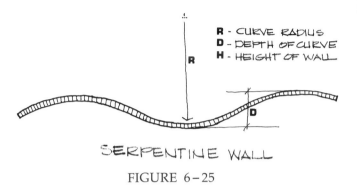

R - CURVE RADIUS
D - DEPTH OF CURVE
H - HEIGHT OF WALL

SERPENTINE WALL

FIGURE 6-25

for pier-and-panel walls are provided in the Reference Manual. The pier-and-panel wall has the advantage of requiring less material and labor to build. On the other hand, its durability is questionable in areas with high wind loads and expansive soils (see Figure 6-24).

Serpentine walls are also single withe masonry or thin concrete walls that rely on their geometric properties for vertical stability as shown in Figure 6-25. The primary concern in designing a serpentine wall is to be sure that the degree of curvature is sufficient to provide support. The rule-of-thumb design method for walls 6 ft or less and subject to no unusual loads is

$$R = 2H \quad \text{and} \quad D = \frac{H}{2}$$

where

R = radius of the curve;
H = height of the wall above grade;
D = depth of curvature measured between a tangent line and the wall face.

This method together with proper reinforcing will provide satisfactory results. However, if it is necessary to design a wall over 6 ft, refer to the design data for serpentine walls in the reference manual.

Retaining Walls

Retaining walls are structures designed to resist soil pressure which is a horizontal force called thrust.

GRAVITY WALL

CANTILEVER WALL

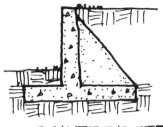
COUNTERFORT WALL

FIGURE 6-26

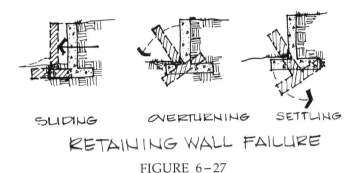
SLIDING   OVERTURNING   SETTLING

RETAINING WALL FAILURE

FIGURE 6-27

FOR MOST SOILS THE ANGLE OF REPOSE CAN BE ASSUMED AS 33°

SOIL   ANGLE OF REPOSE

ANGLE OF REPOSE

FIGURE 6-28

Retaining walls fall into three general categories: gravity walls, cantilever walls, and counterfort walls, as shown in Figure 6-26.

The gravity retaining wall is the simplest of the structures relying only on its mass and weight for stability. The cantilever wall is made of reinforced concrete and utilizes the weight of the soil above the footing to offset any chance of overturning. The counterfort wall works on the same principle as that of the cantilever wall, but also uses buttresses (counterforts) to achieve a more rigid structure.

Gravity retaining walls are the simplest solution for low walls, if a concrete finish is acceptable. Larger walls are usually cantilever walls, since the volume of material required for a gravity wall becomes expensive and cumbersome. Counterfort walls are utilized in extreme conditions where walls 20 ft and higher may be required.

The structural design of a retaining wall depends on the strength of the cross section of the wall. This is the ability of the wall itself to withstand internal stress. The wall must also be laterally stable; that is, it must be able to resist the three types of retaining wall failures, sliding, overturning, and settling at the base of the wall as shown in Figure 6-27.

The usual procedure for the design of a retaining wall is to select a cross section from one of the many technical references or material societies that meet the job requirements and local codes. Then this section is investigated for lateral stability to be sure it will perform under the field conditions. The examples used in this discussion will be taken from material found in the Reference Manual.

Soil Pressure on Retaining Walls

To determine a retaining wall's stability, it is necessary to calculate the weight of the wall and any resultant forces that contribute to its weight and compare this with the soil pressure (thrust). Since the wall section will be selected, first its dimensions and the materials that make it up will be known. This allows you to accurately estimate its weight. The soil pressure, however, is quite another matter.

Soil pressure is the result of several variables: the weight of the soil being retained, the slope of the surface behind the wall, moisture content, and the angle of repose of the retained soil. The weight of most soils is around 100 lb/ft³. Dry sandy soil will, of course, be lighter, and heavy clays will weigh more. On the average, though, 100 lb/ft³ can be used if other data is not available.

The angle of repose refers to the angle between the ground and the surface that a material will maintain without a wall. (See Figure 6-28.) For example, all of us have seen a pile of soil dumped from a truck onto the ground. When the soil is dumped, the top of the pile will continue to slump until the whole pile stabilizes in a cone or prismoid shape. The angle that is made between the side of the pile and the ground is the angle of repose. The angle of repose, like the weight, varies from material to material. However, a safe average is taken to be 33°. This is usually the assumed value for most predesigned cross sections.

It is important that this angle be checked especially if field conditions indicate soil instability.

The only soil that will exert pressure on a retaining wall is the soil that lies outside the angle of repose. This is shown in Figure 6–29. When the surface of the retained soil is level with the wall, the force is assumed to act horizontally on the wall at ⅓ the height. This is because of the traingular cross section of the soil producing the thrust. However, if the soil is sloping up behind the wall, as shown in Figure 6–30, the wall is said to have a surcharge.

Figure 6–31 illustrates the algebraic expressions used to determine the soil pressure P on retaining walls with and without surcharges. You should note here that the thrust acts on the wall parallel to the surface of the ground.

Parallelograms of Force

When a system of two forces acts together, the net effect is a single force acting in a new direction. The new force is called a resultant. The resultant of the two component forces acting in a retaining wall system is best found by drawing a parallelogram of forces. A parallelogram of forces is a graphic technique that can be used to find the resultant of a system of forces. For example, observe the system of forces acting together in Figure 6–32. The retaining wall is exerting a downward force of 1600 lb, while the soil behind the wall is exerting a lateral force of 1200 lb.

To the right of the wall, Figure 6–32b, a force parallelogram has been constructed showing the 1600 lb force acting vertically and the 1200 lb force acting horizontally. Each line is scaled so that 1 unit of measure is equal to 1 pound of force. Thus the vertical line is 1600 units and the horizontal line is 1200 units. The diagonal line of the parallelogram is the resultant which is found by scaling the line. In this case, the resultant equals 2000 lb. Keep in mind that the resultant is the net effect of the two forces acting together. It has its own line, magnitude, and direction.

To be sure that this principle is clear, let's consider another example, illustrated in Figure 6–33 (a and b). Here we have another retaining wall exerting a downward force of 2400 lb and a surcharge pressure of 1800 lb. Remember that the line of action of a force acting on a surcharged retaining wall is parallel to the surface of the soil behind the wall. The force parallelogram for the system of forces described is shown in Figure 6–33b and the resultant is scaled as 3600 lb.

Now, before the stability of the surcharged wall can be properly investigated, it is necessary to find the equivalent horizontal and vertical components of the resultant. This is done by constructing a paral-

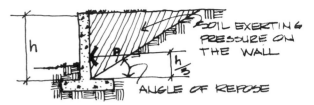

PRESSURE ON RETAINING WALLS

FIGURE 6–29

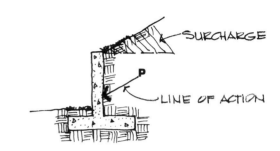

RETAINING WALLS WITH A SURCHARGE

FIGURE 6–30

lelogram of force about the resultant of 3600 lb and finding the equivalent horizontal and vertical components, as illustrated in Figure 6–34.

Observe that the magnitude and line of action of the resultant remain the same. All we have done is translate the actual forces shown in Figure 6–34b to their equivalent horizontal and vertical components.

Investigating Stability

To be considered stable, a retaining wall must be investigated for all three types of failure mentioned earlier. For the sake of simplicity, we will use a plain gravity wall with a trapezoidal cross section for the first illustrations, then work through two other examples of a cantilever wall with and without a surcharge.

First, the wall must be investigated for resistance to overturning. As with a freestanding wall, the righting moment must be greater than the overturning moment. For most retaining wall applications a safety factor of 1.5 to 2 is recommended.

Let's consider the gravity wall shown in Figure 6–35. It is a trapezoid 6 ft tall, 6 in thick at the top, and 3 ft 6 in at the base. Thus, the cross-sectional area is found by the formula

$$A = h \left(\frac{B + b}{2} \right)$$

The next step is to determine the centroid of the wall's cross section. You will recall from earlier discussions that the centroid of a cross section (center of

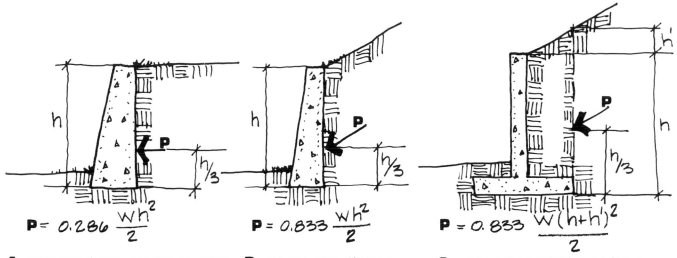

$$P = 0.286 \frac{wh^2}{2}$$

A GRAVITY OR CANTILEVER WALL W/O SURCHARGE

$$P = 0.833 \frac{wh^2}{2}$$

B GRAVITY WALL WITH SURCHARGE

$$P = 0.833 \frac{w(h+h')^2}{2}$$

C CANTILEVER WALL WITH SURCHARGE

FIGURE 6-31

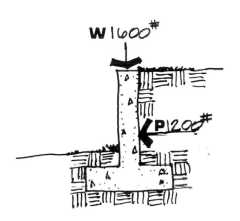

W 1600#

P 1200#

A SYSTEM OF FORCES

1600#

1200#

RESULTANT

B FORCE PARALLELOGRAM

PARALLELOGRAMS OF FORCE

FIGURE 6-32

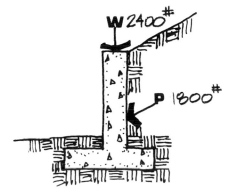

W 2400#

P 1800#

A SYSTEM OF FORCES

P 1800#

W 2400#

R 3400#

B FORCE PARALLELOGRAM

FIGURE 6-33

221

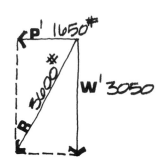

A HORIZONTAL & VERTICAL
COMPONENTS

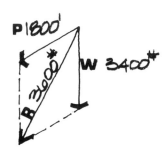

B ORIGINAL FORCE SYSTEM

FINDING EQUIVALENT FORCES

FIGURE 6–34

gravity) is the point through which all forces act. Since we are dealing with an asymetrical shape, it will be necessary to divide it into parts, determine the moments for each, and combine them to find the centroid of the cross section. The easiest way to accomplish this is to tabulate the information as it is calculated, proceeding as follows using a typical 1 ft section of wall (see Table 6–5 and Figure 6–36).

TABLE 6–5

SECTION	WEIGHT	MOMENT ARM	MOMENT
1	9 × 150 = 1350	1.5 ft	2025
2	3 × 150 = 450	.25 ft	112.5
	Total = 1800 lb	Total of moments	2137.5 ft/lb

Next, determine the moment arm for each of the cross-sectional areas around A at the base of the wall. Since the weight is considered to act at the vertical axis of the section, the moment arm for section 1 is 1.5 ft. Remember, the vertical axis of a right triangle lies $\frac{1}{3}$ the length of the base from the apex (Figure 6–37). The moment arm for section 2 is .25 ft. With this information, determine the moments around point A as follows:

Section 1 moment = 1.5 × 1350 = 2025 ft-lb
Section 2 moment = .25 × 450 = 112.5 ft-lb

Now, since the sum of the moments of the parts is equal to the moment of the whole cross section, the location of the vertical axis can be found. If we let X equal the moment arm, then

1800 lb X = 2137.5 ft-lb

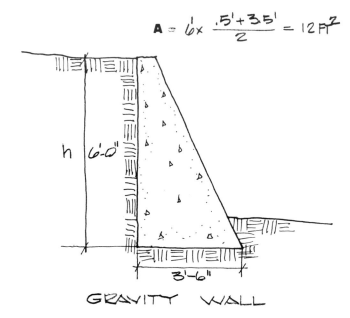

$$A = 6 \times \frac{.5' + 3.5'}{2} = 12 \, FT^2$$

GRAVITY WALL

FIGURE 6–35

$$X = \frac{2137.5 \text{ ft-lb}}{1800 \text{ lb}}$$
$$X = 1.19 \text{ ft}$$

Therefore, the weight of the wall is acting through a point 1.19 ft from the left-hand side of the section as seen in Figure 6–38.

Next, determine the soil pressure P as follows.

$$P = .286 \frac{wh^2}{2}$$

$$P = .286 \times \frac{100 \times 6^2}{2}$$

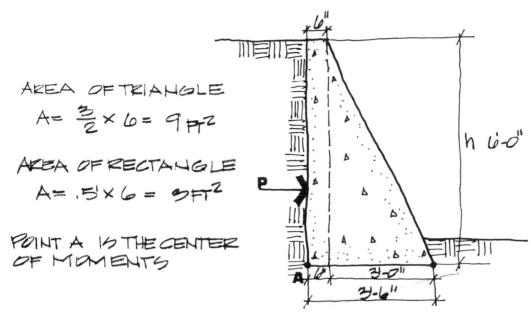

AREA OF TRIANGLE

$A = \dfrac{3}{2} \times 6 = 9\ \text{FT}^2$

AREA OF RECTANGLE

$A = .5' \times 6 = 3\ \text{FT}^2$

POINT A IS THE CENTER OF MOMENTS

FINDING THE CENTROID BY MOMENTS

FIGURE 6-36

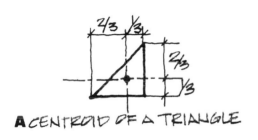

A CENTROID OF A TRIANGLE   **B** CENTROID OF A RECTANGLE

CENTROIDS OF COMMON SECTIONS

FIGURE 6-37

$P = .286 \times \dfrac{100 \times 36}{2}$

$P = .286 \times \dfrac{3600}{2}$

$P = .286 \times 1800$

$P = 514.8\ \text{lb}$

(The value of 100 lb/ft³ is a satisfactory estimate of soil weight when other information is not available.)

The tendency for the wall to overturn will be generated by P (514.8 lb) and its lever arm X. The righting moment is generated by W (1800 lb) and its lever arm Y, as illustrated in Figure 6-38. Therefore, calculate the overturning moment as

$M_o = PX$
$M_o = 514.8 \times 2$
$M_o = 1029.6\ \text{ft-lb}$

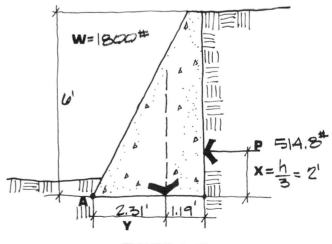

FIGURE 6-38

Find the righting moment as

$$M_r = WY$$
$$M_r = 1800 \times 2.31$$
$$M_r = 4{,}158 \text{ ft-lb}$$

Allowing for safety factor of 2, the righting moment is divided by 2 and checked against the overturning moment.

$$\frac{M_r}{2} = \frac{4158 \text{ ft-lb}}{2} = 2079 \text{ ft-lb}$$

Thus, the wall is not in danger of overturning.

The next consideration is whether the foot pressure exceeds the bearing pressure of the soil. For our example, we will assume a soft clay condition of 2,000 lb/ft². Our first task is to determine where the resultant of the two forces cuts the base of the wall. This is done by constructing the parallelogram of forces and extending the resultant to the base as shown in Figure 6–39.

Note that the resultant cuts the base of the wall 1.6 ft from the left-hand edge; thus the base is eccentrically loaded to the left-hand edge. The load is within the middle third, however. With this known, we can now find the foot pressure as

$$f_A = \frac{P}{A}\left(1 + \frac{6e}{d}\right)$$

$$f_A = \frac{1800^*}{3.5}\left(1 + \frac{6 \times .15}{3.5}\right)$$

$$f_A = 514.29 \times 1.26 = 646.54 \text{ lb/ft}^2$$

Since the allowable limit was 2000 lb/ft², it is within a safety factor of 1.5.

The last possibility to be investigated is the tendency of the wall to creep or slide horizontally. The force that could produce the sliding is the 514.8 lb thrust *(P)*. The force that resists sliding is the 1800 lb load of the wall modified by the friction coefficient of the soil.

The friction coefficient is simply the ability of the soil to resist the tendency of the wall to move horizontally. For example, a coarse material like gravel would have a higher coefficient than soft, moist clay. The average friction coefficients of various soils are given in Table 6–6.

The possibility of creep for the example would be calculated as follows. Assume a wet clay condition. The force that resists creep is

1800 lb × .30 (wet clay friction coefficient) = 540 lb

The thrust times a safety factor of 1.5 is

1.5 × 514.8 lb = 772.2 lb

---

*The value of P in this case is the weight of the wall *(W)*.

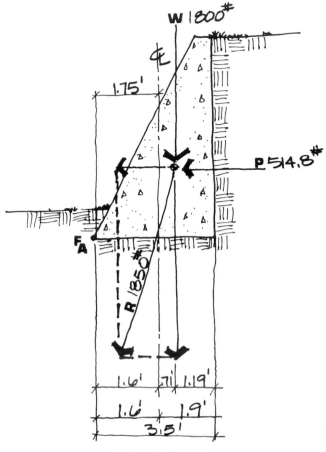

FIGURE 6–39

Thus, the wall is not within acceptable limits. Note, however, that the wall's base has been placed below the frost line. The resisting force in front of the wall generated by the soil is probably sufficient to make up the difference. Another means of countering the creep possibility is to add a key at the base of the wall as shown in Figure 6–40.

Investigating Complex Cross-Section Walls

Now that we have discussed the basic principles of investigating the stability of retaining walls, let's apply these principles to the more complex

TABLE 6–6
Average Friction Coefficients of Various Soils

SOIL TYPE	FRICTION COEFFICIENT
Gravel	0.60
Sand	0.40
Silt/clay, dry	0.50
Clay, wet	0.30

Note: The safety factor recommended against creep is 1.5 × the thrust.

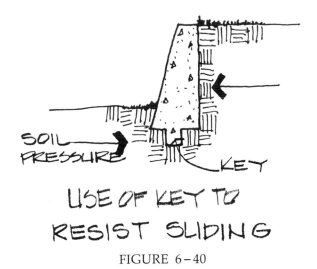

USE OF KEY TO
RESIST SLIDING

FIGURE 6–40

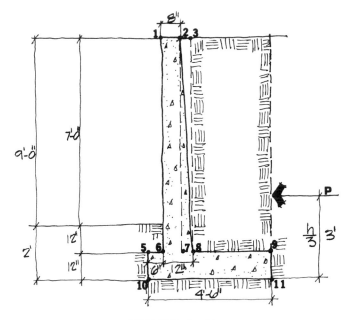

FIGURE 6–41

section of a cantilever retaining wall. The major difference between the cantilever wall and the gravity wall is that the cantilever wall utilizes the weight of the soil acting downward on the footing to achieve a greater righting moment. Now consider the retaining wall in Figure 6–41. This is a predesigned cross section taken from information in the Reference Manual.

The wall is to have an overall height of 9 ft and gives an effective height above the ground of 7 ft 0 in. Notice that P is taken to act at $\frac{1}{3}$ the height of the wall, but the point of action occurs at a line corresponding to the back edge of the footing extended vertically. This is because the soil that lies within rectangles 3, 4, 8, 9, and triangles 2, 3, 8 are actually part of the stabilizing force W.

For the purpose of determining W and the centroid of the section, the wall has been divided into a series of triangles and rectangles described by points 1–11 for which the moments can be calculated. Once again, the easiest way to handle this is in tabular form. Table 6–7 is a summary of these values. The moments are taken about an axis at the left side of the footing.

Next, the righting moment is calculated, letting X equal the moment arm; thus

$$4209X = 10,007.8$$
$$X = \frac{10,007.8}{4,209}$$
$$X = 2.4 \text{ ft}$$

This means that W (4,209 lb) acts through a point 2.4 ft from the left edge of the wall footing. Now P can be calculated and the resultant determined by a force parallelogram as illustrated in Figure 6–42.

Once the information is brought together as shown we are ready to check for the three kinds of failure as before. First calculate the overturning moment as follows.

The moment arm equals 3 ft.

$$P = 1158.3 \text{ lb, thus:}$$
$$M_o = 1158.3 \times 3$$
$$M_o = 3,474.9 \text{ ft-lb}$$

TABLE 6–7
A Summary of the Moment Values for Points 1–11

SECTION DESIGNATION	MATERIAL WEIGHT (lb)	MOMENT ARM	MOMENT
5,9,10,11	$1 \times 4.5 \times 1 \times 150 = 675$	$.5 \times 4.5 = 2.25$	$675 \times 2.25 = 1518.8$
1,2,6,7	$.67 \times 8 \times 1 \times 150 = 804$	$.5 + .35 = .85$	$804 \times .85 = 683.4$
2,7,8	$.33 \times 4 \times 1 \times 150 = 198$	$1.17 + (.33 \times .33) = 1.28$	$198 \times 1.28 = 253.4$
2,3,8	$.33 \times 4 \times 1 \times 100 = 132$	$1.17 + (.33 \times .67) = 1.39$	$132 \times 1.39 = 183.5$
3,4,8,9	$3 \times 8 \times 1 \times 100 = 2400$	$1.5 + .5 \times 3 = 3$	$2400 \times 3 = 7200$
	Sum of the weights = 4209 lb		Sum of the moments = 9839.1 ft-lb

CALCULATE **P** AS:

$$P = 0.286 \frac{wh}{2}$$

$$P = .286 \frac{100 \times 9^2}{2}$$

$$P = .286 \times 4050$$

$$P = 1158.3^\#$$

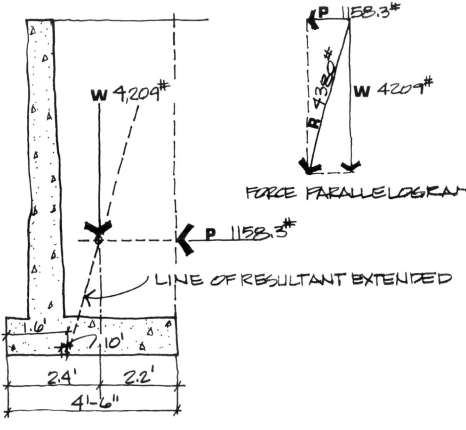

FIGURE 6-42

The righting moment is calculated as (the moment arm equals 2.4 ft)

$$W = 4,209 \text{ lb}$$
$$M_r = 4,209 \times 2.4$$
$$M_r = 10,101.6 \text{ ft-lb}$$

With a safety factor of 2 applied:

$$M_o \times 2 = 3474.9 \times 2 = 6,949.8 \text{ ft-lb}$$

We are well within accepted standards for overturning.

Next, the footing pressure is calculated. We will again assume a soil bearing pressure of 2,000 lb/ft² and a required safety factor of 1.5. Note that the resultant force line cuts the footing 1.6 ft from the left edge. This means that the force acts within the middle third. The greatest footing pressure will occur along the left edge of the footing. The actual pressure is calculated as

$$f_A = \frac{P}{A} \left(1 + \frac{6e}{d}\right)$$

$$f_A = \frac{4209}{4.5} \left(1 + \frac{6 \times .65}{4.5}\right)$$

$$f_A = 935.33 \left(1 + \frac{3.9}{4.5}\right)$$

$$P = 4209 \text{ lb}$$
$$A = 4.5$$
$$e = .75 - .10 = .65$$
$$d = 4.5$$

$$f_A = 935.33 \,(1.867)$$
$$f_A = 1745.95 \text{ lb/ft}^2$$

With the safety factor of 1.5 applied

$$f_A = 1745.95 \times 1.5 = 2,618.92 \text{ lb/ft}^2$$

This value is not within satisfactory limits if the soil bearing pressure is 2,000 lb/ft². The way to correct this is to adjust the footing if possible to reduce the eccentric loading or select and test another cross section. This could be critical to the design if the property line becomes a factor.

Finally, the wall is checked for its resistance to creep. This is found by comparing the weight of the wall multiplied by the friction coefficient with P, the force that would cause sliding. For the sake of illustration again we will use the extreme condition of wet clay having a coefficient of .30.

$$.30 \times 4209 = 1262.7 \text{ lb}$$

Thus the resistance to sliding is 1262.7 lb. Applying a safety factor of 1.5 to P find that

$$1158.3 \times 1.5 = 1737.45 \text{ lb}$$

Once again we find that we have exceeded the acceptable limits. However, the fact that the wall is 2 ft

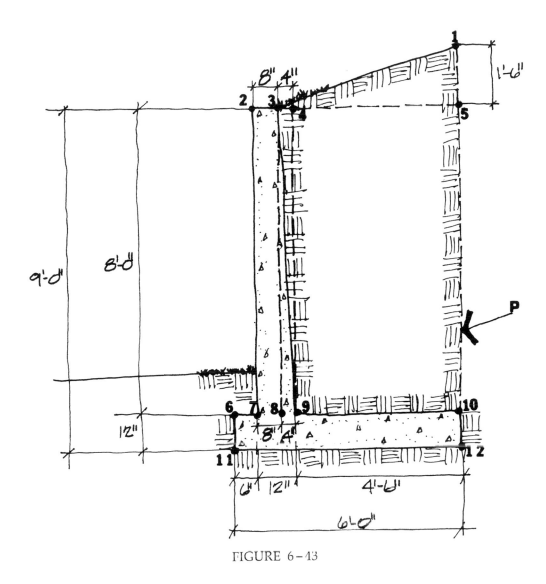

FIGURE 6-43

below grade will be sufficient to counteract the creep. A key can also be added to further resist creeping.

Retaining Walls with a Surcharge

To conclude the section on retaining walls, let's work through the investigation process one more time using a cantilever retaining wall section assuming a 3:1 slope on the soil behind the wall as illustrated in Figure 6-43.

As in the previous examples, the weights, moment arms, and moments were calculated and tabulated as shown in Table 6-8. This information will be used to locate the vertical axis of the section which is the line

TABLE 6-8

SECTION DESIGNATION	MATERIAL WEIGHT (LB)	MOMENT ARM (FT)	MOMENT
6,10,11,12	1 × 6 × 1 × 150 = 900	.5 × 6 = 3	900 × 3 = 2700
2,3,7,8	.67 × 8 × 1 × 150 = 804	.5 + .33 = .83	804 × .83 = 667.3
3,8,9	.33 × 4 × 1 × 150 = 198	.5 + .67 + .11 = 1.28	198 × 1.28 = 253.4
3,4,9	.33 × 4 × 1 × 100 = 132	.5 + .67 + .22 = 1.39	132 × 1.39 = 183.5
4,5,9,10	4.5 × 8 × 1 × 100 = 3600	1.5 + 2.25 = 3.75	3600 × 3.75 = 13500
1,4,5	2.25 × 1.5 × 1 × 100 = 337.5	1.5 + 3 = 4.5	337.5 × 4.5 = 1518.75
	Total weight 5,971.5 lb		Total moments 18,822.95 ft-lb

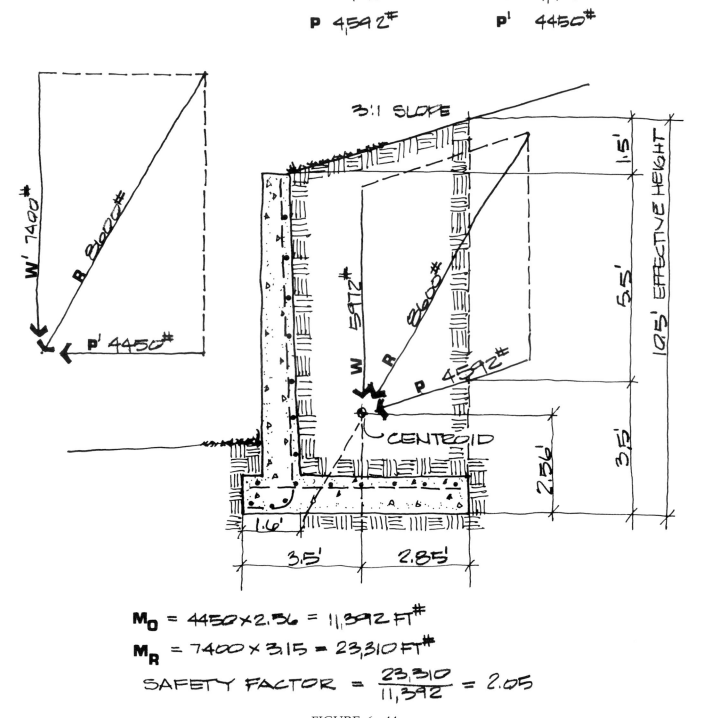

$$M_O = 4450 \times 2.56 = 11,392 \text{ FT}^\#$$

$$M_R = 7400 \times 3.15 = 23,310 \text{ FT}^\#$$

$$\text{SAFETY FACTOR} = \frac{23,310}{11,392} = 2.05$$

FIGURE 6–44

of action for W. This is found by letting the moment arm equal X and we find

$$5,971.5\, X = 18,822.95$$

$$X = \frac{18,822.95}{5,971.5}$$

$$X = 3.15 \text{ ft}$$

Thus, the vertical axis lies 3.15 ft from the left edge of the footing (see Figure 6–44). Next, P is calculated using the formula for cantilever walls with a surcharge

$$P = .833 \frac{W\,(h + h')^2}{2}$$

$$P = .833 \left(\frac{100\,(9 + 1.5)^2}{2} \right)$$

CONCRETE AND MASONRY DESIGN   229

$$P = .833 \left(\frac{11025}{2}\right)$$
$$P = .833 \times 5512.5$$
$$P = 4592 \text{ lb}$$

With this information known, the force parallelograms are constructed to find the resultant force and the equivalent horizontal and vertical components of that resultant as illustrated in Figure 6–44.

There are several things that should be noted with regard to a surcharged wall. First, remember that the thrust, P, acts parallel to the surface of the retained soil at $1/3$ of the effective height of the wall. In this case, the actual height of the wall is 9 ft, but with the surcharge, the effective height is increased by 1.5 ft to 10.5 ft.

Next, notice that when the force parallelogram is constructed, and the resultant is extended throughout the centroid to the base of the footing, it falls outside the middle third. This is no cause for alarm. This is quite a common occurrence for cantilever walls, and the sections have been designed to withstand the tensile stresses that develop in the footing. This can be seen by noting the placement of the steel reinforcement. In the beam portion of the wall, the vertical portion, the steel is placed to the right near the retained soil. In the footing the steel is in the top of the footing to the right and in both the top and bottom to the left.

Lastly, observe that the overturning moment arm is shorter than it would be if the thrust was acting horizontally. This shortening occurs when the resultant is extended to the centroid of the section as illustrated. From the force parallelogram in Figure 6–44 (b) we find that

$$M_o = 4450 \times 2.56 = 11,392 \text{ ft-lb}$$
$$M_r = 7400 \times 3.15 = 23,310 \text{ ft-lb}$$

Since a safety factor of 1.5 is required, we can divide M_r by M_o and find $23,310 \div 11,392 = 2.05$, which is satisfactory.

Next, calculate the bearing pressure on the soil. The greatest pressure is on the left-hand side of the footing and since it is outside the middle third, the pressure will be greater than twice the average unit stress. To find the actual load we use the expression

$$f_A = \frac{W'}{3\frac{d}{2}}$$

where

f_A = the bearing pressure at the loaded side of the footing;
W' = the vertical load equivalent of the resultant;
d = the cross-sectional width of the slab. Note that the length has been omitted from the expression since we are only dealing with a typical 1 ft length of the wall.

Thus

$$f_A = 2\left(\frac{W'}{3\frac{d}{2}}\right)$$
$$f_A = 2\left(\frac{7400}{3\left(\frac{6}{2}\right)}\right)$$
$$f_A = 2\left(\frac{7400}{9}\right)$$
$$f_A = 2 \times 822.22$$
$$f_A = 1644.44 \text{ lb/ft}^2$$

Next, the safety factor is checked by dividing the permissible soil bearing pressure by the calculated load as follows. Assume a 3,000 lb/ft² allowable load.

$$\frac{3000}{1644.44} = 1.82 \text{ lb/ft}^2$$

Since a factor of 1.5 is satisfactory this is within acceptable limits.

Finally, the resistance to creep is calculated. Assume a soil friction coefficient of .60, and find

$$7400 \times .60 = 4440 \text{ lb}$$

The thrust is 4440 lb which would put this outside acceptable limits. But once again, since the wall is below grade the soil in front of the wall will be sufficient to resist any sliding movement.

Keep in mind that all of our discussions regarding the construction of walls has revolved around the use of accepted construction practices. Walls, fences, and retaining walls of moderate height pose no real structural problems if good practices are followed in detailing the work. In the event that some unusual design situations occur that require complex cross sections not covered in a reliable reference manual, then it is best to have the section evaluated by a competent structural engineer. Also keep in mind that investigations of stability are only as reliable as the data they are based on. Always use local data or preferably site specific information if its is available.

PROBLEMS

1. A 6 foot brick masonry wall 10 in thick rests on a 24 in × 8 in footing; the top of the footing is 4 in below grade. If the wall should be designed for a 30 lb/ft² wind load, will the wall be stable? Soil bearing pressure can be taken as 3,500 lb/ft².

2. What is the maximum spacing for piers in a wall that is freestanding for 50 ft and 8 in thick and must sustain a wind load of 30 lb/ft²?

3. What is the lateral pressure on a 7 ft concrete gravity retaining wall with a 14 ft² section? (No surcharge.)

4. What would the lateral pressure be if the wall in Problem 3 had a surcharge?

5. Check the following wall in Figure P6−1 for overturning stability and settling stability. Soil bearing pressure is 4,000 lb/ft².

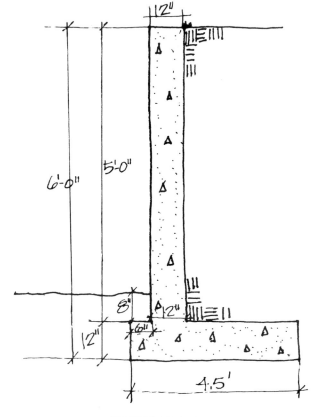

FIGURE P6−1

UNIT III

SPECIAL SYSTEMS

7
Irrigation Design

Irrigation systems have become an increasingly large part of landscape construction budgets. For example, in the case of a golf course it may actually be half the total cost of a golf hole, depending on the sophistication of the system.

Irrigation equipment was originally developed for agricultural purposes and was later applied to residential and commercial projects. Today equipment is available for practically every conceivable job. Each year new equipment is put on the market to do a more efficient job and meet special needs. For this reason it is difficult to discuss irrigation design in specific terms without quickly being dated, especially where equipment is concerned.

Our purpose in this chapter then will be to briefly acquaint you with the agronomic principals of irrigation, and look at a broad classification of equipment and how it can be applied to meet general irrigation needs. It is not possible in a text of this scope to discuss many of the fine points of design since each project will pose different problems. If the problems are carefully thought out in the design, an irrigation system can be an indispensable maintenance tool; but if the system is just thrown together by rule of thumb it will be a useless, expensive, time consuming maintenance headache.

AGRONOMIC PRINCIPLES OF IRRIGATION

When we are discussing irrigation we are usually most concerned with the maintenance of turf area. Large commercial jobs will require irrigation for shrub areas as will residential work, but this is a far less demanding task than designing for turf irrigation. For this reason most of our discussion throughout this chapter is in reference to the maintenance of turf grasses only. However, some consideration will be given to the irrigation of other plant materials in the sections on equipment and design. The objective of any irrigation system is to supply water in usable amounts to the root zone of the plant. To accomplish this it is necessary to consider the soil conditions and the growth characteristics of the turf grass.

Soil Characteristics

Soil has two characteristics of primary importance to the irrigation designer: infiltration rate and field capacity. Infiltration rate refers to the amount of water that can be absorbed by a soil in one hour. The field capacity refers to the volume of water a soil will hold after the natural force of gravity has drained off the excess moisture. Infiltration is measured in inches per hour and field capacity is given in inches.

The infiltration characteristics of a soil depend on the density of the soil and the slope of the surface. Typically sandy soils will have high infiltration rates ranging from .5 in/hr to greater than 3 in/hr. Clay soils will have much lower rates usually from .25 in/hr to being almost impervious. Likewise as the surface slope of a soil increases the surface runoff increases. This has the effect of further reducing the infiltration rate of the soil (see Table 7–1).

TABLE 7–1
Maximum Infiltration Rates for Slope and Soil Type

SLOPE	SANDY SOIL	MEDIUM SOIL	HEAVY SOIL
0–5%	.75 in/hr	.50 in/hr	.25 in/hr
6–8%	.60 in/hr	.40 in/hr	.20 in/hr
9–12%	.55 in/hr	.30 in/hr	.17 in/hr
13–20%	.35 in/hr	.20 in/hr	.10 in/hr
over 20%	.25 in/hr	.15 in/hr	.07 in/hr

Source: Adapted from *Sprinkler Irrigation Handbook*, Crawford Reid, Editor, Rainbird, Glendora, Calif., 1961.

233

Field capacity varies widely from soil to soil depending on its composition and organic content. Of most concern to the irrigation designer is the soil capacity in the top 6 inches, which is the primary root zone. Some approximate values of field capacity for the top 6 inches of depth are sand, .4 in; silt, .9 in; clay, 1.4 in. These values are only estimates and should not be used in lieu of actual field tests.

Even though a soil has a storage capacity of between ¼ to 3 in, all of this water is not available to a plant. For an average soil only about 5–10% of the water volume is available. Once the plant removes the available water it will wilt. Then, if the stress continues and the soil is allowed to dry too much a plant will reach a permanent wilting point and die.

Plant Characteristics

The plant species to be irrigated must be evaluated to determine the amount of water necessary to sustain it during peak growth periods. Water demand is measured by the evapo-transpiration rate of the species. This is the amount of water given up by a plant as a result of normal evaporation and transpiration of the plant. These values will vary a great deal from region to region and can usually be obtained from the county agent or the state extension service.

From this discussion you can see that the designer has some major agronomic questions that must be answered before you are ready to move to the drawing board. The basic questions that must be answered are:

How fast can the water be applied?
This is determined by the infiltration rate of the soil.
How much water needs to be applied?
This depends on the evapo-transpiration rate of the grass species.
How often must water be applied?
This is determined by the field capacity of the soil and the percentage of available moisture.

The answers to these questions will directly determine the type of equipment that should be used and the kind of system. To illustrate how this is applied lets consider a sandy 100-acre park site in Florida that will have a primary turf cover of Bermuda grass.

First we look at infiltration and find that the soil will take .75 in/hr in the lab. But the site has an average slope of 6% so we would reduce the estimated infiltration rate to .60 in/hr in accordance with Table 7–1.

Next we look at the peak evapo-transpiration rate for Bermuda grass in Florida and find that Bermuda has a peak rate of .3 in/day or 2.1 in/week. Thus the system should be designed to provide at least 2.1 in/week even though this will only be required about three months a year.

Finally, we need to determine the frequency of watering. To do this go to Table 7–2 and find that sandy soils will store about .4 in. This means at peak periods we will have to water the whole park everyday to keep the water supply up. If the soil has been clay it would have only been necessary to water every fourth day.

To summarize then, we will want a system that applies water at about .60 in/hr capable of applying at least 2.1 in a week with daily watering. Since such frequent watering is required we would also be wise to consider some type of remote control system as well to reduce the labor required for watering such a large area.

IRRIGATION EQUIPMENT

Irrigation equipment can be broken into six major parts: heads, valves, control devices, pipe, fittings, and pumps. These are the basic parts required to operate most all contemporary irrigation systems. As mentioned in the introduction it is impossible in a text of this kind to cover these materials in depth without becoming dated. So our description of each category will be limited to general characteristics rather than specific performance.

Irrigation Heads

Irrigation heads are the components of the system that distribute the water to the ground. It is comprised of two essential parts: a nozzle and a body. Irrigation heads are classified by their purpose, performance, and the distribution pattern. The purpose classifications are shrub or turf. The performance classifications have to do with how the head oper-

TABLE 7–2
Water Storage Characteristics of Soils

	FIELD CAPACITY (%)	WILTING POINT (%)	AVAILABLE WATER (%)	WATER STORAGE PER 6 IN DEPTH
Sand	8	3	5	0.4 in
Loam	20	10	10	0.9 in
Clay	30	15	15	1.4 in

ates. The distribution classification describes the pattern sprinkled by the head.

Spray Heads

This is the simplest irrigation head. It has only a body and a nozzle, set to spray a fixed area. The patterns available range from square and narrow strip to standard full and part circle patterns. They are relatively inexpensive and have a wide application in all types of irrigation work.

Pop-Up Spray Heads

This is a variation of the spray head. The nozzle is the same but it has been mounted in a body with a riser that will pop up above the ground surface when the water is on. The advantage is that it puts the nozzle above long grass that might interfere with the water distribution. When the water is off it drops flush with the surface again to allow mowing. The major problem with these heads is that some models are frequently clogged by trash that keeps the riser up, and the nozzles are sometimes damaged by people and equipment.

Rotary Heads

Rotary heads have a single nozzle or set of nozzles that rotate to distribute water over an area. The heads come either full or part circle and have application on the smallest residential job to the heaviest agricultural task. There are four common systems used to achieve the rotation: jet action, impact drive, friction drive, and gear drive. The jet action is the simplest. It utilizes the force of the water leaving the nozzle to affect the rotation. The impact drive uses a weighted arm and a spring, the arm overlaps the stream coming from the nozzel and is knocked away then brought back by the spring. The centrifugal force generated by this arm causes the head to rotate. The friction drive head utilizes the water pressure coming into the head directing it against a ball or cam attached to the nozzle shaft. The friction of the water passing the drive mechanism causes the head to rotate. The gear-driven head uses the incoming water to drive an impeller or stator. The energy is then transferred by gears to rotate the nozzle. These various types of rotary heads are illustrated in Figure 7–1.

Rotary Pop-Up Heads

The rotary pop-up is the same as the fixed spray pop-up. It's simply a rotary head of some type that is on a traveling riser that lifts the head out of the body when the water is on. This is probably the most popular head in use today because it is best suited for larger automated irrigation systems.

Specialty Heads

There are two other heads used in special situations that should also be mentioned here, the stream spray head and the bubbler. The stream spray is similar to the fixed spray but it distributes the water in a series of small streams. It is less susceptible to wind influence, requires less pressure and less water. It's not a good head for turf applications, however, since the coverage is less uniform. The bubbler is used to flood areas, like flower beds, where water contact with the foliage is not desirable.

Valves

A valve is any device in the system that is used to control the flow of water in the system. Figure 7–2 illustrates many of the types of valves used in irrigation systems. For most types of irrigation work there are three broad types of valves that you must be familiar with: manual-flow control valves, remote-control valves, and valves for directional flow control.

Manual Valves

Manual valves are used in all systems to control the water supply and shut portions of the system down for maintenance. They can also be used to operate a system with fixed or moveable heads in lieu of remote control valves. Basically there are three kinds of manual valves. globe valves, gate valves, and quick-coupling valves. Globe valves are popular in irrigation work because they are easy to repair and can be used effectively to regulate pressure and flow. Gate valves are a little cheaper than globe valves, but the seats or wedges in the valve are difficult to maintain if there is sand or grit in the water. Some newer gate valves do have removable seats however, which substantially removes the maintenance objections. The quick-coupling valve is used for access to systems under pressure at all times. The main purpose of the quick-coupling valve is for manual irrigation systems that use movable heads. This type of system was very popular in the late forties and fifties but is seldom used today with the development of the rotary pop-up head.

Remote-Control Valves

Remote-control valves are used with automated irrigation systems to turn the water on and off from a central control point. Remote control valves are operated either electrically or hydraulically.

The electrically operated valve uses electricity to open the valve and keep it open during the running period. It is referred to as a normally closed type valve, because if the power source is removed the valve will remain closed.

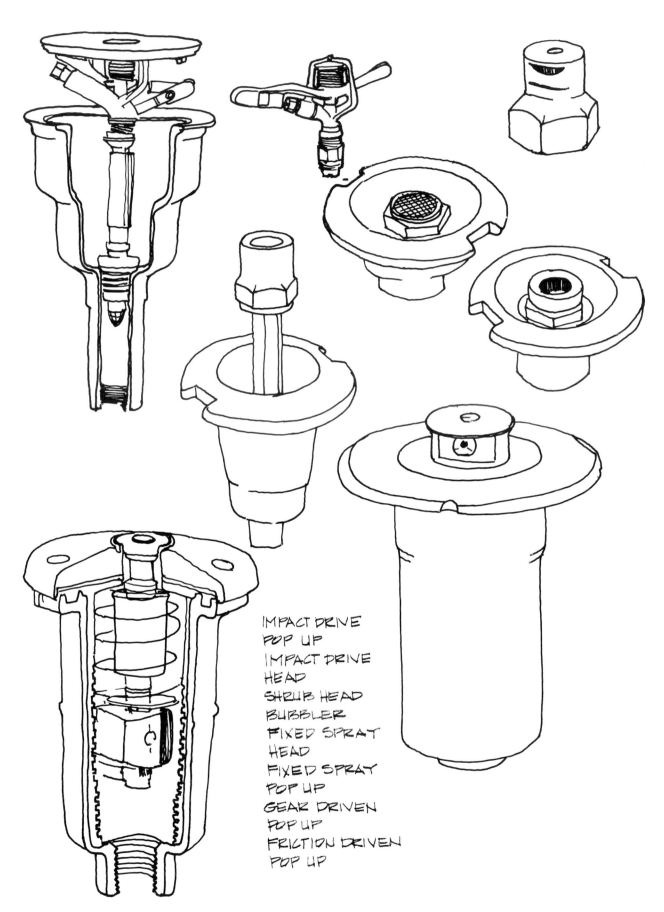

IMPACT DRIVE
POP UP
IMPACT DRIVE
HEAD
SHRUB HEAD
BUBBLER
FIXED SPRAY
HEAD
FIXED SPRAY
POP UP
GEAR DRIVEN
POP UP
FRICTION DRIVEN
POP UP

FIGURE 7-1

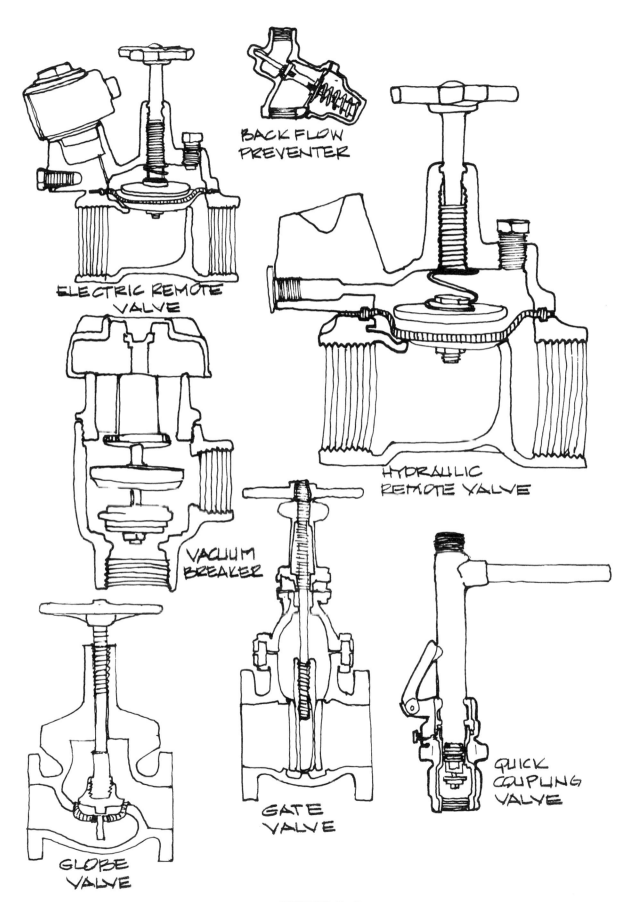

ELECTRIC REMOTE
VALVE

BACK FLOW
PREVENTER

HYDRAULIC
REMOTE VALVE

VACUUM
BREAKER

GLOBE
VALVE

GATE
VALVE

QUICK
COUPLING
VALVE

FIGURE 7-2

237

Hydraulically operated valves rely on a separate water source to close the valve. To open the valve the water pressure to the valve is shut off. Thus, a hydraulically operated valve is called a normally open valve. In other words, when the power source is removed the valve will be open.

The merits of using either the normally open or normally closed valve are largely tied to the design of the system, the soil type, and water condition. Hydraulic valves do have some advantages on large systems like golf courses, whereas the electric valve is usually preferred for more compact or complicated work. Beyond this it is a matter of designer preference.

Direction-Control Valves

Direction-control valves are used to keep water from moving the wrong way in a pipe. There are two types that the irrigation designer uses frequently: the check valve and the atmospheric vacuum breaker.

The check valve is used to prevent portions of a system from draining when the water pressure is removed. There are two reasons for this. First, when heads occur in low places they will continue to drain all the uphill lines generating an undesirable wet spot at the head. Second, if the pipes are allowed to drain when the system is pressurized again, high surge pressure results that can damage the pipe and heads.

Atmospheric vacuum breakers are back-flow prevention devices that prevent contamination of potable water systems. Vacuum breakers are usually required anytime an irrigation system is connected to a potable water supply. The vacuum break is placed at the beginning of a system and must be set 6 in above the elevation of the highest head in the system. The valve will close automatically anytime that the pressure in the supply line drops below normal atmospheric pressure. This prevents contaminated water from being siphoned into the potable water system.

This is a very brief description of valves and by no means covers all of the available equipment. There are valves for all sorts of things such as pressure regulation, flow regulation, pressure relief, velocity control, and so on. Many of these valves have application in irrigation work, but primarily on very large sophisticated systems.

Controllers

Controllers are clock devices used to operate remote-control valves. They can be as simple as a mechanical clock used to operate a single valve or as sophisticated as a computerized system that uses moisture sensors called tensiometers. The primary considerations in selecting a controller are the valves, the number of valves controlled, and the required sophistication of the system.

Controllers are usually designed to be used with the valves manufactured or marketed by the equipment manufacturer. This should always be considered in the initial development of the design. If valves and controllers are mixed, be sure the equipment is compatible. Many controllers will operate only a single valve per control station. This can be a disadvantage on large systems where it might be desirable to operate several valves at one time. This is a very common problem with controllers that operate electric normally closed valves.

Most residential and commercial work will not require a great deal of sophistication in the control system. Usually as long as the system provides for manual operation and control of the watering time over a reasonable range, it is satisfactory. However, where highly manicured conditions are desired, as in the case of a golf course, flexibility becomes very important. Controllers in these situations should be evaluated in light of their application to the overall maintenance program of the facility. One word of caution here: sophisticated equipment is only as good as the people who operate and maintain it. The best equipment can prove no good at all if the personnel using it do not know what they are about. Some typical controllers are illustrated in Figure 7–3.

Pipe

Today pipe is not the problem that it used to be because polyvinyl chloride (PVC) pipe has been much improved and widely accepted by the irrigation industry. In years gone by, all sorts of pipe were used for irrigation work. Even today you will find systems using cast iron, copper, galvanized steel, asbestos-cement, or some combination of these. In some cases one of the other materials may be justified, but for most work some type of PVC pipe will be the best choice.

Determining what type of PVC pipe to use is quite another matter. Much of the confusion over what kind of pipe to use is the misunderstanding caused by the PVC pipe classification system. PVC pipe will always have a code, such as PVC 1120. Then it will either have a designated class, such as class 160, or a schedule, usually schedule 40 or schedule 80.

The code is made up of four elements: the materials, the type of compound, the grade of the compound, and the designed stress of the material. Therefore, the code (PVC) (1) (1) (20) is translated to: PVC material, type 1 compound, grade 1 compound, and a design stress of 2,000 lb. This design stress should not be confused with working pressure; it refers to the material strength only.

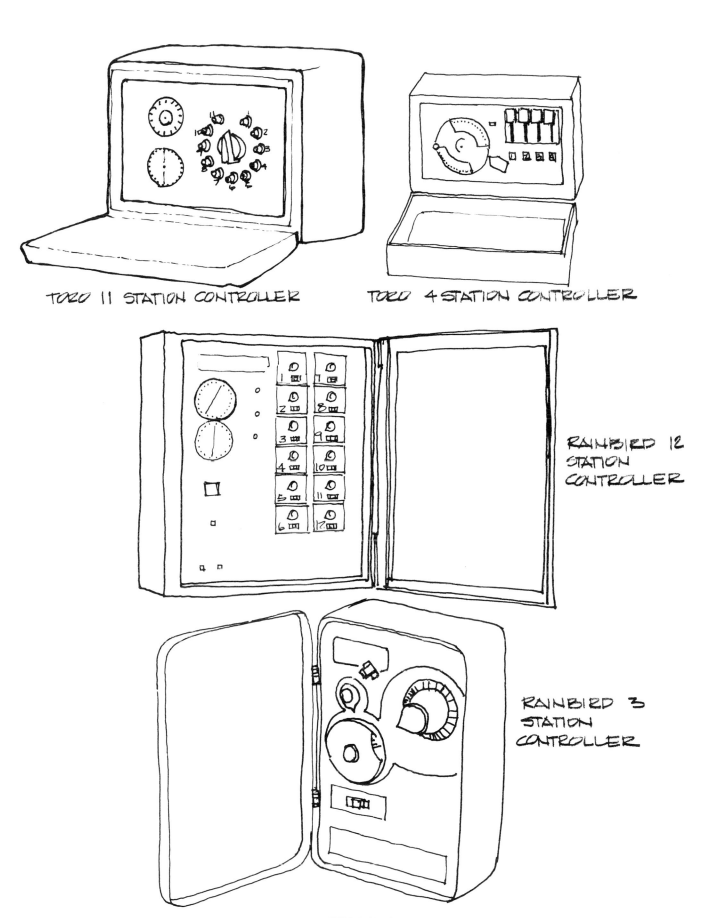

TORO II STATION CONTROLLER

TORO 4 STATION CONTROLLER

RAINBIRD 12
STATION
CONTROLLER

RAINBIRD 3
STATION
CONTROLLER

FIGURE 7-3

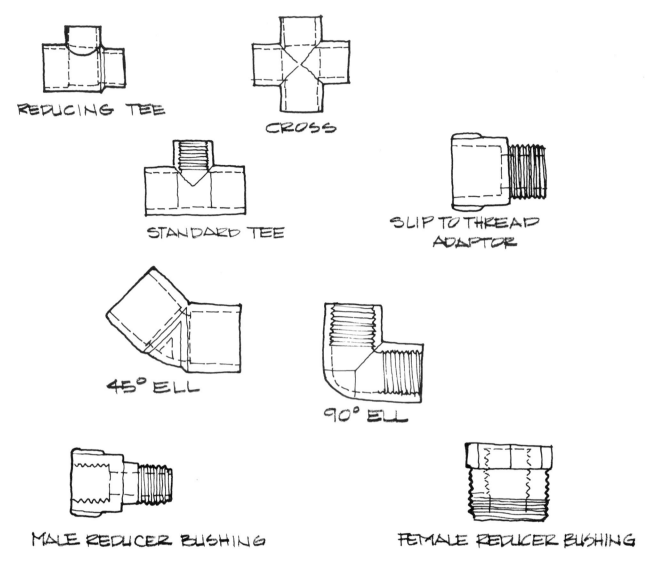

REDUCING TEE

CROSS

STANDARD TEE

SLIP TO THREAD ADAPTOR

45° ELL

90° ELL

MALE REDUCER BUSHING

FEMALE REDUCER BUSHING

FIGURE 7-4

Class is the recommended working pressure of the pipe. So if a PVC pipe is designated as class 160 it has a maximum recommended working pressure of 160 lb/in². The use of a class-rated pipe is in some ways preferable to a schedule-rated pipe because its operational limits are known. These limits have a design safety factor of 2 and allowance has been made for surge pressure in the pipe.

Schedule classification of a pipe refers to wall thickness. The pipe is usually heavier than the class-rated pipes but this does not mean that it necessarily has higher working pressures. The major advantage to heavy wall schedule 40 or schedule 80 pipe is its resistance to damage from sharp objects and abuse from heavy machinery. It can also be threaded and used with threaded pipe fittings.

PVC pipe is manufactured in standard iron pipe sizes (IPS). The IPS of a pipe is the nominal inside diameter (ID) of the pipe. For example, a ¾ in pipe

has an inside diameter not less than ¾ in. The actual ID of a pipe depends on the wall thickness. The outside diameter (OD) of a pipe is always the same regardless of the material. This facilitates joining pipes of different material schedules and class.

For most general irrigation work PVC 1120 or PVC 1220 is used because of the higher design stress. The compound grade has little significance unless used with caustic chemicals. Class 160 pipe is satisfactory for light residential work, but class 250 or schedule 40 is recommended for golf course, park, or commercial projects.

Fittings

Figure 7-4 illustrates many of the common fittings used to join plastic pipe. The important thing to remember with fittings used for plastic pipe is that the fittings must be made of the same material as the pipe if they are to be solvent welded.

Beyond the common fittings like the ell, tee, cross, and coupling, there are some other useful fittings that you should know. All of these are available in PVC and have frequent application in irrigation work.

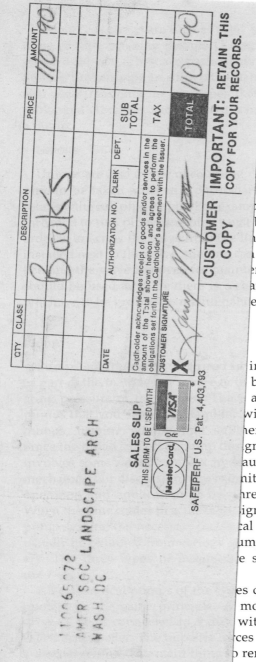

join two sec-
to achieve a
useful for re-
ns. They are
must sustain
rge pipe from

They allow the
place without
le, if a valve is
be removed in
e. If a union is
easily be bro-
nance. Unions
ance that a line
e reasons.

irrigation work
boost the oper-
are three basic
with: centrifugal
ersible pumps.
gn and selection
aulics as well as
nited to the basic
hree basic types.
ign and specify a
al assistance can
ump manufactur-
e shown in Fig-

es discussed here
motor or engine
with blades on it
ces the water into
remember about
that it has very lit-
tle suction capacity. It pushes fluid rather than using suction.

Centrifugal Pumps

The centrifugal pump is the simplest and least expensive of the pumps. The pump and motor are usually mounted together. Water is drawn from a surface reservoir through a short suction line or di-

rectly from a water supply line. They can be used on shallow wells if the lift required is not excessive, generally less than 14 ft. If there is no lift problem involved in obtaining the water, centrifugal pumps are the best all-around pumps.

Turbine Pumps

A turbine pump is actually submersed in the water supply and is connected to an above-ground power source by a long shaft. The turbine is an efficient answer to the lift problem encountered with deeper wells. Maintenance of the motor is still easy because it is above ground, but pump problems require pulling the pump out of the well. The major problem with a turbine pump is that they require a straight well shaft, which is sometimes difficult to achieve.

Submersible Pumps

The submersible pump is a single unit, motor and pump, that is submersed in the water source, connected only by the power cable. Its chief advantage is that it can be placed in a deep well and the shaft does not necessarily have to be straight. Submersible pumps are excellent pumps for jobs that require high water volumes from deep wells. The initial cost of a submersible pump is high and the maintenance cost is higher than for a centrifugal pump. However, since the whole pump unit is submerged in the well it is virtually vandal proof and will add measurably to the appearance of the job.

BASIC IRRIGATION HYDRAULICS

The primary concern of the irrigation designer from a hydraulic standpoint is to deliver a specified volume of water to an irrigation head at a given pressure and at an acceptable velocity. If the designer is to accomplish this goal it is necessary to have some knowledge of how water behaves in a pressurized system. First let's consider the hydraulic elements of concern to be sure they are completely understood.

Pressure

Water pressure is the result of either the application of mechanical energy to the water system or the gravitational force exerted on a column of water. Mechanical pressurization can be accomplished in two ways. First, a pump can be operated continuously to maintain pressure on the system. Second, a pump can be used to force water into an air-filled tank, compressing the air, which in turn pressurizes the system. This is called hydropneumatic pressure and it remains constant until some water is forced out of the system. Once the flow begins the pressure will continue to drop until the air is no longer compressed.

PUMPS FOR IRRIGATION

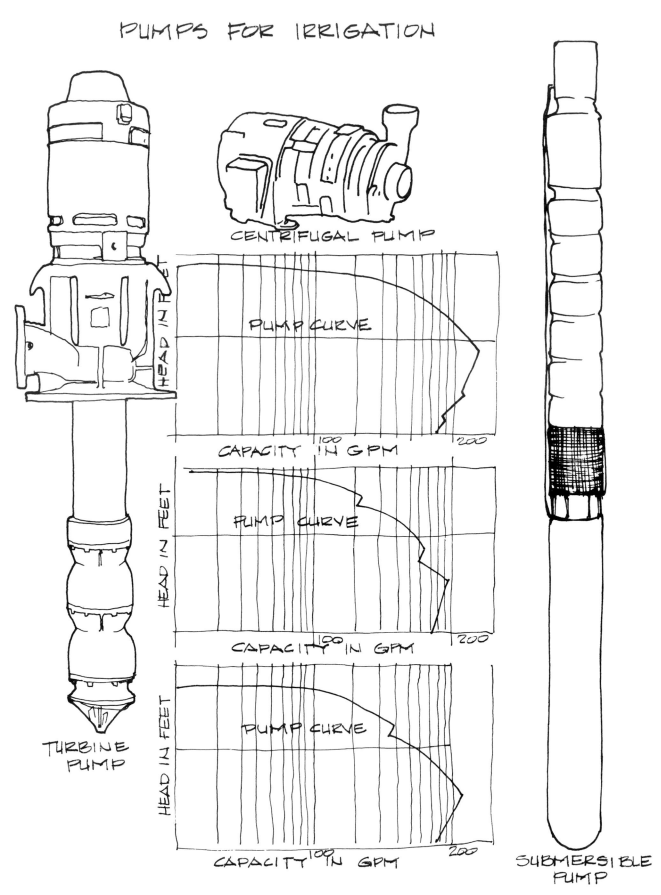

CENTRIFUGAL PUMP

PUMP CURVE

HEAD IN FEET

CAPACITY IN GPM   100   200

PUMP CURVE

HEAD IN FEET

CAPACITY IN GPM   100   200

PUMP CURVE

HEAD IN FEET

CAPACITY IN GPM   100   200

TURBINE PUMP

SUBMERSIBLE PUMP

FIGURE 7-5

242

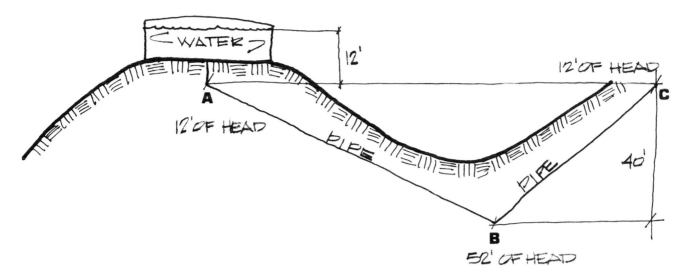

PRINCIPLE OF STATIC HEAD

FIGURE 7-6

Gravity pressure is generated by the gravitational force acting on a column of water above a specific point. Unlike mechanical pressure, gravity pressure will always be a factor in a system, and must be considered.

Pressure is measured in two ways: pounds per square inch (psi), and feet of head. For most pipe and irrigation equipment, pressure is given in psi. Pumps, on the other hand, are usually dimensioned in feet of head. A foot of head refers to the pressure exerted by a column of water 1 foot high. This is a force equal to .433 lb/in².

The real significance of this measure can be quickly illustrated by Figure 7-6. The pressure at point A caused by gravity is 12 ft of head because there is a 12 ft column of water above that point. The pressure at B is 52 ft and the pressure at C is 12 ft, the same as A. To convert these values to psi multiply by .433 as follows.

$$12 \times .433 = 5.20 \text{ psi}$$
$$52 \times .433 = 22.52 \text{ psi}$$

Water Volume

The standard volumetric measure for water is still in gallons for the United States irrigation industry. But since we are concerned with a working volume, water is measured in gallons per minute or gallons per hour delivered to a specific point. For most work, volume measures will be in gallons per minute (GPM). However, some small irrigation pumps will give data in gallons per hour (GPH). Care must be taken to be sure that all volume measures in the system are done in like units.

Velocity

Velocity of travel is a concern in a pressure system just as it is in a gravity system. Several bad things can happen when velocities in a pressure system are high. For example, extreme velocities can cause pipe ruptures, head damage, and inefficient operation of the system. The reason for this is surge pressure or water hammer. A moving stream of water that strikes an object tends to bounce backward. This tendency sets up shock waves that will continue until the energy is dissipated or the driving force is removed. The magnitude of the shock waves increases markedly with an increase in water velocity. Velocity can be calculated by the expression

$$V = \frac{.408 \, q}{D^2}$$

where

V = velocity in feet per second;
q = gallons per minute;
D = diameter of the pipe (ID nominal).

Pressure Loss

When water moves in a closed system the energy causing the motion will be dissipated by the friction between the pipe and the water. The actual amount of pressure loss depends on the water volume, the pipe size, and the roughness of the pipe's surface. This relationship is expressed in the Hazen and Williams formula

$$f = .2083 \frac{(100)^{1.85}}{c} \left(\frac{q^{1.85}}{d^{4.865}} \right)$$

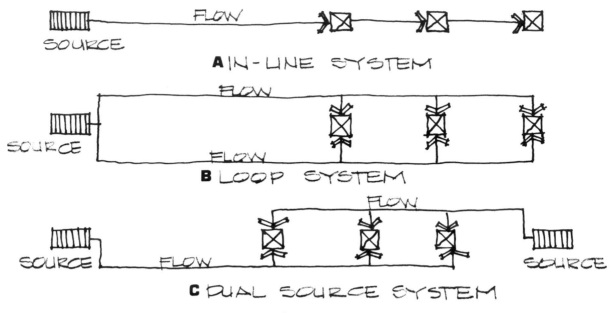

FIGURE 7-7

where

f = friction loss in feet per 100 ft of pipe;
q = water volume in gallons per minute;
d = inside pipe diameter;
c = friction coefficient of the pipe material.

Use of this formula would be cumbersome in figuring friction loss in a system, to say the least, so tables are available for estimating pressure losses in a system. The tables included here were developed by the Toro Company and are handy, since pressure loss is given in increments of 10 ft to 100 ft of pipe. This saves some time in converting from the 100 ft values to distances less than 100 ft. The tables included in this section will allow you to estimate the friction loss in almost any irrigation system. Tables have also been included for pressure loss in valves, fittings, water meters, and other equipment.

Limiting pressure loss to a reasonable figure is a key consideration in the design of a water distribution system. This is accomplished by first selecting a supply and distribution strategy and then selecting a pipe size that will carry the required water volume with a reasonable pressure loss.

Water Distribution Systems

A distribution system is made up of a water source, distribution lines, and demand points. The water source will be rated in terms of its volume capability, given in gallons per minute, and a static pressure value which may be expressed in pounds per square inch or feet of head. The demand points on the system will have a similar rating. The distribution strategy will be selected based on the source, balanced against the demand.

Essentially there are three distribution strategies that can be used: straight-line, loop, and dual source as illustrated in Figure 7-7. The straight-line strategy is most satisfactory for short distances and moderate demands. But the longer the run to the demand point, the greater the friction loss since the effect is cumulative. This means that the in-line strategy will usually require larger pipe.

The loop system has the advantage of providing two paths for the water to move from the source to demand. For example, assume a demand point that requires a supply of 40 gallons per minute (GPM). In the straight-line strategy, all of the 40 GPM must travel in the same line, but in the loop, each line going to the demand point will carry only half the total demand, or 20 GPM per line, as illustrated in Figure 7-8.

This accomplishes two things: It decreases the pipe size required to operate the system and also equalizes the pressure loss over the system. It does require more pipe and more money to install, but this disadvantage is usually overcome by the increase in efficiency.

The third distribution strategy, dual source, is essentially the same as a loop, in that water travels to the demand point from two directions. For the most part, this solution is not usually practical because additional water sources are expensive alternatives.

COMPUTATION OF PRESSURE LOSS AND PIPE SIZING

Total pressure loss in a system is an accumulation of all gains and losses caused by change in elevation

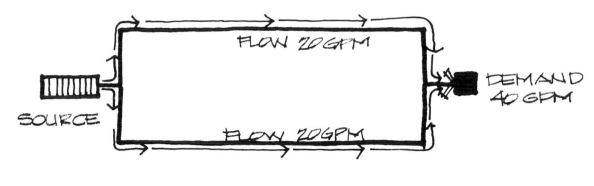

FLOW IN A LOOP SYSTEM

FIGURE 7-8

FIGURE 7-9

and friction loss in pipe, fittings, valves, and other appurtenances. They are usually made on a trial-and-error basis to ensure the most efficient operation of the whole system. The following example is a simple illustration of how pressure loss is determined. Consider Figure 7-9.

To determine the pressure loss, itemize the system elements that contribute to the total pressure loss for a volume of 20 GPM as follows:

water meter
gate valve
165 ft of pipe
1 90° ell

The water pressure loss for 20 GPM can be read directly from the Friction Loss Table on page 256 as 6.5 psi. The gate valve loss must be calculated using the table on page 261. Notice that the values for pressure loss in a gate valve are expressed as an equivalent length of galvanized steel pipe. Therefore, find that a 1½ in gate valve is equal to 1.1 ft of 1½ in galvanized pipe. At 20 GPM a 1½ in pipe loses 2.26 psi per 100 ft. The loss for 1 ft then is

$$\frac{2.26}{100} = .0226, \text{ and } 1.1 \times .0226 = .025 \text{ psi}$$

The pressure loss for the 165 ft of class 160 PVC pipe is found by simply adding the loss for 100 ft + 60 in + 5 ft as follows:

$$100 \text{ ft} = .70 \text{ psi}$$
$$60 \text{ ft} = .42 \text{ psi}$$
$$5 \text{ ft} = .04 \text{ psi}$$
$$\text{Total loss} = 1.16 \text{ psi}$$

The loss in the ell is equal to 3 ft of the same pipe or pressure loss per 100 ft = .70 psi.

$$\text{pressure loss per foot} = \frac{.70}{100} = .007 \text{ psi}$$
$$\text{the loss in the ell} = 3 \times .007 = .021 \text{ psi}$$

The total friction loss then is

1. Meter   6.500
2. Valve   .025
3. Pipe   1.160
4. Fitting   .021
   Total   7.706 psi

The pressure at the base of the head is

$$60 - 7.706 = 52.29 \text{ psi}$$

Now if we think about pressure loss characteristics for just a few minutes it becomes fairly obvious that we cannot expect to deliver water to a group of irrigation heads in the field and have the same pressure at each head. So what the designer usually tries to achieve is a balance. The usual goal is no more than a 10% difference in the operating pressure between

FIGURE 7–10

the first head and the last head on the line. For example, if a system has a residual pressure of 32.6 psi at the first head on the line, the last head should receive at least 29.3 psi. In other words, you could allow a maximum difference of 3.26 psi in that part of the system.

So far, the example we have been working with is an in-line system, typical of the service to a building. But, since the pressure equalization effect of a loop system is usually employed, if at all possible, let us take a look at pressure loss in a loop system. As mentioned previously, a loop system provides two routes of travel for the water from the source to demand point. To illustrate the advantage and effect of the loop consider Figure 7–10. The pressure loss for the meter, elevation and valves has already been figured as shown.

Since water will follow the path of least resistance, 37.5 GPM will be carried by each side of the loop. Note this will only be true if both sides of the loop are equal. This means the lines of the loop can be decreased in size since they are carrying less volume. Referring to the friction loss chart for SCH 40 galvanized pipe, there is no value for 37.5 GPM so it will be necessary to interpolate the values for actual friction loss between 35 GPM and 40 GPM. For the first trial, check the 2 in pipe as follows. The value for 37.5 GPM lies halfway between 35 and 40 GPM:

$$35\,\text{GPM} = 2.4\ \text{psi}/100\,\text{ft}$$
$$40\,\text{GPM} = 3.0\ \text{psi}/100\,\text{ft}$$

The total difference is .6 psi; therefore half of this (.3) added to 2.4 is the friction loss value: 2.4 + .3 = 2.7 psi.

The total run in the loop is 520 ft, so the pressure loss in a 2 in pipe is:

$$5.2 \times 2.7 = 10.40\ \text{psi}$$

This value is within the 14.34 psi loss that is permissible after the loss for the meter and valves are deducted. (See Figure 7–10.) The fact that the other 37.5 GPM loses 10.40 psi is not cumulative since each line of the loop delivers 37.5 GPM to the demand point at the same pressure as illustrated in Figure 7–11.

Pressure loss in top line equals

25.66	psi loss through meter value and elevation
+10.40	psi loss in top line
36.06	total pressure loss

This loss subtracted from the pressure at the source, 90 psi − 36.06 psi = 53.94 psi so the top line delivers 37.5 GPM at 53.94 psi.

Pressure loss in the bottom line equals

25.66	psi loss through meter value and elevation
+10.40	psi loss in lower pipe
36.06	total pressure loss

This loss subtracted from the pressure at the source, 90 psi − 36.06 psi = 53.94 psi so the bottom line delivers 37.5 GPM at the same pressure; therefore the loop delivers a total volume of 75 GPM at a pressure of 53.94 psi. Note that the pipe used in the loop is 1 in smaller than the pipe required to carry the total 75 GPM.

To carry this a step further, what would happen if the demand point was not equidistant from the supply? In this case the loop would simply carry a larger volume the shortest distance compensating for the difference in pressure loss. For example, consider Figure 7–12.

Notice that the long line carries less volume than the short line. Now computing the pressure loss in each line using 1½ in galvanized pipe we find

The Short Line
260 ft @ 24 GPM and a pressure loss of 3.17 psi/100 ft = 2.6 × 3.17 = 8.25 psi pressure loss
The Long Line
550 ft @ 16 GPM and a pressure loss of 1.50 psi/100 ft= 5.5 × 1.50 = 8.25 psi pressure loss

Thus, a loop will always equalize the pressure loss in all parts of the system. The same thing happens if two sources are used.

DESIGNING THE IRRIGATION SYSTEM

The design of an irrigation system takes place in three distinct steps. First the equipment must be se-

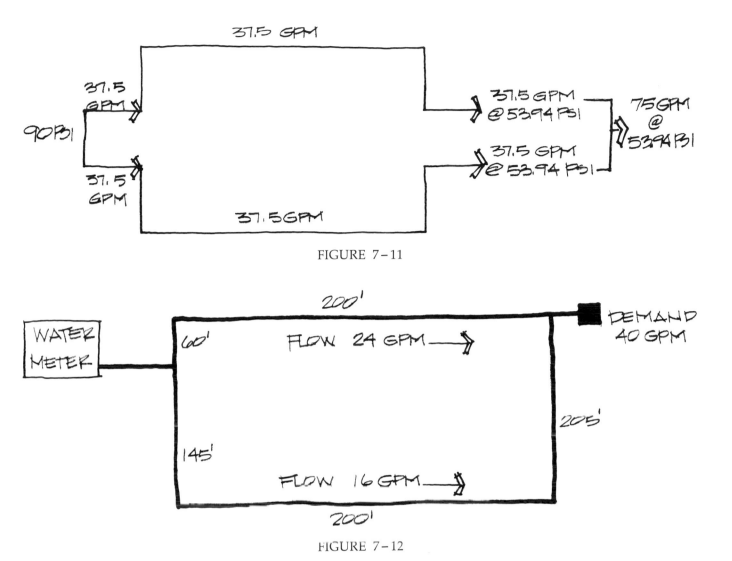

FIGURE 7-11

FIGURE 7-12

lected and laid out on the plan. Then the piping system is worked out. Finally the pipe is sized and the plan is completed. In this section we will work through each one of these steps for the same example. In each case we have tried to touch on most of the major issues, but this brief introduction cannot begin to cover all design problems.

When the time comes to design an irrigation system for a job you should contact several equipment suppliers. They will let you know what equipment is available and who will be able to handle the installation. Discuss the project with them because they generally will have the day-to-day contact with the problems of the area that should be taken into account.

Also contact people in the area to find out what kinds of problems they have had with their systems. Common things to look for are gritty or caustic water, problems with sandy or clayey soils, wind problems, poor installation, or high maintenance costs on equipment.

Equipment Selection and Layout

First consider Figure 7-13. The task is to design an irrigation system for a small professional building. The base sheet for the irrigation system should be prepared from the planting plan as shown.

The equipment should be selected in accordance with the agronomic principles discussed in the first part of this chapter. For example, we have assumed a sandy soil with a high infiltration rate (.96 in/hr). The turf will be Bermuda grass so we need a capacity of about 2 in per week to allow for peak evapo-transpiration rates. Finally the field capacity is low so we will have to water every day to keep up the water supply in the soil.

For this example we have elected to use Toro equipment to make the illustration more realistic. Equipment by other manufacturers would also do a satisfactory job. All of the equipment data was reproduced directly from the Toro 1977 catalog (see Toro Tables at end of chapter).

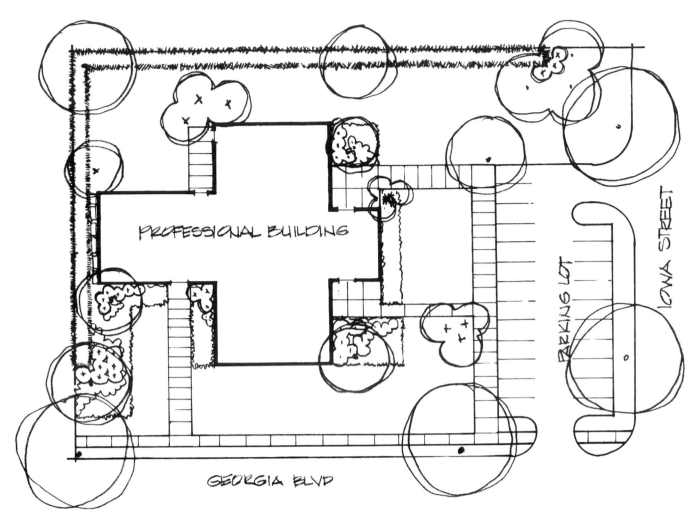

FIGURE 7–13

To cover the area in the example efficiently, we have selected heads of three different series: the 500 series, 590 series, and the 620 series. The 500 series will be used for small turf areas and for shrub beds (Table 7–3). The 590 series heads are brass and have a smaller radius. These were selected for their size and the durability of brass in extreme conditions like parkway strips (Table 7–4). The 620 series heads were selected for the large turf areas. This head is particularly good because it has a low water demand and a moderate pressure requirement (Table 7–5).

Next the spacing for each head was selected. For this we used the accepted rule of thumb spacing method set out in Table 7–6.

A quick glance at the plan and the catalog data seems to indicate that a square spacing will fit the plan easiest. Triangular spacing is more efficient when it will fit the plan but it only works in one place here as we will see later.

The spacings recommended by the manufacturer appear to be for about a 5 mph wind allowance. However, since we have some conflict with plants,

the closer spacing is preferred. Therefore, the 500 series heads were spaced 12 ft, the 590 series heads were spaced 10 ft and the 620 series heads were spaced 30 ft or closer.

Once the spacing was selected the precipitation rate was checked for each head to be sure it was not greater than the .60 design filtration rate of the soil. The precipitation of a head is estimated by the formula:

$$P = \frac{q\,96.3}{A}$$

where

P = the precipitation rate in in/hr;
A = area covered by the heads, which is the spacing;
q = head water demand in GPM.

The calculations were as follows.
The 500 series heads

q = 2 GPM
A = 12^2 = 144 ft²

TABLE 7-3
Series 500—Shrub Sprinklers.

ADJUSTABLE SHRUB SPRAY

MODEL NUMBER	SPACING† △	SPACING† □	G.P.M. AT 25 P.S.I.	RADIUS AT 25 P.S.I.	PATTERN	
510-10*	—	(6'x20')	1.3	4' x 28' PATTERN		STRIP
522-10	6'	5'	.4	4'		180°
531-10	12'	11'	.5	9'		90°
532-10	12'	(10'x12')	1.0	9' x 18' PATTERN		RECT.
534-10*	11'	10'	1.0	8'		360°
541-10	17'	15'	.7	12'		90°
542-10	17'	15'	1.0	12'		180°
544-10*	17'	15'	2.0	12'		360°

*Non adjustable nozzles

For shrub and ground cover areas where sprinkler is elevated

INLET — ½ " I. P. S. Thread
ADJUSTABLE RADIUS
SERVICEABLE SCREEN
MAXIMUM
WORKING PRESSURE — 50 P. S. I.

TABLE 7-4
590 Series—Brass Pop-Up Spray. 90°, 180°, 120°, 360°. 11'-21' Spacing.

APPLICATION- For use in special projects which require brass sprinklers.

MODEL NUMBER STANDARD	MODEL NUMBER HI-POP	SPACING† △	SPACING† □	P.S.I.	G.P.M.	RADIUS	PATTERN	
591-11	591-21	12'	11'	25	1.3	9'		90°
592-11	592-21	12'	11'	25	1.7	9'		180°
593-11	593-21	12'	11'	25	1.5	9'		120°
594-11	594-21	11'	10'	25	2.2	8'		360°
591-12	591-22	17'	15'	25	1.8	12'		90°
592-12	592-22	17'	15'	25	2.2	12'		100°
593-12	593-22	17'	15'	25	2.0	12'		120°
594-12	594-22	17'	15'	25	3.2	12'		360°
591-13	591-23	21'	18'	35	2.2	15'		90°
592-13	592-23	21'	18'	35	3.4	15'		180°
593-13	593-23	21'	18'	35	2.7	15'		120°
594-13	594-23	21'	18'	35	5.2	15'		360°

SPECIFICATIONS
INLET — ½ " I.P.S. Thread
HEIGHT — 2" on standard, 4" on hi-pop
POP-UP — 1" on standard, 2" on hi-pop
ADJUSTABLE RADIUS
MAXIMUM WORKING PRESSURE — 50 P.S.I.

Precipitation rate in pattern is approximately 2" per hour.

†Radius and spacings listed are maximum allowable under ideal conditions and make no allowance for wind, contours, etc.

TABLE 7-5
Series 620—Gear Driven Rotary. Full Circle and Adjustable Part Circle. 30'-45' Spacing.

360° COVERAGE

MODEL NUMBER	SPACING △	SPACING □	***P.S.I.	G.P.M.	RADIUS	PREC.* RATE
624-00-24	40'	35'	35	2.8	38'	.19
	45'	40'	50	3.0	43'	.17
624-00-25	40'	35'	35	4.3	38'	.30
	45'	40'	50	5.0	43'	.28
624-00-26	40'	35'	35	7.0	38'	.48
	45'	40'	50	9.0	43'	.49

ADJUSTABLE FROM 315°-45°

MODEL NUMBER	SPACING △	SPACING □	***P.S.I.	G.P.M.	RADIUS	PREC.* RATE
625-00-24	40'	35'	35	2.8	38'	.39**
	45'	40'	50	3.0	43'	.33**
625-00-25	40'	35'	35	4.3	38'	.59**
	45'	40'	50	5.0	43'	.55**
625-00-26	40'	35'	35	7.0	38'	.97**
	45'	40'	50	9.0	43'	.98**

†Spacing calculated to combat wind to 5 m.p.h. For 5 to 10 m.p.h., derate spacing using .77 factor.
*Precipitation rate is for triangular spacing shown, in inches per hour.

**Precipitation rate varies according to arc set. Figures are for 180° arc.
***Stream breaker screw must be used when operating at 35 P.S.I. to help distribution pattern.

TABLE 7–6
Recommended Head Spacing

WIND SPEED (mph)	□ SPACING	△ SPACING
0	.65D	.75D
5	.60D	.70D
10	.50D	.55D

$$P = \frac{q\ 96.3}{A} = \frac{2 \times 96.3}{144} = \frac{192.6}{144}$$
$$P = 1.33 \text{ in/hr}$$

The 590 series heads

$$q = 2.2 \text{ GPM}$$
$$A = 10^2 = 100 \text{ ft}^2$$
$$P = \frac{q\ 96.3}{A} = \frac{2.2 \times 96.3}{100} = \frac{211.86}{100}$$
$$P = 2.1 \text{ in/hr}$$

The 620 series heads

$$q = 5 \text{ GPM}$$
$$A = 30^2 = 900 \text{ ft}^2$$
$$P = \frac{q\ 96.3}{A} = \frac{5 \times 96.3}{900} = \frac{481.5}{900}$$
$$P = .54 \text{ in/hr}$$

Note the high precipitation rates of the small fixed spray heads. This is almost twice the infiltration rate of the soil which means that there is going to be a certain percentage of water wasted. The high precipitation rate of these small heads is typical of almost all irrigation equipment of this class. In the case of the 620 series head the precipitation rate is very good.

Once the equipment has been selected we proceed to lay out the head pattern. Probably the easiest way to do this is to prepare an overlay template on sketch paper. In this case we made a 10 ft grid, a 12 ft grid, and a 30 ft grid. The templates were moved around on each area to achieve the best possible fit. The fit is never going to be perfect, so as the designer you are going to have to judge what combinations are the best. One rule of thumb that will save a lot of future headaches is Never spread the pattern thin. You can cut a head's performance down much easier than it can be improved. An example of this is at the north property line (Figure 7–14) where the 620 heads are spaced closer than 30 ft.

The final head pattern selected was the result of several trial runs and appears to be as efficient as can be expected. In several places you will note conflicts caused by trees and other plants. The solution to these problems is usually best handled by getting the tree or group of trees inside the head pattern rather than at the edge.

For example in Figure 7–15 the system will oper-ate reasonably well because the pattern is compensated in all directions. In Figure 7–15 head A is almost completely blocked by the group of trees which will cause some problems.

Another criterion that is desirable but not always possible is to avoid throwing water on walks, roads, or against building walls. Buildings in particular should be avoided since the water may stain the finish, and the wall has not usually been properly waterproofed.

Piping the System

The design of an efficient piping system is built around several things: water supply pressure, operating pressure of the equipment, water volume available, and whether the system is to be operated manually or automated. How these considerations fit together is best illustrated by going directly to our example.

The first consideration is the water source itself. You need to know what volume is available and at what pressure. In our example we have a 1½ in water meter servicing the building. The supply has been checked and will deliver a maximum volume of 60 GPM at 65–82 psi. The reason for the pressure variation is the time of measurement. City water lines will always have a pressure fluctuation caused by demand at peak periods. Pressures at a meter should never be assumed in the design. They should always be checked. The methods used in the test are quite simple and reasonably accurate.

This information allows us to make some preliminary decisions regarding how the system can be piped. We know for example that the 620 series head is going to require 40 psi to operate. The 500 and 590 series are designed to operate at 25 psi. Based on the lowest pressure of 64 psi, which is pressure beyond the meter, we can encounter as much as a 24 psi drop in the delivery system and still operate the largest head. The excess pressure going to the smaller heads can be reduced by a manual valve, or it can be lost in the remote control valve. Also, we know that the maximum volume of water available is 60 GPM. This means the system will have to be divided into sections that have demands of less than 60 GPM.

We proceed by studying the plan and grouping the like heads together in a logical manner. It is best to group heads so that they are all performing in similar conditions. For example, the heads next to the house on the north side are not run with the ones to the east even though they are the same heads. This is because the spacing is different, as well as the pattern, which means they have different precipitation rates.

Figure 7–16 shows the nine different groupings selected and the gallonage requirements for each section. They are all less than 60 GPM so this is satisfac-

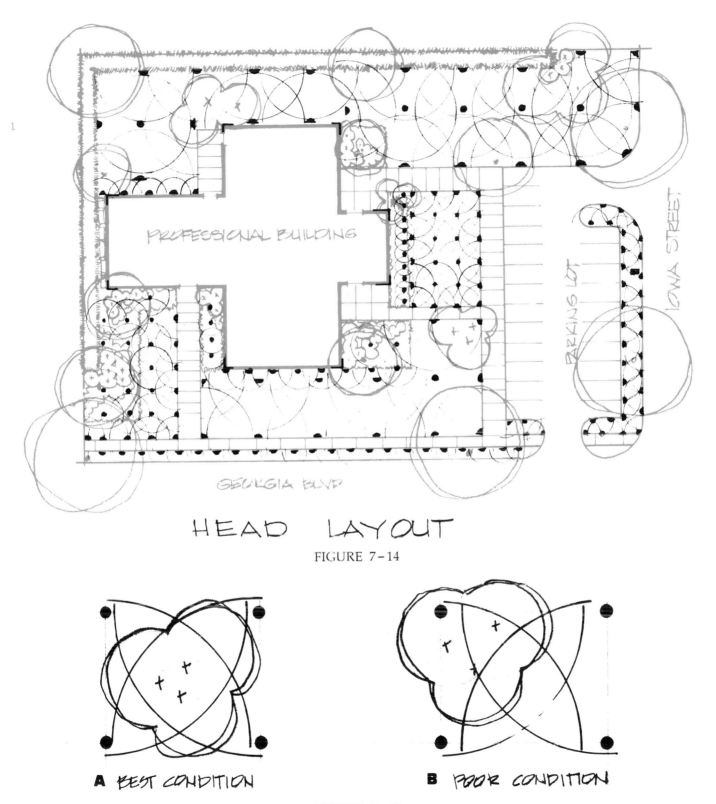

HEAD LAYOUT

FIGURE 7–14

A BEST CONDITION

B POOR CONDITION

FIGURE 7–15

tory. Gallonage demand is calculated by accumulating the GPM required to operate each head.

A word of caution here. You will notice that the water demand ranges from 51.7 GPM, on section 2, to 5 GPM on section 9. This is not a critical problem on this system. But had we been planning to use a pump and well system there would have been a problem with balancing demand. This can be a major efficiency problem on large jobs, but it can usually be handled in the design of the pump system.

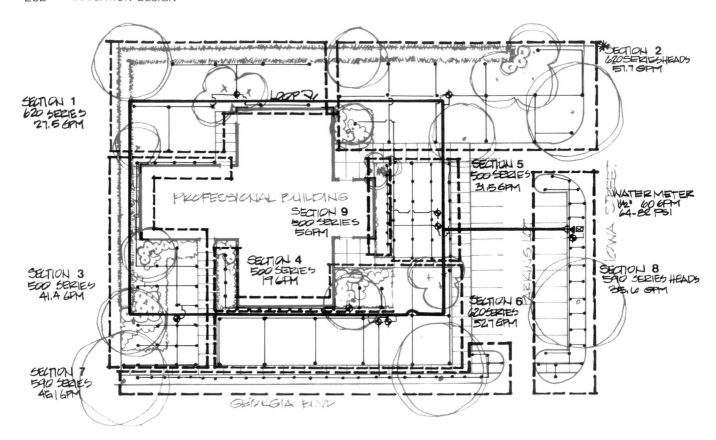

FIGURE 7-16

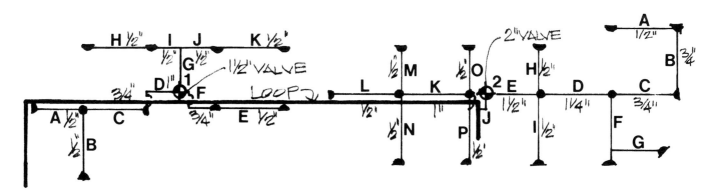

PIPING SCHEMATIC SECTIONS 1 & 2

FIGURE 7-17

Sizing the Pipe

This system is large enough to justify using a loop to distribute the water to each section, so the loop is located as shown. Then a service line is run from the meter. Next the loop and service lines are sized.

The usual method used to size a loop is to take the largest water volume required and increase it by about 10%. This allows for operational differences in the equipment. Then size the loop for ½ of the larg-

est volume (51.7 GPM) based on a length of pipe equal to ½ of the loop.

For example, the highest demand is 51.7 GPM. Adding 10% we have a volume of 55 GPM, and half of this is 27.5 GPM. Half of the loop is equal to 328 ft. So we will size the pipe to carry 27.5 GPM, 328 ft.

Looking at the class 200 PVC tables we find that 1 in pipe would exceed the velocity limits of about 6 ft/second desired. So 1¼ in pipe is the logical choice. Then the pressure loss in the loop is estimated as follows. 328 ft of 1¼ in pipe at a pressure loss of 2.62 lb/100 ft at a flow of 27.5 GPM is

$$3.28 \times 2.62 = 8.60 \text{ psi}$$

Therefore we will use a design value of 8.60 lb/in² as the loss of pressure in the loop. This is assumed as a constant loss anywhere in the loop. Next it is necessary to size the service line from the water meter to the loop. There is total distance of 80 ft and it will have to carry the maximum demand of 55 GPM. Again looking at the class 200 PVC table, we find that 2 in pipe at 55 GPM will lose 1.34 psi in a run of 80 ft. The velocity is less than 6 fps. Thus, 2 in will be satisfactory for the service line.

Now to facilitate sizing the pipe in the rest of the system accumulate the remaining pressure losses in the loop. This will yield the residual pressure available at the valve to each section. The calculations are tabulated here.

Tabulation of Pressure Loss for Loop and Service Line

PIPE OR FITTING DESCRIPTION	PRESSURE AT METER: 64 PSI (PRESSURE LOSS IN PSI)
1. 2 in atmospheric vacuum breaker valve	6.50
2. 2 in gate valve (estimated)	1.00
3. Unions and misc. fittings = 15 ft of 2 in pipe	0.25
4. Ells and tees in loop = 20 ft of 1¼ in pipe	0.64
5. 80 ft of 2 in pipe	1.34
6. Constant loss in loop	8.60
Total loss	18.33 psi

Thus: 64.00 − 18.33 = 45.67 psi residual pressure.

This means that the individual sections that require an operating pressure of 40 psi must be sized to limit pressure loss to a maximum value of 5.67 psi.

To demonstrate the procedure used to size the remaining pipe we will work through sizing the pipe for sections 1 and 2. Figure 7–17 is a schematic of sections 1 and 2 with each section of pipe designated by a letter. In section 1 notice that pipe sections ABCD form one independent section from the valve. EF are independent and so are GHIJK.

First size the valve. This is done using the total water demand then finding the pressure loss from manufacturer's data. For this problem we used Toro 206 series valves. The total gallonage required for section 1 is 27.7, but this should be increased to 30 GPM to allow for differences in operation of the heads. At 30 GPM a 1 in valve will lose 5 psi. This is a little high since we only had 5.67 psi to play with. So

we will use a 1½ in valve at a loss of 1.75 psi. Thus: 45.67 − 1.75 = 43.92 psi entering the section.

At this point the water splits and goes three directions: D carries 12.5 GPM, F carries 5 GPM, and G carries 10 GPM. First itemize A to F.

Section 1 A to D

DESCRIPTION	PRESSURE LOSS IN PSI
D. 20 ft, 1 in pipe @ 12.5 GPM	.37
C. 30 ft, ¾ in pipe @ 10 GPM	1.29
B and A. 30 ft, ½ in pipe @ 2.5 GPM	.22
Fittings. 5 ft of ½ in pipe @ 8 GPM	.49
Total loss	2.37 psi

43.92 − 2.37 = 41.55 psi at the last head.

Section 1 E to F

DESCRIPTION	PRESSURE LOSS (PSI)
F. 20 ft, ½ in pipe @ 5 GPM	.40
E. 30 ft, ½ in pipe @ 2.5 GPM	.33
Fittings. 3 ft, ½ in pipe @ 5 GPM	.15
Total loss	.88 psi

43.92 − .88 = 43.04 psi at last head.

Section 1 G to K

DESCRIPTION	PRESSURE LOSS (PSI)
G. 30 ft, ¾ in pipe @ 10 GPM	1.29
I and J. 15 ft, ½ in pipe @ 5 GPM	.60
H and K. 30 ft, ½ in pipe @ 2.5 GPM	.33
Fittings. 10 ft, ½ in pipe @ 5 GPM	.58
Total loss	2.80 psi

43.92 − 2.80 = 41.12 psi at last head.

The maximum difference in operating pressure is 2.80 which is 6.4% of 43.92. This is within the recommended 10% loss between the first and last head on the line. Section 1 is complete.

One point is worth further comment at this point. We used a 1½ in valve to minimize the pressure loss. This would be an expensive alternative if many valves were required. Here it is best, but when cost enters the picture it might be wise to minimize the constant loss in the loop by increasing its size. This same condition will occur in section 2.

Section 2 calculations are as follows. First, select the valve and find the residual pressure. The section 2 demand is 48.8 GPM or 50 GPM for design purposes. A 2 in valve will give a 1.7 psi loss at 55 GPM. The residual pressure is

$$45.67 - 1.7 = 43.97 \text{ psi entering the section.}$$

Once the valve is passed, the water splits into two

sections, A to I and L to P. The calculations are tabulated as follows:

Section 2 A to I

DESCRIPTION	PRESSURE LOSS (PSI)
E. 20 ft, 1½ in pipe @ 26.7 GPM	.29
D. 30 ft, 1¼ in pipe @ 16.7 GPM	.33
C. 30 ft, ¾ in pipe @ 6.7 GPM	.65
B. 30 ft, ¾ in pipe @ 4.2 GPM	.25
A. 30 ft, ½ in pipe @ 2.5 GPM	.33
Fittings. 15 ft, ¾ in pipe @ 10 GPM	.65
Total loss	2.5 psi

43.97 − 2.5 = 41.47 psi residual at last head.

Note that the pressure loss in pipes F, G and H, I are not included since they will not effect the overall operation.

Section 2 J to P

DESCRIPTION	PRESSURE LOSS (PSI)
L. 10 ft, 1¼ in pipe @ 25 GPM	.23
K. 30 ft, 1 in pipe @ 15 GPM	.27
J,O,P. 30 ft, ½ in pipe @ 2.5 GPM	.33
Fittings. 10 ft, ¾ in pipe @ 10 GPM	.43
Total loss	1.26 psi

43.97 − 1.26 = 42.71 psi residual at last heads.

For section 2 the maximum pressure loss is 2.5 psi, which is 5.7% of the entering pressure. Therefore, the section will operate within acceptable limits.

This same procedure is followed for the other sections and the final plan is drawn up as shown in Figure 7–18. Be sure that the plan is drawn accurately, indicating clearly how you intend the system to work. You will find that most irrigation work is laid out from the scale of the drawing rather than by using written dimensions. In cases where dimensions may be critical it is a good idea to go ahead and shown them on the plan.

Indicating the controller location on the plan and a note as to who will provide the power source is a necessity. Wires and control tubing are not shown. However, usually wire size and location will be called out in the specifications and installed in accordance with the manufacturer's recommendations.

Irrigation design is a subject that will require much more attention than this brief chapter, but if you become involved in a practice that requires irrigation design, a knowledge of these basic elements will help you get the job done. In the final analysis it will take experience to become proficient.

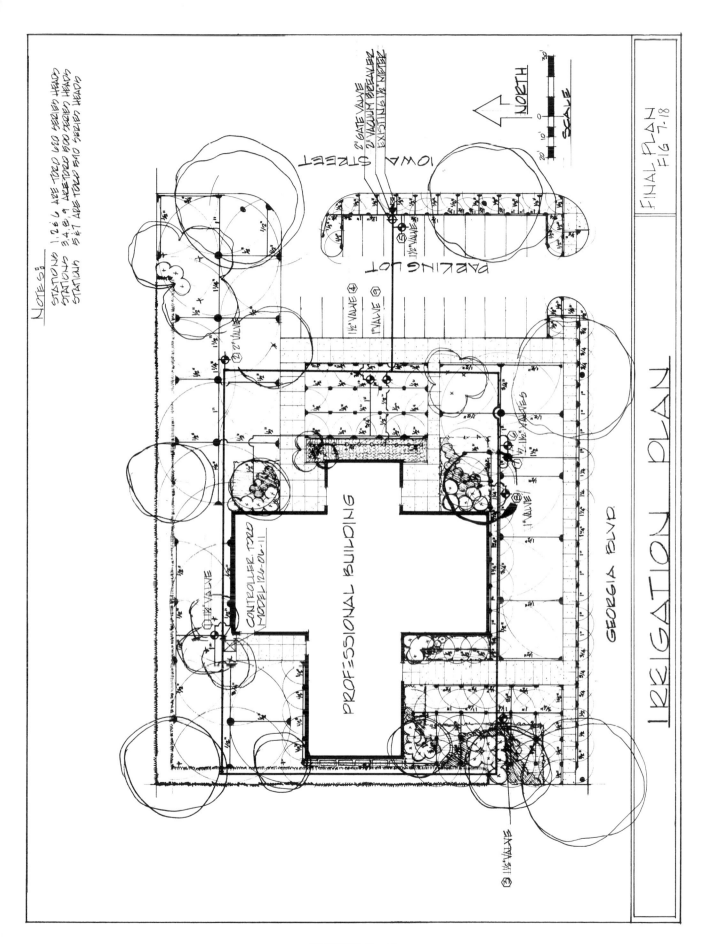

FIGURE 7–18

FRICTION LOSS TABLE
PVC 1120-1220 CLASS 160
P.S.I. LOSS PER PIPE LENGTH NOTED

1/2" — .720" I.D.

GPM	100	90	80	70	60	50	40	30	20	10	5	VEL.
1	.20	.18	.16	.14	.12	.10	.08	.06	.04	.02	.01	.8
2	.74	.67	.59	.52	.44	.37	.30	.22	.15	.07	.04	1.6
3	1.56	1.40	1.25	1.09	.94	.78	.62	.47	.31	.16	.08	2.4
4	2.68	2.41	2.14	1.88	1.61	1.34	1.07	.80	.54	.27	.13	3.2
5	4.04	3.64	3.23	2.83	2.42	2.02	1.62	1.21	.81	.40	.20	4.0
6	5.76	5.18	4.61	4.03	3.46	2.88	2.30	1.73	1.15	.58	.29	4.8
7	7.66	6.89	6.13	5.36	4.60	3.83	3.06	2.30	1.53	.77	.38	5.6
8	9.78	8.80	7.82	6.85	5.87	4.89	3.91	2.93	1.96	.98	.49	6.4

3/4" — .930" I.D.

GPM	100	90	80	70	60	50	40	30	20	10	5	VEL.
2	.22	.20	.18	.15	.13	.11	.09	.07	.04	.02	.01	.9
4	.78	.70	.63	.55	.47	.39	.31	.23	.16	.08	.04	1.9
6	1.66	1.49	1.34	1.16	1.00	.83	.66	.50	.34	.17	.09	2.8
8	2.84	2.56	2.27	1.99	1.70	1.42	1.14	.85	.56	.28	.14	3.7
10	4.30	3.87	3.45	3.01	2.58	2.15	1.72	1.29	.86	.43	.22	4.7
12	6.00	5.40	4.80	4.20	3.60	3.00	2.40	1.80	1.20	.60	.30	5.7
14	8.00	7.20	6.40	5.60	4.80	4.00	3.20	2.40	1.60	.80	.40	6.6

1" — 1.195" I.D.

GPM	100	90	80	70	60	50	40	30	20	10	5	VEL.
6	.48	.44	.39	.34	.29	.24	.20	.15	.10	.05	.03	1.7
8	.84	.76	.67	.59	.50	.42	.34	.25	.16	.08	.04	2.3
10	1.26	1.13	1.02	.88	.76	.63	.50	.38	.26	.13	.07	2.9
12	1.78	1.60	1.43	1.25	1.07	.89	.71	.53	.36	.18	.09	3.4
14	2.36	2.12	1.89	1.65	1.42	1.18	.94	.71	.48	.24	.12	4.0
16	3.04	2.73	2.43	2.12	1.82	1.52	1.21	.91	.60	.30	.15	4.5
18	3.76	3.38	3.01	2.63	2.26	1.88	1.50	1.13	.76	.38	.19	5.1
20	4.56	4.10	3.65	3.19	2.74	2.28	1.82	1.37	.92	.46	.23	5.7
22	5.50	4.95	4.40	3.85	3.30	2.75	2.20	1.65	1.10	.55	.28	6.3
24	6.46	5.81	5.23	4.52	3.88	3.23	2.58	1.94	1.30	.65	.38	6.8

1-1/4" — 1.532" I.D.

GPM	100	90	80	70	60	50	40	30	20	10	5	VEL.
10	.38	.34	.31	.27	.23	.19	.15	.11	.08	.04	.02	1.7
12	.52	.47	.42	.37	.32	.26	.21	.16	.10	.05	.03	2.1
14	.70	.63	.56	.49	.42	.35	.28	.21	.14	.07	.04	2.4
16	.90	.81	.72	.63	.54	.45	.36	.27	.18	.09	.05	2.8
18	1.12	1.01	.90	.78	.67	.56	.45	.34	.22	.11	.06	3.1
20	1.36	1.22	1.09	.95	.82	.68	.54	.41	.28	.14	.07	3.5
22	1.62	1.46	1.30	1.13	.97	.81	.65	.49	.32	.16	.08	3.9
24	1.90	1.71	1.53	1.33	1.14	.95	.76	.57	.38	.19	.10	4.2
26	2.22	2.00	1.78	1.55	1.33	1.11	.89	.67	.44	.22	.11	4.5
28	2.54	2.29	2.04	1.78	1.52	1.27	1.02	.76	.50	.25	.13	4.9
30	2.90	2.61	2.32	2.03	1.74	1.45	1.16	.87	.58	.29	.15	5.2
32	3.26	2.93	2.61	2.28	1.96	1.63	1.30	.98	.66	.33	.17	5.6
34	3.64	3.28	2.91	2.55	2.18	1.82	1.46	1.09	.72	.36	.18	5.9
36	4.04	3.64	3.23	2.83	2.42	2.02	1.62	1.21	.80	.40	.20	6.2
38	4.48	4.03	3.59	3.14	2.69	2.24	1.79	1.34	.90	.45	.23	6.6

Tables on pages 256–261 courtesy of the Toro Company, Irrigation Division, P. O. Box 439, Riverside, California 92502.

1-1/2" 1.754" I.D.

GPM												Vel. (ft/s)
20	.70	.63	.56	.49	.42	.35	.28	.21	.14	.07	.04	2.7
25	1.06	.95	.86	.74	.54	.53	.42	.32	.22	.11	.06	3.3
30	1.50	1.35	1.20	1.05	.90	.75	.60	.46	.30	.15	.08	4.0
35	1.98	1.78	1.59	1.39	1.19	.99	.79	.59	.40	.20	.10	4.7
40	2.54	2.29	2.04	1.78	1.52	1.27	1.02	.76	.51	.25	.13	5.3
45	3.16	2.84	2.53	2.21	1.90	1.58	1.26	.95	.64	.32	.16	6.0
50	3.84	3.46	3.07	2.69	2.30	1.92	1.54	1.15	.75	.38	.19	6.6

2" 2.193" I.D.

GPM												Vel. (ft/s)
30	.50	.45	.40	.35	.30	.25	.20	.15	.10	.05	.03	2.6
35	.68	.61	.54	.47	.40	.34	.27	.20	.13	.07	.04	3.0
40	.86	.77	.69	.60	.52	.43	.34	.26	.17	.09	.05	3.4
45	1.08	.97	.86	.75	.54	.54	.43	.32	.21	.11	.06	3.8
50	1.30	1.17	1.04	.91	.78	.65	.52	.39	.26	.13	.07	4.3
55	1.54	1.39	1.23	1.08	.92	.77	.62	.46	.31	.15	.08	4.7
60	1.80	1.62	1.44	1.26	1.08	.90	.72	.54	.36	.18	.09	5.1
65	2.10	1.89	1.68	1.47	1.26	1.05	.84	.63	.42	.21	.11	5.5
70	2.40	2.16	1.92	1.68	1.44	1.20	.96	.72	.48	.24	.12	6.0
75	2.74	2.47	2.19	1.92	1.64	1.37	1.10	.82	.55	.27	.14	6.4
80	3.10	2.79	2.48	2.17	1.86	1.55	1.24	.93	.62	.31	.16	6.8

2 1/2" 2.655" I.D.

GPM												Vel. (ft/s)
50	.50	.45	.40	.35	.30	.25	.20	.15	.10	.05	.03	2.9
60	.70	.63	.56	.49	.42	.35	.28	.21	.14	.07	.04	3.5
70	.96	.86	.77	.67	.58	.48	.38	.29	.19	.10	.05	4.1
80	1.22	1.10	.98	.85	.73	.61	.49	.37	.24	.12	.06	4.6
90	1.52	1.37	1.22	1.06	.91	.76	.61	.46	.30	.15	.08	5.2
100	1.84	1.66	1.47	1.29	1.10	.92	.74	.55	.37	.18	.09	5.8
110	2.20	1.98	1.76	1.54	1.32	1.10	.88	.66	.44	.22	.11	6.4
120	2.58	2.32	2.06	1.81	1.55	1.29	1.03	.77	.52	.26	.13	7.0

3" 3.230" I.D.

GPM												Vel. (ft/s)
80	.46	.41	.37	.32	.28	.23	.18	.14	.09	.05	.02	3.1
90	.58	.52	.46	.41	.35	.29	.23	.17	.12	.06	.03	3.5
100	.70	.63	.56	.49	.42	.35	.28	.21	.14	.07	.04	3.9
110	.84	.76	.67	.59	.51	.42	.33	.25	.17	.08	.04	4.3
120	.98	.88	.78	.69	.59	.49	.39	.29	.20	.10	.05	4.7
130	1.14	1.03	.91	.80	.68	.57	.46	.34	.23	.11	.06	5.1
140	1.32	1.18	1.05	.92	.79	.66	.52	.39	.26	.13	.07	5.5
150	1.50	1.35	1.20	1.05	.90	.75	.60	.45	.30	.15	.08	5.9
160	1.68	1.51	1.34	1.18	1.01	.84	.67	.50	.34	.17	.09	6.3
170	1.88	1.69	1.51	1.32	1.13	.94	.75	.56	.37	.19	.10	6.7

4" 4.154" I.D.

GPM												Vel. (ft/s)
150	.44	.39	.35	.31	.26	.22	.17	.13	.09	.04	.02	3.6
160	.50	.45	.40	.35	.30	.25	.20	.15	.10	.05	.03	3.8
170	.56	.51	.44	.39	.33	.28	.22	.17	.11	.06	.03	4.0
180	.62	.56	.49	.43	.37	.31	.25	.18	.12	.06	.03	4.3
190	.68	.62	.55	.48	.41	.34	.28	.21	.14	.07	.04	4.5
200	.74	.67	.59	.52	.44	.37	.30	.22	.15	.08	.04	4.7
210	.80	.72	.64	.56	.48	.40	.32	.24	.16	.09	.04	4.9
220	.88	.80	.71	.62	.53	.44	.36	.27	.18	.10	.05	5.2
230	.96	.86	.77	.67	.58	.48	.38	.29	.19	.10	.05	5.4
240	1.04	.94	.83	.73	.62	.52	.42	.31	.21	.11	.05	5.7
250	1.12	1.01	.90	.78	.67	.56	.45	.34	.22	.12	.06	5.9
260	1.20	1.08	.96	.84	.72	.60	.48	.36	.24	.12	.06	6.2
270	1.28	1.16	1.03	.90	.77	.64	.52	.39	.26	.13	.07	6.4
280	1.38	1.24	1.10	.97	.83	.69	.55	.41	.28	.14	.07	6.6

FRICTION LOSS TABLE
PVC 1120-1220 CLASS 200
P.S.I. LOSS PER PIPE LENGTH NOTED

C=150

GPM	VEL.	5	10	20	30	40	50	60	70	80	90	100	PIPE SIZE
1	.8	.01	.02	.04	.06	.08	.10	.12	.14	.16	.18	.20	**1/2"** .720" I.D.
2	1.6	.04	.07	.15	.22	.30	.37	.44	.52	.59	.67	.74	
3	2.4	.08	.16	.31	.47	.62	.78	.94	1.09	1.25	1.40	1.56	
4	3.2	.13	.27	.54	.80	1.07	1.34	1.61	1.88	2.14	2.41	2.68	
5	4.0	.20	.40	.81	1.21	1.62	2.02	2.42	2.83	3.23	3.64	4.04	
6	4.8	.29	.58	1.15	1.73	2.30	2.88	3.46	4.03	4.61	5.18	5.76	
7	5.6	.38	.77	1.53	2.30	3.06	3.83	4.60	5.36	6.13	6.89	7.66	
8	6.4	.49	.98	1.96	2.93	3.91	4.89	5.87	6.85	7.82	8.80	9.78	
2	.9	.01	.02	.04	.07	.09	.11	.13	.15	.18	.20	.22	**3/4"** .930" I.D.
4	1.9	.04	.08	.16	.23	.31	.39	.47	.55	.63	.70	.78	
6	2.8	.09	.17	.34	.50	.66	.83	1.00	1.16	1.34	1.49	1.66	
8	3.8	.14	.28	.56	.85	1.14	1.42	1.70	1.99	2.27	2.56	2.84	
10	4.7	.22	.43	.86	1.29	1.72	2.15	2.58	3.01	3.45	3.87	4.30	
12	5.7	.30	.60	1.20	1.80	2.40	3.00	3.60	4.20	4.80	5.40	6.00	
14	6.6	.40	.80	1.60	2.40	3.20	4.00	4.80	5.60	6.40	7.20	8.00	
6	1.7	.03	.05	.10	.15	.20	.25	.30	.35	.40	.45	.50	**1"** 1.189" I.D.
8	2.3	.05	.09	.17	.26	.34	.43	.52	.60	.69	.77	.86	
10	2.9	.07	.13	.26	.39	.52	.65	.78	.91	1.04	1.17	1.30	
12	3.5	.09	.18	.37	.55	.74	.92	1.10	1.29	1.47	1.66	1.84	
14	4.1	.12	.24	.48	.73	.97	1.21	1.45	1.69	1.94	2.18	2.42	
16	4.7	.16	.31	.62	.93	1.24	1.55	1.86	2.17	2.48	2.79	3.10	
18	5.2	.20	.39	.77	1.16	1.54	1.93	2.32	2.70	3.09	3.47	3.86	
20	5.8	.24	.47	.94	1.40	1.87	2.34	2.81	3.28	3.74	4.21	4.68	
22	6.4	.29	.57	1.13	1.70	2.26	2.83	3.40	3.96	4.53	5.09	5.66	
24	6.9	.33	.66	1.32	1.99	2.65	3.31	3.97	4.63	5.30	5.96	6.62	
10	1.8	.02	.04	.08	.13	.17	.21	.25	.29	.34	.38	.42	**1-1/4"** 1.502" I.D.
12	2.2	.03	.06	.12	.17	.23	.29	.35	.41	.46	.52	.58	
14	2.6	.04	.08	.16	.23	.31	.39	.47	.55	.62	.70	.78	
16	2.9	.05	.10	.20	.30	.40	.50	.60	.70	.80	.90	1.00	
18	3.3	.06	.12	.25	.37	.50	.62	.74	.87	.99	1.12	1.24	
20	3.6	.08	.15	.30	.45	.60	.75	.90	1.05	1.20	1.35	1.50	
22	4.0	.09	.18	.36	.54	.72	.90	1.08	1.26	1.44	1.62	1.80	
24	4.3	.11	.21	.42	.63	.84	1.05	1.26	1.47	1.68	1.89	2.10	
26	4.7	.12	.24	.49	.73	.98	1.22	1.46	1.71	1.95	2.20	2.44	
28	5.1	.14	.28	.56	.84	1.12	1.40	1.68	1.96	2.24	2.52	2.80	
30	5.5	.16	.32	.64	.95	1.27	1.59	1.91	2.23	2.54	2.86	3.18	
32	5.8	.18	.36	.72	1.07	1.43	1.79	2.15	2.51	2.86	3.22	3.58	
34	6.2	.20	.40	.80	1.20	1.60	2.00	2.40	2.80	3.20	3.60	4.00	
36	6.6	.22	.45	.89	1.33	1.78	2.22	2.66	3.11	3.55	4.00	4.44	
15	2.2	.03	.05	.09	.14	.18	.23	.28	.32	.37	.41	.46	**1-1/2"** 1.720" I.D.
20	2.8	.04	.08	.16	.23	.31	.39	.47	.55	.62	.70	.78	
25	3.5	.06	.12	.24	.35	.47	.59	.71	.83	.94	1.06	1.18	
30	4.1	.08	.16	.33	.49	.66	.82	.98	1.15	1.31	1.48	1.64	
35	4.8	.11	.22	.44	.65	.87	1.09	1.31	1.53	1.74	1.96	2.18	
40	5.5	.14	.28	.56	.84	1.12	1.40	1.68	1.96	2.24	2.52	2.80	
45	6.2	.18	.35	.70	1.04	1.39	1.74	2.09	2.44	2.78	3.13	3.48	
50	6.9	.21	.42	.85	1.27	1.70	2.12	2.54	2.97	3.39	3.82	4.24	

2" — 2.149" I.D.

30	.56	.50	.45	.39	.34	.28	.22	.17	.11	.06	.03
35	.74	.67	.59	.52	.44	.37	.30	.22	.15	.07	.04
40	.94	.85	.75	.66	.56	.47	.38	.28	.19	.09	.05
45	1.16	1.04	.93	.81	.70	.58	.46	.35	.23	.12	.06
50	1.40	1.26	1.12	.98	.84	.70	.56	.42	.28	.14	.07
55	1.68	1.51	1.34	1.18	1.01	.84	.67	.50	.34	.17	.08
60	1.96	1.76	1.57	1.37	1.18	.98	.78	.59	.39	.20	.10
65	2.26	2.03	1.81	1.58	1.36	1.13	.90	.68	.45	.23	.12
70	2.60	2.34	2.08	1.82	1.56	1.30	1.04	.78	.52	.26	.13
75	2.98	2.68	2.38	2.09	1.79	1.49	1.13	.89	.60	.30	.15
Vel.	2.7	3.1	3.5	4.0	4.4	4.9	5.3	5.8	6.2	6.7	
	30	35	40	45	50	55	60	65	70	75	

2 1/2" — 2.601" I.D.

50	.56	.50	.45	.39	.34	.28	.22	.17	.11	.06	.03
60	.80	.72	.64	.56	.48	.40	.32	.24	.16	.08	.04
70	1.06	.95	.85	.74	.64	.53	.42	.32	.21	.11	.06
80	1.34	1.21	1.07	.94	.80	.67	.54	.40	.27	.13	.07
90	1.68	1.51	1.34	1.18	1.01	.84	.67	.50	.34	.17	.08
100	2.02	1.82	1.62	1.41	1.21	1.01	.81	.61	.40	.20	.10
110	2.44	2.20	1.95	1.71	1.46	1.22	.98	.73	.49	.24	.12
Vel.	3.0	3.6	4.2	4.8	5.4	6.0	6.6				
	50	60	70	80	90	100	110				

3" — 3.166" I.D.

80	.54	.49	.43	.38	.32	.27	.22	.16	.11	.05	.03
90	.66	.59	.53	.46	.40	.33	.26	.20	.13	.07	.04
100	.80	.72	.64	.56	.48	.40	.32	.24	.16	.08	.04
110	.96	.86	.77	.67	.58	.48	.38	.29	.19	.10	.05
120	1.12	1.01	.90	.78	.67	.56	.45	.34	.22	.11	.06
130	1.32	1.19	1.06	.92	.79	.66	.53	.40	.26	.13	.07
140	1.50	1.35	1.20	1.05	.90	.75	.60	.45	.30	.15	.08
150	1.70	1.53	1.36	1.19	1.02	.85	.68	.51	.34	.17	.09
160	1.92	1.73	1.54	1.34	1.15	.96	.77	.58	.38	.19	.10
170	2.16	1.94	1.73	1.51	1.30	1.08	.86	.65	.43	.22	.11
Vel.	3.3	3.7	4.1	4.5	4.9	5.3	5.7	6.1	6.5	6.9	
	80	90	100	110	120	130	140	150	160	170	

4" — 4.072" I.D.

150	.50	.45	.40	.35	.30	.25	.20	.15	.10	.04	.02
160	.56	.50	.45	.39	.33	.28	.22	.17	.11	.04	.02
170	.62	.56	.50	.43	.37	.31	.25	.19	.12	.06	.03
180	.68	.61	.54	.48	.41	.34	.27	.20	.14	.06	.03
190	.76	.68	.61	.53	.46	.38	.30	.23	.15	.07	.04
200	.84	.76	.67	.59	.50	.42	.34	.25	.17	.08	.04
210	.90	.81	.72	.63	.54	.45	.36	.27	.18	.09	.05
220	.98	.88	.78	.69	.59	.49	.39	.29	.20	.10	.06
230	1.08	.97	.86	.76	.65	.54	.43	.32	.22	.12	.06
240	1.16	1.04	.93	.81	.70	.58	.46	.35	.23	.13	.07
250	1.24	1.12	.99	.87	.74	.62	.50	.37	.25	.14	.07
260	1.34	1.21	1.07	.94	.80	.67	.54	.40	.27	.15	.08
270	1.44	1.30	1.15	1.01	.86	.72	.58	.43	.29		
280	1.54	1.39	1.23	1.08	.92	.77	.62	.46	.31		
Vel.	3.7	3.9	4.2	4.4	4.7	4.9	5.2	5.4	5.7	5.9	6.2
										6.4	6.6	6.9
	150	160	170	180	190	200	210	220	230	240	250	260	270	280

6" — 5.993" I.D.

250	.20	.18	.16	.14	.12	.10	.08	.06	.04	.02	.01
275	.22	.20	.18	.15	.13	.11	.09	.07	.04	.02	.01
300	.28	.25	.22	.18	.17	.14	.11	.08	.06	.03	.02
325	.32	.29	.26	.22	.19	.16	.13	.10	.06	.03	.02
350	.36	.32	.29	.25	.22	.18	.14	.11	.07	.04	.02
375	.42	.38	.34	.29	.25	.21	.17	.13	.08	.04	.02
400	.46	.41	.37	.32	.29	.23	.18	.14	.09	.05	.03
425	.52	.47	.42	.36	.32	.26	.21	.16	.10	.06	.03
450	.58	.52	.46	.41	.35	.29	.23	.17	.12	.06	.03
475	.64	.58	.51	.45	.38	.32	.26	.19	.13	.07	.03
500	.70	.63	.56	.49	.42	.35	.28	.21	.14	.07	.04
525	.76	.68	.61	.53	.46	.38	.30	.23	.15	.08	.04
550	.82	.74	.66	.57	.49	.41	.33	.25	.16	.09	.05
575	.88	.79	.70	.62	.53	.44	.35	.26	.18	.10	.05
600	.96	.86	.77	.67	.58	.48	.38	.29	.19		
Vel.	2.9	3.2	3.5	3.7	4.0	4.3	4.6	4.9	5.2	5.4	5.7
										6.0	6.3	6.6	6.9
	250	275	300	325	350	375	400	425	450	475	500	525	550	575	600

PRESSURE DROP THROUGH STANDARD WATER METER

LOSS GIVEN IN P.S.I.

GALLONS PER MINUTE

METER SIZE	6	8	10	12	14	16	18	20	22	24	26	28	30	35	40	45	50
5/8"	1.3	2.3	3.7	5.1	7.2	9.4	12.0	15.0									
3/4"	.7	1.0	1.6	2.2	3.1	4.1	5.2	6.5	7.9	9.5	11.2	13.0	15.0				
1"	.3	.5	.7	.9	1.1	1.4	1.8	2.2	2.8	3.4	4.0	4.6	5.3	7.3	9.6	12.2	14.9

GALLONS PER MINUTE

	20	25	30	35	40	45	50	55	60	65	70	80	90	100	120	140	160
1 1/2"	.8	1.3	1.8	2.5	3.3	4.0	4.9	5.9	7.2	8.3	9.8	12.8	16.1	20.0			
2"	.4	.5	.7	1.0	1.3	1.6	1.9	2.3	2.7	3.2	3.7	4.9	6.2	7.8	11.3	15.0	20.0

GALLONS PER MINUTE

	60	70	80	90	100	120	140	160	180	200	250	300	350	400	450	500
3"	1.0	1.3	1.6	2.0	2.5	3.4	4.5	5.8	7.2	9.0	14.0	20.0				
4"	.5	.6	.7	.8	.9	1.2	1.6	2.1	2.7	3.2	5.0	7.2	10.0	13.0	16.2	20.0

FLOWS SHOWN IN ABOVE CHART ARE LIMITED TO MAXIMUM SAFE FLOW

COMPARATIVE FLOW CAPACITIES FOR PIPE

PIPE SIZE	1/2"	3/4"	1"	1 1/4"	1 1/2"	2"	2 1/2"	3"	4"	6"	8"
1/2"	1	2½	5	8	13	25					
3/4"		1	2	3	5	10	17	27			
1"			1	2	3	5	9	14	28		
1 1/4"				1	1½	3	5	8	17		
1 1/2"					1	2	3	5	11	28	
2"						1	1½	3	5½	15	29
2 1/2"							1	1½	3	9½	19
3"								1	2	5½	11
4"									1	3	5½
6"										1	2

Figures in this chart represent approximate comparisons to flow at the same pressure loss. As actual inside diameters of pipes vary in comparison in various schedules or ratings, this can only be used as a general guide.

FRICTION LOSSES* THROUGH PIPE FITTINGS AND MANUAL VALVES

PIPE FITTINGS

PIPE SIZE	STANDARD ELBOW OR RUN OF TEE REDUCED BY 1/2	LONG SWEEP ELBOW OR RUN OF STANDARD TEE	SIDE OUTLET OF STANDARD TEE	PIPE SIZE
1/2"	.9	.4	1.8	1/2"
3/4"	1.2	.6	2.5	3/4"
1 "	1.7	.8	3.4	1 "
1 1/4"	2.4	1.2	4.8	1 1/4"
1 1/2"	3.0	1.4	5.8	1 1/2"
2 "	4.0	2.0	7.9	2 "
2 1/2"	5.0	2.5	9.9	2 1/2"
3 "	6.7	3.3	13.1	3 "
4 "	9.2	4.5	18.3	4 "
5 "	12.2	6.0	24.3	5 "
6 "	15.3	7.6	30.5	6 "
8 "	21.7	10.7	43.1	8 "
10 "	28.7	14.1	56.9	10 "

MANUAL VALVES

VALVE SIZE	GATE VALVES	ANGLE VALVES	GLOBE VALVES	VALVE SIZE
1/2"	.3	1.2	2.7	1/2"
3/4"	.5	1.7	3.8	3/4"
1"	.6	2.3	5.1	1"
1 1/4"	.9	3.2	7.2	1 1/4"
1 1/2"	1.1	4.0	8.7	1 1/2"
2"	1.5	5.4	11.9	2"
2 1/2"	1.9	6.7	14.9	2 1/2"
3 "	2.5	8.9	19.7	3 "
4 "	3.4	12.4	27.5	4 "
5 "	4.6	16.5	36.6	5 "
6 "	5.7	20.6	45.0	6 "
8 "	8.1	29.2	64.8	8 "
10"	10.7	38.5	85.6	10"

* Losses are expressed in terms of equivalent lengths of pipe. For figuring losses of pipe fittings, use the friction loss table for the same type of pipe as the fittings. For the manual valves, use the friction loss table for galvanized steel pipe.

261

PROBLEMS

1. What is the pressure in psi at a hose bib 220 ft away from a water tower if the hose bib is at an elevation 212 ft and the water in the tower is at 364.5 ft.

2. Given 7 irrigation heads on a line 50 ft apart that operate at 40 psi and require 7 GPM each, what are the pipe sizes in order from the first to last head on the line? Use PVC 1120 class 200.

3. A loop is proposed for an irrigation system that has total length of 1,400 ft and a high water demand of 200 GPM at 75 psi; what size should the loop be if the water supply provides 120 psi and galvanized pipe is used? What is the constant pressure loss in the loop?

4. What is the residual pressure at a head using 15 GPM if the water has traveled 120 ft of 1½ in 1120 class 200 PVC pipe if it started at 65 psi?

5. For the following problems use PVC 1120 class 200 pipe; assume pressure loss for fittings is 10% of total loss of other elements. Assume pressure loss in valves as given in chart below.
   All heads require 2.5 GPM at 20 psi. Water supply provides 30 GPM at 30 psi. Size the pipe and valves for the following: (a) automatic valve size; (b) gate valve.

6. What should the triangular head spacing be for a head with a 30 ft radius given a 5 mph wind factor? What would the square spacing be?

7. Assuming the heads in Problem 6 use 6.5 GPM, what is the precipitation rate for each spacing?

GATE VALVES (IN)	5 GPM	10 GPM	20 GPM	30 GPM
1	1 psi	2 psi	3 psi	5 psi
2	—	1 psi	2 psi	4 psi

AUTOMATIC VALVES (IN)				
1	2 psi	3 psi	6 psi	10 psi
1.5	—	2 psi	4 psi	6 psi

8
Lighting Design

Lighting is as much a practical consideration as a design consideration. Good lighting can extend the use of outdoor environments, contribute to the safety of many areas, and add charm and drama to the nighttime landscape.

The field of lighting design is actually a highly developed and specialized technology that is constantly changing with new discoveries in optics, light sources, and the understanding of light energy. For these reasons our discussion in this chapter will be limited to those general considerations that are not likely to change rapidly. The objective of this chapter is to present a foundation of basic material that can be expanded to meet the needs of the individual practitioner. The material presented is organized into four sections that discuss the kinds of lighting equipment, basic lighting techniques, the fundamentals of electricity, and the preparation of electrical plans.

LIGHTING EQUIPMENT

The lighting industry produces lighting equipment to serve three functional levels: utility and security lighting, area lighting, and effect lighting. Utility and security lighting is a practical consideration that enters every landscape project, and may be associated with area or effect lighting. The major objective of this level is to increase the efficiency of the driver or pedestrian in the nighttime environment. Characteristically, the light levels are minimal and color and uniformity are minor considerations. Area lighting as used here refers to lighting systems designed to permit the use of an area in near daylight conditions. These are the systems normally associat-

ed with athletic fields, intricate highway interchanges, or high-use public spaces. These kinds of lighting systems typically require special attention to the light distribution pattern, light source, and color. Effect lighting is the most demanding of the three functional lighting levels. Essentially effect lighting has to satisfy the objectives of security and utility lighting with the added objective of creating an exciting visual environment.

The light fixtures used for lighting in the landscape can be classified in two important ways: by the lamp light source and by the light distribution pattern of the light fixtures (luminaire). Within these two broad classifications there are innumerable shapes, sizes, colors, and suggested applications. These are a matter of taste and designer preference. For this reason, specific examples of references to equipment will be avoided in this discussion.

There are two families of light source common to outdoor lighting applications, incandescent filament lamps, and electric-discharge lamps. Within each family there is a host of variation in the lamps themselves. These differences result in a wide variety of light color, lamp life, energy efficiency, and suitability for specific applications.

Incandescent Lamps

Incandescent filament lamps produce light by electric current being transmitted through a filament, usually tungsten, which is heated to an incandescent state. In other words, the filament glows. Incandescent lamps common to landscape applications include the common light bulb, sealed-beam, low-voltage lamps, and tungsten-iodine lamps, frequently called quartz-iodine lamps. Incandescent filament

263

lamps characteristically produce a more pleasing light color and are free of strobe effect.[1] On the other hand, incandescent lamps are less energy efficient and shorter lived when compared to electric-discharge lamps.

The incandescent lamps of the most interest to the landscape architect and site planner are the low voltage incandescent lamps. These lamps are the same as the headlights of an automobile, and operate on 12 volt direct current supplied by a centrally located transformer. Low voltage lamps have the advantage of simple installation, wide availability, and they are much safer than conventional 120 or 240 volt lamps. This is especially true when designs may require that the lights be mounted at or below the ground. In these instances 120 volt lamps are subject to moisture penetration and there is a hazard of electrical shock.

Several companies manufacture a line of low voltage lighting fixtures. The fixtures come in a wide variety of shapes, sizes, and lamp wattages. Color lenses and filters are also available with most low voltage systems; these add another dimension to the design flexibility.

Electric-Discharge Lamps

Electric-discharge lamps are a large family of lamps that produce light by passing an electrical current through a gas or metallic vapor. Lamps most common to landscape applications are mercury vapor, metallic halide, fluorescent, high-pressure sodium, and low-pressure sodium.

The fluorescent lamp is probably the most familiar of these lamps. It is inexpensive and available for a wide range of applications. Its chief disadvantages are the length of the bulb, short life, and low energy efficiency. However, its adaptability, color flexibility, and availability many times make it a good choice for small projects.

The mercury vapor lamp became quite popular in the post-war period in this country and is the primary light source for most highway and general lighting applications. The primary reason for its popularity is its longevity which is about 24 to 26 thousand hours. Its major deficiencies are color and energy efficiency. The light produced is in the green to blue-green spectrum which is not particularly flattering to many natural colors. However, research and development programs have produced several different mercury lamps that have improved color qualities: metal halide is probably the most notable of these. But where purity of color is essential mercury lamps are still lacking.

---

[1]Strobe effect is the flickering of a lamp caused by the cycling of electric current.

TABLE 8–1
Comparison of Life and Efficiency of Various Light Sources

LIGHT SOURCE	ENERGY EFFICIENCY (LUMENS[a]/WATT)	LIFE (HOURS)
Incandescent, standard	10–18	750–1,000
Tungsten-iodine (quartz)	18–20	2,000
Mercury vapor	55	24–26,000
Fluorescent	70	6,000
Metal halide	90	14–15,000
High-pressure sodium	130	16,000
Low-pressure sodium	190	11,000

[a]A lumen is the basic unit of light energy.

You will notice in Table 8–1 that mercury vapor lamps produce fewer lumens per watt than the sodium lamps. This means they are less efficient than the sodium lamps in producing light. This fact, however, must be weighed against its greater longevity.

Sodium lamps are becoming more popular because of their energy efficiency, although they have several distinct disadvantages. Low-pressure sodium lamps are relatively short lived when compared with other sources and the low-pressure sodium bulb is also a disadvantage because of its length, usually 30 inches or more. The high-pressure sodium lamp makes up for most of these objections with only a minimum sacrifice of efficiency. Therefore, most sodium equipment in use now is high-pressure sodium.

The major problem with sodium lamps from a landscape viewpoint is color. Sodium produces a light in the pink to orange spectrum which is even less flattering than mercury vapor light. In years to come, research may improve the color quality of sodium light sources much the same as mercury vapor lights have been improved.

The other important means of classifying lighting equipment is by the light distribution pattern. The light distribution is accomplished by placing the lamp in a luminaire with a refracting lense that distributes the light in some predetermined pattern. Figure 8–1 illustrates the five standard lighting patterns available.

The Type I luminaire is used for overhead applications that might occur in parking facilities or on some athletic facilities such as shuffleboard. It is also used for low-level fixtures that are employed for lighting walks, steps, and planted areas.

Types II, III, and IV are luminaires that are used for street lighting and most general utility lighting applications. The only thing that distinguishes between the three is the ratio of light spread to mounting height. The larger the number the greater the spread.

LIGHT DISTRIBUTION OF LENSES

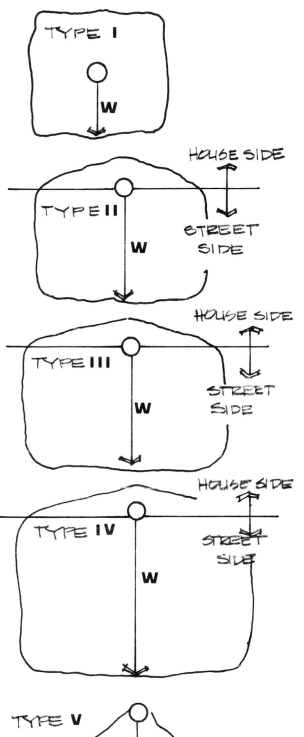

W = 1-2 TIMES MOUNTING HEIGHT

W = 1.5 TIMES THE MOUNTING HEIGHT

W = 2 TIMES THE MOUNTING HEIGHT

W = > 2 TIMES THE MOUNTING HEIGHT

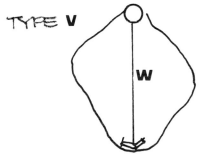

W = 1-5 TIMES THE MOUNTING HEIGHT - FLOOD LIGHT

FIGURE 8-1

The Type V luminaire is most commonly called a floodlight. The light beam is concentrated and can be aimed precisely to control illumination levels. Floodlights are most frequently associated with sports area lighting, buildings, and for effect and decorative lighting. Floodlights are available in an infinite variety of light sources, beam distributions, and lamp wattages, and have a wide variety of applications.

DESIGNING LIGHTING SYSTEMS

Lighting design is a complex technology and many of the detailed concepts are beyond the scope of this text. On the other hand, there are some basic principles of design layout that can be useful to the landscape architect in doing the preliminary work on a project. These principles will provide the background for more detailed study or for discussions with an illumination engineer.

The primary concerns in the design of a lighting system are the level of brightness to be maintained on a surface, the uniformity of the brightness, the color of the light, and the aesthetic value of the lighting scheme.

The illumination level for a project is primarily a function of use. Various standards for lighting levels have been established as guidelines as outlined in Table 8–2.

The primary measure of light intensity used in the field is the footcandle (ft-c). One footcandle equals one lumen per square foot. The metric term that corresponds to this unit is lux, lumens per square meter.

There are several ways of designing light levels, but two of these are particularly significant to this discussion: the point-by-point method and the aver-age-illumination method. The point-by-point method is considered by most lighting specialists to be the best method for determining light levels where accuracy is required. For example, the point-by-point method should be used to design lighting for highways and sports areas. The average illumination method is less accurate, but is a satisfactory means of determining light spacing for most general landscape applications.

Point-by-Point Method

The formula for the point-by-point method is

$$E_h = \frac{I \cos \theta}{d^2}$$

where

E_h = the illumination on the horizontal surface in footcandles;
I = the lamp intensity in lumens;
θ = the angle between the fixture and some known point on the ground;
d = the distance from the luminaire to the point. See Figure 8–2.

To properly apply the point-by-point method several other factors must be considered if the results are to be accurate. First, the light source will not retain its initial lumen output over its entire life. Most lamps will deteriorate as much as 75% during their lifetime. This means that some adjustment for deterioration of the lamp itself should be made. In addition to the lamp deterioration, outdoor fixtures will accumulate dust and oil films on the luminaire lens that will further reduce the output. In addition to these

TABLE 8–2
Recommended Levels of Lighting for Various Activities

USE	RECOMMENDED ILLUMINATION IN FT-CANDLES	
	MAXIMUM	MINIMUM
Utility Lighting		
Minimum Visibility	—	.5
Driving	1	.5
Pedestrian Ways	1	.5
Gardens, General	2	1
Area Lighting		
Parking lots	2	1
Tennis and handball	50	20
Baseball		
infield	150[a]	50[b]
outfield	100[a]	20[b]
Football	100[a]	20[b]

[a]For color telecasts.
[b]These values are sometimes referred to as club class lighting and are preferred by the author. Lower values are frequently used.

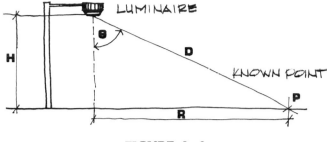

FIGURE 8-2

considerations, the light intensity of a particular fixture will vary within the angle of the vertical plane. This means that the light intensity (I) will be different for each angle θ taken from the lens. This information can be obtained from manufacturer's data.

To illustrate how the point-by-point method is used we will work through a simple problem as shown in Figure 8-3. Let us assume that we want to light a walk area at a maintained level of not less than 2 footcandles. The fixtures will be placed on one side of the walk mounted on 20 ft poles. The fixtures used in this example are Kim 400 watt, metallic halide, Type II luminaires.

To determine the maintained lighting, calculate the illumination intensity contributed by each fixture at points A–J. The illumination data for the fixtures is provided in Figure 8-4. The calculation for point A is worked out in detail and the remaining calculations are summarized in Table 8-3.

TABLE 8-3
Summary of Illumination Intensity Contributed by Each Fixture at Points A-J

POINT	LUMINAIRE 1	LUMINAIRE 2	TOTAL
A	4.80	2.41	7.21
B	2.41	4.80	7.21
C	4.80	.04	4.84
D	3.61	.81	4.42
E	.81	3.61	4.42
F	.04	4.80	4.84
G	2.41	.03	2.44
H	2.21	.53	2.74
I	.53	2.21	2.74
J	.03	2.41	2.44

Notes: Minimum to maximum = 3:1 (2.95:1).
Average to maximum = 2:1 (1.71:1).

Point A is calculated as follows for fixture 1.

$$E_h = \frac{I \cos \theta}{d^2}$$

First find:

$$d^2 = h^2 + R^2$$
$$d^2 = 800$$
$$d = \sqrt{800}$$
$$d = 28.28 \text{ ft}$$

Next find θ where

$$\sin \theta = \frac{R}{d} = \frac{20 \text{ ft}}{28.28 \text{ ft}}$$
$$\sin \theta = 0.7072135$$
$$\theta = 45°$$

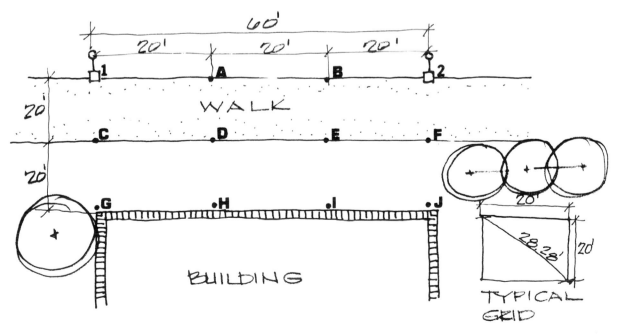

FIGURE 8-3

photometrics

horizontal isolux

400 watt
Metallic Halide
Type II

	Mounting Heights			
	35'	30'	25'	20'
horizontal footcandles	2	2.7	3.9	6.1
	1	1.4	2	3.1
	.5	.7	1	1.5
	.2	.3	.4	.6
	.1	.14	.2	.3
	.05	.07	.1	.2

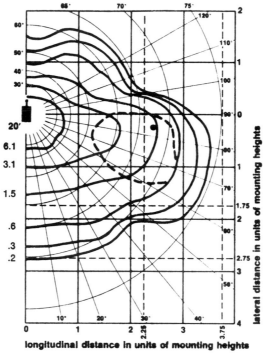
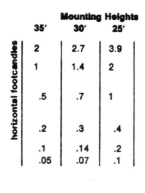

longitudinal distance in units of mounting heights

lateral distance in units of mounting heights

(A)

One Fixture

Catalog numbers
EKG-100 through EKG-104
(type II)

Lamp: 400 Watt Metallic Halide
rated 30,000 lumens horizontal

—— Isolux lines of horizontal footcandles

● Point of maximum candlepower

- - - Half maximum candlepower isocandela trace

ANSI Classification:
Type II, Medium, Cut-off

vertical plane through maximum candela

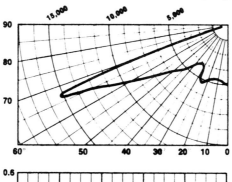

Maximum candela at
67° vertical, 84° horizontal,
15,070 candlepower

Angle	Candela
90°	0
85°	65
75°	572
67°	15070
65°	12490
55°	7540
45°	5430
35°	3630
25°	5770
15°	4840
5°	4770
0°	5490

(B)

coefficients of utilization and flux distribution

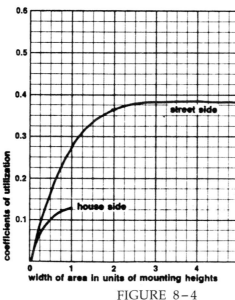

street side

house side

coefficients of utilization

width of area in units of mounting heights

	Lumens
Downward Street Side	11467
Downward House Side	4180
Downward Total	15647
Upward Total	0

(C)

FIGURE 8-4

Then find the light intensity for an angle of 45° from Figure 8–4b as 5430. Then calculate E_h where

$$I = 5430$$
$$\cos \theta = .70699996 \ (\cos 45°)$$
$$d^2 = 800$$
$$E_h = \frac{5430 \times .70699996}{800}$$
$$E_h = 4.80 \ \text{Fc}$$

Notice the minimum to maximum and average to maximum ratios at the bottom of Table 8–3. These are calculated to determine the difference between the lightest and darkest spots. The maximum acceptable ratio is 6 : 1 for most applications and as high as 10 : 1 for some utility lighting projects.

The average maintained lighting for the example is 4.21 footcandles. This figure should be further adjusted for dirt accumulation and lamp depreciation. A good depreciation figure for most work is about 50%. Some highway applications use figures as high as 70% for very dirty conditions. All in all, it is a design decision. The adjusted illumination for the example would be 4.21 ft-c × .50 (depreciation coefficient) = 2.105 ft-c average maintained lighting; thus we have an acceptable solution.

Before leaving this example it should be pointed out that most lighting solutions can be based on a 2 luminaire setup such as the one shown, since the addition of other fixtures 60 ft o.c. will continue to duplicate the pattern calculated for the first two. If other fixtures are placed opposite the first two at 60 ft centers, the light value at each point would be a mirror image.

Average-Illumination Method

The average-illumination method is less exacting than the point-by-point method, but is a satisfactory estimate of the average maintained illumination of a given area. This method can be used to quickly determine lamp spacings for general lighting applications such as pedestrian malls, walks, and some parking areas. The chief disadvantage is that there is no means for checking the maximum and minimum lighting levels. Average illumination is determined by the relationship

$$Fc = \frac{IuM}{LW}$$

where

Fc = average illumination in footcandles;
I = lamp intensity in lumens;
u = the coefficient of utilization;
M = the maintenance depreciation factor;
L = the horizontal distance between fixtures;
W = the width of the area to be illuminated.

The expression solved for L is $L = IuM/FcW$. To illustrate how this expression is used let us apply it to the example used for the point-by-point method and compare the results. All the equipment and conditions remain the same.

First, find the values of the various terms in the expression from Figure 8–4 and from the problem statement as follows. I = 30,000 lumens; this is taken from the lamp specification rating. u = .3625; value taken from Figure 8–4c based on a 40 ft width, 2 mounting heights. M = .50; this is the same factor used to adjust the illumination in the point-by-point method. L = 60 ft o.c.; taken from the problem statement. W = 40 ft; taken from the problem statement. Solve for Fc.

$$Fc = \frac{IuM}{LW} = \frac{30,000 \times .3625 \times .50}{60 \times 40} = \frac{5437.5}{2400} = 2.27$$

Notice that the value from the adjusted point-by-point method (2.41), and the results of the average illumination method are very close, with the average-illumination figure being somewhat more conservative. Once again we have satisfied the 2 footcandle objective set forth in the problem statement.

A second application of the average-illumination method is to determine luminaire spacing to maintain a specified average illumination. Using the expression solved for L, determine the maximum spacing of the fixtures as follows.

$$L = \frac{IuM}{FcW} = \frac{30,000 \times .3625 \times .50}{2 \times 40} = \frac{5437.5}{80} = 67.96 \ \text{ft}$$

This means we could space the luminaires on 68 ft centers and maintain about 2.0 footcandles of illumination on the area. This also agrees with our other figures.

This last application is probably most handy in areas where the growth of plant material will disrupt the light pattern. It allows us to find a desirable spacing and make minor adjustments to allow for plant growth. Critical areas can then be supplemented by low level or effect lighting.

DESIGNING FOR EFFECT

To this point in our discussion we have only considered the principles of light distribution for utility and security lighting and area lighting. The methodology presented works well and it is accurate for the average project. These methods are of little use, however, when lighting for effect is the primary concern. Decorative lighting is a technology that involves controlling the light intensity and direction as well as the color to achieve a desirable composition. The composition perceived in the dark may in fact be quite different from the daylight composition. This is both an advantage and disadvantage.

On the one hand, the lighting designer can develop a system that will emphasize and highlight desirable parts of an outdoor composition and play down others. For example, single plant specimens can be lighted to stand out while the background is played down. Color can also be added as an ingredient to further emphasize mood. The danger comes in designing for only the nighttime environment. A landscape that relies on light to achieve its charm may run the risk of being visually stale in the daylight hours. In some situations this may be valid, but for most situations the landscape composition must work in both daylight and dark.

Effect lighting involves a series of decisions made by a designer to fit specific situations. Like all design there is no absolute, only shades of goodness or badness. Therefore, the objective of this discussion is to provide a palate of basic lighting effects, how they are employed, and how they are accomplished. A basic palate of lighting effect includes the following.

- Uplighting
- Downlighting
- Diffused or moonlighting
- Shadow and texture lighting
- Accent lighting
- Silhouette lighting
- Bounce lighting

Uplighting

Uplighting is one of the most striking of all lighting effects, probably because of the light direction being counter to our normal experience. It is usually used to accent plants or other landscape features. This effect gives a glowing silhouette effect to the object since there is a high contrast between outline and horizontal surfaces.

Downlighting

Downlighting is somewhat less striking than uplighting because the eye is more accustomed to this pattern. Its primary feature is the ability to develop texture pattern on the ground plain by directing the light beam through foliage or other overhead structures. It also gives a high contrast between upper and lower surfaces. The contrast is somewhat less than the contrast developed by uplighting because of light reflection.

Moonlighting

Diffused lighting or moonlighting is usually accomplished by using floodlamps mounted high in trees, on walls, or poles. The light is soft and spread over a large area. It can also be accomplished by using an auxiliary screen to further diffuse the light. The effect is much the same as soft moonlight where objects are visible, but there is a minimum contrast between objects and very little shadow. Diffused lighting effects are useful along paths, in transition spaces, and for intimate spaces like terraces or small view gardens.

Shadow and Texture Lighting

Shadow and texture lighting is accomplished by lighting objects from the side or by downlighting. Many interesting texture effects can be accomplished by directing spot or floodlights through foliage or structures with small openings. This is because shadow size increases with the distance of the object from the background the shadow will be cast on. When distinct shadow patterns are desirable, objects with unique character should be selected and the background placed reasonably close to the subject. As a general rule objects composed of well-spaced slender elements make the best subjects.

Texture lighting can be used to add interest to turf areas, and can be especially interesting on paved surfaces with little natural character. In many cases texture effects are a by-product of downlighting in trees. Texture lighting, however, is an accent effect and must be carefully executed. Many times a shadow effect is lost because the surrounding light levels are too high to achieve the necessary contrast.

Accent Lighting

Accent lighting is most frequently associated with only spotlighting a landscape subject. However, accents can be accomplished by any number of techniques. The chief component of any accent effect is sharp contrast with the surrounding elements. Therefore, accents can be achieved not only by spotlighting, but by uplighting, downlighting or any other method that provides a sharp contrast.

Silhouette Lighting

Silhouette lighting is an effect achieved by lighting the background plane so the objects in the foreground appear as only outlined mass. In order to be effective it usually requires that spotlights or floodlights with concentrated beams be used and that the background be reasonably close to the objects relative to the distance scale. If too much light spills out of the light fixtures used on the background the subjects will lose the silhouette image. Likewise, if the background is too far from the subject it will be difficult to generate the necessary contrast in light and dark.

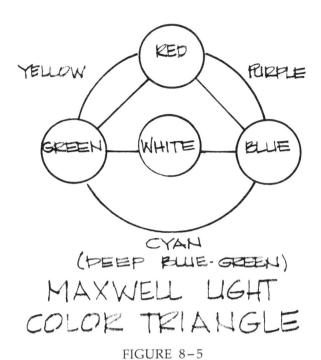

YELLOW — RED — PURPLE

GREEN — WHITE — BLUE

CYAN
(DEEP BLUE-GREEN)
MAXWELL LIGHT
COLOR TRIANGLE

FIGURE 8-5

Bounce Lighting

Bounce lighting refers to the technique of directing a light source against a reflective surface that redistributes the light to the desired area (indirect lighting). Many times this can be a very exciting way to achieve the utility lighting requirements on a project. It can also be used to fill in the areas between other lighting effects without directly exposing the actual light source.

Light Color

The second important component of any effect lighting scheme is color. Color is a powerful tool that can be used to create mood or add emphasis and contrast. It can also be a disaster if it is improperly handled.

The first point that must be made in a discussion of light and light color is that the primary colors in the light spectrum are red, blue, and green. The light colors that result by mixing the various primary colors are illustrated by the Maxwell Color Triangle in Figure 8-5. When the three primary colors are mixed the result is "white light." White light is the apparent absence of color.

Errors and misconceptions about color and light color arise because of the differences between the chromatic relationships of each component. A very simplistic way to get at the relationship between object pigmentation and light color is to remember that object color is the result of its surface reflecting certain colors in the light spectrum.

For example, a leaf appears green in daylight be-

cause most of the reds and blues of the light spectrum are absorbed and the green light is reflected. But if the same leaf is placed in artificial yellow light, the blue light component is not present. Therefore, the leaf is reflecting only green light mixed with red which is perceived as brown.

As a rule, objects look best if they are featured in light of the same color. Foliage looks best in green light, reds look best in red light, and so on. On the other hand, white objects sometimes appear cold and artificial in white light. In most cases, white objects will look better in a yellow or amber light. Amber light is also a good choice for pools and fountains.

The watchword in effect lighting is flexibility. The outdoor setting is in a perpetual state of change because of the season and growth of plant materials. Any lighting system should be designed to recognize these changes and be capable of future adjustment. Even the initial installation will require some tuning to reach the design objectives.

PRINCIPLES OF ELECTRICITY

Electricity is a phenomenon that is still not fully explained. It is now believed that all matter is composed of very small particles called protons and electrons. These small bits of matter make up an atom and the small particles themselves are electricity held together by magnetic attraction.

Protons carry a positive charge and form the nucleus of the atom. Electrons are negative charges that are attracted to the nucleus of positive charges. In the complex structure of some atoms like copper, iron, or aluminum, there are a large number of electrons in the outer shell. Some of these electrons are not held tightly to the nucleus. These are called free electrons. Free electrons will move from one atom to another and they are the basic component of electric current. The materials that have a large number of these free electrons are called conductors. Materials that have very few free electrons are called insulators. A flow of free electrons through a conductor is electric current. This energy can be converted to light, heat, or mechanical energy to accomplish a desired task.

Power Generation

Figure 8-6 is a schematic of a simple generator. When the conductor is rotated in the magnetic field, a flow of free electrons is set up. By convention, the flow is from the positive to the negative pole in a clockwise direction as shown. So long as the line from the generator to the lightbulb is continuous the flow of electricity will be continued. This loop is called a circuit.

Large generators and transformers used to produce electric power for the consumer market are much

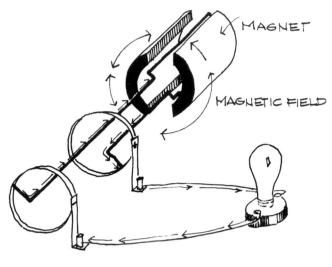

SCHEMATIC GENERATOR

FIGURE 8-6

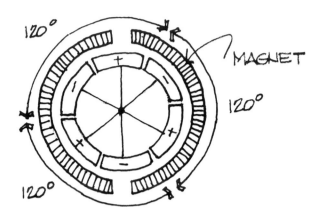

THREE PHASE GENERATOR

FIGURE 8-7

more complex than the one in Figure 8–12, but the basic principles are the same. Commercial power is alternating current (ac). This results from the reversing of the conductor poles as it rotates in the magnetic field.

Figure 8–7 is a simplified schematic diagram of a three-phase alternating current generator. Each conductor loop in the generator produces a current independent of the other, 120° out of phase. The number of cycles per second (hertz, abbreviated Hz) depends on the speed of rotation. The standard cycling rate in this country is 60 Hz.

The advantage of this type of generator is that a number of different power outputs can be obtained by utilizing different combinations of the three phases. When all three phases of the generator are combined it is called three-phase power. If only one phase or some combination of two phases is utilized, it is referred to as single-phase power. This aspect will be important to us in the discussion of distribution and utilization of power.

Electrical Measurement

Electric energy has two variable components called volts and amps. These components are most easily understood by drawing an analogy between electrical systems and hydraulic systems.

The ampere (amp) is a measure of the number of free electrons passing through the cross-sectional area of a conductor. This is analogus to a volume of water flowing through the cross section of a pipe. In a hydraulic system the volume of water would be expressed in cubic feet per second or gallons per minute. In an electrical circuit the intensity of electron flow (volume) is expressed in amps.

The voltage in an electrical system is a measure of the force driving the free electrons. This is called the electromotive force (emf). The emf in an electrical system is similar to pressure in a hydraulic system. The magnitude of the force that moves water through a pipe is expressed in pounds per square inch. In an electrical system the emf is expressed in volts.

Since electric energy is transmitted at the speed of light (186,000 miles per second) the velocity of flow in an electric circuit is taken as a constant. However, there is a natural resistance to the flow of electric current present in any conductor. This resistance is analogous to friction in a pipe. The friction in a pipe will cause a drop in the water pressure as the water moves through the pipe. Likewise, the resistance to the flow of electric current in a conductor will result in a drop in voltage as the current moves through the system. The resistance of a conductor is measured in ohms.

The relationship between these three factors is expressed by Ohm's Law which states the current that will flow through a given resistance is directly proportional to the voltage. This relationship is represented by the expression

$$I = \frac{E}{R}$$

where

I = the intensity of current in amps;
E = the emf in volts;
R = the resistance in ohms.

Electric power is measured in units called watts, or in thousand watt units called kilowatts. The electrical energy input to any electrical device in watts is found by the expression $P = I^2R$ where P = power in

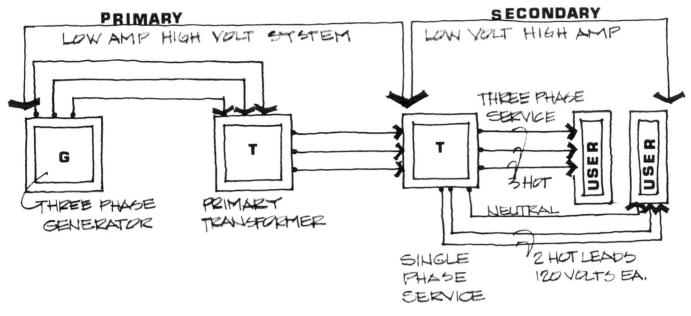

PRIMARY

LOW AMP HIGH VOLT SYSTEM

SECONDARY

LOW VOLT HIGH AMP

G

THREE PHASE
GENERATOR

T

PRIMARY
TRANSFORMER

T

THREE PHASE
SERVICE

3 HOT

NEUTRAL

USER

USER

SINGLE
PHASE
SERVICE

2 HOT LEADS
120 VOLTS EA.

POWER DISTRIBUTION SYSTEM
FIGURE 8-8

watts ($W \times 1000$ equals kilowatts); I = intensity of the current in amps; R = the resistance in ohms. If the basic equation is manipulated it can be expressed as $P = I^2R = I\,(IR)$. Since Ohm's law states that $E = IR$ then it follows that wattage is also the product of volts times amps. Written as an algebraic expression, $P = IE$. This is called the power formula. You will notice that since we are multiplying volts times amps the watt could be expressed in units of volt-amps. The volt-amp (va) is frequently used to express the optimum output of an electric distribution system. Rating a supply in thousands of volt-amps (kVA) is a handy way to describe the maximum power potential, because the power distribution system itself is broken into two parts: the primary distribution system and the secondary distribution system. (See Figure 8-8.)

The primary system for reasons of economy is operated at high voltage and low amperage. The secondary system then steps the power down through secondary transformers to provide working amperages at lower voltage. The kVA rating of the system does not change, however.

For example, assume that the system in Figure 8-8 has a kVA rating of 200 kVA. Its maximum power potential is $200 \times 1000 = 200,000$ volt-amps or 200,000 watts of power maximum. Next assume that the primary distribution portion of the system is operated at 2400 volts. Applying the basic power formula, solving for I we find

$$I = \frac{P}{E} = \frac{200,000 \text{ VA (watts)}}{2400 \text{ V}}$$

$$I = 83.33 \text{ amps}$$

Now that the secondary system is going to be run at 120 volts, what is the amperage in the secondary system? Again using the power formula we find

$$I = \frac{P}{E} = \frac{200,000 \text{ VA}}{120 \text{ V}} = 1,666.66 \text{ amps}$$

As mentioned earlier, most electric power produced for commercial applications is three-phase alternating current, but the power supply that will be available at a site depends on how the distribution system is set up. Many small systems will distribute only single-phase power because of the expense involved in building a secondary three-phase system. However, three-phase power is not usually necessary unless the project requires large appliances or involves some major area lighting.

If three-phase secondary power is available, it will usually be rated at 120/208 volt (4 wire) or 240 V (3 wire). The voltage ratings depend on the type of transformers employed.

Single-phase secondary service is available as 120 V (2 wire), 277 V (2 wire), 120/208 V (3 wire), 277/480 V (3 wire) and as 120/240 V (3 wire). The most common service is the 120/240 V (3 wire) single-phase service, which is the most widely accepted standard for residential and light construction.

The final stage in the power distribution system is the on-site system. This is the component of greatest importance to the landscape architect and site planner. The major components of the on-site system are shown in the schematic diagram, Figure 8-9.

The final step-down transformer may or may not be provided on-site. This will depend on the energy

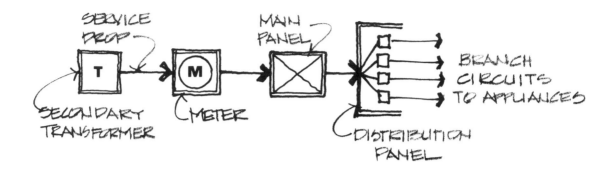

ON SITE ELECTRIC SERVICE

FIGURE 8–9

demand in amps required by the job at hand. Likewise, the voltage and three-phase or single-phase supply will be selected in accordance with the need.

The meter is usually supplied by the power supplier to measure the amount of energy consumed. The consumption is measured in kilowatts times the time in hours (kilowatt-hours). For example, a 100 watt incandescent lamp operated for 10 hours would consume

$$\frac{100 \text{ watts} \times 10 \text{ hours}}{1000} = 1 \text{ kilowatt-hour.}$$

The main breaker or fuse beyond the meter protects the incoming supply from being overloaded, then each branch circuit is protected by its own fuse or circuit breaker. On most small jobs the main breaker will be in the same panel with the branch circuits. On larger jobs the main may be separate with several distribution panels connected to the main panel.

Branch Circuits

The branch circuits distribute electricity to the various fixtures in a system. Figure 8–10 is a schematic diagram of a typical branch circuit that might be used in an outdoor situation.

The system is composed of five 200 watt floodlights and two waterproof duplex outlets. One of the duplex outlets remains hot all the time while the other outlet is switched with the lights. Notice that the wiring utilizes a three-wire system. The wires at the top are the normal service, one hot wire, and the neutral ground. The third wire shown as a dashed line is a system ground that will run the circuit to ground if there should be a failure in any of the fixtures. A three-wire system of this kind is essential outside where the danger of electric shock is very high.

The Three-Wire Grounded Circuit

Figure 8–11 illustrates the principle of the three-wire grounded circuit and a two-wire ungrounded circuit. In Figure 8–11A, if there is a hot wire short to the case of an appliance, current will travel through the case to the girl who completes the circuit to the neutral ground. In Figure 8–11B, the hazard has been reduced, since the case is grounded by the third wire and electricity will follow the path of least resistance.

WIRING AND ELECTRICAL PLANS

In the first part of the chapter we looked at lighting equipment, basic lighting, design considerations, and some principles of electricity and power distribution. In this section we will integrate this basic information into a working vocabulary for preparing electrical plans for landscape construction projects.

Electrical plans are one of the simplest of all the working drawings. The fixtures and appliances are indicated on the plans by symbols, supplemented by equipment schedules. The symbols used for electrical plans are nationally accepted standards. These symbols should always be employed in the prescribed manner to avoid confusion in bidding and construction. Some of the most common symbols are given in Figure 8–12.

The actual wiring is not shown in any detail on the plan, it is simply shown in schematic form. Other information required to finish the work is given in the schedules of materials and supplemented by the technical specifications.

The electrical plans are usually prepared on a schematic site plan, separate from a grading or utility plan. In some cases, where underground utility lines might interfere with the installation of underground conduit, it is wise to indicate them on the electrical

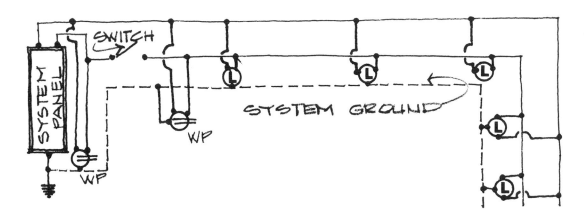

TYPICAL BRANCH CIRCUIT

FIGURE 8-10

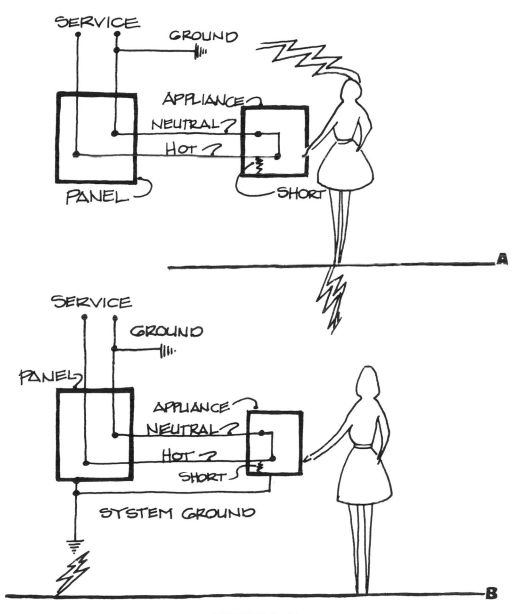

FIGURE 8-11

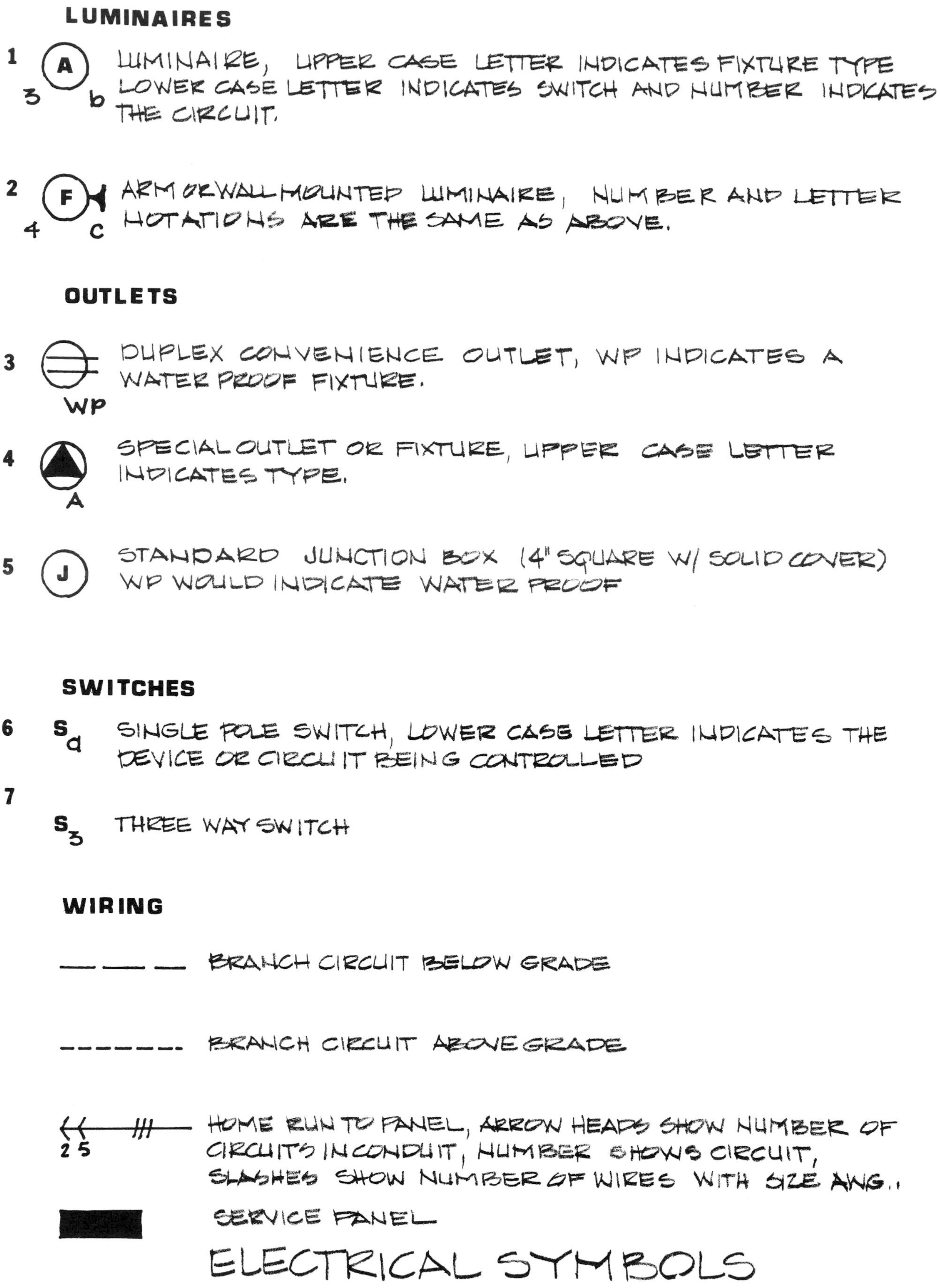

LUMINAIRES

1 (A) LUMINAIRE, UPPER CASE LETTER INDICATES FIXTURE TYPE
3 b LOWER CASE LETTER INDICATES SWITCH AND NUMBER INDICATES
       THE CIRCUIT.

2 (F) ARM OR WALL MOUNTED LUMINAIRE, NUMBER AND LETTER
4 c   NOTATIONS ARE THE SAME AS ABOVE.

OUTLETS

3   DUPLEX CONVENIENCE OUTLET, WP INDICATES A
   WP WATER PROOF FIXTURE.

4   SPECIAL OUTLET OR FIXTURE, UPPER CASE LETTER
   A   INDICATES TYPE.

5 (J) STANDARD JUNCTION BOX (4" SQUARE W/ SOLID COVER)
       WP WOULD INDICATE WATER PROOF

SWITCHES

6 S_d SINGLE POLE SWITCH, LOWER CASE LETTER INDICATES THE
        DEVICE OR CIRCUIT BEING CONTROLLED

7
   S_3 THREE WAY SWITCH

WIRING

——————— BRANCH CIRCUIT BELOW GRADE

- - - - - - - BRANCH CIRCUIT ABOVE GRADE

⟨⟨———///—— HOME RUN TO PANEL, ARROW HEADS SHOW NUMBER OF
2 5   CIRCUITS IN CONDUIT, NUMBER SHOWS CIRCUIT,
            SLASHES SHOW NUMBER OF WIRES WITH SIZE AWG..

▬▬▬ SERVICE PANEL

ELECTRICAL SYMBOLS

FIGURE 8-12

base sheet. In cases where the electricity is only a minor part of the project, the electrical work may appear on other sheets. When this is done be sure that the information is clear and will not be lost in the detail of other systems.

A procedure for preparing electrical plans is outlined below. This procedure can be used as a guide and a checklist for most simple electrical projects.

- Check the local electrical codes and obtain copies of the requirements governing the work.

- Contact the local power distribution company and determine what kind of electrical service will be available at the project site. This is particularly important if there may be a need to use high voltage or three-phase equipment. Also, find out what equipment is furnished by the power company and what will be required of the client. This factor can many times cause budget disasters if it is not taken into account early. Let the power company know what you are doing. Many times they will be able to offer suggestions that can result in substantial savings to the client. Some large companies will also furnish some technical help.

- Check the on-site power supply and determine what new equipment or system revisions might be necessary to operate the new electrical system. This is a very important step if the electrical work is an addition to an existing project.

- Prepare a schematic base map of the site. Indicate any on-site obstructions or other utilities that might interfere with the installation of the electrical work on the base map.

- Locate all of the fixtures, appliance switches, and panels required for the work on the plan by the proper symbols. Be sure that it is clear what equipment is new and what equipment is existing or furnished by others.

- Calculate the wire sizes required by the loads on each circuit and prepare an equipment and panel schedule.

To illustrate how a plan is done we will work through the procedure, using a large residence as the example. Since much of the lighting in the yard is done for effect as well as utility and security, the base map (Figure 8–13) indicates the outline of planting beds and the location of trees.

For the purpose of the example we will assume that we have copies of the local electrical code and that we have cleared our work with the local power company. A check of the existing power panel indicates that there are five additional branch circuits in the panel that are not being used. This means that no revision will be required to the existing distribution

system. We also note that the panel is a 120/240 volt single-phase unit with a system ground already installed.

The equipment selected for the job includes eight 200 watt, 120 volt floodlight fixtures for downlighting in the trees at the front and back of the residence. The downlighting is supplemented by six weatherproof duplex outlets located in the planting beds to operate spike mounted 100 watt floodlamps. These provide flexibility for seasonal change.

In addition to the 120 V system, low voltage lamps have been used in the areas adjacent to the residence. These lamps were selected to do the permanent effect lighting at the entrance and near the terrace. Figure 8–14 shows the schematic layout of the lighting with the equipment legend.

The next step is to calculate the load requirements and work out a panel schedule. To do this we first calculate the amperage required by each device as follows. The amperage of the 200 watt floodlamps is

$$I = \frac{P}{E} = \frac{200W \ (VA)}{120 \ V} = 1.67 \text{ amps (each fixture)}$$

The amperage of the duplex outlets is the same since each duplex outlet will serve two 100 watt lamps.

The next step is to determine the size and load of the transformers that will be used to operate the low voltage lamps. The low voltage system in the back is composed of six 25 watt well lights, a total of 150 watts. The system at the entrance has five 25 watt lamps, a total of 125 watts. The transformers selected are each rated at 126 watts so each transformer represents a load equal to

$$I = \frac{P}{E} = \frac{126}{120} = 1.05 \text{ amps}$$

The total amperage of the backyard fixtures is

8 fixtures @ 1.67 amps	13.36 amps
1 transformer @ 1.05 amps	1.05
Total Load	14.41 amps

The total amperage of the frontyard fixture is

7 fixtures @ 1.67 amps	11.69 amps
1 transformer @ 1.05 amps	1.05
Total Load	12.74 amps

The permissible load on a single-phase branch circuit with #12 or #14 wire is 20 amps. Therefore, two circuits will be required, one for the front and one for the back. You will notice that even though the equipment at the back of the house is on the same branch circuit of the panel, it is wired to allow independent operation of the three components. The operation is controlled by three switches located on the terrace. The front is also designed to be controlled by three switches near the front door.

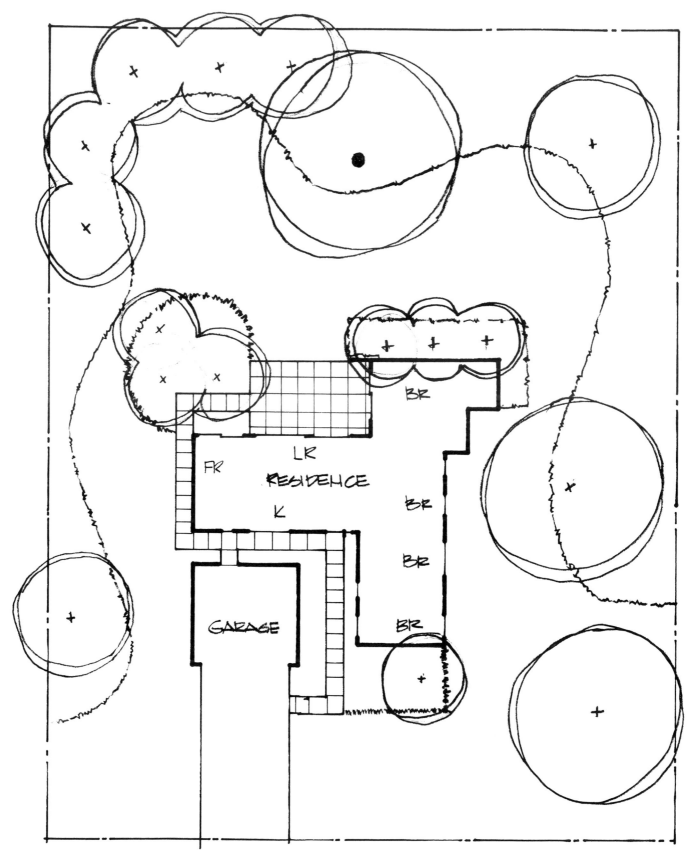

FIGURE 8–13

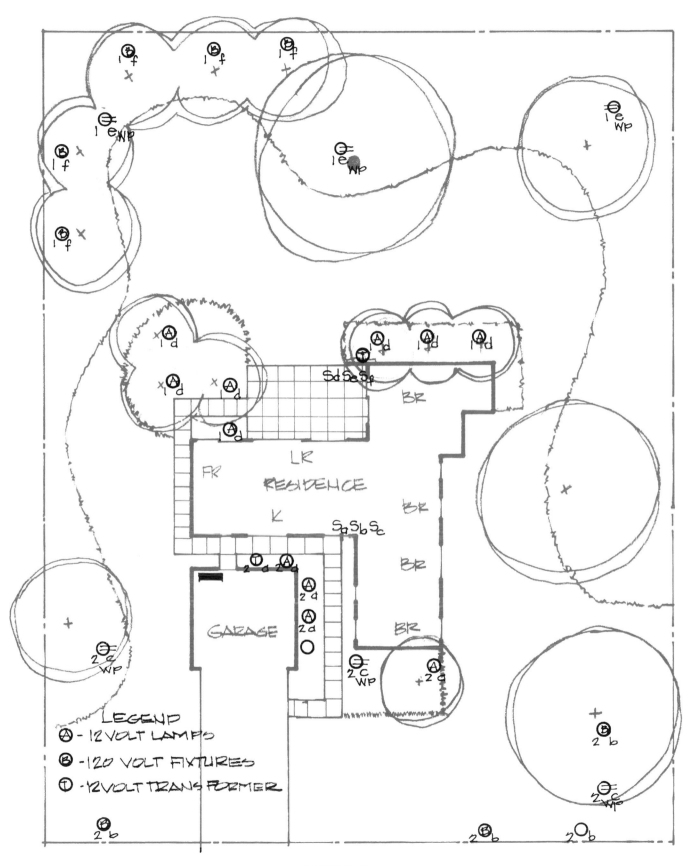

LEGEND
Ⓐ - 12 VOLT LAMPS
Ⓑ - 120 VOLT FIXTURES
Ⓣ - 12 VOLT TRANSFORMER

FIGURE 8-14

TABLE 8–4
Voltage Drops per 100 ft of Copper Wire

WIRE SIZE (AWG)	SIZE IN MILLS	VOLTAGE DROP PER 100 FT PER AMP COPPER
3/0	167,800	.01311
2/0	133,100	.01652
1/0	105,500	.02085
1	83,690	.02628
2	66,370	.03314
3	52,640	.04179
4	41,740	.05270
6	26,250	.08380
8	16,510	.13325
10	10,380	.21194
12	6,530	.33690
14	4,017	.54767

The final step is sizing the wire. The process here is the same as sizing pipe. As noted earlier, as power travels through a conductor there is a voltage drop similar to the pressure drop in a water system. In an electrical system the maximum voltage loss permitted is usually taken as 2% of the operating voltage. This is 2.4 volts for a 120 volt system. Table 8–3 gives the voltage drop in copper wire per 100 feet per amp based on the formula $M = kIL/E$ ($E = kIL/M$) where M = wire size in circular mills; k = resistance coefficient of the wire (copper = 22 ohms, aluminum = 35 ohms); I = amps; E = voltage drop; L = distance in feet.

Now consider Figure 8–15. For the purpose of illustration we have indicated the approximate locations of the wiring for the backyard and the appropriate dimensions. Beginning at the panel branch circuit, one carries a load of 14.41 amps a distance of approximately 100 ft to the switches in the rear. From Table 8–4 find that a #10 wire loses .21194 volts per amp per 100 ft. Therefore, 14.41 × .21194 = 3.05 volts. This is greater than 2% so try a #8 wire at .13325 volts per amp per 100 ft as follows: 14.41 × .13325 volts = 1.92 volts. This is less than 2 volts, so it is satisfactory.

From switch 1 to the first duplex outlet the load will be 3 × 1.67 amps or 5.01 amps. The load must be carried approximately 40 ft. First check a #12 wire. From Table 8–3 a #12 wire loses .33690 volts per amp per 100 ft. Therefore, 5.01 amps × .33690 volts × .40 = .675 volts. This appears to be satisfactory.

From this duplex outlet the line splits and carries 1.67 amps 60 ft to the other duplex outlets. From Table 8–3 find that a #14 wire loses .54767 volts per amp per 100 ft. Therefore, 1.67 amps × .54767 volts × .60 = .54876 volts. The voltage losses for this system are tabulated as follows.

RUN	VOLTAGE DROP	WIRE SIZE
Panel to switch	1.920 volts	#8
Switch to first outlet	.675	#12
First outlet to last outlet	.548	#14
Total	3.143 volts	

The accumulated voltage drop from the panel to the last duplex outlet is 3.14 volts, which is greater than 2%. If #12 wire is used from the first duplex outlet to the last two duplex outlets, the total drop will be 2.93 volts. This is still greater than 2%, but increasing the wire size to #10 wire is not absolutely necessary since the lamps themselves will operate on voltages as low as 115 volts.

The wire sizes for the other areas would be calculated in the same way, holding the voltage drop to less than 3.0 volts. Figure 8–15 is the completed electrical plan.

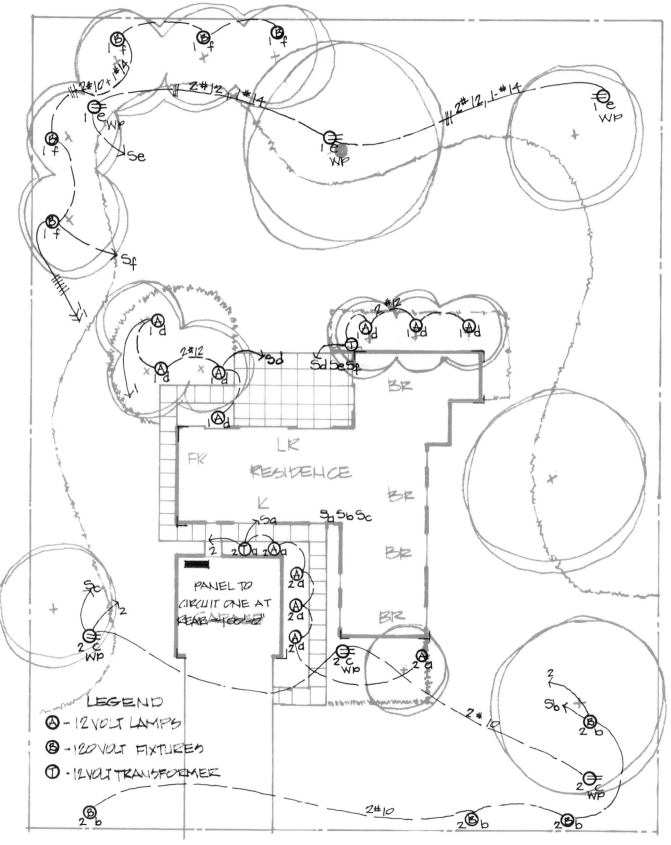

FIGURE 8–15

PROBLEMS

1. Using the point-by-point method, what is the average maintained illumination for two 400 W metallic halide lamps mounted on 30 ft poles 80 ft center-to-center? Use a 20 ft grid and tabulate the points of a 40 ft by 80 ft grid.

2. Using the same fixture as Problem 1 what is the average illumination using the average illumination formula?

3. If you want to light an area approximately 60 ft wide with the same 400 W fixture on 25 ft poles, what should the spacing be if M is assumed to be .5 ft and we need to maintain 2 ft-c?

4. Size the wire for the following 120 volt systems. Remember the maximum voltage drop is 2.4 volts. All fixtures require 2 amps (Figure P8-4).

5. Size the wire for the following 120 volt systems. Remember the maximum voltage drop is 2.4 volts (Figure P8-5).

LOAD = 2 AMPS/FIXTURE

FIGURE P8-4

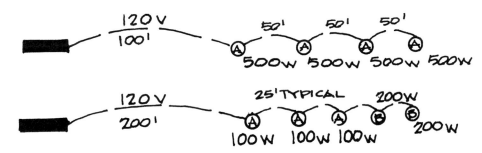

FIGURE P8-5

9
Fountain and Pool Design

The use of water in the landscape is one of the most challenging and delightful ways to add punctuation to almost any project. Water it seems has the ability to attract attention and alter the mood of a space quicker than any other landscape feature. The reflection in a pool tends to lend serenity to a space, the playing sound of running water will cool and cheer a space and the intricate play of water jets adds visual interest that can be accomplished with no other sculptural form.

The design of good water features involves a working knowledge of three basic elements: equipment, basic pool and fountain hydraulics, and the design of basic water holding structures. As with lighting and irrigation, our discussion of equipment will be limited to the basic components used in fountains and pools because the technology is changing so rapidly. Then we will briefly discuss the hydraulics of weirs and water jets and finally look at the design of the pools themselves.

The subject of swimming pools is not considered in this text because the development of the pool industry is, in our opinion, at a point that will allow the designer to select a pool package to meet almost any commercial or residential need. Large swimming pools on the other hand require some rather sophisticated design considerations beyond the scope of this discussion, and these kinds of projects are best accomplished in association with competent engineers.

EQUIPMENT FOR FOUNTAINS AND POOLS

Nozzles

The heart of any fountain display is the spray nozzle used to distribute the water. The effect that is obtained is directly related to the design of the nozzle itself and this component requires precission engineering. Some of the more basic kinds of nozzles will be discussed in the following paragraphs.[1]

Smooth-Bore Nozzles

Smooth-bore nozzles are used to achieve clear, smooth water columns. If a smooth bore nozzle is placed in a vertical position it will give the appearance of a crystal or glasslike shaft supporting a frothing cascade at its summit. This is a particularly interesting effect when lighted but lacks visual appeal in daylight. Smooth-bore nozzles placed at an angle maintain a clear shaft over the first part of the trajectory gradually breaking into a finer spray in its downward path. These basic effects are illustrated in Figure 9–1.

Aerating Nozzles

Aerating nozzles generate water columns mixed with thousands of air bubbles. The diameter of the water column is usually larger than a comparable smooth-bore nozzle and they require higher operating pressures. The aerated water column has much greater visibility in daylight or in other forms of high illumination. For this reason it is usually preferred if only a single jet is used in a water display or if the display is designed to be seen from a great distance.

The aerating nozzle operates by discharging water through several small jets near its base, or by an aeration sleeve. The streams pick up air, incorporate it into the water, and are discharged as a single stream at the top. To achieve a proper air–water mix-

---

[1]The illustrations of equipment were provided by Kim Lighting, City of Industry, California.

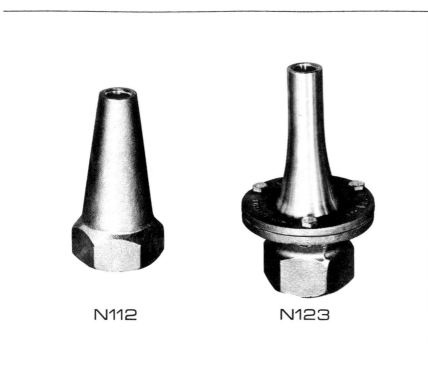
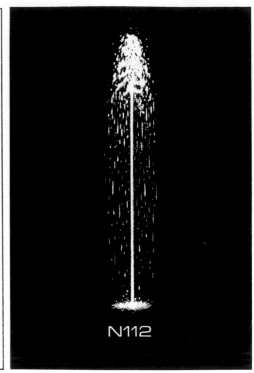

N112   N123

N112

FIGURE 9–1

ture, the water level around the nozzle is critical. At low levels proper aeration will not take place and at high levels the column height will be markedly reduced. Since the water-level tolerance is usually less than 2 in, some kind of water level control is essential for any fountain that will utilize aerating nozzles. A typical aerating nozzle is shown in Figure 9–2.

Multi-Jet Nozzles

Multi-jet nozzles are used to sculpture the water into a pattern or they can be grouped to give the appearance of a large single stream. Multi-jet nozzles can be most effective when water sound and pattern are the primary design objectives. Since the water pattern is controlled and more compact these nozzles are frequently used where wind could be a limiting factor in the design, or where space is a limiting factor. A variety of multi-jet nozzles are shown in Figure 9–3.

Pumps

Pumps used for foutains and pools are similar to those discussed in irrigation. A fountain system will employ either a centrifugal pump or a submersible pump, since the water is taken directly from the pool and recirculated through the system.

For fountains that require high operating pressure and large volumes of water, a centrifugal pump is

usually the best choice. The major difficulty with the centrifugal pump system is that the pump must be housed somewhere near the pool and this may be objectionable as well as expensive.

Submersible pumps are usually employed for small fountains that have moderate pressure and water volume requirements. They are most convenient because they require no special housing or equipment other than a waterproof electrical service. One disadvantage of a submersible pump is that they cannot be operated at low water levels usually less than 16 in. If the pump should be operated at a low level, a vortex will develop over the intake orifice, the pump will loose its prime, and subsequently burn the motor up. This problem can easily be avoided by providing a water level control device.

Water Level Control Devices

There are two kinds of water level control devices used for pools and fountains: electronic and float type. The electronic device is a small sensor that operates an electric solenoid value to keep the pool full. The float type device is similar to the assembly in a water closet. Water pressure acting on the float keeps the valve closed but if the water level drops the pressure is no longer on the float and the valve opens.

The electronic device is usually used on pools that have volumes greater than 1000 cubic feet. For pools less than 1000 cubic feet the float valve is usually sat-

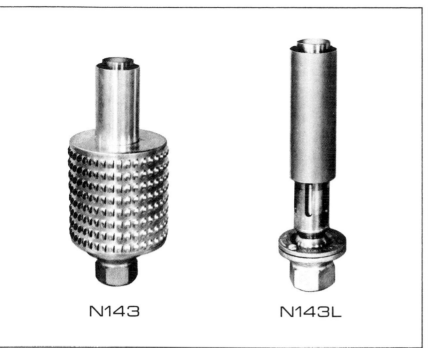
N143

N143L

N143

FIGURE 9–2

N365

N360

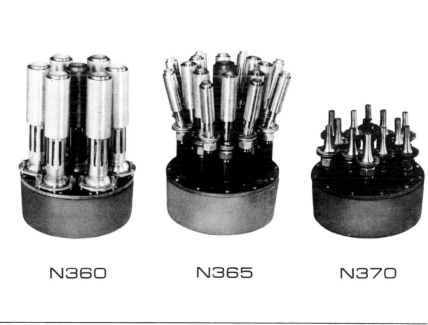
N360

N365

N370

FIGURE 9–3

285

R50　　　　R55C　　　　R55

FIGURE 9–4

isfactory. Water level control devices are shown in Figure 9–4.

Filters

Large pools and fountains usually require the use of a filter system to reduce the frequency of maintenance. These filters are the same as those used for swimming pools and use sand, charcoal, or diatomaceous earth as the filter material. Figure 9–5 illustrates a typical package pool filter.

Lighting

Pool lighting equipment is available in both 120 volt and 12 volt systems. The 12 volt system has the obvious safety advantage of providing little shock hazard; however they do not have the wattage flexibility of the 120 volt fixtures. The maximum bulb wattage for a 12 volt system is about 300 watts while a 120 volt system can provide wattages in excess of 1000 watts and the bulbs are longer lived.

The bulbs used for underwater lighting are not the same as those used above ground. They are designed to operate at higher temperatures taking advantage of the water for cooling. This is important because pool lights will burn out if they are operated above the water surface.

Other Fountain Equipment

In major urban centers where a fountain may generate mist that can be carried by high winds it is usually desirable to install a wind control. This device has a calibrated wind sensor that will automatically shut the fountain down if a specified wind speed is reached. In most cases the switch will stay

R-62-1

FIGURE 9–5

off until the wind velocity drops below the specified value or for 30 minutes, which ever is greater.

Many fountain displays are designed to display several different water patterns. In these situations they are controlled by an automatic sequencing device similar to an irrigation controller. These devices operate the valves and lighting to achieve the desired effect.

Fittings such as junction boxes, cord and cable seals, drains, stand pipes, and mounting brackets are also an integral part of the equipment to be incorporated into a pool. Most pool equipment manufacturers and contractors recommend that the fittings be cast or machined from red brass to insure longevity

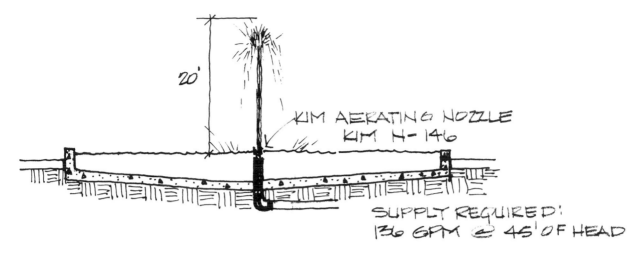

KIM AERATING NOZZLE
KIM H-146

SUPPLY REQUIRED:
136 GPM @ 45' OF HEAD

POOL & FOUNTAIN

FIGURE 9-6

and prevent leaking. While the expense of these fittings is initially high the serviceability justifies the cost.

BASIC HYDRAULICS OF FOUNTAINS AND POOLS

There are two basic effects that are used in the design of ornamental fountains: water jets and water cascades over weirs. Each of these effects involves a different set of hydraulic principles to ensure the proper operation, and each effect will be discussed.

Water Jets

Water jets are the result of forcing water through a restricted orifice (nozzle) to increase its velocity and generate a uniform stream. As we have noted in the brief discussion on equipment there are several types of nozzles available to the designer to achieve a variety of effects in the water stream.

When the initial design of a fountain has been completed with respect to the size of the pool and the character and height of the water display, the major design task involves selecting and sizing the pump and necessary control equipment. To illustrate this process consider the following example (Figure 9-6).

A pool is to have a single aerating nozzle that will operate at a height of 20 ft. From manufacturer's data we have determined that the nozzle requires a pump that will deliver 136 GPM at 45 ft of head. This pressure and water volume is probably best handled by a centrifugal pump rather than a submersible pump.

Figure 9-7 illustrates a series of pump curves from a Kim Equipment Catalog. Notice that the required gallonage and head is a point that lies below the

curve for a model KP 500-3 pump. The KP-200-3 would be too small for the job so the KP 500-3 should be specified.

Notice that the pump is rated at a much higher volume and pressure than required to operate the nozzle as designed. This means that height of the water stream will be higher than specified or some measure must be taken to reduce the water volume and pressure produced by the pump. This situation is not at all unusual and can be handled simply by installing a throttling valve at the pump. The pump will then have to work against the valve and the valve can be adjusted to achieve the desired performance at the fountain nozzle.

Weirs and Cascades

A water cascade falling from one level to another is an interesting detail that is frequently employed in water displays. Several different visual effects can be obtained with the cascade depending on the design detail of the weir and the water volume. For example, water that passes over a smooth-faced weir will form a clear sheet; but if the surface of the weir is rough, the water will break up and fall as an aerated sheet.

Water falling away from a weir begins to accelerate under the influence of gravity and at some point will begin to break up rather than remain in a uniform sheet. The point at which the breakup will occur is a function of the water volume and the velocity as it approaches the weir. Small water volumes that just cover the weir will break up quickly and tend to dance or trickle over the weir. As water depths increase at the weir the discharge velocity will increase and the sheet will remain intact much longer. Since the actual point of break-

KP SERIES DRY TYPE PUMPS

Kim dry type pumps are furnished standard trimmed with brass or bronze. Designed for continuous operation they represent the highest quality available. If the pumps to fill your specific need are not listed, write Kim your requirements.

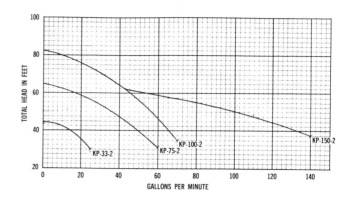

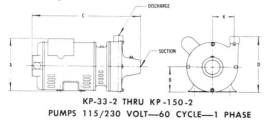

KP-33-2 THRU KP-150-2
PUMPS 115/230 VOLT—60 CYCLE—1 PHASE

PUMP DIMENSIONS

PUMP NO.	H.P.	A	B	C	D	K	Discharge	Suction
KP-33-2	1/3	7 1/2	3 1/2	15 3/8	7	3	3/4 N.P.T.	1 1/4 N.P.T.
KP-75-2	3/4	7 1/2	3 1/2	15 3/16	8	3 3/8	1 N.P.T.	1 1/4 N.P.T.
KP-100-2	1	7 1/2	3 1/2	15 11/16	8	3 3/8	1 N.P.T.	1 1/4 N.P.T.
KP-150-2	1 1/2	8 3/4	3 1/2	16 11/16	8 11/16	3 3/8	1 1/2 P.N.T.	2 N.P.T.

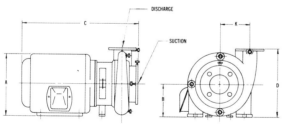

KP-200-3 THRU KP-750-3 PUMPS
208/220/440 VOLT — 60 CYCLE — 3 PHASE

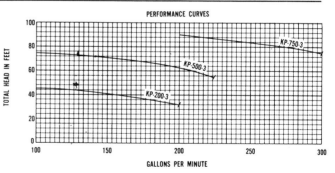

PUMP DIMENSIONS

PUMP NO.	H.P.	A	B	C	D	K	Discharge	Suction
KP-200-3	2	9	4 1/2	19 5/16	10 1/2	4 11/16	2 1/2 FLG	3 FLG
KP-500-3	5	10 1/2	5 1/4	22 1/4	12 1/4	5 7/8	2 FLG	2 1/2 FLG
KP-750-3	7 1/2	12 1/2	6 1/4	25	13	6	2 1/2 FLG	3 FLG

FIGURE 9-7

POOL & CASCADE

FIGURE 9-8

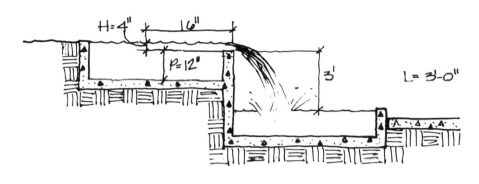

POOL & CASCADE

FIGURE 9-9

up is difficult to predict accurately and is frequently a major design consideration it is suggested that the mechanical equipment be designed to allow fine tuning of the system after it is completed.

Estimating Water Volume over Weirs

The critical design consideration of a water cascade display is determining the water volume required to maintain a continuous flow and achieve the desired effect. Water volume over a rectangular weir can be estimated by Bazin's formula:

$$Q = \left(.405 + \frac{.00984}{H}\right) \left[1 + .55 \frac{H^2}{(P + H)^2}\right] LH \, (2gH)^{.5}$$

where

Q = Water volume in cubic feet per second;
H = Head in feet (the water depth above the weir taken at a distance of $4H$ from the weir, see Figure 9-8);
P = The height of the weir above the upper pool level in feet;

L = The length of the weir in feet;
g = 32.17 (The universal gravity constant).

To illustrate how the formula is applied consider the water cascade shown in Figure 9-9. A water cascade has been designed to flow over a 3 ft wide weir at a depth of 3 in to 4 in and fall as a continuous sheet to a lower pool; the water volume required is found as follows.

$$Q = \left(.405 + \frac{.00984}{H}\right) \left[1 + .55 \frac{H^2}{(P + H)^2}\right] LH \, (2gH)^{.5}$$

$$Q = \left(.405 + \frac{.00984}{.33}\right) \left[1 + .55 \frac{.33^2}{(1 + .33)^2}\right] 3$$
$$\times .33 \, (2 \times 32.17 \times .33)^{.5}$$

$Q = .4348 \times (1.55 \times .61564) \times .99 \times (21.23)^{.5}$
$Q = .4348 \times .9542 \times .99 \times 4.608$
$Q = 1.89$ cfs

To convert cubic feet per second (cfs) to gallons per minute (GPM) multiply by 448.831. Thus,

$$1.89 \times 448.831 = 848.29 \text{ GPM}$$

Therefore, to operate this cascade as designed it will require a pump that will circulate 850 gallons per minute. The water volume requirement is high but the head requirement is low. The pump selected should only generate enough pressure to raise the water from the lower pool to the upper pool. For the example the pump will only have to lift the water 3 ft 4 in so a pump that generates 5 to 6 feet of head will do the job.

POOL CONSTRUCTION

The pool is the heart of any successful water feature in the landscape. A well-designed pool can reduce maintenance, complement the active water display and accent the overall landscape composition, but if the pool is not properly designed the water feature will almost certainly fail.

The most common failure that results in abandoning a water feature is pool leakage. Mechanical equipment can be repaired or replaced but a pool leak is very difficult to trace or repair. For this reason no expense should be spared in the design of the pool. The major points that should be considered in developing a pool detail are water depth, surfacing, structural material, water level control, and drain.

Water Depth

The most commonly used pool depth is 16 in. This seems to be the best depth to achieve a good reflective surface, prevent excessive algae growth, and it will satisfy the requirements of most domestic fountain equipment. Water depth less than 16 in should be used advisedly since algae will develop quickly in shallow warm water and quickly become a maintenance problem. Similarly, deeper pools seem to offer no great advantage unless there is some specific reason for the greater depth, such as a pump that might require more water over the intake orifice.

Pool Surfacing

The pool surfacing should be selected with two things in mind: the ease of cleaning and the desired appearance of the water surface. For ease of maintenance the interior surface of the pool should be as smooth as possible with rounded corners that can be cleaned easily. The best materials are probably ceramic tile or steel troweled concrete.

The appearance of the water surface is a function of the color of the surfacing material. Light reflective colors will make the water appear clear and transparent, dark colors cause the surface to be reflective. In most situations the dark color is preferred particularly when there are vertical structures that could be reflected to good advantage. Keep in mind that light-colored finish materials will expose any equipment in the pool.

Structural Materials

There are several materials that have been used for pool construction including copper, PVC, fiberglass, and concrete. Copper is an interesting material that is frequently employed for small indoor pools. PVC has been used as a liner on sand to generate large free-form pools. While the results obtained with this material are very photogenic their durability must be questioned. Fiberglass has been employed in the manufacture of prefabricated pools for residential and commercial applications. For small jobs fiberglass is an excellent alternative to concrete especially where weight might be a critical consideration.

Concrete is still the most widely utilized material for pool construction and is probably best for most situations because it is durable and can be formed and finished in a wide range of shapes and colors. While concrete offers distinct advantages, keep in mind that it is not waterproof unless it is properly proportioned and finished. For most pool work it is recommended that 3,000 lb material be specified at least 4 in thick and the pool should be treated with a waterproofing agent to ensure it will not leak.

Water Level Controls

In many small pools the provision of a special water fill connection is not necessary. But for most large pools, over 35 cubic feet, a special fill line and an automatic water level control device should be provided. The size of the fill line is a function of the volume of the pool. For medium-sized pools, 40 to 80 cubic feet, a ³⁄₄ in line is satisfactory; for larger pools a $1 - 1\frac{1}{2}$ in line should be provided.

The fill line should be brought into the pool next to the automatic level control valve, at a point that is easily accessible for maintenance. If a float valve device is used it is best located in the front edge of the pool since this is the part of the pool that is least obvious to the viewer, as seen in Figure 9–10.

All pools should include an overflow control. This is accomplished simply by providing a standpipe that is threaded into the pool drain. To drain the pool the standpipe is removed. When the standpipe is in place excess water will run over it into the drain system, as shown in Figure 9-11.

The pool drain system should be connected to a storm sewer, sanitary sewer or some approved drainage outlet. Always be sure to check the elevation of the pool and the drainage outlet. Pools are often located in low places that prevent the use of a gravity drain. In these situations a pump must be used to drain the pool. This is not a big problem if a filter or a

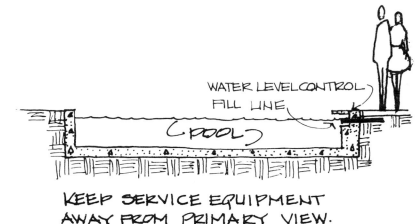

KEEP SERVICE EQUIPMENT
AWAY FROM PRIMARY VIEW.

FIGURE 9–10

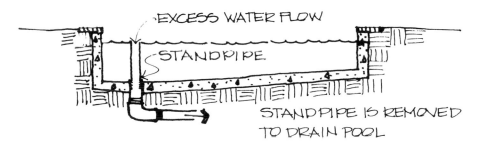

FIGURE 9–11

dry pump is used for fountain equipment because the same equipment can be used to drain the pool.

In cold climates where pools must be shut down in the winter it is essential that all piping be designed so that it can be drained when the pool is drained. Residual water left in pipes or in pump and filter equipment can cause considerable freeze damage.

The structural design and details of water features are largely a matter of designer preference. For this reason there is no lengthy discussion included here about the structural design of pools. The Reference Manual covers many essential structural features that should be considered in all pools, and suggests some general finish details.

PROBLEMS

1. What is the volume of water required to maintain a 2 in flow over a weir 8 ft wide that drops 2.5 ft?

2. If a smooth-bore nozzle requires 1.2 ft of head for each ft of height, what is the pump pressure in psi required to life a stream 12 ft high?

3. What is the total demand in GPM if a fountain has 4 nozzles that require 34 GPM each and a ring that requires 20 GPM?

4. If the ring in the previous problem requires 7 psi and the nozzles require 23 psi, what pressure will the pump have to produce?

UNIT
IV

LANDSCAPE CONSTRUCTION
MANUAL

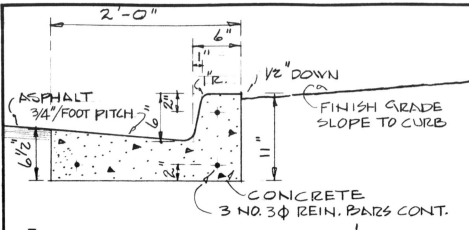

A SECTION · MONOLITHIC CURB & GUTTER
SCALE   1" = 1'-0"

A ONE OF THE MOST USED CURB & GUTTER DETAILS. WORKS WELL TO CONTROL VEHICLES. SLOPE ON FACE OF CURB PREVENTS WEAR ON TIRES. SQUARE EDGE ON BACK OF CURB ALLOWS A TURF EDGER TO BE USED.

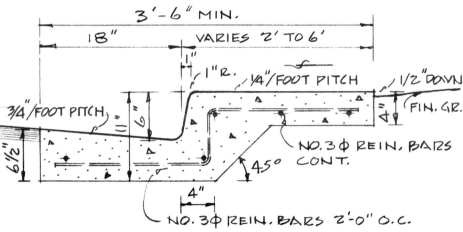

B SECTION · MONOLITHIC CURB, GUTTER AND LANDING OR WALK 1"=1'-0"

B A MINIMUM TWO FOOT WIDTH AT THE TOP OF THE CURB WILL PERMIT MOWING WHILE CARS ARE PARKED. THIS WILL ALSO PROVIDE A REASONABLE LOCATION FOR SPRINKLER HEADS FOR TURF OR GROUND COVER. THE TOP PORTION MAY BE EXTENDED TO PROVIDE WALK SPACE ALONG THE CURB. THE MONOLITHIC POUR ELIMINATES A JOINT BETWEEN WALK AND CURB; THUS WALK AND CURB STAY EVEN. MORE SKILL WILL BE REQUIRED TO INSTALL A MONOLITHIC POUR.

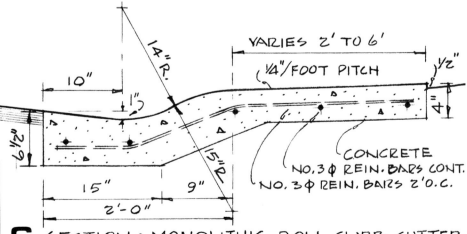

C SECTION · MONOLITHIC ROLL CURB, GUTTER AND LANDING OR WALK 1"=1'-0"

C THIS DETAIL PROVIDES ACCESS ALONG ITS ENTIRE EDGE, ALLOWING DRIVES TO BE ADDED WITHOUT BREAKING CURB. IT DOES NOT CONTROL TRAFFIC VERY WELL (SHOULD NOT BE USED FOR HEAD IN PARKING) AND WILL NOT CARRY THE WATER VOLUME OF VERTICAL CURBS.

LANDSCAPE CONSTRUCTION – MANUAL

D THIS DETAIL IS USED FREQUENTLY WITH ALL TYPES OF CONCRETE PAVING. THE EDGE OF THE PAVING CAN BE DOWELED AND THE CURB IS ADDED AFTER PAVING HAS HARDENED. THIS CURB WILL CONTROL VEHICLES AND PROVIDE A CHANNEL FOR STORM WATER.

6"

1" R.

1"

1/2" DOWN

FINISH GRADE SLOPE TO CURB

NO. 3 ∅ REIN. BAR CONT.

CONC. PAVING

1 1/2" R.

6"

2"

11"

NO. 3 ∅ REIN. BARS 12" O.C. B.W.

D SECTION · MONOLITHIC CURB & PAVING

SCALE   1" = 1'-0"

E A 6" HIGH ROLL CURB WILL CONTROL VEHICLES TO SOME DEGREE, YET ALLOW ACCESS OVER IT. STORM WATER CAPACITY WILL ALMOST EQUAL THAT OF THE VERTICAL CURB.

2'-0"

12"   12"

7 1/2" R.

7 1/2" R.

SLOPE FIN. GR. TO CURB

1/2" DOWN

ASPHALT

6"

6"

1 1/2"

11"

5 1/2"

3 NO. 3 ∅ REIN. BARS CONT.

CONCRETE

E SECTION · ROLL CURB & GUTTER

SCALE   1" = 1'-0"

F THIS DETAIL SHOULD ONLY BE USED WHERE THE SLOPE IS DIRECTED AWAY FROM THE CURB. WHEN USED AS A GUTTER, THE JOINT BETWEEN THE ASPHALT PAVING AND CONCRETE CURB WILL ALLOW WATER TO MOVE UNDER THE PAV- ING AND CURB CAUS- ING BOTH TO FAIL.

3" 5"

1" R.

1/2" DOWN

6"

SLOPE FROM CURB

SLOPE FIN. GR. TO CURB

ASPHALT

CONCRETE

18"

3 NO. 3 ∅ REIN. BARS

8"

F SECTION · CURB W/OUT GUTTER

SCALE   1" = 1'-0"

CONCRETE CURB & GUTTER DETAILS

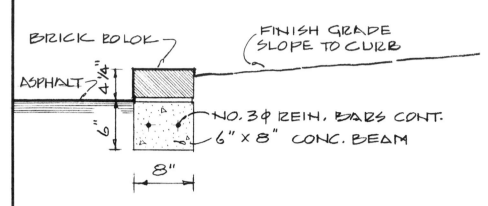

BRICK BOLOK

ASPHALT

FINISH GRADE
SLOPE TO CURB

4 ¼"

6"

8"

NO. 3∅ REIN. BARS CONT.
6" X 8" CONC. BEAM

A SECTION · BRICK CURB ON BEAM
SCALE   1" = 1'-0"

A THE USE OF ANY
ASPHALT TYPE PAVING
WILL REQUIRE A STRUCT-
URAL EDGE TO KEEP IT
FROM BREAKING OFF
AND PRODUCING AN
EDGE THAT IS DIFFICULT
TO MAINTAIN. WHERE
BRICK IS DESIRED, THIS
DETAIL SHOWS A CURB
OF BRICK THAT WILL
ALSO HELP TO CONTROL
WATER RUN OFF.

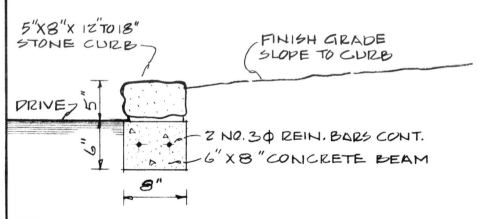

5"X8"X 12" TO 18"
STONE CURB

DRIVE

FINISH GRADE
SLOPE TO CURB

5"

6"

8"

2 NO. 3∅ REIN. BARS CONT.
6" X 8" CONCRETE BEAM

B SECTION · STONE CURB ON BEAM
SCALE   1" = 1'-0"

B ANY MATERIAL
MAY BE USED FOR THE
CURB IF IT WILL WITH-
STAND THE FORCE OF
A TIRE BUMPING IT.
DUE TO THE CRACK
THAT WILL FORM BE-
TWEEN THE CONCRETE
BEAM AND ASPHALT,
IT IS RECOMMENDED
THAT WATER NOT BE
DIRECTED TO THIS CURB.

BRICK BOLOK

CONC.

FINISH GRADE
SLOPE TO CURB

4 ¼"

2.5"

7"

8"

NO. 3∅ REIN. BARS 12" O.C. B.W.

C SECTION · BRICK CURB AT CONC. PAVING
SCALE   1" = 1'-0"

C THIS DETAIL WILL
WORK WELL AS AN EDGE
TO A DRIVE WAY OR A
MAJOR WALK WAY.
FOR A WALK 4" OF
CONCRETE IS ENOUGH
FOR MOST SITUATIONS.

LANDSCAPE CONSTRUCTION - MANUAL

D CURBS WITHIN A LARGE PAVED AREA WILL HELP FACILITATE GRADING FOR DRAINAGE, IN THAT THE CURB WILL NOT ALLOW THE WATER TO FLOW INTO PLANTED AREAS. WEEPS ARE IMPORTANT IN THESE CURBS FOR AN AREA OF HIGH RAIN FALL.

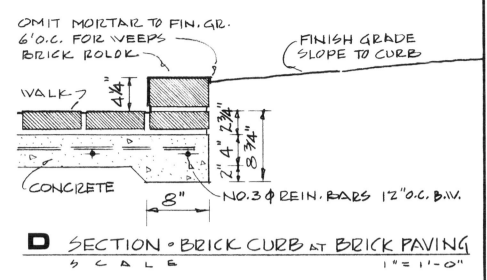

OMIT MORTAR TO FIN. GR. 6'O.C. FOR WEEPS
BRICK ROLOK
FINISH GRADE SLOPE TO CURB
WALK
4¼"
2" 4" 2¾"
8¾"
CONCRETE
8"
NO.3 ∅ REIN. BARS 12"O.C. B.W.

D SECTION · BRICK CURB AT BRICK PAVING
SCALE   1" = 1'-0"

E A MONOLITHIC CONCRETE CURB AND PAVING LOOKS NEAT AND WILL PROHIBIT WATER FLOWING INTO PLANTED AREAS. FINISH SHOULD BE THE SAME FOR CURB AND PAVING. SAND FILL UNDER CONCRETE SHOULD BE USED ON ALL OF THESE DETAILS WHERE HEAVY CLAY SOILS OCCUR.

EXPOSED AGGREGATE CONC. FIN. WALK.
ROLL CURB (EXP. AGGR. FINISH)
4"
3½"R
1"R.
4"
4"
¾" P.V.C. PIPE WEEP 6'O.C.
NO.3 ∅ REIN. BAR CONT.
NO.3 ∅ REIN. BARS 12"O.C. BOTHWAYS
2" SAND FILL

E SECTION · CURB AT CONCRETE WALK.
SCALE   1" = 1'-0"

F THIS SHOULD BE CONSIDERED AS A MINIMUM DETAIL TO ACHIEVE A RAISED PLANT BED. IT IS LIMITED AS A GUTTER AND WOULD NOT WITHSTAND MUCH FORCE AS FROM LAWN MOWERS, ETC.

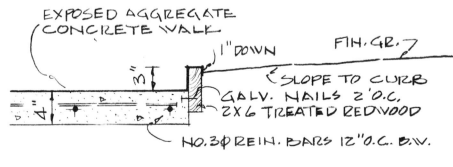

EXPOSED AGGREGATE CONCRETE WALK
1" DOWN
FIN. GR.
3"
4"
SLOPE TO CURB
GALV. NAILS 2'O.C.
2 X 6 TREATED REDWOOD
NO.3 ∅ REIN. BARS 12"O.C. B.W.

F SECTION · WOOD CURB AT CONC. WALK
SCALE   1" = 1'-0"

CURB DETAILS

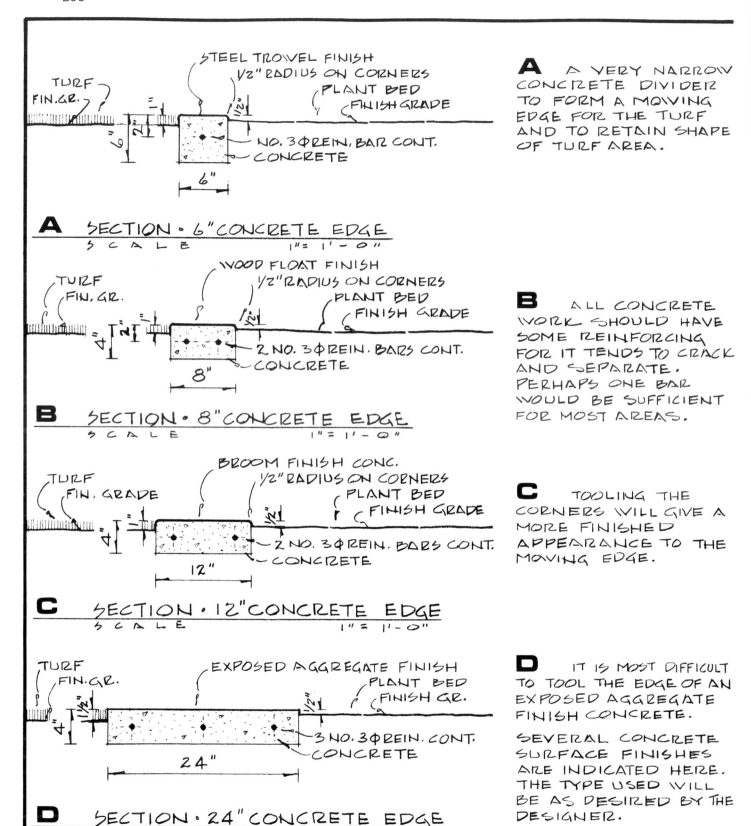

A STEEL TROWEL FINISH
½" RADIUS ON CORNERS
PLANT BED
FINISH GRADE
TURF FIN. GR.
NO. 3 Ø REIN. BAR CONT.
CONCRETE
6"

A SECTION · 6" CONCRETE EDGE
SCALE 1" = 1'-0"

B WOOD FLOAT FINISH
½" RADIUS ON CORNERS
PLANT BED
FINISH GRADE
TURF FIN. GR.
2 NO. 3 Ø REIN. BARS CONT.
CONCRETE
8"

B SECTION · 8" CONCRETE EDGE
SCALE 1" = 1'-0"

C BROOM FINISH CONC.
½" RADIUS ON CORNERS
PLANT BED
FINISH GRADE
TURF FIN. GRADE
2 NO. 3 Ø REIN. BARS CONT.
CONCRETE
12"

C SECTION · 12" CONCRETE EDGE
SCALE 1" = 1'-0"

D EXPOSED AGGREGATE FINISH
PLANT BED
FINISH GR.
TURF FIN. GR.
3 NO. 3 Ø REIN. CONT.
CONCRETE
24"

D SECTION · 24" CONCRETE EDGE
SCALE 1" = 1'-0"

A A VERY NARROW CONCRETE DIVIDER TO FORM A MOVING EDGE FOR THE TURF AND TO RETAIN SHAPE OF TURF AREA.

B ALL CONCRETE WORK SHOULD HAVE SOME REINFORCING FOR IT TENDS TO CRACK AND SEPARATE. PERHAPS ONE BAR WOULD BE SUFFICIENT FOR MOST AREAS.

C TOOLING THE CORNERS WILL GIVE A MORE FINISHED APPEARANCE TO THE MOVING EDGE.

D IT IS MOST DIFFICULT TO TOOL THE EDGE OF AN EXPOSED AGGREGATE FINISH CONCRETE.

SEVERAL CONCRETE SURFACE FINISHES ARE INDICATED HERE. THE TYPE USED WILL BE AS DESIRED BY THE DESIGNER.

E SHOWING A TYPICAL SECTION FOR A WALK WAY. 4" THICKNESS SHOULD BE CONSIDERED MINIMUM BUT WILL BE SUFFICIENT FOR MOST SITUATIONS WHERE HEAVY VEHICLES WILL NOT DRIVE OVER IT.

THE 2" SAND FILL MAY BE USED IN AREAS WITH VERY ACTIVE SOILS OR TO ASSURE FOUR FULL INCHES OF CONCRETE.

F SHOWING A 1X4 DOWELED JOINT. WITH OUT THE DOWEL THE CONCRETE WILL OFTEN SHIFT, PRODUCING TWO LEVELS AT THE JOINT.

ALL REDWOOD JOINTS TO BE SELECT HEART, AND TREATED WITH A WOOD PRESERVATIVE.

G USING A 2X4 FOR MORE DEFINITION OF THE JOINTS IN THE DESIGN.

H SHOWING A TYPICAL SECTION FOR A DRIVE WAY. IN MOST AREAS THE ADDITIONAL INCH OF CONCRETE IS ALL THAT IS NECESSARY FROM A WALK DETAIL TO A DRIVE.

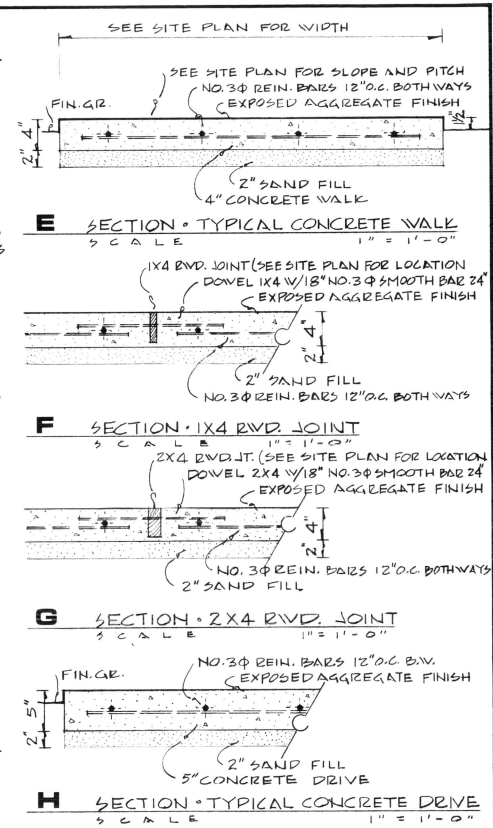

SEE SITE PLAN FOR WIDTH

SEE SITE PLAN FOR SLOPE AND PITCH
NO. 3 φ REIN. BARS 12" O.C. BOTH WAYS
EXPOSED AGGREGATE FINISH
FIN. GR.
2" SAND FILL
4" CONCRETE WALK

E SECTION · TYPICAL CONCRETE WALK
SCALE 1" = 1'-0"

1X4 RWD. JOINT (SEE SITE PLAN FOR LOCATION
DOWEL 1X4 W/18" NO.3 φ SMOOTH BAR 24"
EXPOSED AGGREGATE FINISH
2" SAND FILL
NO. 3 φ REIN. BARS 12" O.C. BOTH WAYS

F SECTION · 1X4 RWD. JOINT
SCALE 1" = 1'-0"

2X4 RWD. JT. (SEE SITE PLAN FOR LOCATION
DOWEL 2X4 W/18" NO.3 φ SMOOTH BAR 24"
EXPOSED AGGREGATE FINISH
NO. 3 φ REIN. BARS 12" O.C. BOTH WAYS
2" SAND FILL

G SECTION · 2X4 RWD. JOINT
SCALE 1" = 1'-0"

NO. 3 φ REIN. BARS 12" O.C. B.W.
EXPOSED AGGREGATE FINISH
FIN. GR.
2" SAND FILL
5" CONCRETE DRIVE

H SECTION · TYPICAL CONCRETE DRIVE
SCALE 1" = 1'-0"

CONCRETE EDGES AND PAVING DETAILS

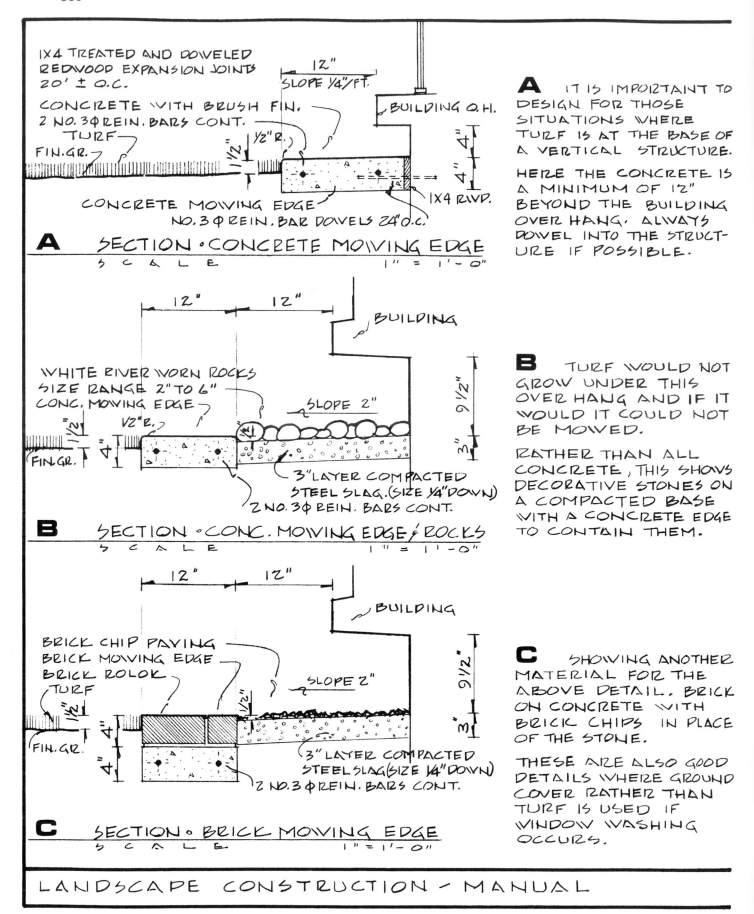

IX4 TREATED AND DOWELED
REDWOOD EXPANSION JOINTS
20' ± O.C.

CONCRETE WITH BRUSH FIN.
2 NO.3 Ø REIN. BARS CONT.

TURF

FIN.GR.

12"

SLOPE 1/4"/FT.

BUILDING O.H.

1/2" R.

4" 4"

IX4 RWD.

CONCRETE MOWING EDGE
NO.3 Ø REIN. BAR DOWELS 24" O.C.

A SECTION · CONCRETE MOWING EDGE
SCALE   1" = 1'-0"

A IT IS IMPORTANT TO DESIGN FOR THOSE SITUATIONS WHERE TURF IS AT THE BASE OF A VERTICAL STRUCTURE.

HERE THE CONCRETE IS A MINIMUM OF 12" BEYOND THE BUILDING OVER HANG. ALWAYS DOWEL INTO THE STRUCTURE IF POSSIBLE.

12"   12"

BUILDING

WHITE RIVER WORN ROCKS
SIZE RANGE 2" TO 6"
CONC. MOWING EDGE

1/2" R.

SLOPE 2"

9 1/2"

3"

FIN.GR.

4"

3" LAYER COMPACTED
STEEL SLAG. (SIZE 1/4" DOWN)
2 NO.3 Ø REIN. BARS CONT.

B SECTION · CONC. MOWING EDGE & ROCKS
SCALE   1" = 1'-0"

B TURF WOULD NOT GROW UNDER THIS OVER HANG AND IF IT WOULD IT COULD NOT BE MOWED.

RATHER THAN ALL CONCRETE, THIS SHOWS DECORATIVE STONES ON A COMPACTED BASE WITH A CONCRETE EDGE TO CONTAIN THEM.

12"   12"

BUILDING

BRICK CHIP PAVING
BRICK MOWING EDGE
BRICK ROLOK
TURF

SLOPE 2"

9 1/2"

1/2"

3"

FIN.GR.

4" 4"

3" LAYER COMPACTED
STEEL SLAG (SIZE 1/4" DOWN)
2 NO.3 Ø REIN. BARS CONT.

C SECTION · BRICK MOWING EDGE
SCALE   1" = 1'-0"

C SHOWING ANOTHER MATERIAL FOR THE ABOVE DETAIL. BRICK ON CONCRETE WITH BRICK CHIPS IN PLACE OF THE STONE.

THESE ARE ALSO GOOD DETAILS WHERE GROUND COVER RATHER THAN TURF IS USED IF WINDOW WASHING OCCURS.

LANDSCAPE CONSTRUCTION - MANUAL

D SHOWING A MINIMUM WIDTH FOR MOWING AND WINDOW WASHING.

USE 8d GALV. NAILS 24" O.C. PROJECTING FROM THE 1X4 WHERE BUILDINGS CAN NOT BE DOWELED.

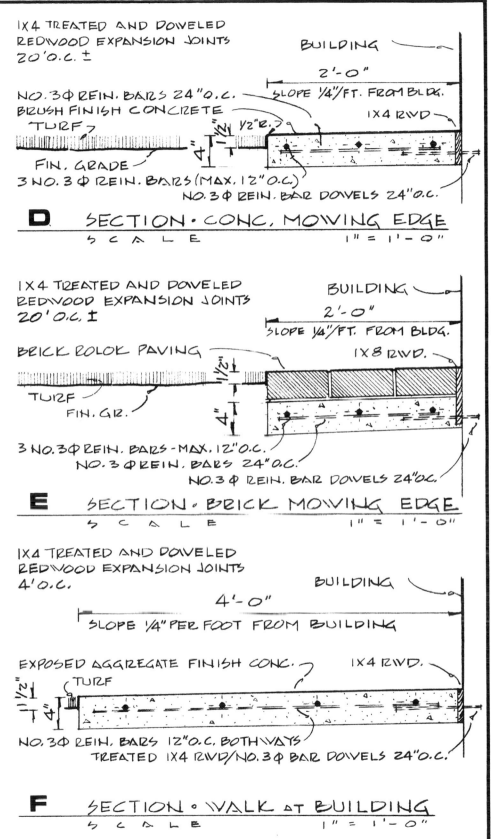

1X4 TREATED AND DOWELED REDWOOD EXPANSION JOINTS 20' O.C. ±

BUILDING

2'-0"

NO. 3ϕ REIN. BARS 24" O.C.
BRUSH FINISH CONCRETE
TURF
SLOPE 1/4"/FT. FROM BLDG.
1X4 RWD
1/2"R.
FIN. GRADE
3 NO. 3ϕ REIN. BARS (MAX. 12" O.C.)
NO. 3ϕ REIN. BAR DOWELS 24" O.C.

D SECTION · CONC. MOWING EDGE
SCALE   1" = 1'-0"

E SAME DETAIL AS ABOVE WITH BRICK PAVING ON TOP. THIS CHANGE OF MATERIAL COULD ALSO INCLUDE FLAG STONE, SLATE, ETC.,

1X4 TREATED AND DOWELED REDWOOD EXPANSION JOINTS 20' O.C. ±

BUILDING

2'-0"

SLOPE 1/4"/FT. FROM BLDG.

BRICK BOLOK PAVING
1X8 RWD.
1/2"
TURF
FIN. GR.
4"
3 NO. 3ϕ REIN. BARS - MAX. 12" O.C.
NO. 3ϕ REIN. BARS 24" O.C.
NO. 3ϕ REIN. BAR DOWELS 24" O.C.

E SECTION · BRICK MOWING EDGE
SCALE   1" = 1'-0"

F THIS WOULD SERVE AS A HARD SURFACE FOR A LADDER USED FOR WASHING HIGH WINDOWS.

4' WIDTH ADJACENT TO A STRUCTURE WOULD NOT ALLOW TWO PEOPLE TO PASS COMFORTABLY WHEN USED AS A WALK.

1X4 TREATED AND DOWELED REDWOOD EXPANSION JOINTS 4' O.C.

BUILDING

4'-0"

SLOPE 1/4" PER FOOT FROM BUILDING

EXPOSED AGGREGATE FINISH CONC.
1X4 RWD.
TURF
1/2"
4"
NO. 3ϕ REIN. BARS 12" O.C. BOTH WAYS
TREATED 1X4 RWD/NO. 3ϕ BAR DOWELS 24" O.C.

F SECTION · WALK AT BUILDING
SCALE   1" = 1'-0"

MOWING EDGE DETAILS

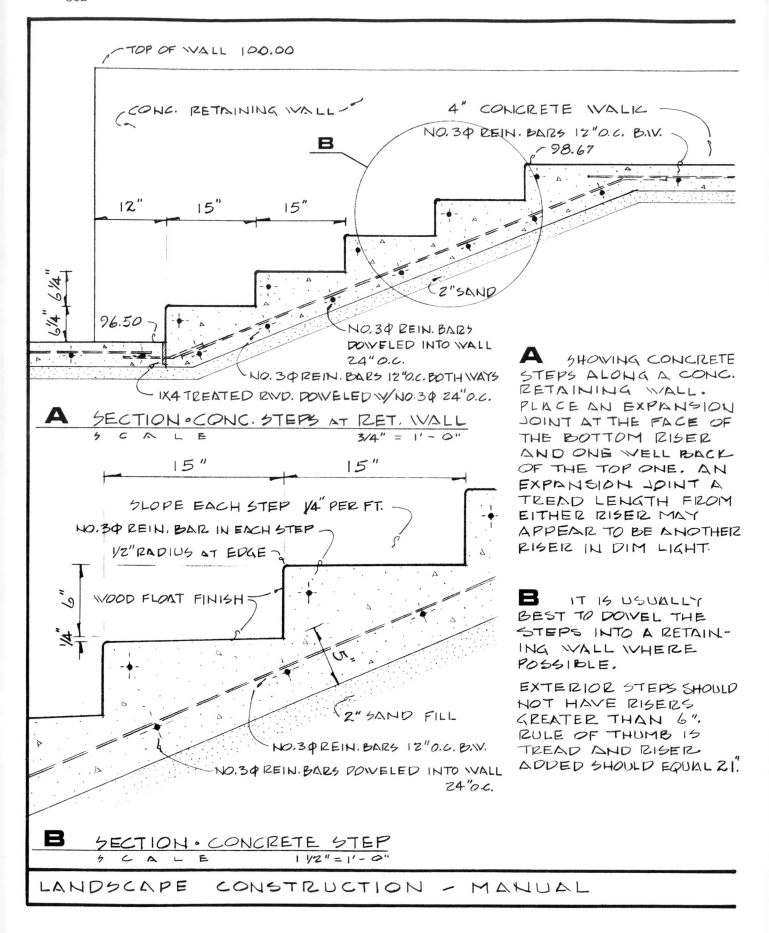

TOP OF WALL 100.00

CONC. RETAINING WALL

4" CONCRETE WALK

B

NO.3⌀ REIN. BARS 12"O.C. B.W.

98.67

12"   15"   15"

2" SAND

6¼" 6¼"

96.50

NO.3⌀ REIN. BARS DOWELED INTO WALL 24"O.C.

NO.3⌀ REIN. BARS 12"O.C. BOTH WAYS

1X4 TREATED RWD. DOWELED W/NO.3⌀ 24"O.C.

A SECTION · CONC. STEPS AT RET. WALL
SCALE   3/4" = 1'-0"

15"   15"

SLOPE EACH STEP ¼" PER FT.

NO.3⌀ REIN. BAR IN EACH STEP

½" RADIUS AT EDGE

6"

WOOD FLOAT FINISH

¼"

5"

2" SAND FILL

NO.3⌀ REIN. BARS 12"O.C. B.W.

NO.3⌀ REIN. BARS DOWELED INTO WALL 24"O.C.

B SECTION · CONCRETE STEP
SCALE   1½" = 1'-0"

A SHOWING CONCRETE STEPS ALONG A CONC. RETAINING WALL. PLACE AN EXPANSION JOINT AT THE FACE OF THE BOTTOM RISER AND ONE WELL BACK OF THE TOP ONE. AN EXPANSION JOINT A TREAD LENGTH FROM EITHER RISER MAY APPEAR TO BE ANOTHER RISER IN DIM LIGHT.

B IT IS USUALLY BEST TO DOWEL THE STEPS INTO A RETAINING WALL WHERE POSSIBLE.

EXTERIOR STEPS SHOULD NOT HAVE RISERS GREATER THAN 6". RULE OF THUMB IS TREAD AND RISER ADDED SHOULD EQUAL 21".

LANDSCAPE   CONSTRUCTION — MANUAL

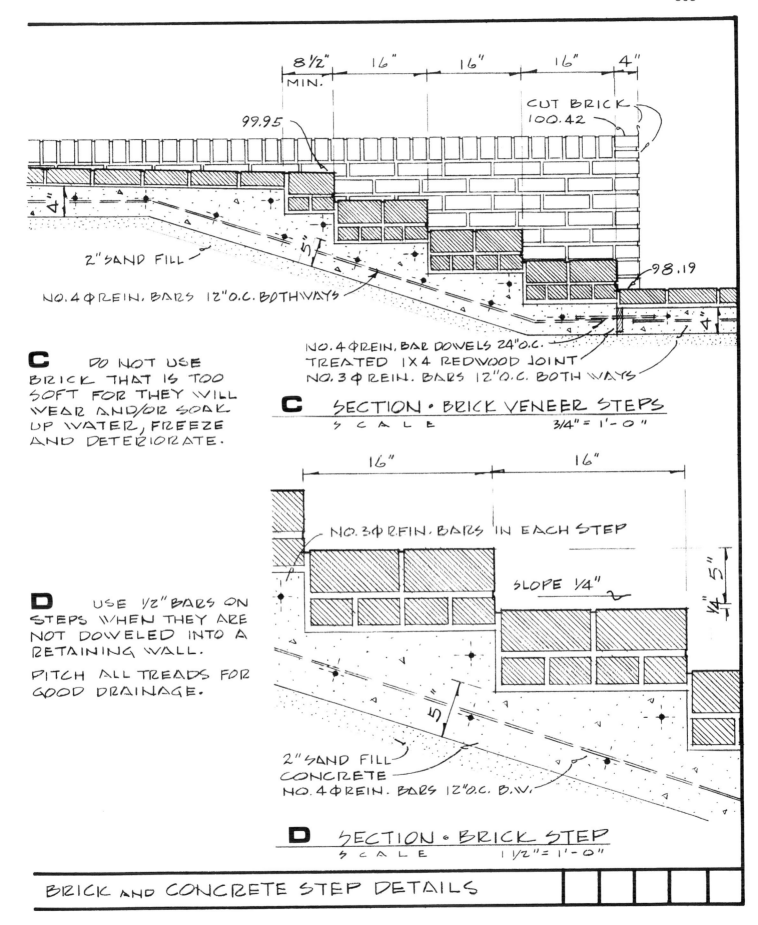

8½" MIN. 16" 16" 16" 4"

99.95

CUT BRICK 100.42

2" SAND FILL

NO. 4 φ REIN. BARS 12" O.C. BOTHWAYS

5"

98.19

4"

NO. 4 φ REIN. BAR DOWELS 24" O.C.
TREATED 1X4 REDWOOD JOINT
NO. 3 φ REIN. BARS 12" O.C. BOTH WAYS

C DO NOT USE BRICK THAT IS TOO SOFT FOR THEY WILL WEAR AND/OR SOAK UP WATER, FREEZE AND DETERIORATE.

C SECTION • BRICK VENEER STEPS
SCALE   3/4" = 1'-0"

16" 16"

NO. 3 φ REIN. BARS IN EACH STEP

SLOPE ¼"

5" ¼"

D USE ½" BARS ON STEPS WHEN THEY ARE NOT DOWELED INTO A RETAINING WALL.

PITCH ALL TREADS FOR GOOD DRAINAGE.

5"

2" SAND FILL
CONCRETE
NO. 4 φ REIN. BARS 12" O.C. B.W.

D SECTION • BRICK STEP
SCALE   1½" = 1'-0"

BRICK AND CONCRETE STEP DETAILS

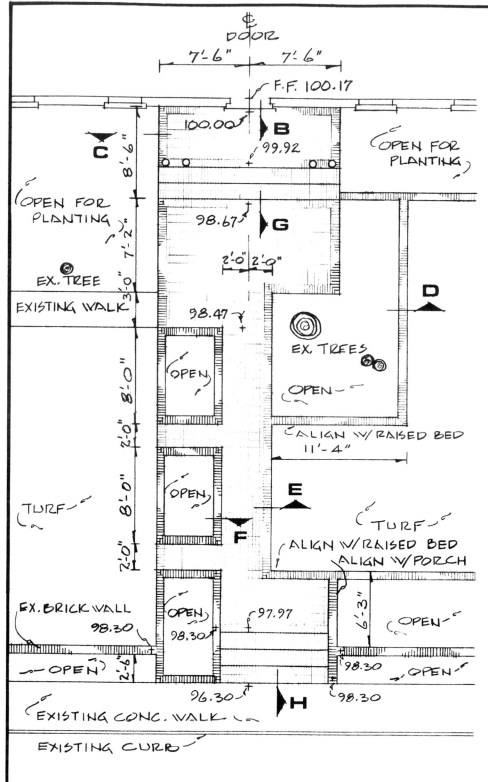

A SHOWING A PORCH WITH STEPS TO THE WALK AND STEPS AT THE EXISTING SIDE WALK. ALSO SHOWING RAISED PLANT BEDS AND BRICK MOVING EDGES.

THE SECTIONS, INDICATED BY REFERENCE SYMBOLS ON THE PLAN, WILL OCCUR ON THE NEXT THREE PAGES.

THIS PLAN IS SIGNIFICANT ONLY IN SHOWING A METHOD OF LAYOUT AND TO INDICATE SECTION DRAWINGS.

Door

7'-6"   7'-6"

F.F. 100.17

100.00

B   99.92

OPEN FOR PLANTING

C

8'-6"

OPEN FOR PLANTING

7'-2"

98.67   G

EX. TREE

3'-0"

EXISTING WALK

2'-0" 2'-0"

98.47

D

EX. TREES

OPEN

8'-0"   2'-0"

OPEN

ALIGN W/ RAISED BED
11'-4"

TURF

8'-0"

OPEN

E

F

TURF

ALIGN W/ RAISED BED
ALIGN W/ PORCH

EX. BRICK WALL

98.30

OPEN   98.30

97.97

6'-3"

OPEN

2'-0"

2'-6"

OPEN

96.30   H

98.30

98.30   OPEN

EXISTING CONC. WALK

EXISTING CURB

A PLAN • FRONT BRICK WALK
SCALE   1/8" = 1'-0"

LANDSCAPE CONSTRUCTION - MANUAL

B EVEN THOUGH THE PORCH IS DOWELED INTO THE FOUNDATION OF THE HOUSE IT IS IMPORTANT THAT THE CONCRETE ALSO BE CARRIED DOWN BELOW EXISTING GRADE FOR ADDITIONAL SUPPORT.

FOR A SMALL AREA SUCH AS THIS THE CONTRACTOR MAY WANT TO POUR THE CONCRETE LEVEL AND HAVE A THICKER MORTAR BED UNDER THE FLAT PAVERS.

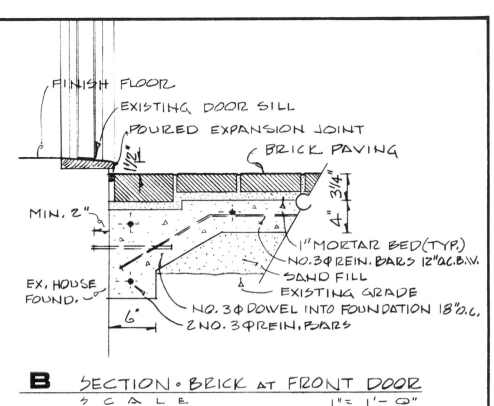

FINISH FLOOR
EXISTING DOOR SILL
POURED EXPANSION JOINT
BRICK PAVING
MIN. 2"
EX. HOUSE FOUND.
6"
1" MORTAR BED (TYP.)
NO. 3Φ REIN. BARS 12" O.C. B.W.
SAND FILL
EXISTING GRADE
NO. 3Φ DOWEL INTO FOUNDATION 18" O.C.
2 NO. 3Φ REIN. BARS

B SECTION · BRICK AT FRONT DOOR
SCALE 1" = 1'-0"

C SHOWING THE TWO SIDES OF THE PORCH WITH ITS PAVING, BOLOK EDGE AND VENEER ON THE SIDE.

THE STEEL MAY ALSO BE BENT AND CARRIED DOWN RATHER THAN A CUT PIECE AS SHOWN.

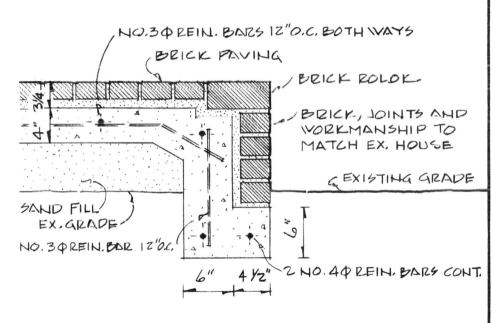

NO. 3Φ REIN. BARS 12" O.C. BOTH WAYS
BRICK PAVING
BRICK ROLOK
BRICK, JOINTS AND WORKMANSHIP TO MATCH EX. HOUSE
EXISTING GRADE
SAND FILL
EX. GRADE
NO. 3Φ REIN. BAR 12" O.C.
6" 4½"
2 NO. 4Φ REIN. BARS CONT.

C SECTION · PORCH EDGE
SCALE 1" = 1'-0"

PLAN AND DETAILS FOR BRICK PAVING

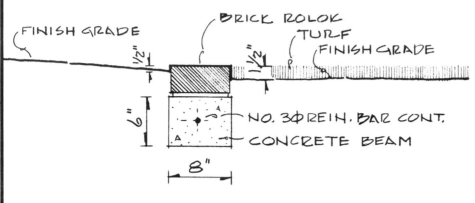

D FINISH GRADE

BRICK ROLOK
TURF
FINISH GRADE

1½"

1½"

6"

NO. 3∅ REIN. BAR CONT.

CONCRETE BEAM

8"

D SECTION · BRICK MOWING EDGE
S C A L E   1" = 1'-0"

D A BRICK DIVIDER BETWEEN A GROUND COVER BED AND TURF. THIS MOWING EDGE MUST SLOPE TO GIVE A CONSTANT 1½" ABOVE FINISH GRADE ON THE TURF SIDE. THIS ALLOWS THE LAWN MOWER WHEEL TO ROLL ON THE BRICK.

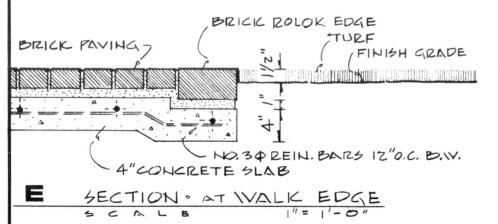

BRICK PAVING

BRICK ROLOK EDGE
TURF
FINISH GRADE

1½"

1"

4"

NO. 3∅ REIN. BARS 12" O.C. B.W.

4" CONCRETE SLAB

E SECTION · AT WALK EDGE
S C A L E   1" = 1'-0"

E SHOWING A TYPICAL BRICK WALK EDGE WHERE A ROLOK IS USED IN THE PATTERN.

A ONE INCH MORTAR BED IS TYPICAL BUT NOT CRITICAL UNLESS IT BECOMES TOO LITTLE AND THE BRICK MUST BE CUT.

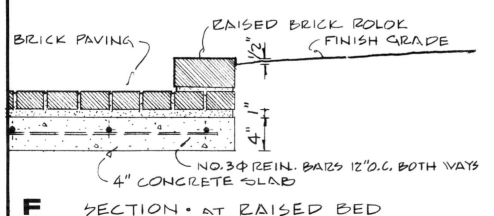

BRICK PAVING

RAISED BRICK ROLOK
FINISH GRADE

½"

1"

4"

NO. 3∅ REIN. BARS 12" O.C. BOTH WAYS

4" CONCRETE SLAB

F SECTION · AT RAISED BED
S C A L E   1" = 1'-0"

F FOR DRAINAGE IT IS OFTEN DESIRABLE TO RAISE PLANTING AREAS THAT OCCUR IN THE WALK.

THE CONCRETE AND ITS REINFORCING WILL BE THE SAME AS FOR A CONCRETE FINISH WALK. A ROUGH FINISH TO THE CONCRETE IS PREFERRED FOR IT WILL ASSURE BOND WITH THE BRICK.

G A TYPICAL BRICK VENEERED STEP WITH BRICK PAVING CONTINUING AT THE BOTTOM AND TOP.

A DOWELED EXPANSION JOINT IS BEST PLACED AT THE BOTTOM AND IN LINE OF THE FACE OF THE RISER.

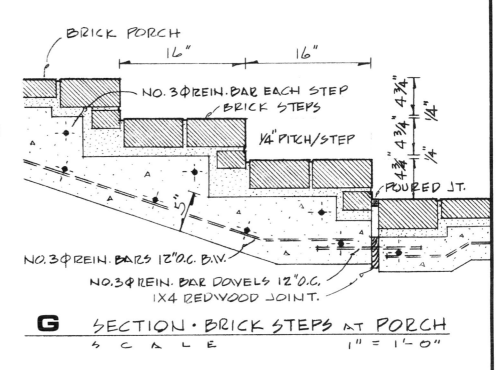

BRICK PORCH
16"   16"
NO. 3Ø REIN. BAR EACH STEP
BRICK STEPS
4¾" 4¾" ¼"
4¾" ¼"
¼" PITCH/STEP
POURED JT.
5"
NO. 3Ø REIN. BARS 12"O.C. B.W.
NO. 3Ø REIN. BAR DOWELS 12"O.C.
1X4 REDWOOD JOINT.

G SECTION · BRICK STEPS AT PORCH
SCALE   1" = 1'-0"

H UNDER CUT AT JOINING WITH EXISTING PAVING WHEN DOWELING IS NOT PRACTICAL. THIS WILL KEEP THE STEP FROM SHIFTING UP OR THE EXISTING PAVING FROM SINKING.

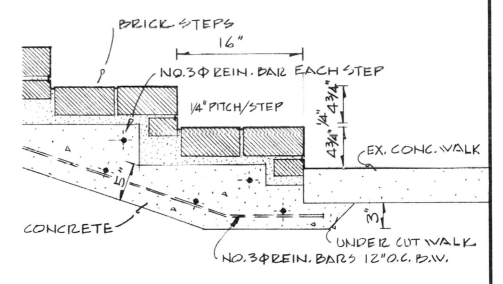

BRICK STEPS
16"
NO. 3Ø REIN. BAR EACH STEP
¼" PITCH/STEP
¼" 4¾"
4¾"
EX. CONC. WALK
5"
CONCRETE
3"
UNDER CUT WALK
NO. 3Ø REIN. BARS 12"O.C. B.W.

H SECTION · BRICK STEPS AT EX. WALK
SCALE   1" = 1'-0"

BRICK STEP AND PAVING DETAILS

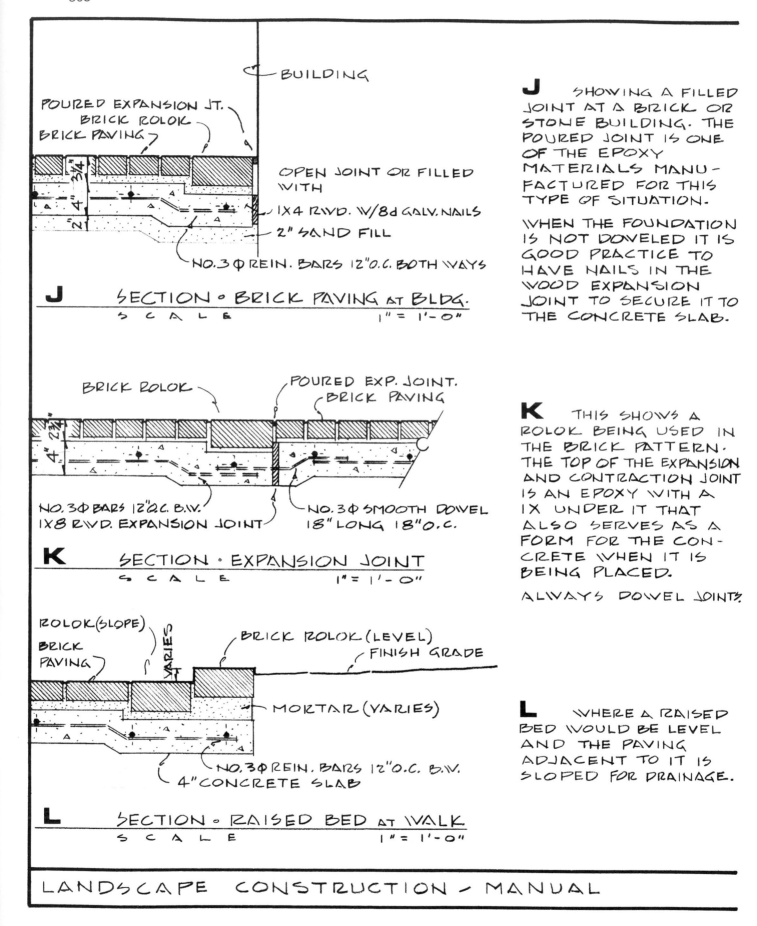

BUILDING

POURED EXPANSION JT.
BRICK ROLOK
BRICK PAVING

OPEN JOINT OR FILLED
WITH

1X4 RWD. W/8d GALV. NAILS

2" SAND FILL

NO. 3φ REIN. BARS 12"O.C. BOTH WAYS

J SECTION · BRICK PAVING AT BLDG.
SCALE 1" = 1'-0"

J SHOWING A FILLED JOINT AT A BRICK OR STONE BUILDING. THE POURED JOINT IS ONE OF THE EPOXY MATERIALS MANUFACTURED FOR THIS TYPE OF SITUATION.

WHEN THE FOUNDATION IS NOT DOVELED IT IS GOOD PRACTICE TO HAVE NAILS IN THE WOOD EXPANSION JOINT TO SECURE IT TO THE CONCRETE SLAB.

BRICK ROLOK

POURED EXP. JOINT.
BRICK PAVING

NO. 3φ BARS 12"O.C. B.W.
1X8 RWD. EXPANSION JOINT

NO. 3φ SMOOTH DOWEL
18" LONG 18" O.C.

K SECTION · EXPANSION JOINT
SCALE 1" = 1'-0"

K THIS SHOWS A ROLOK BEING USED IN THE BRICK PATTERN. THE TOP OF THE EXPANSION AND CONTRACTION JOINT IS AN EPOXY WITH A 1X UNDER IT THAT ALSO SERVES AS A FORM FOR THE CONCRETE WHEN IT IS BEING PLACED.

ALWAYS DOWEL JOINTS

ROLOK (SLOPE)
BRICK PAVING

VARIES

BRICK ROLOK (LEVEL)
FINISH GRADE

MORTAR (VARIES)

NO. 3φ REIN. BARS 12"O.C. B.W.
4" CONCRETE SLAB

L SECTION · RAISED BED AT WALK
SCALE 1" = 1'-0"

L WHERE A RAISED BED WOULD BE LEVEL AND THE PAVING ADJACENT TO IT IS SLOPED FOR DRAINAGE.

LANDSCAPE CONSTRUCTION - MANUAL

M THE JOINT BEHIND THE ROLOK MAY EITHER BE OPEN OR FILLED WITH MORTAR. THIS DETAIL DOES NOT ALLOW FOR INDEPENDENT MOVEMENT BETWEEN THE HOUSE AND PAVING.

HOUSE SIDING

GYPBOARD

2X4 STUD
2X4 BOTTOM PLATE
F.F. FLOOR

1X6 RWD. BASE BOARD
BRICK ROLOK
BRICK PAVING

OPEN JOINT
1" MORTAR JOINT
1X4 RWD. EXP. JOINT
NO.3 Ø SMOOTH DOWEL 2' O.C.
CONCRETE SLAB
NO.3 Ø REIN. BARS 12" O.C. BOTH WAYS

M SECTION · BRICK PAVING at HOUSE
S C A L E   1" = 1'-0"

N A BRICK VENEER DOWN THE SIDE OF THE CONCRETE IS NOT NECESSARY FOR IT WILL NOT BE VIEWED BECAUSE OF THE DECK.

IT IS NOT NECESSARY TO TIE THE PAVING AND DECK TOGETHER, BUT BE SURE THAT THEY MAINTAIN THE SAME LEVEL.

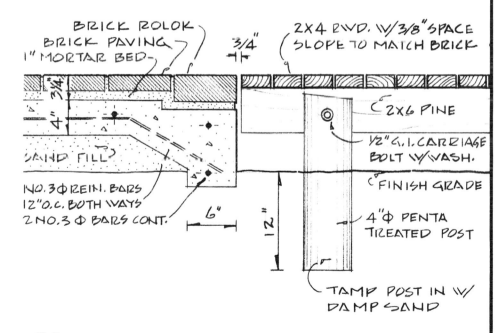

BRICK ROLOK
BRICK PAVING
1" MORTAR BED
3/4"

2X4 RWD. W/3/8" SPACE
SLOPE TO MATCH BRICK

3/4"
4"

SAND FILL

2X6 PINE

1/2" G.I. CARRIAGE BOLT W/WASH.

FINISH GRADE

4" Ø PENTA TREATED POST

NO.3 Ø REIN. BARS 12" O.C. BOTH WAYS
2 NO.3 Ø BARS CONT.
6"
12"

TAMP POST IN W/ DAMP SAND

N SECTION · BRICK PAVING at DECK
S C A L E   1" = 1'-0"

BRICK PAVING DETAILS

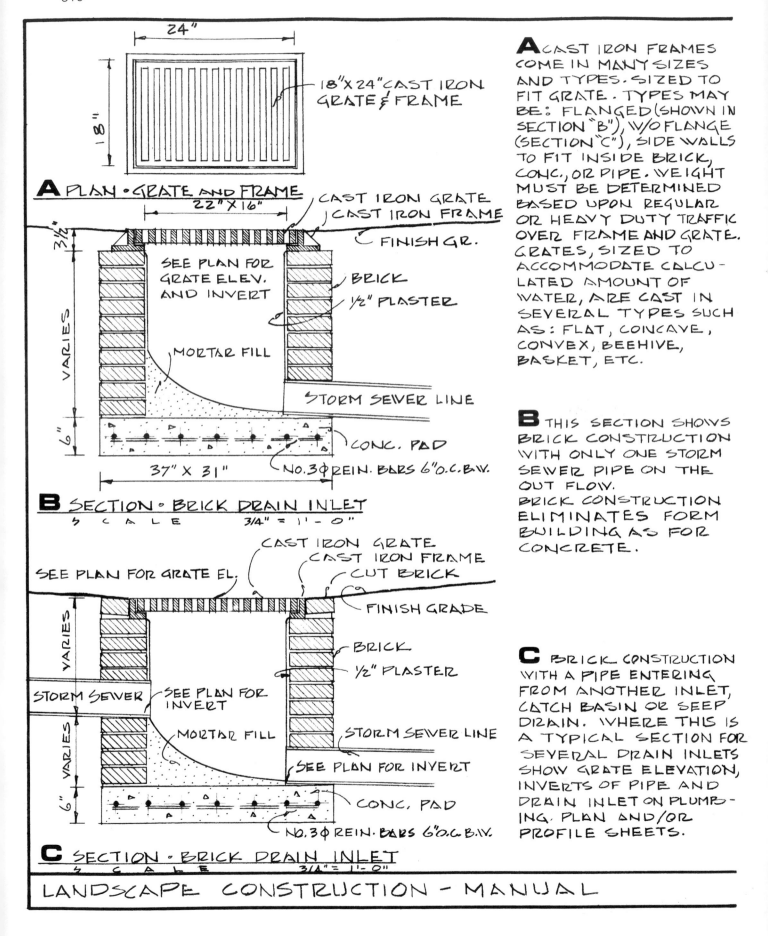

24"

18"

18"X24"CAST IRON
GRATE & FRAME

A PLAN · GRATE AND FRAME
22"X16"

A CAST IRON FRAMES COME IN MANY SIZES AND TYPES. SIZED TO FIT GRATE. TYPES MAY BE: FLANGED (SHOWN IN SECTION "B"), W/O FLANGE (SECTION "C"), SIDE WALLS TO FIT INSIDE BRICK, CONC., OR PIPE. WEIGHT MUST BE DETERMINED BASED UPON REGULAR OR HEAVY DUTY TRAFFIC OVER FRAME AND GRATE. GRATES, SIZED TO ACCOMMODATE CALCULATED AMOUNT OF WATER, ARE CAST IN SEVERAL TYPES SUCH AS: FLAT, CONCAVE, CONVEX, BEEHIVE, BASKET, ETC.

CAST IRON GRATE
CAST IRON FRAME
FINISH GR.

3½"

VARIES

SEE PLAN FOR GRATE ELEV. AND INVERT

BRICK
½" PLASTER

MORTAR FILL

STORM SEWER LINE

6"

CONC. PAD

NO.3∅ REIN. BARS 6"O.C.B.W.

37" X 31"

B SECTION · BRICK DRAIN INLET
SCALE   3/4" = 1'-0"

B THIS SECTION SHOWS BRICK CONSTRUCTION WITH ONLY ONE STORM SEWER PIPE ON THE OUT FLOW. BRICK CONSTRUCTION ELIMINATES FORM BUILDING AS FOR CONCRETE.

CAST IRON GRATE
CAST IRON FRAME
CUT BRICK

SEE PLAN FOR GRATE EL.

FINISH GRADE

VARIES

BRICK
½" PLASTER

STORM SEWER

SEE PLAN FOR INVERT

VARIES

MORTAR FILL

STORM SEWER LINE

SEE PLAN FOR INVERT

6"

CONC. PAD

NO.3∅ REIN. BARS 6"O.C.B.W.

C SECTION · BRICK DRAIN INLET
SCALE   3/4" = 1'-0"

C BRICK CONSTRUCTION WITH A PIPE ENTERING FROM ANOTHER INLET, CATCH BASIN OR SEEP DRAIN. WHERE THIS IS A TYPICAL SECTION FOR SEVERAL DRAIN INLETS SHOW GRATE ELEVATION, INVERTS OF PIPE AND DRAIN INLET ON PLUMBING PLAN AND/OR PROFILE SHEETS.

LANDSCAPE CONSTRUCTION - MANUAL

D CONSIDERATION FOR GRATE DESIGN SHOULD BE GIVEN TO BICYCLES WHERE THEY ARE ALLOWED. SOME SUGGESTIONS ARE: 1. DIAGONAL BARS AT 45° 2. BARS TRANSVERSE TO DIRECTION OF TRAFFIC. 3. SLOTTED GRATES WITH SLOTS 1¼" TO 2¼" AND CROSS BAR SPACING 9" MAXIMUM.

E THIS SECTION SHOWS CONCRETE BOTTOM AND SIDES. THE KEY INDICATES TWO POURS (BOTTOM AND THEN THE SIDES). THE BOX COULD BE A MONOLITHIC POUR BUT FORMING IS MORE DIFFICULT. THE RAISED FRAME ON EITHER BRICK OR CONCRETE WILL ALLOW PAVING AROUND THE INLET.

F SHOWING A PIPE INTO INLET BOX AND PIPE TAKING WATER OUT. PIPE DEPTH WILL DEPEND UPON OVERALL SUBSURFACE DRAINAGE PLAN; BUT CARE SHOULD BE TAKEN TO PLACE THEM BELOW A MINIMUM DEPTH TO AVOID DAMAGE FROM ACTIVITY ON THE GROUND SURFACE.

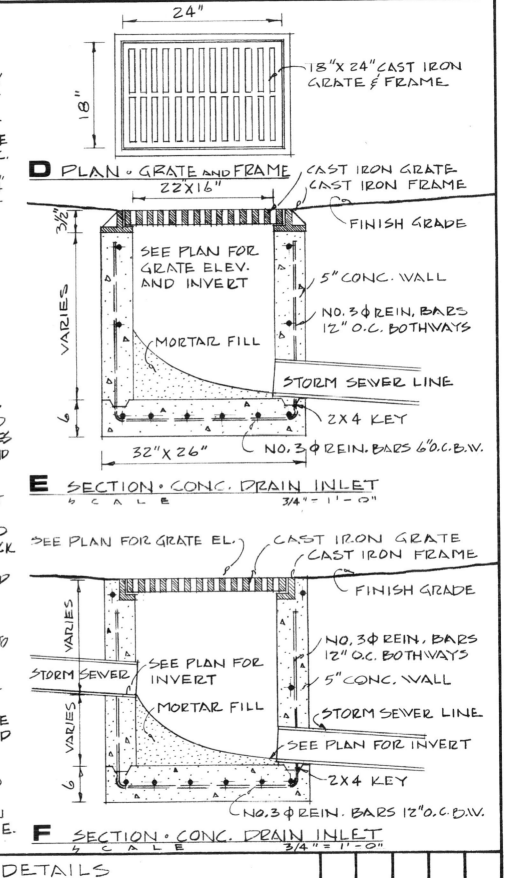

24"

18"

18"X 24" CAST IRON GRATE & FRAME

D PLAN · GRATE and FRAME

22"X16"

CAST IRON GRATE
CAST IRON FRAME
FINISH GRADE

3½"

SEE PLAN FOR GRATE ELEV. AND INVERT

5" CONC. WALL

NO. 3 ⌀ REIN. BARS 12" O.C. BOTHWAYS

VARIES

MORTAR FILL

STORM SEWER LINE

6"

2 X 4 KEY

32" X 26"

NO. 3 ⌀ REIN. BARS 6" O.C. B.W.

E SECTION · CONC. DRAIN INLET
SCALE   3/4" = 1'-0"

SEE PLAN FOR GRATE EL.

CAST IRON GRATE
CAST IRON FRAME
FINISH GRADE

VARIES

STORM SEWER

SEE PLAN FOR INVERT

NO. 3 ⌀ REIN. BARS 12" O.C. BOTHWAYS

5" CONC. WALL

STORM SEWER LINE

VARIES

MORTAR FILL

SEE PLAN FOR INVERT

6"

2 X 4 KEY

NO. 3 ⌀ REIN. BARS 12" O.C. B.W.

F SECTION · CONC. DRAIN INLET
SCALE   3/4" = 1'-0"

DRAIN INLET DETAILS

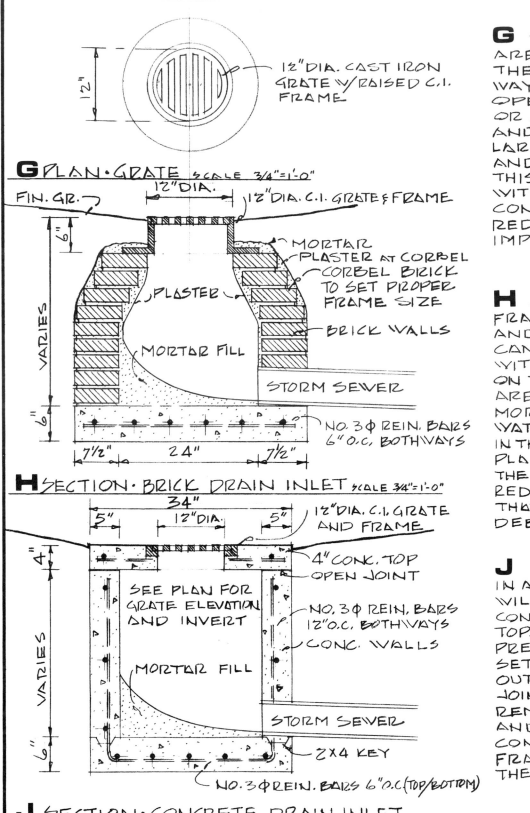

12" DIA. CAST IRON GRATE w/ RAISED C.I. FRAME

G PLAN·GRATE SCALE 3/4"=1'-0"

FIN. GR.

12"DIA.

12"DIA. C.I. GRATE & FRAME

MORTAR PLASTER AT CORBEL

CORBEL BRICK TO SET PROPER FRAME SIZE

PLASTER

BRICK WALLS

MORTAR FILL

STORM SEWER

VARIES

NO.3 ⌀ REIN. BARS 6" O.C. BOTH WAYS

7 1/2"   24"   7 1/2"

H SECTION·BRICK DRAIN INLET SCALE 3/4"=1'-0"

34"

5"   12"DIA.   5"

12"DIA. C.I. GRATE AND FRAME

4" CONC. TOP OPEN JOINT

SEE PLAN FOR GRATE ELEVATION AND INVERT

NO.3 ⌀ REIN. BARS 12" O.C. BOTH WAYS

CONC. WALLS

MORTAR FILL

VARIES

STORM SEWER

2X4 KEY

NO.3 ⌀ REIN. BARS 6" O.C. (TOP/BOTTOM)

J SECTION·CONCRETE DRAIN INLET

SCALE   3/4" = 1'-0"

LANDSCAPE CONSTRUCTION - MANUAL

G WHERE LARGE GRATES ARE NOT NECESSARY, THERE ARE SEVERAL WAYS TO REDUCE THE OPENING OF AN INLET OR A CATCH BASIN AND STILL RETAIN A LARGE AREA TO COLLECT AND MOVE WATER. THIS SMALL GRATE WITH NO BRICK OR CONCRETE SHOWING REDUCES THE VISUAL IMPACT.

H GRATES AND FRAMES OF LARGER AND SMALLER DIA. CAN ALSO BE USED WITH THE SECTIONS ON THIS PAGE. THE AREA SHOWN AS MORTAR FILL KEEPS WATER FROM REMAINING IN THE INLET BOX. THE PLASTER WILL SMOOTH THE WALLS, THUS REDUCING ROUGH SPOTS THAT WILL COLLECT DEBRIS.

J A REDUCED GRATE IN A CONCRETE INLET WILL CALL FOR A CONCRETE SLAB ON TOP. THIS IS USUALLY PRECAST AND THEN SET IN PLACE WITH OUT FILLING THE JOINT. IT CAN BE REMOVED FOR REPAIR AND ADDITIONAL CONSTRUCTION. THE FRAME IS CAST INTO THE TOP SLAB.

K FOUNDRIES CAST SEVERAL SIZES AND TYPES OF THE GRATE AND FRAME SHOWN HERE. THE FRAME FITS INTO THE BELL OF A PIPE. A DETAIL WOULD SHOW, IN ADDITION TO THAT INFORMATION SHOWN HERE, A FOUNDRY CATALOG NUMBER FOR BOTH THE GRATE AND FRAME. (THIS WOULD BE TYPICAL FOR ALL GRATES AND FRAMES SHOWN IN THIS DOCUMENT.)

L THIS DETAIL MAY OCCUR AT THE END OF A CAST IRON DRAIN LINE. CAST IRON DRAIN PIPE SHOULD BE USED WHERE IT RUNS UNDER A STRUCTURE, SUCH AS FROM AN INTERIOR COURT.

M CAST IRON GRATES THAT WILL FIT INTO THE BELL OF A DRAIN PIPE ARE AVAILABLE FROM 3¾" DIA. TO OVER 32" IN DIA.

N SOMETIMES REFERRED TO AS A "YARD DRAIN", THESE SMALL SIMPLE DRAIN INLET DETAILS WORK WELL IN MANY SITUATIONS ON RESIDENTIAL PROJECTS.

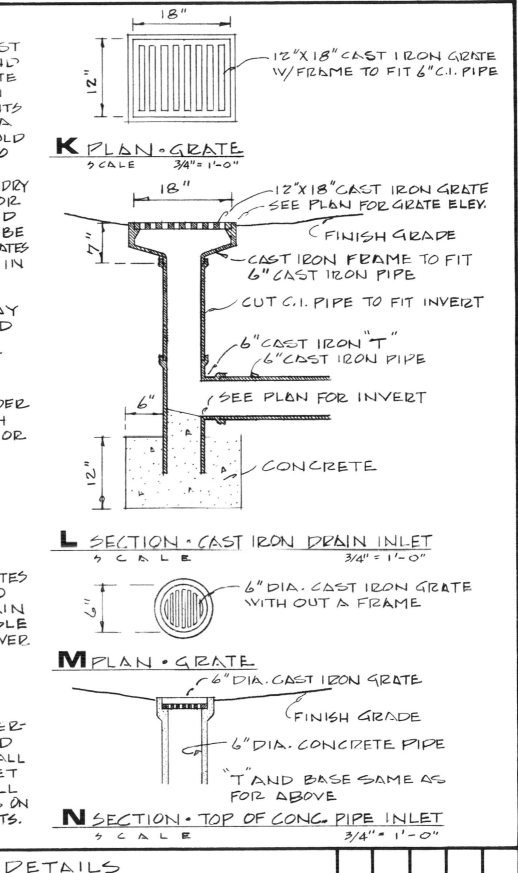

18"

12"

12"×18" CAST IRON GRATE W/ FRAME TO FIT 6" C.I. PIPE

K PLAN · GRATE
SCALE   3/4" = 1'-0"

18"

7"

12"

6"

12"×18" CAST IRON GRATE SEE PLAN FOR GRATE ELEV.

FINISH GRADE

CAST IRON FRAME TO FIT 6" CAST IRON PIPE

CUT C.I. PIPE TO FIT INVERT

6" CAST IRON "T"
6" CAST IRON PIPE

SEE PLAN FOR INVERT

CONCRETE

L SECTION · CAST IRON DRAIN INLET
SCALE   3/4" = 1'-0"

6"

6" DIA. CAST IRON GRATE WITH OUT A FRAME

M PLAN · GRATE

6" DIA. CAST IRON GRATE

FINISH GRADE

6" DIA. CONCRETE PIPE

"T" AND BASE SAME AS FOR ABOVE

N SECTION · TOP OF CONC. PIPE INLET
SCALE   3/4" = 1'-0"

DRAIN INLET DETAILS

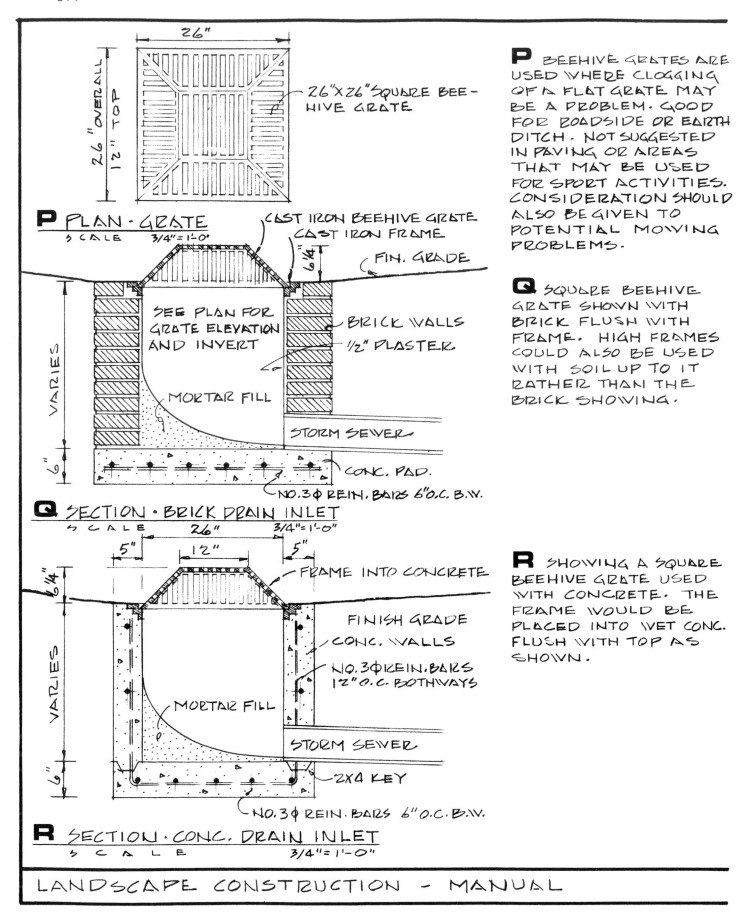

26"

26" OVERALL
24" TOP

26"x26" SQUARE BEE-HIVE GRATE

P PLAN · GRATE
SCALE   3/4"=1'-0"

CAST IRON BEEHIVE GRATE
CAST IRON FRAME

FIN. GRADE

SEE PLAN FOR GRATE ELEVATION AND INVERT

BRICK WALLS
1/2" PLASTER

MORTAR FILL

STORM SEWER

VARIES

6"

CONC. PAD.

NO. 3ø REIN. BARS 6" O.C. B.W.

Q SECTION · BRICK DRAIN INLET
SCALE   3/4"=1'-0"

26"
5"   12"   5"

FRAME INTO CONCRETE

FINISH GRADE
CONC. WALLS

NO. 3ø REIN. BARS 12" O.C. BOTHWAYS

MORTAR FILL

STORM SEWER

2X4 KEY

VARIES

6"

NO. 3ø REIN. BARS 6" O.C. B.W.

R SECTION · CONC. DRAIN INLET
SCALE   3/4"=1'-0"

P BEEHIVE GRATES ARE USED WHERE CLOGGING OF A FLAT GRATE MAY BE A PROBLEM. GOOD FOR ROADSIDE OR EARTH DITCH. NOT SUGGESTED IN PAVING OR AREAS THAT MAY BE USED FOR SPORT ACTIVITIES. CONSIDERATION SHOULD ALSO BE GIVEN TO POTENTIAL MOWING PROBLEMS.

Q SQUARE BEEHIVE GRATE SHOWN WITH BRICK FLUSH WITH FRAME. HIGH FRAMES COULD ALSO BE USED WITH SOIL UP TO IT RATHER THAN THE BRICK SHOWING.

R SHOWING A SQUARE BEEHIVE GRATE USED WITH CONCRETE. THE FRAME WOULD BE PLACED INTO WET CONC. FLUSH WITH TOP AS SHOWN.

LANDSCAPE CONSTRUCTION - MANUAL

S THE ROUND BEEHIVE GRATE WILL WORK FOR SITUATIONS DESCRIBED FOR SQUARE ONES.

T ALTHOUGH ROUND GRATES AND FRAMES ARE NOT ONLY FOR USE AS SHOWN, THIS ONE IS SIZED TO FIT INTO THE BELL OF A 24" SEWER PIPE.

U A GRATE FOR THE SMALL PRECAST DRAIN INLETS NEED NOT BE VERY HEAVY FOR THE BOX ITSELF WILL NOT WITHSTAND MUCH WEIGHT.

V THERE ARE MANY TYPES OF SMALL PRECAST CONCRETE DRAIN INLETS. THEY CAN BE ORDERED WITH HOLE SIZES AND DIRECTIONS AS DESIRED. THE GRATE FITS INTO A SPACE IN THE CONCRETE WITHOUT A FRAME. USE FOR SMALL YARD INLETS ONLY.

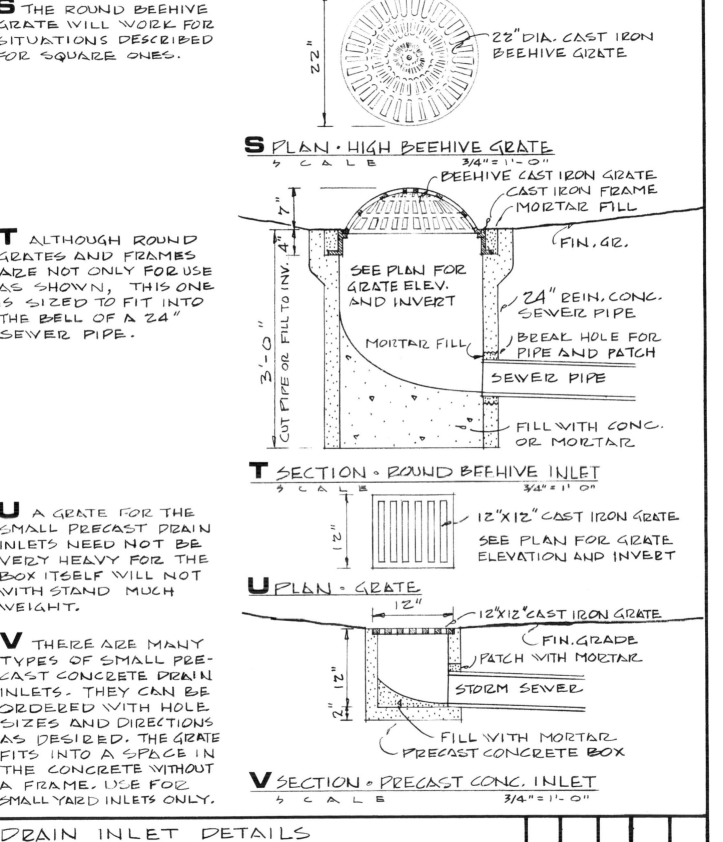

S PLAN · HIGH BEEHIVE GRATE
SCALE 3/4"=1'-0"

22" DIA. CAST IRON BEEHIVE GRATE

BEEHIVE CAST IRON GRATE
CAST IRON FRAME
MORTAR FILL
FIN. GR.
24" REIN. CONC. SEWER PIPE
BREAK HOLE FOR PIPE AND PATCH
SEWER PIPE
FILL WITH CONC. OR MORTAR
SEE PLAN FOR GRATE ELEV. AND INVERT
MORTAR FILL
CUT PIPE OR FILL TO INV.

T SECTION · ROUND BEEHIVE INLET
SCALE 3/4"=1'0"

12"X12" CAST IRON GRATE
SEE PLAN FOR GRATE ELEVATION AND INVERT

U PLAN · GRATE

12"X12" CAST IRON GRATE
FIN. GRADE
PATCH WITH MORTAR
STORM SEWER
FILL WITH MORTAR
PRECAST CONCRETE BOX

V SECTION · PRECAST CONC. INLET
SCALE 3/4"=1'-0"

DRAIN INLET DETAILS

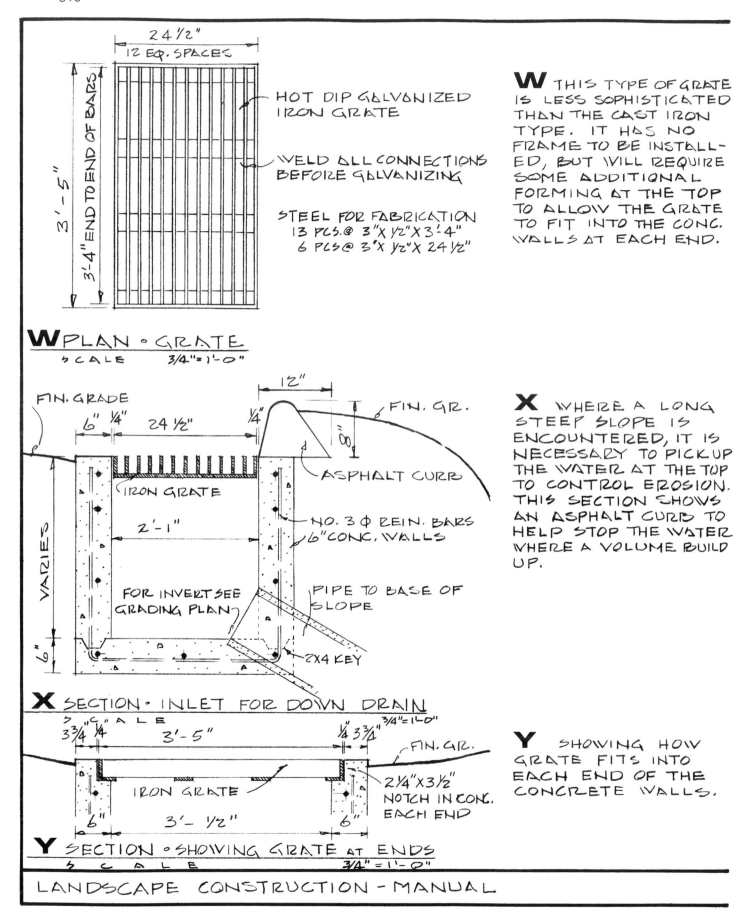

24 1/2"
12 EQ. SPACES

3'-5" END TO END OF BARS
3'-4" END TO END OF BARS

HOT DIP GALVANIZED
IRON GRATE

WELD ALL CONNECTIONS
BEFORE GALVANIZING

STEEL FOR FABRICATION
13 PCS.@ 3"X 1/2"X 3'-4"
6 PCS @ 3"X 1/2"X 24 1/2"

W THIS TYPE OF GRATE
IS LESS SOPHISTICATED
THAN THE CAST IRON
TYPE. IT HAS NO
FRAME TO BE INSTALL-
ED, BUT WILL REQUIRE
SOME ADDITIONAL
FORMING AT THE TOP
TO ALLOW THE GRATE
TO FIT INTO THE CONC.
WALLS AT EACH END.

W PLAN · GRATE
SCALE   3/4"=1'-0"

FIN. GRADE
6" 1/4"   24 1/2"   1/4"
12"
FIN. GR.
8"
ASPHALT CURB

IRON GRATE
2'-1"
NO. 3 ∅ REIN. BARS
6"CONC. WALLS

VARIES
FOR INVERT SEE
GRADING PLAN
PIPE TO BASE OF
SLOPE
6"
2X4 KEY

X SECTION · INLET FOR DOWN DRAIN
SCALE   3/4"=1'-0"

X WHERE A LONG
STEEP SLOPE IS
ENCOUNTERED, IT IS
NECESSARY TO PICKUP
THE WATER AT THE TOP
TO CONTROL EROSION.
THIS SECTION SHOWS
AN ASPHALT CURB TO
HELP STOP THE WATER
WHERE A VOLUME BUILD
UP.

3 3/4" 1/4"   3'-5"   1/4" 3 3/4"
FIN. GR.
IRON GRATE
2 1/4"X3 1/2"
NOTCH IN CONC.
EACH END
6"   3'-1/2"   6"

Y SECTION · SHOWING GRATE AT ENDS
SCALE   3/4"=1'-0"

Y SHOWING HOW
GRATE FITS INTO
EACH END OF THE
CONCRETE WALLS.

LANDSCAPE CONSTRUCTION - MANUAL

Z HERE SPACE ALLOWS A MOUND OF EARTH BEHIND THE INLET. THE "V" TYPE GRATE FITS WELL IN THIS TYPE OF DRAINAGE SWALE. INLETS ARE PLACED PARALLEL TO THE TOP OF THE SLOPE AT LOW POINTS WITH HIGH POINTS IN BETWEEN.

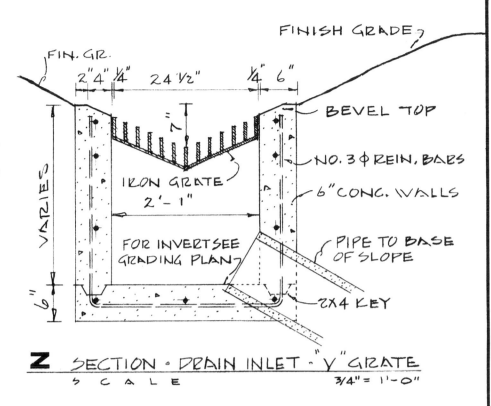

FINISH GRADE

FIN. GR.

2"4" 1/4" 24 1/2" 1/4" 6"

BEVEL TOP

NO. 3 Ø REIN. BARS

6" CONC. WALLS

IRON GRATE 2'-1"

FOR INVERT SEE GRADING PLAN

PIPE TO BASE OF SLOPE

2X4 KEY

VARIES

6"

Z SECTION • DRAIN INLET • "V" GRATE
SCALE   3/4" = 1'-0"

ZZ THIS LONGITUDINAL SECTION OF THE INLET WITH A "V" TYPE GRATE SHOWS 1/2 OF THE GRATE AND HOW END WALLS MUST SLOPE. THIS TYPE INLET WORKS WELL IN LARGE OPEN FIELDS, PARKS, ETC.

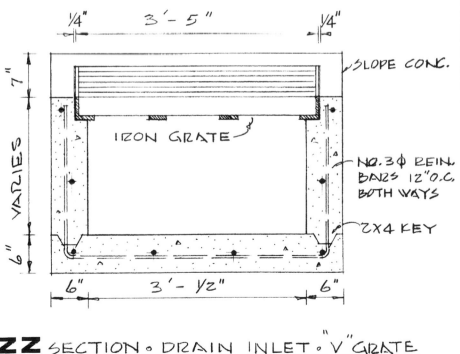

1/4" 3'-5" 1/4"

7"

SLOPE CONC.

IRON GRATE

NO. 3 Ø REIN. BARS 12" O.C. BOTH WAYS

2X4 KEY

VARIES

6"

6" 3'-1/2" 6"

ZZ SECTION • DRAIN INLET • "V" GRATE
SCALE   3/4" = 1'-0"

DRAIN INLET DETAILS

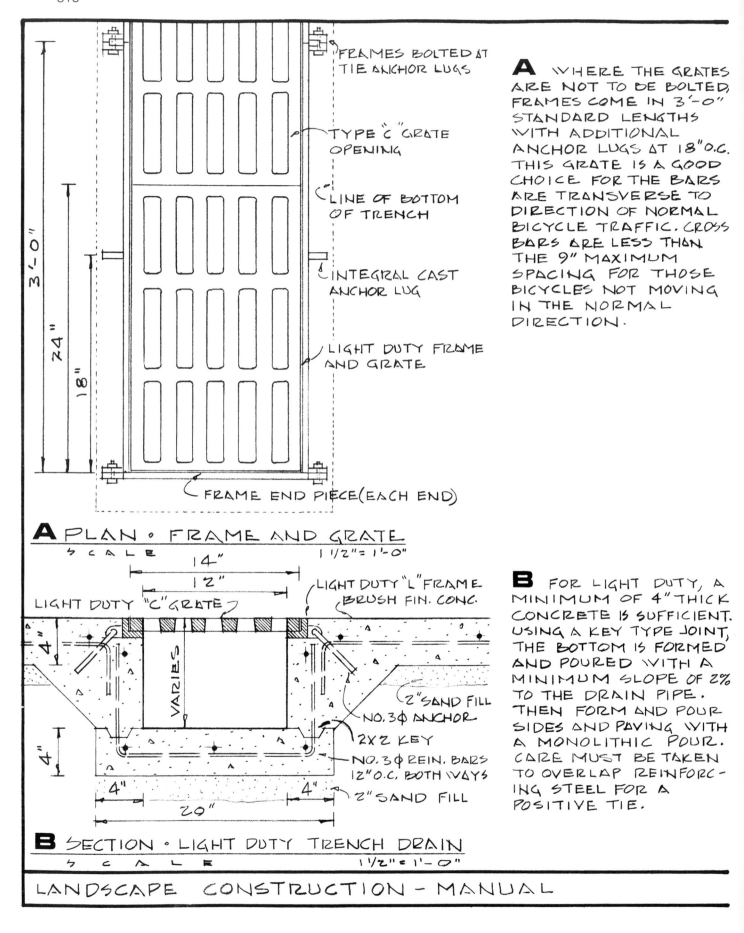

FRAMES BOLTED AT TIE ANCHOR LUGS

TYPE "C" GRATE OPENING

LINE OF BOTTOM OF TRENCH

INTEGRAL CAST ANCHOR LUG

LIGHT DUTY FRAME AND GRATE

3'-0"

24"

18"

FRAME END PIECE (EACH END)

A WHERE THE GRATES ARE NOT TO BE BOLTED, FRAMES COME IN 3'-0" STANDARD LENGTHS WITH ADDITIONAL ANCHOR LUGS AT 18"O.C. THIS GRATE IS A GOOD CHOICE FOR THE BARS ARE TRANSVERSE TO DIRECTION OF NORMAL BICYCLE TRAFFIC. CROSS BARS ARE LESS THAN THE 9" MAXIMUM SPACING FOR THOSE BICYCLES NOT MOVING IN THE NORMAL DIRECTION.

A PLAN · FRAME AND GRATE
SCALE   1 1/2" = 1'-0"

14"
12"

LIGHT DUTY "C" GRATE
LIGHT DUTY "L" FRAME BRUSH FIN. CONC.

4"

VARIES

4"

4"   4"

20"

2" SAND FILL
NO. 3∅ ANCHOR
2X2 KEY
NO. 3∅ REIN. BARS 12"O.C. BOTH WAYS
2" SAND FILL

B FOR LIGHT DUTY, A MINIMUM OF 4" THICK CONCRETE IS SUFFICIENT. USING A KEY TYPE JOINT, THE BOTTOM IS FORMED AND POURED WITH A MINIMUM SLOPE OF 2% TO THE DRAIN PIPE. THEN FORM AND POUR SIDES AND PAVING WITH A MONOLITHIC POUR. CARE MUST BE TAKEN TO OVERLAP REINFORCING STEEL FOR A POSITIVE TIE.

B SECTION · LIGHT DUTY TRENCH DRAIN
SCALE   1 1/2" = 1'-0"

LANDSCAPE CONSTRUCTION - MANUAL

C IT IS NOT A GOOD IDEA TO ATTEMPT A MONOLITHIC POUR OF TRENCH WALLS AND A RETAINING WALL (WHERE IT OCCURS AS SHOWN). IT IS, HOWEVER, IMPORT- ANT THAT THE TWO BE TIED TOGETHER. DOWELING, AS SHOWN, IS ONE GOOD WAY TO ACCOMPLISH THIS. TRENCH DEPTHS WILL BE THE SAME AS SUGGESTED IN THE HEAVY DUTY TRENCH DETAILS.

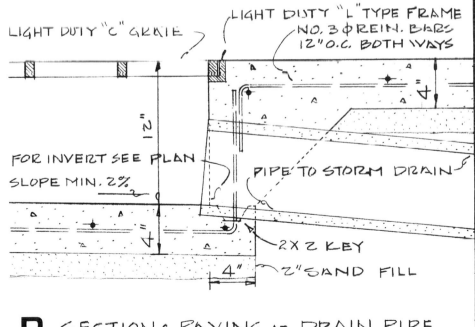

RETAINING WALL

LIGHT DUTY "L" FRAME
LIGHT DUTY "C" GRATE

4"

NO. 3 ∅ DOWEL 2'0.C.

2"

FOR INVERT SEE PLAN MIN. 2% SLOPE

PIPE TO STORM DRAIN

4"

2 X 2 KEY
NO. 3 ∅ REIN. BARS 12" O.C. BOTH WAYS
2" SAND FILL

C SECTION · RET. WALL AT DRAIN PIPE
SCALE   1 1/2" = 1'-0"

D WHERE PAVING EXISTS AT AN END OF THE TRENCH, THE DETAIL WOULD BE SIMULAR TO THAT OF THE CROSS- SECTION, WITH THE DRAIN PIPE SHOWN. SEVERAL TYPES OF GRATES AND FRAMES ARE AVAILABLE FOR LIGHT DUTY TRENCH DRAINS. CHECK WITH THE MANUFACTURERS CATALOG FOR ADDITIONAL INFORMATION.

LIGHT DUTY "C" GRATE

LIGHT DUTY "L" TYPE FRAME
NO. 3 ∅ REIN. BARS 12" O.C. BOTH WAYS

2"

FOR INVERT SEE PLAN
SLOPE MIN. 2%

PIPE TO STORM DRAIN

4"

4"

2 X 2 KEY
2" SAND FILL

D SECTION · PAVING AT DRAIN PIPE
SCALE   1 1/2" = 1'-0"

DRAIN INLET DETAILS (TRENCH)

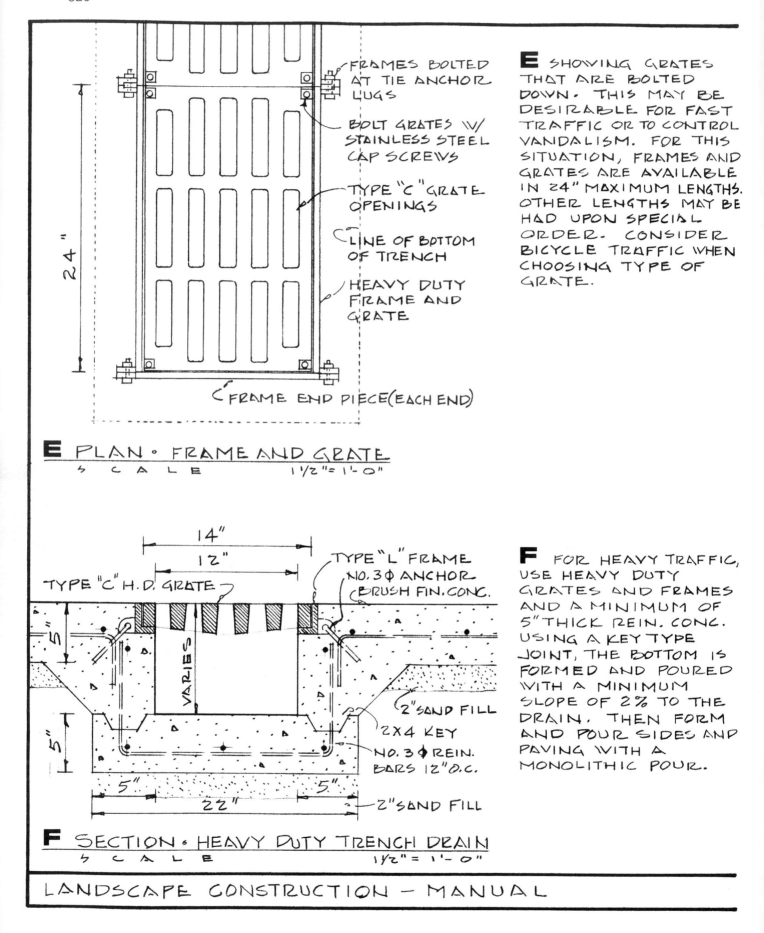

FRAMES BOLTED AT TIE ANCHOR LUGS

BOLT GRATES W/ STAINLESS STEEL CAP SCREWS

TYPE "C" GRATE OPENINGS

LINE OF BOTTOM OF TRENCH

HEAVY DUTY FRAME AND GRATE

24"

FRAME END PIECE(EACH END)

E PLAN · FRAME AND GRATE
SCALE 1½" = 1'-0"

E SHOWING GRATES THAT ARE BOLTED DOWN. THIS MAY BE DESIRABLE FOR FAST TRAFFIC OR TO CONTROL VANDALISM. FOR THIS SITUATION, FRAMES AND GRATES ARE AVAILABLE IN 24" MAXIMUM LENGTHS. OTHER LENGTHS MAY BE HAD UPON SPECIAL ORDER. CONSIDER BICYCLE TRAFFIC WHEN CHOOSING TYPE OF GRATE.

14"

12"

TYPE "C" H.D. GRATE

TYPE "L" FRAME
NO. 3⌀ ANCHOR
BRUSH FIN. CONC.

5"

VARIES

5"

2" SAND FILL

2X4 KEY

NO. 3⌀ REIN. BARS 12" O.C.

5"   5"

22"

2" SAND FILL

F SECTION · HEAVY DUTY TRENCH DRAIN
SCALE 1½" = 1'-0"

F FOR HEAVY TRAFFIC, USE HEAVY DUTY GRATES AND FRAMES AND A MINIMUM OF 5" THICK REIN. CONC. USING A KEY TYPE JOINT, THE BOTTOM IS FORMED AND POURED WITH A MINIMUM SLOPE OF 2% TO THE DRAIN. THEN FORM AND POUR SIDES AND PAVING WITH A MONOLITHIC POUR.

LANDSCAPE CONSTRUCTION — MANUAL

G CURBS MAY BE POURED MONOLITHIC OR DOWELED AND POURED SEPARATELY. THE PIPE (SIZED DEPENDING UPON CALCULATED VOLUME OF FLOW) WILL BE PLACED BEFORE THE BOTTOM OF THE TRENCH IS POURED. DEPTH OF TRENCH WILL BE A MINIMUM OF 6" AT THE HIGH END AND DEEP ENOUGH AT THE LOW END TO ACCOMMODATE ALL OF THE FOLLOWING: MINIMUM 2% SLOPE, PIPE SIZE, AND SPECIAL DEPTH REQUIREMENTS FOR THE PIPE.

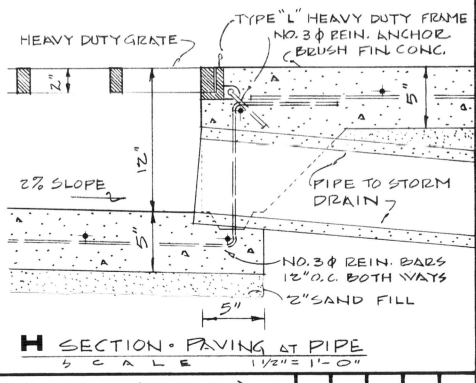

HEAVY DUTY "L" FRAME
HEAVY DUTY GRATE
2" SLOPE
5" 6"
1"
6"
8"
12"
5"
3 NO. 3∅ CONT.
NO. 3∅ @ 24" O.C.
PIPE TO STORM DRAIN
NO. 3∅ REIN. BARS 12" O.C. BOTH WAYS
2" SAND FILL

G SECTION · CURB AT PIPE
SCALE   1½" = 1'-0"

H PAVING OCCURRING AT ENDS OR SIDES OF THE TRENCH SHOULD BE A MONOLITHIC POUR WITH THE WALLS. CHECK WITH MANUFACTURERS TO DETERMINE THE VARIOUS TYPES OF FRAMES AND GRATES AND THEIR STANDARD DIMENSIONS.

HEAVY DUTY GRATE
TYPE "L" HEAVY DUTY FRAME
NO. 3∅ REIN. ANCHOR
BRUSH FIN. CONC.
2"
12"
5"
5"
2% SLOPE
PIPE TO STORM DRAIN
NO. 3∅ REIN. BARS 12" O.C. BOTH WAYS
2" SAND FILL
5"

H SECTION · PAVING AT PIPE
SCALE   1½" = 1'-0"

DRAIN INLET DETAILS (TRENCH)

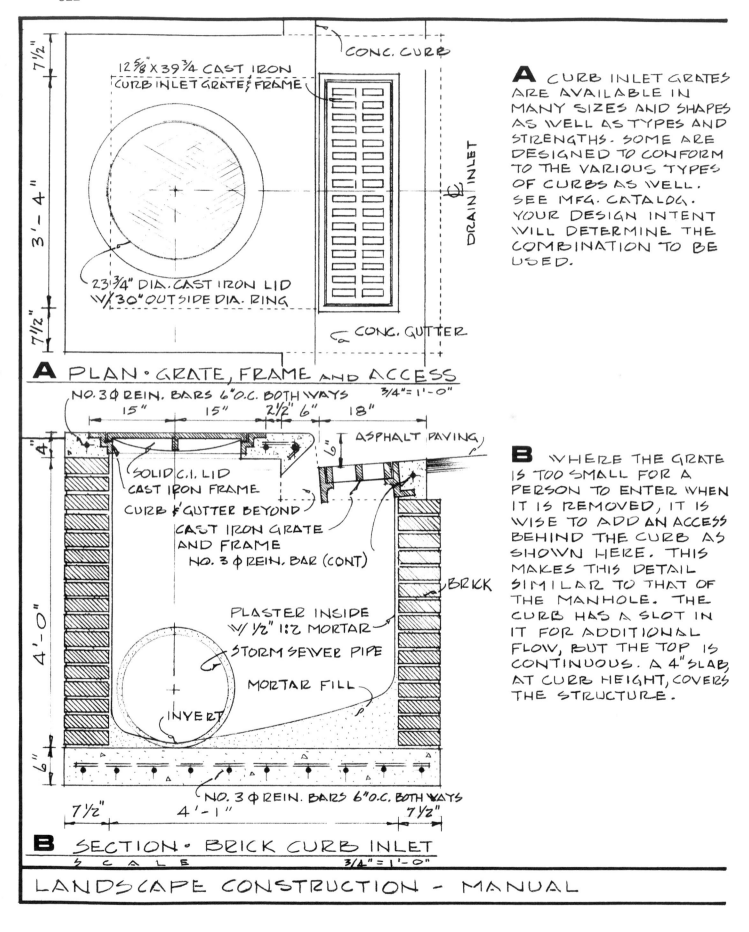

7½"

3'-4"

7½"

12⅝" X 39¾ CAST IRON CURB INLET GRATE & FRAME

CONC. CURB

DRAIN INLET

23¾" DIA. CAST IRON LID W/ 30" OUTSIDE DIA. RING

CONC. GUTTER

A PLAN • GRATE, FRAME AND ACCESS

NO. 3 Φ REIN. BARS 6" O.C. BOTH WAYS   ¾"=1'-0"

15"   15"   2½" 6"   18"

4"

6"

ASPHALT PAVING

SOLID C.I. LID
CAST IRON FRAME
CURB & GUTTER BEYOND
CAST IRON GRATE AND FRAME
NO. 3 Φ REIN. BAR (CONT)

BRICK

PLASTER INSIDE W/ ½" 1:2 MORTAR
STORM SEWER PIPE
MORTAR FILL

4'-0"

INVERT

6"

NO. 3 Φ REIN. BARS 6" O.C. BOTH WAYS

7½"   4'-1"   7½"

B SECTION • BRICK CURB INLET

SCALE   ¾"=1'-0"

A CURB INLET GRATES ARE AVAILABLE IN MANY SIZES AND SHAPES AS WELL AS TYPES AND STRENGTHS. SOME ARE DESIGNED TO CONFORM TO THE VARIOUS TYPES OF CURBS AS WELL. SEE MFG. CATALOG. YOUR DESIGN INTENT WILL DETERMINE THE COMBINATION TO BE USED.

B WHERE THE GRATE IS TOO SMALL FOR A PERSON TO ENTER WHEN IT IS REMOVED, IT IS WISE TO ADD AN ACCESS BEHIND THE CURB AS SHOWN HERE. THIS MAKES THIS DETAIL SIMILAR TO THAT OF THE MANHOLE. THE CURB HAS A SLOT IN IT FOR ADDITIONAL FLOW, BUT THE TOP IS CONTINUOUS. A 4" SLAB AT CURB HEIGHT, COVERS THE STRUCTURE.

LANDSCAPE CONSTRUCTION - MANUAL

C ALWAYS CONSIDER SAFETY STANDARDS FOR BICYCLES WHEN CHOOSING A GUTTER GRATE. WHERE BICYCLES ARE NOT ALLOWED, SUCH AS FREEWAYS, ETC. THIS IS OF NO CONCERN. THIS DETAIL SHOWS THE CURB WIDTH CHANGED TO COVER THE STRUCTURE. THIS WILL PRESENT A PROBLEM WHERE TURF IS TO BE EDGED.

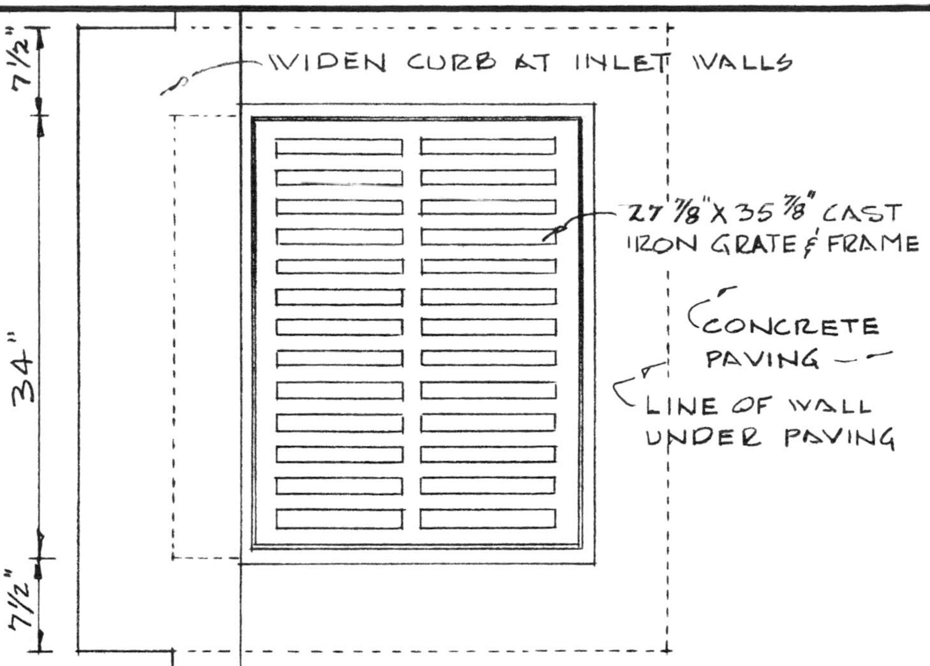

D DUE TO THE WIDTH OF THIS GRATE AND FRAME, THE DETAIL WILL ONLY WORK WHERE THE STREET OR PARKING AREA IS PAVED WITH CONCRETE. WHEN USING MORE THAN ONE GRATE IN LINE, OR WHERE HEAVY VEHICLES ARE ANTICIPATED, AN IRON "I" BEAM WOULD BE ADDED UNDER THE INSIDE EDGE OF THE FRAME. PIPE SIZES AND DIRECTIONS WILL BE INDICATED ON THE GRADING PLAN. HOWEVER, IT IS DESIRABLE TO SHOW SOME ON THE DETAIL AS TYPICAL TO INDICATE HOW THEY FIT INTO THE DETAIL.

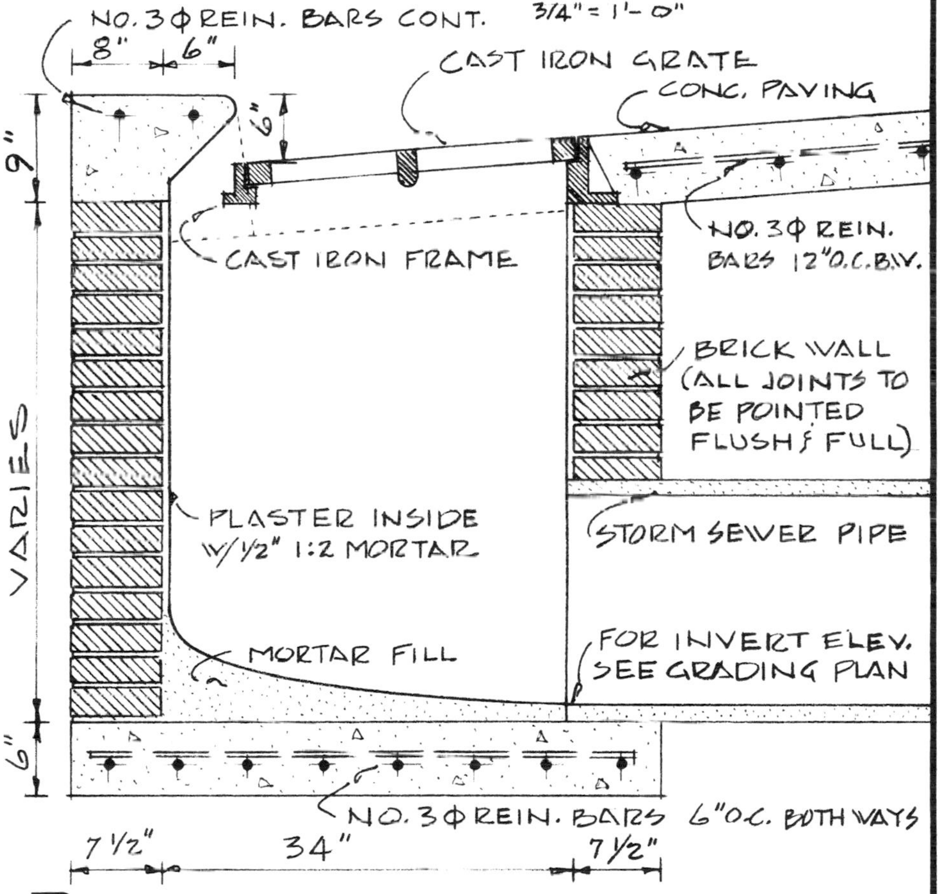

WIDEN CURB AT INLET WALLS

27⅞" X 35⅞" CAST IRON GRATE & FRAME

CONCRETE PAVING

LINE OF WALL UNDER PAVING

7½"

34"

7½"

C PLAN · GRATE AND FRAME   3/4" = 1'-0"

NO. 3φ REIN. BARS CONT.

8"   6"

9"

6"

CAST IRON GRATE

CONC. PAVING

NO. 3φ REIN. BARS 12" O.C. B.W.

CAST IRON FRAME

BRICK WALL (ALL JOINTS TO BE POINTED FLUSH & FULL)

VARIES

PLASTER INSIDE W/ ½" 1:2 MORTAR

STORM SEWER PIPE

MORTAR FILL

FOR INVERT ELEV. SEE GRADING PLAN

6"

NO. 3φ REIN. BARS 6" O.C. BOTH WAYS

7½"   34"   7½"

D SECTION · BRICK CURB INLET
SCALE   3/4" = 1'-0"

CURB INLET DETAILS

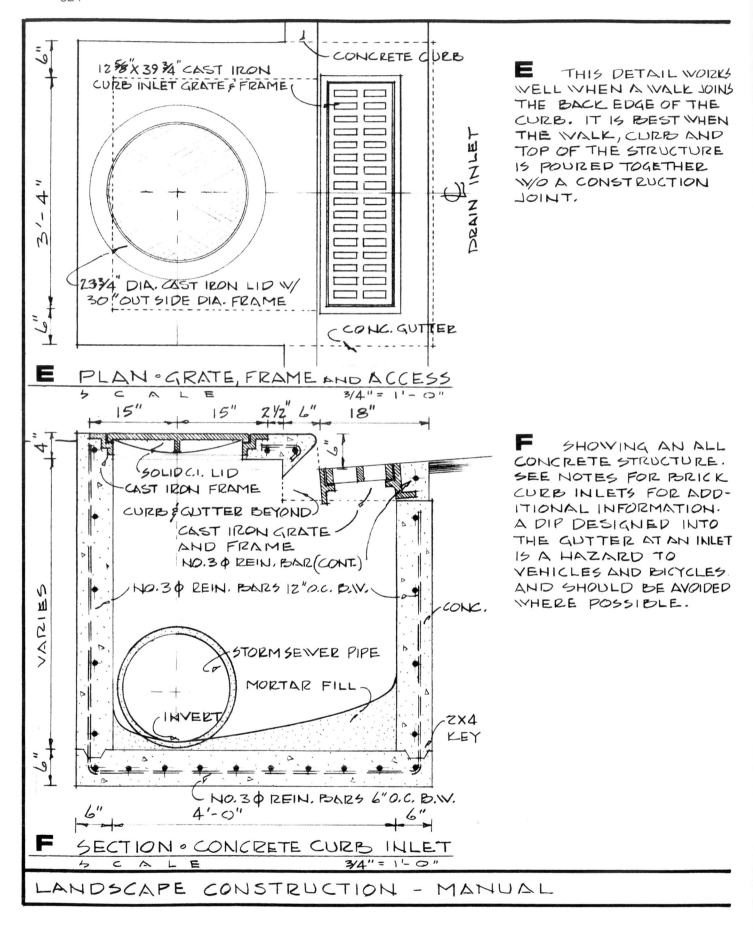

12⅝" X 39¾" CAST IRON CURB INLET GRATE & FRAME

CONCRETE CURB

23¾" DIA. CAST IRON LID W/ 30" OUTSIDE DIA. FRAME

DRAIN INLET

CONC. GUTTER

6"   3'-4"   6"

E PLAN ○ GRATE, FRAME AND ACCESS
S C A L E   3/4" = 1'-0"

E THIS DETAIL WORKS WELL WHEN A WALK JOINS THE BACK EDGE OF THE CURB. IT IS BEST WHEN THE WALK, CURB AND TOP OF THE STRUCTURE IS POURED TOGETHER W/O A CONSTRUCTION JOINT.

15"   15"   2½" 6"   18"

4"

SOLID C.I. LID
CAST IRON FRAME
CURB & GUTTER BEYOND
CAST IRON GRATE AND FRAME
NO. 3 ∅ REIN. BAR (CONT.)
NO. 3 ∅ REIN. BARS 12" O.C. B.W.

CONC.

STORM SEWER PIPE
MORTAR FILL
INVERT

2X4 KEY

VARIES

6"

NO. 3 ∅ REIN. BARS 6" O.C. B.W.
6"   4'-0"   6"

F SECTION ○ CONCRETE CURB INLET
S C A L E   3/4" = 1'-0"

F SHOWING AN ALL CONCRETE STRUCTURE. SEE NOTES FOR BRICK CURB INLETS FOR ADDITIONAL INFORMATION. A DIP DESIGNED INTO THE GUTTER AT AN INLET IS A HAZARD TO VEHICLES AND BICYCLES AND SHOULD BE AVOIDED WHERE POSSIBLE.

LANDSCAPE CONSTRUCTION - MANUAL

G THIS WOULD BE A GOOD CHOICE OF A GRATE WHERE BICYCLES WILL BE ON THE STREET. REMEMBER GRATE SIZES ARE SET BY THE CALCULATED VOLUME OF WATER AT THAT POINT.

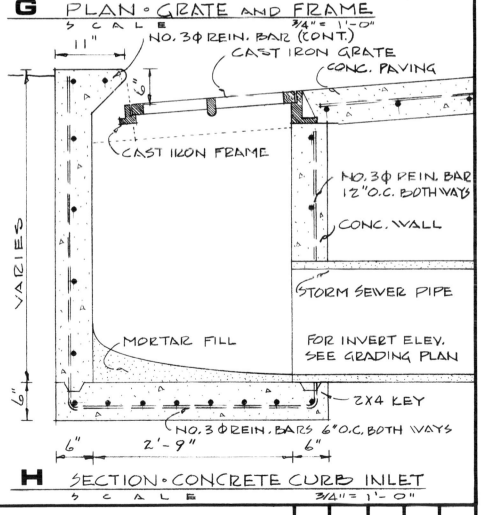

WIDEN CURB AT INLET WALLS

27⅞" X 35⅞" CAST IRON GRATE & FRAME

LINE OF WALL UNDER PAVING

CONCRETE PAVING

6"

2'-10"

6"

G PLAN · GRATE AND FRAME
SCALE ¾" = 1'-0"

H 1. POUR THE BOTTOM 2. SET PIPE OR PIPES 3. POUR WALLS 4. SET GRATE FRAME 5. POUR STREET PAVING AND CURB 6. MORTAR FILL.

11"

NO. 3∅ REIN. BAR (CONT.)

CAST IRON GRATE

CONC. PAVING

6"

CAST IRON FRAME

NO. 3∅ REIN. BAR 12" O.C. BOTH WAYS

CONC. WALL

STORM SEWER PIPE

FOR INVERT ELEV. SEE GRADING PLAN

VARIES

MORTAR FILL

6"

2X4 KEY

NO. 3∅ REIN. BARS 6" O.C. BOTH WAYS

6"   2'-9"   6"

H SECTION · CONCRETE CURB INLET
SCALE ¾" = 1'-0"

CURB INLET DETAILS

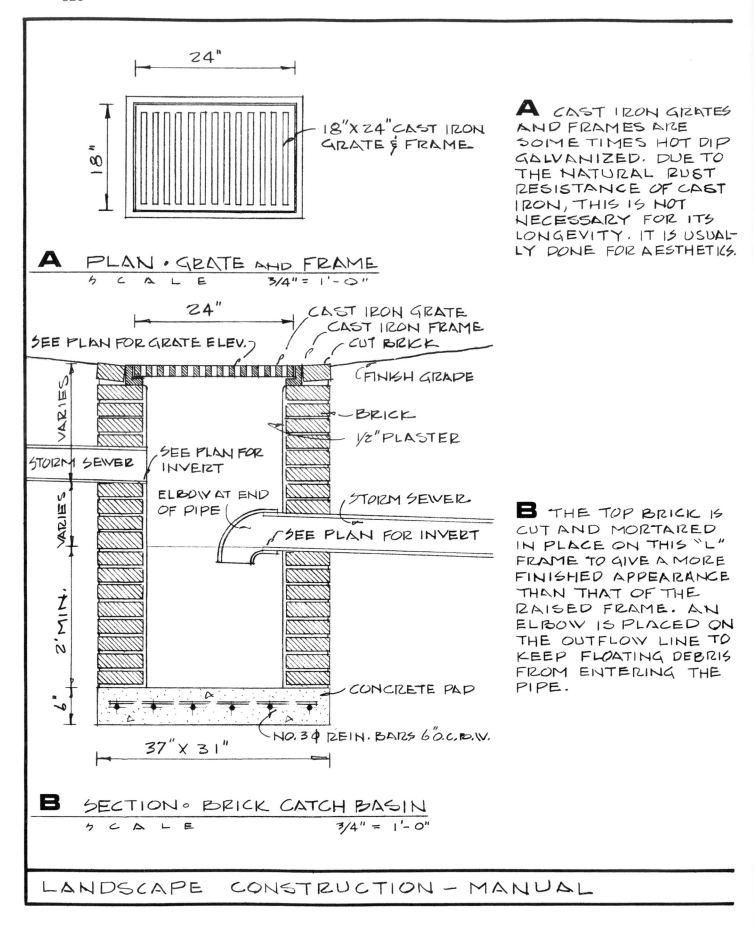

24"

18"

18" X 24" CAST IRON GRATE & FRAME

A PLAN • GRATE AND FRAME
SCALE   3/4" = 1'-0"

24"

CAST IRON GRATE
CAST IRON FRAME
CUT BRICK

SEE PLAN FOR GRATE ELEV.

FINISH GRADE

BRICK

1/2" PLASTER

VARIES

STORM SEWER

SEE PLAN FOR INVERT

VARIES

ELBOW AT END OF PIPE

STORM SEWER

SEE PLAN FOR INVERT

2' MIN.

6"

CONCRETE PAD

NO. 3 ∅ REIN. BARS 6" O.C. B.W.

37" X 31"

B SECTION • BRICK CATCH BASIN
SCALE   3/4" = 1'-0"

A CAST IRON GRATES AND FRAMES ARE SOME TIMES HOT DIP GALVANIZED. DUE TO THE NATURAL RUST RESISTANCE OF CAST IRON, THIS IS NOT NECESSARY FOR ITS LONGEVITY. IT IS USUALLY DONE FOR AESTHETICS.

B THE TOP BRICK IS CUT AND MORTARED IN PLACE ON THIS "L" FRAME TO GIVE A MORE FINISHED APPEARANCE THAN THAT OF THE RAISED FRAME. AN ELBOW IS PLACED ON THE OUTFLOW LINE TO KEEP FLOATING DEBRIS FROM ENTERING THE PIPE.

LANDSCAPE CONSTRUCTION - MANUAL

C GRATE ELEVATIONS AS WELL AS ALL INVERT ELEVATIONS AND PIPE SIZES ARE USUALLY GIVEN ON THE GRADING PLAN AND STORM DRAIN PROFILES. WHERE MORE THAN ONE DRAIN INLET OR CATCH BASIN OCCURS ON THE PROJECT, IT WOULD BE DIFFICULT TO EXPRESS THESE VARIOUS ELEVATIONS AND INVERTS ON THE DETAIL.

D CARE MUST BE TAKEN TO ASSURE THAT THE CATCH BASIN IS LARGE ENOUGH TO CLEAN OUT THE PIT. ALTHOUGH ONLY ONE IN-FLOWING PIPE IS SHOWN, SEVERAL MAY FLOW TO ONE UNIT AS A COLLECTING POINT IN SOME SITUATIONS.

THE FRAME MUST BE CAST INTO THE CONC.

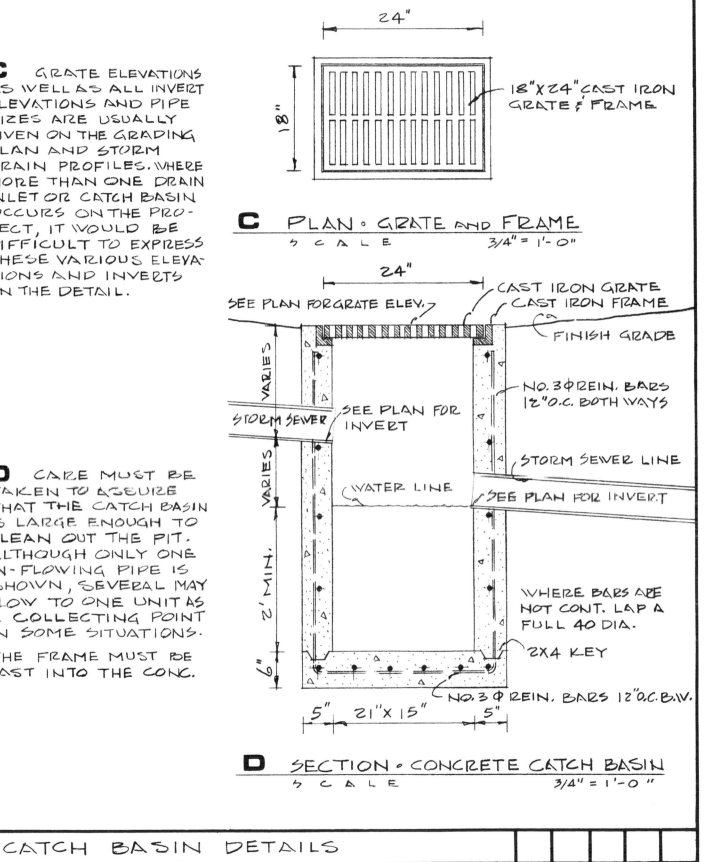

C PLAN · GRATE AND FRAME
SCALE   3/4" = 1'-0"

18"X24" CAST IRON GRATE & FRAME

SEE PLAN FOR GRATE ELEV.
CAST IRON GRATE
CAST IRON FRAME
FINISH GRADE
STORM SEWER
NO. 3 Φ REIN. BARS 12" O.C. BOTH WAYS
SEE PLAN FOR INVERT
STORM SEWER LINE
WATER LINE
SEE PLAN FOR INVERT
WHERE BARS ARE NOT CONT. LAP A FULL 40 DIA.
2X4 KEY
NO. 3 Φ REIN. BARS 12" O.C. B.W.
VARIES
VARIES
2' MIN.
6"
5"   21"X 15"   5"

D SECTION · CONCRETE CATCH BASIN
SCALE   3/4" = 1'-0"

CATCH BASIN DETAILS

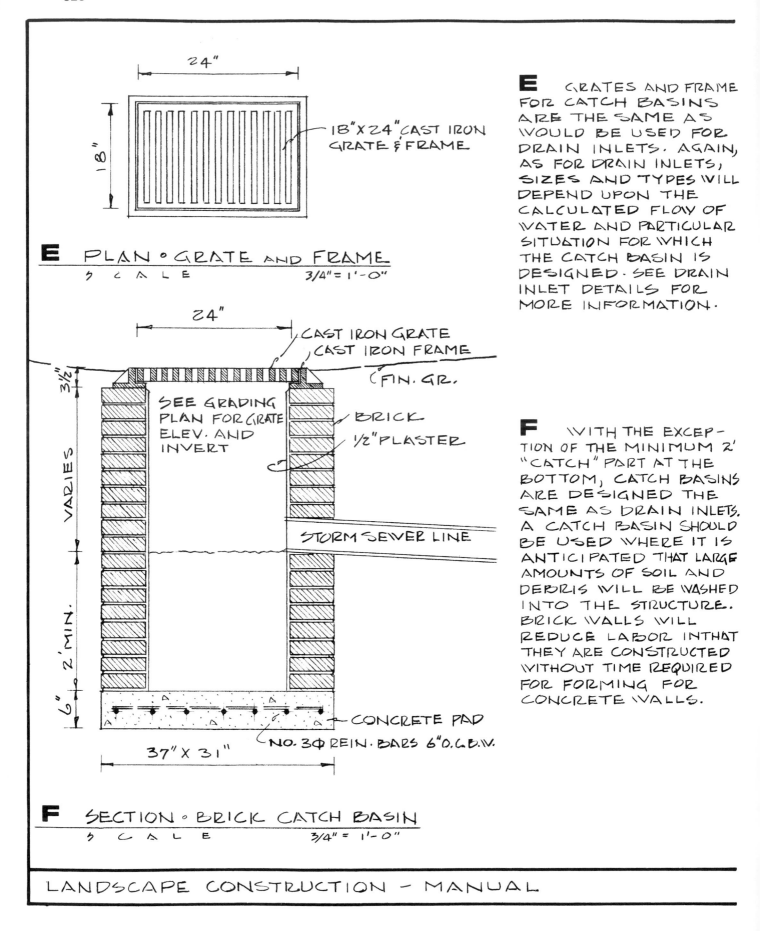

24"

18"

18"X24" CAST IRON GRATE & FRAME

E PLAN ∘ GRATE AND FRAME
SCALE   3/4" = 1'-0"

E GRATES AND FRAME FOR CATCH BASINS ARE THE SAME AS WOULD BE USED FOR DRAIN INLETS. AGAIN, AS FOR DRAIN INLETS, SIZES AND TYPES WILL DEPEND UPON THE CALCULATED FLOW OF WATER AND PARTICULAR SITUATION FOR WHICH THE CATCH BASIN IS DESIGNED. SEE DRAIN INLET DETAILS FOR MORE INFORMATION.

24"

CAST IRON GRATE
CAST IRON FRAME

3½"

FIN. GR.

SEE GRADING PLAN FOR GRATE ELEV. AND INVERT

BRICK
½" PLASTER

VARIES

STORM SEWER LINE

2' MIN.

6"

CONCRETE PAD
NO. 3∅ REIN. BARS 6"O.C.E.W.

37" X 31"

F WITH THE EXCEPTION OF THE MINIMUM 2' "CATCH" PART AT THE BOTTOM, CATCH BASINS ARE DESIGNED THE SAME AS DRAIN INLETS. A CATCH BASIN SHOULD BE USED WHERE IT IS ANTICIPATED THAT LARGE AMOUNTS OF SOIL AND DEBRIS WILL BE WASHED INTO THE STRUCTURE. BRICK WALLS WILL REDUCE LABOR IN THAT THEY ARE CONSTRUCTED WITHOUT TIME REQUIRED FOR FORMING FOR CONCRETE WALLS.

F SECTION ∘ BRICK CATCH BASIN
SCALE   3/4" = 1'-0"

G THIS MAY BE A BETTER GRATE CHOICE WHERE BICYCLES WILL CROSS IT AT VARIOUS ANGLES. SEE DRAIN INLET DETAILS FOR SUGGESTIONS ON BICYCLE CONSIDERATIONS.

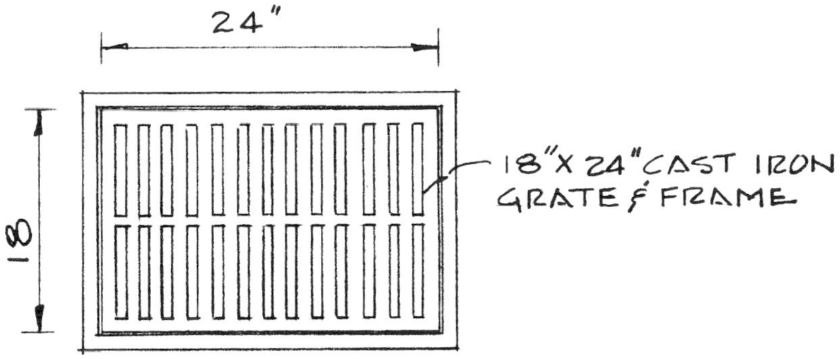

24"

18"

18" X 24" CAST IRON GRATE & FRAME

G PLAN · GRATE AND FRAME
SCALE 3/4" = 1'-0"

H ALTHOUGH BRICK CATCH BASINS ARE EASIER TO CONSTRUCT, WHERE ADDITIONAL WALL STRENGTH IS NECESSARY, CONCRETE SHOULD BE USED. EXPANSIVE TYPE SOILS AND HEAVY LOADS OF VEHICLES OVER THE TOP WILL PRESENT SOME PROBLEMS WITH BRICK WALLS. CONCRETE MUST BE FORMED AND REASONABLY ACCESSABLE TO THE CONCRETE TRUCK.

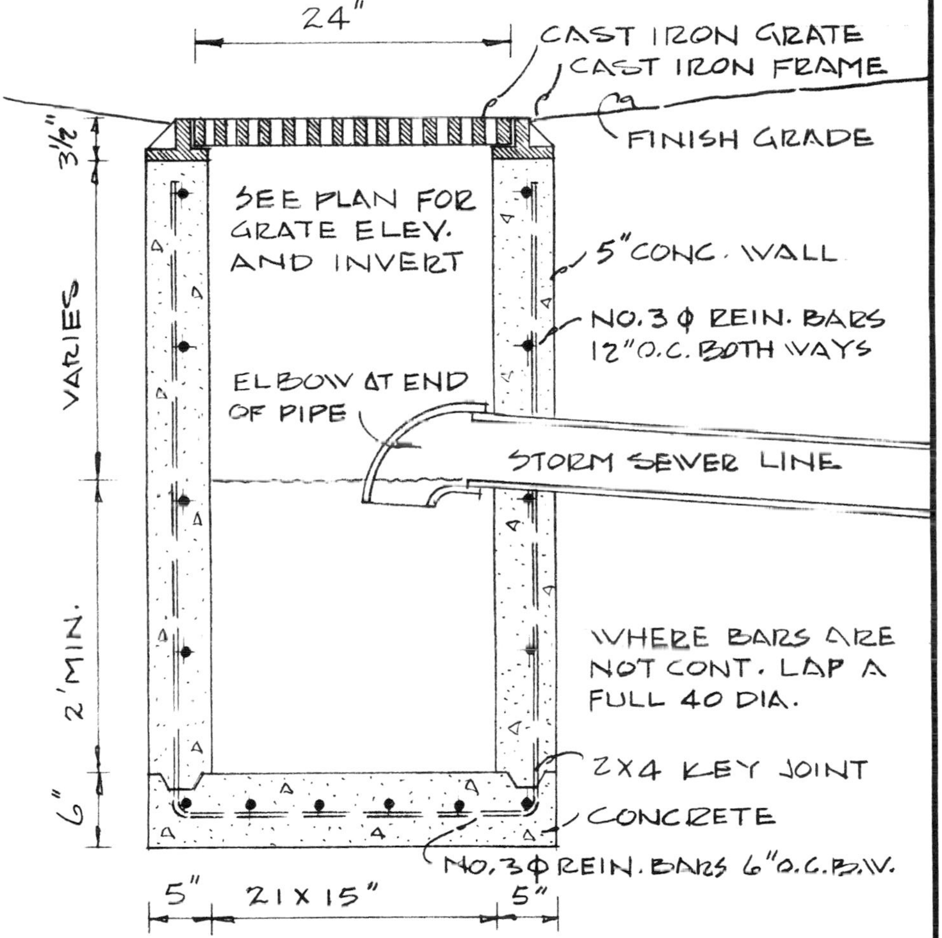

24"

CAST IRON GRATE
CAST IRON FRAME
FINISH GRADE

3½"

SEE PLAN FOR GRATE ELEV. AND INVERT

5" CONC. WALL

NO. 3 ∅ REIN. BARS 12" O.C. BOTH WAYS

ELBOW AT END OF PIPE

STORM SEWER LINE

VARIES

2' MIN.

WHERE BARS ARE NOT CONT. LAP A FULL 40 DIA.

6"

2X4 KEY JOINT
CONCRETE

5" 21 X 15" 5"

NO. 3 ∅ REIN. BARS 6" O.C. B.W.

H SECTION · CONCRETE CATCH BASIN
SCALE 3/4" = 1'-0"

CATCH BASIN DETAILS

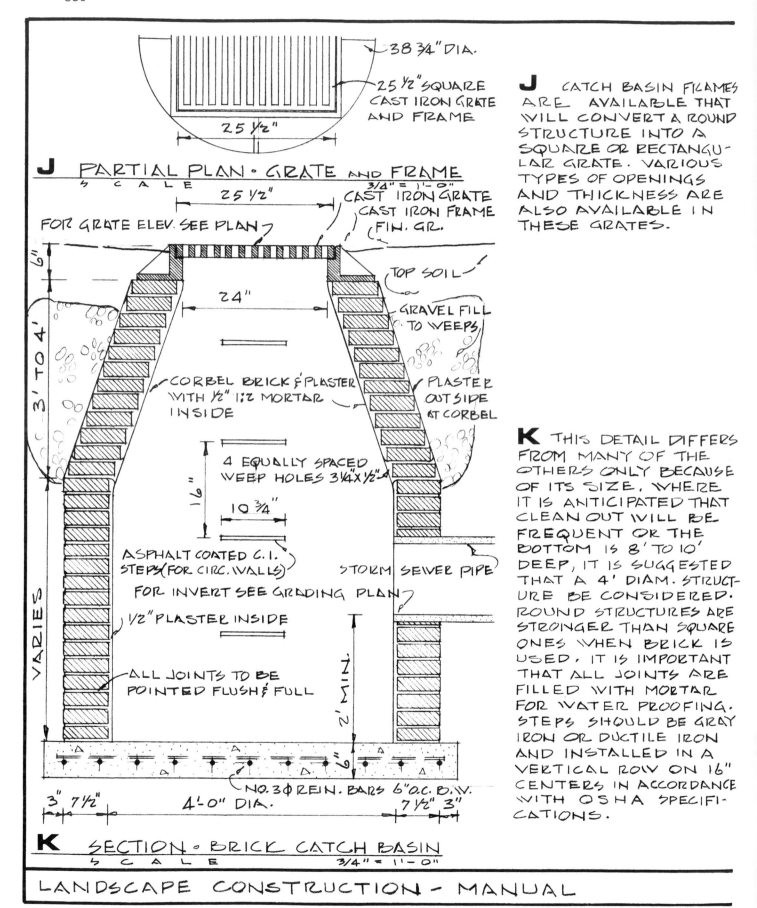

38 ¾" DIA.

25 ½" SQUARE CAST IRON GRATE AND FRAME

25 ½"

J PARTIAL PLAN · GRATE AND FRAME
SCALE ¾" = 1'-0"

25 ½"

FOR GRATE ELEV. SEE PLAN

CAST IRON GRATE
CAST IRON FRAME
FIN. GR.

6"

TOP SOIL

GRAVEL FILL TO WEEPS

24"

3' TO 4'

CORBEL BRICK & PLASTER WITH ½" 1:2 MORTAR INSIDE

PLASTER OUTSIDE AT CORBEL

4 EQUALLY SPACED WEEP HOLES 3¼" X ½"

16"

10 ¾"

ASPHALT COATED C.I. STEPS (FOR CIRC. WALLS)
FOR INVERT SEE GRADING PLAN

STORM SEWER PIPE

½" PLASTER INSIDE

VARIES

ALL JOINTS TO BE POINTED FLUSH & FULL

2' MIN.

6"

NO. 3Ø REIN. BARS 6" O.C. B.W.

3" 7½"

4'-0" DIA.

7½" 3"

K SECTION · BRICK CATCH BASIN
SCALE ¾" = 1'-0"

J CATCH BASIN FRAMES ARE AVAILABLE THAT WILL CONVERT A ROUND STRUCTURE INTO A SQUARE OR RECTANGULAR GRATE. VARIOUS TYPES OF OPENINGS AND THICKNESS ARE ALSO AVAILABLE IN THESE GRATES.

K THIS DETAIL DIFFERS FROM MANY OF THE OTHERS ONLY BECAUSE OF ITS SIZE. WHERE IT IS ANTICIPATED THAT CLEAN OUT WILL BE FREQUENT OR THE BOTTOM IS 8' TO 10' DEEP, IT IS SUGGESTED THAT A 4' DIAM. STRUCTURE BE CONSIDERED. ROUND STRUCTURES ARE STRONGER THAN SQUARE ONES WHEN BRICK IS USED. IT IS IMPORTANT THAT ALL JOINTS ARE FILLED WITH MORTAR FOR WATER PROOFING. STEPS SHOULD BE GRAY IRON OR DUCTILE IRON AND INSTALLED IN A VERTICAL ROW ON 16" CENTERS IN ACCORDANCE WITH OSHA SPECIFICATIONS.

LANDSCAPE CONSTRUCTION · MANUAL

L CONCRETE STRUCTURES ARE MORE EASILY FORMED SQUARE RATHER THAN ROUND. THUS A SQUARE GRATE AND FRAME IS USED HERE.

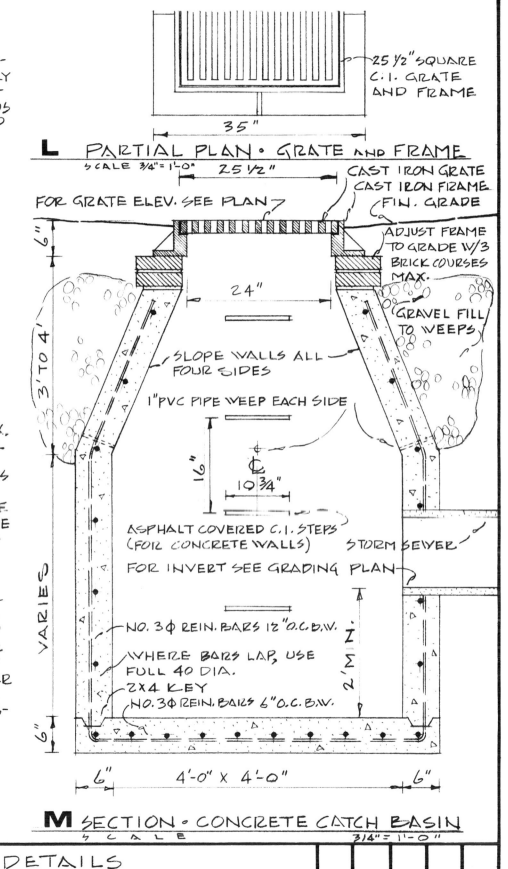

25 ½" SQUARE C.I. GRATE AND FRAME

35"

L PARTIAL PLAN · GRATE AND FRAME
SCALE ¾"=1'-0" 25 ½"

CAST IRON GRATE
CAST IRON FRAME
FIN. GRADE

FOR GRATE ELEV. SEE PLAN

ADJUST FRAME TO GRADE W/3 BRICK COURSES MAX.

6"

24"

GRAVEL FILL TO WEEPS

3' TO 4'

SLOPE WALLS ALL FOUR SIDES

1" PVC PIPE WEEP EACH SIDE

16"

10 ¾"

ASPHALT COVERED C.I. STEPS (FOR CONCRETE WALLS)

STORM SEWER

FOR INVERT SEE GRADING PLAN

VARIES

NO. 3∅ REIN. BARS 12" O.C. B.W.

2'±

WHERE BARS LAP, USE FULL 40 DIA.

2X4 KEY

NO. 3∅ REIN. BARS 6" O.C. B.W.

6"

6"

4'-0" X 4'-0"

6"

M THIS DETAIL WILL BE GOOD UP TO APPROX. 10' DEEP FOR THE TOTAL STRUCTURE. WEEP HOLES ARE NOT ALWAYS NECESSARY, BUT WILL HELP ASSURE THAT THE SOIL DOES NOT BECOME SATURATED AROUND THE CATCH BASIN WHEN THE SOIL IS SANDY OR VERY LOAMY. WHERE EXPANSIVE SOILS ARE ENCOUNTERED, 12" TO 18" OF SAND FILL UNDER THE STRUCTURE MAY BE NECESSARY. NEVER ALLOW A STRUCTURE TO BE PLACED ON DISTURBED SOIL THAT HAS NOT BEEN COMPACTED TO 90%.

M SECTION · CONCRETE CATCH BASIN
SCALE ¾"=1'-0"

CATCH BASIN DETAILS

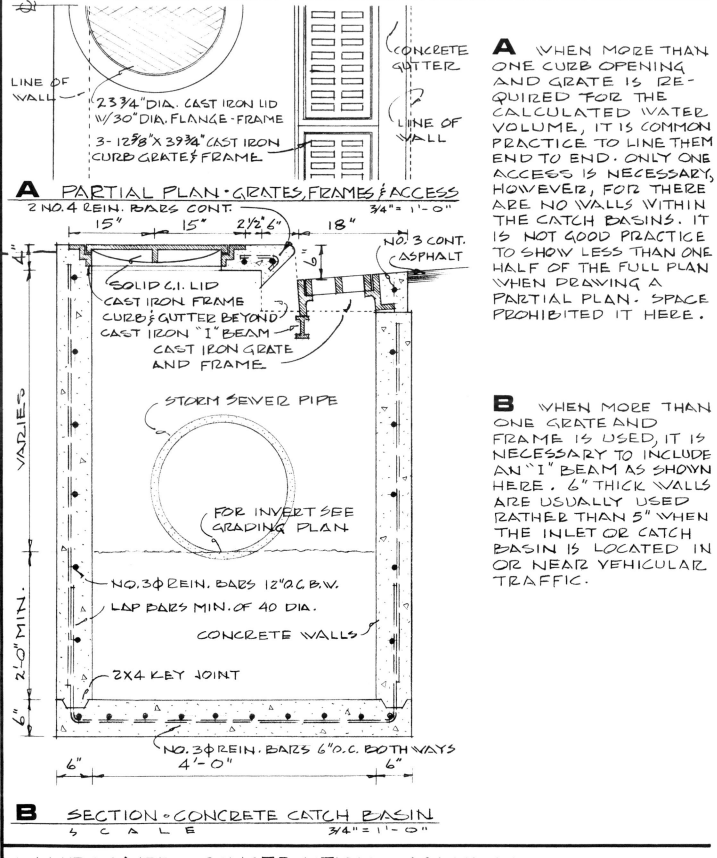

LINE OF WALL

23¾" DIA. CAST IRON LID W/ 30" DIA. FLANGE - FRAME

3 - 12⅝" X 39¾" CAST IRON CURB GRATE & FRAME

CONCRETE GUTTER

LINE OF WALL

A PARTIAL PLAN · GRATES, FRAMES & ACCESS   ¾" = 1'-0"

2 NO. 4 REIN. BARS CONT.

15"   15"   2½" 6"   18"

4"

NO. 3 CONT.
ASPHALT

SOLID C.I. LID
CAST IRON FRAME
CURB & GUTTER BEYOND
CAST IRON "I" BEAM
CAST IRON GRATE
AND FRAME

STORM SEWER PIPE

FOR INVERT SEE
GRADING PLAN

VARIES

2'-0" MIN.

NO. 3 Ø REIN. BARS 12" O.C. B.W.
LAP BARS MIN. OF 40 DIA.
CONCRETE WALLS

2X4 KEY JOINT

6"

NO. 3 Ø REIN. BARS 6" O.C. BOTH WAYS

6"   4'-0"   6"

B SECTION · CONCRETE CATCH BASIN

SCALE   ¾" = 1'-0"

LANDSCAPE CONSTRUCTION - MANUAL

A WHEN MORE THAN ONE CURB OPENING AND GRATE IS REQUIRED FOR THE CALCULATED WATER VOLUME, IT IS COMMON PRACTICE TO LINE THEM END TO END. ONLY ONE ACCESS IS NECESSARY, HOWEVER, FOR THERE ARE NO WALLS WITHIN THE CATCH BASINS. IT IS NOT GOOD PRACTICE TO SHOW LESS THAN ONE HALF OF THE FULL PLAN WHEN DRAWING A PARTIAL PLAN. SPACE PROHIBITED IT HERE.

B WHEN MORE THAN ONE GRATE AND FRAME IS USED, IT IS NECESSARY TO INCLUDE AN "I" BEAM AS SHOWN HERE. 6" THICK WALLS ARE USUALLY USED RATHER THAN 5" WHEN THE INLET OR CATCH BASIN IS LOCATED IN OR NEAR VEHICULAR TRAFFIC.

C VARIOUS TYPES OF CAST IRON CURB INLET FRAME, GRATE AND CURB BOX COMBINATIONS ARE AVAILABLE. SEE MFG. CATALOG FOR THE ONE THAT FITS BEST YOUR PARTICULAR SITUATION.

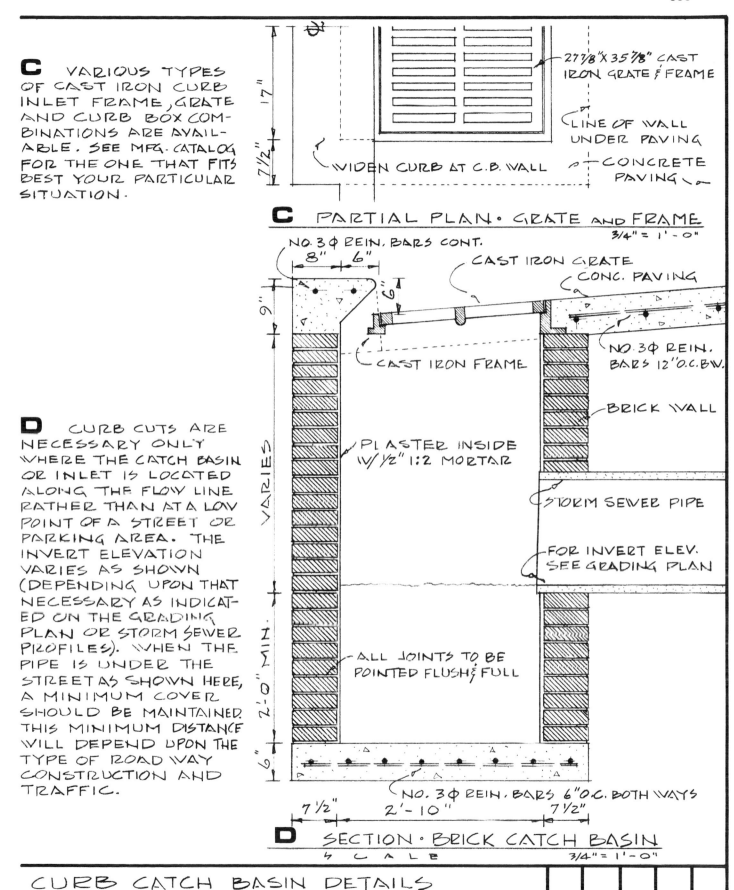

27⅞" X 35⅞" CAST IRON GRATE & FRAME

LINE OF WALL UNDER PAVING

CONCRETE PAVING

WIDEN CURB AT C.B. WALL

17"

7½"

C PARTIAL PLAN · GRATE AND FRAME
¾" = 1'-0"

NO. 3∅ REIN. BARS CONT.
8" 6"

CAST IRON GRATE
CONC. PAVING

CAST IRON FRAME

NO. 3∅ REIN. BARS 12" O.C. B.W.

BRICK WALL

PLASTER INSIDE W/ ½" 1:2 MORTAR

STORM SEWER PIPE

FOR INVERT ELEV. SEE GRADING PLAN

ALL JOINTS TO BE POINTED FLUSH & FULL

9"

VARIES

2'-0" MIN.

6"

NO. 3∅ REIN. BARS 6" O.C. BOTH WAYS

7½" 2'-10" 7½"

D CURB CUTS ARE NECESSARY ONLY WHERE THE CATCH BASIN OR INLET IS LOCATED ALONG THE FLOW LINE RATHER THAN AT A LOW POINT OF A STREET OR PARKING AREA. THE INVERT ELEVATION VARIES AS SHOWN (DEPENDING UPON THAT NECESSARY AS INDICATED ON THE GRADING PLAN OR STORM SEWER PROFILES). WHEN THE PIPE IS UNDER THE STREET AS SHOWN HERE, A MINIMUM COVER SHOULD BE MAINTAINED. THIS MINIMUM DISTANCE WILL DEPEND UPON THE TYPE OF ROADWAY CONSTRUCTION AND TRAFFIC.

D SECTION · BRICK CATCH BASIN
SCALE ¾" = 1'-0"

CURB CATCH BASIN DETAILS

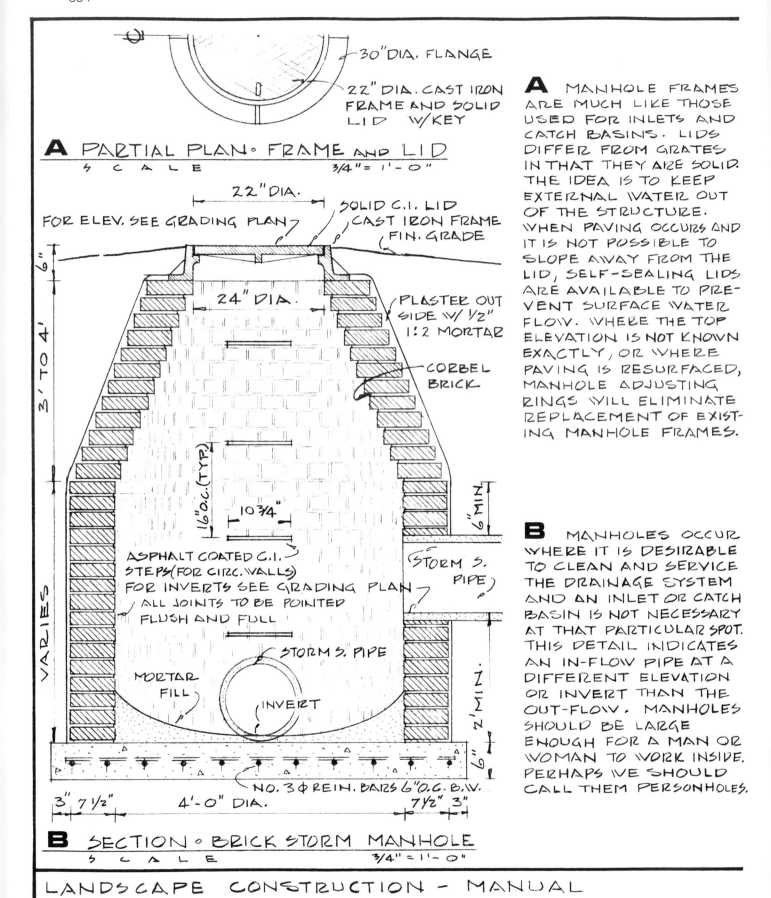

30" DIA. FLANGE

22" DIA. CAST IRON FRAME AND SOLID LID W/KEY

A PARTIAL PLAN ∘ FRAME AND LID

SCALE   3/4" = 1'-0"

22" DIA.

FOR ELEV. SEE GRADING PLAN

SOLID C.I. LID
CAST IRON FRAME
FIN. GRADE

6"

3' TO 4'

24" DIA.

PLASTER OUT SIDE W/ 1/2" 1:2 MORTAR

CORBEL BRICK

16" O.C. (TYP.)

10 3/4"

6" MIN.

ASPHALT COATED C.I. STEPS (FOR CIRC. WALLS) FOR INVERTS SEE GRADING PLAN ALL JOINTS TO BE POINTED FLUSH AND FULL

(STORM S. PIPE)

VARIES

STORM S. PIPE

MORTAR FILL

INVERT

12" MIN.

6"

NO. 3 ⌀ REIN. BARS 6" O.C. B.W.

3" 7 1/2"   4'-0" DIA.   7 1/2" 3"

B SECTION ∘ BRICK STORM MANHOLE

SCALE   3/4" = 1'-0"

A MANHOLE FRAMES ARE MUCH LIKE THOSE USED FOR INLETS AND CATCH BASINS. LIDS DIFFER FROM GRATES IN THAT THEY ARE SOLID. THE IDEA IS TO KEEP EXTERNAL WATER OUT OF THE STRUCTURE. WHEN PAVING OCCURS AND IT IS NOT POSSIBLE TO SLOPE AWAY FROM THE LID, SELF-SEALING LIDS ARE AVAILABLE TO PREVENT SURFACE WATER FLOW. WHERE THE TOP ELEVATION IS NOT KNOWN EXACTLY, OR WHERE PAVING IS RESURFACED, MANHOLE ADJUSTING RINGS WILL ELIMINATE REPLACEMENT OF EXISTING MANHOLE FRAMES.

B MANHOLES OCCUR WHERE IT IS DESIRABLE TO CLEAN AND SERVICE THE DRAINAGE SYSTEM AND AN INLET OR CATCH BASIN IS NOT NECESSARY AT THAT PARTICULAR SPOT. THIS DETAIL INDICATES AN IN-FLOW PIPE AT A DIFFERENT ELEVATION OR INVERT THAN THE OUT-FLOW. MANHOLES SHOULD BE LARGE ENOUGH FOR A MAN OR WOMAN TO WORK INSIDE. PERHAPS WE SHOULD CALL THEM PERSONHOLES.

C MANHOLE FRAMES AND LIDS ARE AVAILABLE IN ROUND OR SQUARE, VARIOUS SIZES, AND VARIOUS HEIGHTS. CHECK MFG. CATALOGS.

30" SQUARE FLANGE

22" SQUARE CAST IRON FRAME AND SOLID LID

C PARTIAL PLAN · FRAME AND LID
SCALE 3/4" = 1'-0"

22" X 22"

SEE PLAN FOR ELEV.

SOLID CAST IRON LID
CAST IRON FRAME
FIN. GRADE

6"

3' MIN. TO 4' MAX.

24"

PLASTER OUTSIDE W/ ½" 1:2 MORTAR

CORBEL BRICK ON 3 SIDES

16" O.C. (TYP.)

ASPHALT COATED C.I. STEPS (FOR BRICK)

ALL JOINTS TO BE POINTED FLUSH AND FULL

STORM SEWER

MORTAR FILL

INVERT

VARIES

6"

3" 7½"

4'-0" X 4'-0"

7½" 3"

NO. 3 Ø REIN. BARS 6" O.C. B.W.

D THIS DETAIL SHOWS A SQUARE MANHOLE WITH THREE SIDES SLOPING AND THE FOURTH SIDE VERTICAL, WHICH RECEIVES THE STEPS. MANHOLES SHOULD BE PLASTERED ON THE OUTSIDE TO PREVENT WATER SEEPING IN. FOR STRUCTURAL SAFETY, DO NOT ALLOW THE BRICK TO BE CORBELED 24" IN LESS THAN 3' MINIMUM. SEE NOTES ON 4' WIDE CATCH BASINS FOR ADDITIONAL INFORMATION.

D SECTION · BRICK STORM MANHOLE
SCALE 3/4" = 1'-0"

STORM MANHOLE DETAILS

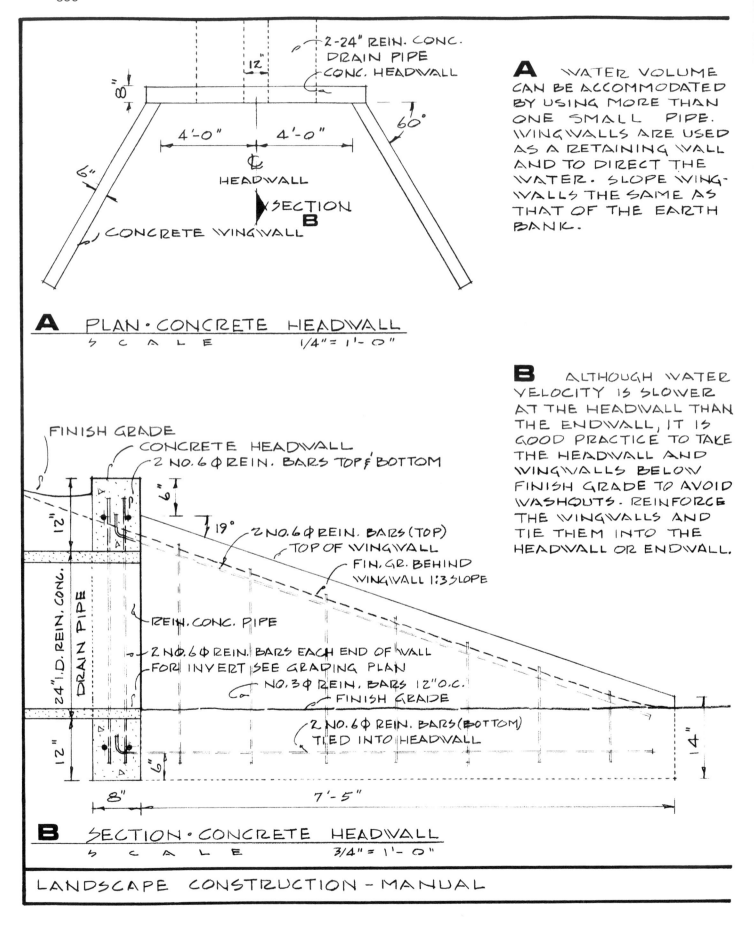

2-24" REIN. CONC.
DRAIN PIPE
CONC. HEADWALL

12"

8"

4'-0"   4'-0"

60°

6"

HEADWALL

SECTION
B

CONCRETE WINGWALL

A PLAN · CONCRETE HEADWALL
SCALE   1/4" = 1'-0"

A WATER VOLUME CAN BE ACCOMMODATED BY USING MORE THAN ONE SMALL PIPE. WINGWALLS ARE USED AS A RETAINING WALL AND TO DIRECT THE WATER. SLOPE WINGWALLS THE SAME AS THAT OF THE EARTH BANK.

B ALTHOUGH WATER VELOCITY IS SLOWER AT THE HEADWALL THAN THE ENDWALL, IT IS GOOD PRACTICE TO TAKE THE HEADWALL AND WINGWALLS BELOW FINISH GRADE TO AVOID WASHOUTS. REINFORCE THE WINGWALLS AND TIE THEM INTO THE HEADWALL OR ENDWALL.

FINISH GRADE
CONCRETE HEADWALL
2 NO. 6 ⌀ REIN. BARS TOP & BOTTOM

6"

12"

19°

2 NO. 6 ⌀ REIN. BARS (TOP)
TOP OF WINGWALL
FIN. GR. BEHIND
WINGWALL 1:3 SLOPE

24" I.D. REIN. CONC.

DRAIN PIPE

REIN. CONC. PIPE

2 NO. 6 ⌀ REIN. BARS EACH END OF WALL
FOR INVERT SEE GRADING PLAN
NO. 3 ⌀ REIN. BARS 12" O.C.
FINISH GRADE

12"

6"

2 NO. 6 ⌀ REIN. BARS (BOTTOM)
TIED INTO HEADWALL

14"

8"   7'-5"

B SECTION · CONCRETE HEADWALL
SCALE   3/4" = 1'-0"

LANDSCAPE CONSTRUCTION - MANUAL

C DUE TO THE ADDED VELOCITY OF THE WATER AS IT FLOWS OUT OF THE CULVERTS, AN APRON IS DESIGNED INTO THE ENDWALL DETAIL.

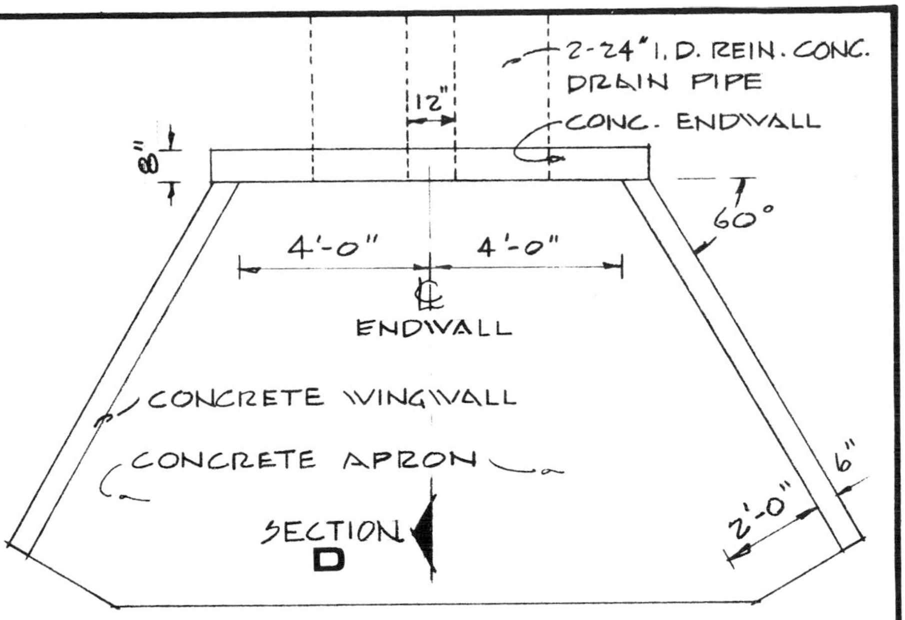

2-24" I.D. REIN. CONC. DRAIN PIPE

CONC. ENDWALL

12"

8"

4'-0"   4'-0"

60°

℄ ENDWALL

CONCRETE WINGWALL

CONCRETE APRON

SECTION D

6"

2'-0"

C PLAN · CONCRETE ENDWALL

SCALE   1/4" = 1'-0"

D THE DROP FROM THE PIPE TO THE APRON IS NOT CRITICAL, BUT A MINIMUM OF 8" WILL SERVE TO KEEP THE WATER FROM BACKING UP INTO THE CULVERT. THE WING-WALL COULD BE EXTENDED IN THIS DETAIL TO ALLOW FOR THE SLOPE OF THE FIN. GRADE. DO NOT SLOPE THE SOIL MORE THAN 1:3 IF TURF IS TO BE MOWED.

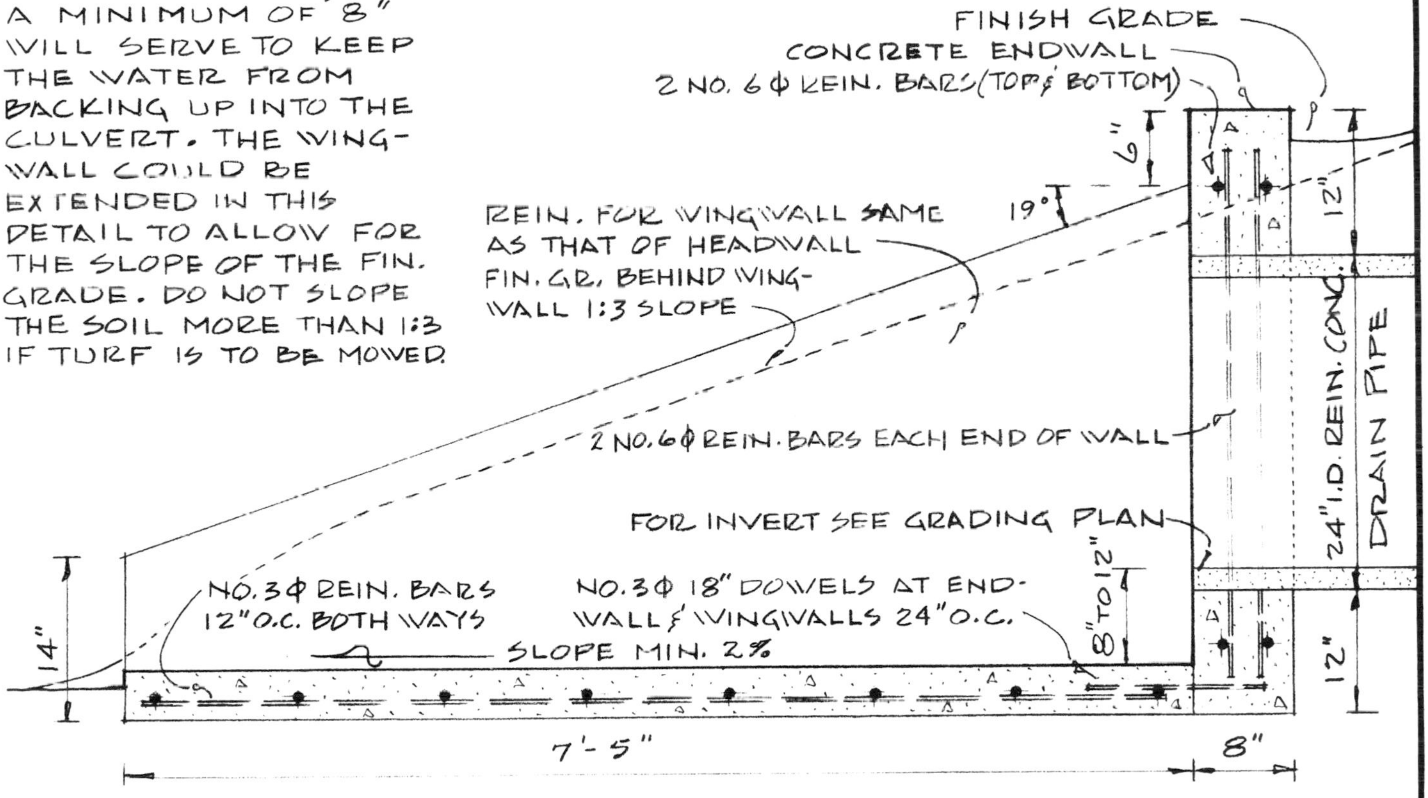

FINISH GRADE

CONCRETE ENDWALL

2 NO. 6 Ø REIN. BARS (TOP & BOTTOM)

6"

12"

REIN. FOR WINGWALL SAME AS THAT OF HEADWALL FIN. GR. BEHIND WING-WALL 1:3 SLOPE

19°

24" I.D. REIN. CONC. DRAIN PIPE

2 NO. 6 Ø REIN. BARS EACH END OF WALL

FOR INVERT SEE GRADING PLAN

NO. 3 Ø REIN. BARS 12" O.C. BOTH WAYS

NO. 3 Ø 18" DOWELS AT END-WALL & WINGWALLS 24" O.C.

SLOPE MIN. 2%

8" TO 12"

14"

12"

7'-5"   8"

D SECTION · CONCRETE ENDWALL

SCALE   3/4" = 1'-0"

CONCRETE HEADWALL/ENDWALL DETAILS

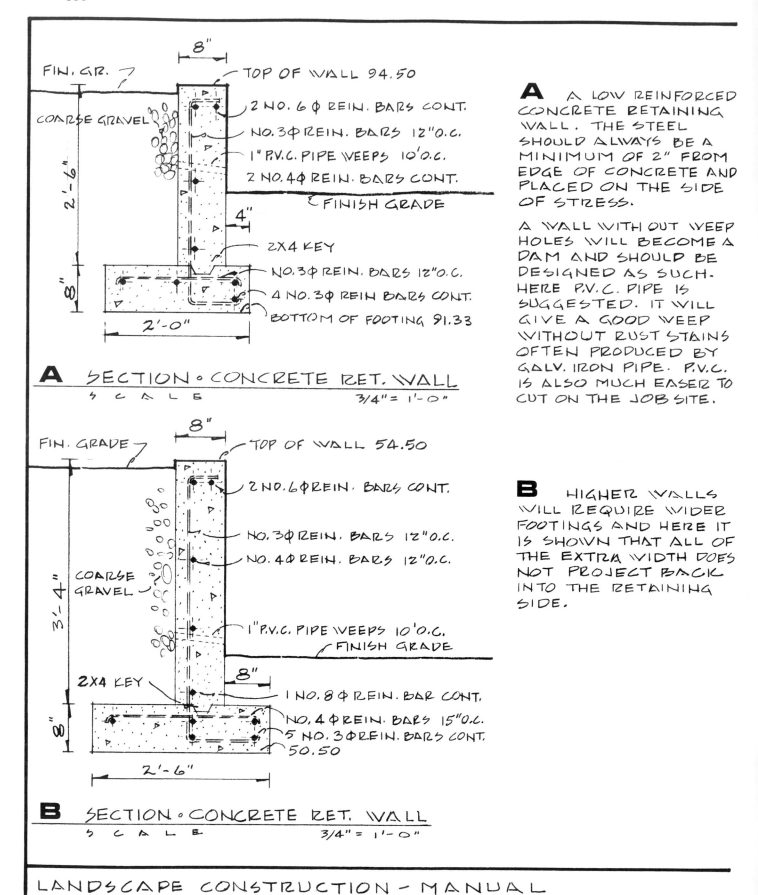

FIN. GR.

COARSE GRAVEL

2'-6"

8"

8"

TOP OF WALL 94.50

2 NO. 6 φ REIN. BARS CONT.

NO. 3 φ REIN. BARS 12" O.C.

1" P.V.C. PIPE WEEPS 10' O.C.

2 NO. 4 φ REIN. BARS CONT.

FINISH GRADE

4"

2X4 KEY

NO. 3 φ REIN. BARS 12" O.C.

4 NO. 3 φ REIN BARS CONT.

BOTTOM OF FOOTING 91.33

2'-0"

A SECTION ∘ CONCRETE RET. WALL

SCALE   3/4" = 1'-0"

A   A LOW REINFORCED CONCRETE RETAINING WALL. THE STEEL SHOULD ALWAYS BE A MINIMUM OF 2" FROM EDGE OF CONCRETE AND PLACED ON THE SIDE OF STRESS.

A WALL WITHOUT WEEP HOLES WILL BECOME A DAM AND SHOULD BE DESIGNED AS SUCH. HERE P.V.C. PIPE IS SUGGESTED. IT WILL GIVE A GOOD WEEP WITHOUT RUST STAINS OFTEN PRODUCED BY GALV. IRON PIPE. P.V.C. IS ALSO MUCH EASIER TO CUT ON THE JOB SITE.

FIN. GRADE

COARSE GRAVEL

3'-4"

8"

TOP OF WALL 54.50

2 NO. 6 φ REIN. BARS CONT.

NO. 3 φ REIN. BARS 12" O.C.

NO. 4 φ REIN. BARS 12" O.C.

1" P.V.C. PIPE WEEPS 10' O.C.

FINISH GRADE

2X4 KEY

8"

1 NO. 8 φ REIN. BAR CONT.

NO. 4 φ REIN. BARS 15" O.C.

5 NO. 3 φ REIN. BARS CONT.

50.50

2'-6"

B SECTION ∘ CONCRETE RET. WALL

SCALE   3/4" = 1'-0"

B   HIGHER WALLS WILL REQUIRE WIDER FOOTINGS AND HERE IT IS SHOWN THAT ALL OF THE EXTRA WIDTH DOES NOT PROJECT BACK INTO THE RETAINING SIDE.

LANDSCAPE CONSTRUCTION - MANUAL

C EVEN A VERY LOW WALL MUST HAVE SOME REINFORCING AND WEEP HOLES.

THIS WALL NEED NOT BE 8" WIDE, BUT IS DESIGNED SO HERE FOR CONSISTENCY.

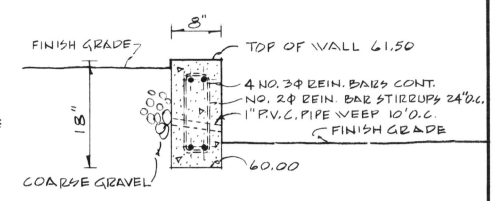

FINISH GRADE

8"

TOP OF WALL 61.50

4 NO. 3⌀ REIN. BARS CONT.

NO. 2⌀ REIN. BAR STIRRUPS 24" O.C.

1" P.V.C. PIPE WEEP 10' O.C.

FINISH GRADE

18"

COARSE GRAVEL

60.00

C SECTION · CONCRETE RET. WALL

SCALE   3/4" = 1'-0"

D THE STRUCTURES SHOWN ON THIS AND THE NEXT FEW PAGES WERE DESIGNED FOR AN AREA OF VERY ACTIVE SOIL CONDITIONS. IT IS WISE, IF INDEED NOT IMPERATIVE, THAT EACH PROJECT USING CONCRETE RETAINING WALLS BE REVIEWED BY A STRUCTURAL ENGINEER.

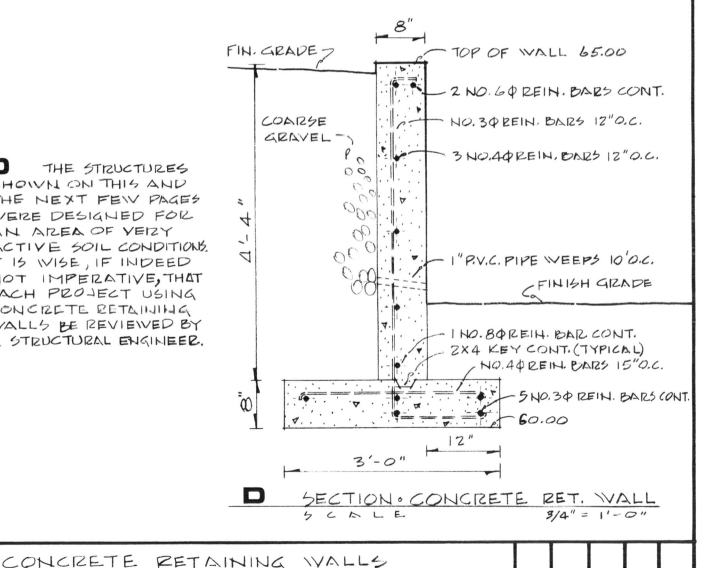

FIN. GRADE

8"

TOP OF WALL 65.00

2 NO. 6⌀ REIN. BARS CONT.

NO. 3⌀ REIN. BARS 12" O.C.

3 NO. 4⌀ REIN. BARS 12" O.C.

COARSE GRAVEL

1" P.V.C. PIPE WEEPS 10' O.C.

FINISH GRADE

4'-4"

1 NO. 8⌀ REIN. BAR CONT.

2X4 KEY CONT. (TYPICAL)

NO. 4⌀ REIN. BARS 15" O.C.

5 NO. 3⌀ REIN. BARS CONT.

60.00

8"

12"

3'-0"

D SECTION · CONCRETE RET. WALL

SCALE   3/4" = 1'-0"

CONCRETE RETAINING WALLS

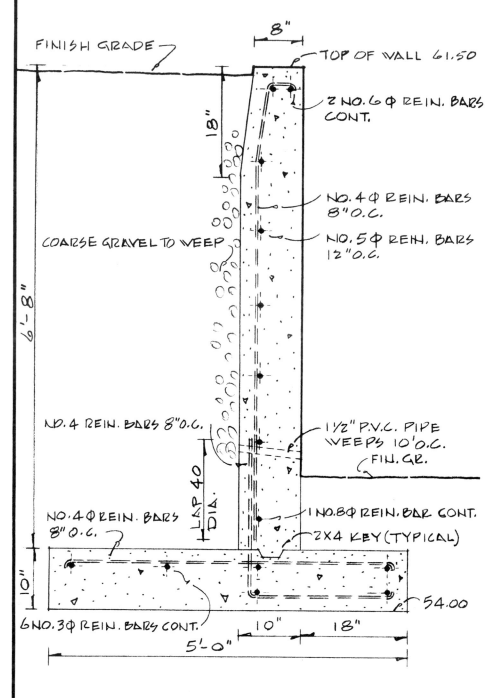

FINISH GRADE

8"

TOP OF WALL 61.50

2 NO. 6 ⌀ REIN. BARS CONT.

18"

NO. 4 ⌀ REIN. BARS 8" O.C.

NO. 5 ⌀ REIN. BARS 12" O.C.

COARSE GRAVEL TO WEEP

6'-8"

NO. 4 REIN. BARS 8" O.C.

1½" P.V.C. PIPE WEEPS 10' O.C.
FIN. GR.

LAP 40 DIA.

NO. 4 ⌀ REIN. BARS 8" O.C.

1 NO. 8 ⌀ REIN. BAR CONT.

2 X 4 KEY (TYPICAL)

10"

54.00

6 NO. 3 ⌀ REIN. BARS CONT.

10" 18"

5'-0"

E SECTION · CONCRETE RET. WALL

SCALE   3/4" = 1'-0"

E A MEDIUM HEIGHT RETAINING WALL WITH A 10" WIDTH AT THE BASE REDUCED TO 8" AT THE TOP. THIS IS ONLY TO KEEP THE WALL FROM APPEARING TOO BULKY.

DEPENDING UPON WHAT HAPPENS ON THE UPPER LEVEL, A HAND RAILING MAY BE ATTACHED TO THE TOP OF THE WALL OR BY EXTENDING THE WALL AND IT'S REINFORCING A PARAPET COULD EXIST.

BAR LAP IS SHOWN IN THIS DETAIL FOR AT THIS HEIGHT A CONTINUOUS BAR WOULD BE TOO DIFFICULT TO INSTALL.

LANDSCAPE CONSTRUCTION - MANUAL

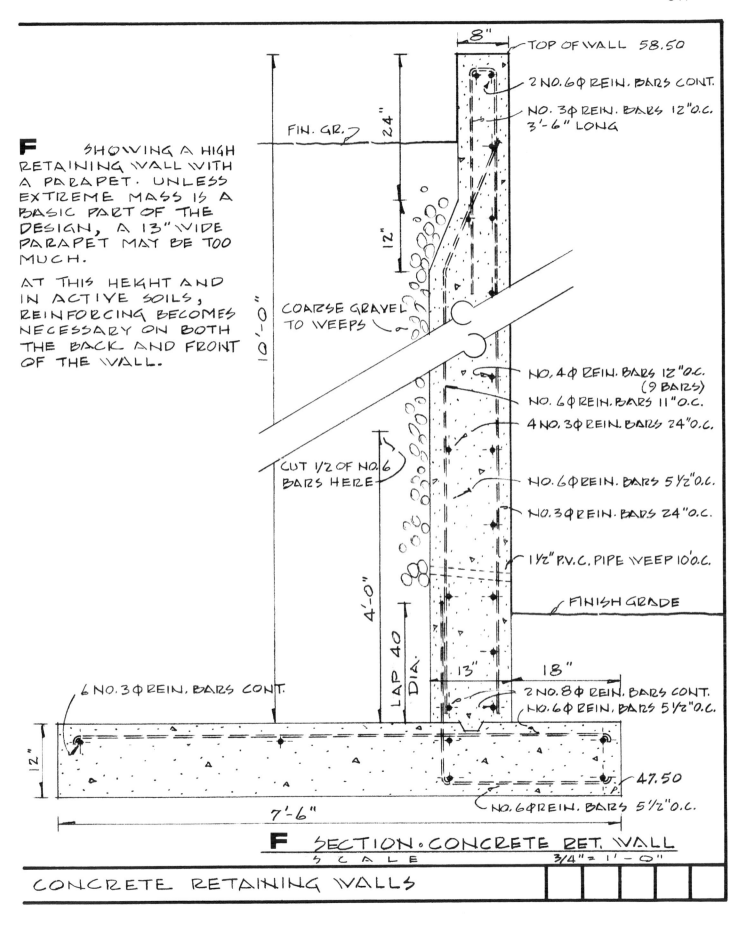

F SHOWING A HIGH RETAINING WALL WITH A PARAPET. UNLESS EXTREME MASS IS A BASIC PART OF THE DESIGN, A 13" WIDE PARAPET MAY BE TOO MUCH.

AT THIS HEIGHT AND IN ACTIVE SOILS, REINFORCING BECOMES NECESSARY ON BOTH THE BACK AND FRONT OF THE WALL.

8"
TOP OF WALL 58.50
2 NO. 6φ REIN. BARS CONT.
NO. 3φ REIN. BARS 12"O.C. 3'-6" LONG
FIN. GR.
24"
12"
COARSE GRAVEL TO WEEPS
NO. 4φ REIN. BARS 12"O.C. (9 BARS)
NO. 6φ REIN. BARS 11"O.C.
4 NO. 3φ REIN. BARS 24"O.C.
NO. 6φ REIN. BARS 5½"O.C.
NO. 3φ REIN. BARS 24"O.C.
1½" P.V.C. PIPE WEEP 10'O.C.
FINISH GRADE
CUT ½ OF NO. 6 BARS HERE
10'-0"
4'-0"
LAP 40 DIA.
13" 18"
2 NO. 8φ REIN. BARS CONT.
NO. 6φ REIN. BARS 5½"O.C.
6 NO. 3φ REIN. BARS CONT.
12"
47.50
NO. 6φ REIN. BARS 5½"O.C.
7'-6"

F SECTION • CONCRETE RET. WALL
SCALE 3/4"=1'-0"

CONCRETE RETAINING WALLS

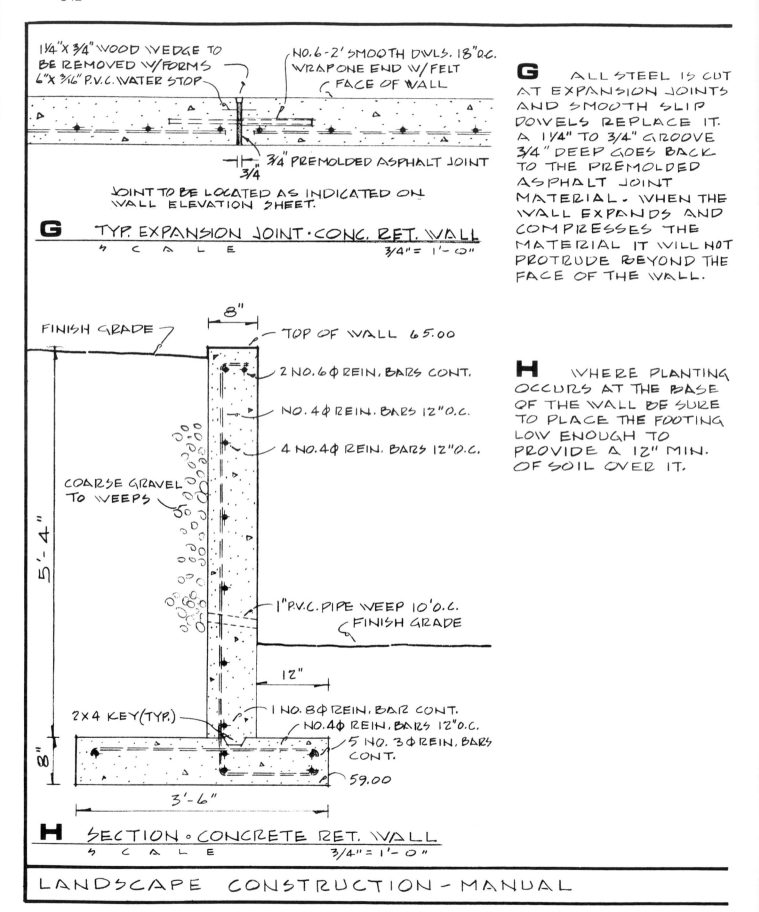

1¼"X ¾" WOOD WEDGE TO BE REMOVED W/FORMS
6"X 3/16" P.V.C. WATER STOP

NO.6-2' SMOOTH DWLS. 18"O.C. WRAP ONE END W/FELT
FACE OF WALL

¾ ¾" PREMOLDED ASPHALT JOINT

JOINT TO BE LOCATED AS INDICATED ON WALL ELEVATION SHEET.

G   TYP. EXPANSION JOINT·CONC. RET. WALL
SCALE   ¾" = 1'-0"

G   ALL STEEL IS CUT AT EXPANSION JOINTS AND SMOOTH SLIP DOWELS REPLACE IT. A 1¼" TO ¾" GROOVE ¾" DEEP GOES BACK TO THE PREMOLDED ASPHALT JOINT MATERIAL. WHEN THE WALL EXPANDS AND COMPRESSES THE MATERIAL IT WILL NOT PROTRUDE BEYOND THE FACE OF THE WALL.

FINISH GRADE

8"

TOP OF WALL 65.00

2 NO.6φ REIN. BARS CONT.

NO.4φ REIN. BARS 12"O.C.

4 NO.4φ REIN. BARS 12"O.C.

COARSE GRAVEL TO WEEPS

5'-4"

1"P.V.C. PIPE WEEP 10'0.C.
FINISH GRADE

12"

2X4 KEY (TYP.)

1 NO.8φ REIN. BAR CONT.
NO.4φ REIN. BARS 12"O.C.
5 NO.3φ REIN. BARS CONT.

59.00

8"

3'-6"

H   SECTION·CONCRETE RET. WALL
SCALE   ¾" = 1'-0"

H   WHERE PLANTING OCCURS AT THE BASE OF THE WALL BE SURE TO PLACE THE FOOTING LOW ENOUGH TO PROVIDE A 12" MIN. OF SOIL OVER IT.

LANDSCAPE CONSTRUCTION - MANUAL

J CONTROL JOINTS, UNLIKE EXPANSION JOINTS, DO NOT ALLOW FOR THE WALL TO MOVE. IT IS TO ASSURE AN EVEN CRACK IF THE WALL SHOULD DO SO.

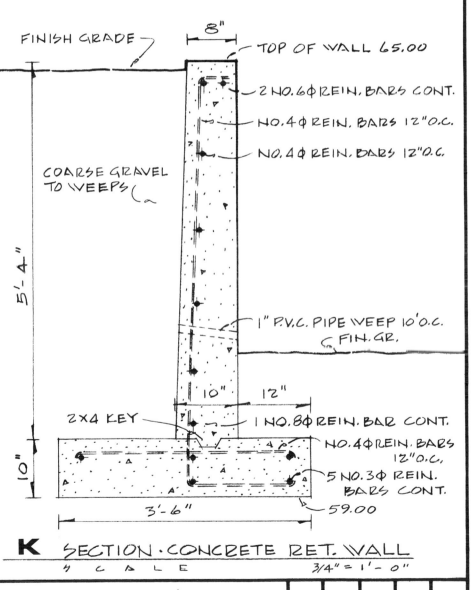

1/4" GROOVE JOINT AT ALL EXPOSED SURFACE OF WALL

FACE OF WALL

1/4"   1/8"

CUT 1/2 OF HORIZ. WALL REIN. (DO NOT CUT BOTTOM BAR)

3/4"X 3/4 WOOD AGAINST EARTH.

SEE WALL ELEVATION SHEET FOR JOINT LOCATIONS

J   TYP. CONTROL JOINT·CONC. RET. WALL
SCALE   3/4" = 1'-0"

K NOTE THAT THIS DETAIL IS VERY SIMILAR TO THAT ON THE PRECEDING PAGE. WHEN SOIL CONDITIONS DICTATE A HEAVIER WALL, YET AN 8" TOP WIDTH IS DESIRED, THE BACK SIDE CAN BE INSTALLED AT AN ANGLE.

THIS AMOUNT OF ADD- ITIONAL WEIGHT MAY ALSO REQUIRE THE 10" THICK FOOTING.

FINISH GRADE

8"

TOP OF WALL 65.00

2 NO.6∅ REIN. BARS CONT.

NO.4∅ REIN. BARS 12"O.C.

NO.4∅ REIN. BARS 12"O.C.

COARSE GRAVEL TO WEEPS

5'-4"

1" P.V.C. PIPE WEEP 10'O.C. ⊊ FIN. GR.

10"   12"

2X4 KEY

1 NO.8∅ REIN. BAR CONT.

NO.4∅REIN. BARS 12"O.C.

5 NO.3∅ REIN. BARS CONT.

10"

59.00

3'-6"

K   SECTION·CONCRETE RET. WALL
SCALE   3/4" = 1'-0"

CONCRETE RETAINING WALLS

344

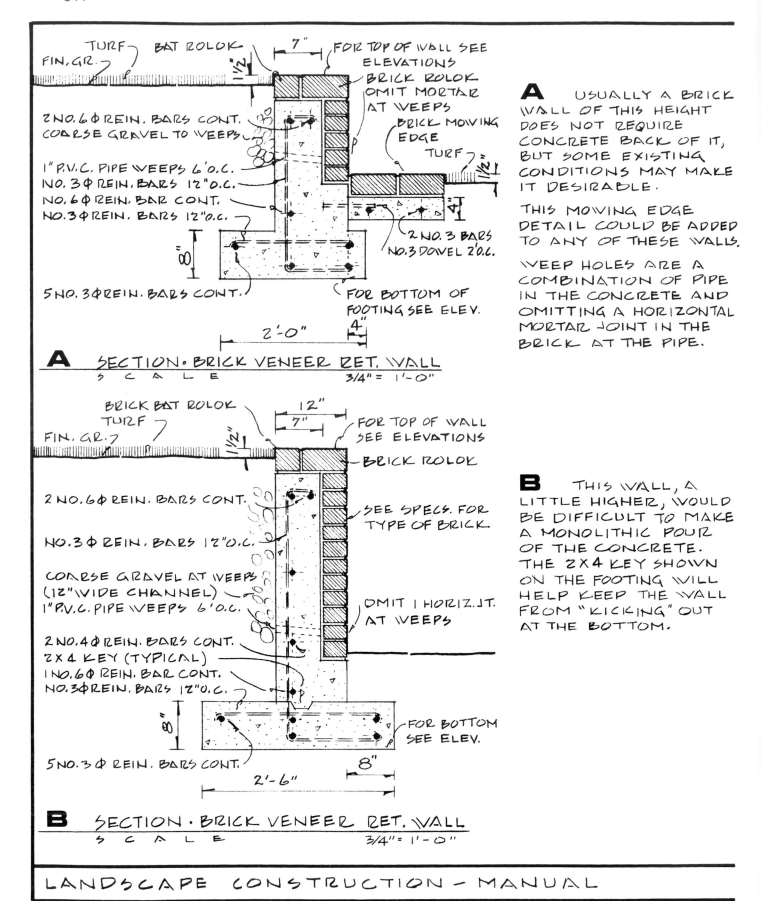

A USUALLY A BRICK WALL OF THIS HEIGHT DOES NOT REQUIRE CONCRETE BACK OF IT, BUT SOME EXISTING CONDITIONS MAY MAKE IT DESIRABLE.

THIS MOWING EDGE DETAIL COULD BE ADDED TO ANY OF THESE WALLS.

WEEP HOLES ARE A COMBINATION OF PIPE IN THE CONCRETE AND OMITTING A HORIZONTAL MORTAR JOINT IN THE BRICK AT THE PIPE.

B THIS WALL, A LITTLE HIGHER, WOULD BE DIFFICULT TO MAKE A MONOLITHIC POUR OF THE CONCRETE. THE 2X4 KEY SHOWN ON THE FOOTING WILL HELP KEEP THE WALL FROM "KICKING" OUT AT THE BOTTOM.

A SECTION • BRICK VENEER RET. WALL
SCALE 3/4" = 1'-0"

B SECTION • BRICK VENEER RET. WALL
SCALE 3/4" = 1'-0"

LANDSCAPE CONSTRUCTION - MANUAL

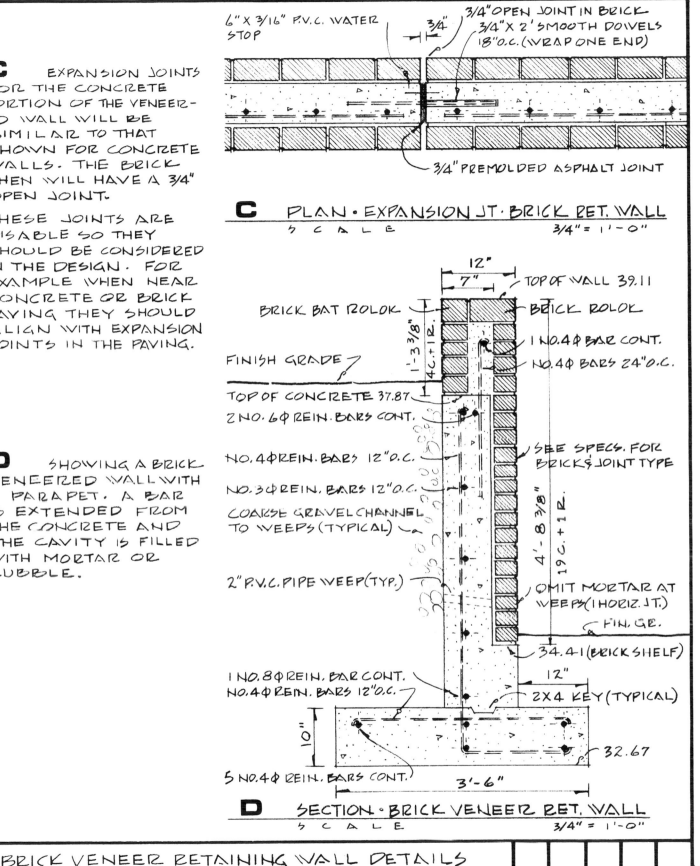

C EXPANSION JOINTS FOR THE CONCRETE PORTION OF THE VENEERED WALL WILL BE SIMILAR TO THAT SHOWN FOR CONCRETE WALLS. THE BRICK THEN WILL HAVE A 3/4" OPEN JOINT.

THESE JOINTS ARE VISABLE SO THEY SHOULD BE CONSIDERED IN THE DESIGN. FOR EXAMPLE WHEN NEAR CONCRETE OR BRICK PAVING THEY SHOULD ALIGN WITH EXPANSION JOINTS IN THE PAVING.

D SHOWING A BRICK VENEERED WALL WITH A PARAPET. A BAR IS EXTENDED FROM THE CONCRETE AND THE CAVITY IS FILLED WITH MORTAR OR RUBBLE.

6" X 3/16" P.V.C. WATER STOP

3/4"

3/4" OPEN JOINT IN BRICK
3/4" X 2' SMOOTH DOWELS
18" O.C. (WRAP ONE END)

3/4" PREMOLDED ASPHALT JOINT

C PLAN · EXPANSION JT · BRICK RET. WALL
SCALE 3/4" = 1'-0"

12"
7"
TOP OF WALL 39.11
BRICK BAT ROLOK
BRICK ROLOK
1 NO. 4∅ BAR CONT.
NO. 4∅ BARS 24" O.C.
FINISH GRADE
1'-3 3/8" 4C. + 1R.
TOP OF CONCRETE 37.87
2 NO. 6∅ REIN. BARS CONT.
NO. 4∅ REIN. BARS 12" O.C.
NO. 3∅ REIN. BARS 12" O.C.
SEE SPECS. FOR BRICK & JOINT TYPE
COARSE GRAVEL CHANNEL TO WEEPS (TYPICAL)
4'-8 3/8" 19C. + 1R.
2" P.V.C. PIPE WEEP (TYP.)
OMIT MORTAR AT WEEPS (1 HORIZ. JT.)
FIN. GR.
34.41 (BRICK SHELF)
12"
2X4 KEY (TYPICAL)
1 NO. 8∅ REIN. BAR CONT.
NO. 4∅ REIN. BARS 12" O.C.
32.67
10"
5 NO. 4∅ REIN. BARS CONT.
3'-6"

D SECTION · BRICK VENEER RET. WALL
SCALE 3/4" = 1'-0"

BRICK VENEER RETAINING WALL DETAILS

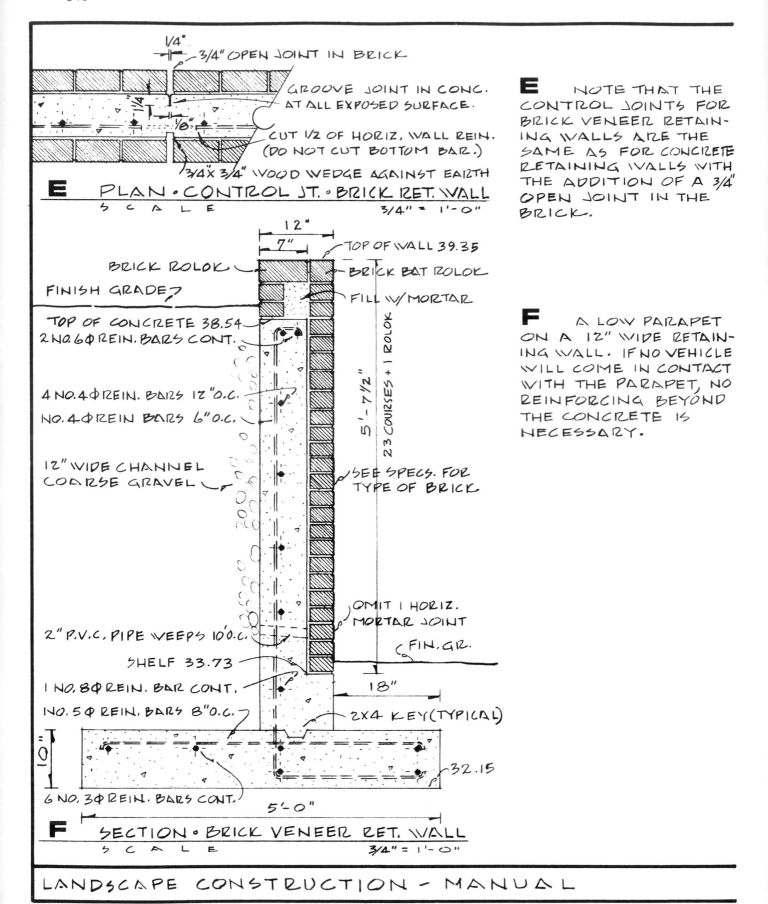

1/4"
3/4" OPEN JOINT IN BRICK

GROOVE JOINT IN CONC. AT ALL EXPOSED SURFACE.

CUT 1/2 OF HORIZ. WALL REIN. (DO NOT CUT BOTTOM BAR.)

1/4"
1/8"

3/4" X 3/4" WOOD WEDGE AGAINST EARTH

E   PLAN · CONTROL JT. · BRICK RET. WALL
SCALE   3/4" = 1'-0"

12"
7"
TOP OF WALL 39.35

BRICK ROLOK
BRICK BAT ROLOK

FINISH GRADE
FILL W/ MORTAR

TOP OF CONCRETE 38.54
2 NO. 6Φ REIN. BARS CONT.

4 NO. 4Φ REIN. BARS 12" O.C.
NO. 4Φ REIN BARS 6" O.C.

12" WIDE CHANNEL
COARSE GRAVEL

SEE SPECS. FOR TYPE OF BRICK

5'-7½"   23 COURSES + 1 ROLOK

OMIT 1 HORIZ. MORTAR JOINT
FIN. GR.

2" P.V.C. PIPE WEEPS 10' O.C.
SHELF 33.73
1 NO. 8Φ REIN. BAR CONT.
NO. 5Φ REIN. BARS 8" O.C.

18"
2X4 KEY (TYPICAL)

10"

32.15

6 NO. 3Φ REIN. BARS CONT.
5'-0"

F   SECTION · BRICK VENEER RET. WALL
SCALE   3/4" = 1'-0"

E NOTE THAT THE CONTROL JOINTS FOR BRICK VENEER RETAINING WALLS ARE THE SAME AS FOR CONCRETE RETAINING WALLS WITH THE ADDITION OF A 3/4" OPEN JOINT IN THE BRICK.

F A LOW PARAPET ON A 12" WIDE RETAINING WALL. IF NO VEHICLE WILL COME IN CONTACT WITH THE PARAPET, NO REINFORCING BEYOND THE CONCRETE IS NECESSARY.

LANDSCAPE CONSTRUCTION - MANUAL

G A HIGH RETAINING WALL BECOMES RATHER HEAVY APPEARING AT THE TOP. THIS 16" WIDE TOP CAN BE REDUCED IN SCALE BY THE ROLOK CAP.

THE STEEL IS PROJECTED UP INTO THE PARAPET WITH ONE CUT TO FORM A BRICK SHELF. THIS TOP WILL RESIST DAMAGE MUCH BETTER THAN THE ONE ON THE OPPOSITE PAGE.

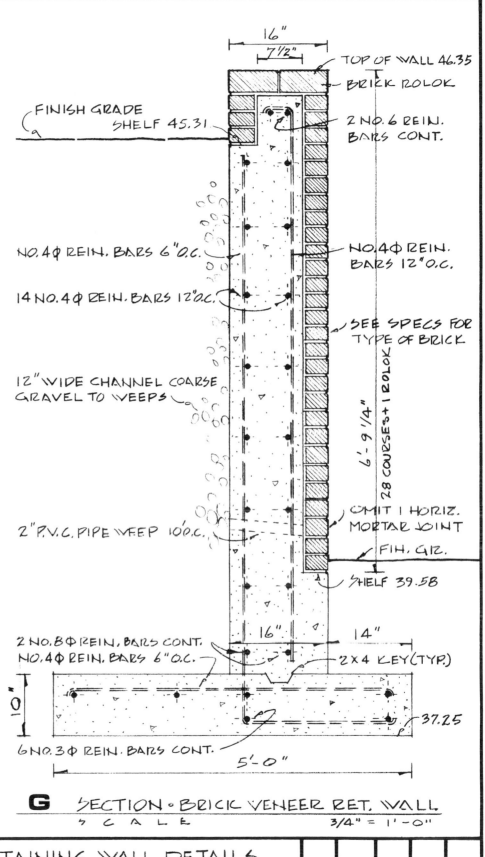

16"

7 1/2"

TOP OF WALL 46.35

BRICK ROLOK

FINISH GRADE
SHELF 45.31

2 NO. 6 REIN. BARS CONT.

NO. 4 ∅ REIN. BARS 6" O.C.

NO. 4 ∅ REIN. BARS 12" O.C.

14 NO. 4 ∅ REIN. BARS 12" O.C.

SEE SPECS FOR TYPE OF BRICK

6'- 9 1/4"

28 COURSES + 1 ROLOK

12" WIDE CHANNEL COARSE GRAVEL TO WEEPS

OMIT 1 HORIZ. MORTAR JOINT

FIN. GR.

2" P.V.C. PIPE WEEP 10' O.C.

SHELF 39.58

2 NO. 8 ∅ REIN. BARS CONT.
NO. 4 ∅ REIN. BARS 6" O.C.

16"

14"

2 X 4 KEY (TYP.)

10"

37.25

6 NO. 3 ∅ REIN. BARS CONT.

5'- 0"

G SECTION · BRICK VENEER RET. WALL

SCALE   3/4" = 1'-0"

BRICK VENEER RETAINING WALL DETAILS

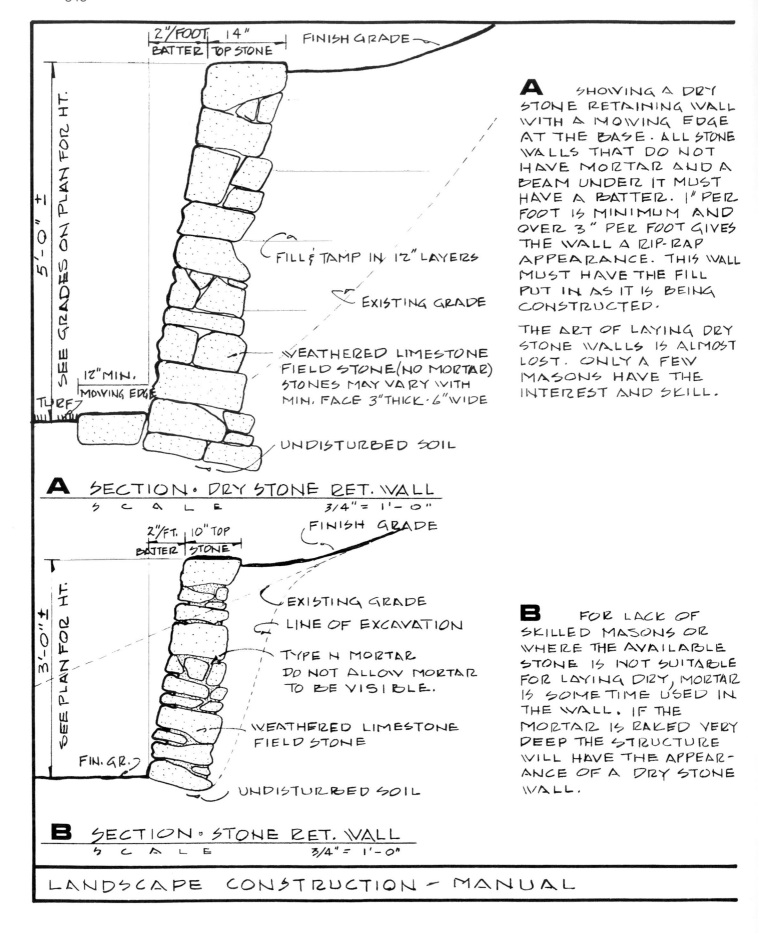

2"/FOOT | 14"
BATTER | TOP STONE

FINISH GRADE

5'-0" ± SEE GRADES ON PLAN FOR HT.

FILL & TAMP IN 12" LAYERS

EXISTING GRADE

WEATHERED LIMESTONE FIELD STONE (NO MORTAR) STONES MAY VARY WITH MIN. FACE 3" THICK · 6" WIDE

12" MIN. MOWING EDGE

TURF

UNDISTURBED SOIL

A SECTION · DRY STONE RET. WALL
SCALE   3/4" = 1'-0"

2"/FT. | 10" TOP
BATTER | STONE

FINISH GRADE

3'-0" ± SEE PLAN FOR HT.

EXISTING GRADE
LINE OF EXCAVATION

TYPE N MORTAR
DO NOT ALLOW MORTAR TO BE VISIBLE.

WEATHERED LIMESTONE FIELD STONE

FIN. GR.

UNDISTURBED SOIL

B SECTION · STONE RET. WALL
SCALE   3/4" = 1'-0"

A SHOWING A DRY STONE RETAINING WALL WITH A MOWING EDGE AT THE BASE. ALL STONE WALLS THAT DO NOT HAVE MORTAR AND A BEAM UNDER IT MUST HAVE A BATTER. 1" PER FOOT IS MINIMUM AND OVER 3" PER FOOT GIVES THE WALL A RIP-RAP APPEARANCE. THIS WALL MUST HAVE THE FILL PUT IN AS IT IS BEING CONSTRUCTED.

THE ART OF LAYING DRY STONE WALLS IS ALMOST LOST. ONLY A FEW MASONS HAVE THE INTEREST AND SKILL.

B FOR LACK OF SKILLED MASONS OR WHERE THE AVAILABLE STONE IS NOT SUITABLE FOR LAYING DRY, MORTAR IS SOMETIME USED IN THE WALL. IF THE MORTAR IS RAKED VERY DEEP THE STRUCTURE WILL HAVE THE APPEARANCE OF A DRY STONE WALL.

LANDSCAPE CONSTRUCTION - MANUAL

C A TWO BRICK WIDE RETAINING WALL WITH A BRICK MOWING EDGE AT THE BASE. A LOW WALL SUCH AS SHOWN HERE WILL RETAIN SOIL WITH ONLY REINFORCING IN THE CONCRETE BEAM.

FIN. GR.
BRICK ROLOK
COARSE GRAVEL TO WEEPS
OMIT 1 VERT. JT. FOR WEEPS 4'O.C.
BRICK ROLOK
FINISH GR. TURF
TOP OF BEAM 99.50
CONC. BEAM
2 NO.4 ⌀ REIN. BARS
2 NO.3 ⌀ REIN. BARS CONC. BEAM
8"   16"
6 C. 1 R.   20 3/4"

C   SECTION · BRICK RET. WALL
SCALE   3/4" = 1'-0"

D FOR A STRONGER VISUAL APPEARANCE, THE LOW BRICK WALL MAY NEED TO BE WIDER. HERE IS SHOWN A 12" WIDE WALL WITH A ONE AND ONE HALF BRICK ROLOK ON TOP.

FIN. GR.
BRICK BAT ROLOK
BRICK ROLOK
COARSE GRAVEL TO WEEPS
USE COMMON BRICK INSIDE
OMIT 1 VERT. JT. FOR WEEPS 4'0.C.
TOP OF BEAM 99.50
FINISH GRADE
2 NO.4 ⌀ REIN. BARS CONT. CONCRETE BEAM
6 C. 1 R.   20 3/4"
8"
12"

D   SECTION · BRICK RET. WALL
SCALE   3/4" = 1'-0"

E THE SAME DETAIL AS ABOVE WITH RUBBLE FILL RATHER THAN LAID BRICK.

ALL SOLID RETAINING WALLS MUST HAVE WEEP HOLES.

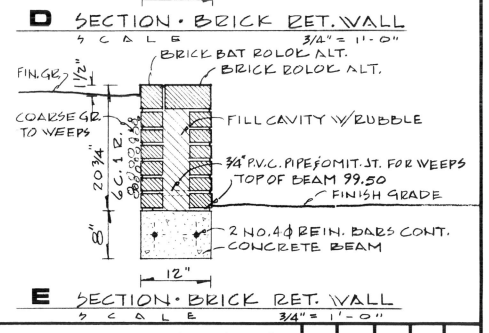

FIN. GR.
BRICK BAT ROLOK ALT.
BRICK ROLOK ALT.
COARSE GR. TO WEEPS
FILL CAVITY W/ RUBBLE
3/4" P.V.C. PIPE & OMIT JT. FOR WEEPS
TOP OF BEAM 99.50
FINISH GRADE
2 NO.4 ⌀ REIN. BARS CONT. CONCRETE BEAM
6 C. 1 R.   20 3/4"
8"
12"

E   SECTION · BRICK RET. WALL
SCALE   3/4" = 1'-0"

NON-REINFORCED MASONRY RET. WALLS

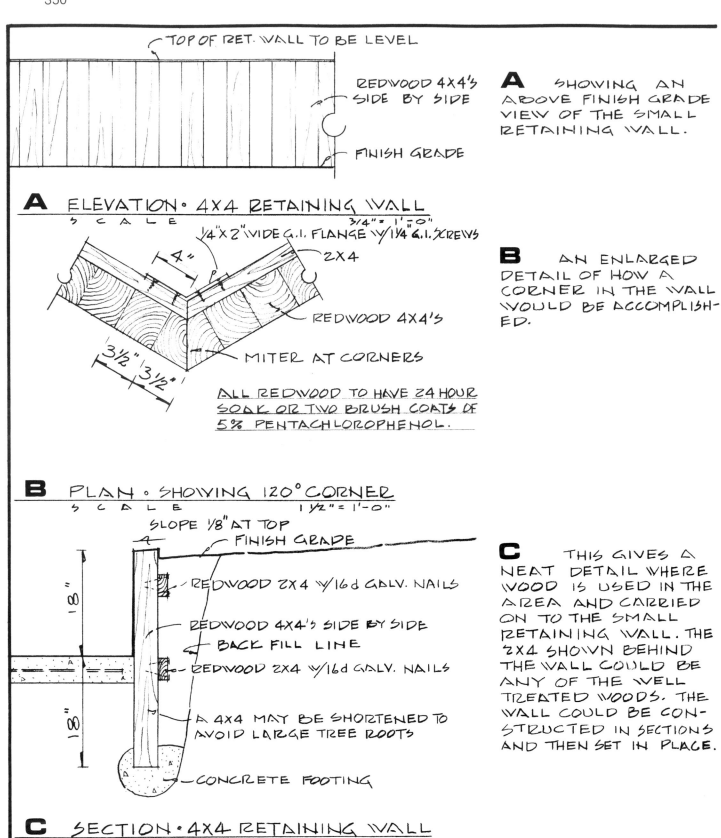

TOP OF RET. WALL TO BE LEVEL

REDWOOD 4X4'S SIDE BY SIDE

FINISH GRADE

A ELEVATION · 4X4 RETAINING WALL
SCALE 3/4" = 1'-0"

A SHOWING AN ABOVE FINISH GRADE VIEW OF THE SMALL RETAINING WALL.

1/4" X 2" WIDE G.I. FLANGE W/ 1 1/4" G.I. SCREWS

2X4

4"

REDWOOD 4X4'S

MITER AT CORNERS

3 1/2" 3 1/2"

ALL REDWOOD TO HAVE 24 HOUR SOAK OR TWO BRUSH COATS OF 5% PENTACHLOROPHENOL.

B AN ENLARGED DETAIL OF HOW A CORNER IN THE WALL WOULD BE ACCOMPLISHED.

B PLAN · SHOWING 120° CORNER
SCALE 1 1/2" = 1'-0"

SLOPE 1/8" AT TOP
FINISH GRADE

18"

REDWOOD 2X4 W/ 16d GALV. NAILS

REDWOOD 4X4'S SIDE BY SIDE
BACK FILL LINE
REDWOOD 2X4 W/ 16d GALV. NAILS

18"

A 4X4 MAY BE SHORTENED TO AVOID LARGE TREE ROOTS

CONCRETE FOOTING

C SECTION · 4X4 RETAINING WALL
SCALE 3/4" = 1'-0"

C THIS GIVES A NEAT DETAIL WHERE WOOD IS USED IN THE AREA AND CARRIED ON TO THE SMALL RETAINING WALL. THE 2X4 SHOWN BEHIND THE WALL COULD BE ANY OF THE WELL TREATED WOODS. THE WALL COULD BE CONSTRUCTED IN SECTIONS AND THEN SET IN PLACE.

LANDSCAPE CONSTRUCTION - MANUAL

D A PLAN SHOWING PLACEMENT OF POSTS IN LINE AND AT CORNERS. THE PLAN IS FOR THE SECTION BELOW ONLY.

E SHOWING A SECTION THRU THE PLAN ABOVE. THIS IS A GOOD RUSTIC APPEARING WOOD RETAINING WALL DETAIL.

F A VARIATION OF THE RUSTIC WOOD RETAINING WALL IS TO PLACE ALL OF THE TIES ON END, SIDE BY SIDE AND SECURE FROM THE BACK.

WHERE TURF OCCURS AT THE BASE OF THE WALL, IT IS DESIRABLE TO DESIGN A MOWING EDGE.

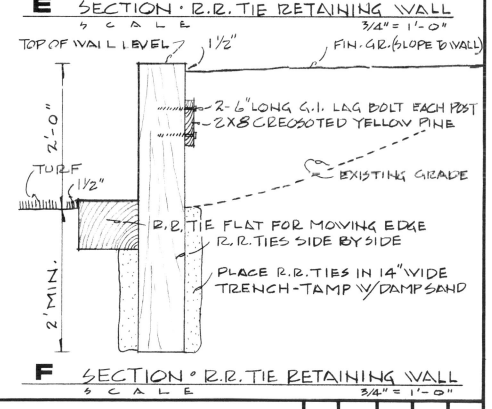

D PLAN · R.R. TIE RETAINING WALL ¼"=1'-0"

- R.R. TIE CORNER
- RAIL ROAD TIE
- R.R. TIE CORNER POST
- R.R. TIE POST AT EACH JOINT (8'-0.C.)

TOP OF WALL LEVEL 1" FIN. GR.
SLOPE TO WALL
FILL
R.R. TIES FLAT
R.R. TIE POST 8'-0" O.C.
FIN. GR.
EXISTING GRADE
14" DIA. HOLE W/ POST SET IN WELL TAMPED DAMP SAND
2' MIN.

E SECTION · R.R. TIE RETAINING WALL
SCALE 3/4" = 1'-0"

TOP OF WALL LEVEL 1½" FIN. GR. (SLOPE TO WALL)
2'-0"
TURF
1½"
2 - 6" LONG G.I. LAG BOLT EACH POST
2 X 8 CREOSOTED YELLOW PINE
EXISTING GRADE
R.R. TIE FLAT FOR MOWING EDGE
R.R. TIES SIDE BY SIDE
PLACE R.R. TIES IN 14" WIDE TRENCH - TAMP W/ DAMP SAND
2' MIN.

F SECTION · R.R. TIE RETAINING WALL
SCALE 3/4" = 1'-0"

WOOD RETAINING WALL DETAILS

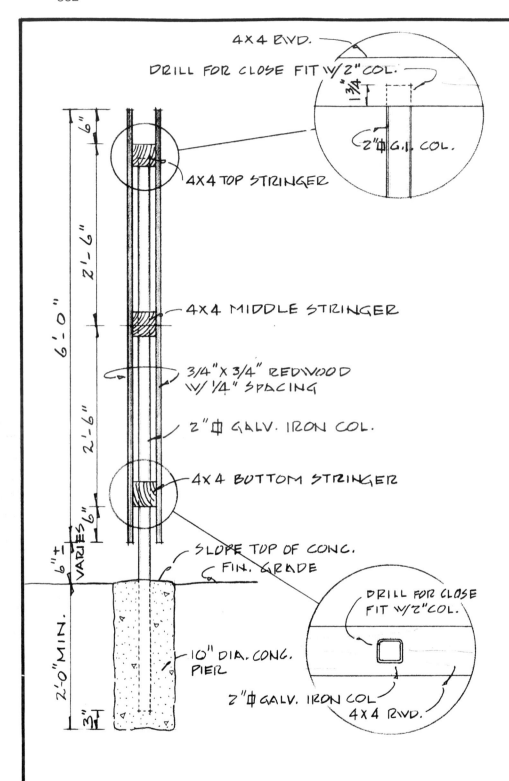

4X4 RVD.

DRILL FOR CLOSE FIT W/2"COL.

1¾"

2"Ø G.I. COL.

4X4 TOP STRINGER

4X4 MIDDLE STRINGER

3/4"X 3/4" REDWOOD W/ 1/4" SPACING

2"Ø GALV. IRON COL.

4X4 BOTTOM STRINGER

SLOPE TOP OF CONC.

FIN. GRADE

10" DIA. CONC. PIER

DRILL FOR CLOSE FIT W/2"COL.

2"Ø GALV. IRON COL.

4X4 RVD.

6" 2'-6" 2'-6" 6" 6'-0"

VARIES 6"±

2'-0"MIN. 3"

A SECTION • WOOD SCREEN
SCALE 3/4"= 1'-0"

A THIS DETAIL USES A GALVANIZED IRON TUBE COLUMN FOR DURABILITY, YET DOES NOT REQUIRE DRILLING THE COLUMN FOR BOLTING. THE TOP STRINGER IS CUT ONLY 1½" AND RESTS ON TOP OF THE COLUMN. THE OTHER STRINGERS ARE DRILLED AND SLIPPED OVER THE COLUMN, TEMPORARILY HELD IN PLACE UNTIL 1X1 STRIPS ARE NAILED. COLUMN AND STRINGER DETAIL WOULD BE THE SAME IF ONLY ONE SIDE OF THE SCREEN IS FINISHED.

THIS SCREEN DETAIL IS TIME CONSUMING TO CONSTRUCT, THUS EXPENSIVE. IT WILL NOT TAKE A LOT OF ABUSE, BUT WILL GIVE A FINE TEXTURED, HANDSOME SCREEN.

LANDSCAPE CONSTRUCTION - MANUAL

B THE 4X4 ARE ALL 10' IN LENGTH. THE JOINTS ALIGN AND IS BEST IF AN OPEN JOINT OF 3/4" TO 1" IS ALLOWED WITH NO ATTEMPT TO CONNECT THEM. THE SCREEN COULD BE CONSTRUCTED IN THESE PANELS AND THEN SET IN PLACE. NO FINISH IS SUGGESTED HERE BUT THE REDWOOD COULD BE ALLOWED TO WEATHER A SILVER GRAY OR STAINED WITH A PENETRATING STAIN.

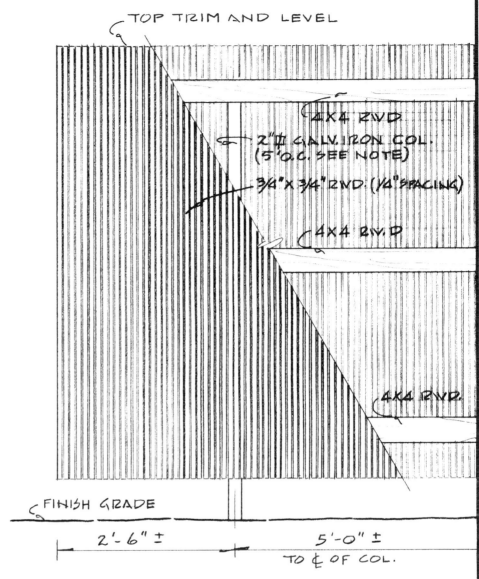

TOP TRIM AND LEVEL

4X4 RWD

2"⌀ GALV. IRON COL. (5'O.C. SEE NOTE)

3/4"X 3/4" RWD. (1/4" SPACING)

4X4 RWD

4X4 RWD.

FINISH GRADE

2'-6" ±   5'-0" ±
              TO ₵ OF COL.

NOTE: COL. SPACING AND LENGTH DIM. CAN VARY SLIGHTLY TO ACCOMMODATE SCREEN SECTIONS SLIGHTLY MORE OR LESS THAN 10'-0".

USE ONLY HOT DIP GALV. NAILS.

B ELEVATION · WOOD SCREEN
S C A L E   3/4" = 1'-0"

VISUAL SCREEN DETAILS

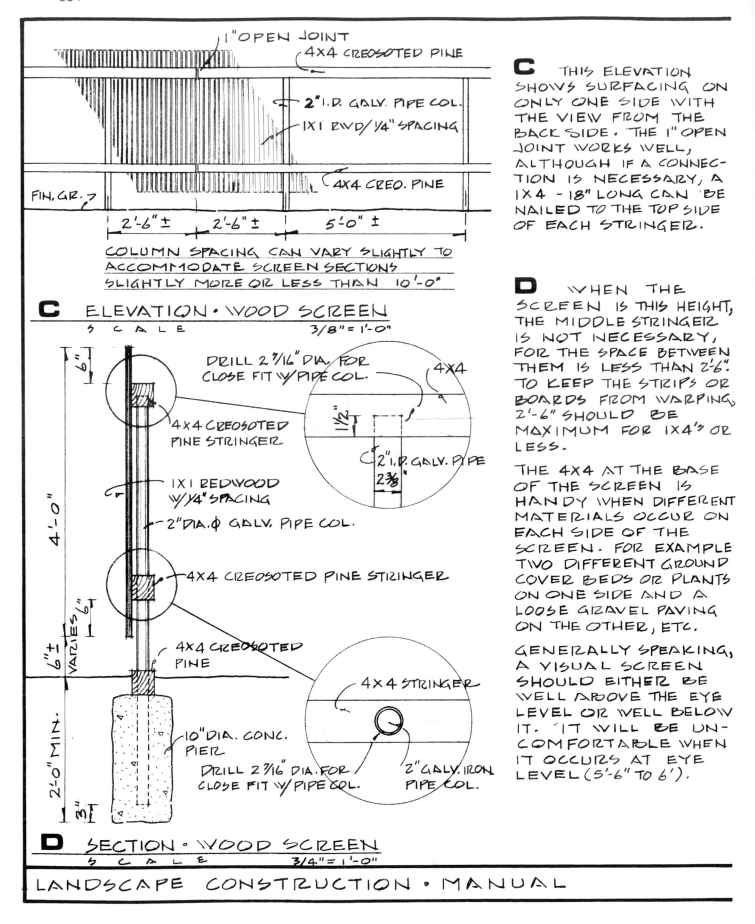

I" OPEN JOINT
4X4 CREOSOTED PINE
2" I.D. GALV. PIPE COL.
IXI RWD/ ¼" SPACING
4X4 CREO. PINE
FIN. GR.

2'-6" ±   2'-6" ±   5'-0" ±

COLUMN SPACING CAN VARY SLIGHTLY TO
ACCOMMODATE SCREEN SECTIONS
SLIGHTLY MORE OR LESS THAN 10'-0"

C ELEVATION · WOOD SCREEN
SCALE   3/8" = 1'-0"

6"
4'-0"
6"
VARIES 6"
6" ±
2'-0" MIN.
3"

DRILL 2 7/16" DIA. FOR
CLOSE FIT W/ PIPE COL.
4X4

1½"
2 3/8"
2" I.D. GALV. PIPE

4X4 CREOSOTED
PINE STRINGER

IXI REDWOOD
W/ ¼" SPACING

2" DIA. Φ GALV. PIPE COL.

4X4 CREOSOTED PINE STRINGER

4X4 CREOSOTED
PINE

10" DIA. CONC.
PIER

DRILL 2 7/16" DIA. FOR
CLOSE FIT W/ PIPE COL.

4X4 STRINGER

2" GALV. IRON
PIPE COL.

D SECTION · WOOD SCREEN
SCALE   3/4" = 1'-0"

LANDSCAPE CONSTRUCTION · MANUAL

C THIS ELEVATION SHOWS SURFACING ON ONLY ONE SIDE WITH THE VIEW FROM THE BACK SIDE. THE I" OPEN JOINT WORKS WELL, ALTHOUGH IF A CONNECTION IS NECESSARY, A IX4 - 18" LONG CAN BE NAILED TO THE TOP SIDE OF EACH STRINGER.

D WHEN THE SCREEN IS THIS HEIGHT, THE MIDDLE STRINGER IS NOT NECESSARY, FOR THE SPACE BETWEEN THEM IS LESS THAN 2'-6". TO KEEP THE STRIPS OR BOARDS FROM WARPING, 2'-6" SHOULD BE MAXIMUM FOR IX4'S OR LESS.

THE 4X4 AT THE BASE OF THE SCREEN IS HANDY WHEN DIFFERENT MATERIALS OCCUR ON EACH SIDE OF THE SCREEN. FOR EXAMPLE TWO DIFFERENT GROUND COVER BEDS OR PLANTS ON ONE SIDE AND A LOOSE GRAVEL PAVING ON THE OTHER, ETC.

GENERALLY SPEAKING, A VISUAL SCREEN SHOULD EITHER BE WELL ABOVE THE EYE LEVEL OR WELL BELOW IT. IT WILL BE UN-COMFORTABLE WHEN IT OCCURS AT EYE LEVEL (5'-6" TO 6').

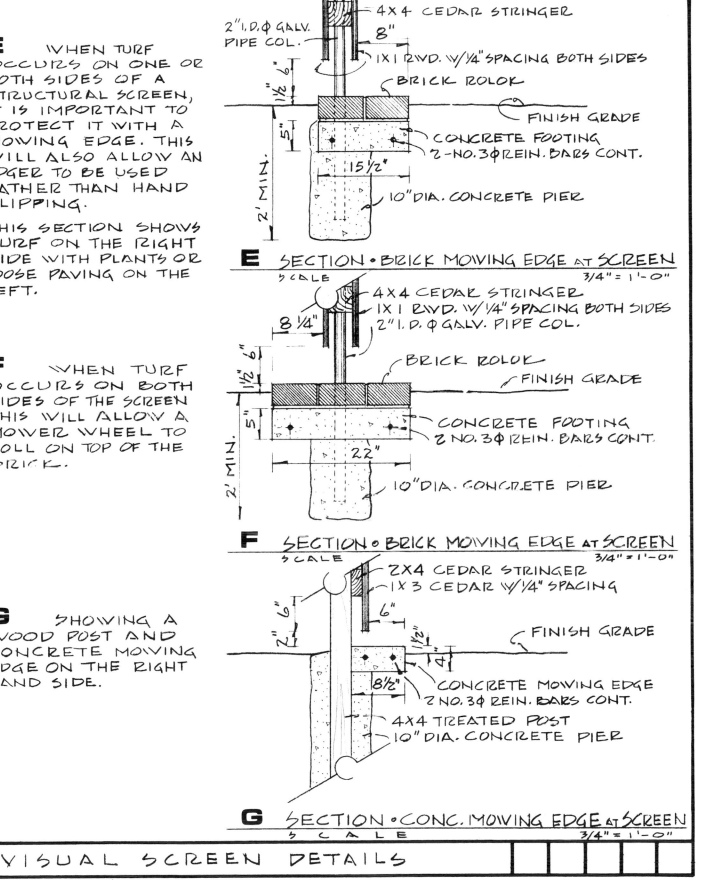

E WHEN TURF OCCURS ON ONE OR BOTH SIDES OF A STRUCTURAL SCREEN, IT IS IMPORTANT TO PROTECT IT WITH A MOWING EDGE. THIS WILL ALSO ALLOW AN EDGER TO BE USED RATHER THAN HAND CLIPPING.

THIS SECTION SHOWS TURF ON THE RIGHT SIDE WITH PLANTS OR LOOSE PAVING ON THE LEFT.

4×4 CEDAR STRINGER
2" I.D. φ GALV. PIPE COL.
8"
1×1 R.WD. W/¼" SPACING BOTH SIDES
BRICK ROLOK
FINISH GRADE
CONCRETE FOOTING
2-NO.3φ REIN. BARS CONT.
10" DIA. CONCRETE PIER
1½"   6"   5"   2' MIN.   15½"

E SECTION • BRICK MOWING EDGE AT SCREEN
SCALE   3/4" = 1'-0"

F WHEN TURF OCCURS ON BOTH SIDES OF THE SCREEN THIS WILL ALLOW A MOWER WHEEL TO ROLL ON TOP OF THE BRICK.

4×4 CEDAR STRINGER
1×1 R.WD. W/¼" SPACING BOTH SIDES
2" I.D. φ GALV. PIPE COL.
8¼"
BRICK ROLOK
FINISH GRADE
CONCRETE FOOTING
2 NO.3φ REIN. BARS CONT.
10" DIA. CONCRETE PIER
1½"   6"   5"   2' MIN.   22"

F SECTION • BRICK MOWING EDGE AT SCREEN
SCALE   3/4" = 1'-0"

G SHOWING A WOOD POST AND CONCRETE MOWING EDGE ON THE RIGHT HAND SIDE.

2×4 CEDAR STRINGER
1×3 CEDAR W/¼" SPACING
6"
FINISH GRADE
CONCRETE MOWING EDGE
2 NO.3φ REIN. BARS CONT.
4×4 TREATED POST
10" DIA. CONCRETE PIER
2"   6"   1½"   4"   8½"

G SECTION • CONC. MOWING EDGE AT SCREEN
SCALE   3/4" = 1'-0"

VISUAL SCREEN DETAILS

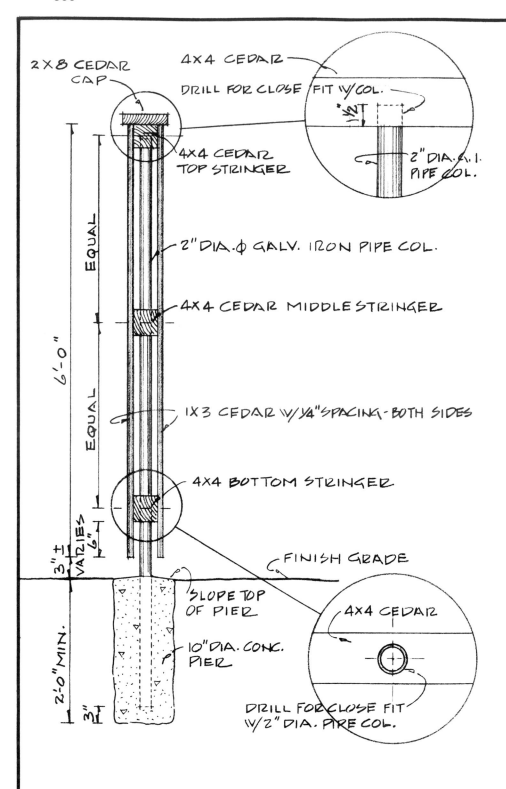

2 X 8 CEDAR CAP

4X4 CEDAR

DRILL FOR CLOSE FIT W/COL.

4X4 CEDAR TOP STRINGER

2" DIA. G.I. PIPE COL.

EQUAL

2" DIA. ∅ GALV. IRON PIPE COL.

4X4 CEDAR MIDDLE STRINGER

EQUAL

6'-0"

1X3 CEDAR W/¼" SPACING - BOTH SIDES

4X4 BOTTOM STRINGER

6"

3"±

VARIES

FINISH GRADE

SLOPE TOP OF PIER

10" DIA. CONC. PIER

4X4 CEDAR

2'-0" MIN.

3"±

DRILL FOR CLOSE FIT W/2" DIA. PIPE COL.

H WHEN A SCREEN IS TO BE VIEWED FROM BOTH SIDES, IT IS BEST TO DESIGN A DETAIL THAT CAN BE SURFACED ON BOTH SIDES WITHOUT CREATING AN EXTRA WIDE STRUCTURE. THIS DETAIL DOES THAT AND IS PLEASANT LOOKING FROM THE BACK EVEN WHEN SURFACED ON ONLY THE FRONT SIDE. A GALVANIZED IRON PIPE COLUMN IS USED FOR DURABILITY. THE PIPE DOES NOT REQUIRE DRILLING OR BOLTING. THE TOP STRINGER IS CUT ONLY 1½" AND RESTS ON TOP OF THE COLUMN. THE OTHER STRINGERS ARE DRILLED AND SLIPPED OVER THE COLUMN, TEMPORARILY HELD IN PLACE UNTIL 1X3'S ARE NAILED.

H SECTION · WOOD SCREEN

SCALE   3/4" = 1'-0"

LANDSCAPE CONSTRUCTION - MANUAL

J THE 1×3'S GIVE A FINE TO MEDIUM TEXTURE IN THE DESIGN. S4S LUMBER WILL GIVE A FINER TEXTURE THAN ROUGH CUT. THE CAP AND END PIECE GIVE A FINISHED APPEARANCE TO THE DESIGN.

NO FINISH IS SUGGESTED HERE BUT THE CEDAR COULD BE ALLOWED TO WEATHER A SILVER GRAY OR STAINED WITH A PENETRATING STAIN.

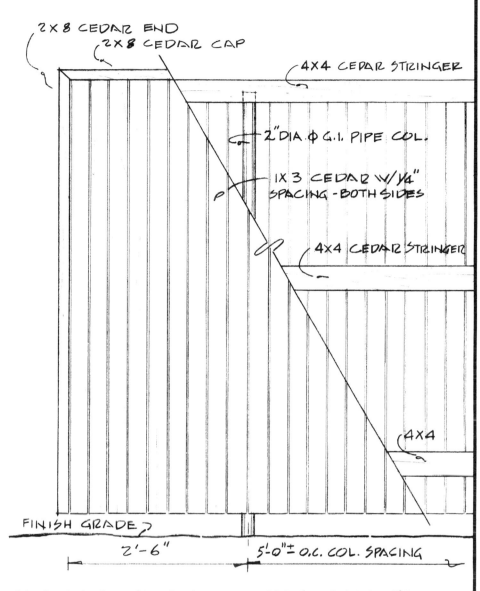

2×8 CEDAR END
2×8 CEDAR CAP
4×4 CEDAR STRINGER
2" DIA. ∅ G.I. PIPE COL.
1×3 CEDAR W/ ¼" SPACING - BOTH SIDES
4×4 CEDAR STRINGER
4×4
FINISH GRADE
2'-6"
5'-0"± O.C. COL. SPACING

COLUMN SPACING CAN VARY SLIGHTLY TO ACCOMMODATE SCREEN SECTIONS SLIGHTLY MORE OR LESS THAN 10'-0".

ALL CEDAR TO BE ROUGH FINISH AND FREE OF UNSOUND KNOTS.
USE ONLY HOT DIP GALV. NAILS.
POST TO BE GALV. IRON PIPE (NOT TUBING)

J ELEVATION · WOOD SCREEN
SCALE   3/4" = 1'-0"

VISUAL SCREEN DETAILS

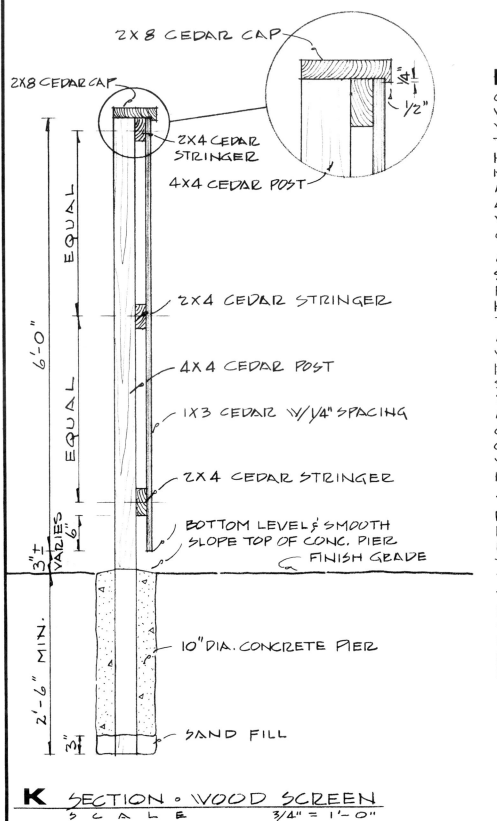

2 X 8 CEDAR CAP

2X8 CEDAR CAP

1/4"
1/2"

2X4 CEDAR STRINGER

4X4 CEDAR POST

EQUAL

6'-0"

EQUAL

EQUAL

2X4 CEDAR STRINGER

4X4 CEDAR POST

1X3 CEDAR W/ 1/4" SPACING

2X4 CEDAR STRINGER

6"

VARIES

BOTTOM LEVEL & SMOOTH SLOPE TOP OF CONC. PIER

FINISH GRADE

3"±

2'-6" MIN.

10" DIA. CONCRETE PIER

3"

SAND FILL

K SECTION • WOOD SCREEN

SCALE   3/4" = 1'-0"

K   THIS DETAIL COULD BE USED WITH VARIOUS DIMENSION WOOD ON THE SURFACE. THE 2X8 CAP IS ROUTED HERE SO THAT THE 1X3's NEED NOT BE AS ACCURATE AT THE TOP AS IT WOULD IF THERE WAS NO CAP OR THE CAP WAS NOT ROUTED.

ALWAYS NAIL THE 2X4 STRINGER ONTO THE FACE OF THE POST. NEVER TOE NAIL IT INTO THE SIDE, AS THIS MAKES A WEAK JOINT, EVEN WHEN A BLOCK IS NAILED UNDER THE STRINGER. KEEP THE 2X4 STRINGER ON EDGE AND NOT FLAT AS IT COULD OCCUR ON TOP OF THE POST, FOR IT WILL RESIST SAGGING MUCH MORE.

WHEN A CONCRETE PIER IS USED, BRING IT ABOVE GROUND LEVEL AND PROJECT THE POST BELOW IT. THIS WILL HELP KEEP WATER OUT OF THE PIER AS THE WOOD SHRINKS, AND WILL LET WATER THAT ENTERS OUT THE BOTTOM.

LANDSCAPE CONSTRUCTION - MANUAL

This detail works well where only one side of the screen is of primary concern. If 2x4 stringers and 1x3 boards were added to the back side, the screen would be eleven inches wide. This gives a pretty heavy looking structure.

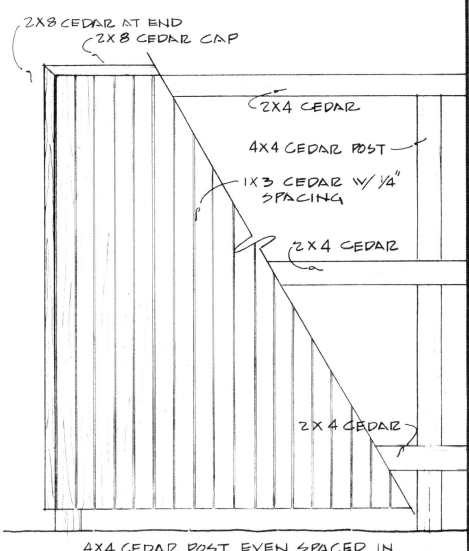

2x8 CEDAR AT END
2x8 CEDAR CAP
2x4 CEDAR
4x4 CEDAR POST
1x3 CEDAR W/ 1/4" SPACING
2x4 CEDAR
2x4 CEDAR

4x4 CEDAR POST EVEN SPACED IN EACH SECTION · MAX. OF 5'-0" O.C.

ALL CEDAR TO BE ROUGH FINISH, FREE OF UNSOUND KNOTS.

ALL POSTS TO HAVE 24 HR. SOAK OF 5% PENTACHLOROPHENOL. MIN. OF 36" FROM BOTTOM END.

USE ONLY HOT DIP GALV. NAILS.

L ELEVATION · WOOD SCREEN
SCALE   3/4" = 1'-0"

VISUAL SCREEN DETAILS

360

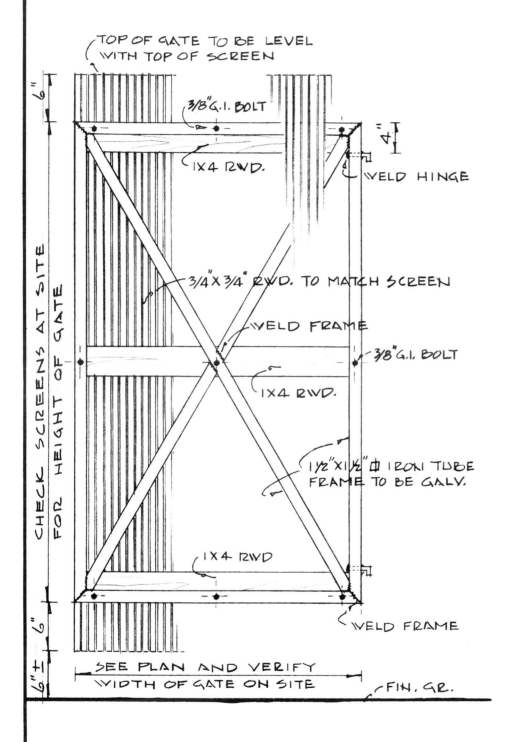

TOP OF GATE TO BE LEVEL
WITH TOP OF SCREEN

3/8"G.I. BOLT

1X4 RWD.

WELD HINGE

6"

4"

CHECK SCREENS AT SITE
FOR HEIGHT OF GATE

3/4"X 3/4" RWD. TO MATCH SCREEN

WELD FRAME

3/8"G.I. BOLT

1X4 RWD.

1 1/2"X1 1/2" ⌷ IRON TUBE
FRAME TO BE GALV.

1X4 RWD

WELD FRAME

6"   4"   6"

SEE PLAN AND VERIFY
WIDTH OF GATE ON SITE

FIN. GR.

A THIS IS A VERSATILE GATE DETAIL IN THAT IT COULD BE USED FOR ALL WOOD SCREENS. THE SURFACING (ONE OR BOTH SIDES) COULD BE CHANGED TO MATCH THE SURFACE ON THE SCREEN. MOST WOOD FRAME GATES SAG AFTER A SHORT TIME; THIS DETAIL WILL NOT. THERE ARE MANY STANDARD LATCHES (BOTH PLAIN AND THOSE THAT WILL LOCK) MANUFACTURED THAT WILL WORK WELL WITH THIS DETAIL.

A ELEVATION ○ METAL FRAME WOOD GATE

SCALE   1"= 1'-0"

LANDSCAPE CONSTRUCTION - MANUAL

B THE EXPANDED SECTION AT THE TOP SHOWS HOW SURFACING BOTH SIDES IS ACCOMPLISHED AND THE ONE AT THE BOTTOM SHOWS ONE SIDE ONLY. IT IS IMPORTANT THAT GATE FRAMES BE DELIVERED TO THE SITE BEFORE THE SCREEN IS CONSTRUCTED OR THAT AN ACCURATE MEASUREMENT BE MADE ON THE SITE IF THE SCREENS ARE CONSTRUCTED FIRST.

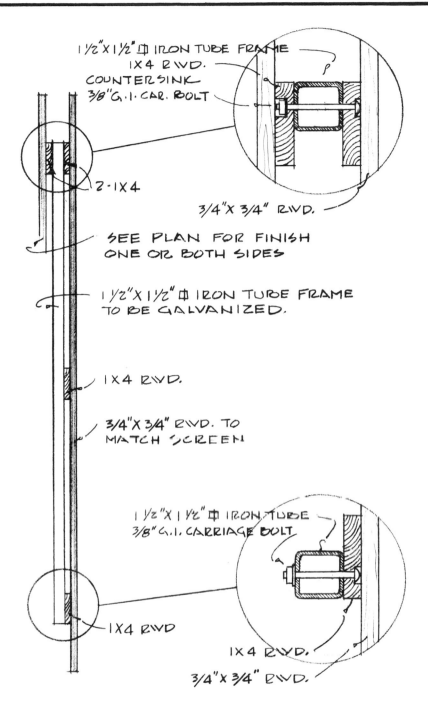

1½" X 1½" ⊡ IRON TUBE FRAME
1X4 RWD.
COUNTERSINK
3/8" G.I. CAR. BOLT

2-1X4

3/4" X 3/4" RWD.

SEE PLAN FOR FINISH ONE OR BOTH SIDES

1½" X 1½" ⊡ IRON TUBE FRAME TO BE GALVANIZED.

1X4 RWD.

3/4" X 3/4" RWD. TO MATCH SCREEN

1½" X 1½" ⊡ IRON TUBE
3/8" G.I. CARRIAGE BOLT

1X4 RWD

1X4 RWD.

3/4" X 3/4" RWD.

TUBE FRAME TO BE HOT DIP GALV. AFTER FAB.
CLEAR CEDAR MAY BE USED FOR RWD.
USE HOT DIP GALV. OR ALUMINUM NAILS ONLY.
STAIN TO MATCH SCREEN.

B SECTION · METAL FRAME WOOD GATE
SCALE   1" = 1'-0"

GATE DETAILS

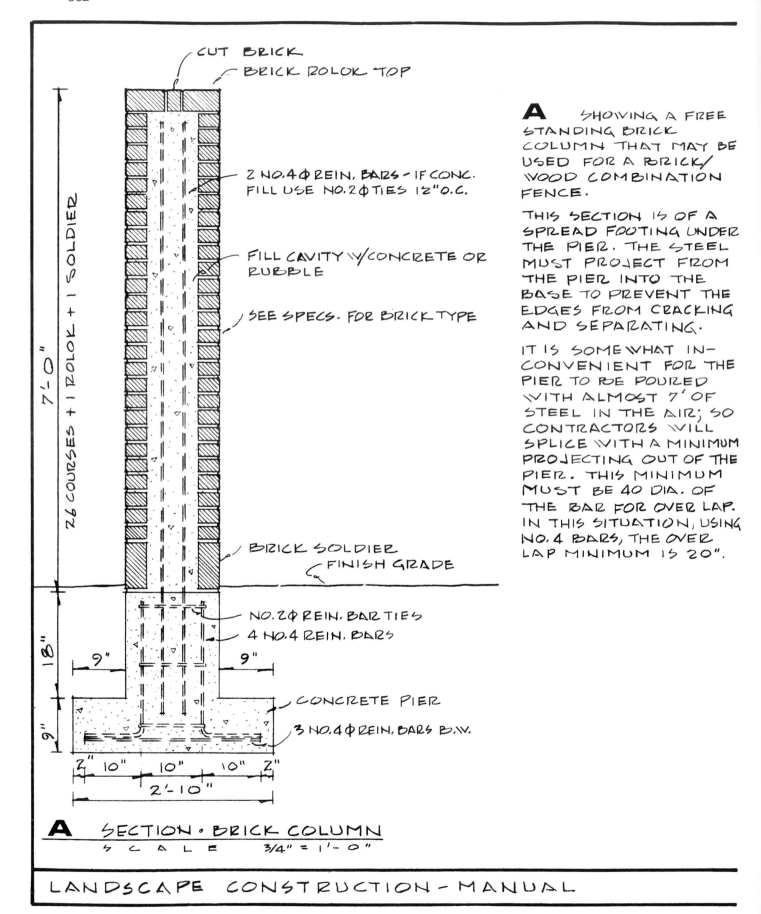

CUT BRICK

BRICK ROLOK TOP

2 NO. 4 φ REIN. BARS - IF CONC. FILL USE NO. 2 φ TIES 12" O.C.

FILL CAVITY W/CONCRETE OR RUBBLE

SEE SPECS. FOR BRICK TYPE

7'-0"

26 COURSES + 1 ROLOK + 1 SOLDIER

BRICK SOLDIER

FINISH GRADE

NO. 2 φ REIN. BAR TIES
4 NO. 4 REIN. BARS

18"

9"

9"

9"

CONCRETE PIER

3 NO. 4 φ REIN. BARS B.W.

2" 10"   10"   10" 2"

2'-10"

A   SECTION · BRICK COLUMN

SCALE   3/4" = 1'-0"

A   SHOWING A FREE STANDING BRICK COLUMN THAT MAY BE USED FOR A BRICK/WOOD COMBINATION FENCE.

THIS SECTION IS OF A SPREAD FOOTING UNDER THE PIER. THE STEEL MUST PROJECT FROM THE PIER INTO THE BASE TO PREVENT THE EDGES FROM CRACKING AND SEPARATING.

IT IS SOMEWHAT IN-CONVENIENT FOR THE PIER TO BE POURED WITH ALMOST 7' OF STEEL IN THE AIR; SO CONTRACTORS WILL SPLICE WITH A MINIMUM PROJECTING OUT OF THE PIER. THIS MINIMUM MUST BE 40 DIA. OF THE BAR FOR OVER LAP. IN THIS SITUATION, USING NO. 4 BARS, THE OVER LAP MINIMUM IS 20".

LANDSCAPE CONSTRUCTION - MANUAL

B MANY INTEREST-
ING BRICK PATTERNS
CAN BE DEVELOPED
FOR THE COLUMN. ALL
OF THE WOOD SCREENS
SHOWN HEREIN COULD
BE USED BETWEEN
THIS BRICK COLUMN.

COLUMN SPACING COULD
BE OF THE DESIGNERS
CHOICE INTHAT THEY
ARE NOT STRUCTURALLY
INTERRELATED.

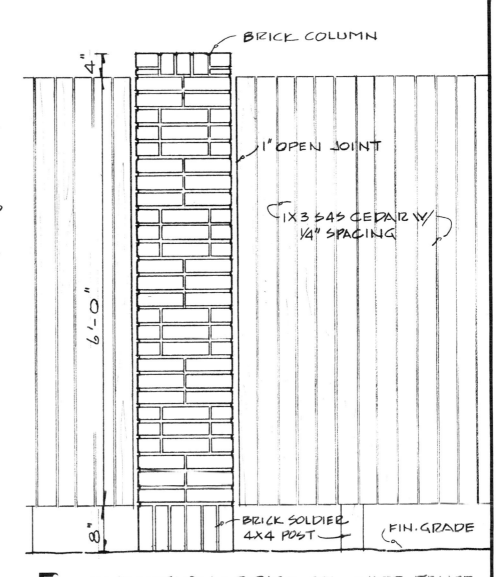

- BRICK COLUMN
- 1" OPEN JOINT
- 1X3 S4S CEDAR W/ 1/4" SPACING
- BRICK SOLDIER 4X4 POST
- FIN. GRADE

6'-0" 4" 8"

B ELEVATION · BRICK COL. · WOOD FENCE
SCALE   3/4" = 1'-0"

C SHOWING THE
WOOD FENCE BETWEEN
THE BRICK COLUMNS
ALTERNATING FROM
FRONT TO BACK.

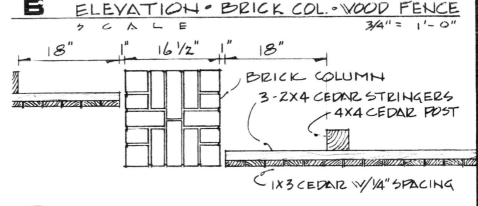

18" 1" 16 1/2" 1" 18"

- BRICK COLUMN
- 3-2X4 CEDAR STRINGERS
- 4X4 CEDAR POST
- 1X3 CEDAR W/ 1/4" SPACING

C PLAN · BRICK COL. · WOOD FENCE
SCALE   3/4" = 1'-0"

BRICK AND WOOD FENCE DETAILS

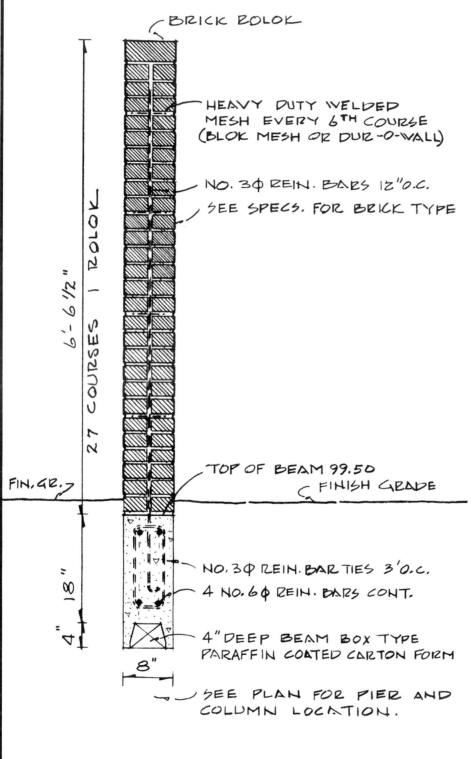

BRICK ROLOK

HEAVY DUTY WELDED MESH EVERY 6TH COURSE (BLOK MESH OR DUR-O-WALL)

NO. 3Ø REIN. BARS 12"O.C.

SEE SPECS. FOR BRICK TYPE

27 COURSES 1 ROLOK

6'-6½"

FIN. GR.

TOP OF BEAM 99.50

FINISH GRADE

18"

4"

NO. 3Ø REIN. BAR TIES 3' O.C.

4 NO. 6Ø REIN. BARS CONT.

4" DEEP BEAM BOX TYPE PARAFFIN COATED CARTON FORM

8"

SEE PLAN FOR PIER AND COLUMN LOCATION.

A SECTION · BRICK WALL
SCALE   3/4" = 1'-0"

A   THIS TWO BRICK WIDE WALL IS SHOWN HERE IN TWO SECTIONS, THIS PAGE AND THE NEXT.

THE REINFORCED BEAM CONTINUOUS UNDER THE WALL AND ON TOP OF THE PIERS, HAVE A PARAFFIN COATED HEAVY PAPER FORM UNDER IT THAT WILL HOLD UP WHILE THE CONCRETE IS BEING PLACED AND THEN WILL DETERIORATE, THUS PREVENTING UP-HEAVAL OF THE SOIL FROM EXERTING PRESSURE ON THE BEAM. ALWAYS CHECK THE JOB SITE TO ASSURE THAT THE STEEL REINFORCING BARS ARE CONTINUOUS FROM THE BEAM TO TOP OF WALL AS SHOWN IN THIS SECTION.

LANDSCAPE CONSTRUCTION - MANUAL

B SHOWING A SECTION AT THE COLUMN AND PIER. WHERE THE DESIGN PERMITS, THE COLUMN AND PIER SHOULD OCCUR AT THE SAME LOCATION. PLACING CONCRETE INTO THE CAVITY OF A COLUMN IS DIFFICULT AND OFTEN PRODUCES VOIDS OR BRICK DISPLACEMENT. IT IS GOOD PRACTICE TO HAVE THE BRICK MASONS FILL THE CAVITY WITH RUBBLE MORTARED IN AS THE BRICK WORK GOES UP.

TOP OF PIER IS EXPANDED TO SERVE AS A BASE FOR THE BRICK COLUMN. NOTE THAT THE REINFORCING BARS IN THE BEAM CONTINUES THRU THE PIER.

A BELL AT THE BOTTOM OF THE PIER IS TO ADD BEARING SURFACE. PIER DEPTH IS CRITICAL AND SHOULD BE CALCULATED FOR EACH PROJECT WITH RESPECT TO SUBSOIL CONDITION.

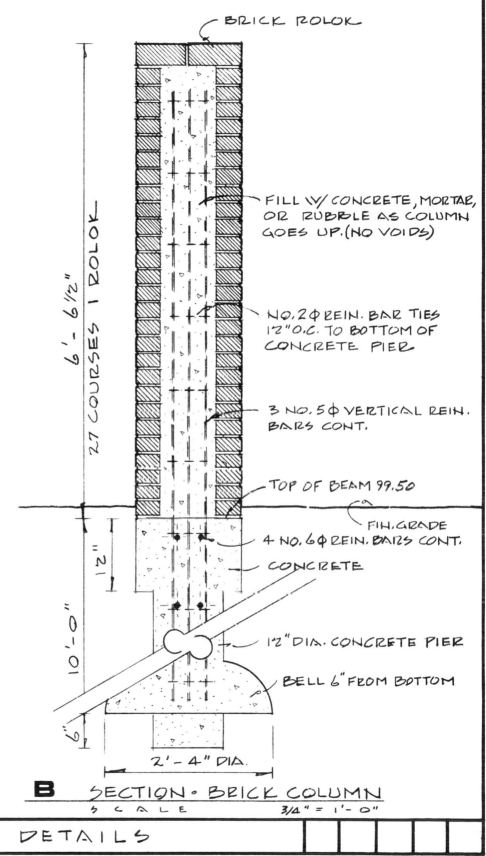

BRICK ROLOK

FILL W/ CONCRETE, MORTAR, OR RUBBLE AS COLUMN GOES UP. (NO VOIDS)

NO. 2 Ø REIN. BAR TIES 12" O.C. TO BOTTOM OF CONCRETE PIER

3 NO. 5 Ø VERTICAL REIN. BARS CONT.

TOP OF BEAM 99.50

FIN. GRADE

4 NO. 6 Ø REIN. BARS CONT.

CONCRETE

12" DIA. CONCRETE PIER

BELL 6" FROM BOTTOM

6' - 6½"

27 COURSES 1 ROLOK

12"

10'-0"

6"

2' - 4" DIA.

B SECTION · BRICK COLUMN
SCALE   3/4" = 1'-0"

BRICK WALL DETAILS

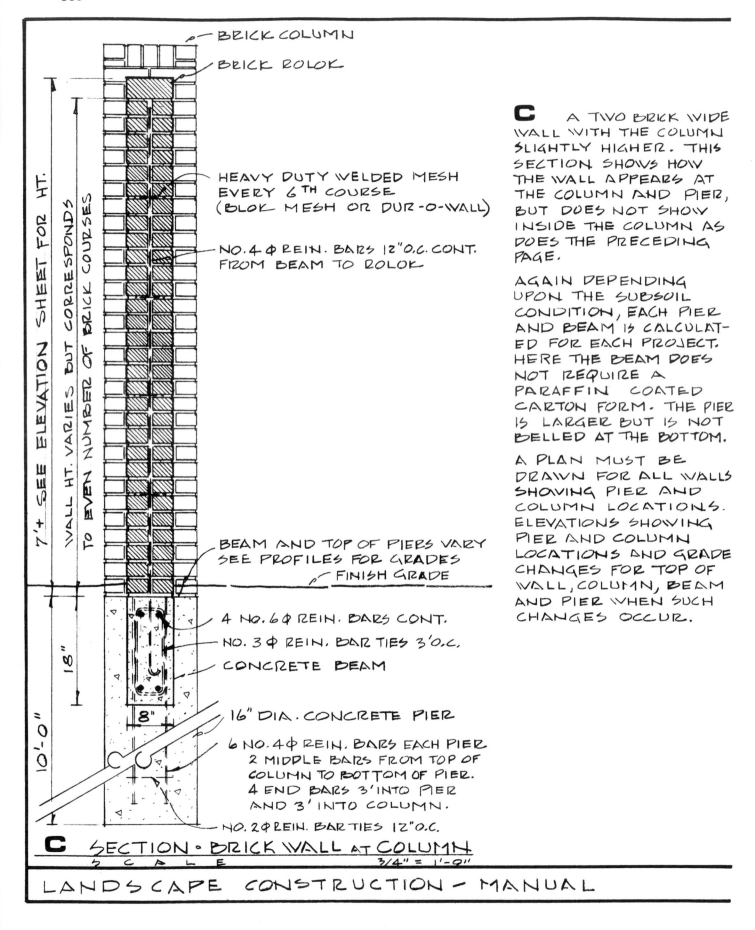

BRICK COLUMN

BRICK ROLOK

HEAVY DUTY WELDED MESH EVERY 6TH COURSE (BLOK MESH OR DUR-O-WALL)

NO. 4 Ø REIN. BARS 12"O.C. CONT. FROM BEAM TO ROLOK

7'± SEE ELEVATION SHEET FOR HT.

WALL HT. VARIES BUT CORRESPONDS TO EVEN NUMBER OF BRICK COURSES

BEAM AND TOP OF PIERS VARY SEE PROFILES FOR GRADES

FINISH GRADE

18"

10'-0"

8"

4 No. 6 Ø REIN. BARS CONT.

NO. 3 Ø REIN. BAR TIES 3' O.C.

CONCRETE BEAM

16" DIA. CONCRETE PIER

6 NO. 4 Ø REIN. BARS EACH PIER 2 MIDDLE BARS FROM TOP OF COLUMN TO BOTTOM OF PIER. 4 END BARS 3' INTO PIER AND 3' INTO COLUMN.

NO. 2 Ø REIN. BAR TIES 12"O.C.

C SECTION · BRICK WALL AT COLUMN
SCALE   3/4" = 1'-0"

C A TWO BRICK WIDE WALL WITH THE COLUMN SLIGHTLY HIGHER. THIS SECTION SHOWS HOW THE WALL APPEARS AT THE COLUMN AND PIER, BUT DOES NOT SHOW INSIDE THE COLUMN AS DOES THE PRECEDING PAGE.

AGAIN DEPENDING UPON THE SUBSOIL CONDITION, EACH PIER AND BEAM IS CALCULATED FOR EACH PROJECT. HERE THE BEAM DOES NOT REQUIRE A PARAFFIN COATED CARTON FORM. THE PIER IS LARGER BUT IS NOT BELLED AT THE BOTTOM.

A PLAN MUST BE DRAWN FOR ALL WALLS SHOWING PIER AND COLUMN LOCATIONS. ELEVATIONS SHOWING PIER AND COLUMN LOCATIONS AND GRADE CHANGES FOR TOP OF WALL, COLUMN, BEAM AND PIER WHEN SUCH CHANGES OCCUR.

LANDSCAPE CONSTRUCTION - MANUAL

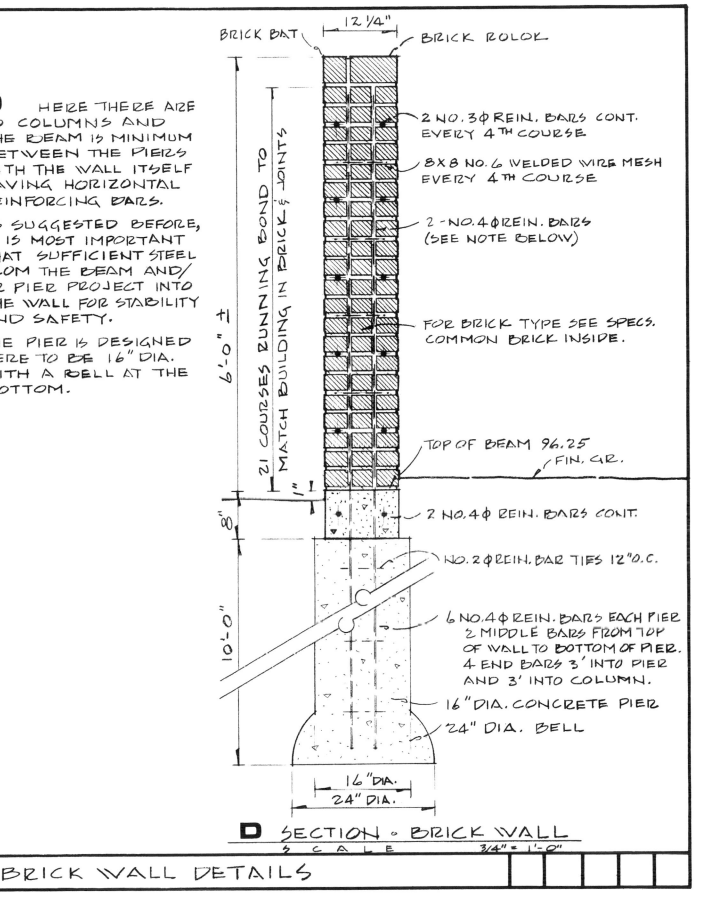

D HERE THERE ARE NO COLUMNS AND THE BEAM IS MINIMUM BETWEEN THE PIERS WITH THE WALL ITSELF HAVING HORIZONTAL REINFORCING BARS.

AS SUGGESTED BEFORE, IT IS MOST IMPORTANT THAT SUFFICIENT STEEL FROM THE BEAM AND/OR PIER PROJECT INTO THE WALL FOR STABILITY AND SAFETY.

THE PIER IS DESIGNED HERE TO BE 16" DIA. WITH A BELL AT THE BOTTOM.

BRICK BAT

12 1/4"

BRICK ROLOK

2 NO. 3 φ REIN. BARS CONT. EVERY 4TH COURSE

8X8 NO. 6 WELDED WIRE MESH EVERY 4TH COURSE

2 - NO. 4 φ REIN. BARS (SEE NOTE BELOW)

FOR BRICK TYPE SEE SPECS. COMMON BRICK INSIDE.

21 COURSES RUNNING BOND TO MATCH BUILDING IN BRICK & JOINTS

6'-0" ±

1"

TOP OF BEAM 96.25
FIN. GR.

2 NO. 4 φ REIN. BARS CONT.

8"

NO. 2 φ REIN. BAR TIES 12" O.C.

10'-0"

6 NO. 4 φ REIN. BARS EACH PIER 2 MIDDLE BARS FROM TOP OF WALL TO BOTTOM OF PIER. 4 END BARS 3' INTO PIER AND 3' INTO COLUMN.

16" DIA. CONCRETE PIER

24" DIA. BELL

16" DIA.

24" DIA.

D SECTION · BRICK WALL
SCALE   3/4" = 1'-0"

BRICK WALL DETAILS

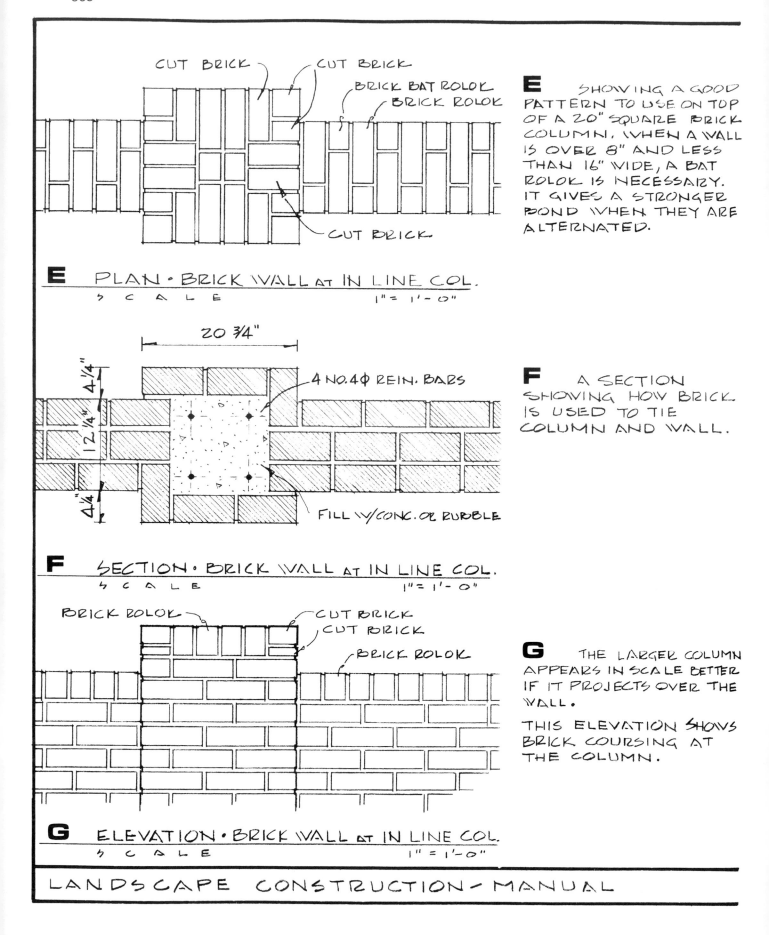

CUT BRICK   CUT BRICK
BRICK BAT ROLOK
BRICK ROLOK

CUT BRICK

E SHOWING A GOOD PATTERN TO USE ON TOP OF A 20" SQUARE BRICK COLUMN, WHEN A WALL IS OVER 8" AND LESS THAN 16" WIDE, A BAT ROLOK IS NECESSARY. IT GIVES A STRONGER BOND WHEN THEY ARE ALTERNATED.

E PLAN · BRICK WALL AT IN LINE COL.
SCALE   1" = 1'-0"

20 3/4"

4 1/4"
12 1/4"
4 1/4"

4 NO.4Ø REIN. BARS

FILL W/CONC. OR RUBBLE

F A SECTION SHOWING HOW BRICK IS USED TO TIE COLUMN AND WALL.

F SECTION · BRICK WALL AT IN LINE COL.
SCALE   1" = 1'-0"

BRICK ROLOK   CUT BRICK
CUT BRICK
BRICK ROLOK

G THE LARGER COLUMN APPEARS IN SCALE BETTER IF IT PROJECTS OVER THE WALL.

THIS ELEVATION SHOWS BRICK COURSING AT THE COLUMN.

G ELEVATION · BRICK WALL AT IN LINE COL.
SCALE   1" = 1'-0"

LANDSCAPE CONSTRUCTION · MANUAL

H SHOWING A SECTION OF THE COL. AT A GATE. MORE REINFORCING IS NEEDED AND THE GATE HINGES MUST BE INSTALLED AS THE COLUMN IS BEING CONSTRUCTED.

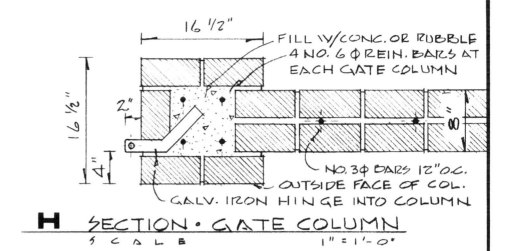

16 ½"

16 ½"

2"

4"

FILL W/CONC. OR RUBBLE 4 NO. 6 ∅ REIN. BARS AT EACH GATE COLUMN

8"

NO. 3∅ BARS 12" O.C. OUTSIDE FACE OF COL.

GALV. IRON HINGE INTO COLUMN

H SECTION · GATE COLUMN
SCALE 1" = 1'-0"

I HINGE LOCATION IS IMPORTANT. HINGES THAT ARE TOO CLOSE TO-GETHER MAKE A WEAK AND SAGGING GATE. IF IT IS TOO CLOSE TO THE TOP OF THE COLUMN IT MAY BREAK OUT.

IT IS NECESSARY TO MEASURE THE HINGES AFTER INSTALLATION AND BEFORE THE GATE IS CONSTRUCTED TO ASSURE A GOOD FIT.

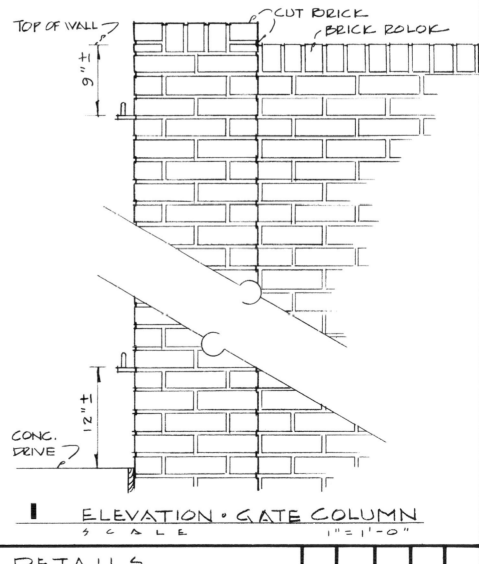

TOP OF WALL

9" ±

CUT BRICK
BRICK ROLOK

12" ±

CONC. DRIVE

I ELEVATION · GATE COLUMN
SCALE 1" = 1'-0"

BRICK WALL DETAILS

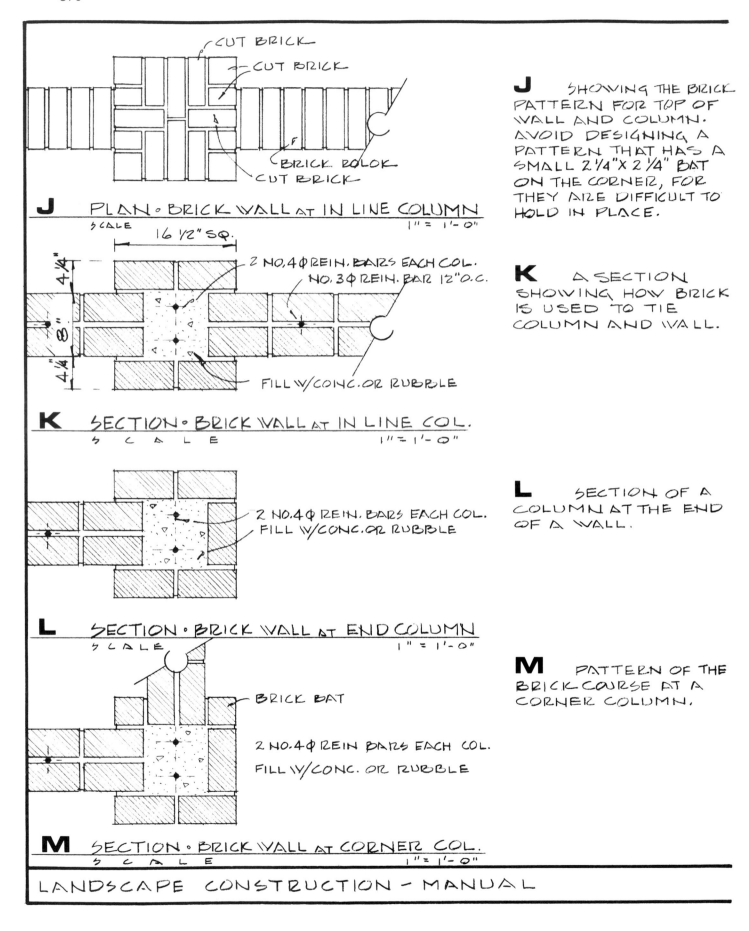

J — PLAN • BRICK WALL AT IN LINE COLUMN
SCALE   1" = 1'-0"

- CUT BRICK
- CUT BRICK
- BRICK BOLOK
- CUT BRICK

16 ½" SQ.

4 ¼"

8"

4 ¼"

2 NO. 4∅ REIN. BARS EACH COL.
NO. 3∅ REIN. BAR 12" O.C.

FILL W/CONC. OR RUBBLE

K — SECTION • BRICK WALL AT IN LINE COL.
SCALE   1" = 1'-0"

2 NO. 4∅ REIN. BARS EACH COL.
FILL W/CONC. OR RUBBLE

L — SECTION • BRICK WALL AT END COLUMN
SCALE   1" = 1'-0"

BRICK BAT

2 NO. 4∅ REIN BARS EACH COL.
FILL W/CONC. OR RUBBLE

M — SECTION • BRICK WALL AT CORNER COL.
SCALE   1" = 1'-0"

J SHOWING THE BRICK PATTERN FOR TOP OF WALL AND COLUMN. AVOID DESIGNING A PATTERN THAT HAS A SMALL 2¼"X 2¼" BAT ON THE CORNER, FOR THEY ARE DIFFICULT TO HOLD IN PLACE.

K A SECTION SHOWING HOW BRICK IS USED TO TIE COLUMN AND WALL.

L SECTION OF A COLUMN AT THE END OF A WALL.

M PATTERN OF THE BRICK COURSE AT A CORNER COLUMN.

LANDSCAPE CONSTRUCTION - MANUAL

N FOR AESTHETICS, THE COLUMN SHOULD BE SLIGHTLY HIGHER THAN THE WALL.

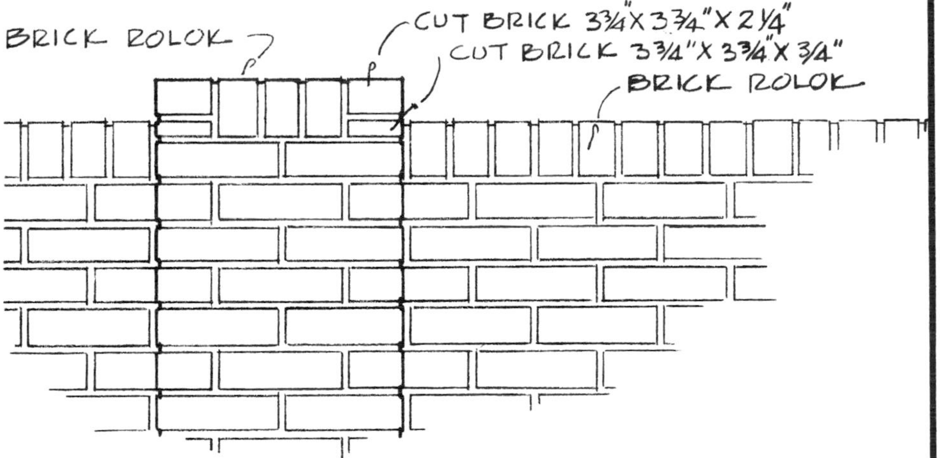

BRICK ROLOK

CUT BRICK 3¾" X 3¾" X 2¼"
CUT BRICK 3¾" X 3¾" X ¾"
BRICK ROLOK

N ELEVATION • COLUMN W/ LEVEL WALL
SCALE   1" = 1'-0"

O WHEN DIMENSIONS ARE GIVEN ON ELEVATIONS, PROFILES OR GRADES AS SPOT ELEVATIONS ON PLANS, MAKE SURE TO GIVE DIFFERENCES IN EVEN BRICK COURSES TO AVOID CUTTING.

DO NOT SLOPE BRICK WALLS WHEN COLUMNS ARE USED.

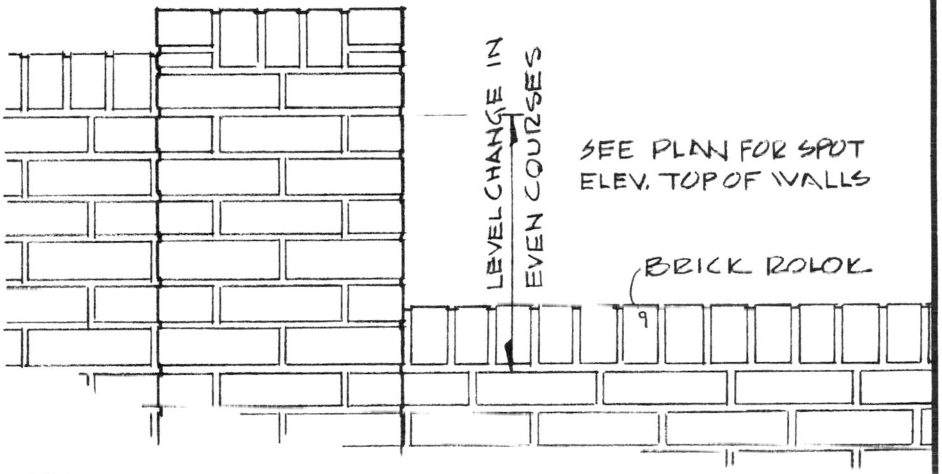

LEVEL CHANGE IN EVEN COURSES

SEE PLAN FOR SPOT ELEV. TOP OF WALLS

BRICK ROLOK

O ELEVATION • COLUMN W/ WALL CHANGE
SCALE   1" = 1'-0"

P AN ALTERNATE DETAIL FOR WALL HEIGHT CHANGE AT A COLUMN.

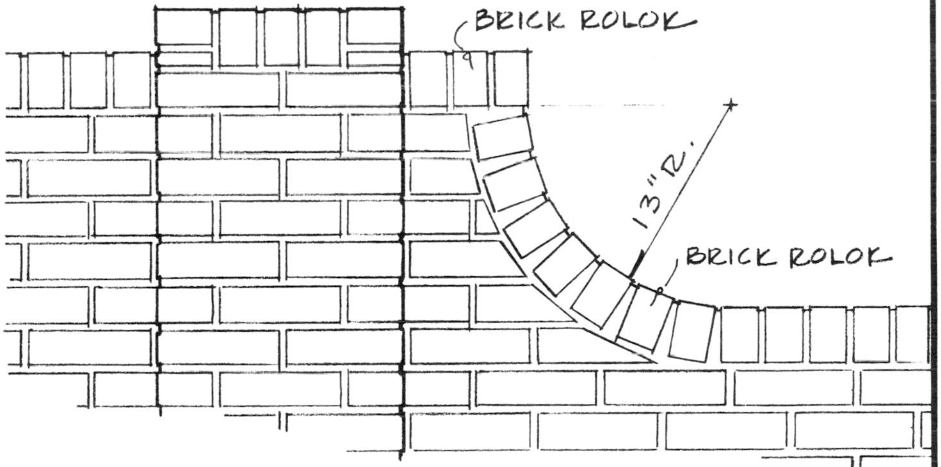

BRICK ROLOK

13" R.

BRICK ROLOK

P ELEVATION • COLUMN W/ WALL CHANGE
SCALE   1" = 1'-0"

BRICK WALL DETAILS

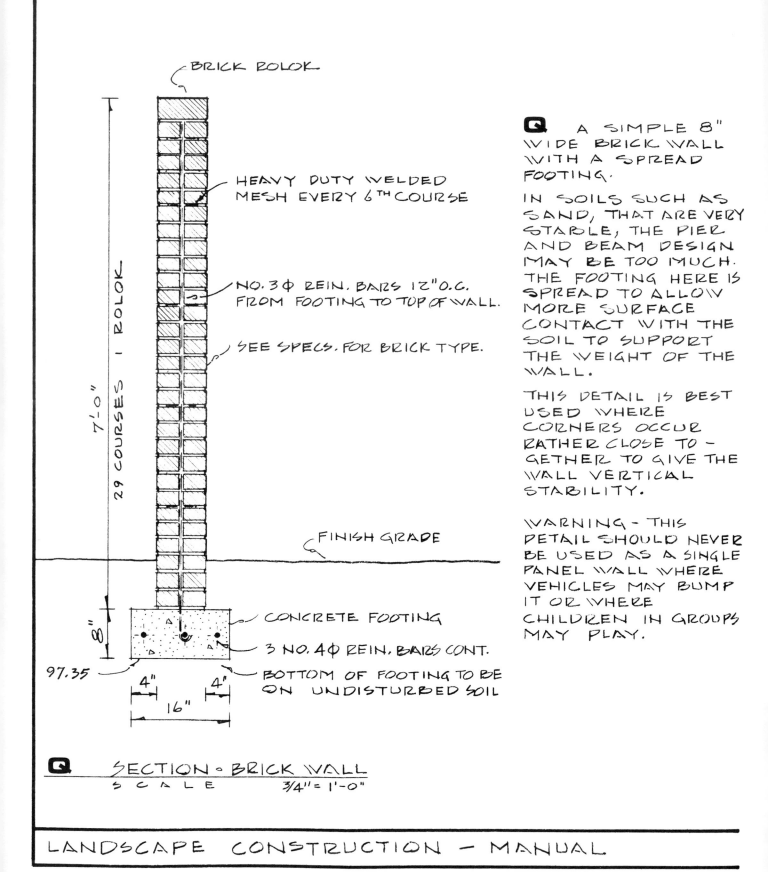

BRICK ROLOK

HEAVY DUTY WELDED
MESH EVERY 6TH COURSE

NO. 3Φ REIN. BARS 12" O.C.
FROM FOOTING TO TOP OF WALL.

SEE SPECS. FOR BRICK TYPE.

7'-0"
29 COURSES = ROLOK

FINISH GRADE

8"

CONCRETE FOOTING

3 NO. 4Φ REIN. BARS CONT.

BOTTOM OF FOOTING TO BE
ON UNDISTURBED SOIL

97.35

4"   4"

16"

Q SECTION - BRICK WALL
   S C A L E   3/4" = 1'-0"

Q A SIMPLE 8"
WIDE BRICK WALL
WITH A SPREAD
FOOTING.

IN SOILS SUCH AS
SAND, THAT ARE VERY
STABLE, THE PIER
AND BEAM DESIGN
MAY BE TOO MUCH.
THE FOOTING HERE IS
SPREAD TO ALLOW
MORE SURFACE
CONTACT WITH THE
SOIL TO SUPPORT
THE WEIGHT OF THE
WALL.

THIS DETAIL IS BEST
USED WHERE
CORNERS OCCUR
RATHER CLOSE TO -
GETHER TO GIVE THE
WALL VERTICAL
STABILITY.

WARNING - THIS
DETAIL SHOULD NEVER
BE USED AS A SINGLE
PANEL WALL WHERE
VEHICLES MAY BUMP
IT OR WHERE
CHILDREN IN GROUPS
MAY PLAY.

LANDSCAPE CONSTRUCTION - MANUAL

R A 12" OR THREE BRICK WIDE WALL WITH A SPREAD FOOTING.

CARE SHOULD BE TAKEN NOT TO USE A SPREAD TYPE FOOTING IN OTHER THAN STABLE SOILS.

THE "RULE OF THUMB" FOR A SPREAD FOOTING IS TWO TIMES THE WIDTH OF THE WALL.

ALL FOOTING TYPE WALLS MUST HAVE THE BOTTOM OF THE FOOTING PLACED ON UNDISTURBED SOIL AND BELOW THE FROST LINE. FOR AESTHETICS, IT IS SUGGESTED THAT THE TOP OF THE FOOTING BE BELOW FINISH GRADE.

THIS DETAIL WILL HAVE THE SAME GENERAL LIMITATIONS AS SUGGESTED ON THE PRECEEDING PAGE.

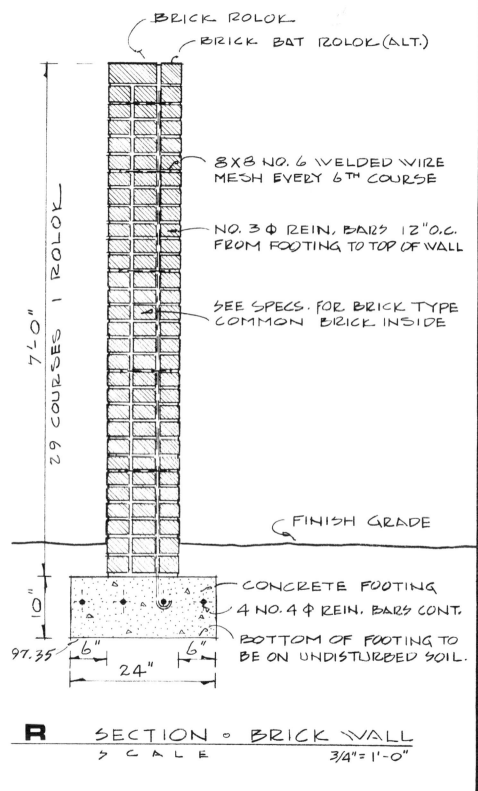

BRICK ROLOK
BRICK BAT ROLOK (ALT.)

7'-0"
29 COURSES 1 ROLOK

8X8 NO. 6 WELDED WIRE MESH EVERY 6TH COURSE

NO. 3 Φ REIN, BARS 12" O.C. FROM FOOTING TO TOP OF WALL

SEE SPECS. FOR BRICK TYPE COMMON BRICK INSIDE

FINISH GRADE

10"

97.35   6"   24"   6"

CONCRETE FOOTING
4 NO. 4 Φ REIN. BARS CONT.
BOTTOM OF FOOTING TO BE ON UNDISTURBED SOIL.

R SECTION ○ BRICK WALL
SCALE   3/4" = 1'-0"

BRICK WALL DETAILS

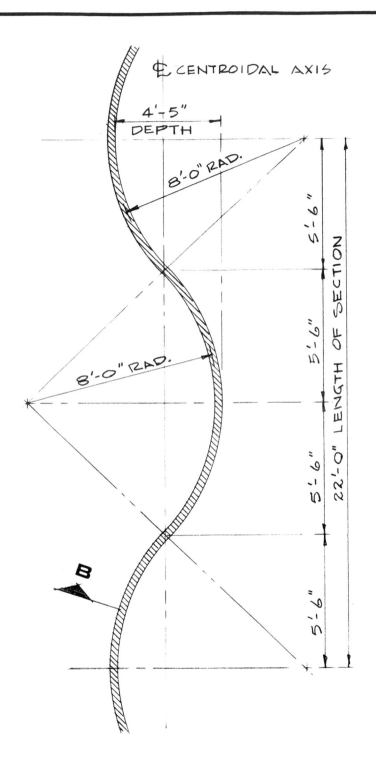

℄ CENTROIDAL AXIS

4'-5"
DEPTH

8'-0" RAD.

8'-0" RAD.

5'-6"

5'-6"

5'-6"

5'-6"

22'-0" LENGTH OF SECTION

B

A THIS TECHNIQUE OF GARDEN WALL CONSTRUCTION HAS BEEN USED IN THIS COUNTRY FOR ALMOST 200 YEARS. THE SERPENTINE SHAPE PROVIDES LATERAL STRENGTH TO THE WALL SO THAT IT NORMALLY CAN BE BUILT ONLY ONE BRICK WIDE WITHOUT ADDITIONAL LATERAL SUPPORT.

SINCE THE WALL DEPENDS ON ITS SHAPE FOR STRENGTH, IT IS IMPORTANT THAT THE CONFIGURATION DOES NOT VARY TOO MUCH FROM THE FOLLOWING LIMITATIONS.

THE RADIUS OF CURVATURE OF A SINGLE BRICK WIDTH WALL SHOULD BE NO MORE THAN TWICE THE HEIGHT OF THE WALL EXTENDING ABOVE FINISH GRADE.

THE DEPTH OF CURVATURE SHOULD BE NO LESS THAN ONE HALF OF THE HEIGHT ABOVE FINISH GRADE.

A PARTIAL PLAN ○ 4" WALL
SCALE
1/4" = 1'-0"

LANDSCAPE CONSTRUCTION – MANUAL

B SECTION SHOW-
ING A SERPENTINE
GARDEN WALL WITH-
OUT A COPING, BUT
WITH A REINFORCED
CONCRETE FOOTING.

SINCE GARDEN WALLS
GENERALLY DO NOT
CARRY ANY VERTICAL
LOADS OTHER THAN
THEIR OWN WEIGHT,
THE FOUNDATIONS OR
FOOTINGS IN STABLE
SOILS MAY BE OF BRICK
OR CONCRETE.

AS SHOWN HERE, THE
FOOTING SHOULD BE OF
REINFORCED CONCRETE
IN AREAS WITH ACTIVE
SOILS.

ALL FOOTINGS MUST BE
PLACED   UNDISTURB-
ED EARTH AND AT A
DEPTH BELOW THE
FROST LINE.

C A COPING WILL
CHANGE THE APPEAR-
ANCE AND CHARACTER
OF A WALL AS WELL
AS HELP PREVENT
FREEZING DAMAGE
WHEN IT PROVIDES
AN OVERHANG FOR A
DRIP LINE.

HERE IS SHOWN A
BRICK THAT IS CUT TO
FIT OR ONE THAT IS
SPECIAL MOLDED.

D AN ALL BRICK
FOOTING HAS BEEN
USED WITH MUCH
SUCCESS FOR A
GREAT NUMBER OF
YEARS WHERE THE
SOIL IS NOT ACTIVE.

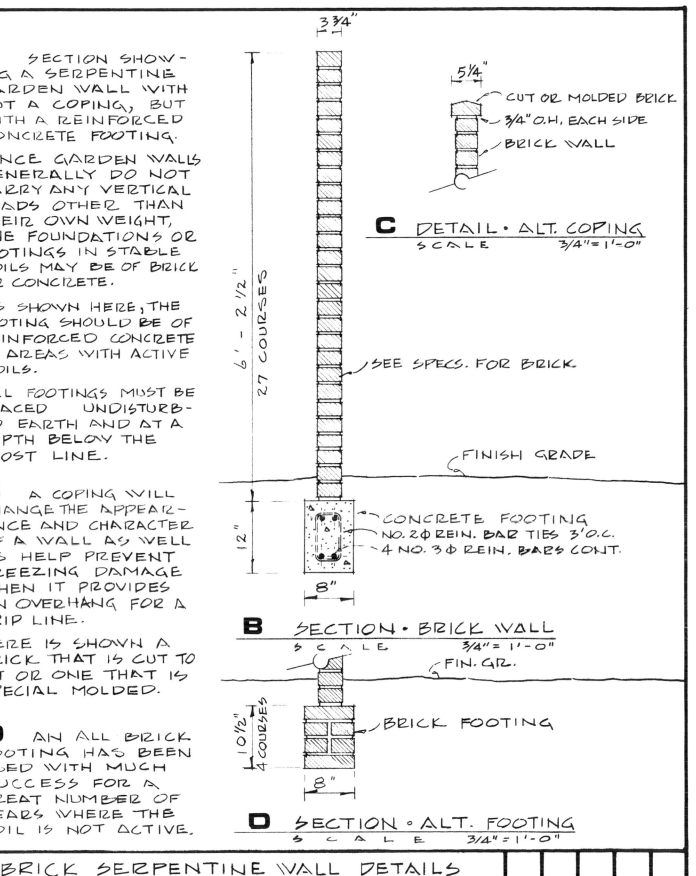

3 ¾"

6' - 2 ½"
27 COURSES

5 ¼"
CUT OR MOLDED BRICK
¾" O.H. EACH SIDE
BRICK WALL

C DETAIL · ALT. COPING
SCALE   ¾" = 1'-0"

SEE SPECS. FOR BRICK

FINISH GRADE

12"

8"

CONCRETE FOOTING
NO. 2 Ø REIN. BAR TIES 3' O.C.
4 NO. 3 Ø REIN. BARS CONT.

B SECTION · BRICK WALL
SCALE   ¾" = 1'-0"

FIN. GR.

10 ½"
4 COURSES

BRICK FOOTING

8"

D SECTION · ALT. FOOTING
SCALE   ¾" = 1'-0"

BRICK SERPENTINE WALL DETAILS

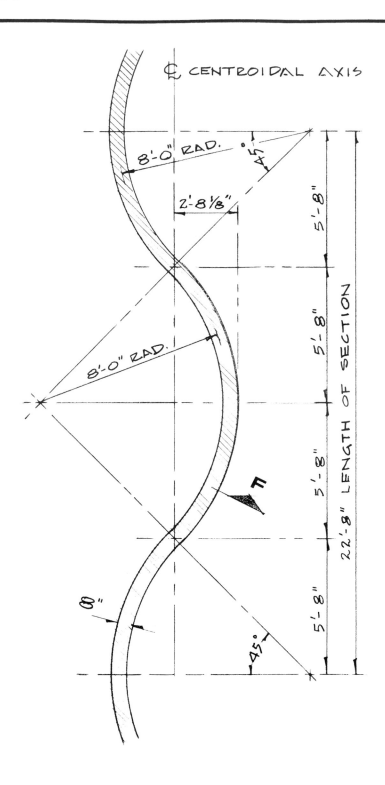

℄ CENTROIDAL AXIS

8'-0" RAD.

2'-8⅛"

45°

8'-0" RAD.

5'-8"

5'-8"

5'-8"

5'-8"

22'-8" LENGTH OF SECTION

8"

45°

F

E   THERE WILL BE
OCCASIONS WHEN A
SERPENTINE WALL
WILL BE DESIRABLE
AND THE THIN GARDEN
WALL WILL NOT SERVE
THE PURPOSE. A
LOADBEARING OR NON-
LOADBEARING BUILD-
ING WALL, A RETAIN-
ING WALL, A HIGH
GARDEN WALL, ETC.

THE "RULE OF THUMB"
SUGGESTED ON THE
PRECEEDING DETAIL
WILL NOT APPLY TO
THESE CONDITIONS,
BUT WILL REQUIRE
AN ENGINEERED
DESIGN.

E   PARTIAL PLAN ∘ 8" WALL
SCALE   ¼" = 1'-0"

LANDSCAPE CONSTRUCTION - MANUAL

F SECTION SHOWING A SERPENTINE WALL THAT IS 8" IN WIDTH, BRICK ROLOK CAP OR COPING, AND A REINFORCED CONCRETE FOOTING OR FOUNDATION.

FOR ACTIVE SOILS, THE FOOTING MUST BE OF HIGH STRENGTH CONCRETE, SIZED AND REINFORCED AS NECESSARY.

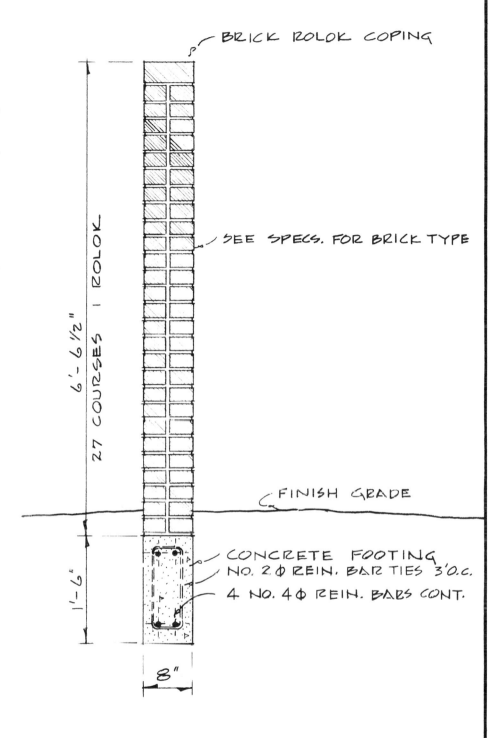

BRICK ROLOK COPING

SEE SPECS. FOR BRICK TYPE

6'-6½"

27 COURSES 1 ROLOK

FINISH GRADE

1'-6"

CONCRETE FOOTING
NO. 2 φ REIN. BAR TIES 3' O.C.
4 NO. 4 φ REIN. BARS CONT.

8"

F SECTION · BRICK WALL
SCALE   3/4"= 1'-0"

BRICK SERPENTINE WALL DETAILS

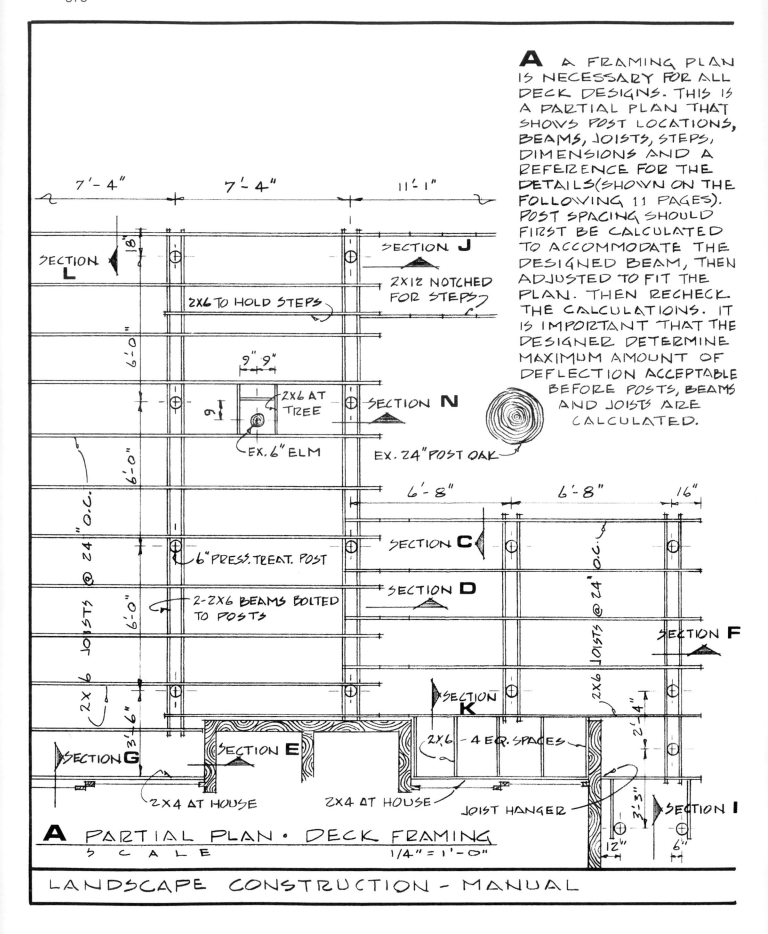

A A FRAMING PLAN IS NECESSARY FOR ALL DECK DESIGNS. THIS IS A PARTIAL PLAN THAT SHOWS POST LOCATIONS, BEAMS, JOISTS, STEPS, DIMENSIONS AND A REFERENCE FOR THE DETAILS(SHOWN ON THE FOLLOWING 11 PAGES). POST SPACING SHOULD FIRST BE CALCULATED TO ACCOMMODATE THE DESIGNED BEAM, THEN ADJUSTED TO FIT THE PLAN. THEN RECHECK THE CALCULATIONS. IT IS IMPORTANT THAT THE DESIGNER DETERMINE MAXIMUM AMOUNT OF DEFLECTION ACCEPTABLE BEFORE POSTS, BEAMS AND JOISTS ARE CALCULATED.

7'-4"   7'-4"   11'-1"

SECTION L   8"

SECTION J

2X12 NOTCHED FOR STEPS

2X6 TO HOLD STEPS

6'-0"

9" 9"

2X6 AT TREE

SECTION N

9"

EX. 6" ELM   EX. 24" POST OAK

6'-0"

6'-8"   6'-8"   16"

2X6 JOISTS @ 24" O.C.

SECTION C

6" PRESS. TREAT. POST

SECTION D

2-2X6 BEAMS BOLTED TO POSTS

6'-0"

2X6 JOISTS @ 24" O.C.

SECTION F

2X6 JOISTS @ 24" O.C.

SECTION K

2X6 - 4 EQ. SPACES

2'-4"

3'-6"

SECTION G

SECTION E

2X4 AT HOUSE   2X4 AT HOUSE   JOIST HANGER

3'-3"

SECTION I

A PARTIAL PLAN · DECK FRAMING

SCALE   1/4" = 1'-0"

12"   6"

LANDSCAPE CONSTRUCTION - MANUAL

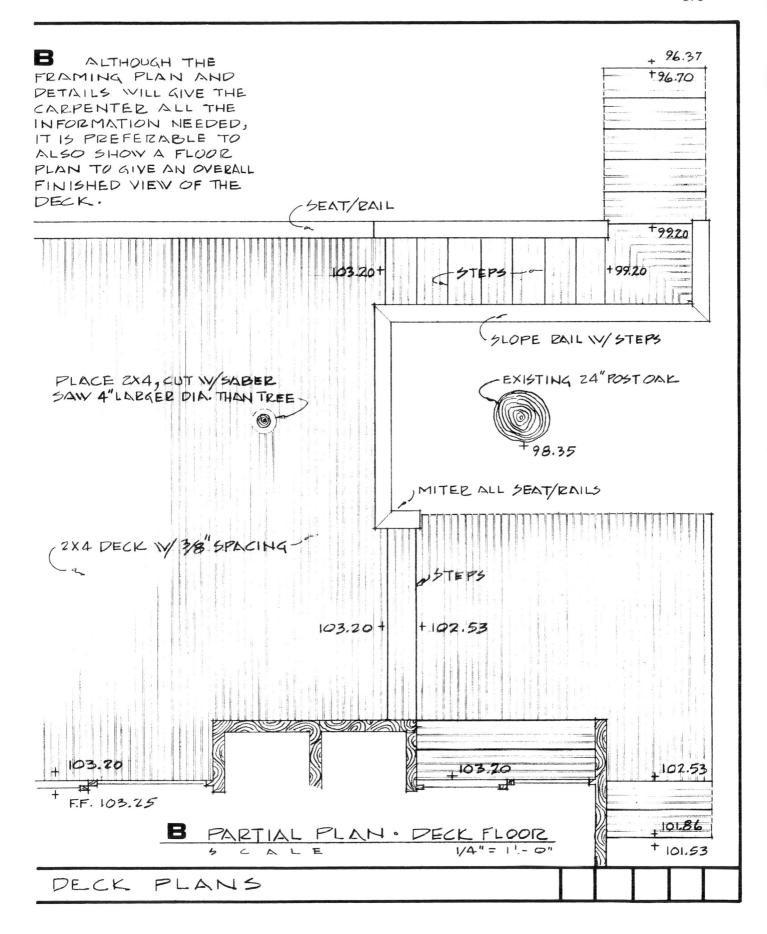

B ALTHOUGH THE FRAMING PLAN AND DETAILS WILL GIVE THE CARPENTER ALL THE INFORMATION NEEDED, IT IS PREFERABLE TO ALSO SHOW A FLOOR PLAN TO GIVE AN OVERALL FINISHED VIEW OF THE DECK.

SEAT/RAIL

+ 96.37

+ 96.70

+ 99.20

103.20 +

STEPS

+ 99.20

SLOPE RAIL W/ STEPS

PLACE 2X4, CUT W/ SABER SAW 4" LARGER DIA. THAN TREE

EXISTING 24" POST OAK

+ 98.35

MITER ALL SEAT/RAILS

2X4 DECK W/ 3/8" SPACING

STEPS

103.20 +

+ 102.53

+ 103.20

+ F.F. 103.25

+ 103.20

+ 102.53

+ 101.86

+ 101.53

B PARTIAL PLAN · DECK FLOOR
SCALE   1/4" = 1'-0"

DECK PLANS

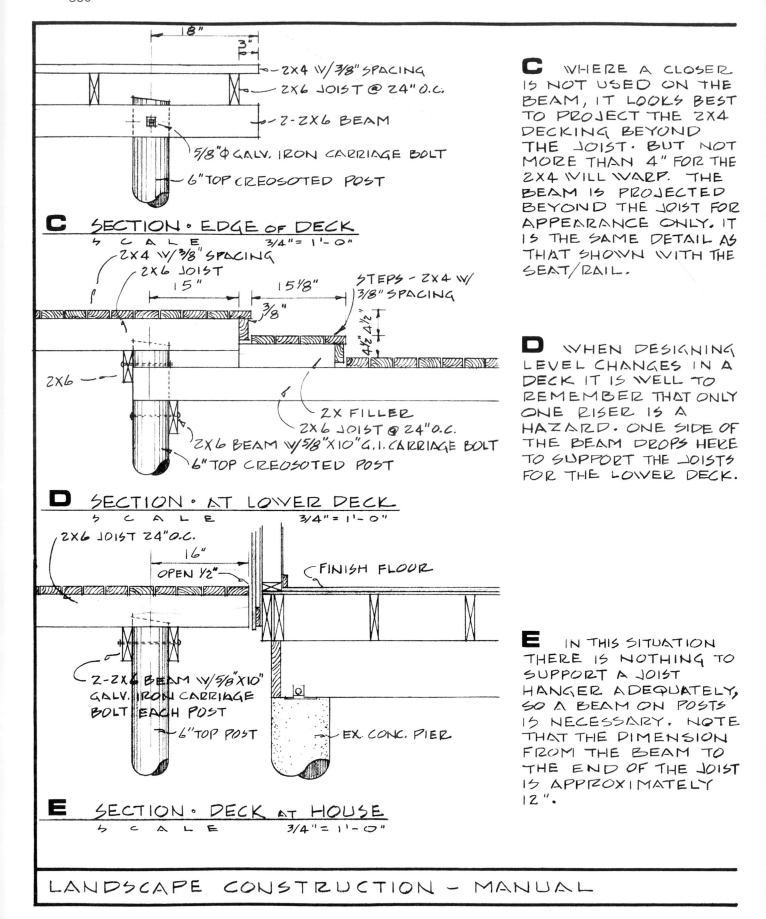

18"

3"

2x4 w/ 3/8" SPACING

2x6 JOIST @ 24" O.C.

2-2x6 BEAM

5/8"Ø GALV. IRON CARRIAGE BOLT

6" TOP CREOSOTED POST

C SECTION · EDGE of DECK
SCALE   3/4" = 1'-0"

2x4 w/ 3/8" SPACING

2x6 JOIST

15"

15 1/8"

3/8"

STEPS - 2x4 w/ 3/8" SPACING

4 1/2" 4 1/2"

2x6

2X FILLER

2x6 JOIST @ 24" O.C.

2x6 BEAM w/ 5/8"x10" G.I. CARRIAGE BOLT

6" TOP CREOSOTED POST

D SECTION · AT LOWER DECK
SCALE   3/4" = 1'-0"

2x6 JOIST 24" O.C.

16"

OPEN 1/2"

FINISH FLOOR

2-2x6 BEAM w/ 5/8"x10" GALV. IRON CARRIAGE BOLT EACH POST

6" TOP POST

EX. CONC. PIER

E SECTION · DECK at HOUSE
SCALE   3/4" = 1'-0"

C WHERE A CLOSER IS NOT USED ON THE BEAM, IT LOOKS BEST TO PROJECT THE 2x4 DECKING BEYOND THE JOIST. BUT NOT MORE THAN 4" FOR THE 2x4 WILL WARP. THE BEAM IS PROJECTED BEYOND THE JOIST FOR APPEARANCE ONLY. IT IS THE SAME DETAIL AS THAT SHOWN WITH THE SEAT/RAIL.

D WHEN DESIGNING LEVEL CHANGES IN A DECK IT IS WELL TO REMEMBER THAT ONLY ONE RISER IS A HAZARD. ONE SIDE OF THE BEAM DROPS HERE TO SUPPORT THE JOISTS FOR THE LOWER DECK.

E IN THIS SITUATION THERE IS NOTHING TO SUPPORT A JOIST HANGER ADEQUATELY, SO A BEAM ON POSTS IS NECESSARY. NOTE THAT THE DIMENSION FROM THE BEAM TO THE END OF THE JOIST IS APPROXIMATELY 12".

LANDSCAPE CONSTRUCTION – MANUAL

F AT THIS EDGE A CLOSER IS USED TO GIVE A FINISHED APPEARANCE. SPACING BETWEEN THE 2X4'S SHOULD BE 3/8" AS SHOWN. 1/4" IS TOO TIGHT AND HARD TO WORK. 1/2" IS WIDE ENOUGH TO LOOK BEYOND THE FLOOR AND GIVE AN UNEASY FEELING. TOE NAIL ALL DECKING.

G THIS DETAIL SHOWS THE USE OF A NAILER ON THE BUILDING WHERE SIDING DOES NOT OCCUR. THE POST LOCATION ALLOWS FOR ENOUGH OF A CANTILEVER ON THE BEAM TO SUPPORT THE FIRST JOIST.

H AN ALTERNATE DETAIL OF THE ABOVE. WHERE NO POST IS USED WITHIN 4', THE BEAM ATTACHED TO THE HOUSE WITH GALVANIZED JOIST HANGERS. EVEN WITH THIS, THE 2X4 NAILED TO THE HOUSE IS SUFFICIENT TO SUPPORT THE DECKING.

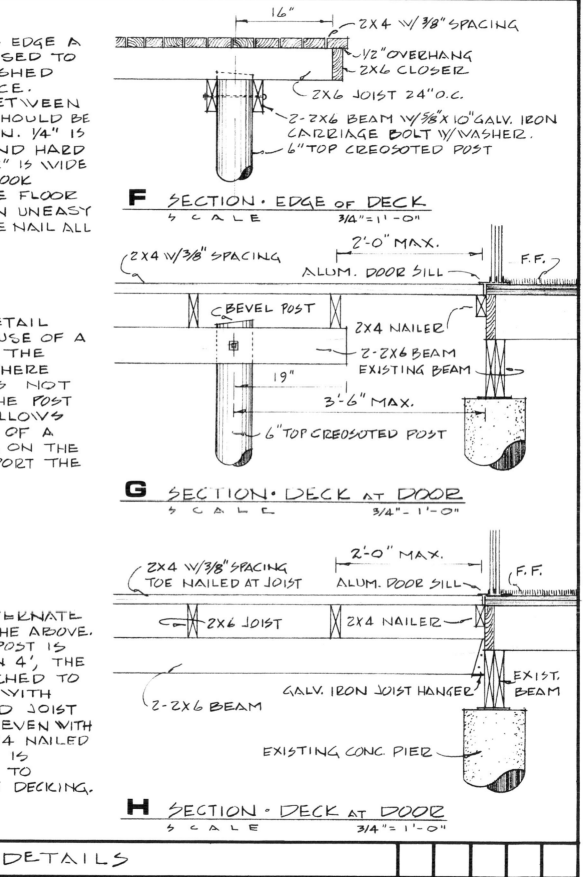

16"
2X4 W/ 3/8" SPACING
1/2" OVERHANG
2X6 CLOSER
2X6 JOIST 24" O.C.
2-2X6 BEAM W/5/8"X10" GALV. IRON CARRIAGE BOLT W/WASHER.
6" TOP CREOSOTED POST

F SECTION · EDGE of DECK
SCALE   3/4"=1'-0"

2X4 W/3/8" SPACING
2'-0" MAX.
ALUM. DOOR SILL
F.F.
BEVEL POST
2X4 NAILER
2-2X6 BEAM
EXISTING BEAM
19"
3'-6" MAX.
6" TOP CREOSOTED POST

G SECTION · DECK AT DOOR
SCALE   3/4"-1'-0"

2X4 W/3/8" SPACING TOE NAILED AT JOIST
2'-0" MAX.
ALUM. DOOR SILL
F.F.
2X6 JOIST
2X4 NAILER
GALV. IRON JOIST HANGER
EXIST. BEAM
2-2X6 BEAM
EXISTING CONC. PIER

H SECTION · DECK AT DOOR
SCALE   3/4"=1'-0"

DECK DETAILS

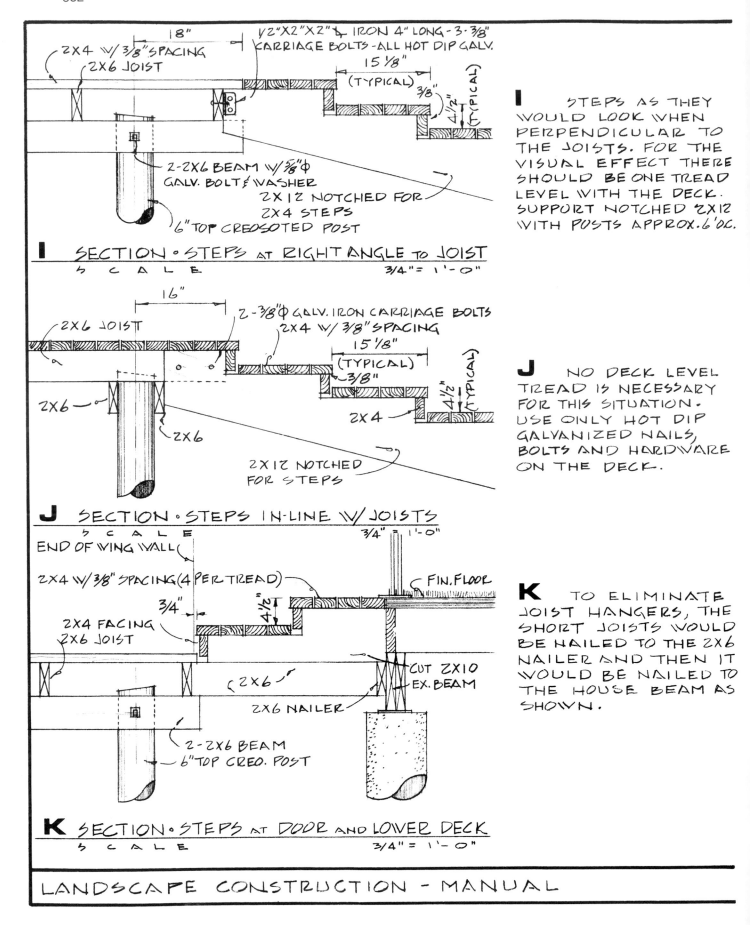

2X4 W/ 3/8" SPACING
2X6 JOIST
18"
1/2"X2"X2" ∠ IRON 4" LONG - 3-3/8"
CARRIAGE BOLTS - ALL HOT DIP GALV.
15 1/8"
(TYPICAL)
3/8"
4 1/2" (TYPICAL)

2-2X6 BEAM W/ 5/8"∅
GALV. BOLT & WASHER
2X12 NOTCHED FOR
2X4 STEPS
6" TOP CREOSOTED POST

I SECTION • STEPS AT RIGHT ANGLE TO JOIST
SCALE   3/4" = 1'-0"

I STEPS AS THEY WOULD LOOK WHEN PERPENDICULAR TO THE JOISTS. FOR THE VISUAL EFFECT THERE SHOULD BE ONE TREAD LEVEL WITH THE DECK. SUPPORT NOTCHED 2X12 WITH POSTS APPROX. 6' OC.

16"
2X6 JOIST
2 - 3/8"∅ GALV. IRON CARRIAGE BOLTS
2X4 W/ 3/8" SPACING
15 1/8"
(TYPICAL)
3/8"
4 1/2" (TYPICAL)
2X6
2X6
2X4
2X12 NOTCHED FOR STEPS

J SECTION • STEPS IN-LINE W/ JOISTS
SCALE   3/4" = 1'-0"

J NO DECK LEVEL TREAD IS NECESSARY FOR THIS SITUATION. USE ONLY HOT DIP GALVANIZED NAILS, BOLTS AND HARDWARE ON THE DECK.

END OF WING WALL
2X4 W/ 3/8" SPACING (4 PER TREAD)
3/4"
4 1/2"
FIN. FLOOR
2X4 FACING
2X6 JOIST
2X6
CUT 2X10 EX. BEAM
2X6 NAILER
2-2X6 BEAM
6" TOP CREO. POST

K SECTION • STEPS AT DOOR AND LOWER DECK
SCALE   3/4" = 1'-0"

K TO ELIMINATE JOIST HANGERS, THE SHORT JOISTS WOULD BE NAILED TO THE 2X6 NAILER AND THEN IT WOULD BE NAILED TO THE HOUSE BEAM AS SHOWN.

LANDSCAPE CONSTRUCTION - MANUAL

L   THIS IS A SIMPLE BUT GOOD SEAT/RAIL COMBINATION. FOR DECKS OVER 5' OR 6' OFF THE GROUND, ANOTHER DETAIL MAY BE DESIRABLE. THE BOLTS GOING BOTH WAYS WILL GIVE A VERY STURDY SEAT THAT WILL ADD TO THE SECURE FEELING.

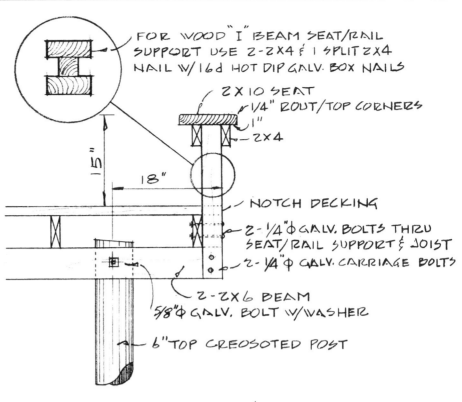

FOR WOOD "I" BEAM SEAT/RAIL SUPPORT USE 2-2X4 & 1 SPLIT 2X4 NAIL W/16d HOT DIP GALV. BOX NAILS

2X10 SEAT
1/4" ROUT/TOP CORNERS
1"
2X4

15"

18"

NOTCH DECKING

2-1/4"⌀ GALV. BOLTS THRU SEAT/RAIL SUPPORT & JOIST

2-1/4"⌀ GALV. CARRIAGE BOLTS

2-2X6 BEAM
5/8"⌀ GALV. BOLT W/WASHER

6" TOP CREOSOTED POST

L   SECTION • SEAT/RAIL
SCALE   3/4" = 1'-0"

M   USE ONLY TREATED WOOD FOR DECK CONSTRUCTION. STAIN AS DESIRED. SOME OF THE SILVER GRAY STAINS WILL GIVE THE APPEARANCE OF WEATHERED WOOD.

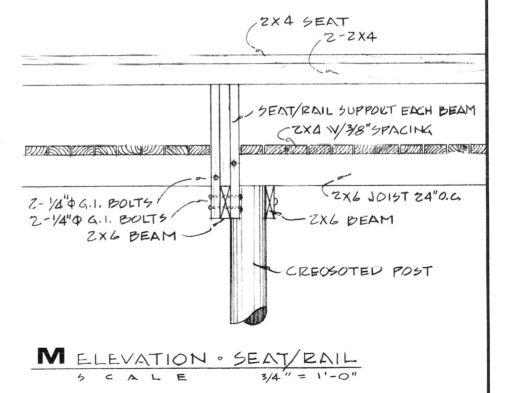

2X4 SEAT
2-2X4

SEAT/RAIL SUPPORT EACH BEAM
2X4 W/3/8" SPACING

2-1/4"⌀ G.I. BOLTS
2-1/4"⌀ G.I. BOLTS
2X6 BEAM

2X6 JOIST 24" O.C.
2X6 BEAM

CREOSOTED POST

M ELEVATION • SEAT/RAIL
SCALE   3/4" = 1'-0"

DECK DETAILS

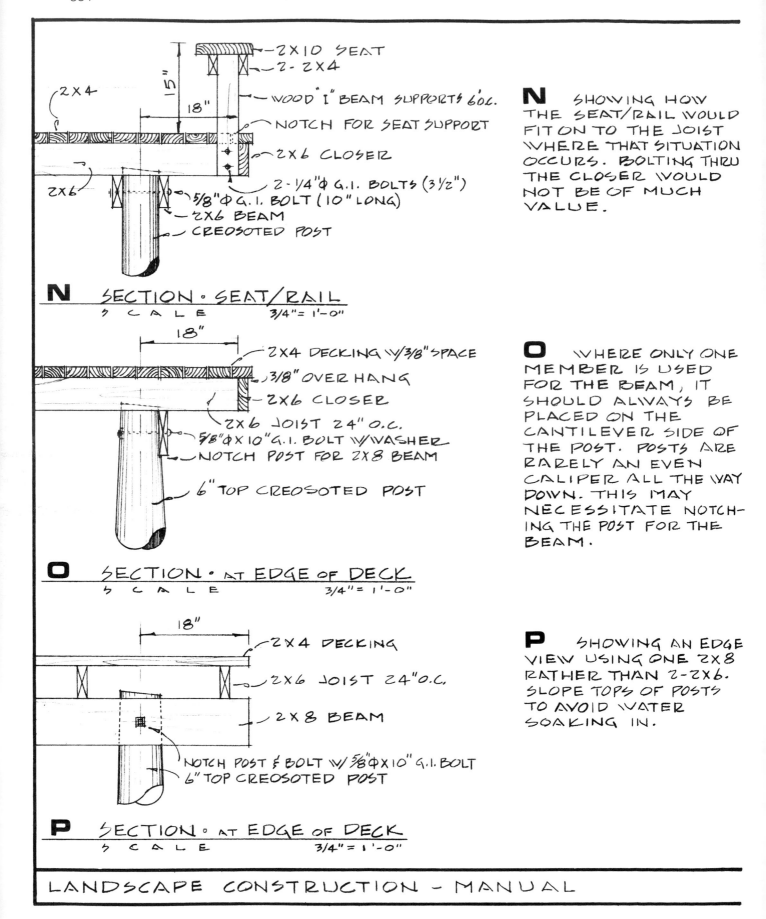

N SECTION · SEAT/RAIL
SCALE   3/4" = 1'-0"

- 2X10 SEAT
- 2-2X4
- WOOD "I" BEAM SUPPORTS 6'O.C.
- NOTCH FOR SEAT SUPPORT
- 2X6 CLOSER
- 2-1/4"ø G.I. BOLTS (3½")
- 5/8"ø G.I. BOLT (10" LONG)
- 2X6 BEAM
- CREOSOTED POST

2X4
2X6

15"
18"

N SHOWING HOW THE SEAT/RAIL WOULD FIT ON TO THE JOIST WHERE THAT SITUATION OCCURS. BOLTING THRU THE CLOSER WOULD NOT BE OF MUCH VALUE.

O SECTION · AT EDGE OF DECK
SCALE   3/4" = 1'-0"

18"
- 2X4 DECKING W/3/8" SPACE
- 3/8" OVER HANG
- 2X6 CLOSER
- 2X6 JOIST 24" O.C.
- 5/8"øX10" G.I. BOLT W/WASHER
- NOTCH POST FOR 2X8 BEAM
- 6" TOP CREOSOTED POST

O WHERE ONLY ONE MEMBER IS USED FOR THE BEAM, IT SHOULD ALWAYS BE PLACED ON THE CANTILEVER SIDE OF THE POST. POSTS ARE RARELY AN EVEN CALIPER ALL THE WAY DOWN. THIS MAY NECESSITATE NOTCHING THE POST FOR THE BEAM.

P SECTION · AT EDGE OF DECK
SCALE   3/4" = 1'-0"

18"
- 2X4 DECKING
- 2X6 JOIST 24" O.C.
- 2X8 BEAM
- NOTCH POST & BOLT W/ 5/8"øX10" G.I. BOLT
- 6" TOP CREOSOTED POST

P SHOWING AN EDGE VIEW USING ONE 2X8 RATHER THAN 2-2X6. SLOPE TOPS OF POSTS TO AVOID WATER SOAKING IN.

Q THIS IS JUST ONE OF MANY DESIGNS THAT MAY BE USED AT THE EDGE OF A DECK. THIS GIVES A SEAT WITH A BACK REST. NOTE THAT THIS DETAIL WILL BLOCK SOME OF THE VIEW FROM INSIDE THE HOUSE.

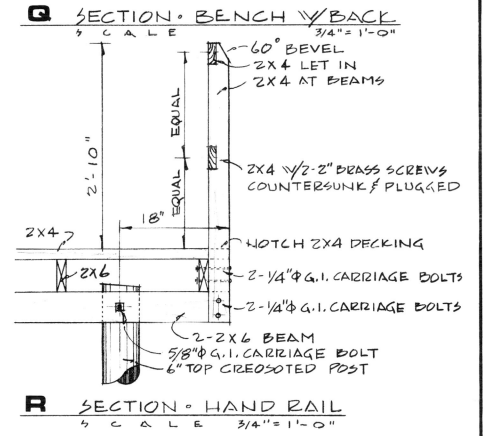

18°

2X4
2X2

SAND TOP & SEAT 2X4
2X4
2X4 LET IN

18"

15"

10°

LET 2X4 IN & COUNTERSINK
2" BRASS SCREWS
2X4

15"

NOTCH DECKING
2X GUSSET
2-1/4"⌀ G.I. BOLTS
2-1/4"⌀ G.I. BOLTS

1/4"⌀ G.I. BOLT

2-2X6 BEAM

17"

6" TOP CREOSOTED POST

Q SECTION · BENCH W/ BACK
SCALE   3/4" = 1'-0"

R FOR A HIGH DECK SOME TYPE OF SAFETY PROVISIONS MUST BE MADE. THIS COULD HAVE A NYLON FISH NET ATTACHED FOR BABIES. THIS ALSO WILL BLOCK VIEW TO SOME EXTENT.

60° BEVEL
2X4 LET IN
2X4 AT BEAMS

2'-10"

EQUAL
EQUAL
EQUAL

2X4 W/2-2" BRASS SCREWS
COUNTERSUNK & PLUGGED

2X4

18"

NOTCH 2X4 DECKING

2X6

2-1/4"⌀ G.I. CARRIAGE BOLTS

2-1/4"⌀ G.I. CARRIAGE BOLTS

2-2X6 BEAM
5/8"⌀ G.I. CARRIAGE BOLT
6" TOP CREOSOTED POST

R SECTION · HAND RAIL
SCALE   3/4" = 1'-0"

DECK DETAILS

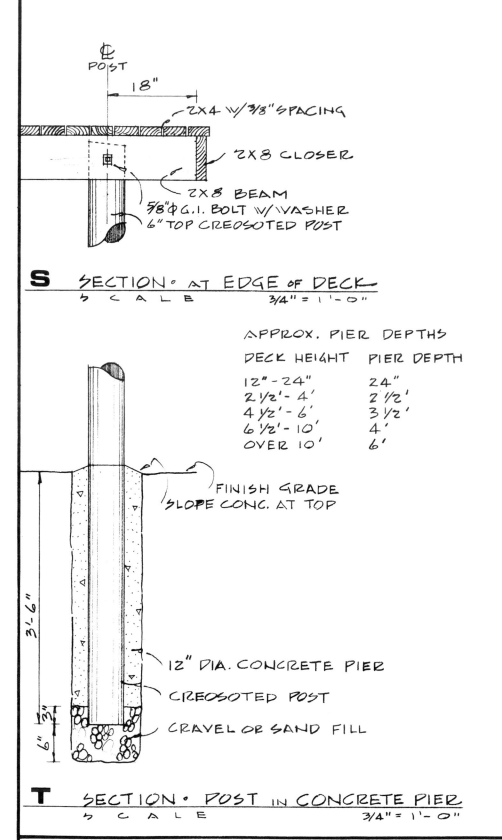

℄
POST

18"

2X4 W/3/8" SPACING

2X8 CLOSER

2X8 BEAM
5/8" Ø G.I. BOLT W/ WASHER
6" TOP CREOSOTED POST

S SECTION• AT EDGE OF DECK
SCALE   3/4" = 1'-0"

APPROX. PIER DEPTHS

DECK HEIGHT	PIER DEPTH
12" - 24"	24"
2 1/2' - 4'	2 1/2'
4 1/2' - 6'	3 1/2'
6 1/2' - 10'	4'
OVER 10'	6'

FINISH GRADE
SLOPE CONC. AT TOP

3'-6"

3"

6"

12" DIA. CONCRETE PIER

CREOSOTED POST

GRAVEL OR SAND FILL

T SECTION• POST IN CONCRETE PIER
SCALE   3/4" = 1'-0"

S THIS DETAIL IS OFTEN REFERRED TO AS PLANK AND BEAM CONSTRUCTION. THE JOIST IS OMITTED AND THE 2X8 IN THIS DETAIL SERVES BOTH AS A BEAM AND A JOIST. THE POSTS ALONG THE BEAM ARE SPACED AS INDICATED ON THE BASIC SYSTEM; BUT THE BEAMS MUST BE CLOSER TOGETHER (4' MAX. FOR 2X4 DECKING), THUS MORE POSTS ARE NECESSARY. MOST OFTEN USED WHERE DECK IS TOO LOW TO ACCOMMODATE BOTH BEAM AND JOIST.

T SHOWING ONE OF THE BETTER METHODS OF SECURING DECK POST INTO GROUND. THIS GIVES A MOST STABLE DECK THAT IS FREE OF SWAY OR RACKING. PROJECT THE POST THRU THE CONCRETE TO AVOID WATER RUNNING DOWN THE POST AND COLLECTING. GRAVEL OR SHARP SAND WILL ALSO HELP KEEP THE END OF THE POST DRY. TAMPING THE ENTIRE BACK FILL FOR THE POST WITH A DAMP FILL SAND WILL WORK ABOUT AS WELL AS USING CONCRETE AS A BACK FILL.

LANDSCAPE CONSTRUCTION - MANUAL

U CONCRETE PIER/POST ARE TOO "HEAVY" FOR MOST DECK CONSTRUCTION. FOR SHEAR, SOME REINFORCING BARS ARE NECESSARY WHERE DECK HEIGHTS ARE ABOVE 4'.

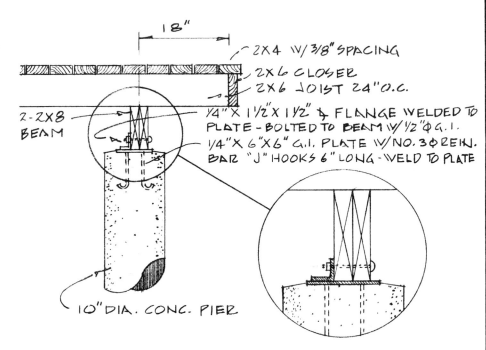

2X4 W/3/8" SPACING
2X6 CLOSER
2X6 JOIST 24"O.C.
2-2X8 BEAM
1/4"X 1 1/2"X 1 1/2" & FLANGE WELDED TO PLATE - BOLTED TO BEAM W/1/2"Ø G.I.
1/4"X 6"X 6" G.I. PLATE W/NO.3Ø REIN. BAR "J" HOOKS 6" LONG - WELD TO PLATE
10"DIA. CONC. PIER

U SECTION · CONC. PIER W/WOOD BEAM
SCALE 3/4" = 1'-0"

V WHEN METAL BEAMS ARE USED, POSTS CAN BE SPACED MUCH FARTHER APART. PERHAPS EVEN AS A CANTIVEVERED DECK. A NAILER MUST BE BOLTED TO THE TOP OF THE BEAM SO THAT EACH JOIST CAN BE TOE NAILED INTO IT.

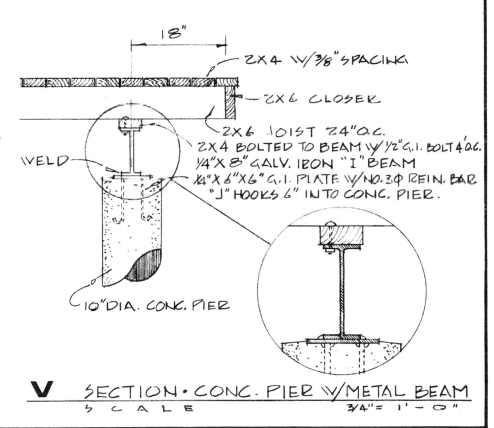

2X4 W/3/8" SPACING
2X6 CLOSER
WELD
2X6 JOIST 24"O.C.
2X4 BOLTED TO BEAM W/1/2"G.I. BOLT 4 O.C.
1/4"X 8" GALV. IRON "I" BEAM
1/4"X 6"X 6" G.I. PLATE W/NO.3Ø REIN. BAR "J" HOOKS 6" INTO CONC. PIER.
10"DIA. CONC. PIER

V SECTION · CONC. PIER W/METAL BEAM
SCALE 3/4" = 1'-0"

DECK DETAILS

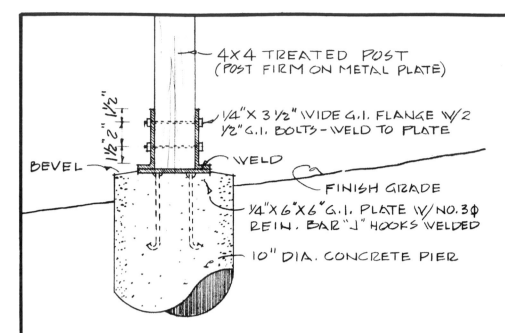

4X4 TREATED POST
(POST FIRM ON METAL PLATE)

1/4" X 3 1/2" WIDE G.I. FLANGE W/2
1/2" G.I. BOLTS - WELD TO PLATE

BEVEL

WELD

FINISH GRADE

1/4" X 6" X 6" G.I. PLATE W/NO. 3∅
REIN. BAR "J" HOOKS WELDED

10" DIA. CONCRETE PIER

W SECTION · CONC. FTG. W/FLANGES
SCALE   1 1/2" = 1'-0"

W WHERE THERE IS SOME REASON TO PLACE A POST ON A CONCRETE FOOTING, IT IS EASIER TO USE A CUT POST (4X4, 4X6, 6X6, ETC.) THAN A ROUND POST. A ROUND POST COULD BE NOTCHED AT THE BOTTOM, HOWEVER. THE DETAILS ON THIS AND THE NEXT PAGE ARE NOT SUGGESTED WHERE RACKING MAY OCCUR.

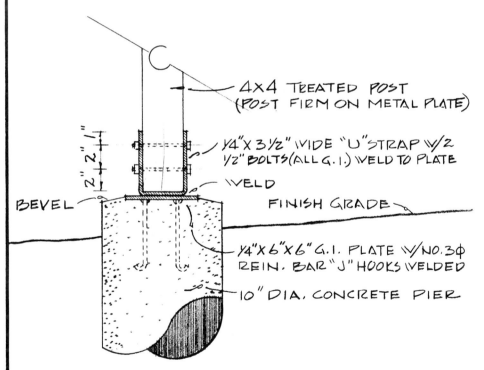

4X4 TREATED POST
(POST FIRM ON METAL PLATE)

1/4" X 3 1/2" WIDE "U" STRAP W/2
1/2" BOLTS (ALL G.I.) WELD TO PLATE

BEVEL

WELD

FINISH GRADE

1/4" X 6" X 6" G.I. PLATE W/NO. 3∅
REIN. BAR "J" HOOKS WELDED

10" DIA. CONCRETE PIER

X SECTION · CONC. FTG. W/"U" STRAP
SCALE   1 1/2" = 1'-0"

X THIS DETAIL DIFFERS VERY LITTLE FROM THAT ABOVE. IT IS IMPORTANT IN BOTH DETAILS TO HAVE THE POST RESTING ON THE BOTTOM AND NOT ON THE BOLTS. FOOTING DEPTH WILL DEPEND UPON SOIL CONDITIONS, ETC.

LANDSCAPE CONSTRUCTION - MANUAL

Y FOR VERY LOW DECKS A SIMPLE PRE-CAST FOOTING WITH A NAILER CAST INSIDE MAY SERVE THE PURPOSE.

12" SQ. BOTTOM - 8" SQ. TOP PRECAST CONCRETE

4 X 4 NAILER CAST IN CONC.

BEVEL TOP TO SHED WATER

Y PLAN · PRECAST CONC. FOOTING

SCALE   1 1/2" = 1'-0"

Z A BEAM COULD BE PLACED ON TOP OF THIS AND TOE NAILED TO THE 4 X 4. IF POSTS ARE USED AND TOE NAILED TO THE 4 X 4, RACKING COULD BE A PROBLEM.

2"   8"   2"

BEVEL TOP OF FOOTING

4X4 TREATED NAILER W/ 16d GALV. COMMON NAILS

CONCRETE

FINISH GRADE

8"

ON UNDISTURBED SOIL

Z SECTION · PRECAST CONC. FOOTING

SCALE   1 1/2" = 1'-0"

AA SAME AS ABOVE EXCEPT DEEPER. IT MAY BE USED WHERE FILL HAS OCCURRED OR TO GET BELOW THE FROST LINE.

4"   8"   4"

BEVEL TOP OF FOOTING

4X4 TREATED NAILER W/ 16d GALV. COMMON NAILS

FINISH GRADE

14"

CONCRETE

ON UNDISTURBED SOIL

AA SECTION · PRECAST CONC. FOOTING

SCALE   1 1/2" = 1'-0"

DECK   DETAILS

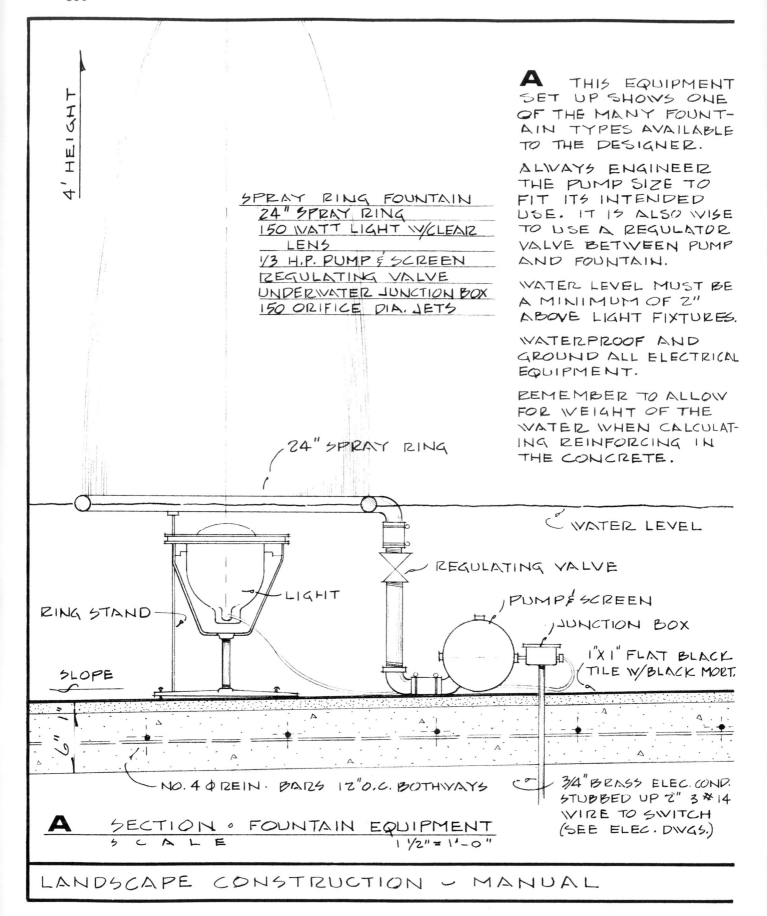

4' HEIGHT

SPRAY RING FOUNTAIN
24" SPRAY RING
150 WATT LIGHT W/CLEAR
    LENS
1/3 H.P. PUMP & SCREEN
REGULATING VALVE
UNDERWATER JUNCTION BOX
150 ORIFICE DIA. JETS

A   THIS EQUIPMENT SET UP SHOWS ONE OF THE MANY FOUNTAIN TYPES AVAILABLE TO THE DESIGNER.

ALWAYS ENGINEER THE PUMP SIZE TO FIT ITS INTENDED USE. IT IS ALSO WISE TO USE A REGULATOR VALVE BETWEEN PUMP AND FOUNTAIN.

WATER LEVEL MUST BE A MINIMUM OF 2" ABOVE LIGHT FIXTURES.

WATERPROOF AND GROUND ALL ELECTRICAL EQUIPMENT.

REMEMBER TO ALLOW FOR WEIGHT OF THE WATER WHEN CALCULATING REINFORCING IN THE CONCRETE.

24" SPRAY RING

WATER LEVEL

REGULATING VALVE

PUMP & SCREEN

JUNCTION BOX

RING STAND

LIGHT

SLOPE

1" X 1" FLAT BLACK TILE W/BLACK MORT.

6" 1"

NO. 4 Ø REIN. BARS 12" O.C. BOTH WAYS

3/4" BRASS ELEC. COND. STUBBED UP 2" 3 #14 WIRE TO SWITCH (SEE ELEC. DWGS.)

A   SECTION ○ FOUNTAIN EQUIPMENT
SCALE   1 1/2" = 1'-0"

LANDSCAPE CONSTRUCTION ○ MANUAL

B NO POOL SHOULD BE BUILT WITH OUT AN AUTOMATIC WATER FEED AND AN EASY METHOD FOR DRAINING.

WHERE THE POOL CAN NOT BE CONSTRUCTED WITH A MONOLITHIC POUR, A KEY JOINT WILL HELP TO WATERPROOF IT.

CONCRETE IS TOO POROUS FOR THE POOL FINISH AND IT IS SUGGESTED THAT 1" STIFF MORTAR BE APPLIED TO THE INSIDE SURFACE TO CONTAIN THE WATER.

BLACK TILE WILL GIVE THE POOL A MIRROR LIKE QUALITY, THUS KEEPING THE EQUIPMENT FROM BECOMING TOO OBVIOUS. TILE OR A LIKE SMOOTH SURFACE IS NECESSARY FOR A POOL IF IT IS TO BE MAINTAINED WITH EASE.

OVERFLOW DRAIN TO BE CAST IRON OVERFLOW DRAIN WITH WATERPROOFING FLANGE - 2" I.P.S. OUTLET 17" HT. BRASS STANDPIPE THREADED INTO GROUND JOINT ADAPTER WHICH FITS INTO BRASS ADJUSTABLE COLLAR AND BRASS LIFT OFF DOME

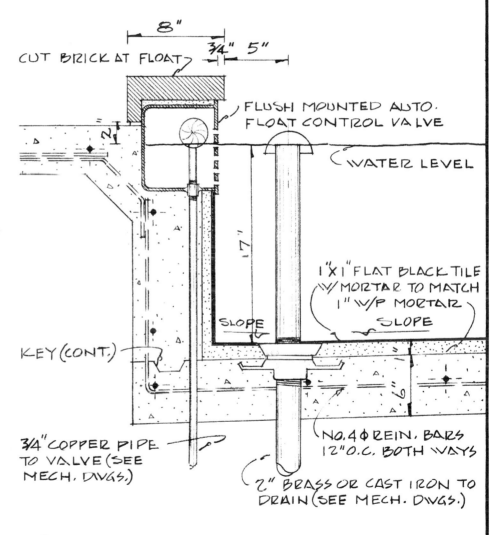

8"

3/4" 5"

CUT BRICK AT FLOAT

FLUSH MOUNTED AUTO. FLOAT CONTROL VALVE

WATER LEVEL

17"

1"X1" FLAT BLACK TILE W/ MORTAR TO MATCH 1" W/P MORTAR

SLOPE

SLOPE

KEY (CONT.)

3/4" COPPER PIPE TO VALVE (SEE MECH. DWGS.)

NO.4 Ø REIN. BARS 12" O.C. BOTH WAYS

2" BRASS OR CAST IRON TO DRAIN (SEE MECH. DWGS.)

B SECTION • POOL FOUNTAIN
SCALE 1 1/2" = 1'-0"

POOL FOUNTAIN DETAILS

LIGHT TO BE MERCURY
VAPOR SEMI-RECESSED
UP LIGHT WITH 100 WATT
M.V. LAMP. COMPLETE
WITH TRANSFORMER
ENCLOSED IN WATERPROOF
JUNCTION BOX - FULL 360
DEGREE SHIELD.

A TO AVOID THE MAINTENANCE TIME INVOLVED IN TRIMMING PLANTS AT LIGHT FIXTURES WHEN THEY OCCUR IN PLANT BEDS, A SHIELD TO THE HEIGHT OF THE PLANTS SHOULD BE A PART OF THE DESIGN.

MERCURY VAPOR HAS A LIGHT SPECTRUM THAT TENDS TO MAKE GREEN FOLIAGE APPEAR EVEN GREEN-ER.

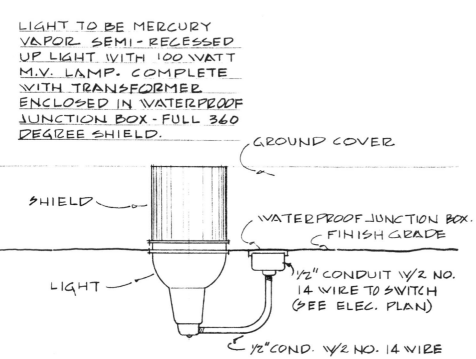

GROUND COVER

SHIELD

WATERPROOF JUNCTION BOX.
FINISH GRADE

LIGHT

1/2" CONDUIT W/2 NO.
14 WIRE TO SWITCH
(SEE ELEC. PLAN)

1/2" COND. W/2 NO. 14 WIRE

A SEMI-RECESSED UP LIGHT IN PLANT BED
S C A L E   1 1/2" = 1'-0"

200 WATT P.A.R. LAMP

ALL BRONZE LIGHT
WITH 3/8" THICK
TEMPERED IMPACT
RESISTING FLAT LENS,
WITH NEOPRENE
GASKET

B FOR LIGHTING THE FACADE OF A STRUCTURE, A LIGHT RECESSED INTO AN EXTENDED MOWING EDGE FROM THE STRUCTURE WILL SECURE IT AS WELL AS REDUCE MAINTEN- ANCE REQUIRED WITH FIXTURES IN TURF AREAS.

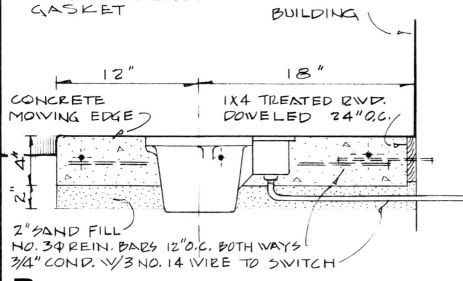

BUILDING

12"   18"

CONCRETE
MOWING EDGE

1X4 TREATED RWD.
DOWELED 24" O.C.

4"

2"

2" SAND FILL
NO. 3Φ REIN. BARS 12" O.C. BOTH WAYS
3/4" COND. W/3 NO. 14 WIRE TO SWITCH

B ADJUSTABLE LIGHT IN CONCRETE
S C A L E   1 1/2" = 1'-0"

LANDSCAPE CONSTRUCTION - MANUAL

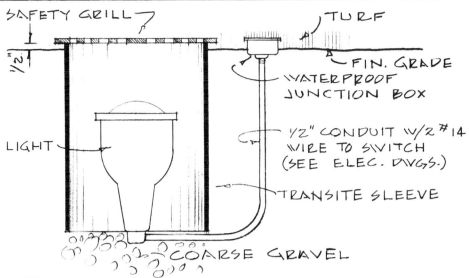

C USING A SLEEVE TO RECESS UP LIGHTS THAT OCCUR IN TURF AREAS. MAY BE USED UNDER TREES, ETC.

SAFETY GRILL

TURF

FIN. GRADE

LIGHT

WATERPROOF JUNCTION BOX

½" CONDUIT W/2 #14 WIRE TO SWITCH (SEE ELEC. DWGS.)

TRANSITE SLEEVE

COARSE GRAVEL

C RECESSED UP LIGHT IN TURF
S C A L E   1 ½" = 1'-0"

LIGHT TO BE MERCURY VAPOR WITH 100 WATT M.V. LAMP COMPLETE WITH TRANSFORMER ENCLOSED IN WATERPROOF JUNCTION BOX. COPPER AND BRONZE WATERPROOF UNIT WITH HEAT RESISTANT CLEAR LENS AND MOLDED SILICONE GASKET - TRANSITE SLEEVE WITH GRILL.

D SAME FIXTURE AS ABOVE BUT OCCURING WITHIN A MAINTENANCE BORDER ADJACENT TO A STRUCTURE.

DRAIN AWAY FROM FIXTURE AND PLACE GRAVEL UNDER IT.

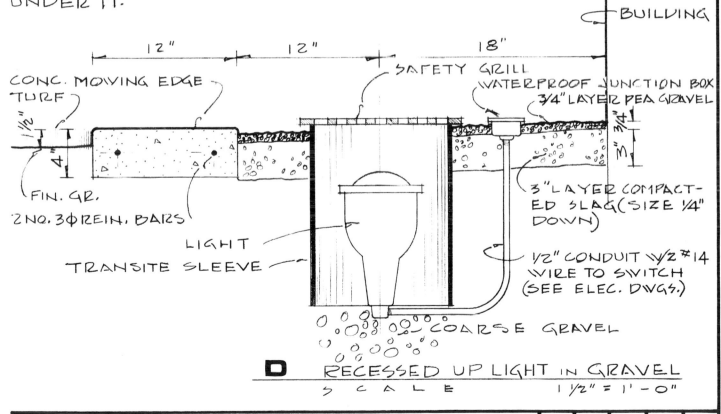

CONC. MOWING EDGE
TURF

FIN. GR.
2 NO. 3 ∅ REIN. BARS

LIGHT

TRANSITE SLEEVE

12"

12"

18"

SAFETY GRILL

BUILDING

WATERPROOF JUNCTION BOX

¾" LAYER PEA GRAVEL

3" LAYER COMPACTED SLAG (SIZE ¼" DOWN)

½" CONDUIT W/2 #14 WIRE TO SWITCH (SEE ELEC. DWGS.)

COARSE GRAVEL

D RECESSED UP LIGHT IN GRAVEL
S C A L E   1 ½" = 1'-0"

LIGHT   DETAILS

393

394

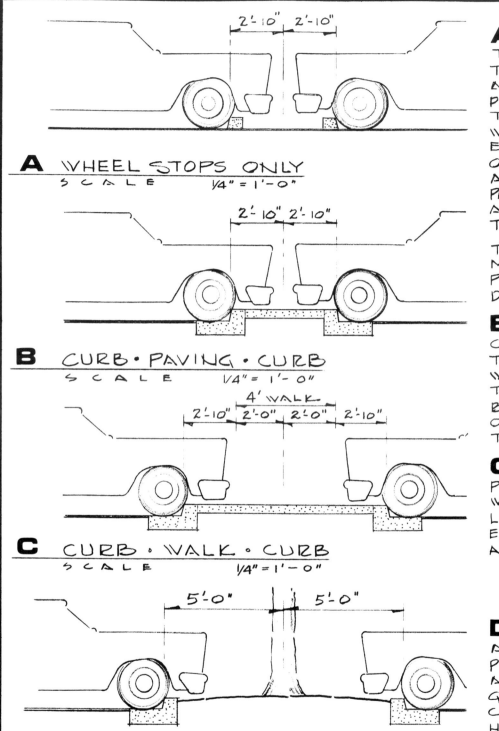

A WHEEL STOPS ONLY
S C A L E   1/4" = 1'-0"

B CURB · PAVING · CURB
S C A L E   1/4" = 1'-0"

C CURB · WALK · CURB
S C A L E   1/4" = 1'-0"

D CURB · GROUND COVER & TREE · CURB
S C A L E   1/4" = 1'-0"

A THE SIMPLEST THING FOR PARKING IS TO PAVE THE AREA WITH ASPHALT AND INSTALL PRECAST WHEEL STOPS. THE BARS HOLDING THE WHEEL STOPS DOWN WILL EVENTUALLY BE PUSHED OUT, TEARING UP THE ASPHALT, REQUIRING PATCHING OF THE PAVING AND REPLACEMENT OF THE WHEEL STOPS.

TRASH AND SNOW REMOVAL IS ALSO A PROBLEM WITH THIS DETAIL.

B GUTTERS ON THE CURB WILL HELP HOLD THEM UPRIGHT FOR THE WEIGHT OF THE FRONT OF THE CAR WILL HELP BALANCE THE FORCE OF THE TIRE STRIKING THE CURB.

C THIS AND THE PRECEDING SECTION WOULD BEST BE A MONOLITHIC POUR WITH EXPANSION JOINTS APPROX. 20' APART.

D THE OVERHANG OF AN AUTO WILL NOT PERMIT TURF IN THIS AREA. INDEED THE GROUND COVER COULD NOT BE VERY HIGH ITSELF THE 5' MINIMUM IS TO PROTECT THE TREE FROM THOSE WHO WILL BACK INTO A PARKING SPACE.

LANDSCAPE CONSTRUCTION — MANUAL

E   THIS EXTENTION AT TOP OF THE CURB WILL ALLOW TURF TO BE PLANTED AND A REASONABLE LOCATION FOR SPRINKLER HEADS FOR BOTH TURF OR GROUND COVER.

F   FOR A MINIMUM WALK ALONG ONE SIDE OF THE PARKING ROWS.

CARS BACKING IN WILL BLOCK THIS WALK.

G   SHOWING AN APPROXIMATELY 4' WIDE PLANT SCREEN.

H   MINIMUM DISTANCE FOR A TREE ROW AND TWO WALKS.

NOTE: ALL SECTIONS ON THESE TWO PAGES MUST HAVE STEEL REINFORCING AS HERE-IN-BEFORE SHOWN.

LANDINGS OR WALKS ADJACENT TO CURBS SHOULD BE MONOLITHIC OR BE DOVELED AS SHOWN ON THE FOLLOWING PAGE.

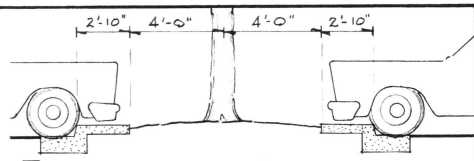

2'-10"   4'-0"   4'-0"   2'-10"

E   CURB · PAVING · G.C. & TREE · PAVING · CURB
SCALE   1/4" = 1'-0"

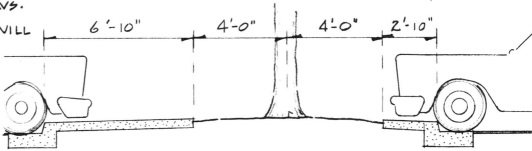

6'-10"   4'-0"   4'-0"   2'-10"

F   CURB · WALK · G.C. & TREE · PAVING · CURB
SCALE   1/4" = 1'-0"

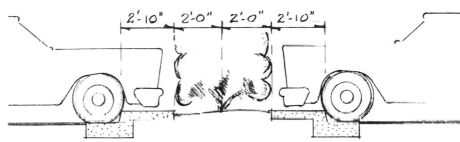

2'-10"   2'-0"   2'-0"   2'-10"

G   CURB · PAVING · SHRUB · PAVING · CURB
SCALE   1/4" = 1'-0"

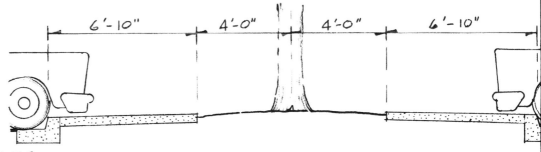

6'-10"   4'-0"   4'-0"   6'-10"

H   CURB · WALK · G.C. & TREE · WALK · CURB
SCALE   1/4" = 1'-0"

PARKING STANDARDS (90°)

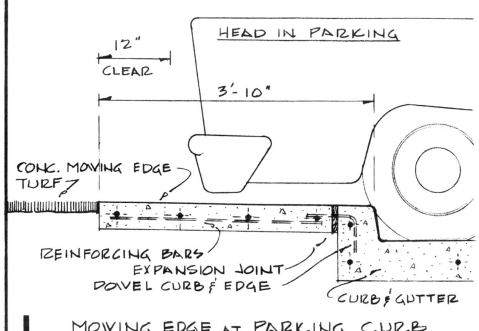

HEAD IN PARKING

12" CLEAR

3'-10"

CONC. MOVING EDGE
TURF

REINFORCING BARS
EXPANSION JOINT
DOWEL CURB & EDGE

CURB & GUTTER

I MOWING EDGE AT PARKING CURB
SCALE   3/4" = 1'-0"

I 10" TO 12" BEYOND THE OVERHANG WILL ALLOW A MOWER OR EDGER WHEEL TO RIDE ON THE CONCRETE WHILE THE CAR IS PARKED.

2'-10" FROM THE FACE OF THE CURB IS SUFFICIENT WHERE GROUND COVER RE-PLACES THE TURF.

THIS SECTION SHOWS AN EXPANSION JOINT BETWEEN THE CURB AND MOWING EDGE. IT IS IMPORTANT THAT IT BE DOWELED.

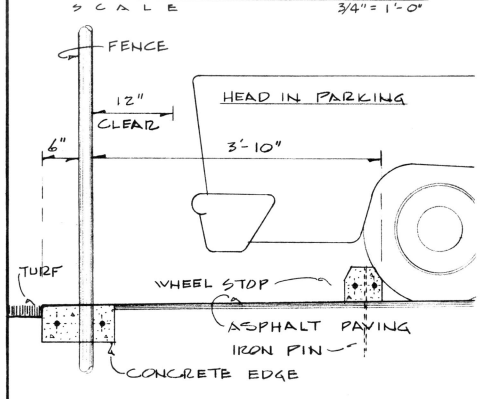

FENCE

HEAD IN PARKING

12" CLEAR

6"

3'-10"

TURF

WHEEL STOP

ASPHALT PAVING
IRON PIN

CONCRETE EDGE

J WHEEL STOP AT FENCE
SCALE   3/4" = 1'-0"

J ASPHALT MUST ALWAYS HAVE A PERMANENT STRUCT-URAL EDGE; HERE THE EDGE ALSO SERVES AS A MOWING AND TRIMMING LINE BEYOND THE FENCE.

12" BEYOND THE FENCE WOULD BE A BETTER SITUATION.

LANDSCAPE CONSTRUCTION - MANUAL

K HEAD IN PARK-
ING WHERE A
STRUCTURAL WALL
OCCURS. THIS WOULD
BE MINIMUM AND
WOULD NOT ALLOW
FOR THE CAR BEING
BACKED INTO THE
PARKING SPACE.

THE MONOLITHIC
CURB, GUTTER AND
PAVING AT TOP OF
CURB IS DESIRABLE
OVER AN EXPANSION
JOINT AT THE BACK
SIDE OF THE CURB.

AN EXPANSION JOINT
IS NECESSARY AT THE
WALL.

L SHOWING THE
SAME SECTION AS
ABOVE AS IT MUST
BE ADAPTED TO
BACKING THE CAR
INTO THE PARKING
SPACE.

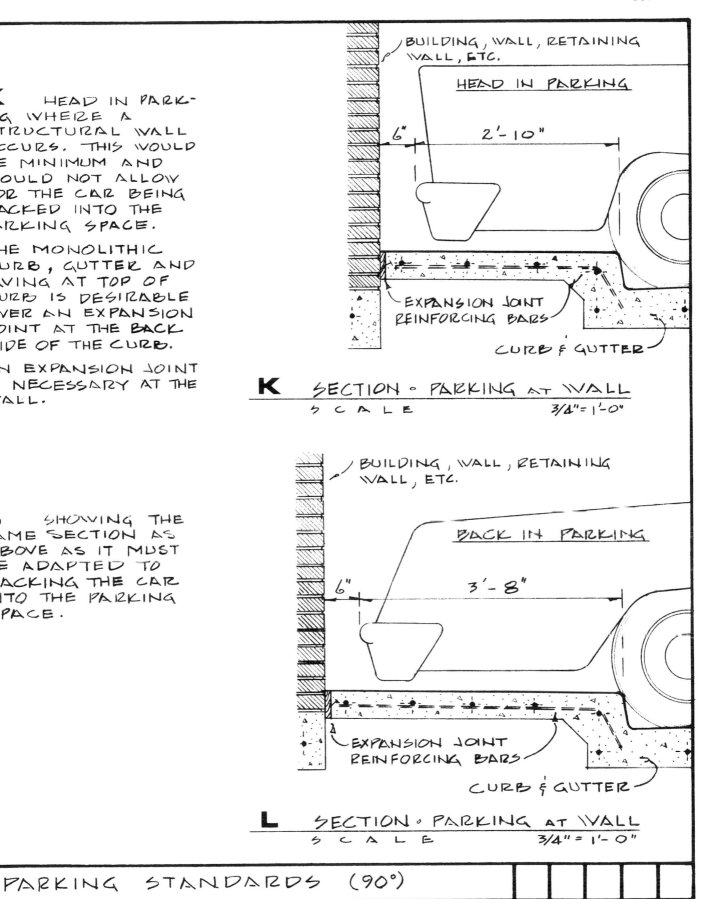

BUILDING, WALL, RETAINING WALL, ETC.

HEAD IN PARKING

6" 2'-10"

EXPANSION JOINT
REINFORCING BARS

CURB & GUTTER

K SECTION · PARKING AT WALL
SCALE   3/4"=1'-0"

BUILDING, WALL, RETAINING WALL, ETC.

BACK IN PARKING

6" 3'-8"

EXPANSION JOINT
REINFORCING BARS

CURB & GUTTER

L SECTION · PARKING AT WALL
SCALE   3/4"=1'-0"

PARKING STANDARDS (90°)

Appendix

Contract Documents and Specifications

The final step in completing the work on a project is the preparation of the contract document package. While this is customarily the last thing to be accomplished on a project it is by no means the least important. In fact, a good set of construction documents will do much to guarantee the success of a job.

With the exception of the working drawings, the package of materials that makes up the contract documents is usually bound together in a single volume. This volume is referred to by many as the specifications or "specs." This term is misleading, however, since the specifications are only one part of the package. For this reason some have proposed that this document be referred to as the "project manual."

THE PROJECT MANUAL

While our primary concern in this brief discussion is the development of the technical specifications, it is helpful to briefly look at the other contract documents and how they relate to the technical specifications. The materials that constitute a full set of contract documents can be grouped into five separate catagories.

The Bidding Documents
  Legal advertisement or invitation to bid
  Instructions to bidders
  Bid forms
  Bid bond forms
Contract Forms
  The agreement
  Bond and insurance forms
Contract Conditions
  General conditions
  Supplementary conditions

The Technical Specifications
Working Drawings[1]

All of the materials together constitute a complete set of contract documents. By definition all of these documents are mutually supportive and no single document takes precedence. Notice that in this list of materials the working drawings are included. Sometimes it's easy to forget that the working drawings are in fact a part of the contract documents.

Bidding Documents

Depending on the office or agency the first pages in a project manual will be the bidding documents. The legal advertisement, or bid invitation, is a brief description of the work and describes how copies of the contract documents can be obtained for submitting a bid.

The instructions to bidders is a more detailed description of what is required for a bid submission. Some of the topics common to most instructions to bidders are how the contract will be awarded, when and where bids will be opened, site visit requirements, bid security requirements, methods for submitting material substitutions and modification of proposals and the owners right of acceptance or rejection. The amount of detail in this section depends a great deal on the client and the scope of the project. Government contracts typically require more detail than work in the private sector.

The bid forms are tailored to each job. They may require a simple lump sum bid for the job or they may require detailed unit price bids for various parts

---

[1]These are not usually bound into the project manual.

399

of the project. In addition, to the dollar figures the bid form will also require information about the time of execution and pledge to execute the agreement if offered.

For many contracts a bid bond is required as a part of the bid submission. This is usually in the form of a surety certificate or check in the amount of some specified percentage of the bid price. Bid bond forms are usually prepared and included as a part of the bidding documents.

Contract Forms

The contract forms are placed behind the bidding documents or, sometimes, in the last section of the project manual. The first form is the agreement. This is the actual contract which is the legal basis for the work.

In addition to the actual agreement form several bonds and proof of insurance may be required as a part of the contract. The kinds of bonds and insurance forms depend once again on the scope and complexity of the project.

Two bonds frequently required are the performance bond and the materials and labor bond. The performance bond is to insure that the contractor will faithfully perform the work required in the contract in accordance with the plans and specifications. Should the contractor fail to live up to the terms of the agreement the bonding agent is held responsible for completion of the work. The materials and labor bond is to insure that the contractor will pay for all the materials and labor incorporated in the project. This protects the owner from any claims that might be filed against the project as a result of nonpayment by the contractor.

Contract Conditions

The next section in the project manual is usually the contract conditions section. The contract conditions set the legal ground rules that will govern the execution of the work. Most offices and agencies utilize a standard form general conditions that is tailored to their type of practice. The AIA, ASLA, CSI and AGC publish a standard form general conditions that can be purchased from each organization at a nominal cost. There are twelve articles that are common to most forms of general conditions listed below.

- Definition and status of the contract documents;
- Administrative function of the landscape architect;
- Rights and responsibilities of the owner;
- Rights and responsibilities of the contractor;
- Subcontracting procedures;

- Arbitration of disputes;
- Insurance, performance, and payment bonds;
- Contract time, delays, and extension of time;
- Payments;
- Changes to the scope of work;
- Inspection and correction of work;
- Termination of the contract.

These articles are not necessarily found in all forms of general conditions, but it serves to illustrate the nature of the conditions section. All designers should be familar with the provisions of the general conditions that will be used in their particular situation because this section spells out the administrative procedures to be followed during construction.

Some projects are of such a nature that a standard form general conditions section will not satisfy all of the project requirements. This is frequently encountered on projects that are being partially financed by the federal government. In these situations it is customary to provide a second section called supplementary conditions. Typically this section will include articles that prohibit discrimination in employment, descriptions of material sources, and required wage and hour schedules. In other cases the supplementary conditions may set requirements for on site sanitation, furnishing of utilities such as power and water, provision of on-site security and other matters of a nontechnical nature. While this information will appear in the supplementary conditions the trend today seems to be toward putting it in the scope statement of each section in the technical specification as well.

TECHNICAL SPECIFICATIONS

The specifications provide information that concerns the type and quality of building materials, equipment, fixtures, and furniture that are to be incorporated into a project. The format of technical specifications for many years was a function of professional preference. However, the wide variation in form and language can result in costly errors and bitter lawsuits. Recognizing these wide variations in construction specifying the Construction Specifications Institute (CSI) and the American Institute (AIA) initiated a study aimed at developing an industry-wide standard specification form. Published in 1963, the construction specifications have become generally known as "the uniform system."

Shortly after its publication the uniform system was adopted by all the major organizations involved in the building industry, including ASLA. The transition to the uniform system format has been slow, but it appears that it is fast becoming the industry standard. The format of the uniform system and the development of the technical specifications is the subject of our discussion for the remainder of this section.

THE UNIFORM SYSTEM

The full title of the document known as the uniform system is The Uniform System for Construction Specifications, Data Filling and Cost Accounting. As we mentioned, this system was developed in response to the need for a more efficient data handling system. The first move toward the development of the Uniform System was generated when the AIA invited the Construction Specifications Institute to join with them in an effort to develop a standardized data-filing system for building products. This effort resulted in the concept of a filing system based on specifications practice. This idea led directly to the expansion of the concept to include a specification outline and a system for cost accounting.

All three systems are based on the specifications outline which organizes all information into sixteen groups designated as divisions. Each of the sixteen divisions is based on the close associations that exist between construction timing, trade, functional requirement, and materials.

The Specification Outline

The specification outline is developed around two principles. First, that the sixteen divisions are constant. They are broad and describe the relationships between units of work. For example division 2 is site work. Units of work under this division are such things as clearing, earth work, drainage, etc. The units of work are referred to as sections. The sections will vary according to the job, but they should always occur under the proper division.

Work units that are common to most projects, like earth work, are called broad scope sections. These titles should always be the same and follow in the order of the outline. It is also recommended that broad scope sections be typed in capital letters. Narrow scope sections are those work units that are less typical on a job such as dewatering. These titles are typed with initial capitals and lowercase letters. In some cases narrow scope sections can take precedence over a broad scope section. For instance, site grading is frequently used as a broad scope section rather than making it subordinate to earthwork.

The sixteen divisions of the uniform system and the broad scope sections for each division are shown in Figure A–1. You will notice that some of the divisions and many of the sections do not have wide application to landscape construction. Under the uniform system this poses no problem. If a division or section does not apply to a job it is simply omitted from the specifications. However, division titles and the order of the sections will not change. For example, if a project involved only site work, carpentry, and some painting the technical specifications outline would be General Requirements—Division 1, Site Work—Division 2, Carpentry—Division 6, and Finishes—Division 9. Under each of the appropriate divisions the pertinent broad scope and narrow scope sections would be included in order as they appear in the outline.

The advantages of having a widely accepted standard outline for technical specifications are numerous. The chance for errors or misunderstandings between the designers and contractors is minimized because each one is more familiar with the system. The time for writing is reduced and the system lends itself to computer adaptation and the use of automated typing equipment.

Writing Technical Specifications

The technical specifications for a project are seldom written from scratch. Most agencies and offices have extensive collections of project specifications from previous work. In addition to these materials there are several reference manuals that provide detailed specifications for almost any imaginable project. Some of the more useful references for landscape architects are publications by ASLA, CSI, AIA, and the American Association of Nurserymen (AAN).

Regardless of the manual that is selected as a specification guide it is usually necessary to modify the specification to fit the job at hand. This is very important. Many of the costly errors made in construction specifying are the result of poor editing rather than an actual error or omission in the writing. What follows is a suggested procedure that can be used as a guide to specification writing.

Collect the materials that will be required to write the specifications. A typical list would include:

- A set of working drawings;
- Catalogs and manufacturer's literature;
- A specification outline, old specifications or an appropriate specification guide;
- A materials takeoff (if this is not already available it should be done as a preparation to writing).
- A list of site conditions, restrictions, permit requirements or other information that might effect the work flow;
- A list of available construction materials, local suppliers, and sales representatives.

CSI FORMAT

DIVISION 1 — GENERAL REQUIREMENTS
- 01010 SUMMARY OF WORK
- 01100 ALTERNATIVES
- 01150 MEASUREMENT & PAYMENT
- 01200 PROJECT MEETINGS
- 01300 SUBMITTALS
- 01400 QUALITY CONTROL
- 01500 TEMPORARY FACILITIES & CONTROLS
- 01600 MATERIAL & EQUIPMENT
- 01700 PROJECT CLOSEOUT

DIVISION 2 — SITE WORK
- 02010 SUBSURFACE EXPLORATION
- 02100 CLEARING
- 02110 DEMOLITION
- 02200 EARTHWORK
- 02250 SOIL TREATMENT
- 02300 PILE FOUNDATIONS
- 02350 CAISSONS
- 02400 SHORING
- 02500 SITE DRAINAGE
- 02550 SITE UTILITIES
- 02600 PAVING & SURFACING
- 02700 SITE IMPROVEMENTS
- 02800 LANDSCAPING
- 02850 RAILROAD WORK
- 02900 MARINE WORK
- 02950 TUNNELING

DIVISION 3 — CONCRETE
- 03100 CONCRETE FORMWORK
- 03150 FORMS
- 03200 CONCRETE REINFORCEMENT
- 03250 CONCRETE ACCESSORIES
- 03300 CAST-IN-PLACE CONCRETE
- 03350 SPECIALLY FINISHED (ARCHITECTURAL) CONCRETE
- 03360 SPECIALLY PLACED CONCRETE
- 03400 PRECAST CONCRETE
- 03500 CEMENTITIOUS DECKS
- 03600 GROUT

DIVISION 4 — MASONRY
- 04100 MORTAR
- 04150 MASONRY ACCESSORIES
- 04200 UNIT MASONRY
- 04400 STONE
- 04500 MASONRY RESTORATION & CLEANING
- 04550 REFRACTORIES

DIVISION 5 — METALS
- 05100 STRUCTURAL METAL FRAMING
- 05200 METAL JOISTS
- 05300 METAL DECKING
- 05400 LIGHTGAGE METAL FRAMING
- 05500 METAL FABRICATIONS
- 05700 ORNAMENTAL METAL
- 05800 EXPANSION CONTROL

DIVISION 6 — WOOD & PLASTICS
- 06100 ROUGH CARPENTRY
- 06130 HEAVY TIMBER CONSTRUCTION
- 06150 TRESTLES
- 06170 PREFABRICATED STRUCTURAL WOOD
- 06200 FINISH CARPENTRY
- 06300 WOOD TREATMENT
- 06400 ARCHITECTURAL WOODWORK
- 06500 PREFABRICATED STRUCTURAL PLASTICS
- 06600 PLASTIC FABRICATIONS

DIVISION 7 — THERMAL & MOISTURE PROTECTION
- 07150 DAMPPROOFING
- 07200 INSULATION
- 07200 INSULATION
- 07300 SHINGLES & ROOFING TILES
- 07400 PREFORMED ROOFING & SIDING
- 07500 MEMBRANE ROOFING
- 07570 TRAFFIC TOPPING
- 07600 FLASHING & SHEET METAL
- 07800 ROOF ACCESSORIES
- 07900 SEALANTS

DIVISION 8 — DOORS & WINDOWS
- 08100 METAL DOORS & FRAMES
- 08200 WOOD & PLASTIC DOORS
- 08300 SPECIAL DOORS
- 08400 ENTRANCES & STOREFRONTS
- 08500 METAL WINDOWS
- 08600 WOOD & PLASTIC WINDOWS
- 08650 SPECIAL WINDOWS
- 08700 HARDWARE & SPECIALTIES
- 08800 GLAZING
- 08900 WINDOW WALLS/ CURTAIN WALLS

DIVISION 9 — FINISHES
- 09100 LATH & PLASTER
- 09250 GYPSUM WALLBOARD
- 09300 TILE
- 09400 TERRAZZO
- 09500 ACOUSTICAL TREATMENT
- 09540 CEILING SUSPENSION SYSTEMS
- 09550 WOOD FLOORING
- 09650 RESILIENT FLOORING
- 09680 CARPETING
- 09700 SPECIAL FLOORING
- 09760 FLOOR TREATMENT
- 09800 SPECIAL COATINGS
- 09900 PAINTING
- 09950 WALL COVERING

DIVISION 10 — SPECIALTIES
- 10100 CHALKBOARDS & TACKBOARDS
- 10150 COMPARTMENTS & CUBICLES
- 10200 LOUVERS & VENTS
- 10240 GRILLES & SCREENS
- 10260 WALL & CORNER GUARDS
- 10270 ACCESS FLOORING
- 10280 SPECIALTY MODULES
- 10290 PEST CONTROL
- 10300 FIREPLACES
- 10350 FLAGPOLES
- 10400 IDENTIFYING DEVICES
- 10450 PEDESTRIAN CONTROL DEVICES
- 10500 LOCKERS
- 10530 PROTECTIVE COVERS
- 10550 POSTAL SPECIALTIES
- 10600 PARTITIONS
- 10650 SCALES
- 10670 STORAGE SHELVING
- 10700 SUNCONTROL DEVICES (EXTERIOR)
- 10750 TELEPHONE ENCLOSURES
- 10800 TOILET & BATH ACCESSORIES
- 10900 WARDROBE SPECIALTIES

DIVISION 11 — EQUIPMENT
- 11050 BUILT-IN MAINTENANCE EQUIPMENT
- 11100 BANK & VAULT EQUIPMENT
- 11150 COMMERCIAL EQUIPMENT
- 11170 CHECKROOM EQUIPMENT
- 11180 DARKROOM EQUIPMENT
- 11200 ECCLESIASTICAL EQUIPMENT

FIGURE A–1

11300 EDUCATIONAL EQUIPMENT
11400 FOOD SERVICE EQUIPMENT
11480 VENDING EQUIPMENT
11500 ATHLETIC EQUIPMENT
11550 INDUSTRIAL EQUIPMENT
11600 LABORATORY EQUIPMENT
11630 LAUNDRY EQUIPMENT
11650 LIBRARY EQUIPMENT
11700 MEDICAL EQUIPMENT
11800 MORTUARY EQUIPMENT
11830 MUSICAL EQUIPMENT
11850 PARKING EQUIPMENT
11860 WASTE HANDLING EQUIPMENT
11870 LOADING DOCK EQUIPMENT
11880 DETENTION EQUIPMENT
11900 RESIDENTIAL EQUIPMENT
11970 THEATER & STAGE EQUIPMENT
11990 REGISTRATION EQUIPMENT

DIVISION 12—FURNISHINGS
12100 ARTWORK
12300 CABINETS & STORAGE
12500 WINDOW TREATMENT
12550 FABRICS
12600 FURNITURE
12670 RUGS & MATS
12700 SEATING
12800 FURNISHING ACCESSORIES

DIVISION 13—SPECIAL CONSTRUCTION
13010 AIR SUPPORTED STRUCTURES
13050 INTEGRATED ASSEMBLIES
13100 AUDIOMETRIC ROOM
13250 CLEAN ROOM
13350 HYPERBARIC ROOM
13400 INCINERATORS
13440 INSTRUMENTATION
13450 INSULATED ROOM
13500 INTEGRATED CEILING
13540 NUCLEAR REACTORS
13550 OBSERVATORY
13600 PREFABRICATED STRUCTURES
13700 SPECIAL PURPOSE ROOMS & BUILDINGS
13750 RADIATION PROTECTION
13770 SOUND & VIBRATION CONTROL
13800 VAULTS
13850 SWIMMING POOLS

DIVISION 14—CONVEYING SYSTEMS
14100 DUMBWAITERS
14200 ELEVATORS
14300 HOISTS & CRANES
14400 LIFTS
14500 MATERIAL HANDLING SYSTEMS
14570 TURNTABLES
14600 MOVING STAIRS & WALKS
14700 TUBE SYSTEMS

14800 POWERED SCAFFOLDING

DIVISION 15—MECHANICAL
15010 GENERAL PROVISIONS
15050 BASIC MATERIALS & METHODS
15180 INSULATION
15200 WATER SUPPLY & TREATMENT
15300 WASTE WATER DISPOSAL & TREATMENT
15400 PLUMBING
15500 FIRE PROTECTION
15600 POWER OR HEAT GENERATION
15650 REFRIGERATION
15700 LIQUID HEAT TRANSFER
15800 AIR DISTRIBUTION
15900 CONTROLS & INSTRUMENTATION

DIVISION 16—ELECTRICAL
16010 GENERAL PROVISIONS
16100 BASIC MATERIALS & METHODS
16200 POWER GENERATION
16300 POWER TRANSMISSION
16400 SERVICE & DISTRIBUTION
16500 LIGHTING
16600 SPECIAL SYSTEMS
16700 COMMUNICATIONS
16850 HEATING & COOLING
16900 CONTROLS & INSTRUMENTATION

FIGURE A-1 (*Continued*)

Make a careful review of the working drawings, noting dimensions, material specifications that may appear on the plans. The preparation of a materials list is an excellent vehicle for this review. Visit the site with the working drawings if possible. Be alert for anything that might affect the work adversely.

Subdivide the work to be specified into the required number of divisions according to the uniform system. Then prepare an outline of the appropriate sections for each division.

Prepare a paste-up draft of each division and check each division against the working drawings. Be alert for any disagreement between the plans and specifications. Double check all dimensions and size references. Have the draft typed, and if possible get another person to review the work.

Selected Bibliography

Chapter 1: Introduction to Grading
1. Carpenter, Jot D. *The Landscape Construction Workbook.* McLean, Virginia: American Society of Landscape Architects Foundation, 1971.
2. Carpenter, Jot D., Ed. *The Handbook of Landscape Architectural Construction.* McLean, Virginia: American Society of Landscape Architects Foundation, 1976.
3. DeChiara, Joseph and Koppelman, Lee. *Planning and Design Criteria*, 2nd edit. New York: McGraw-Hill Book Co., 1975.
4. Hayslett, Jack J. *Architectural Drawing & Planning*, 2nd edit. New York: McGraw-Hill Book Co., 1972.
5. Lynch, Kevin. *Site Planning*, 2nd edit. Cambridge, Massachusetts: The M.I.T. Press, 1971.
6. Merritt, Fredrick S., Ed. *Standard Handbook for Civil Engineers.* New York: McGraw-Hill Book Co., 1968.
7. Munson, Albe E. *Construction Design for Landscape Architects.* New York: McGraw-Hill Book Co., 1974.
8. Nathan, Kurt. *Basic Site Engineering for Landscape Designers.* New York: MSS Information Corp., 1973.
9. Parker, Harry and MacGuire, John W. *Simplified Site Engineering for Architects and Builders.* New York: John Wiley & Sons, 1954.
10. Rubenstein, Harvey M. *A Guide to Site and Environmental Planning.* New York: John Wiley & Sons, 1969.
11. Seelye, Elwin E. *Design: Data Book for Civil Engineers*, Vol. 1, 3rd edit. New York: John Wiley & Sons, 1960.
12. Unterman, Richard K. *Grade Easy.* McLean, Virginia: American Society of Landscape Architects Foundation, 1973.

Chapter 2: Circulation Design
1. American Association of State Highway Officials, "A Policy on Geometric Design of Rural Highways", Washington, D.C., 1954.
2. Carpenter, Jot D. *Landscape Construction Workbook.* McLean, Virginia: American Society of Landscape Architects Foundation, 1971.
3. Carpenter, Jot D. *The Handbook of Landscape Architec-

tural Construction.* McLean, Virginia: American Society of Landscape Architects Foundation, 1976.
4. DeChiara, Joseph and Koppelman, Lee. *Planning & Design Criteria*, 2nd edit. New York: McGraw-Hill Book Co., 1975.
5. Lynch, Kevin. *Site Planning*, 2nd edit. Cambridge, Massachusetts: The M.I.T. Press, 1971.
6. Merritt, Fredrick S., Ed. *Standard Handbook for Civil Engineers.* New York: McGraw-Hill Book Co., 1968.
7. Munson, Albe E. *Construction Design for Landscape Architects.* New York: McGraw-Hill Book Co., 1974.
8. Nathan, Kurt. *Basic Site Engineering for Landscape Designers.* New York: MSS Information Corp., 1973.
9. Parker, Harry and MacGuire, John W. *Simplified Site Engineering for Architects and Builders.* New York: John Wiley & Sons, 1954.
10. Rubenstein, Harvey M. *A Guide to Site & Environmental Planning.* New York: John Wiley & Sons, 1969.
11. Seelye, Elwin E. *Design: Data Book for Civil Engineers*, 3rd edit. New York: John Wiley & Sons, 1960.
12. Unterman, Richard K. *Grade Easy.* McLean, Virginia: American Society of Landscape Architects Foundation, 1973.

Chapter 3: Drainage Design
1. American Concrete Pipe Association. *Concrete Pipe Design Manual.* Arlington, Virginia, 1974.
2. Callender, John H., Ed. *Time Saver Standards*, 4th edit. New York: McGraw-Hill Book Co., 1966.
3. Carpenter, Jot D., Ed. *The Handbook of Landscape Architectural Construction.* McLean, Virginia: American Society of Landscape Architects Foundation, 1976.
4. DeChiara, Joseph and Koppelman, Lee. *Planning and Design Criteria*, 2nd edit. New York: McGraw-Hill Book Co., 1975.
5. Lynch, Kevin. *Site Planning*, 2nd edit. Cambridge, Massachusetts: The M.I.T. Press, 1971.
6. Merritt, Fredrick S., *Standard Handbook for Civil Engineers.* New York: McGraw-Hill Book Co., 1968.

7. Munson, Albe E. *Construction Design for Landscape Architects.* New York: McGraw-Hill Book Co., 1974.
8. Nathan, Kurt. *Basic Site Engineering for Landscape Designers.* New York: MSS Information Corp., 1973.
9. Parker, Harry and MacGuire, John W. *Simplified Site Engineering for Architects and Builders.* New York: John Wiley & Sons, 1954.
10. National Clay Pipe Institute. *Clay Pipe Engineering Manual.* Chicago, Illinois, 1974.
11. Schwab, Glen O., Frevert, Richard, Edminster, Talcott, and Barnes, Kenneth. *Soil and Water Conservation Engineering.* New York: John Wiley & Sons, 1966.
12. Seelye, Elwin E. *Design: Data Book for Civil Engineers,* Vol. 1, 3rd edit. New York: John Wiley & Sons, 1960.
13. Unterman, Richard K. *Grade Easy.* McLean, Virginia: American Society of Landscape Architects Foundation, 1973.
14. U.S. Department of Agriculture, Soil Conservation Service, "Urban Hydrology for Small Watersheds", Technical Release No. 55, 1975.
15. "Ponds for Water Supply and Recreation," Agriculture Handbook No. 387, 1971.

Chapter 4: Basic Principles of Statics and Mechanics
1. Huntington, Whitney C. *Building Construction: Materials and Types of Construction,* 3rd edit. New York: John Wiley & Sons, 1963.
2. McKaig, Thomas H. *Applied Structural Design of Buildings.* New York: McGraw-Hill Book Co., 1965.
3. Munson, Albe E. *Construction Design for Landscape Architects.* New York: McGraw-Hill Book Co., 1974.
4. National Board of Fire Underwriters. *The National Building Code,* Golden Anniversary Edition. New York: 1955.
5. Parker, Harry. *Simplified Engineering for Architects and Builders,* 4th edit. New York: John Wiley & Sons, 1967.
6. ———*Simplified Mechanics and Strength of Materials,* 2nd edit. New York: John Wiley & Sons, 1965.
7. Ramsey, Charles G. and Sleeper, Harold R. *Architectural Graphic Standards,* 5th edit. New York: John Wiley & Sons, 1956.
8. Roark, Raymond J. *Formulas for Stress and Strain,* 4th edit. New York: McGraw-Hill Book Co., 1965.
9. Shedd, Thomas C. and Vawter, Jamison. *Theory of Simple Structures,* 2nd edit. New York: John Wiley & Sons, 1941.

Chapter 5: Carpentry and Design with Wood
1. Callender, John H. *Time Saver Standards,* 4th edit. New York: McGraw-Hill Book Co., 1966.
2. Hoyle, R. J. *Wood Technology in the Design of Structures,* 3rd edit. Missoula, Montana: Mountain Press Publishing Co., 1973.
3. Huntington, Whitney C. *Building Construction: Materials and Types of Construction,* 3rd edit. New York: John Wiley & Sons, 1963.
4. Munson, Albe E. *Construction Design for Landscape Architects.* New York: McGraw-Hill Book Co., 1974.
5. Newman, Morton. *Standard Structural Details for Build-*

ing Construction. New York: McGraw-Hill Book Co., 1968.
6. National Board of Fire Underwriters. *The National Building Code,* Golden Anniversary Edition. New York: 1955.
7. Parker, Harry. *Simplified Engineering for Architects and Builders,* 4th edit. New York: John Wiley & Sons, 1967.
8. Ramsey, Charles G. and Sleeper, Harold R. *Architectural Graphic Standards,* 5th edit. New York: John Wiley & Sons, 1956.
9. Smith, Ronald C. *Principles and Practices of Light Construction,* 2nd edit. Englewood Cliffs, New Jersey: Prentice-Hall, Inc., 1963.
10. Southern Forest Products Association. *Design With Wood.* Atlanta, Georgia: 1970.
11. Virey, Harry F. *Carpentry and Building.* Indianapolis, Indiana: Theodore Audel and Co., 1971.

Chapter 6: Concrete and Masonry Design
1. Callender, John H. *Time Saver Standards,* 4th edit. New York: McGraw-Hill Book Co., 1966.
2. Carpenter, Jot D., Ed. *The Handbook of Landscape Architectural Construction.* McLean, Virginia: American Society of Landscape Architects Foundation, 1976.
3. Dalzell, J. Ralph. *Simplified Concrete Masonry Planning and Building,* 2nd edit. New York: McGraw-Hill Book Co., 1972.
4. Huntington, Whitney C. *Building Construction: Materials and Types of Construction,* 3rd edit. New York: John Wiley & Sons, 1963.
5. Plummer, Harry G. *Brick and Tile Engineering.* McLean, Virginia: Structural Clay Products Institute, 1950.
6. Ramsey, Charles G. and Sleeper, Harold R. *Architectural Graphic Standards,* 5th edit. New York: John Wiley & Sons, 1956.
7. Portland Cement Association. *Basic Concrete Construction Practices.* New York: John Wiley & Sons, 1975.
8. Seelye, Elwin E. *Design: Data Book for Civil Engineers,* 3rd edit. New York: John Wiley & Sons, 1960.
9. Structural Clay Products Institutes. *Recommended Practice for Brick Masonry.* McLean, Virginia: 1969.

Chapter 7: Irrigation Design
1. Hanson, A.A. and Jurka, F.V., eds. *Turf Grass Science.* Madison, Wisconsin: American Society of Agronomy, Inc., 1969.
2. Watkins, J.A. and Snoddy, M.E. *Turf Irrigation Manual.* Dallas, Texas: Telsco Industries, 1965.
3. ———. *Architect—Engineer Turf Sprinkler Manual.* Glendora, California: Rain Bird Sprinkler Manufacturing Co., 1972.
4. ———. *Design Information for Large Turf Irrigation Systems.* Riverside, California: The Toro Co., 1973.

Chapter 8: Lighting Design
1. Adams, James E. *Electrical Principles and Practices,* 2nd edit. New York: McGraw-Hill Book Co., 1971.
2. Flynn, John E. and Mills, Samuel M. *Architectural Lighting Graphics.* New York: Reinhold Publishing Co., 1962.

3. Henderson, S.T. and Marsden, A.M. *Lamps and Lighting*, 2nd edit. New York: Crane Russak and Co., 1972.

4. Horne, Bob, Ed. *Outdoor Lighting.* Menlo, California: Lane Books, 1969.

5. Kaufman, John E., Ed. *I.E.S. Lighting Handbook,* 5th edit. New York: Illuminating Engineering Society, 1976.

6. McGuinness, William J. and Stein, Benjamin, *Mechanical and Electrical Equipment for Buildings*, 5th edit. New York: John Wiley & Sons, 1971.

7. Wilson, Robert F. *Colour and Light at Work*. London: Seven Oaks Press, Ltd., 1953.

Appendix: Contract Documents and Specifications

1. Hauf, Harold D. *Building Contracts for Design and Construction*. New York: John Wiley & Sons, 1968.

2. Seelye, Elwin E. *Specifications and Costs: Data Book for Civil Engineers*, 3rd edit. New York: John Wiley & Sons, 1960.

3. ————. *The Handbook of Professional Practice*. McLean, Virginia: American Society of Landscape Architects Foundation, 1970.

4. ————. *The Uniform System for Construction Specifications, Data Filing and Cost Accounting*. Washington, D.C.: The Construction Specifications Institute, Inc., 1966.

Solutions to Problems

1. (a) .01
   (b) .07
   (c) .05
   (d) .05
   (e) .01

2. (a) 1,400 m
   (b) 500 m
   (c) 233.33 ft
   (d) 133.33 ft
   (e) 250 ft

3. (a) 3.75 ft
   (b) 1.0 ft
   (c) 10.35 m
   (d) .60 ft
   (e) 172 ft

4. The contours form a symmetrical W pattern around the intersection 30 ft from the 60.40 elevation. The points of the W point downhill.

5. Depending on how you number the contours, the swale will point to the high elevation. The contours adjacent to the slab must be parallel and 10 ft apart. On the back slope they are parallel and 6.67 ft apart.

6. 32.14 in²,   86.02 in²,   11.86 in²,   26.58 in²
   32,140 mm²   86,020 mm²   11,860 mm²   26,580 mm²

7. 1 in² = 900 ft² (30 × 30 = 900)

Cut		Fill	
A = 32.14 × 900	28,926 ft³	C = 11.86 × 900	10,674
B = 86.02 × 900	77,418 ft³	D = 26.58 × 900	23,922
	106,344		34,596

   Cut = 3,938.66 yd³   Fill = 1,281.33 yd³

8. Conversion = 50 mm × 500 mm = $\dfrac{25,000 \text{ mm}^2}{1,000,000 \text{ mm}^2}$ = .025 m²

   Thus write

   $$V = \left(10 \times \frac{A}{2}\right) + \left(10\,\frac{A + B}{2}\right) + \left(10 \times \frac{B + C}{2}\right) + \left(10\,\frac{C + D}{2}\right) + \left(10\,\frac{D}{2}\right)$$

   Areas converted to meters²
   A = 32,140 × .025 = 803.5
   B = 86,020 × .025 = 2,150.5
   C = 11,860 × .025 = 296.5
   D = 26,580 × .025 = 664.5

   $$V = \frac{803.5}{2} + \frac{803.5 + 2150.5}{2} + \frac{2150.5 + 296.5}{2} + \frac{296.5 + 664.5}{2}$$
   $$+ \frac{664.5}{2} \times 10 = 39,150 \text{ m}^2$$

9. Scale conversion: $in^2 = 500 \ ft^2$

ft² of section areas

A
Fill	1	$7.21 \times 500 = 3,605$
Fill	2	$8.53 + 500 = 4,265$
Cut	3	$9.86 \times 500 = 4,930$

B
Cut	4	$6.12 \times 500 = 3,060$
Fill	5	$10.55 \times 500 = 5,275$

C
Cut	6	$5.23 \times 500 = 2,615$
Fill	7	$9.26 \times 500 = 4,630$

D
Cut	8	$7.51 \times 500 = 3,755$
Fill	9	$13.69 \times 500 = 6,845$

E
Cut	10	$7.51 \times 500 = 3,755$
Fill	11	$14.76 \times 500 = 7,380$
Cut	12	$9.98 \times 500 = 4,990$

Accumulate Sections

	CUT (ft²)	FILL (ft²)
A	4,930	7,870
B	3,060	5,275
C	2,615	4,360
D	3,755	6,845
E	8,745	7,380

Cut

$$V = \left(\frac{4,930}{2} + \frac{4,930 + 3,060}{2} + \frac{3,060 + 2,615}{2} + \frac{2,615 + 3,755}{2}\right.$$

$$\left. + \frac{3,755 + 8,745}{2} + \frac{8,745}{2}\right) \times 50 \ ft = 1,155,025 \ ft^3$$

Total Cut $= 42,778 \ yd^3$

Fill

$$V = \left(\frac{7,870}{2} + \frac{7,870 + 5,275}{2} + \frac{5,275 + 4,360}{2} + \frac{4,360 + 6,845}{2}\right.$$

$$\left. + \frac{6,845 + 7,330}{2} + \frac{7,380}{2}\right) \times 50 \ ft = 1,585,250 \ ft^3 = \frac{1,585,250}{27}$$

$$= 58,712.9 \ yd^3$$

10. Scale Conversion: $(50 \ mm)^2 = 2500 \ mm^2$

$$(50 \ mm)^2 \ (\text{Conversion to } m^2) = \frac{2,500}{1,000,000} = .0025 \ m^2$$

AREAS IN M²		VOLUME IN M³	
		Cut	Fill
Fill A	$12,160 \times .0025$		30.4
Cut B	$9,530 \times .0025$	23.83	
Cut C	$15,210 \times .0025$	38.03	
Fill D	$7,220 \times .0025$		18.05
Cut E	$16,230 \times .0025$	40.58	
Fill F	$5,200 \times .0025$		13.00
Cut G	$8,750 \times .0025$	21.88	
		124.3m³	61.5m³

CHAPTER 2

1. I of Curve #1 = 70°. I of Curve #2 = 25°.

Tangent curve #1 = $T = 200 \tan 35°$

$T = 140.04$ ft

PC curve #1 = $400 - 140.04 = 259.96$

PC #1 = 2 + 59.96

$$L \text{ #1} = \frac{70 \times 200}{57.3} = \frac{14,000}{57.3} = 244.33 \text{ ft}$$

PT = 259.96 + 244.33 = 504.29 ft

PT station = 5 + 04.29

Tangent curve #2 = $T = 200 \tan 12.5$

$T = 44.34$ ft

PC #2 = 44.33 + 140.04 = 184.39 ft

400 − 184.39 = 215.61 ft

PC #2 = 504.29 + 215.61 = 719.9 ft

PC #2 = 7 + 19.90

$$L \text{ #2} = \frac{25 \times 200}{57.3} = \frac{5,000}{57.3} = 87.26 \text{ ft}$$

PT #2 = 719.90 + 87.26 = 807.16 ft

PT #2 = 8 + 07.16

Terminus station = 400 − 44.33 = 355.67

Terminus = 807.16 + 355.67 = 1,162.83

Terminus station = 11 + 62.83

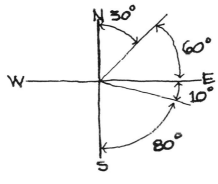 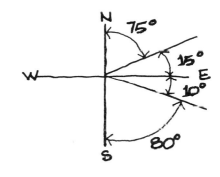

2. Tangent curve #1 = $T = 300 \tan 10°$

$T = 52.90$

PC #1 = 500 − 52.90 = 447.10 ft

PC #1 = 4 + 47.10

$$L \text{ #1} = \frac{20 \times 300}{57.3} = \frac{6,000}{57.3} = 104.71 \text{ ft}$$

PT #1 = 551.81

PT #1 = 5 + 51.81

Tangent curve #2 = $T = 300 \tan 31°$

$T = 180.26$ ft

PC #2 = 180.26 + 52.90 = 233.16 ft

PC #2 = 400 − 233.16 = 166.84 ft

PC #2 = 5 + 51.81 + 166.84 = 718.65 ft

PC #2 = 7 + 18.65

$$L \text{ #2} = \frac{62 \times 300}{57.3} = 324.61 \text{ ft}$$

PT #2 = 718.65 + 324.61 = 1,043.26 ft

PT #2 = 10 + 43.26

$T_3 = 300 \text{ TAN } 18°$

$T_3 = 97.48'$

$PC_3 = 97.48' + 180.26' = 277.74$

$PC_3 = 600 = 277.74 = 322.26$

$PC_3 = 1043.26 + 322.26 = 1365.52$

$PC_3 = 13 + 65.52$

$L_3 = \dfrac{36 \times 300}{57.3} = 188.48$

$PT_3 = 1365.52 + 188.48 = 1554.00$

$PT_3 = 15 + 54.00$

Terminus $= 400 - 97.48 = 302.52$

Terminus $= 1554.00 + 302.52 = 1856.52$

Terminus $= 18 + 56.52$

3. Bearing line #2 = N 65°E. (25 + 40 = 65°). I for line #3 = 53° (65° − 12° = 53°).

Radius of the curves $= R = \dfrac{1{,}746.5}{D} = \dfrac{1{,}746.5}{10}$

$R = 174.65$ m

Tangent curve #1 $= T = 174.65 \tan 20°$

$T = 63.57$ m

PC curve #1 = 155 m − 63.57 m = 91.43 m

PC curve #1 = station 91.430 m

L curve #1 $= \dfrac{40 \times 174.65\text{m}}{174.650} = \dfrac{6{,}986}{174.650} = 40$ m

PT curve #1 = 91.430 + 40 = 131.430 m

PT curve #1 = 131.430

Tangent curve #2 $= T = 174.65 \tan 26.5°$

$T = 87.077$ m

PC curve #2 = 63.570 + 87.077 = 150.647 m

220 m − 150.647 m = 69.353 m

PC curve #2 = 131.430 + 69.353 = 200.783 m

PC curve #2 = 200.783

L curve #2 $= \dfrac{53 \times 174.65}{174.65} = \dfrac{9{,}256.450}{174.65} = 53$ m

PT curve #2 = 200.783 + 53 = 253.783 m

Terminus = 215 − 87.077 = 127.923 m

Terminus = 253.783 + 127.923 = 381.706 m

Terminus station = 381.706

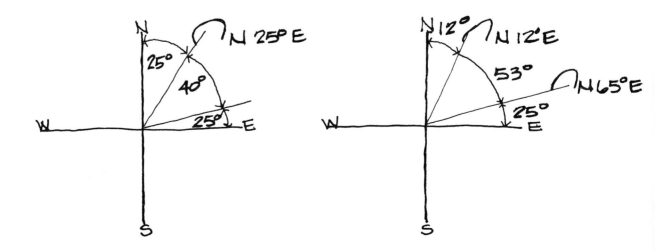

4.

STATION	CURVE ELEVATION
3 + 74	200.91
4 + 00	200.57
4 + 50	200.16
4 + 86.5	200.06
5 + 00	200.07
5 + 50	200.34
6 + 00	200.93
6 + 50	201.49
6 + 74	202.41

5.

STATION	CURVE ELEVATION
5 + 95	201.44
6 + 00	201.73
6 + 50	203.94
7 + 00	204.82
7 + 08.21	205.01
7 + 50	204.37
8 + 00	202.60
8 + 45	199.88

6.

STATION	CURVE ELEVATION
4 + 00	116.52
4 + 50	117.80
4 + 93.33	118.16
5 + 00	118.14
5 + 50	117.55
6 + 00	116.02

7.

STATION	CURVE ELEVATION
56.5	22.254
60	22.391
80	23.068
100	23.564
120	23.878
140	24.009
144.5	24.014
160	23.959
180	23.728
200	23.314
220	22.718
240	21.941
243.5	21.787

8. $e + f = \dfrac{40^2}{477.5 \times 15} = .22$

   $e = .22 \quad .15 = .07 \quad e = 7\%$

9. $e + f = \dfrac{50^2}{750 \times 15} = .22$

   $e = .22 - .14 = .08 \quad e = 8\%$

10. $e + f = \dfrac{70^2}{1910 \times 15} = .17$

   $e = .17 - .12 = .05 \quad e = 5\%$ (does not exceed maximum of .10)

11. $e + f = \dfrac{80^2}{249.5 \times 127.4} = .20$

$e = .20 - .14 = .06 \qquad e = 6\%$

12. $e + f = \dfrac{95^2}{335 \times 127.4} = .21$

$e = .21 - .13 = .08 \qquad e = 8\%$

CHAPTER 3

1. Find average runoff coefficient

$.35 \times .90 = .315$
$.40 \times .95 = .380$
$.25 \times .35 = \underline{.08}$
$\qquad C = .775 \ (.78).$

Find

$tc = .619 \ (1.1 - C) \ L^{.5} \ S^{-.33}$
$tc = .619 \ (1.1 - .78) \ 425^{.5} \ .032^{-.33}$
$tc = .19808 \times 20.62 \times 3.11$
$tc = 12.70 \text{ min}$

Find i by the Steel formula. Columbus is in region and so for a 5 year storm:

$i = \dfrac{k}{t + b} \qquad i = \dfrac{131}{19 + 12.7} = 4.13 \text{ in/hr}$

Next find Q for each area and accumulate as follows:

$Q \ = \ C \qquad i \qquad A$
$Q_1 = .90 \times 4.13 \times (.35 \times 10) = 13.00 \text{ cfs}$
$Q_2 = .95 \times 4.13 \times (.40 \times 10) = 15.69 \text{ cfs}$
$Q_3 = .35 \times 4.13 \times (.25 \times 10) = \underline{3.61 \text{ cfs}}$
$\qquad\qquad\qquad\qquad\qquad \text{Total} = 32.3 \ \ \text{cfs}$

Notice that this is the same as using the average C of .78.
$Q = .78 \times 4.13 \times 10 = 32.214 \text{ cfs}.$

2. Find i by the Steel formula:

$i = 25.4 \left(\dfrac{k}{t + b} \right)$

$i = 25.4 \left(\dfrac{111}{18 + 17} \right) = 25.4 \times 3.17$

$i = 80.52 \text{ mm/hr}$
Find $Q = .00277 \ CiA$
$Q = .00277 \times .78 \times 80.52 \times 5 = .867 \text{m}^3/\text{sec}$

3. $Q = VA$
$4 \ = 7.5 \ V$
$V = \dfrac{4}{7.5} = .53 \text{ ft/sec}$
No siltation may be a problem.

4. The area of the ditch is:
$A = .5 \times 16 \times 2 = 16 \text{ ft}^2$

$Q = VA$
$Q = 4 \times 16$
$Q = 64 \text{ cfs}^*$

5. Ditch D-7A
Dimensions: 2 ft deep, 8 ft wide

---

*This allows no freeboard and no allowance for "n".

Velocity is as follows:

$$V = \frac{1.486}{.025} r^{.67} s^{.5}$$

$$V = 59.44 \times .895^{.67} \times .008^{.5}$$

$$V = 59.44 \times .93 \times .09 \qquad V = 4.98$$

The velocity is satisfactory.

6. Since the area of the ditch in Problem 5 was 8 ft², try a triangular ditch 16 ft wide by 1 ft deep maintaining the 8 ft² area.

Find:

$$P \text{ as } 2\sqrt{8^2 + 1^2} \qquad P = 16.12$$

Find r as:

$$r = \frac{A}{P} \qquad r = \frac{8}{16.12} = .5$$

Find V as:

$$V = \frac{1.486}{.025} \times .5^{.67} \times .008^{.5}$$

$$V = 59.44 \times .63 \times .09$$

$$V = 3.37 \text{ fps}$$

Check:

$$Q = \frac{V}{A} \qquad Q = 3.37 \times 8 \text{ ft}^2 = 26.96 \text{ cfs}$$

7. Find P to be 8.32 ft

Find A to be 5.0 ft²

Find r as:

$$r = \frac{A}{P} = \frac{5}{8.32} \qquad r = .60$$

Next using the Manning formula find:

$$V = \frac{1.486}{.025} \times r^{.67} \times s^{.5}$$

$$4 = 59.44 \times .60^{.67} \times s^{.5}$$

$$4 = 42.21 s^{.5} \qquad s^{.5} = \frac{4}{42.21}$$

$$s^{.5} = .09 \qquad S = .01$$

The maximum slope is 1%.

8. If $Q = VA$, then:

$$7 = 4A \qquad A = 7/4 = 1.75 \text{ ft}^2$$

For a trial, it is best to increase the ditch size to allow free board; thus a 2 ft² was selected. This gives a ditch 4 ft wide and 1 ft deep to get the required 2 ft² area.

Find P and r as follows:

$$P = 2\sqrt{2^2 + 1^2}$$

$$P = 4.47 \qquad r = \frac{A}{P} = \frac{2}{4.47} \qquad r = .45$$

Find V:

$$V = \frac{1.486}{.025} .45^{.67} \times .012^{.5}$$

$$V = 59.44 \times .59 \times .11 = 3.86$$

Check Q:

$$Q = VA \qquad Q = 3.86 \times 2 = 7.72$$

This ditch is satisfactory.

9. The *HG* is assumed to be the crown elevation of the pipe so the diameter is added to the invert.

(a) 126.49 ft + 1 ft = 127.49 ft

(b) 3.263 mm + 600 mm = 3.863 mm

(c) 152.97 ft + 3 ft = 155.97 ft
(d) 5.873 mm + 300 mm + 6.173 mm

10. The discharge pipe should be .008 ft lower or 246.97 − .008 = 246.96.

11. (a) 18 in pipe; (b) 42 in pipe; (c) 24 in pipe; (d) 48 in pipe.

12. Only (b) is acceptable. All other velocities are too high.

13. (a) 15 in pipe; (b) 21 in pipe; (c) 24 in pipe.

14. The hydraulic gradient of the discharge line is taken as the crown elevation; therefore, 116.72 + 3.5 = 120.22. This should be the invert of the entering pipe.

15. 126.92

16. An 18 in pipe flowing full carries 7 cfs at a .006 slope.
The Q/Q ratio is 6/7 = .86
From the table of hydraulic elements find V = 1.12, approximately.
From the nomograph find the velocity at 6 cfs is 3.8 ft sec. Thus:
3.8 × 1.12 = 4.26 ft sec

CHAPTER 4

1. $16R_2 = (4 \times 200) + (8 \times 400)$

$$R_2 = \frac{800 + 3{,}200}{16} \qquad R_2 = 250 \text{ lb}$$

$16R_1 = (8 \times 400) + (12 \times 200)$

$$R_1 = \frac{3{,}200 + 2{,}400}{16} \qquad R_1 = 350 \text{ lb}$$

Check: 350 + 250 = 400 + 200
600 = 600

2. $15R_2 = (3 \times 400) + (6 \times 800) + (9 \times 200)$

$$R_2 = \frac{1{,}200 + 4{,}800 + 1{,}800}{15} \qquad R_2 = 520 \text{ lb}$$

$15R_1 = (6 \times 200) + (9 \times 800) + (12 \times 400)$

$$R_1 = \frac{1{,}200 + 7{,}200 + 4{,}800}{15} \qquad R_1 = 880 \text{ lb}$$

Check: 800 + 520 = 400 + 800 + 200
1,400 = 1,400

3. $16R_2 = (200 \times 4) + (10 \times 1{,}000)$

$$R_2 = \frac{800 + 10{,}000}{16} \qquad R_2 = 675 \text{ lb}$$

$16R_1 = (6 \times 1{,}000) + (12 \times 200)$

$$R_1 = \frac{6{,}000 + 2{,}400}{16} \qquad R_1 = 525 \text{ lb}$$

Check: 525 + 675 = 1,000 + 200
1,200 = 1,200

4. $16R_2 = (6 \times 800) + (8 \times 800)$

$$R_2 = \frac{4{,}800 + 6{,}400}{16} \qquad R_2 = 700 \text{ lb}$$

$16R_1 = (8 \times 800) + (10 \times 800)$

$$R_1 = \frac{6,400 + 8,000}{16} \qquad R_1 = 900 \text{ lb}$$

Check: $700 + 900 = 800 + 800$
$$1,600 = 1,600$$

5. $12R_2 = (4 \times 400) + (10 \times 1,000) + (-2 \times 200)$

$$R_2 = \frac{1,600 + 10,000 - 400}{12}$$

$$R_2 = \frac{11,200}{12} \qquad R_2 = 933.33 \text{ lb}$$

$$12R_1 = (2 \times 1,000) + (10 \times 600)$$

$$R_1 = \frac{2,000 + 6,000}{12} \qquad R_1 = 666.67 \text{ lb}$$

Check: $933.33 + 666.67 = 1,000 + 600$
$$1,600 = 1,600$$

6. $16\,R_1 = (7.5' \times 15' \times 20\#) + (22 \times 200) - (4 \times 600)$

$$16\,R_1 = 2250 + 4400 - 2400$$

$$R_1 = \frac{4250}{16}$$

$$R_1 = 265.62\#$$

$$16\,R_2 = (8.5 \times 15 \times 20) + (20 \times 600) - (6 \times 200)$$

$$16\,R_2 = 2550 + 12000 - 1200$$

$$R_2 = \frac{13350}{16}$$

$$R_2 = 834.38\#$$

Check: $834.38 + 265.62 = 200 + 300 + 600$
$$1100\# = 1100\#$$

7. $I = \dfrac{2.5 \times 9.5^3}{12} = \dfrac{2.5 \times 857.375}{12}$

$\quad I = 178.62 \text{ in}^4$

8. $I = \dfrac{4.5 \times 5.5^3}{12} = \dfrac{4.5 \times 166.375}{12}$

$\quad I = 62.39 \text{ in}^4$

9. $I = \dfrac{bd^3}{12} = \dfrac{3.5 \times 11.5^5}{12} = 443.59 \text{ in}^4$

10. $I = \dfrac{5.5 \times 5.5^3}{12} = \dfrac{5.5 \times 166.375}{12}$

$\quad I = 76.26 \text{ in}^4$

11. $S = \dfrac{bd^2}{6} = \dfrac{1.5 \times 9.5^2}{6} = 22.56 \text{ in}^3$

12. $S = \dfrac{6 \times 5.5^2}{6} = \dfrac{6 \times 30.25}{6}$

$\quad S = 30.25 \text{ in}^3$

13. $S = \dfrac{5.5 \times 5.5^2}{6} = \dfrac{5.5 \times 30.25}{6}$

$S = 27.73 \text{ in}^3$

14. $S = \dfrac{1.5 \times 11.5^2}{6} = \dfrac{1.5 \times 132.25}{6}$

$S = 33.06 \text{ in}^3$

15. $S = \dfrac{M}{fb}$

$M = \dfrac{WL}{8} = \dfrac{350 \times 10 \times 10}{8} = \dfrac{35000}{8}$

$M = 4375 \text{ ft\#}$

$fb = 1600 \text{ \#/in}^2$

$S = \dfrac{4375 \times 12}{1600} = 32.81 \text{ in}^3$

16. Note: this is still taken as a simple beam

$M = \dfrac{WL}{8} = \dfrac{400 \times 16 \times 16}{8} = 12800 \text{ ft}$

$S = \dfrac{M}{fb} = \dfrac{12800 \text{ ft\#} \times 12}{1600} = 96 \text{ in}^3$

$S = 96 \text{ in}^3$

17. $M = \dfrac{WL}{8} = \dfrac{600 \times 14 \times 14}{8} = 14700 \text{ ft\#}$

$S = \dfrac{M}{fb} = \dfrac{14700 \times 12}{1600} = 110.25 \text{ in}^3$

4, 2 × 12

$S = \dfrac{bd^3}{6} = \dfrac{6'' \times 11.25''^2}{6} = 126.56 \text{ in}^3$

$3 - 2 \times 12 = \dfrac{6'' \times 9.5^2}{6} = 90.25$

18. $M = \dfrac{PL}{4} = \dfrac{5000 \times 12}{4} = 15000 \text{ ft\#}$

$S = \dfrac{M}{fb} = \dfrac{15000 \times 12}{1600} = 112.50 \text{ in}^3$

A 6 × 12 timber $S = 21.23 \text{ in}^3$

19. $M = \dfrac{WL}{8} = \dfrac{150 \times 13.5 \times 13.5}{8} = 3417.19$

$S = \dfrac{M}{fb} = \dfrac{3417.19 \times 12}{1600} = 25.63 \text{ in}^3$

REQUIRED S

$$S = \frac{bd^2}{6} = \frac{1.5'' \times 9.5^2}{C} = 22.56 \text{ in}^3$$

A 2 × 10 will not work

20. $$S = \frac{bd^2}{6} = \frac{1.5 \times 9.5^2}{6} = 22.56 \text{ in}^3$$

$$S = \frac{M}{fb} = 22.56 = \frac{M}{1600 \text{ \#/in}^2}$$

$$22.56 \text{ in}^3 \times 1600 \text{\#/in}^2 = 36096.00 \text{ in/lb}$$

Since $M = \dfrac{WL}{8}$ then $36096 = \dfrac{2000 \text{ lb} \times L}{8}$

$$L = \frac{288768}{2000} = 144.38'' = 12' - \text{3/8}''$$

21. $$f_c = \frac{.3 \, E}{\dfrac{(12 \, l)^2}{d}} = \frac{.3 \times 1,600,000}{\dfrac{(12 \times 8)^2}{3.5}}$$

$$f_c = \frac{480,000}{2633.14}$$

$$f_c = 182.29 \text{ lb/in}^2$$

22. $$f_c = \frac{.3 \, E}{\dfrac{(12 \, l)^2}{d}} = \frac{.3 \times 1,600,000}{\dfrac{(12 \times 6)^2}{3.5}}$$

$$f_c = \frac{480,000}{1481.14}$$

$$f_c = 324.07$$

The unit stress on the column is:

$$f = \frac{P}{A} = \frac{13,000}{12.25}$$

$$f = 1061.22 \text{ lb/in}^2$$

The column would not support the load.

23. $$f_c = \frac{.3E}{\dfrac{(12 \, l)^2}{d}} = \frac{.3 \times 1,600,000}{\dfrac{(12 \times 9)^2}{5.5}}$$

$$f_c = \frac{480,000}{2,120.73} \qquad f_c = 226.34$$

Since

$$f = \frac{P}{A} \qquad 226.34 = \frac{P}{5.5^2}$$

$$P = 226.34 \times 30.25 \qquad P = 6,846.79 \text{ lb total load}$$

24. Find the reaction at R_1 by writing:

$$16\,R_1 = 12 \times 15000 \qquad R_1 = \frac{180,000}{16} \qquad R_1 = 11,250 \text{ lb.}$$

Then by trial find that a 4×4, 6 ft long has an allowable f_c buckling of 324.07 lb/in².

$$f = \frac{P}{A} \qquad \frac{11,250 \text{ lb}}{3.52} = 918.37 \text{ lb/in}^2$$

The column would buckle.

25. R for each column is ½ the total load so

$$\frac{18 \times 400}{2} = 3,600 \text{ lb}$$

Each column must carry 3,600 lb.
Check the 4 ft column.

$$f_c = \frac{.3 \times 1,600,000}{\dfrac{(12 \times 4)^2}{3.5}} = \frac{480,000}{658.29}$$

$$f_c = 729.17 \text{ lb/in}^2$$

$$f = \frac{P}{A} = \frac{3,600}{12.25} = 293.88$$

The 4 ft column is quite safe.
Check the 12 ft column.

$$f_c = \frac{.3 \times 1,600,000}{\dfrac{(12 \times 12)^2}{3.5}}$$

$$f_c = \frac{480,000}{5924.57} = 81.02 \text{ lb/in}^2$$

A 12 ft 4×4 will not support the 3,600 lb load.

CHAPTER 5

1. Table 5–8   **2 in $\times$ 10 in**
2. Table 5–8   **It is not possible.**
3. The area of the deck is $16 \times 16 = 256$ ft²
   Total load $= 40 \times 256 = 10,240$ lb
   Each beam carries half the load so each beam carries 5,120 lb.

4. $M = \dfrac{WL}{8} = \dfrac{5,120 \times 16}{8} = 10,240$ ft/lb

5. $S = \dfrac{M}{f} = \dfrac{10,240 \times 12}{1,600} = 76.80$ in³

   Remember f is in inches and M is in ft/lb.

6. First find $I = \dfrac{bd^3}{12} = \dfrac{5.5 \text{ in} \times 9.5^3}{12}$

   $$I = \frac{4,715.56}{12} = 392.96 \text{ in}^4$$

   Find $D = \dfrac{5\,WL^3}{384\,EI} = \dfrac{5 \times 5,120 \text{ lb} \times (16 \times 12)^3}{384 \times 1,600,000 \times 392.96}$

   $D = .75$ in

7. $\dfrac{12 \times 16}{360} = .53$

8. The load on each column is ¼ the total load.
18 ft × 12 ft × 60 lb/ft² × .25 = 3,240 lb

Unit Stress $f = \dfrac{P}{A}$

$f = \dfrac{3240}{3.5^2} = \dfrac{3240}{12.25} = 264.49 \text{ lb/in}^2$

9. The two center posts are assumed to carry half the load of each panel resting on them so one post carries half the weight of the 16 ft × 16 ft panel or:
16 ft × 16 ft × 100 lb/ft² × .5 = 12,800 lb.

10. The middle beam carries half the load of each 10 ft × 10 ft panel or half the total load, therefore:
10 ft × 20 ft × 70 lb/ft² × .5 = 7000 lb

CHAPTER 6   1. Calculate M_o and M_r — Assume no eccentric loading from wind load so f for footing load will be

$f = \dfrac{P}{A}$

Masonry = 120 lb/ft³
Concrete = 150 lb/ft³
W = (.83 ft × 6 ft × 120 lb) + (.67 × 2 × 150)
W = 597.6 lb + 201 lb = 796.60
M_u = 4 ft × 5.67 ft × 30 lb/ft² = 680.40 ft/lb
M_r = 1 × 796.60   = 796.60 ft/lb

Safety factor $\dfrac{796.6}{680.4} = 1.17$

This is probably satisfactory if no unusual conditions exist.

Foot Pressure $f - \dfrac{P}{A} = \dfrac{796.60}{(.67 \times 2)} = 594.48 \text{ lb/ft}^2$

2. From Table 6−5 find maximum L/T ratio = 14. Thus

$14 = \dfrac{L}{8 \text{ in}}$ $L = 14 \times 8 \text{ in} = 112 \text{ in}$

$L = 9.33$ ft
Recommend 6 piers 8 ft − 4 in o.c.

3. $P = .286 \dfrac{Wh^2}{2} = 2.86 \times \dfrac{150 \text{ lb} \times 49}{2}$

$P = .286 \times \dfrac{7,350}{2} = 1051.05$ lb

4. $P = .833 \dfrac{Wh^2}{2} = .833 \dfrac{150 \times 49}{2}$

$P = .833 \times \dfrac{7,350}{2} = 3,061.28$ lb

5. Calculate and tabulate weight of each segment as follows:
Figure P6−1
Footing   4.5 ft × 1 ft × 150 lb = 675 lb
Wall   1 ft × 5 × 150 lb   = 750 lb
Soil   3 ft × 5 ft × 100   = 1500 lb

Find moment of individual sections and tabulate. We used left edge of footing as center of moments

SECTION	MOMENT ARM	WEIGHT	MOMENT
Footing	2.25	675	1,518.75 ft/lb
Wall	1	750	750.00 ft/lb
Soil	3	1,500	4,500.00 ft/lb
Total		2,925 lb	6,768.75 ft/lb

$$\text{Moment Arm of Section} = \frac{6,768.75 \text{ ft/lb}}{2,925 \text{ lb}} = 2.31 \text{ ft}$$

$$P = .286 \frac{Wh^2}{2} = .286 \frac{100 \times 6^2}{2}$$

$$P = .286 \frac{3,600}{2} = 514.8 \text{ lb}$$

Check overturning stability

$$M_o = P \times \frac{h}{3} = 514.8 \times 2 = 1,029.6 \text{ ft/lb}$$

$M_r = W \times$ the moment arm of the total section
$M_r = 2,925 \text{ lb} \times 2.31 = 6,756.75 \text{ ft/lb}$

$$\text{Safety factor} = \frac{6,756.75}{1,029.6} = 6.56$$

To check for settling stability construct a force parallelogram and find that the resultant cuts the base $\pm$ 1.15 ft from the left edge of the footing; thus

$$f_a = \frac{P}{A}\left(1 + \frac{6e}{d}\right) = \frac{2,925}{4.5}\left(1 + \frac{6 \times 1.16}{4.5}\right)$$

$$f_a = 650\left(1 + \frac{6.96}{4.5}\right) = 650 \times 2.55$$

$$f_a = 1,657.5 \text{ lb per ft}^2$$

$$\text{Safety factor} \frac{4,000}{1,657.5} = 2.41$$

CHAPTER 7

1. 364.5 − 220 = 144.5 feet of head
   144.5 × .433 = 62.57 psi

2. There will be six lengths of pipe 50 ft each
   (1)   42 GPM−2 in pipe   .63 psi Loss
   (2)   35 GPM−2 in   .44
   (3)   28 GPM−1.5 in pipe   .70 psi Loss
   (4)   21 GPM−1.25 in pipe   .80
   (5)   14 GPM−1.25 in   .39
   (6)   7 GPM−1 in   .34
   _____
   3.30 psi
   Maximum Pressure Loss is 4 psi

3. 4 in pipe is required to hold the velocity below 5 ft/sec. The pressure loss per 100 ft is .54 psi. The total loss then is:
   7 × .54 = 3.78 psi

4. 1.2 × .46 = .55 psi
   65.0 − .55 = 64.45 psi

5. (a)

COMPONENT SIZE (in)		PRESSURE LOSS (psi)
Valve = 1		6
a = 1.25		.30
b = 1.25		.33
c = 1		.39
d = .75		.36
e = .25		.34

(b)

	SIZE (in)	PRESSURE LOSS
Gate Valve	2	2.5
Automatic Valve (1)	1.5	3.0
Automatic Valve (2)	1.5	4.5 @ 22.5 GPM
Pipe A	1.5	.69
B	1	.55
C	1	.55
D	1	.26
E	.75	.36
F	.5	.23
G	1.5	.20
H	1.5	.20
I	1	.55
J	.75	.53
K	.75	.30
L	.5	.23

6. .70 D for triangular
.7 × 60 = 42 ft spacing
.65 D for square
.65 × 60 − 39 ft spacing

7. Precipitation for triangular spacing is:

$$P = \frac{q\ 96.3}{A} = \frac{6.5 \times 96.3}{36.37 \times 21}$$

$$P = \frac{625.95}{763.83} = .82 \text{ in/hr}$$

Precipitation for square spacing is:

$$P = \frac{q\ 96.3}{A} = \frac{6.5 \times 96.3}{1521.}$$

$$P = \frac{625.95}{1521} = .41 \text{ in/hr}$$

CHAPTER 8   1.

POINT	LUMINAIRE 1	LUMINAIRE 2	TOTAL
A	2.56	1.19	3.75
B	1.68	1.68	3.36
C	1.19	2.56	3.75
D	2.56	.32	2.88
E	2.14	1.09	3.23
F	1.53	1.53	3.06
G	1.09	2.14	3.23
H	.32	2.56	2.88

1. *(continued)*

POINT	LUMINAIRE 1	LUMINAIRE 2	TOTAL
I	1.68	.028	1.71
J	1.53	.94	2.47
K	1.14	1.14	2.28
L	.94	1.53	2.47
M	.028	1.68	1.71

	A and D	B and I	C	E	F and J	G	H	K	L	M
$r =$	20	40	60	28.28	44.72	63.24	85.44	56.56	72.11	89.44
$d^2 =$	1,300	2,500	4,500	1,699.75	2,899.88	4,899.3	8,200	4,099.03	6,099.85	8,900
$d =$	36.05	50	67.08	41.22	53.85	69.99	90.55	64.02	78.10	94.33
$\theta =$	33.69	53.13	63.43	43.37	56.14	64.62	70.65	62.06	67.41	71.47
$I =$	4,000	7,000	12,000	5,000	8,000	12,490	7,800	10,000	15070	800
$E_H =$	2.56	1.68	1.19	2.14	1.53	1.09	.32	1.14	.94	.028

Maximum to Minimum
2.19 : 1

2. $Fc = \dfrac{1\ \mu M}{L\ w} = \dfrac{30{,}000 \times .33 \times .5}{80 \times 40}$

$Fc = 1.54$

3. $L = \dfrac{I\ \mu M}{Fc\ W} = \dfrac{30{,}000 \times .375 \times .5}{2 \times 60}$

$L = \dfrac{5{,}625}{120} = 46.88\ \text{ft}$

4. (top) 130 ft run   8 amps = #10 Wire
   #10 Wire = .21194 × 8 × 1.3 = 2.20 loss
   #8 Wire = .13325 × 8 × 1.3 = 1.39 loss
   First 20 ft run 6 amps
   # Wire .21194 × 6 × .20 = .25 loss
   Second 20 ft run 4 amps
   #10 Wire .21194 × 4 × .20 = .17 loss
   Third 20 ft run 2 amps
   #10 Wire .21194 × 2 × .20 = .08 loss
      Total Loss   1.89 volts

4. (bottom) 260 ft run at 10 amps
   #8 Wire = .13325 × 10 × 2.6 = 3.46 loss
   #6 Wire = .08380 × 10 × 2.6 = 2.18 loss
   #4 Wire = .05270 × 10 × 2.6 = 1.37 loss
   First 30 ft run 8 amps
   #8 Wire = .13325 × 8 × .3 = .32 loss
   Second 30 ft run 6 amps
   #8 Wire = .13325 × 6 × .3 = .24 loss
   Third 30 ft run 4 amps
   #8 Wire = .13325 × 4 × .3 = .16 loss
   Fourth 30 ft run 2 amps
   #10 Wire = .21194 × 2 × .3 = .13 loss
      Total Loss   2.21 volts

5. (top) First find total load in amps.

$I = \dfrac{P}{E} = \dfrac{2{,}000}{120} = 16.67\ \text{amps}$

4.167 amps per fixture
100 ft run at 16.66 amps
#6 Wire = .08380 × 16.66 × 1 = 1.4
First 50 ft run at 12.5 amps
#6 Wire = .08380 × 12.5 × .5 = .52
Second 50 ft run at 8.34 amps
#6 Wire = .08380 × 8.34 × .5 = .35
Third 50 ft run at 4.16 amps
#6 Wire = .08380 × 4.16 × .5 = .17
Total Loss   2.4 volts

5. (bottom) Total load in AMPS is:

$$I = \frac{P}{E} = \frac{700}{120} = 5.83 \text{ amps}$$

100 W fixtures = .83 amps
200 W fixture = 1.66 amps
200 ft run at 5.83 amps
#6 Wire = .08380 × 5.83 × 2 = .98
First 25 ft run at 5 amps
#10 Wire = .21194 × 5 × .25 = .26
Second 25 ft run at 4.17 amps
#10 Wire = .21194 × 4.17 × .25 = .22
Third 25 ft run at 3.34 amps
#12 Wire = .33690 × 3.34 × .25 = .28
Fourth 25 ft run at 1.67 amps
#12 Wire = .33690 × 1.67 × .25 = .14
Total Loss   1.88 volts

CHAPTER 9   1. $Q = \left(.405 + \dfrac{.00984}{H}\right)\left[1 + .55 \dfrac{H^2}{(P + H)^2}\right] LH \, (2qH)^{.5}$

$Q = \left(.405 + \dfrac{.00984}{.166}\right)\left[1 + .55 \dfrac{.166^2}{(2.5 + .166)^2}\right] 8 \times .166 \, (2 \times 32.17 \times .166)^{.5}$

$Q = .464 \times 1.0021 \times 1.328 \times 4.34$
$Q = 2.68$ cfs
Q in GPM is: $2.68 \times 448.83 = 1{,}203$ GPM

2. $1.2 \times 12 = 14.4$
$14.4 \times .433 = 6.23$ psi

3. $(34 \times 4) + 20 = 156$ GPM

4. 23 psi the ring will require the use of a pressure regulator valve.

Index

A

ADT, 76
Alignment, street, 77
  horizontal, 77
  vertical, 77
Angle of repose, 219
Arterial street, 76
Asphalt, 204
  cold mix, 204
  hot mix, 204
  materials, 204
  pavements, 204
Axial loading, columns, 170

B

Bay, 17
Bazin's formula, 289
Beam failure, 164
Beams, 165
  cantilever, 165
  continuous, 165
  maximum moment, 166
  overhanging, 165
  simple, 165
Bearing capacity, soil, 210
Bending, 164
Bending moment, 164
Bicycle ways, design considerations, 107, 108
Bidding documents, 293
Bituminous concrete, 204
Blind nailing, 197
Board, 176
Board foot, 177
Board measure, 177
Bolts, 183, 184
  length, 184
  size, 184
Branch circuits, 274
Brick, 202
  clinkers, 202
  dimensions, 203
  grades, 202, 203
  modular, 203
  soft, 202
Buckling, 170
Buildings
  grading around, 46
  grading for, 27
Butt joint, 194
Butte, 17

C

Camel back, 17
Cantilever beam, 165
Cantilever wall, 219
Catch basin, 143
Cedar, 175
Cement, portland, 200
Center of moments, 160
Centroids
  of common sections, 223
  by moments, 223
Chamfer, 197
Circular curves, geometry of, 90
  chord, 91
  curve length (L), 90
  deflection angle, 91
  degree of curve, 90
  delta (Δ), 90
  included angle (I), 90
  point of curvature, 90
  point of intersection, 91
  point of tangency, 90
  radius (R), 90
  tangent, 91
Circular curves, see Horizontal alignment
Circular pipe, properties of, 128
Clay units, 202
Clinker, 202
Collector street, 76
Column failure, 170
Columns, 164
  maximum loading, 170

Concrete, 199
  aggregates, 201
  composition, 200
  plain, 199
  reinforced, 199
  steel reinforced, 199
  strength of, 201
  types, 200
Concrete block, 203
Concrete masonry units, 200
Concrete units, 203
Connections, 193
  post to beam, 193, 194
  joist to beam, 193, 195
Construction joint, 208
Contours, 110
  interpretation, 12
  laws of, 23
  manipulation, 27
  signature, 12
Contract conditions, 400
Contract forms, 400
Control joint, 208
  placement, 209
Controllers, irrigation, 238
Coping, 213
Counterfort wall, 219
Countersink, 197
Crest, 23
Cross bridging, 186
Crushing, 170
Cul-de-sac, 76
Curb inlet, 143
Curbs, 80, 81
Cut and fill, calculation of, 64
  average end area method, 66
  planimeter method, 68
Cypress, 175

D

Dams, earth, 149, 151
Datum, 10
Decking, 186–188
Deflection, 164
  maximum in beams, 166
Degree of curve, 77
Depth of flow, 122
Design speed
  roads, 77
  streets, 77
Design storm, 116, 118
DHV, 76
Distance, horizontal calculation, 37
Ditch sections, properties of, 124, 125
Doweling, 197
Drain inlets, 142
  size, 142
Drainage
  access structures, 141
  channels, kinds, 121
  design of surface systems, 120
  flood control, 114
  grading, 37
  issues, 113
  properties of sections, 122
  runoff estimation, 116

sheet, 31
structures for, 141
volumes of flow, 121

E

Eccentric loads, 213, 214
Elastic limit, 164
Electrical measurement, 272
Electrical plans, 274
Electrical symbols, 276
Electricity, principles of, 271
Elevation
  calculation of, 37
  difference, 37
Endwall, 141
Equilibrium, 160
Equivalent forces, 222
Erosion, 115
Evapo-transpiration rate, 234
Expansion joint, 208
  placement, 209
Explosive driven fasteners, 185
Expressway, 76
Extreme fiber stress, 163

F

Fan, 23
Fasteners
  specialized, 184
  wood, 177
Fence, 212
Field capacity, 233, 234
Finish details, 193
Fir, douglas, 176
Flexible pavements, 204
Flexure formula, 168
Flood control, 114
Flood insurance, 114
Flood plain, 17
Flood plane, 115
Fluid behavior, 120
Footings, 209
Force, 159
  properties of, 159
  types of, 159
  units of, 159
Force parallelogram, 220
Foundations, 209
Fountain equipment
  filters, 286
  nozzles, 283
  pumps, 284
Fountain hydraulics, 287
Framing, 186
  plank and beam system, 188
  platform system, 187
Freestanding walls, 210
Freeway, 76
Friction coefficient (n), 122, 123
  of soils, 224

G

Girder, 164
Glen, 17

Grades, calculation of, 37
Gradient, 37
Grading, 59
    basic equation, 37
    standards for, 36
Granites, 202
Grate inlet, 143
Gravity wall, 219

H

Hachures, 10
Hardwood, 176
Haunch footing, 211
Head, 243
    loss, compensation for, 132
Headwall, 141
Hog's back, 17
Hollow wall fasteners, 185
Horizontal alignment, streets,
    calculation of, 90
    control of, 89
    curves for, 89
    layout of, 91
Horizontal shear,
Hurricane brace, 185
Hydraulic gradient, 122, 131
    matching of, 131
Hydraulic radius, 122
Hydraulic sections, properties of, 122
Hydraulic surface, 122
Hydraulics, 120
Hydropneumatic pressure, 241

I

Inertia, moment of, 167
Infiltration, soil, 233
Intermediate regional flood, 115
Intersections, 83
    at grade, 83
    channelized, 83
    grade separated, 83
    turning radii for, 89
Invert, 122
Irrigation, 233
    agronomic principles, 233
    controllers, 238
    design, 246
    equipment, 234
    fittings, pipe, 240
    heads, 234, 235
    hydraulics, 241
    pipe, 238
    principles, 233
    pumps, 241
    valves, 235

J

Joints, 194
Joist, 164
    maximum span, 191
Joist hanger, 185

K

Key, 225
Kilowatt-hour, 274
Knob, 17
Knoll, 17

L

L, Horizontal distance, 37
Laminar flow, 121
Lamp efficiency, 264
Lamps
    electric discharge, 264
    incandescent, 263
Landform, 15
    character, 15
    representation, 10
Lateral stability, 216
Lateral support, walls, 217
Length to thickness ratio, 217
Lighting, 266
    average illumination, 269
    design of, 266
    distribution, 265
    effect, 269
    equipment, 263
    levels, 266
    light color, 271
    plans, 274
    point by point method, 266
Limestone, 202
Live load, 189
Lumber, 176
    common yard, 176
    grading, 176
    measurement, 177
Lumen, 264

M

Manning formula, 122
Manholes, 142, 145
Maps, 7
    availability, 10
    scales, 7
Masonry paving, 208
Mass, 163
Materials
    strength of, 163
    weight of, 210
Maximum moment, in beams, 166
Meadow, 23
Mechanics, 159
Middle third, principle of, 212
Military crest, 17
Miter, 197
Modulus of elasticity, 163
Moment, 160
    of inertia, 167
Mortar, 201
    proportioning, 201
    strength of, 201
    types, 201

N

n, values of, 123
Nailing technique, 193
Nails, 177
    kinds and quantity, 181, 182
    withdrawal, 177
Neutral surface, 164
Nomograph, for circular pipe, flowing full, 135
Non-loadbearing walls, 210

O

Ohm's law, 272
One hundred year flood, 115
Open drainage channel, 121
Optimum density, 204
Overland flow times, 117
Overturning, retaining walls, 220
Overturning moment, 215

P

Parabolic curves, see Vertical alignment
Parking,
    design considerations, 84
    layout of, 86, 87
    turning radii for, 89
Paths, grading of, 37
Pavement, bituminous, 204
Pedestrian circulation systems, 104
Pedestrian ways, design considerations, 104–106
Photometrics, 268
Pier, 164
    and beam, foundation, 212
    and footing, details, 193, 194
Piling, 164
Pine, southern yellow, 176
Pipe,
    asbestos cement, 145
    bedding, 145
    concrete, 145
    corrugated steel, 145
    fittings, 240
    irrigation, 238
        sizing, 252
    shape, 138
    vitrified clay, 145
Planimeter, 64
Plans, grading, 59
Plate, 164, 187
Plugged, 197
Pool construction, 290
Portland cement, 200
Post, 164
Power
    formula, 273
    generation, 271
Preservatives, wood, 184
Pressure loss, 243
    computation of, 244
    tables, 256–261
Pressure treatment, 186
Primary distribution, power, 273
Profile, 11
Project manual, 399
Promontory, 17

Pumps, irrigation, 241
Purlin, 164
PVC pipe, 238

R

Rabbet, 194
Racking, 177
Rainfall intensity, 116
Rational formula, 116
Ravine, 17
Reactions, 161
    for combined loads, 161
    for evenly distributed loads, 161
    overhanging beams, 161
Rebars, 206
Recharge of aquifer, 115
Redwood, 176
Reinforcing steel, 206
Reinforcing walls, 218
Resultant, 220
Retaining walls, 218
    centroid of, 222
    complex sections, 224
    failure of, 218
    footing pressure, 224
    overturning, 220
    pressure on, 219
    sliding, 224
    stability of, 220
    surcharge of, 227
Retention structures, 148
Ridge lines, 12–17
Righting moment, 215
Rigid pavements, 205
Roads, grading for, 30
Routed joint, 194
Runoff
    control of, 148
    estimating volume, 116
Runoff coefficient, 116
    values of, 119

S

Saddle, 23
Sandstone, 202
Scab, 195
Screws, wood, 177
    sizes, 183
Secondary distribution, power, 273
Section, 11
Section modulus, 167
Serpentine wall, 212, 213, 218
Sight distance, 77
Sizing beams, 168
Slabs, 204
    concrete, 205
        base preparation, 205
        center lift damage, 207
        end life damage, 207
        placing and finishing, 206
        reinforcing of, 206
    grading for, 30
Slenderness ratio, 170
Slope, 37
    standards of, 38–41

Slotted joint, 194
Slump test, 201
Softwood, 175
Soil, 4
  bearing capacity of, 210
  characteristics, irrigation, 233
  classification, 5
  formation, 4
  friction coefficients of, 224
  infiltration rates, 233
Special conditions, 300
Spillways, 150, 151
Spot elevations, calculations of, 37
Stability, of retaining walls, 219
Standard project flood, 115
Standards, for grading, 36
Static head, 243
Statics, 159
Stationing, 90
Steel formula, 118
Steel placement, 210, 211
Stone, 201
Storm drain, 128
  computation sheet, 134
Streets, 76
  alignment of, 77
  classification of, 76
  cross section of, 80
  intersections, 83
  location of, 81
  maximum gradient of, 77
  sight distance, 77
  standards for, 76
  width of, 79
Strength of materials, 163
  ultimate strength, 163
Stress, 159
  patterns, in beams, 165
  properties of, 159
  types of, 159
  units of, 159
  working stress, 163
Stringer, 164, 187
Strobe effect, 264
Structural properties of materials, 163
Structures, grading around, 37
Stud, 164
Sub-base, 204
Sub-drainage, 116, 152
  layout of, 153, 154
  materials for, 153
  pipe depth and spacing, 153
Subsidence, 116
Subsurface drainage, 115
Subsurface runoff, 115
Super elevation, 104
  calculation of, 104
  metric measure, use of, 104
  values of f, 104
Surcharge, retaining walls, 227
Swale, 17
System ground, 274

T

Technical specifications, 924
Thermal control, reinforcing, 208

Thrust, 218
Ticksheet, 99
Timber, 176
Time of concentration, 117
Toe of slope, 23
Toe-nailing, 197
Tongue and groove, 194, 197
Tread, 187
Trip-L-Grip fastener, 185
Turbulence,
  compensation for, 130
  in pipe, 129

U

Ultimate strength, 163
Uniform flow, 121
Uniform system, 301
Unit force, 159, 160
Unit stress, 159, 160
  allowable for lumber, 178
USGS Map, 12, 14

V

Valleys, 12, 24
Valves, irrigation, 235
Vehicular circulation systems, 75
Velocity
  of flow, drainage channels, 120, 125
  of runoff, 122
Velocity head, 122
Vertical alignment, streets, 96, 97
  algebraic difference (d), 97
  calculation of, 96
  curve data sheet, 100
  design considerations, 96
  geometry of, 97
  high point of, 98
  horizontal offset (x), 97
  length of curve, 97
  low point of, 98
  middle ordinant of curves, 97-98
  point of vertical curvature, 97
  point of vertical intersection, 97
  point of vertical tangency, 97
  vertical offset (y), 97
Vertical curve, computation sheet, 100
Vertical shear, 164
Volt-amperes, 273
Voltage drop, copper wire, 280
Volume, of flow in drainage channels, 121

W

Wall failure, 212, 214
Water
  distribution, 244
  jets, 287
  properties of, 120
  storage, soil, 234
  volumes over weirs, 289
Watering frequency, 234
Watershed, 116
Weathering, 177
Weight of materials, 210
Weirs, 287
Wetted perimeter, 122

Wind loading
  fences, 215
  walls, 215
Wind loads, 216
Wire reinforcing mesh, 206
Wire sizes, 280
Withe, 213
Wood
  grading, 176

preservatives, 184
  application of, 184
structures, detailing of, 192
structural design of, 189
Working stress, 163

Z
Zero runoff, 114